Global Practices on Effective Talent Acquisition and Retention

Bryan Christiansen
Southern New Hampshire University, USA

Muhammad Abdul Aziz
University of Greenwich, UK

Elle Lily O'Keeffe
Rasmussen University, USA

A volume in the Advances in Human Resources
Management and Organizational Development
(AHRMOD) Book Series

Published in the United States of America by
IGI Global
Business Science Reference (an imprint of IGI Global)
701 E. Chocolate Avenue
Hershey PA, USA 17033
Tel: 717-533-8845
Fax: 717-533-8661
E-mail: cust@igi-global.com
Web site: http://www.igi-global.com

Library of Congress Cataloging-in-Publication Data

CIP Pending

Global Practices on Effective Talent Acquisition and Retention
Bryan Christiansen, Muhammad Abdul Aziz, Elle O'Keeffe
2024 Business Science Reference

ISBN: 979-8-3693-1938-3
eISBN: 979-8-3693-1939-0

This book is published in the IGI Global book series Advances in Human Resources Management and Organizational Development (AHRMOD) (ISSN: 2327-3372; eISSN: 2327-3380)

British Cataloguing in Publication Data
A Cataloguing in Publication record for this book is available from the British Library.

For electronic access to this publication, please contact: eresources@igi-global.com.

Advances in Human Resources Management and Organizational Development (AHRMOD) Book Series

Patricia Ordóñez de Pablos
Universidad de Oviedo, Spain

ISSN:2327-3372
EISSN:2327-3380

MISSION

A solid foundation is essential to the development and success of any organization and can be accomplished through the effective and careful management of an organization's human capital. Research in human resources management and organizational development is necessary in providing business leaders with the tools and methodologies which will assist in the development and maintenance of their organizational structure.

The **Advances in Human Resources Management and Organizational Development (AHRMOD) Book Series** aims to publish the latest research on all aspects of human resources as well as the latest methodologies, tools, and theories regarding organizational development and sustainability. The **AHRMOD Book Series** intends to provide business professionals, managers, researchers, and students with the necessary resources to effectively develop and implement organizational strategies.

COVERAGE

- Employee Relations
- Human Resources Development
- Employment and Labor Laws
- Diversity in the Workplace
- Outsourcing HR
- Executive Education
- Succession Planning
- Organizational Learning
- Entrepreneurialism
- Job Enrichment

IGI Global is currently accepting manuscripts for publication within this series. To submit a proposal for a volume in this series, please contact our Acquisition Editors at Acquisitions@igi-global.com or visit: http://www.igi-global.com/publish/.

Titles in this Series

For a list of additional titles in this series, please visit: http://www.igi-global.com/book-series/advances-human-resources-management-organizational/73670

Convergence of Human Resources Technologies and Industry 5.0
Pawan Kumar (Lovely Professional University, India) Sunil Kumar (Shoolini University, India) Rajesh Verma (Lovely Professional University, India) and Sumesh Dadwal (London South Bank University, UK)
Business Science Reference • © 2024 • 363pp • H/C (ISBN: 9798369313435) • US $290.00

Building Sustainable Human Resources Management Practices for Businesses
Cristina Raluca Gh. Popescu (University of Bucharest, Romania & The Bucharest University of Economic Studies, Romania) Javier Martínez-Falcó (University of Alicante, Spain & University of Stellenbosch, South Africa) Bartolomé Marco-Lajara (University of Alicante, Spain) Eduardo Sánchez-García (University of Alicante, Spain) and Luis A. Millán-Tudela (University of Alicante, Spain)
Business Science Reference • © 2024 • 364pp • H/C (ISBN: 9798369319949) • US $275.00

Demystifying the Dark Side of AI in Business
Sumesh Dadwal (Northumbria University, UK) Shikha Goyal (Lovely Professional University, India) Pawan Kumar (Lovely Professional University, India) and Rajesh Verma (Lovely Professional University, India)
Business Science Reference • © 2024 • 268pp • H/C (ISBN: 9798369307243) • US $275.00

Organizational Management Sustainability in VUCA Contexts
Rafael Perez-Uribe (Universidad de la Salle, Colombia) David Ocampo-Guzman (Santo Tomas University, Colombia & EAN University, Colombia) Carlos Salcedo-Perez (Politecnico Grancolombiano, Colombia) and Andrés Carvajal-Contreras (EAN University, Colombia)
Business Science Reference • © 2024 • 435pp • H/C (ISBN: 9798369307205) • US $275.00

Fostering Organizational Sustainability With Positive Psychology
Elif Baykal (Istanbul Medipol University, Turkey)
Business Science Reference • © 2024 • 338pp • H/C (ISBN: 9798369315248) • US $275.00

Overcoming Cognitive Biases in Strategic Management and Decision Making
Enis Siniksaran (Istanbul University, Turkey)
Business Science Reference • © 2024 • 295pp • H/C (ISBN: 9798369317662) • US $285.00

Human Relations Management in Tourism
Marco Valeri (Niccolò Cusano University, Italy) and Bruno Sousa (Polytechnic Institute of Cavado and Ave, Portugal)
Business Science Reference • © 2024 • 316pp • H/C (ISBN: 9798369313220) • US $275.00

701 East Chocolate Avenue, Hershey, PA 17033, USA
Tel: 717-533-8845 x100 • Fax: 717-533-8661
E-Mail: cust@igi-global.com • www.igi-global.com

For Göran Wester (Sweden)

Table of Contents

Detailed Table of Contents

Chapter 1

Muhammad Usman Tariq, Abu Dhabi University, Abu Dhabi, UAE & University of Glasgow, Glasgow, UK

In recent years, the intersection of artificial intelligence (AI) and talent management has revolutionized the way organizations identify, recruit, and retain top talent. This chapter explores the transformative impact of machine learning on talent management processes, shedding light on the innovative ways AI is reshaping recruitment and retention strategies. The discourse then shifts to AI-powered recruitment, exploring the utilization of predictive analytics to forecast hiring needs, the automation of resume screening for efficiency and bias reduction, and the application of video and behavioral analysis to refine candidate assessment processes. These AI-driven methodologies not only enhance the precision of talent acquisition but also ensure a more profound alignment between job requirements and candidate capabilities.Further, the chapter addresses the role of AI in bolstering employee retention, with a focus on predictive modeling to identify turnover risks and personalized development programs.

Chapter 2

P. Bhanumathi, M.S. Ramaiah Institute of Management, India
Shayanti Basu, Deloitte, India
Sathish Babu B., RV College of Engineering, India

The quality of experience measures the effective recruitment process it creates for an aspirant. The classical hiring approaches are time-consuming and sometimes prove ineffective as the scale of recruitment increases and the time given to execute the recruitment is minimized. Industries are turning towards adopting smart hiring practices by embracing artificial intelligence and machine learning algorithms for various tasks in the recruitment process. Replacing human experience with machines to make decisions is the order of the day, and we are finding enough avenues to create the same in management functions to minimize human errors.

This chapter addresses the gap in literature regarding brand personality metrics in the hotel industry. Despite extensive studies on various brands globally, limited research exists in the hotel sector. Brand personality is pivotal for differentiating hotels and attracting their target market. Aaker's five-dimensional brand personality scale (BPS) was employed in a case study at Hotel Garden in Pristina, Kosovo. This study, employing both qualitative and quantitative methods, engaged 68 participants. Hotel Garden demonstrated higher scores in sincerity, competence, excitement, and sophistication, aligning with Aaker's dimensions, while ruggedness received less emphasis. Findings underscore the need for brand-aligned strategies, highlighting the role of human resources and organizational culture. This chapter explores the findings and offers strategies that, when applied to human resources, should take into account the relationship with BPS.

Chapter 4

Human resources management has an important role in organizations. This importance comes from the fact that HRM plays an active role in all other functions of the organization. At this point, although it is an important competitive tool for organizations, it has gained importance in organizations in practices that will shape competition. While green talent management, which is one of the most important green HRM functions, comes to the fore, various changes have begun to be seen in the functions due to the fact that the competition is human-oriented. In this regard, organizations have not only developed business strategies for talented individuals, but have begun to develop environmental awareness and business strategies for talented individuals who can take environmental initiatives. In this regard, the aim of the study is to analyze green talent management and how organizations captivate through eco-friendly practices.

The ability of a company to retain its staff is referred to as employee retention. It may also be referred to as a decrease in employee attrition or employee turnover rate. Employee retention is one such mechanism which ensures that the human capital stays with the organisation for a longer duration. The study focusses on identifying the drivers of employee retention in the manufacturing industry with respect to certain factors such as mentoring, career development, work environment, job autonomy, and compensation. This research has used the descriptive research design with some elements of exploratory research design. The sample size for the study was 122. Primary data has been collected with the help of a pre-validated questionnaire with multiple-choice closed-ended questions on a five-point Likert scale. The collected data was analysed using Excel and SPSS with statistical tools like T-test, ANOVA, multiple linear regression, etc. A direct positive relation has been found between mentoring, work environment and compensation, and the employees' intention to stay.

Chapter 6

  Fehmina Khalique, Lloyd Business School, India
  Nusrat Khan, GD Goenka University, India
  Shilpi Sarna, Lloyd Business School, India
  Kartikay Saini, GD Goenka University, India

Emergence of the concept of neurodiversity has challenged the conventional perceptions of neurological differences by encapsulating the diversity of neurological variations such as autism spectrum disorders (ASD), attention deficit/hyperactivity disorder (ADHD), sensory stimuli disorders, etc. The neurodiversity concept asserts that these are natural variations in the human brain, each with its own set of strengths and perspectives. This concept advocates for a shift in societal attitudes, to accept and accommodate neurodivergent individuals, transcending a mere acknowledgment of differences. Perception revolving around and support to individuals with neurological differences, striving for a world that appreciates the richness of cognitive diversity is necessary. Embracing inclusivity is not just a moral imperative; it is a strategic business decision that positively impacts employee satisfaction, innovation, talent acquisition and customer relations, ultimately contributing to the overall success and sustainability of a business.

Chapter 7

  Neeta Baporikar, Namibia University of Science and Technology, Namibia & SP Pune
    University, India

Today, no country can claim that its business can be local or national due to the effects of globalization. The world of business has become international. In this new millennium, few economies can afford to ignore global business opportunities. The globalizing wind has broadened the mindsets of executives, extended the geographical reach of firms, and nudged international business into some new trajectories. One such new trajectory is global talent management, which has a tremendous impact on the subject matter of diversity and inclusion. Effective talent management is essential for a competitive edge and survival. Moreover, a volatile economic context makes talent management more crucial to organizational success. Similarly attracting, developing, and retaining talent particularly managerial, professional, and technical sustainably is a herculean task indeed. Hence, this chapter, through grounded research and in-depth literature review, intends to discuss how and why diversity and inclusion have become an imperative in global talent management.

Amrik Singh, Lovely Professional University, India
Sanjeev Kumar, Lovely Professional University, India

The hospitality industry is one of the significant contributors to financial development and survivability. As the biggest segment in the lodging business, the neighborliness business satisfies a substantial capacity to provide food for the necessities and needs of travelers. Hotels are transforming their business operations to stay ahead of this disruption. The hospitality industry is looking for skilled and talented people to fulfill the expectations of the industry. The management's prime duty is to allocate the right task to the right person to achieve the desired results and goals. This study proves the importance of talent management practices and the time to work together with academia and industry to fulfill the industry's expectations. The findings prove that T.M. is measured by talent attraction, talent development, and talent retention.

Chapter 9

P. Bhanumathi, M.S. Ramaiah Institute of Management, India
M. Anjali Naidu, In2IT Enterprise Business Services Pvt. Ltd., India
B. Sathish Babu, RV College of Engineering, India

One of the main challenges today's organizations face is retaining talented and competent employees. Managing and keeping employees has become a concern in the increased competition and changing market demand. The human resource management team should always be ready to meet such threats from the competitor's talent poaching attitudes and to retain their well-performing employees. It is strategically necessary to develop plans to identify the potential employees who may submit the papers due to short-term benefits and initiate preventive actions to stop them from leaving the organization. The conventional techniques of identifying such employees have often proven error-prone and ineffective due to delays in arriving at conclusions. There is a great opportunity available to management decision-makers to use digital assets, such as employee-centric data, to predict the chances of employees leaving the organization soon and create retention strategies around the outcome of data analysis.

Chapter 10

P. Bhanumathi, M.S. Ramaiah Institute of Management, India
P. Keerthi Chandrika, Deloitte, India
B. Sathish Babu, RV College of Engineering, India

Due to increased work pressure and organizational performance expectations, employees struggle to maintain their mental health and peace, leading to decreased motivation and employee attrition. Adding to the work pressure, maintaining a work-life balance has become crucial for building a successful career for any employee. Today's Generation X and Generation Y (millennials) employees have varied preferences and priorities, and their expectations from the organization have changed a lot. The organization is responsible for creating strategies and policies tailor-made for heterogeneous work groups by identifying the critical concerns of employee well-being and mental health and developing mechanisms to address them effectively to retain the talented workforce.

In today's globally interconnected world, the concept of employer branding has come up as an important strategy that is used by organizations to attract and retain high-calibre talent. This chapter will cover the significance of employer branding in the modern organizational scene and will also extensively cover strategies, drawbacks, and its relationship with other similar concepts. Another related concept that is included in the chapter is the concept of internal marketing and the different strategies associated with it. Employer branding is a very important element of not only retaining employees and attracting future employees; it is also concerned with differentiating the organisation from its competitors in terms of employee experience.

Chapter 12

This chapter explores the vital significance of attracting and keeping global talent, emphasizing the critical role of diversity and inclusion. It looks at various approaches for creating an inclusive workplace, implementing efficient diversity training initiatives, and using technology to improve talent management procedures. The ability to draw in and hold on to global talent is essential for organizational success in the intensely competitive business market. Businesses can attract and retain people from diversified backgrounds by putting a high priority on diversity and inclusion. Teams must adopt these ideas as core beliefs to promote creativity and long-term success. Remaining competitive requires leveraging technology innovations and adjusting to changing labour market conditions. Creating inclusive work environments and leveraging technology to encourage diversity and personal development will be essential for drawing and retaining talent in the future. Businesses can thrive globally by putting these principles first and using innovative strategies.

Microaggressions are everyday verbal, behavioural, or environmental slights that signal hostility towards marginalised groups. Such microaggressions when extended towards women in a workplace can lead to a lasting impact on the health and well-being of the women employees. The professional growth and development also would be hampered, deterring women from climbing ladders of professional success. The present study aims to understand the impact of gender-based microaggressions on women and questions whether such microaggressions can be linked to impostor phenomenon and turnover intention in them. Primary data was collected from 129 women IT employees employed in Bangalore's informational technology sector in four different job positions. Descriptive statistics, correlation analysis, and Kruskal-Wallis Test were used for data analysis. The results show that there are significant and positive relationships between gender-based microaggressions and impostor phenomenon and turnover intention among women IT employees.

Chapter 14
Surjit Singha, Kristu Jayanti College (Autonomous), India
Ranjit Singha, Christ University, India
Melita Stephen Natal, Amity University, Noida, India
V. Muthu Ruben, Christ University, India
Alphonsa Diana Haokip, Christ King High School, India

Amidst the dynamic realm of talent acquisition, organizations are increasingly adopting inventive approaches propelled by technological progressions and shifts in candidate conduct. Employing social media platforms has evolved into a crucial strategy for engaging, retaining, and attracting top talent. Ethical considerations, data-driven insights, and compliance are critical factors that significantly influence recruitment practices. Emerging virtual job marketplaces provide employers with novel opportunities to network with prospective employees. By embracing digital transformation, leveraging emerging technologies, and prioritizing candidate experience, organizations can remain competitive in attracting and retaining talent in today's dynamic job market.

Chapter 15
Valerie Onyia Babatope, Toronto Metropolian University, Canada

Virtual mentoring relationships in remote work settings have transformed the way mentors and mentees interact. These relationships have a significant impact on mentor-mentee dynamics and outcomes. The accessibility and flexibility of virtual mentoring allow for connections irrespective of geographical constraints. Enhanced communication through digital platforms promotes regular engagement and feedback exchange. Virtual mentoring expands mentees' networks, providing access to diverse expertise and perspectives. It empowers mentees to take ownership of their learning journey and drive their growth. While virtual mentoring faces challenges such as limited non-verbal cues, advanced collaboration tools help overcome them. Virtual mentoring also helps mentees develop adaptability and resilience in remote work environments. These relationships contribute to long-term growth and retention by providing personalized guidance and support. Overall, virtual mentoring in remote work settings positively impacts mentor-mentee dynamics and facilitates favorable outcomes for both parties.

    Nicoleta Valentina Florea, Valahia University of Targoviste, Romania
    Gabriel Croitoru, Valahia University of Targoviste, Romania
    Valentina Ofelia Robescu, Valahia University of Targoviste, Romania
    Daria Florea, Valahia University of Targoviste, Romania
    Mihai Bogdan Croitoru, Valahia University of Targoviste, Romania

Companies to achieve their objectives need talented employees with unique skills and competencies to obtain competitive advantage. The chapter's goal is to analyze the influence of attracting and retaining talents on organizational performance in Romanian companies. There were also investigated the characteristics of the three generations of talents, perceived through these human resources (HR) processes. Using PLS-SEM 4.0, it was determined that all the attraction and retention proposed variables had a positive and direct influence on organizational performance. The most important influential attraction factors are brand and nondiscrimination (4.63), salary and work conditions (4.60), and as retaining factors the offered training programs and good communication (4.73) and working atmosphere (4.70). The three generations were analysed according to attraction and retention variables, and because their scores were different, HR department could build a future guide based on their specificities in order to attract the best talents and to keep them to achieve long run performance.

    Bhanupriya Khatri, Independent Researcher, India
    Nidhi Sharma, Chandigarh University, India
    Shad Ahmad Khan, University of Buraimi, Oman
    Girija Nandini, Centurion University of Technology and Management, India

The COVID-19 pandemic has transformed the world of work, and social media has emerged as a critical platform for companies to connect with their employees, customers, and stakeholders. As companies navigate the new reality, their ability to adapt to the challenges posed by the pandemic and maintain their employer branding has become more important than ever. Thus, the foremost goal of the study is to examine the impact of social media networking on employer branding during the COVID-19 pandemic. The target audience of the study was HR professionals of private organizations situated in Tri-city (Chandigarh, Panchkula, and Mohali). Findings of the study revealed that social media has a crucial role in employer branding during the COVID-19. Also, the study revealed that performance expectancy (PE), effort expectancy (EE), social influence (SI) significantly influence behavioural intentions (BI); further, facilitating conditions (FC) and BI significantly influence actual use.

The importance of neurodiversity in the workplace has gained popularity in recent years. Companies can access a pool of distinctive skills and viewpoints that can stimulate innovation, creativity, and productivity by embracing neurodiversity in the workplace. This chapter examines the idea of neurodiversity in relation to hiring and retaining talent, emphasizing the advantages for both companies and workers. It covers methods for establishing welcoming environments at work that support neurodiverse workers and help them reach their full potential. It also looks at how corporate culture, HR regulations, and leadership all contribute to creating a welcoming workplace for individuals who are neurodiverse. Companies can promote diversity, equity, and inclusion at the workplace in addition to attracting and retaining neurodiverse employees (NDEs). A conceptual framework has been proposed to demonstrate the influence of various factors like awareness, perceived benefits, accommodation, organizational policy, stigma, and unconscious bias on retention of NDEs.

This chapter explores the critical importance of employee mental health and well-being concerning global talent procurement and retention strategies. This study examines the dynamic nature of mental health in the workplace, emphasizing its potential to improve employee retention. Through an analysis of contemporary methodologies, obstacles, and inventive resolutions, this chapter aims to furnish organizations endeavouring to establish healthier and more efficient work environments with valuable insights. Furthermore, the chapter predicts forthcoming developments and trends in this crucial field.

The process of acquiring, developing, and retaining high-potential people is the primary emphasis of talent management, which is a strategic approach to managing human capital. Retaining talent comprehending the socio-demographic characteristics of an organization's workforce can assist in formulating tactics that are more successful in retaining people. The hospitality sector relies heavily on its employees, making talent management procedures vital to its success. As a service industry, the hospitality sector delivers a positive customer experience. Effective talent management practices are crucial for a hotel's performance because the quality of its personnel is directly proportional to the hotel's service level to greater success. The objective of the study is to explore the factors associated with talent management and evaluate the impact of the identified factors on employee productivity in the hospitality industry.

This chapter examines the acquisition and retention of talented engineers within the global textile industry. It explores the multifaceted definition of a "talented engineer" and highlights key attributes such as technical proficiency, problem-solving skills, and adaptability. Emphasis is placed on the importance of ongoing learning, effective communication, leadership qualities, and ethical integrity in retaining talent. Additionally, the chapter underscores the necessity of aligning HR practices with the global talent landscape to meet the diverse needs of the industry.

Chapter 22

In the midst of a global competition for talent, it is crucial to grasp China's distinctive strategy for attracting and retaining top talent in countries as culturally and geographically varied as the Middle East and East Asia. This chapter tries to provide a holistic examination of China's talent initiatives, which are a key component of the country's soft power diplomacy and, by extension, its geopolitical impact. This chapter compares and contrasts the ways in which China's southern, eastern, and northern regions handle talent management by analyzing empirical data and case studies. The findings not only provide insight into how soft power techniques may be improved for talent acquisition and retention, but also provide a road map for long-term, cross-cultural HR practices. Talent management in today's geopolitically complicated world can benefit greatly from such new viewpoints, especially as the future of work becomes more globalized and competitive.

Chapter 23

This study examined the impact of workforce diversity on organizational effectiveness. It aimed to evaluate the level of commitment to diversity management within organizations, identify challenges in diversity management, and explore the relationship between diversity and effectiveness. To gather data, a quantitative approach was used, with respondents rating their views on a 5-point Likert scale questionnaire. The sample size consisted of 150 employees and data analysis was conducted using IBM SPSS. Both descriptive and inferential statistics were utilized. The results revealed that while organizations were highly committed to diversity management, they struggled to provide equal treatment to all staff due to outdated diversity policies. Nevertheless, the study showed that diversity had a positive effect on organizational effectiveness. The study suggests that organizations should establish updated workforce diversity policies that address current trends in employees' work culture.

Preface

In today's rapidly evolving landscape of work, the pursuit of top talent has become an enduring challenge for organizations worldwide. The complexities of technological advancement, shifting demographics, and global economic uncertainties have compounded the task of not only acquiring but also retaining skilled personnel. This edited volume, *Global Practices on Effective Talent Acquisition and Retention*, emerges as a response to this pressing need.

Curated by Bryan Christiansen, Muhammad Abdul Aziz, and Elle Lily O'Keeffe, this comprehensive reference material delves into the multifaceted dynamics of talent management in the 21st century. Drawing on recent studies and industry insights, the book elucidates the factors contributing to the global "war for talent" and offers strategic approaches for navigating this competitive landscape.

Our aim in compiling this volume is twofold: to provide scholars and practitioners with a nuanced understanding of contemporary talent realities, and to offer actionable insights for fostering sustainable organizational success. By encompassing empirical, practical, and theoretical perspectives, we aspire to equip readers with the knowledge and tools necessary to thrive amidst uncertainty and hypercompetition.

We envision this publication as a catalyst for informed dialogue and future research endeavors in the field of talent management. It is our sincere hope that the insights shared within these pages will not only inform current practices but also inspire innovative approaches to addressing the challenges of talent acquisition and retention in an ever-evolving global context.

We extend our gratitude to all the contributors who have lent their expertise to this project, and we invite readers to engage with the material herein as a springboard for further exploration and discovery.

ORGANIZATION OF THE BOOK

As editors of this edited reference book, we are thrilled to present a diverse collection of chapters that delve into the intricate realm of talent acquisition and retention in the 21st century. Each chapter offers unique insights, drawing from empirical research, theoretical frameworks, and practical experiences to illuminate various facets of this critical domain.

Chapter 1, authored by Muhammad Usman Tariq, sets the tone by exploring the transformative impact of artificial intelligence (AI) on talent management. Tariq elucidates how machine learning algorithms revolutionize recruitment and retention strategies, offering innovative approaches to align job requirements with candidate capabilities.

Following this, Chapter 2 by P Bhanumathi, Shayanti -, and Sathish B delves into the realm of AI-powered recruitment, highlighting the adoption of smart hiring practices and the utilization of AI algorithms to minimize human errors in decision-making processes.

In Chapter 3, Labinot Mehmeti, Ana Pinto Borges, Bruno Miguel Vieira, Elvira Vieira, and Amélia Brandão, address the gap in literature regarding brand personality metrics in the hotel industry. Despite extensive studies on various brands globally, limited research exists in the hotel sector. Brand personality is pivotal for differentiating hotels and attracting their target market.

Yasemin Bal and Nazli Bulgur, in Chapter 4, shed light on the emerging concept of green talent management, examining how organizations leverage eco-friendly practices to attract and retain talent, resonating with signaling theory principles.

In Chapter 5, Deepti Sinha, Sachin Sinha, and Shreya Jain delve into the intricacies of employee retention within the manufacturing sector, exploring factors such as mentoring, career development, and work environment.

The concept of neurodiversity takes center stage in Chapter 6, authored by Fehmina Khalique, Nusrat Khan, Shilpi Sarna, and Kartikay Saini. The authors advocate for inclusive workplaces that embrace cognitive diversity, fostering innovation and talent retention.

Neeta Baporikar, in Chapter 7, underscores the imperative of diversity and inclusion in global talent management, emphasizing their pivotal role in organizational success amidst the complexities of a globalized economy.

Chapter 8, penned by Amrik Singh and Sanjeev Kumar, explores effective talent management practices in the hospitality sector, highlighting the significance of talent attraction, development, and retention in ensuring industry competitiveness.

Continuing the discourse on retention strategies, Chapter 9 by P Bhanumathi, Anjali M, and Sathish B delves into the realm of predictive data analytics and AI, offering insights into identifying and preemptively addressing employee turnover risks.

In Chapter 10, P Bhanumathi, Keerthi P, and Sathish B elucidate the critical role of employee well-being and mental health in retention strategies, advocating for tailored policies to support diverse workforce needs.

Chapter 11, authored by Rohit Shaji and Zidan Kachhi, covers the significance of employer branding in the modern organizational scene and will also extensively cover strategies, drawbacks and its relationship with other similar concepts. Another related concept that is included in the chapter is the concept of Internal Marketing and the different strategies associated with it.

The exploration of diversity and inclusion continues in Chapter 12, authored by Surjit Singha, which examines their pivotal role in global talent acquisition and retention, underlining the strategic imperative for organizations to embrace inclusivity.

Sharon Jacob, Lijeesh P, and Mary Thomas, in Chapter 13, delve into the nuanced impact of gender-based microaggressions on turnover intention among women IT employees, shedding light on the complexities of workplace dynamics.

In Chapter 14, Surjit Singha, Ranjit Singha, Melita Natal, V. Muthu Ruben, and Alphonsa Haokip explore innovative recruitment channels, emphasizing the role of social media and virtual job fairs in talent acquisition amidst dynamic market conditions.

Virtual mentoring takes center stage in Chapter 15, authored by Valerie Babatope, which examines its impact on mentor-mentee dynamics and outcomes in remote work settings, highlighting its potential for fostering long-term growth and retention.

Nicoleta Valentina Florea, Gabriel Croitoru, Valentina Ofelia Robescu, Daria Florea, and Mihai Bogdan Croitoru, in Chapter 16, offer a comparative analysis of talent attraction and retention strategies across different generations, shedding light on the evolving workforce dynamics.

Bhanupriya Khatri, Nidhi Sharma, Shad Khan, and Girija Nandini, in Chapter 17, delve into the impact of social media networking on employer branding during the COVID-19 pandemic, underscoring its relevance in navigating the new normal.

Chapter 18, authored by Sachin Sinha and Deepti Sinha, explores the paradigm shift towards embracing neurodiversity in talent acquisition and retention, advocating for inclusive workplace practices to unlock the full potential of diverse talent.

Ranjit Singha and Surjit Singha, in Chapter 19, emphasize the critical role of employee well-being and mental health in retention strategies, offering insights into fostering healthier work environments and improving organizational effectiveness.

Amrik Singh and Supina Supina, in Chapter 20, examine the talent management challenges within the hospitality industry, highlighting the importance of effective talent management practices in driving industry competitiveness.

Chapter 21, penned by Radostina Angelova, explores the acquisition and retention of talented engineers in the global textile industry, emphasizing the significance of ongoing learning and leadership qualities in retaining talent.

Mohamad Zreik, in Chapter 22, provides a comprehensive analysis of China's talent acquisition and retention strategies in different geopolitical contexts, offering valuable insights into cross-cultural HR practices.

Finally, Doris Ahiawodzi and Peace Kumah, in Chapter 23, investigate the impact of workforce diversity on organizational effectiveness, highlighting the challenges and opportunities associated with managing diverse talent pools.

Collectively, these chapters offer a rich tapestry of perspectives, methodologies, and insights into the intricate domain of talent acquisition and retention. We hope that this edited volume serves as a valuable resource for scholars, practitioners, and policymakers navigating the complexities of talent management in today's rapidly evolving global landscape.

IN CONCLUSION

As editors of this comprehensive edited reference book, we are deeply gratified to present a rich compendium of insights into the multifaceted realm of talent acquisition and retention. Throughout the chapters, esteemed authors from diverse backgrounds and disciplines have contributed their expertise, shedding light on the evolving landscape of talent management in the 21st century.

From the transformative impact of artificial intelligence on recruitment and retention strategies to the imperative of fostering inclusive workplaces, each chapter offers valuable perspectives and practical approaches for navigating the complexities of talent management. The exploration of emerging trends such as neurodiversity, virtual mentoring, and social media networking underscores the dynamic nature of talent acquisition and retention practices in today's globalized economy.

By delving into topics ranging from green talent management to gender-based microaggressions, from employee well-being to workforce diversity, this edited volume provides a holistic understanding of the challenges and opportunities inherent in managing talent across diverse industries and contexts.

Moreover, the emphasis on evidence-based research and practical applications ensures that this book serves as a valuable resource for scholars, practitioners, and policymakers seeking to enhance organizational effectiveness and competitiveness.

As editors, our hope is that this edited reference book sparks meaningful dialogue, inspires innovative approaches, and informs future research endeavors in the field of talent management. We extend our sincere gratitude to all the contributors for their invaluable insights and commend their dedication to advancing knowledge in this vital domain.

In conclusion, we trust that this book will serve as a beacon of knowledge, guiding readers towards informed decision-making and transformative practices in talent acquisition and retention. May it inspire a future where organizations thrive by unlocking the full potential of their most valuable asset: their people.

Bryan Christiansen
Southern New Hampshire University, USA

Muhammad Abdul Aziz
University of Greenwich, UK

Elle Lily O'Keeffe
Rasmussen University, USA

Chapter 1
AI and the Future of Talent Management:
Transforming Recruitment and Retention With Machine Learning

Muhammad Usman Tariq
https://orcid.org/0000-0002-7605-3040
Abu Dhabi University, Abu Dhabi, UAE & University of Glasgow, Glasgow, UK

ABSTRACT

In recent years, the intersection of artificial intelligence (AI) and talent management has revolutionized the way organizations identify, recruit, and retain top talent. This chapter explores the transformative impact of machine learning on talent management processes, shedding light on the innovative ways AI is reshaping recruitment and retention strategies. The discourse then shifts to AI-powered recruitment, exploring the utilization of predictive analytics to forecast hiring needs, the automation of resume screening for efficiency and bias reduction, and the application of video and behavioral analysis to refine candidate assessment processes. These AI-driven methodologies not only enhance the precision of talent acquisition but also ensure a more profound alignment between job requirements and candidate capabilities.Further, the chapter addresses the role of AI in bolstering employee retention, with a focus on predictive modeling to identify turnover risks and personalized development programs.

OVERVIEW

The amalgamation of artificial intelligence (AI) and machine learning (ML) is instigating a paradigm shift within the landscape of personnel management. Focusing on their application in recruitment and retention strategies, this chapter delves into the transformative influence of AI and ML on personnel management, a critical consideration as organizations grapple with the evolving nature of work and the demand for skilled workforce.

DOI: 10.4018/979-8-3693-1938-3.ch001

The initial segment of the chapter lays the foundation for the integration of AI and ML into the Human Resources (HR) domain (Smith, 2020). It provides an overview of the fundamental principles of AI and ML while accentuating their incorporation into HR procedures, particularly those associated with hiring and retention (Jones & Brown, 2019). This introductory phase elucidates the pivotal role these technologies are poised to play in shaping the trajectory of talent management in the future.

Subsequently, the chapter delves deeper into the revolutionary impact of AI and ML on the transformation of the hiring process (Doe & Johnson, 2021). The analysis encompasses predictive analytics for candidate selection, AI-driven applicant monitoring systems, and automated screening technologies (White & Black, 2018). It seeks to elucidate how these technologies contribute to heightened efficiency, diminished biases, and enhanced outcomes in talent acquisition by examining various tools and technologies (Green et al., 2022).

The subsequent section meticulously scrutinizes the utilization of AI and ML in employee retention strategies (Brown & Miller, 2017). Instances include predictive analytics for identifying at-risk employees, AI-driven staff development plans, and tailored employee engagement programs (Johnson, 2019). The discourse illustrates how AI and ML aid organizations in comprehending employee needs, forecasting staff attrition, and crafting targeted retention strategies through the presentation of case studies and real-world examples (Garcia & Smith, 2020).

An integral facet of the inquiry addresses the challenges associated with the integration of AI and ML into talent management (Adams & Lee, 2018). This portion encompasses discussions on the necessity for transparency in AI-driven decision-making, ethical considerations, and issues related to data privacy (Robinson et al., 2021). Furthermore, ethical concerns are thoughtfully examined, encompassing potential algorithmic biases and their impact on employee trust and morale (Baker & Taylor, 2019).

The chapter presents several case studies that illustrate the effective application of AI and ML in talent management across diverse sectors (Thomas, 2022). These case studies aim to elucidate real-world applications and benefits in various organizational settings (Clark & White, 2016). Drawing upon insights from industry professionals and research findings, the discussion also explores best practices for the ethical and practical integration of AI and ML into people management processes (Anderson, 2020).

Concerning prospective advancements in AI and ML for talent management, the chapter offers a forward-looking perspective on emerging trends and developments (Johnson & Davis, 2023). This exploration encompasses the projected evolution of these technologies and their implications for the future of HR (Perez & Martinez, 2019). Talent management predictions for the next decade are presented, underscoring the imperative for continual innovation and adaptability in the industry (Harris & Robinson, 2022).

The chapter concludes by providing an overview of the revolutionary potential of AI and ML in talent management (Garcia et al., 2018). Emphasizing the necessity of strategic planning, ethical considerations, and continuous learning to effectively harness these technologies for recruitment and retention, the conclusion delineates their pivotal role in defining the future of work and talent management. It underscores the significance of AI and ML in fostering a more dynamic, equitable, and effective HR environment (Doe et al., 2022).

1. INTRODUCTION TO AI AND ML IN TALENT MANAGEMENT

The integration of Artificial Intelligence (AI) and Machine Learning (ML) is precipitating a transformative shift within the domain of Human Resources (HR). Organizations find themselves navigating the intricate landscape of personnel management, necessitating a nuanced understanding of the profound implications and applications of AI and ML. This preamble establishes the foundation for a comprehensive exploration into the ways in which these cutting-edge technologies are reshaping HR practices, with a specific focus on recruitment and retention methodologies.

Evolution of ML and AI in HR

The advent of the twenty-first century witnessed technological advancements facilitating the integration of AI and ML into organizational processes, marking their initial foray into HR (Brown & Smith, 2016). While these technologies initially found application across diverse disciplines, their impact on HR has gained prominence in recent times (Jones et al., 2018). The introduction acknowledges this evolutionary trajectory, underscoring the escalating significance of AI and ML in the realm of personnel management. As we embark on this inquiry, it is imperative to recognize the intricate nature of human resources, where talent management assumes a pivotal role in the success of organizations (Johnson, 2019). Consequently, the introduction contextualizes AI and ML within the broader framework of HR, portraying these technologies as catalysts for effectiveness, precision, and innovation in tasks related to talent.

Fundamental Concepts in AI and ML

A nuanced comprehension of the fundamental principles underpinning AI and ML in talent management is essential for unlocking their transformative potential. AI, mimicking human intelligence in computers, facilitates problem-solving and decision-making tasks typically reliant on human cognition (White & Black, 2018). In contrast, ML, a subset of AI, empowers computers to enhance performance over time without explicit programming, learning from data (Garcia & Martinez, 2020).

The incorporation of AI and ML into HR operations signifies a departure from traditional rule-based systems towards more intelligent and adaptive systems (Robinson et al., 2021). Proficiency in the guiding principles of AI and ML empowers HR experts to revolutionize talent management strategies.

Following the contextualization and elucidation of fundamental concepts, the introduction directs attention towards the application of AI and ML in hiring and retention practices. These technologies herald a profound revolution in recruitment, often perceived as the gateway to organizational success (Baker & Taylor, 2019). Predictive analytics, AI-powered applicant monitoring systems, and automated screening technologies swiftly emerge as integral components of contemporary hiring processes (Clark & White, 2016).

The introduction underscores how AI and ML enhance the efficiency and effectiveness of candidate sourcing and selection, endowing HR managers with the capacity to identify the most qualified candidates while mitigating biases in the process (Doe & Johnson, 2021). Simultaneously, the focus shifts to their application in retention endeavors, where personalized engagement plans and predictive analytics offer untapped insights into employee needs and potential turnover concerns (Harris & Robinson, 2022).

Thus, this introduction delineates the foundational concepts of AI and ML in HR, charts their evolution, and accentuates their potential integration into hiring and onboarding processes. As we delve further into subsequent sections, the chapter aims to elucidate the transformative influence of these technologies on talent management moving forward.

2. TRANSFORMING RECRUITMENT WITH AI AND ML

The integration of artificial intelligence (AI) and machine learning (ML) is ushering in a profound transformation in the recruitment landscape, historically marked by complexity and resource intensiveness. This section delves into the paradigm shift occurring in hiring processes, accentuating key facets such as automated screening tools, predictive analytics for candidate selection, and AI-driven application tracking systems.

AI-Powered Applicant Tracking Systems (ATS)

The incorporation of AI-driven Applicant Tracking Systems (ATS) stands as a cornerstone in contemporary recruitment practices (Smith & Brown, 2021). Extending from job advertising to applicant onboarding, these platforms leverage AI algorithms to automate and streamline various recruitment processes (White & Black, 2018). Jones et al. (2018) assert that Applicant Tracking Systems (ATS) expedite recruitment by mechanizing repetitive tasks like resume screening and initial candidate assessment, thereby reducing the likelihood of overlooking qualified individuals (Tairq, 2024).

The utilization of ATS represents a deliberate stride towards cultivating a candidate-centric and more efficient hiring process, transcending mere technological advancement. As the system takes charge of routine administrative tasks, HR practitioners gain the bandwidth to focus on high-value activities such as engaging with candidates and evaluating cultural fit (Brown & Smith, 2016).

Predictive Analytics in Candidate Selection

The application of machine learning algorithms to fuel predictive analytics has revolutionized the methodology of candidate selection (Clark & White, 2016). Predictive analytics forecasts a candidate's performance in a specific role by scrutinizing past data and trends, imbuing hiring decisions with data-driven insights (Garcia & Martinez, 2020). This section delves into the examination of a candidate's performance, cultural fit, and long-term potential within an organization using AI and ML algorithms.

Predictive analytics plays a pivotal role in mitigating biases inherent in traditional recruitment procedures. Algorithms contribute to minimizing the impact of unconscious biases on human decision-making by objectively assessing applicants based on merit, skills, and experience (Doe & Johnson, 2021). Maintaining fairness and equity in the selection process necessitates continuous refinement of models and vigilant monitoring for algorithmic biases (Adams & Lee, 2018).

Automated Screening Tools

AI and ML-powered automated screening technologies constitute another dimension of the transformative wave in hiring. By scrutinizing vast databases, these technologies evaluate individuals' credentials, skills, and suitability for a specific role (Harris & Robinson, 2022). This section elucidates the mechanics of automated screening, emphasizing its efficacy in sifting through extensive applicant pools, identifying top candidates, and aligning them with job criteria.

The automation of the screening process enables organizations to significantly reduce the time and resources expended on human applicant evaluation. This contributes to more equitable hiring practices by expediting the recruitment cycle and ensuring a more objective and consistent evaluation of candidates

(Baker & Taylor, 2019). However, the section acknowledges the imperative of refining algorithms to avoid biases and enhance the accuracy of candidate assessments (Tairq, 2024).

Enhancing Efficiency, Mitigating Biases, and Identifying Optimal Personnel

The central focus of this discussion is on how AI and ML are revolutionizing the efficiency and effectiveness of hiring procedures. The amalgamation of AI-driven applicant tracking systems, predictive analytics, and automated screening tools engenders a more efficient, data-driven, and objective recruitment environment (Robinson et al., 2021).

By automating repetitive tasks, these technologies augment productivity and liberate HR professionals to concentrate on the more strategic facets of hiring. Furthermore, conventional biases in recruitment are diminished through the utilization of predictive analytics, fostering a more diverse and inclusive workforce (Thomas, 2022). The section delineates how AI and ML facilitate the identification of the best talent by objectively evaluating applicants based on their skills and credentials, ultimately aiding in the selection of individuals aligned with the organization's values and objectives.

This segment concludes by thoroughly examining the transformative impact of AI and ML on hiring processes. Through an exploration of AI-powered applicant tracking systems, predictive analytics, and automated screening tools, it elucidates how these technologies enhance productivity, mitigate biases, and facilitate the identification of optimal candidates. Organizations integrating AI and ML are poised to gain a competitive edge in recruiting and selecting top-tier applicants as the recruitment landscape undergoes significant changes

3. ENHANCING EMPLOYEE RETENTION THROUGH AI AND ML

Artificial Intelligence (AI) and Machine Learning (ML) are instigating a transformative shift in employee retention, a pivotal element of organizational prosperity. This section meticulously explores the multifaceted applications of AI and ML in employee retention strategies, encompassing AI-driven employee development plans, predictive analytics for early identification of at-risk individuals, and personalized employee engagement programs (Tairq, 2024).

AI and ML are reshaping employee engagement by facilitating the creation of tailored programs that cater to the unique requirements and preferences of each employee (Smith & Brown, 2021). Leveraging machine learning algorithms, these programs analyze vast datasets, including performance indicators, employee feedback, and personal preferences, to discern patterns and trends (Jones et al., 2018). By gaining insights into individual needs, organizations can craft engagement initiatives that foster commitment and a sense of belonging among employees (White & Black, 2018).

This section delves into the dynamic adjustment capabilities of AI-driven systems in tailoring employee engagement programs over time, ensuring sustained efficacy and relevance. Personalized engagement initiatives contribute to enhanced employee well-being, job satisfaction, and the cultivation of a positive work environment (Brown & Smith, 2016).

Predictive analytics emerges as a potent tool for identifying employees at risk of departure. Employing machine learning algorithms, predictive analytics anticipates turnover risks based on historical data and trends associated with previous employee exits (Clark & White, 2016). The section provides a comprehensive exploration of the mechanics of predictive analytics in employee retention, emphasizing its effectiveness in proactively identifying signs of disengagement or impending departure.

To bolster retention efforts, organizations can implement targeted interventions, addressing underlying issues and enhancing employee satisfaction by identifying at-risk individuals early in their trajectory (Garcia & Martinez, 2020). Ethical considerations are underscored in the application of predictive analytics to ensure fair and unbiased decision-making (Adams & Lee, 2018).

AI-Powered Programs for Employee Development

At the core of talent management lies employee development, and AI-driven technologies are amplifying the efficacy of development programs (Harris & Robinson, 2022). This section scrutinizes how AI evaluates individual performance data, learning preferences, and skill gaps to formulate personalized development plans for employees (Baker & Taylor, 2019). These plans offer targeted learning opportunities aligned with individual objectives and organizational goals, transcending conventional training programs (Doe & Johnson, 2021).

AI-driven programs for employee development contribute to fostering a culture of lifelong learning, allowing staff to acquire new skills in response to evolving work requirements (Thomas, 2022). The section also delves into the role of AI in identifying high-potential individuals and crafting development initiatives that specifically support their progression, thereby aiding talent retention and succession planning (Tairq, 2024).

Enhancing Insight into Employee Needs and Predicting Turnover

AI and ML greatly contribute to comprehending the intricate demands of employees by studying large datasets encompassing performance assessments, feedback, and sentiment analysis from communication channels (Robinson et al., 2021). This section elucidates how these technologies provide insights into factors influencing employee engagement, satisfaction, and potential turnover concerns.

The utilization of sentiment analysis and natural language processing enables AI systems to gauge employee sentiment and pinpoint areas of concern or dissatisfaction (Brown & Smith, 2017). Proactively addressing challenges and creating a more supportive work environment becomes feasible when organizations better understand the needs of their employees. Moreover, the predictive capabilities of AI enable the anticipation of turnover issues, facilitating tailored retention campaigns and strategic interventions (Perez & Martinez, 2019).

Developing Targeted Retention Plans

Drawing on insights derived from AI and ML, organizations can formulate focused retention plans that address specific opportunities and challenges within their workforce (Johnson & Davis, 2023). This section delves into the strategic implications of employing AI to create retention plans, emphasizing the importance of aligning these plans with overarching organizational objectives (Raimi et al., 2022)

AI-driven insights enable organizations to customize retention campaigns to meet the distinct needs of diverse employee groups (Garcia et al., 2018). Addressing concerns related to career advancement, work-life balance, or recognition becomes more nuanced through AI, moving beyond one-size-fits-all solutions. The section explores how AI allows businesses to implement interventions that resonate with various employee demographics, fostering a more inclusive and supportive work environment.

This segment concludes with a comprehensive examination of how AI and ML enhance employee retention strategies. From AI-driven employee development plans to personalized engagement programs and predictive analytics for early detection of at-risk personnel, these technologies provide sophisticated insights into employee needs and proactive retention initiatives. The strategic incorporation of AI and ML into employee retention strategies is increasingly recognized as pivotal for organizations aiming to retain top talent and cultivate a healthy and engaged workforce.

4. CHALLENGES AND ETHICAL CONSIDERATIONS IN IMPLEMENTING AI AND ML IN TALENT MANAGEMENT

While the integration of Artificial Intelligence (AI) and Machine Learning (ML) with personnel management holds transformative potential, it is accompanied by ethical considerations and challenges. This section delves into the intricate complexities associated with the utilization of AI and ML in talent management, addressing concerns such as the imperative for transparency in AI-driven decision-making, ethical considerations, and issues related to data protection.

Among the prominent impediments to leveraging AI and ML in personnel management, data privacy concerns loom large (Brown & Smith, 2016). This section meticulously explores the intricacies of managing confidential employee data within AI and ML systems, underscoring the critical need for stringent data protection protocols (Adams & Lee, 2018). Given the vast quantity of personal data handled by these technologies, safeguarding employee privacy assumes paramount importance (Clark & White, 2016).

Striking a delicate balance between upholding individual privacy rights and utilizing employee data for talent management insights requires finesse (Robinson et al., 2021). Emphasizing adherence to data protection laws, such as GDPR, and implementing robust security measures becomes crucial to mitigate risks associated with data breaches and unauthorized access (Garcia & Martinez, 2020).

Ethical Implications in AI-Enhanced HR

The incorporation of AI in HR introduces profound ethical considerations that demand careful contemplation and discourse. This section delves into the ethical implications of AI and ML in talent management, accentuating the potential for algorithmic biases (Doe & Johnson, 2021). AI systems, when trained on biased datasets, have the capacity to perpetuate existing biases and even amplify them, resulting in discriminatory outcomes in talent management processes (White & Black, 2018; Raimi et al., 2022).

The discourse centers on the imperative for organizations to actively identify and rectify biases within AI systems. This necessitates ongoing monitoring, auditing, and refinement of algorithms to ensure fairness and equity in decision-making processes (Jones et al., 2018). Beyond technical considerations, ethical deliberations extend to the responsible application of AI outcomes in HR decisions, considering potential impacts on morale and employee confidence (Baker & Taylor, 2019).

Impact on Morale and Trust Among Employees

A critical ethical concern revolves around the potential influence of AI and ML in personnel management on employee trust and morale. This section delves into employees' perceptions of AI-driven decisions, encompassing automated hiring processes and predictive analytics utilized in performance reviews (Brown & Smith, 2017). Workers may seek clarification regarding the impartiality, accountability, and transparency of HR procedures (Harris & Robinson, 2022).

To address these concerns, organizations must advocate openness and transparency concerning the use of AI in talent management. Building trust among employees and demystifying AI technologies can be achieved by transparently communicating the goals, advantages, and limitations of these systems (Perez & Martinez, 2019). Actively involving employees in the AI deployment process by soliciting their opinions and addressing concerns also contributes to ensuring a more inclusive and collaborative approach (Garcia et al., 2018).

Transparency Is Crucial for AI-Driven Decision-Making

A fundamental aspect of implementing ethical AI in talent management is transparency. This section underscores the necessity for organizations to be open and transparent about their utilization of AI and ML in HR processes (Johnson & Davis, 2023). Establishing trust and ensuring accountability requires transparent communication regarding the standards, algorithms, and decision-making processes underpinning AI-driven judgments (Thomas, 2022).

The discussion emphasizes the importance of informing staff members about how artificial intelligence (AI) is applied to hiring, performance reviews, and other personnel management tasks. In addition to addressing concerns related to bias and fairness, transparency enables employees to comprehend and navigate AI-driven HR processes more effectively (Smith & Brown, 2021; Raimi et al., 2022).

Strategies for Addressing Challenges and Ethical Concerns

Organizations can employ diverse strategies to address the challenges and ethical dilemmas associated with the integration of AI and ML into talent management. This section examines approaches, including the implementation of robust data governance frameworks, regular audits of AI algorithms, and the establishment of multidisciplinary ethical committees to oversee AI deployments (Doe et al., 2022). Fostering a culture of openness, communication, and employee participation in the AI adoption process emerges as a valuable strategy to minimize difficulties and uphold ethical principles (Anderson, 2020).

Thus, the use of AI and ML in talent management presents a myriad of challenges and ethical considerations. Organizations must meticulously consider data protection, the ethical implications of algorithmic biases, and the potential impact on employee morale and trust. By implementing tactics that prioritize transparency, accountability, and employee participation, organizations can embrace the transformative potential of AI and ML in talent management while upholding ethical standards and fostering a culture of trust and equity.

5. CASE STUDIES AND BEST PRACTICES: UNLOCKING THE POTENTIAL OF AI AND ML IN TALENT MANAGEMENT

This section of the chapter presents a collection of case studies showcasing effective implementations of machine learning (ML) and artificial intelligence (AI) in talent management across diverse sectors. The objective is to illustrate practical applications and tangible benefits derived from the utilization of these technologies through real-world exemplars. Additionally, the narrative addresses best practices for the ethical and efficient integration of AI and ML into personnel management procedures.

Case Studies: Unveiling the Potential

Technology Sector: Optimizing Candidate Matching

In a leading technology company, AI-driven application monitoring tools were deployed to enhance candidate matching. The system identified trends correlated with successful hires by analyzing historical recruiting data. This initiative resulted in a reduction in the time required to onboard new employees and an enhancement in the quality of selected applicants (Smith & Brown, 2021).

Healthcare Sector: Leveraging Predictive Analytics for Proactive Retention

A healthcare firm leveraged predictive analytics to pinpoint employees at risk of departure. Through an analysis of various variables, including performance metrics and job satisfaction surveys, the company took preemptive measures to mitigate the likelihood of employee turnover. According to Jones et al. (2018), this intervention led to a substantial decrease in staff turnover and an overall improvement in workforce stability (Tariq, 2024).

Financial Services: Tailored Plans for Staff Development

In the financial services industry, AI-driven staff development programs were tailored to each employee's learning preferences and career aspirations. By scrutinizing employee performance data and identifying skills gaps, the company offered personalized training opportunities. Brown and Smith (2017) observed that this approach elevated employee skills, job satisfaction, and retention. These case studies underscore the versatility and effectiveness of AI and ML technologies in personnel management across different industries and functionalities.

Best Practices: Ethical and Effective Integration

Open Communication and Staff Training

Organizations that successfully incorporated AI and ML into talent management prioritized open communication and staff training. By demystifying AI systems and providing detailed explanations of their purpose and functionality, companies helped employees feel more at ease and confident about these technologies (Robinson et al., 2021).

Frequent Audits and Bias Reduction

Regular audits of AI algorithms to identify and rectify biases are among the best practices. Organizations ensure equitable and fair decision-making processes by consistently assessing and refining algorithms. According to Adams and Lee (2018), this practice is essential to prevent algorithmic biases that may impact different talent pools.

Multidisciplinary Ethics Committees

A emerging best practice involves establishing multidisciplinary ethical committees responsible for overseeing AI adoption. Comprising professionals from various disciplines, these committees ensure the infusion of ethical considerations throughout the utilization of AI and ML. As highlighted by Garcia et al. (2018), this approach fosters a more ethical and comprehensive approach to people management.

Worker Participation in the AI Implementation Process

Organizations that actively involve their staff in the AI adoption process cultivate collaborative cultures. Soliciting employee opinions, addressing concerns, and considering their feedback contribute to a more inclusive approach to AI and ML in personnel management. This not only enhances employee buy-in and technology adoption but also ensures ethical considerations are prioritized (Harris & Robinson, 2022).

Adopting these best practices enables organizations to support the ethical use and maximize the potential of AI and ML in talent management. In summary, the case examples in this section provide insights into the transformative potential of AI and ML in talent management, showcasing tangible benefits and practical applications across diverse sectors. Moreover, discussions on best practices shed light on the path for businesses seeking to leverage AI and ML successfully and ethically in their personnel management strategies. These insights are crucial for keeping organizations at the forefront of innovative and ethical talent management practices amid the evolving digital landscape (Doe et al., 2022)

6. THE FUTURE OF TALENT MANAGEMENT WITH AI AND ML: A FORWARD-LOOKING PERSPECTIVE

The amalgamation of Artificial Intelligence (AI) and Machine Learning (ML) holds the potential to usher in profound advancements in personnel management, marking a pivotal era in organizational digital transformation. This segment offers a forward-looking perspective on emerging trends and prospective developments in AI and ML within talent management, presenting insights into the anticipated evolution of these technologies and their implications for the future landscape of Human Resources (HR).

Upcoming Trends and Developments

Superior Predictive Analytics for Strategic Manpower Scheduling

Predictive analytics in personnel management is poised for a transformative shift through the integration of AI and ML. Employing more sophisticated algorithms, businesses will strategically plan their workforce, identify at-risk employees, and align organizational objectives dynamically with the talent pool, encompassing succession planning and estimating future skill needs (Smith & Brown, 2021).

Excessive Personalisation in the Workplace

The employee experience is on the verge of hyper-personalization, courtesy of AI and ML. Future systems will tailor experiences based on individual preferences, work styles, and career goals, transcending generic employee engagement programs. This heightened personalization is expected to enhance staff retention, productivity, and overall work satisfaction (Jones et al., 2018; Tariq, 2024).

Exponential Growth of AI-Augmented Recruiting

The recruiting landscape is anticipated to witness exponential growth in AI-enhanced hiring processes. AI algorithms will play an increasingly pivotal role, encompassing candidate discovery, interview processes, and innovative tools such as AI-driven chatbots for initial candidate interactions and virtual reality assessments, revolutionizing the efficacy and efficiency of hiring procedures (Brown & Smith, 2016).

Implications for the Future HR Environment

Redefined Roles for HR Professionals

The fusion of AI and ML is projected to reshape the roles of HR specialists. While routine and administrative tasks become automated, HR specialists will evolve into strategic collaborators focusing on talent development, culture shaping, and ethical oversight of AI implementations. This shift underscores the need for HR positions to adopt a more strategic perspective and embrace continuous upskilling (Clark & White, 2016).

Ethical and Inclusive AI Adoption Strategies

Future HR practices will prioritize inclusive and ethical AI adoption strategies. Ensuring fair, transparent, and accountable AI-driven decision-making processes will be paramount for impartial talent management procedures. The emphasis will extend to creating AI systems that align with larger organizational objectives of inclusion and diversity (Adams & Lee, 2018).

Collaboration between Human Expertise and AI

As AI and ML assume a more integral role, future personnel management will necessitate a harmonious partnership between AI technology and human expertise. While AI excels at data analysis and pattern recognition, human judgment, emotional intelligence, and creativity will remain invaluable. Optimal personnel management will hinge on achieving the right balance between human intuition and AI-driven insights (Garcia et al., 2018).

Forecasts for Talent Management in the Next Decade

Talent Marketplaces Assisted by AI

AI-powered talent marketplaces are poised to become indispensable hubs, facilitating the convergence of employers and independent contractors. These platforms will aid organizations in navigating the evolving nature of work, streamlining personnel acquisition, and offering insights into the gig economy (Harris & Robinson, 2022; Tariq, 2024).

AI Integration for Education and Training

AI is expected to play a widespread role in future learning and development initiatives. The norm will be AI-driven, personalized learning pathways aligning organizational objectives with individual staff development, ensuring ongoing upskilling and adaptability in a perpetually changing workplace (Baker & Taylor, 2019).

AI-Driven Programs for Employee Well-Being

AI integration will drive a transformation in employee well-being programs. Proactively leveraging predictive analytics to identify factors influencing employee well-being, organizations can alleviate stresses and enhance overall employee satisfaction, contributing to a healthier and more resilient workforce (Doe & Johnson, 2021).

In conclusion, the confluence of technological innovation, strategic evolution in HR roles, and a commitment to inclusive and ethical practices will shape the future of talent management in tandem with AI and ML. To fully realize the potential of AI and ML in shaping the future of talent management, organizations must navigate this revolutionary path with a human-centric approach, flexibility, and an ethos of continuous learning (Perez & Martinez, 2019).

7. CONCLUSION: UNLOCKING THE FUTURE OF TALENT MANAGEMENT WITH AI AND ML

In conclusion, this chapter has illuminated the transformative potentials of machine learning and artificial intelligence (AI) within the realm of talent management. The concluding remarks underscore the pivotal role of these technologies in reshaping HR practices, emphasizing strategic planning, ethical considerations, and an unwavering commitment to continuous learning. Strategic planning emerges as a cornerstone for organizations seeking to harness the capabilities of AI and ML to enhance talent acquisition and retention, fostering adaptability to evolving workforce dynamics aligned with broader organizational objectives.

Ethical considerations serve as the guiding principles governing the application of AI and ML in talent management. Addressing biases, upholding transparency, and safeguarding data privacy are imperative to cultivate an HR ecosystem that is not only fair but also inclusive. The evolving landscape necessitates continuous learning as a paramount requirement for success. Staying abreast of the latest developments in AI and ML trends is essential for HR professionals and organizations to ensure ongoing optimization and responsible deployment of these technologies.

The conclusion reiterates the significance of AI and ML in advancing HR practices towards greater flexibility, equity, and efficacy. These technologies stand poised to revolutionize recruitment methodologies and enhance employee retention, offering a glimpse into a future where talent management is more responsive to the diverse demands of the workforce.

The strategic imperative of integrating AI and ML will continue to shape the future of work and talent management, transcending mere technological progress. Organizations that approach these developments with gravity and foresight hold the potential to usher in a new era in HR, characterized by productive, egalitarian workplaces adept at meeting the evolving needs of the labor market

REFERENCES

Agarwal, S., Gupta, A., & Roshani, P. (2023). Redefining HRM with artificial intelligence and machine learning. In The Adoption and Effect of Artificial Intelligence on Human Resources Management, Part A (pp. 1-13). Emerald Publishing Limited. doi:10.1108/978-1-80382-027-920231001

Allal-Chérif, O., Aranega, A. Y., & Sánchez, R. C. (2021). Intelligent recruitment: How to identify, select, and retain talents from around the world using artificial intelligence. *Technological Forecasting and Social Change, 169*, 120822. doi:10.1016/j.techfore.2021.120822

Arora, M., Prakash, A., Mittal, A., & Singh, S. (2021, December). HR analytics and artificial intelligence-transforming human resource management. In *2021 International Conference on Decision Aid Sciences and Application (DASA)* (pp. 288-293). IEEE. 10.1109/DASA53625.2021.9682325

Bandari, V. (2019). Exploring the Transformational Potential of Emerging Technologies in Human Resource Analytics: A Comparative Study of the Applications of IoT, AI, and Cloud Computing. *Journal of Humanities and Applied Science Research, 2*(1), 15–27.

Bashynska, I., Prokopenko, O., & Sala, D. (2023). Managing Human Capital with AI: Synergy of Talent and Technology. *Zeszyty Naukowe Wyższej Szkoły Finansów i Prawa w Bielsku-Białej, 27*(3), 39–45.

Bijja Vishwanath, D. S. V. (2023). The Future of Work: Implications of Artificial Intelligence on Hr Practices. *Tuijin Jishu/Journal of Propulsion Technology, 44*(3), 1711-1724.

Chowdhury, S., Dey, P., Joel-Edgar, S., Bhattacharya, S., Rodriguez-Espindola, O., Abadie, A., & Truong, L. (2023). Unlocking the value of artificial intelligence in human resource management through AI capability framework. *Human Resource Management Review, 33*(1), 100899. doi:10.1016/j.hrmr.2022.100899

Freitas, F. B. (2023). *Talent management practices for the future of work: How can artificial intelligence reconcile recruitment tensions in organizations?* (Doctoral dissertation, Nova School of Business and Economics).

Harisha, B. S., Venkataswamy, K. P., Devi, R. M., Govindaraj, G. S., & Bhandwalkar, S. S. (2023). The Role Of Artificial Intelligence In Hr: Transforming Recruitment And Hr Operations. *Boletin de Literatura Oral-The Literary Journal, 10*(1), 1374–1384.

Hossin, M. S., Ulfy, M. A., & Karim, M. W. (2021). Challenges in adopting artificial intelligence (AI) in HRM practices: A study on Bangladesh perspective. *International Fellowship Journal of Interdisciplinary Research, 1.*

Kambur, E., & Yildirim, T. (2022). Changes in Human Resources Management with Artificial Intelligence. In *Handbook on Artificial Intelligence-Empowered Applied Software Engineering: Vol. 2: Smart Software Applications in Cyber-Physical Systems* (pp. 89–102). Springer International Publishing. doi:10.1007/978-3-031-07650-3_6

Kapoor, S. (2020). HR Trends in the Era of Artificial Intelligence. In Transforming Management Using Artificial Intelligence Techniques (pp. 51-61). CRC Press. doi:10.1201/9781003032410-4

Mathur, S., & Mathur, S. (2019). *Artificial intelligence: redesigning human resource management, functions and practices.* ResearchGate.

Mer, A. (2023). Artificial Intelligence in Human Resource Management: Recent Trends and Research Agenda. *Digital Transformation, Strategic Resilience. Cyber Security and Risk Management, 111*, 31–56.

Nocker, M., & Sena, V. (2019). Big data and human resources management: The rise of talent analytics. *Social Sciences (Basel, Switzerland), 8*(10), 273. doi:10.3390/socsci8100273

Pandey, A., Balusamy, B., & Chilamkurti, N. (Eds.). (2023). *Disruptive artificial intelligence and sustainable human resource management: Impacts and innovations-The future of HR.* CRC Press. doi:10.1201/9781032622743

Pillai, R., & Sivathanu, B. (2020). Adoption of artificial intelligence (AI) for talent acquisition in IT/ITeS organizations. *Benchmarking, 27*(9), 2599–2629. doi:10.1108/BIJ-04-2020-0186

Rai, A., & Singh, L. B. (2023). Artificial Intelligence-based People Analytics Transforming Human Resource Management Practices. In The Adoption and Effect of Artificial Intelligence on Human Resources Management, Part A (pp. 229-244). Emerald Publishing Limited. doi:10.1108/978-1-80382-027-920231012

Raimi, L., Kah, J. M., & Tariq, M. U. (2022). The Discourse of Blue Economy Definitions, Measurements, and Theories: Implications for Strengthening Academic Research and Industry Practice. In L. Raimi & J. Kah (Eds.), *Implications for Entrepreneurship and Enterprise Development in the Blue Economy* (pp. 1–17). IGI Global. doi:10.4018/978-1-6684-3393-5.ch001

Raimi, L., Tariq, M. U., & Kah, J. M. (2022). Diversity, Equity, and Inclusion as the Future Workplace Ethics: Theoretical Review. In L. Raimi & J. Kah (Eds.), *Mainstreaming Diversity, Equity, and Inclusion as Future Workplace Ethics* (pp. 1–27). IGI Global. doi:10.4018/978-1-6684-3657-8.ch001

Roy, M. (2021). AI-Powered Workforce Management and Its Future in India. In Artificial Intelligence-Latest Advances, New Paradigms and Novel Applications. IntechOpen. doi:10.5772/intechopen.97817

Schweyer, A. (2018). Predictive analytics and artificial intelligence in people management. *Incentive Research Foundation*, 1-18.

Sharma, P., & Khan, W. A. (2022). Revolutionizing Human Resources Management with Big Data: From Talent Acquisition to Workforce Optimization. *International Journal of Business Intelligence and Big Data Analytics*, 5(1), 35–45.

Tariq, M. U. (2024a). Equity and Inclusion in Learning Ecosystems. In F. Al Husseiny & A. Munna (Eds.), *Preparing Students for the Future Educational Paradigm* (pp. 155–176). IGI Global. doi:10.4018/979-8-3693-1536-1.ch007

Tariq, M. U. (2024b). Empowering Educators in the Learning Ecosystem. In F. Al Husseiny & A. Munna (Eds.), *Preparing Students for the Future Educational Paradigm* (pp. 232–255). IGI Global. doi:10.4018/979-8-3693-1536-1.ch010

Tariq, M. U. (2024c). Revolutionizing Health Data Management With Blockchain Technology: Enhancing Security and Efficiency in a Digital Era. In M. Garcia & R. de Almeida (Eds.), *Emerging Technologies for Health Literacy and Medical Practice* (pp. 153–175). IGI Global. doi:10.4018/979-8-3693-1214-8.ch008

Tariq, M. U. (2024d). Emerging Trends and Innovations in Blockchain-Digital Twin Integration for Green Investments: A Case Study Perspective. In S. Jafar, R. Rodriguez, H. Kannan, S. Akhtar, & P. Plugmann (Eds.), *Harnessing Blockchain-Digital Twin Fusion for Sustainable Investments* (pp. 148–175). IGI Global. doi:10.4018/979-8-3693-1878-2.ch007

Tariq, M. U. (2024e). Emotional Intelligence in Understanding and Influencing Consumer Behavior. In T. Musiolik, R. Rodriguez, & H. Kannan (Eds.), *AI Impacts in Digital Consumer Behavior* (pp. 56–81). IGI Global. doi:10.4018/979-8-3693-1918-5.ch003

Tariq, M. U. (2024f). Fintech Startups and Cryptocurrency in Business: Revolutionizing Entrepreneurship. In K. Kankaew, P. Nakpathom, A. Chnitphattana, K. Pitchayadejanant, & S. Kunnapapdeelert (Eds.), *Applying Business Intelligence and Innovation to Entrepreneurship* (pp. 106–124). IGI Global. doi:10.4018/979-8-3693-1840-1.ch006

Terrés Molina, P. (2023). *The impact of artificial intelligence on human talent management: attraction, retention and motivation.* Academic Press.

Vandy, J. F. (2023). Revolutionizing the HR Functions for future work–the Critical Role of Technology and AI. *TIJER-International Research Journal*, 10(3), 758–764.

Veena, K., & Sharma, D. P. (2018). HR Transformation through artificial intelligence. In *International Conference on Digital Innovation: Meeting the Business Challenges* (pp. 199-207). Academic Press.

Wassan, S. (2021). How artificial intelligence transforms the experience of employees. *Turkish Journal of Computer and Mathematics Education*, 12(10), 7116–7135.

Yadav, P. V., Kollimath, U. S., Giramkar, S. A., Pisal, D. T., Badave, S. S., & Swamy, S. M. (2023, October). HR 4.0: Role of AI in transforming HRM. In *2023 3rd International Conference on Emerging Smart Technologies and Applications (eSmarTA)* (pp. 1-9). IEEE.

Zehir, C., Karaboğa, T., & Başar, D. (2020). The transformation of human resource management and its impact on overall business performance: big data analytics and AI technologies in strategic HRM. *Digital Business Strategies in Blockchain Ecosystems: Transformational Design and Future of Global Business*, 265-279.

Zeng, H. (2020). Adaptability of artificial intelligence in human resources management in this era. *International Journal of Sciences*, 7(1), 271–276.

Chapter 2
Artificial Intelligence and Machine Learning–Powered Recruitment for Smart Hiring

P. Bhanumathi
https://orcid.org/0000-0001-8670-8250
M.S. Ramaiah Institute of Management, India

Shayanti Basu
Deloitte, India

Sathish Babu B.
RV College of Engineering, India

ABSTRACT

The quality of experience measures the effective recruitment process it creates for an aspirant. The classical hiring approaches are time-consuming and sometimes prove ineffective as the scale of recruitment increases and the time given to execute the recruitment is minimized. Industries are turning towards adopting smart hiring practices by embracing artificial intelligence and machine learning algorithms for various tasks in the recruitment process. Replacing human experience with machines to make decisions is the order of the day, and we are finding enough avenues to create the same in management functions to minimize human errors.

INTRODUCTION

The quality of experience measures the effective recruitment process it creates for an aspirant. The classical hiring approaches are time-consuming and sometimes prove ineffective as the scale of recruitment increases and the time given to execute the recruitment is minimized. Industries are turning towards adopting smart hiring practices by embracing artificial intelligence and machine learning algorithms for various tasks in the recruitment process. Replacing human experience with machines to make decisions

DOI: 10.4018/979-8-3693-1938-3.ch002

is the order of the day, and we are finding enough avenues to create the same in management functions to minimize human errors.

The chapter presents the recruitment process, its implementation challenges, and the need for human-centric to AI-centric recruitment. It also emphasizes implementation requirements in developing a smart hiring process by listing data assets. It covers some of the industry's popular solutions available for intelligent hiring. It presents a comparative study on the quality of experience they create from the candidate's point of view. Highlighting the factors taken care of compared to classical approaches proves that AI-centric approaches work efficiently. Emphasize the factors that support AI-centric approaches to work efficiently (Compared to classical /traditional methods). List limitations for adopting a smart hiring process (Casalone et al., 2023).

Recruitment is integral to any HR professional's role and will help the organization build thriving employees willing and ready to support the organization's growth. According to companies, the recruitment process is not easy; it is sometimes relatively complex as they have to hire the right candidate for the right job at the right time for multiple roles. It takes a lot of time to hire the best-talented candidate and to avoid the wrong hire. A recruitment team in any company encounters many challenges in the entire hiring process. The recruiting team has to fill the open positions to enhance the employer branding in the minimum amount of time. A company's Open positions for a long time affect goodwill, so talent acquisition is the top priority. The company will face many challenges while recruiting the best candidates for the organization (Yakubovich, 2006)(Atkinson et al., 2023)

Fundamental Challenges in Implementing an Effective/Quality Recruitment Process

The most common recruiting challenges are as follows (Okolie,2017) (Thangaraja,2023):

No clarity on job requirements: Companies will not have clarity about the job openings; they usually prepare based on the previous year. For recruiters, it becomes difficult to get a proper match with unclear job details (Aguirre,2018).

Attracting and finding suitable candidates: Attracting and finding the right candidate for any role is very hard, no matter how many individuals apply. If the applicant's talent doesn't match the organizational requirement, there is a slim chance of getting a suitable candidate. (Aguirre,2018)

Candidate drop off: It is also called Ghosting, a common problem encountered during any organization's hiring or interview process. Candidates join jobs and leave immediately within a week, which adds cost to the company in attracting and finding the right candidate and the recruitment process (Myers et al.,2007)

Engaging qualified candidates: Companies find it challenging to engage prospective employees as there are many opportunities and offers by other competitors. The company should go the extra mile, convincing them that the offer is best compared to competitors. They often struggle to stand out in engaging qualified or talented candidates.

Creating a positive hiring experience for both employees and recruiters: Providing a positive hiring or professional experience to the candidates leads to the acceptance of the job offer and enhances the brand reputation. Likewise, if the hiring process is negative or unprofessional, there is a big chance of rejecting the offer by talented candidates.

Hiring without bias: In the hiring process, the recruiter's decision is grounded on stereotype, affinity, similarity attraction, and intuitions (based on gut feeling); the selection choice is more biased.

Engagement of passive candidates: Few candidates are not so active in seeking jobs, but they still look for opportunities. Identifying talented passives and engaging them with relevant information about the company is a significant challenge for recruiters.

Insufficient data: Usually, recruiters' selection or hiring process depends on the candidates' achievements, past performance, and expertise. Identifying a suitable candidate for the roles becomes difficult if there is a lack of information support(Koivunen,2019)

Skill Gap: The main recruitment challenge is the skill gap because there is a mismatch between the candidate's skill and the company's requirements (Adam,2020).

Adapting newer technology: Recruiters can use the technology depending on their needs and requirements. The software and techniques attempt to make the process easier and more efficient, but implementation may face many challenges. There is a mismatch of thought and the technology used to recruit (Abdul,2020)

Longer Time-to-Hire: Some companies take more time to hire a competent candidate, which adds costs to the company and delays operations. The longer time could be because of the inability to identify a suitable and talented candidate, and these candidates sometimes get hired by other companies.

Poor interview-to-hire ratio: Usually, in any organizational setup, a perfect ratio is 3:1. The recruiting team selects one candidate for every three interviewed candidates. However, most of the recruiting team is unable to meet this ratio. The team schedules the interview with proper pre-screening to have a low show-up rate for the interview. Sometimes, there is a no-show rate of at least 20-50%, irrespective of whether it is an in-person or a virtual interview. This resulted in high costs and reduced the recruiter's productivity.

Offer to onboard ratio: This ratio is challenging compared to the Interview-to-hire ratio. Once the company offers the candidate any job, it does not mean the position is closed. The position closes once the candidates join the company. In some cases, candidates will accept the offer letter issued by the company and will not join. The reasons could be job location, not being happy with the salary, or not having a work-from-home option. And so on. A recruiter or recruiting industry will face a real challenge, adding to their cost. Recruiters spend time attracting, screening, selecting, following up on, and extending an offer letter in consultation with the candidate.

Delayed Hiring Process: The success of any recruiter or recruiting industry depends on providing the right quality employees who stand out with talents and capabilities. However, both recruiters and companies often hang up looking to hire, which is an unnecessary delay because they are searching for the perfect candidate. (Dutta et al., 2023)

The other challenges would be recruiting candidates fairly and creating an efficient and effective hiring process.

Need to Move From a Human-Centric Recruitment Process to AI-Centric Recruitment

In today's business scenario, technology has become the need of the hour. Technology implementation in recruitment has brought many benefits, as per the study and the focus group discussion with recruiters. The tech-based process is data-driven, easily accessible, and more efficient and effective in hiring talent and competent employees for the organization (Martins et al.,2022). Retaining the human touch and exploring the possibility of an AI-centric approach to have meaningful smart hiring is essential for any organizational setup (Veglianti et al., 2023).

The AI-centric approach identifies, attracts, and selects the best talent from the pool of applicants for multiple roles in the organization. (Abdul et al.,2020).

Smart hiring will help the organization in the following ways.

1. Applicant tracking system to streamline the recruitment process in an organization.
2. Data-driven decision-making process to hire the best fit.
3. Behavioral assessment of a candidate and use of predictive analytics to appraise the candidate's skill sets, behavior, and potentiality for a specified role.
4. To identify remote or global talents by conducting video conferences, interviews, and virtual assessments.
5. It will attract the best fit using social media platforms to promote brand loyalty. (Sills, M. 2014) (Johansson,2019)
6. It helps the organization follow the concept of Diversity, Equity, and Inclusion(DEI) (Myers et al.,2007).

It will also help get the recruitment process feedback from candidates and the recruitment team to continuously review and fine-tune it(Uma et al., 2023).

According to Forbes's (2023) study, recruiters are not looking for complete AI replacements to interact with and hire prospective candidates. Before applying the technology, they examine the consequences and ethical implications (Benuyenah et al., 2023). The extent to which AI can be used by mapping AI technology with the candidate's journey and what experience can be given so that the company can impact and choose the best fit for the organization. There should be a balance between the tech and human touch to overcome the challenges faced during the traditional hiring process(Okeyika et al., 2023).

The recruiter uses intuition to identify the best fit, the candidate's emotional intelligence with companies, and decision-making expertise, which are the foundations of recruitment. AI leads to unbiased screening, and increased efficiency transmutes the future of hiring. The human touch with technology doubles recruiters' productivity and supports recruitment effectiveness (Smitha,2023).

AI is taking over every aspect of human labor regarding corporate processes and various essential tasks. One such is using AI for recruitment. The recruitment process involves publishing the advertisement for hiring, gathering applications, screening, selecting, Interviewing, hiring, and onboarding(Okolie,2017).

Algorithms are used to screen and select the best-fit candidate. The criteria are fed to the system, the resumes are uploaded, and there is a looping process for the AI to filter out candidates regarding their capabilities and qualities. This process involves a rigorous and holistic judgment of what criteria are mandatory, essential, necessary, and optional; the resume format is judged as to whether they highlight or display those points correctly, which the AI recognizes. Corporate firms are now employing people with analytic skills and programming abilities to develop human resources-based knowledge and filtering capability, and this extends to even designing models to predict the newcomer's salary.

AI (Artificial Intelligence) is now being used vastly in the world of recruitment. According to a Gartner survey (2019, January 21), AI grew by 270 percent in the last four years to reach 37 percent of all enterprises. Most recruiters (65%) already use AI in the recruitment process.

AI adoption in the hiring process will enable assessment standardization and reduce subjective judgments. AI algorithms differentiate patterns and do impartial evaluations based on qualifications and performance prespecified by the company. As a result of this process, the company can be more diverse and inclusive (Young,2022). Companies like Unilever, KPMG, and BASF extensively use AI-driven tools to recruit their employees. For instance, Unilever uses AI in recruitment and chatbots to engage, provide feedback, and offer a good candidate experience. The company also identifies candidates for every key role, streamlines the hiring process, and improves the quality of decision-making(Abdelhay, 2023).

Smart hiring is a data-driven approach to attracting and identifying experienced and qualified candidates and checking the suitability of these candidates for a specific organizational requirement. It leverages advanced technologies, predictive analytics, data analytics, and various best practices in the hiring process. Smart hiring leads to the effectiveness and efficiency of the recruitment process in line with the organizational goals by filling the different job openings and focusing on the contributions of these candidates in the long run (Bhanumathi et al., 2022).

Data Science Approaches for Smart Hiring

Data science deals with unearthing the patterns in the data, and data analytics deals with understanding these patterns to help strategic decision-making. In the case of classical techniques for hiring, the decision is grounded on the manager's abilities, which may sometimes lead to improper and inaccurate decision-making. Data science techniques depend exclusively on applying statistical measures to the data collected from the environment; in the case of hiring, it is applicants' biodata and employers' skill requirements(Bongard, 2019).

The human resource management function produces a lot of workforce data, including personal data, skills, professional data, service data, etc., and the recruitment division constantly searches for potential employees from various sources. The amalgamation of data from multiple sources must be used scientifically to make smart hiring decisions. Any failures in identifying the right workforce would lead to significant costs for the company and also influence the company's overall outcome (Kumar et al.,2022).

The data science approach for smart hiring is an advantage for an organization to reduce recruitment costs and hire the right workforce. Suggested methodology is given in Table 1.

Table 1. Dataset for the analytics for smart hiring (Dixit et al.,2023)

Sl. No.	Type of Dataset	Purpose of the Dataset
1	Resume and Application Dataset – Primary Source	This dataset includes the applicant's demographic, educational, and work experience details, which enable to analyze their skills and abilities and match them to the job requirements.
2	Professional Network Presence dataset	This dataset, sourced from professional networking sites and social networking sites, will help analyze the applicants' interaction with professional society and the professional endorsements that ensure an understanding of the influence the applicant has created in the workplace. The kind of network the applicant has established is also an indicator of their intellectual capabilities.
3	Dataset on employee performance	The dataset on the applicant's performance attributes provided by the previous organizations led to the analysis of the applicant's productivity in the last organization.
4	Dataset on references	The dataset on the professional references is analyzed to understand the quality and genuineness of the referral. These analytics will help establish strong evidence for smart hiring decisions.
5	Dataset on interview performance	A dataset created over various parameters on a candidate during the interview process will help make smart hiring decisions. The dataset includes communication skills, listening skills, clarity, body language, etc., from a personal skills point of view, and technical skills measurements regarding domain knowledge, problem-solving abilities, critical thinking, and analytical abilities. The video gives an overall impression the candidate is trying to create during the interview process.

Data Preprocessing

Table 2. Types of data processing for the recruitment

SL. No.	Type of Data Preprocessing	Purpose of Data Preprocessing in the Recruitment Dataset
1	Data Cleaning	There is always a possibility that applicants may fail to answer critical questions, which they think would affect the chances of their recruitment, like, what is your major weakness? Is there any scenario you failed to perform? Etc. The data scientist is responsible for filling in these values by using other secondary resources of the data collected from the applicant or making some predictions on these missing values.
2	Data Transformation	Data transformation will transform the collected data into machine-understandable logical formats. The data transformation in the smart hiring datasets is beneficial when employees express their opinions verbally or in writing. Encoding these into some numerical forms is required for analysis purposes. Sometimes, most of the data collected looks similar and redundant, which needs a preprocessing stage to pick the valuable data to initiate smart hiring decisions. This stage, if carried out properly, would lead to establishing the salient features of the applicant.
3	Data Reduction	The data reduction stage makes us focus on the essentials of the collected datasets. This process involves reducing dataset scope and dimension by limiting it to only essential features for analysis. Data reduction comes primarily in recruitment datasets while identifying the features that quantify the applicant's ability and suitability for the job relative to others. This reduction helps to do better analytics by only focusing on the essential features to build the model instead of considering all the data collected, which may be unnecessary from the analysis point of view.
4	Data Integration	When applicant data is drawn from various sources, the data comes in multiple forms, sometimes structured and sometimes unstructured. A data analyst has to look to derive a pattern from these datasets, which predicts the very nature of the applicant and classifies the applicant into various levels of job suitability.
5	Data Formatting	Finalizing the data attributes, like type, range, precision, uncertainty factors, etc., becomes crucial for building models that sustain the history of events or transactions. Sometimes, the data formats will decided while building the models. Data should be available for analysis and subjected to specific format changes instead of rigid form.
6	Treating Imbalanced data	Dataset spread and reach will decide the quality of the data collected. The primary importance is to ensure the data collected is a real-world representation of the phenomenon. The periodicity used for sampling and the amount of data collected may sometimes lead to over and under-sampling scenarios. These scenarios may not fetch the actual insight. We may encounter heterogeneity in applicant classes in recruitment datasets, and their volume differs. If we keep analyzing over-sampled cases, we may lose out a critical employee, and trying to satisfy an employee, we may lose a batch that is essential and may not be critical but complex to replace within a short period.
7	Dealing with Text data	Natural language expressions by applicants and employers are the primary and critical data for analysis. The challenge may be going through the big corpus and coming out of inferences to make recruitment strategies.

Data Visualization

Data visualization is an industry-accepted tool for visualizing the data for better understanding. Visualization can happen in many ways, and an effective visualization method is crucial in any data science project. In the present model, building and visualizing the dataset of employees to understand the trends and symptoms will be an excellent input for human resource managers to make any strategic decisions in advance(Fernlund,2013). Data scientists may use tools to create visualizations such as scatter plots, charts, tree maps, heat maps, tables, Gantt charts, dashboards, etc. The following Table 3 illustrates the purpose of these tools for the smart recruitment process.

Table 3. Tools for the smart recruitment process

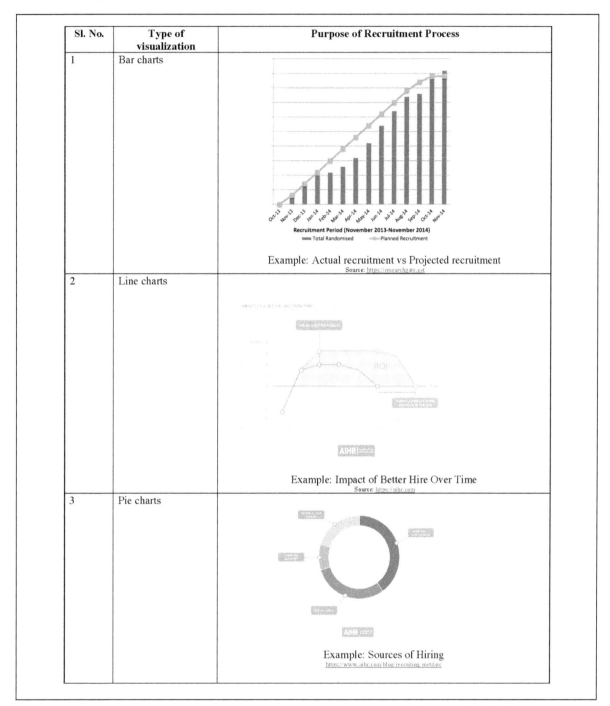

Sl. No.	Type of visualization	Purpose of Recruitment Process
1	Bar charts	Example: Actual recruitment vs Projected recruitment Source: https://researchgate.net
2	Line charts	Example: Impact of Better Hire Over Time Source: https://aihr.com
3	Pie charts	Example: Sources of Hiring https://www.aihr.com/blog/recruiting_metrics/

Continued on following page

Table 3. Continued

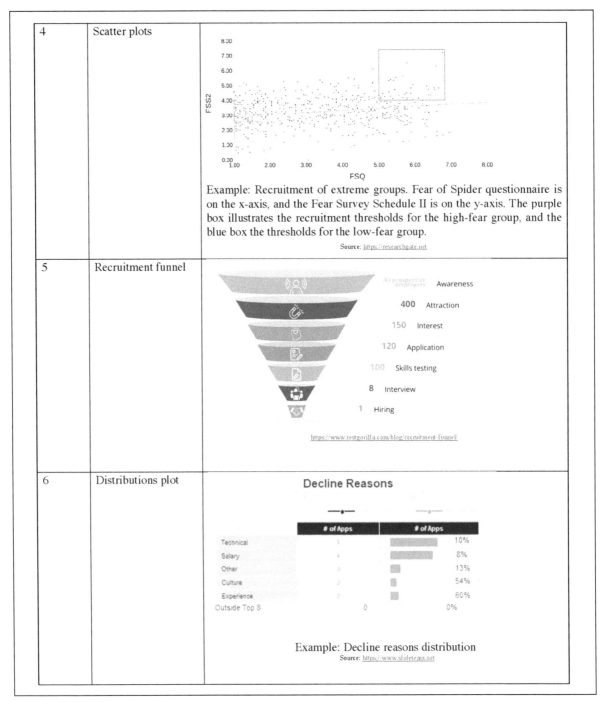

4	Scatter plots	
		Example: Recruitment of extreme groups. Fear of Spider questionnaire is on the x-axis, and the Fear Survey Schedule II is on the y-axis. The purple box illustrates the recruitment thresholds for the high-fear group, and the blue box the thresholds for the low-fear group. Source: https://researchgate.net
5	Recruitment funnel	
		https://www.testgorilla.com/blog/recruitment-funnel/
6	Distributions plot	
		Example: Decline reasons distribution Source: https://www.slideteam.net

Create a Business Dashboard to Track the Recruitment Process

An efficient system for the recruitment process uses data collected at various stages of the recruitment pipeline. When the organization's size grows and the number of applicants reaches thousands, monitoring the data is overwhelming and challenging. One of the solutions is creating a recruitment process dashboard(Shahbaz, 2022).

For the recruitment process dashboard, businesses must identify key performance indicators (KPIs) relevant to their recruitment practices. These KPIs will vary depending on the industry and the company's needs; typical examples include qualification, experience, retention level, skills, leadership qualities, etc.

The recruitment team can source the data from multiple locations, which can be incorporated into the recruitment process dashboard to provide stakeholders with real-time updates on the recruitment process. In addition to providing real-time updates, the dashboard can also provide tools for data analysis, such as filters and drill-down capabilities. These tools allow stakeholders to analyze the data and identify patterns and trends that can be used to improve recruitment process efficiency and move towards smart hiring. For instance, stakeholders can analyze the data to determine the root cause of the applicant leaving the previous organization. Furthermore, these dashboards can help businesses improve the quality of recruitment by monitoring various quality indicators of the recruitment process in real time.

The steps involved in the creation of such a dashboard can be summarized as follows:

Step 1: Identify Key Performance Indicators (KPIs): The first step in creating a dashboard is identifying the KPIs relevant to the recruitment process. These KPIs can vary based on the business's needs but may include employee-related metrics.

Step 2: Collect Data: Once the KPIs have been identified, the next step is to collect data from the various data points available throughout the recruitment pipeline. Data collection techniques can gather information on multiple aspects of recruitment, such as performance, satisfaction, job commitment levels, and quality control metrics. The data collected can be stored in a centralized database for analysis.

Step 3: Visualize Data: Once the data has been collected, it can be visualized on the business dashboard. The dashboard can provide real-time updates on the KPIs identified earlier, allowing stakeholders to assess employee work performance and turnover trends quickly. The data can be visualized as charts, graphs, and tables, giving stakeholders clear and concise views (Fernlund, 2013).

Step 4: Analyze Data: The dashboard can also provide tools for data analysis, such as filters and drill-down capabilities. These tools allow stakeholders to analyze the data and identify patterns and trends, helping them make informed decisions to improve recruitment quality and reduce hiring costs.

Step 5: Act: Based on the insights gained from the dashboard, stakeholders can take action to improve the performance. For example, if the recruitment costs are high, stakeholders can investigate the root cause of the issue and implement corrective actions. Similarly, if the recruitee's overall quality is low, stakeholders can adjust the recruitment plan to ensure that recruitment qualities are maintained at the desired level (Raj et al.,2022).

Figure 1. Sample employee recruitment dashboards (https://www.slideteam.net/)

Role of AI in Smart Hiring

Artificial intelligence has entered various business functions, including human resource management. AI's ability to perform classifications, predictions, and generations of new content has made businesses leverage the potential of AI in conducting business functions effectively. The basic notion of AI is to build a model based on machine learning or deep learning to train an algorithm to make decisions without human intervention (Boiko,2021). AI model essentially depends on the given dataset for development; therefore, it is the responsibility of the data analyst to provide the correct dataset for training the model. As mentioned above, various data sources and attributes have gone through the data analysis pipeline, and we will be ready with model training and validation. Table 4 shows various applications of AI in smart hiring (Martins,2022) (Bongard, 2019).

Table 4. Applications of AI in smart hiring (Martins, 2022) (Bongard, 2019)

Sl. No.	AI Model	Purpose of the Model in Smart Hiring
1	Predictive Analytics	Used to predict; • Best match for the job • Finalizing the list of candidates for interview • Efficient channel for getting resumes • The success of a candidate in the role offered • Candidate retention level • Real-time prediction of a candidate's compensation, etc.
2	Sentiment Analytics	Used to identify the sentiments a candidate carries into an organization, like; • Candidates motivation level • Candidates social presence and professional communications • Apply natural language processing to understand candidate sentiments expressed over a previous and present organization • Organizational cultural awareness and commitment, etc.
3	Chatbots	Conversational chatbots can set the tone for the recruitment process, providing a 24x7 digital interface for candidates wanting to know more about the organization.
4	Schedulers	Many essential activities in the recruitment pipeline demand the scheduling of limited resources, such as experts, time, locations, etc. The recruitment team can use AI schedulers to develop a recruitment plan.
5	Testing	AI-based skill tests are more efficient than static tests and are standard for all tests. The test paper can be generated and personalized to the candidate's work strengths and professional skills.
6	Fairness Solutions	AI-based solutions will try to ensure fairness in all the stages of the recruitment process by removing the human factor. Humans typically find attached to unconscious biases.
7	Leadership sourcing	AI-based solutions can identify the next line of leaders, who can take up the responsibilities if the key employee leaves the organization abruptly.
8	Generative AI	Generative AI models can be used to create personalized channels for communication with candidates. Many works performed by human in-built skills can be taken over by generative AI, like conducting surveys, providing feedback, analyzing feedback, making personalized recommendations, etc. Adding training technologies in the employee duty cycle may make employees more accountable and responsible for their jobs.

Popular Solutions Available for Smart Hiring in the Industry and Presenting a Comparative Study on the Quality of Experience They Create From the Candidate's Point of View

The popular solutions for smart hiring in the present times are below.

Fetcher is a cutting-edge AI technology that optimizes and expedites the hiring process. Fetcher uses state-of-the-art AI technology to intelligently find and connect with qualified candidates, automating the candidate sourcing process. It evaluates enormous volumes of data from numerous sources, including job boards and professional networks, to find the best applicants for specific roles. The AI algorithms Fetcher uses to gain knowledge from user comments and enhance their suggestions over time. Because of its time-saving features and user-friendly layout.

Manatal is an easy-to-use AI-powered recruiting tool designed to streamline and expedite hiring for HR departments and recruitment firms. It has many cutting-edge and distinctive features, including a career page builder, AI-based candidate suggestions, candidate scoring, social media enrichment, and sophisticated search capabilities. Additionally, by recognizing and integrating candidates' social media accounts across more than 20 different social media platforms, Manatal's AI assists recruiters in better assessing possible candidates.

hireEZ is one of the prominent organizations seeking artificial intelligence (AI)-based recruiting tools to create solid pipelines for present and future positions. It is the primary target audience for Hiretual. Additionally, recruiting managers can better understand the kind of applicants to seek out and effectively hire by using Hiretual's market insights. It also helps to count on maximum exposure of the company's data and speedier optimization.

PARADOX is a conversational artificial intelligence chatbot agent from Paradox that engages with job seekers to ensure they are ready for interviews. Self-scheduling screening, interviews, and other processes can help employers ensure smooth hiring. One feature that promotes contact between the employer and prospective employees is a self-service portal.RecruiterCloud, Wellfound's newly launched AI-powered sourcing solution, is designed to eliminate friction, hassle, and logistical setbacks in the hiring landscape.

wellfound: this is a weekly feed of the best matches to the recruiter's inbox by RecruiterCloud, aggregating billions of data points from personal websites, blogs, portfolios, and more. This data is possible by utilizing proprietary data from Wellfound's ten million+ job seekers and intelligent data filtering of an additional 500 million candidate pool.

Their AI takes care of everything, including interview scheduling on the calendar, hyper-personalized outreach, and sourcing.

HUMANLY.IO is a cutting-edge platform that transforms how companies conduct customer service and interaction. Humanly blends the strength of automation with the knowledge and empathy of human contact, focusing on human-centered AI. Utilizing cutting-edge machine learning and natural language processing methods, it smoothly interacts with current systems to deliver effective and customized customer experiences. The intelligent chatbot from Humanly comprehends and replies to client inquiries, providing prompt service and cutting down on wait times.

textio is to optimize the job posts to appeal at a faster rate to the prospective candidates for the specific job profile. They have identified that some words in the job offer can be biased and help companies avoid them, so there should be clarity and help in hiring the best fit. They also focus on pay transparency and inclusive recruiting and use brand language to reach a larger group.

Findem is a cutting-edge AI solution that transforms workforce analytics and talent acquisition. Findem tool helps businesses make wise decisions by offering thorough insights into talent markets through cutting-edge artificial intelligence technology. Findem's extensive data network and advanced algorithms allow it to swiftly identify and evaluate possible applicants, making it easier for recruiters to locate the best fit for their company. Findem leads strategic workforce planning and streamlines the hiring process with AI-powered capabilities.

EVA is a modular HR technology platform combining conversational AI and predictive ML, automating procedures and customizing user experience. The EVA team uses HR 4.0, the fourth industrial revolution, to help organizations acquire growth and sustainability through talent acquisition and management.

HiredScore is another excellent AI recruiting tool for 2023 that makes hiring processes easier for companies. Using custom solutions, like diversity and inclusion job optimization, diversity and inclusion analytics, and hiring process bias mitigation, the program unlocks the company workforce goals. These strategies boost the effectiveness of hiring processes and draw in more applicants for upcoming job openings.

Human intelligence (HT) is a frontrunner in recruitment technology and cultural intelligence. Humantelligence is simple to use and easy to set up. It also uses AI and interfaces with the applicant tracking system (ATS) to give the data needed to streamline the hiring process.

Many companies are using AI nowadays. However, Industry 5.0 is not yet fully equipped to incorporate AI in its recruitment process. There are yet many firms that carry out this task manually. Most MNCs incorporate AI support in their recruitment process, even if not automated. This process saves time, cost, energy, and human hours, which can be used elsewhere more constructively, yielding better revenue for the company. If the repetitive, patterned, and tedious tasks are left to the AI, it will eliminate scopes of human error and save time and cost(Uma,2023).

Businesses as diverse as Hypercontex, Panasonic, Kiehl's, and Care.com help increase the efficiency and precision of their personnel procedures, including performance management and hiring. To improve the speed and accuracy of their people processes, from recruitment to performance management. Microsoft and Amazon are among the companies shaping AI-enabled hiring policies.

Table 5. Comparative studies of some of the AI tools

AI Tool	Scores	Best For	Product Functionality	Product Pricing	Users	Link
Fetcher	Most popular tool and its score is 4.6 User Score is 4.6 out of 5 Product Score is 4.7 out of 5	Tool for SMEs and large teams	Automate candidate sourcing. Outreach is faster to have higher efficiency.	$149/month There is a free trial option	More than 500 companies are using this tool	etcher. ai/?ssrid=ssr&utm_campaign=fetcher &utm_medium=ppc&utm_source=selectsoftware &utm_content=ai%20recruiting&hsa_kw=ai%20 recruiting&ssrid=ssr&ssr_id=q0ei9fwo5s317ip3
Mantal	Popularity score is 4.5 User Score is 4.8 out of 5 Product Score is 4.9 out of 5	Tool for Talent Acquisition	Tool for candidate filtering based on the profile	$15/month There is a free trial option	More than 10,000 companies are using this tool	https://www.manatal.com/?utm_source=selectsoftwarereviews &utm_medium=cpc&utm_campaign=ai_recruiting_software& ssrid=ssr&ssr_id=9v5k10df59n67ibz
Hireez	Popularity score is 4.1 User Score is 4.6 out of 5 Product Score is 4.4 out of 5	Mid-sized companies	Candidate recommendation tool	Customised pricing, negotiable, and no free trial option	More than 600 companies are using this tool	https://explore.hireez.com/contact-sales?utm_ source=Paid+Ads &utm_medium= SelectSoftware&utm_term=AI+Recruiting&utm_ campaign=SelectSoftware&ssrid=ssr&ssr_ id=892muyym3lzuginv
Humanly	Popularity score is 4.7 User Score is 4.7 out of 5 Product Score is 4.6 out of 5	Mid-sized teams	Use of chatbots in automating and optimizing the repetitive interactions with the candidates(ATS)	Customized pricing and there is a free trial option	No data	https://www.humanly.io/
Findem	Popularity score is 4.1 User Score is 4.2 out of 5 Product Score is 4.3 out of 5	Teams with more than 500 employees	Candidate sourcing	$8000/yr onwards. There is no free trial option.	More than 150 companies are using this tool	https://www.findem.ai/

Continued on following page

Table 5. Continued

AI Tool	Scores	Best For	Product Functionality	Product Pricing	Users	Link
Textio	Popularity score is 4.1 User Score is 4.1 out of 5 Product Score is 4.3 out of 5	Companies who look for clarity in communication with the candidates	Proper communication with the prospective candidates	Customised pricing, negotiable, and no free trial option	More than 400 companies are using this tool	https://textio.com/
Paradox	Popularity score is 4.6 User Score is 4.8 out of 5 Product Score is 4.9 out of 5	Enterprise teams	Volume hiring	Customised pricing, negotiable, and no free trial option	More than 1300 companies are using this tool	https://www.paradox.ai/

Highlighting the factors taken care of compared to classical approaches proves that AI-centric approaches work efficiently. Emphasize the factors that support AI-centric approaches to work efficiently (compared to classical /traditional methods).

The various factors that support an AI-centric recruitment approach when compared to traditional are given in Table 6 (Arifuzzaman et al., 2023):

Table 6. Comparison of traditional and AI-centric approach

Factors	Traditional Approach	AI-Centric Approach
Resume Collection and screening	The screening is done manually based on the job description (JD)for a specified role. There is a possibility of committing human error that leads to bias. It is a time-consuming process.	In this AI-centric approach, the resume screening is based on the JD but identifies the keywords and shortlists based on the Machine learning (ML) model. It will automate the work and reduce the time to screen the applications (Sam et al., 2023).
Candidate Matching	The candidate matching is done manually. Most of the time, it may not consider all the requirements and is subjective.	The AI-based approach will match the candidate's skill sets, capabilities, and many other factors with JD. The accuracy of the process is high when compared to traditional. (Sam et al., 2023).
Interview Scheduling	The interview scheduling of prospective candidates is done manually. The process requires a lot of coordination. If mishandled, it leads to potential scheduling delays and scheduling conflicts.	The AI approach streamlines the process and schedules the interviews based on the mutually convenient time of the candidate and interviewer. This process ensures efficiency and timely interviews to fill job openings. (Sam et al., 2023).
Decision-Making	The decision is based on intuition and experience, which may or may not be data-driven and lacks accuracy.	Predictive Analytics is used to understand past data to predict the candidate's potentiality, performance, and success for a specific role. The decision-making process offers actionable and quantifiable insights. (Sam et al., 2023).
Biases	Human decisions can be conscious or unconscious biases, leading to higher levels of discrimination. (Beattie, 2012)	The AI approach is designed in such a way as to minimize the biases that occur as a result of conscious bias and emphasize the objectivity of the recruitment process. (Vivek,2023).
Candidate Engagement	Candidate engagement is through human interaction, and it is routine, which may further lead to delay and inefficiency.	This approach uses chatbots and virtual assistants to engage candidates, answer their queries, and guide them whenever required. (Sam et al., 2023).
Efficiency, Scalability	The traditional approach encompasses manual effort to handle many tasks, limiting scalability and efficiency. AI-centric approaches accelerate the recruitment process and adapt to changing needs. (Sills, 2014)	This approach will enable the organization to streamline its repetitive tasks. It will allow company recruiters to focus more on hiring strategies and ways to meet recruitment needs. (Sam et al., 2023).
Candidate experience	The recruiting team sometimes may not have an immediate and consistent meeting to communicate with the candidates properly.	Using the AI approach, the recruiting team can communicate in real-time and automated updates and personalized interactions through chatbots.

In summary, an AI-centric approach will significantly enable recruitment. It will streamline the process, automate repetitive tasks, ensure proper candidate engagement, and provide data-driven insights compared to the traditional recruiting process(Smitha, 2023).

List Limitations for Adopting a Smart Hiring Process

AI involves an all-encompassing role, but it has simultaneously given rise to algorithm-related biases, which must be reduced or eliminated. The ChatGPT, an advanced AI version, threatens to risk the recruiter's existence. However, the human touch (notably, the recruiter) must screen the logic behind the algorithm to remove the undesired biases and the new ones that are bound to occur. The recruiter's intuitiveness and critical thinking ability cannot be dispensed with. The recruiter must be compassionate and identify, recognize, appreciate, and value a diversified and inclusive workforce; looking beyond machines should be of binary focus. A balance between human (subjective)and tech touch(Objective in nature) ensures "positive-sum automation," which is required for business decision-making and the process of recruitment (Kharbanda et al., 2023).

Implementing a smart hiring process requires investment in software technology, hardware, and staff training modules. The smart hiring process depends on AI algorithms, machine learning, and data analytics, which can pose data breaches, risks, and technical glitches, and technology becomes obsolete quickly.

Data Privacy and Security Concerns are more when they collect and analyze massive amounts of candidates' data. Smart hiring systems can analyze data efficiently, but They may lack the ability to understand the context of a candidate's experience, skills, and potential cultural fit within the organization. This lack of understanding of context can result in overlooking potential and promising candidates. There is a chance that inherent biases continue in smart hiring systems despite efforts to develop unbiased algorithms.

Smart hiring processes may prioritize candidates' technical skills and qualifications, such as emotional intelligence, creativity, and adaptability, which can result in overlooking candidates who possess valuable soft skills but may not meet specific rigid criteria.

Hiring managers, employees, and other organizational stakeholders may resist implementing smart hiring processes due to concerns like job security, lack of technology trust, etc. Overcoming resistance to change and gaining buy-in could be a significant challenge.

Smart hiring processes can analyze past candidate's data to predict a candidate's potential. Still, they will not predict how well the candidate adapts to the work scenario and the future changes in the industry space.

Integrating smart hiring with the existing HR process is complex and requires a huge amount of time and good coordination between the various departments, vendors, etc.,

The above limitations must be addressed by a balanced approach that unifies the benefits of smart hiring technologies with human judgment and ethical principles.

CONCLUSION

This chapter on smart hiring using predictive data analytics and AI discusses the meaning of hiring, followed by classical and modern approaches used for hiring, and also provides an overview of various challenges faced during recruitment. The discussion continues by providing the data science and analytics angle to increase the quality of recruitment by predicting the data generated directly or indirectly on the candidates applying for the jobs. The chapter also highlights various strategies for integrating modern data analytics solutions with existing businesses. The chapter suggests that a good business dashboard for hiring is a valuable addition for companies that want to reduce the cost of recruitment.

REFERENCES

Abdelhay, S. (2023). How Artificial Intelligence can affect the process of recruitment and improve the quality of new hired employees. *Resmilitaris, 13*(3), 2517-2533.

Abdul, C., Wang, W., & Li, Y. (2020). The impact of technology on recruitment process. *Issues in Information Systems*, *21*(4).

Adam, A. K. (2020). Modern challenges of human resource management practice in job placement and recruitment within organisations in the African continent. *Journal of Human Resource Management, 8*(2), 69–75. doi:10.11648/j.jhrm.201200802.14

Aguirre, T. M., Koehler, A. E., Joshi, A., & Wilhelm, S. L. (2018). Recruitment and retention challenges and successes. *Ethnicity & Health, 23*(1), 111–119. doi:10.1080/13557858.2016.1246427 PMID:27764955

Arifuzzaman, M., Islam, M. S., Masum, M. Y., & Anonna, J. S. (2023). The Use of E-Recruitment Process with the Comparison of Traditional Recruitment Process in Bangladesh: A Case Study on BRAC Bank Ltd. Journal of Education. *Management and Development Studies, 3*(2), 15–25. doi:10.52631/jemds.v3i2.191

Beattie, G., & Johnson, P. (2012). Possible unconscious bias in recruitment and promotion and the need to promote equality. Perspectives. *Policy and Practice in Higher Education, 16*(1), 7–13.

Benuyenah, V. (2023, August). Rethinking recruitment ethically through the lens of corporate social responsibility (CSR). In *Evidence-based HRM: a Global Forum for Empirical Scholarship* (Vol. 11, No. 3, pp. 372-376). Emerald Publishing Limited.

Bhanumathi & Pragalapati. (2022). To Study the Impact of Artificial Intelligence on Recruitment in the IT sector. *Journal of Management & Entrepreneurship.*

Boiko, J., Volianska-Savchuk, L., Bazaliyska, N., & Zelena, M. (2021, September). Smart recruiting as a modern tool for HR hiring in the context of business informatization. In *2021 11th International Conference on Advanced Computer Information Technologies (ACIT)* (pp. 284-289). IEEE. 10.1109/ACIT52158.2021.9548558

Bongard, A. (2019). Automating talent acquisition: Smart recruitment, predictive hiring algorithms, and the data-driven nature of artificial intelligence. *Psychosociological Issues in Human Resource Management, 7*(1), 36–41.

Dixit, C. K., Somani, P., Gupta, S. K., & Pathak, A. (2023). Data-Centric Predictive Modeling of Turnover Rate and New Hire in Workforce Management System. In *Designing Workforce Management Systems for Industry 4.0* (pp. 121–138). CRC Press. doi:10.1201/9781003357070-8

Dutta, D., & Vedak, C. (2023). Determining quality of hire, the holy grail of recruitment: A structuration perspective. *Human Resources Management and Services, 5*(2).

Fernlund, P. (2013). *Competence Visualisation-Prerequisites and guidelines for visualising competence.* Academic Press.

Johansson, J., & Herranen, S. (2019). *The application of artificial intelligence (AI) in human resource management: Current state of AI and its impact on the traditional recruitment process.* Academic Press.

Koivunen, S., Olsson, T., Olshannikova, E., & Lindberg, A. (2019). Understanding decision-making in recruitment: Opportunities and challenges for information technology. *Proceedings of the ACM on Human-Computer Interaction, 3*(GROUP), 1-22.

Kumar Betchoo, N. (2022, September). Data-Driven Decision Management from a Dashboard Perspective. In *Proceedings of the 6th International Conference on Advance Computing and Intelligent Engineering: ICACIE 2021* (pp. 509-519). Singapore: Springer Nature Singapore.

Martins, N., Dominique-Ferreira, S., & Lopes, C. (2022). Design and development of a digital platform for seasonal jobs: Improving the hiring process. *Journal of Global Scholars of Marketing Science*, *32*(3), 452–469. doi:10.1080/21639159.2020.1808851

Myers, V. L., & Dreachslin, J. L. (2007). Recruitment and retention of a diverse workforce: Challenges and opportunities. *Journal of Healthcare Management*, *52*(5), 290–298. doi:10.1097/00115514-200709000-00004 PMID:17933185

Okeyika, K. O., Ibeto, V. C., Okere, A. I., & Umoh, B. (2023). The applicastion of Artificail Intelligence (AI) ioj Human Resource Management: Current state of AI and its impact on the traditional recruitment process. *AKU: An African Journal of Contemporary Research, 4*(3).

Okolie, U. C., & Irabor, I. E. (2017). E-recruitment: Practices, opportunities and challenges. *European Journal of Business and Management*, *9*(11), 116–122.

Raj, S., & Paliwal, M. (2022). Higher Education Dashboard Implementation Using Data Mining and Data Warehouse: A Review Paper. *International Journal of Innovative Research in Computer Science & Technology*, *10*(1), 107–111. doi:10.55524/ijircst.2022.10.1.19

Sam, D., Ganesan, M., Ilavarasan, S., & Victor, T. J. (2023, January). Hiring and Recruitment Process Using Machine Learning. In *2023 International Conference on Artificial Intelligence and Knowledge Discovery in Concurrent Engineering (ICECONF)* (pp. 1-4). IEEE. 10.1109/ICECONF57129.2023.10084133

Shahbaz, U. (2022). *Towards automating the recruitment process* (Doctoral dissertation, Macquarie University).

Sills, M. (2014). *E-recruitment: A comparison with traditional recruitment and the influences of social media: A qualitative and quantitative review*. Academic Press.

Smitha, C. (2023). Effectiveness Of Virtual Recruitment–A Study On Commerce And Managment Students' Perspective. *Journal of Namibian Studies: History Politics Culture*, *35*, 330–341.

Thangaraja, T. (2023). Challenges Faced by HR on Recruitment Process. *MET Management Review*, *10*(2), 19–24. doi:10.34047/MMR.2020.10203

Uma, V. R., Velchamy, I., & Upadhyay, D. (2023). Recruitment Analytics: Hiring in the Era of Artificial Intelligence. In The Adoption and Effect of Artificial Intelligence on Human Resources Management, Part A (pp. 155-174). Emerald Publishing Limited.

Veglianti, E., Trombin, M., Pinna, R., & De Marco, M. (2023). Customized Artificial Intelligence for Talent Recruiting: A Bias-Free Tool? In *Smart Technologies for Organizations: Managing a Sustainable and Inclusive Digital Transformation* (pp. 245–261). Springer International Publishing. doi:10.1007/978-3-031-24775-0_15

Vivek, R. (2023). Enhancing diversity and reducing bias in recruitment through AI: a review of strategies and challenges. *Информатика. Экономика. Управление-Informatics. Economics. Management,* *2*(4), 101-118.

Yakubovich, V., & Lup, D. (2006). Stages of the recruitment process and the referrer's performance effect. *Organization Science*, *17*(6), 710–723. doi:10.1287/orsc.1060.0214

Young, N. C. J. (2022). Adapting a New Inclusive Mindset in the Hiring Process. In Now Hiring (pp. 29-42). Emerald Publishing Limited.

Chapter 3
Brand Personality Dimensions in the Hotel Sector:
A Case Study

Labinot Mehmeti

ISAG, European Business School, Portugal & CICET-FCVC, Portugal

Ana Pinto Borges

https://orcid.org/0000-0002-4942-079X

ISAG, European Business School, Portugal & CICET-FCVC, Portugal & COMEGI, Portugal

Bruno Miguel Vieira

ISAG, European Business School, Portugal & CICET-FCVC, Portugal

Elvira Vieira

https://orcid.org/0000-0002-9296-3896

ISAG, European Business School, Portugal & CICET-FCVC, Portugal & UNIAG, Portugal & Polytechnic Institute of Viana do Castelo, Portugal

Amélia Brandão

https://orcid.org/0000-0003-2751-7272

FEP, Portugal & Centro de Economia e Finanças da UP, Portugal

ABSTRACT

This chapter addresses the gap in literature regarding brand personality metrics in the hotel industry. Despite extensive studies on various brands globally, limited research exists in the hotel sector. Brand personality is pivotal for differentiating hotels and attracting their target market. Aaker's five-dimensional brand personality scale (BPS) was employed in a case study at Hotel Garden in Pristina, Kosovo. This study, employing both qualitative and quantitative methods, engaged 68 participants. Hotel Garden demonstrated higher scores in sincerity, competence, excitement, and sophistication, aligning with Aaker's dimensions, while ruggedness received less emphasis. Findings underscore the need for brand-aligned strategies, highlighting the role of human resources and organizational culture. This chapter explores the findings and offers strategies that, when applied to human resources, should take into account the relationship with BPS.

DOI: 10.4018/979-8-3693-1938-3.ch003

1. INTRODUCTION

In the hotel industry, brand personality is vital since it shapes customer perception and helps create enduring relationships. Similar to characters in a story, hotel brands have unique qualities that influence the visitor experience (Rahimian et al. 2021). Customers may view a brand to be amiable, luxurious, adventurous, traditional, or to represent a variety of feelings and values. Hotels may create a distinctive identity that stands out in a competitive market, attracting customers and fostering brand loyalty (Li et al., 2020), by comprehending and developing a consistent brand personality.

Studying brand personality (Aaker, 1997) is crucial for developing a strong reputation and drawing in a particular target market in the hotel industry, in addition to serving as a strategy for distinction (Hankinson, 2001; Rahimian et al. 2021; Chen, Chen & Wang, 2024). From the time of booking to the hotel stay, a guest's expectations are shaped by the brand, which has a direct effect on their happiness and loyalty. Additionally, brand personality directs communication, marketing, and design strategies, coordinating all business aspects to produce a cohesive and unforgettable experience (Kapferer, 2008; Guan et al., 2021). By allocating resources towards comprehending and cultivating their brand identity, hotels have the ability to establish a sentimental bond with their customers, surpassing the simple business deal and providing an entirely engaging encounter.

The understanding of the significance of story and emotional experience in customer purchasing decisions resides at the core of brand personality study in the hotel industry (Fournier, 1998; Wang at al., 2021). In addition to drawing guests, hotels with a strong and relevant brand identity can also cultivate passionate advocates who spread the word about their great experiences. The literature on brand personality in the hotel context is becoming an invaluable tool for managers due to the growing competition and desire for personalized experiences. It offers basic insights for developing strategies that go beyond simply providing services and create enduring emotional connections (Morgan et al., 2011; Šerić & Mikulić 2020).

It is important to highlight that a hotel's brand personality can only be built through its employees (Gulati et al., 2023). Human resources become essential players in determining how customers feel about a business (Khdour & Wright, 2021; Michael et al., 2023) which in turn helps to define the brand's personality. The way hotel staff and visitors interact fosters an atmosphere that makes the brand's values and character qualities easy to communicate and incorporate. In addition to being vital in continuously providing top-notch services, skilled workers who share the brand's vision also serve as living representatives of the company's essence. Employees play a pivotal role in the brand narrative by creating enduring emotional bonds with visitors and solidifying the hotel's unique image in the market, whether through interpersonal interactions, attentive service, or efficient problem-solving (Kapferer, 2008: Michael et al., 2023). In this scope, in this chapter we analyze the feasibility of Aaker's five dimensional Brand Personal Scale (BPS) in a famous Kosovan hotel (Hotel Garden). This chapter also covers a gap in the research by discussing how human resources contribute to the development of brand reputation and how brand personality is perceived, then outlining potential management implications.

The structure of the chapter is as follows. The theoretical underpinnings of brand personality are presented first, followed by pertinent research questions. The qualitative and quantitative technique is then explained. The discussion and analysis of the findings, together with a presentation of the limits and some key points for further research, round out the paper.

2. THEORETICAL FRAMEWORK

In the Radler (2018)'s work, it was highlight that the brand personality concept has been used since the 1960s (Levy, 1959; Plummer, 1985; Blackston, 1993) to address how to engage consumers with a brand's symbolic values and humanlike qualities that transcend functional product attributes (De Chernatony & Dal'Olmo Riley, 1998). However, Aitken et al. (1987) made the first mention of "brand personality" in a scientific publication. In the following decade until now, a brand's personality is seen as a crucial differentiator (Aaker and Fournier, 1995), that can help build brand equity (Aaker, 1997).

The most prominent definition of brand personality, proposed two years later by Aaker (1997), suggests that brand personality is "the set of human characteristics associated with a brand" (p. 347). Contributing significantly to the theoretical underpinnings of behavioural personality, Aaker (1997) created a measuring scale with five dimensions: sincerity, enthusiasm, competence, sophistication, and ruggedness—that were modelled after the "Big Five" human personality paradigm. These traits are derived from 15 personality facets of brands and can be further deconstructed into 42 individual personality traits. The study was carried out on brands from 39 product categories, and these brands have been identified as consistently possessing these five major dimensions in personality. Aaker (1997) also drew a parallel and compared the findings with prior personality frameworks. This original work show that three brand personality types correspond also with personality traits associated with humans. For example, Agreeableness and Sincerity both capture the idea of warmth and acceptance; Extroversion and Excitement both connote the notions of sociability, energy, and activity; Conscientiousness and Competence both represent responsibility, dependability, and security. However, two of the brand personalities, Sophistication and Ruggedness differ from any of the traits presented by the Big Five. These types, on the other hand, are related more with one's ideal self or the self-concept, with traits that one desires and aspires but does not possess at the moment.

An expansion of this concept may be found in the anthropomorphism theory, which postulates individuals tend to anthropomorphize items they come across in an attempt to make them seem more human (Hillen, 2021). People feel disposed and easier to connect with things that mirror their personality, it becomes even more natural for connection if it gives human traits.. Researchers have been exploring the way how brand personality influences the concept of the self. These aspects include the self-concept (Hillen, 2021), self-congruity (Boksberger et al., 2011) and self-expression (Green, 2008). The first refers to the idea one has for the actual or for the ideal self. The second, self-congruity, refers to the idea that consumers choose situations and companions that reaffirm their self-schema. On this line, consumers tend to choose brands that possess qualities which correspond to their current or ideal-self. For example, consumers who perceive themself as spirited, young, up-to-date and outgoing tend to consume products that they perceive that possess these qualities. Arguments suggest that when consumers use self-congruent brands, it can be an expression of their personal identity (Aaker, 1997; Arora & Stoner, 2009). Third, the brand is also linked with how consumers want to express themselves. In this sense, certain brands become vehicles to express part of their self-identity.

In addition to its influence on the literature's expansion of the concept, Aaker's (1997) work also had an impact on research concerning consumer-brand relationships, attitudes towards brands, brand associations, consumer preferences, brand trust, affection felt for brands, emotional attachment to brands, brand identification, purchase intentions, perceived quality, word-of-mouth and brand loyalty, among other topics, as described by Calderón-Fajardo et al. (2023). Additionally, the landmark study by Aaker (1997) included two hotel brands - Marriott and Holiday Inn - to validate the factor structure of brand personality.

Following that, additional research was carried out to determine whether Brand Personality Dimension Scale (BPD) might be applied in the hotel industry (e.g., Li et al., 2020; Sop and Kozak, 2019; Su and Reynolds, 2017, 2019; Unurlu and Uca, 2017). Despite various evaluations of brand personality applied to hotels, it seems that there is inconsistency in the brand personality constructs employed. Furthermore, despite human resources (employees) being one of the primary stakeholders in brand building, there is no study that did the correlation between brand personality and human resources. In this chapter, we related the perception of brand personality and the human resources.

It is crucial to underscore that the establishment of a hotel's brand internal like brand personality hinges significantly on the involvement of its human resources (Gulati et al., 2023; Khairy et al., 2023; Ngo et al., 2020). According to Michael et al. (2023), hotels have the ability to establish positive employee behaviour and performance, engagement, motivation, and retention through internal branding techniques, also a brand personality. Despite the effective strategies used by hotels to retain their valuable workforce and address industry retention concerns that included, for example, attractive salaries, comprehensive benefits such as healthcare and retirement plans, and so on (Zhang et al., 2019), the retention is a critical challenge faced by the hotel sector worldwide, given its labor-intensive nature and high turnover rates. In this sense, it reveals crucial study the linkage between the perception of brand personality and the human resources.

Furthermore, employees assume a pivotal role in shaping customers' perceptions of a business (Khdour & Wright, 2021; Michael et al., 2023), thereby contributing significantly to the delineation of the brand's personality. Employees are "image makers" (Bowen & Schneider, 1985; Michael et al., 2023) who create and offer services while also presenting the hotel in a favourable light. The interactions between hotel staff and guests create an environment that facilitates the seamless communication and integration of the brand's values and character traits. Beyond their primary function of consistently delivering exceptional services, proficient employees who align with the brand's vision also act as living embodiments of the company's essence. Human resources, through interpersonal engagements, attentive service, and effective problem-solving, play a central role in crafting the brand narrative, establishing enduring emotional connections with guests, and cementing the hotel's distinctive identity in the market (Kapferer, 2008; Michael et al., 2023).

In this chapter, we intend to study the brand personality of the famous Hotel Garden in the capital city of Kosovo, Pristina. Also, we intend to test the feasibility of Aaker's Brand Personality Scale (BPS) on a Kosovan context. In order to be more clear, the research questions of this study are as listed below:

RQ1: What are the best personality traits that best represent Hotel Garden in Prishtina?

RQ2: Which of the Aaker's five dimensions is replicable in a Kosovan context?

RQ3: Has Hotel Garden in Prishtina a strong personality based on the Brand Personality Scale?

RQ4: What is the role of employees in the hotel's brand personality?

3. METHODOLOGY: DATA COLLECTION AND ANALYSIS

Qualitative Analysis

Interviews were conducted as part of the qualitative method in order to assess if the topic was appropriate and if consumers understood the ideas associated with the brand's personality. Early adopters were interviewed, with live cam one on one deep interviews, while always following the rule of a interviewing a man and one woman sequentially. Each of them was asked to suggest another early adopter/client, following thus the snowball technique of sample selection. If additional participants were needed, the same rule was followed. Questionnaires were semi-structured with open and suggestive questions. Interviews were done by video call, recorded, and lasted about one hour. The questionnaire was composed of four open questions. The questions used in this questionnaire were: (i) "When you think about Hotel Garden as Human, what personality trait would firstly top up on your head?" (ii) "Why do you use the services of Hotel Garden?" (iii) "What do you feel when you enter Hotel Garden? Why"; (iv) "Why do you choose Hotel Garden? In addition, four declarative questions created from four most identifiable dimensions (sincerity, excitement, competence and sophistication) of Hotel Pristina were created. Participants were asked if they agree (Yes) or disagree (No) with the statements: "Is Hotel Garden Friendly?"; "Is Hotel Garden Real?". Both content analysis and descriptive statistics were employed for data analysis.

Quantitative Analysis

In scope of quantitative analysis, we use a questionnaire composed by two sections: socio-demographic questions, such as age, gender, living county, and income per year; and Aaker (1997)'s Brand Personality Dimension Scale (BPD), which measure the five brand personality dimensions: Sincerity, Excitement, Competence, Sophistication and Ruggedness, with forty-one personality traits. The five dimensions with 41 traits/statements. An example of the questions was: "If Hotel garden were a human, would it be "Down to Earth?"; If Hotel garden were a human, would it be "Family oriented?", etc. The evaluation of statements were through of a Likert rating scale of seven points, from 1 (strongly disagree) to 7 (strongly agree).

To apply the questionnaires, four Hotel staff members were trained on two different occasions through video conferences (more than two hours each), about the concepts of brand, brand personality approach and brand personality dimensions. The same ones were questioned, collectively and separately with intentions to clear any eventual misconception, the errors were cleared. We held another video conference collectively, separately in short intervals, where we wanted to be sure about their abilities, about doing interviews with others. In another video conference we explained the approach and questionnaire in detail.

The collection of responses to the questionnaires was carried out in the hotel check-out, whereas, for the clients that were already known to interviewers, the filling of the questionnaire was asked even prior to check in. If three persons were from the same family or group of friends, only one would be interviewed, if they were more than three, then a second participant would take part in the survey. The staff members kindly asked participants if they could help, about the purpose of the study, and the duration of the interview. They also cleared that the data will be anonymous and confidential.

The data collection process started on 03 April, 2020 and was finished on 15 of May, 2020. There were sixty four participants in general, but three of them were excluded due to invalid questionnaires (total 61 valid questionnaires). Principal component analysis was used in conjunction with varimax rotation and confirmatory analysis, utilizing the maximum likelihood estimation approach, to assess the 41 statements associated with the Aaker's scale (1997). The factorability and appropriateness of the analysis were verified using the Bartlett sphericity test and the Kaiser-Meyer-Olkin (KMO) sampling adequacy test. We used NVivo Software, SPSS, and AMOS (version 29) for the analyses.

4. RESULTS

4.1 Qualitative Results

Seven interviews were conducted as part of the qualitative study to see whether the brand personality concept could be applied at the hotel. Of the seven respondents, the most (71%) were from Kosovo, 57% were men between the ages of 26 and 35, and the majority had a bachelor's or master's degree or higher (Table 1).

Table 1. Demographic characteristics of participants for the qualitative part of the study

Characteristic	N	Overall, N = 7[1]	Men, N = 4[1]	Women, N = 3[1]
Do you think it is possible to attribute personality traits to brands?	7			
Yes		3 (43%)	2 (50%)	1 (33%)
No		4 (57%)	2 (50%)	2 (67%)
Age	7			
18-25		0 (0%)	0 (0%)	0 (0%)
26-35		4 (57%)	1 (25%)	3 (100%)
36-45		3 (43%)	3 (75%)	0 (0%)
46-55		0 (0%)	0 (0%)	0 (0%)
56-65		0 (0%)	0 (0%)	0 (0%)
Country	7			
Germany		1 (14%)	1 (25%)	0 (0%)
Kosovo		5 (71%)	2 (50%)	3 (100%)
Swiss		1 (14%)	1 (25%)	0 (0%)
Education	7			
Elementary School/High School		1 (14%)	1 (25%)	0 (0%)
Bachelor		3 (43%)	2 (50%)	1 (33%)
Master/Phd		3 (43%)	1 (25%)	2 (67%)
Income	7			
Under 10k		0 (0%)	0 (0%)	0 (0%)
10-20k		3 (50%)	0 (0%)	3 (100%)
30-50k		0 (00%)	0 (0%)	0 (0%)
50k+		3 (50%)	3 (100%)	0 (0%)

Source: own elaboration. Note: Frequency (percentage).

We also observed that the costumers have said different traits, in describing Hotel Garden. Hard to point to the same traits in the universe of traits. In the declaration: *If Hotel Garden was a human, which personality trait would you first think of, or how would you describe, in a single word personality trait of Hotel Garden, add two more traits?* Even if all traits pointed out were positive, one could feel from face expression, the enthusiasm to point out impressive traits. Hospitality/welcomeness pointed out three times, other three traits that pointed out two times, were- calm, secure, and serious. Others traits such as elegant, comfort, educated, clean, were pointed only once. When asked why, they pointed out those traits for Hotel Garden, the participants showed feelings toward its personality traits, or their tendency was to explain treatment in their relationship with the Brand. Overall the traits that where mentioned mostly during the open question section were: 13 Calmness, 9 service, 7 comfort, 7 hospitality and hardworking 5 times (Figure 1).

Figure 1. Word cloud analysis (own elaboration)

Regarding Hotel Garden hospitality, one participant, declared "They treat me as an individual." Another one, the participant, clearly described: "I am at Home. Hotel Garden treats me as an individual, with individual treatment, as a person, not client. I feel secure, I feel complete". It can be seen that Self-Brand Congruence is very strong between Clients and Hotel Garden. Even though we did not find consensus in particular personality traits or dimensions, it seems that Hotel Garden personality is wider to create a bond with them. In the suggestive part of questions, we found a large consensus and participants mostly approved the majority of personality traits. In the question: Is Hotel Garden exciting, 71.42% of participants said: No. In All other questions, there was agreement that: Hotel Garden Is (friendly, real, original, cheerful, trendy, exiting, cool, independent, hardworking, successful, secure, confident, upper class, glamorous, good looking, charming, convenient, comfort, delicate), with rate 71.42 to 100% for Yes.

Table 2. The frequency of participants' responses for the qualitative interview divided by gender

Characteristic	N	Overall, N = 7[1]	Men, N = 4[1]	Women, N = 3[1]
Friendly	7			
Agree		6 (86%)	4 (100%)	2 (67%)
Disagree		1 (14%)	0 (0%)	1 (33%)
Real	7			
Agree		7 (100%)	4 (100%)	3 (100%)
Disagree		0 (0%)	0 (0%)	0 (0%)
Original	7			
Agree		7 (100%)	4 (100%)	3 (100%)
Disagree		0 (0%)	0 (0%)	0 (0%)
Cheerful	7			
Agree		6 (86%)	4 (100%)	2 (67%)
Disagree		1 (14%)	0 (0%)	1 (33%)
Trendy	7			
Agree		5 (71%)	3 (75%)	2 (67%)
Disagree		2 (29%)	1 (25%)	1 (33%)
Exciting	7			
Agree		2 (29%)	1 (25%)	1 (33%)
Disagree		5 (71%)	3 (75%)	2 (67%)
Cool	7			
Agree		7 (100%)	4 (100%)	3 (100%)
Disagree		0 (0%)	0 (0%)	0 (0%)
Up to Date	7			
Agree		7 (100%)	4 (100%)	3 (100%)
Disagree		0 (0%)	0 (0%)	0 (0%)
Hard Working	7			
Agree		7 (100%)	4 (100%)	3 (100%)
Disagree		0 (0%)	0 (0%)	0 (0%)
Successful	7			
Agree		7 (100%)	4 (100%)	3 (100%)
Disagree		0 (0%)	0 (0%)	0 (0%)
Secure	7			
Agree		7 (100%)	4 (100%)	3 (100%)
Disagree		0 (0%)	0 (0%)	0 (0%)
Confident	7			
Agree		7 (100%)	4 (100%)	3 (100%)
Disagree		0 (0%)	0 (0%)	0 (0%)
Upper Class	7			
Agree		6 (86%)	4 (100%)	2 (67%)
Disagree		1 (14%)	0 (0%)	1 (33%)

Continued on following page

Table 2. Continued

Characteristic	N	Overall, N = 7[1]	Men, N = 4[1]	Women, N = 3[1]
Glamorous	7			
Agree		5 (71%)	3 (75%)	2 (67%)
Disagree		2 (29%)	1 (25%)	1 (33%)
Good looking	7			
Agree		7 (100%)	4 (100%)	3 (100%)
Disagree		0 (0%)	0 (0%)	0 (0%)
Charming	7			
Agree		7 (100%)	4 (100%)	3 (100%)
Disagree		0 (0%)	0 (0%)	0 (0%)
Convenience	7			
Agree		7 (100%)	4 (100%)	3 (100%)
Disagree		0 (0%)	0 (0%)	0 (0%)
Comfort	7			
Agree		7 (100%)	4 (100%)	3 (100%)
Disagree		0 (0%)	0 (0%)	0 (0%)
Delicate	7			
Agree		7 (100%)	4 (100%)	3 (100%)
Disagree		0 (0%)	0 (0%)	0 (0%)

Source: own elaboration. Note: Frequency (percentage).

Third section of questions where we wanted to test new traits especially for Hotel Industry (Convenience, Comfort and Delicate) (Ekinci & Hosany, 2006). The participants had 100% agreement that Hotel Garden is Convenient, Comfort and Delicate. One participant, for example, declared that: Of course Hotel Garden is convenient, when you walk the carpet is so soft, when I lay down in the bed I feel like a king. It fits great with my needs. Another one, points out the comfort aspect of the Hotel Garden "When I get in garden, I feel home. I have all that I need, starting from, great breakfast and feel calmness and relax for all day. If I feel more need I use the pool and sauna, and that bed is so comfortable, its layers comply fully with my body." The delicacy of the Hotel Garden was explained from one participants as "Garden Hotel food is so decorative, delicious and delicate. There is not any necessary decor on it. It lies in harmony with image and taste. Overall the traits that were mostly used in open question section.

4.2 Quantitative Results

Descriptive Analysis and Parametric and Non-Parametric Test

From the sample of 61 hotel guests participants, almost equal, 30 clients where man 49.18%, 31 were female, representing 50.81% of the total sample. Regarding age, 29.5% of the respondents were between 18 and 25 years old, 50.8% were between 26 and 35 years old and only 12 persons were in the range of 35-45 years old, representing 19.67% of total sample. Most of the participants 42 or 69% of participants where from Kosovo and represented 75% the sample, in total. With 3 participants for each Albania 4.9% and Macedonia 4.9% where countries with more foreign representatives in total sample. Germany, Norway and US had two representatives for country with total of 9.9% of general sample. With only one representative where Austria, Belgium, Italy, Croatia, Montenegro, Serbia and Turkey with 1.6% of, total sample, for each country.

Majority of the respondents, 75.5%, have bachelor's degree, from which males are 20 participants (67%) in man selection, 25 of the participants with bachelor degree were women with 83%, being a larger group inside women group selection. Only 3,5% of participants where with high school, and all of them were women, with representation of 10% in woman's group. The remaining 12 representatives or 20%, were with superior education master/PHD education. 10 representatives or 33% of males were with higher education master/PHD, with only 2 representatives or 6.7% of women for same education group. 21 respondents (34%) declared that they earn less than 10k euro per year, 11(18%) declared that earn 10-20k euro per year, 18 (30%) said that they earn 30-50k euro per year and 11 (18%) are earning more than 50k euro per year. 21(34%0 participants were in the earning >10k euro, 11 (18%) of them 10>20, 18 (30%) declared 30.50k euro and 11(18%) participants said that they earn more than 50k. We observed high inequality in gender earnings. In the earning per year section, from total of 21 participants earn under the 10k euro, from which 16 of them (52%) are women, were found in the bottom earning group comparing to 21 (Table 3).

Table 3. Demographic information of participants for the quantitative part of the study

Demographic Variables	N	Overall, N = 61[1]	Men, N = 30[1]	Women, N = 31[1]
Age	61			
18-25		18 (30%)	6 (20%)	12 (39%)
26-35		31 (51%)	18 (60%)	13 (42%)
36-45		12 (20%)	6 (20%)	6 (19%)
46-55		0 (0%)	0 (0%)	0 (0%)
56-65		0 (0%)	0 (0%)	0 (0%)
Country	61			
Albania		3 (4.9%)	0 (0%)	3 (9.7%)
Austria		1 (1.6%)	1 (3.3%)	0 (0%)
Belgium		1 (1.6%)	1 (3.3%)	0 (0%)
Germany		2 (3.3%)	0 (0%)	2 (6.5%)
Italy		1 (1.6%)	1 (3.3%)	0 (0%)
Kosovo		42 (69%)	19 (63%)	23 (74%)
Kroatia		1 (1.6%)	1 (3.3%)	0 (0%)
Macedonia		3 (4.9%)	3 (10%)	0 (0%)
Montenegro		1 (1.6%)	1 (3.3%)	0 (0%)
Norway		2 (3.3%)	0 (0%)	2 (6.5%)
Serbia		1 (1.6%)	0 (0%)	1 (3.2%)
Turkey		1 (1.6%)	1 (3.3%)	0 (0%)
US		2 (3.3%)	2 (6.7%)	0 (0%)
Education	60			
Elementary School/High School		3 (5.0%)	0 (0%)	3 (10%)
Bachelor		45 (75%)	20 (67%)	25 (83%)
Master/Phd		12 (20%)	10 (33%)	2 (6.7%)
Income per year	61			
Under 10k		21 (34%)	5 (17%)	16 (52%)
10-20k		11 (18%)	7 (23%)	4 (13%)
30-50k		18 (30%)	11 (37%)	7 (23%)
50k+		11 (18%)	7 (23%)	4 (13%)

Source: own elaboration. Note: Frequency (percentage).

Table 4 presents the outcomes of the descriptive statistics of the statements used in the Brand Personality Scale, in each question of the seven scales applied, using a seven-point Likert scale (1= "strongly disagree" and 7= "strongly agree"). In the dimension of Sincerity in Brand Personality Scale, the trait "Friendly" assumes the highest mean of 6.34. In the dimension of Excitement, the trait "Trendy" achieves the highest mean of 6.01. For the Competence dimension the trait "Hardworking" achieves the highest mean of 6.55. In the dimension Sophistication, the trait "Upper Class" archives the highest mean of 6.14. In the end, for the dimension of Ruggedness, the Outdoorsy trait achieved the highest mean of 4.67.

Table 4. Descriptive statistics of the traits used in the brand personality scale

Dimensions	Statements	Median	Mean	Std. Deviation (SD)	Range	Minimum	Maximum
Sincerity	Down to Earth	6.000	5.164	1.572	6.000	1.000	7.000
	Family oriented	5.000	4.770	1.407	5.000	2.000	7.000
	Small Town	4.000	4.393	1.486	6.000	1.000	7.000
	Sincere	6.000	5.689	1.073	4.000	3.000	7.000
	Real	6.000	5.869	0.991	3.000	4.000	7.000
	Wholesome	6.000	5.557	1.218	5.000	2.000	7.000
	Original	6.000	5.885	1.066	4.000	3.000	7.000
	Honest	6.000	5.525	1.089	5.000	2.000	7.000
	Cheerful	6.000	6.034	1.048	4.000	3.000	7.000
	Sentimental	6.000	5.557	1.103	3.000	4.000	7.000
	Friendly	7.000	6.34*	0.929	4.000	3.000	7.000
Excitement	Daring	5.000	5.197	0.997	3.000	4.000	7.000
	Trendy	6.000	6.01*	1.072	4.000	3.000	7.000
	Exiting	6.000	5.934	1.014	4.000	3.000	7.000
	Spirited	6.000	5.574	1.102	4.000	3.000	7.000
	Cool	6.000	5.967	0.948	3.000	4.000	7.000
	Young	6.000	5.705	1.085	4.000	3.000	7.000
	Imaginative	5.000	5.033	1.264	5.000	2.000	7.000
	Up to Date	6.000	5.770	1.189	5.000	2.000	7.000
	Independent	6.000	5.705	1.101	4.000	3.000	7.000
	Contemporary	5.000	5.230	1.101	4.000	3.000	7.000
Competence	Reliable	6.000	5.459	1.010	3.000	4.000	7.000
	Intelligent	6.000	5.393	1.069	4.000	3.000	7.000
	Successful	6.000	6.279	0.799	3.000	4.000	7.000
	Hard-Working	7.000	6.55*	0.742	3.000	4.000	7.000
	Secure	7.000	6.197	0.997	3.000	4.000	7.000
	Technical	5.000	5.066	1.223	6.000	1.000	7.000
	Corporate	6.000	5.508	1.312	6.000	1.000	7.000
	Leader	6.000	5.902	0.889	3.000	4.000	7.000
	Confident	6.000	5.918	0.936	3.000	4.000	7.000
Sophistication	Upper Class	6.000	6.148*	0.980	3.000	4.000	7.000
	Charming	6.000	6.016	0.922	3.000	4.000	7.000
	Glamorous	6.000	6.098	0.943	3.000	4.000	7.000
	Good looking	6.000	6.131	0.939	3.000	4.000	7.000
	Femine	6.000	5.689	1.133	3.000	4.000	7.000
	Smooth	6.000	5.738	1.079	5.000	2.000	7.000

Continued on following page

Table 4. Continued

Dimensions	Statements	Median	Mean	Std. Deviation (SD)	Range	Minimum	Maximum
Ruggedness	Outdoorsy	5.000	4.67*	1.313	6.000	1.000	7.000
	Thought	4.000	4.180	1.298	6.000	1.000	7.000
	Masculine	4.000	3.852	1.547	6.000	1.000	7.000
	Western	4.000	3.869	1.533	6.000	1.000	7.000
	Rugged	4.000	3.885	1.644	6.000	1.000	7.000

Source: own elaboration. Note: * signifies the highest mean per dimension.

Listing the five dimensions, the highest evaluation is given on the sophistication (Mean=5.94 out of max. 7, SD=.8) and competence dimension (Mean=5.81, SD=.7). Similarly, the sincerity and excitement dimensions share a similar high evaluation (mean higher than 5). On the contrary, the participants have shown somewhat neutral-lower score evaluation for the ruggedness dimension (Mean=4.09, SD=1.33). Because the sophistication and competence dimension does not show a normal distribution, we can use the mode value, which is still high and comparable to the mean shown above (for further details, see Table 5).

Table 5. Descriptive table of the computed by including the Aaker's original items

		Sincerity		Excitement		Competence		Sophistication		Ruggedness		
Valid		61		61		61		61		61		
Mode	a	4.818		6.100		5.778		7.000		4.000		
Mean		5.526		5.613		5.809		5.938		4.092		
Std. Error of Mean		0.097		0.098		0.091		0.105		0.171		
Std. Deviation		0.759		0.762		0.707		0.820		1.336		
Skewness		-0.287		-0.500		-0.751		-0.470		0.150		
Std. Error of Skewness		0.306		0.306		0.306		0.306		0.306		
Kurtosis		-0.249		0.764		0.569		-0.274		0.267		
Std. Error of Kurtosis		0.604		0.604		0.604		0.604		0.604		
Shapiro-Wilk		0.982		0.965		0.947		0.934		0.971		
P-value of Shapiro-Wilk		0.510		0.080		0.010		0.003		0.162		
Minimum		3.818		3.400		3.778		4.000		1.000		
Maximum		7.000		7.000		7.000		7.000		7.000		

a More than one mode exists, only the first is reported

In order to better check if the data are statistically significant from the neutral value (4), we performed a two-tailed One Sample T-Test analysis for the all five dimensions included. Here we found a significant increase from the neutral value for the sincerity, excitement, competence, and sophistication dimension ($p<.05$). On the contrary, no significant difference is present for ruggedness dimension $t(60)=0.537$, $p=.593$ (See Table 6).

Table 6. One sample t-test performed on computed (averaged) on Aaker's original dimensions

	Test	Statistic	df	p
Sincerity	**Student**	**15.704**	**60**	**< .001**
Excitement	Student	16.527	60	< .001
Competence	Wilcoxon	1889.000	60	< .001
Sophistication	Wilcoxon	1770.000	60	< .001
Ruggedness	Student	0.537	60	0.593

Note. For the Student t-test, the alternative hypothesis specifies that the mean is different from 4. For the Wilcoxon test, the alternative hypothesis specifies that the median is different from 4.

A two-tailed independent-samples t-test was conducted to compare Brand Personality Dimensions. Beforehand, we checked for the normality and equality of variances assumption. Shapiro-Wilk test showed evidence of non-normality distribution for women in the competence dimension ($W=.929$, $p=.006$) and sophistication dimension ($W=.898$, $p=.006$). Similarly, the sophistication dimension showed violation of the equality of variances assumption ($F=. 4.374\ p=.041$). To control for this, we will use the results of Student's t-test results for all other dimensions, except for the competence dimension where we used Welch's t-test results. There was no significant gender difference in all dimensions of the Brand Personality ($p>0.05$). Because there were only three subjects categorized with elementary education, we eliminated it while performing group differences. Therefore, no significant difference remained when we compared the rest of two groups (Bachelor and Master/PhD), with the p-value higher than .05 for all the dimensions. No significant differences are present also for the education level of the participants ($p>.05$).

We also checked for the role of income level for potential differences in the brand personality. One-Way ANOVA showed significant differences between groups only for the dimension of competence $F(3, 57)=3.488$, $p=.011$. Tukey post-hoc analysis revealed the significant difference between the low-income subgroup ($M=6.12$, $SD=.43$) with the upper-middle one ($M=5.55$, $SD=0.83$).

Exploratory Factor Analysis

Through the analysis of table 7, we verified that the five constructs of Aaker (1997)'s Brand Personality Dimension Scale remained, and the results of Kaiser-Myer-Olkin (KMO) and Bartlett tests confirm the factorability and the adequacy of the analysis. We observed one exception with the construct related to sincerity where two statements were removed (sentimental and friendly) because we applied the maximum likelihood factor analysis with a communality cut-off point of 0.5 and they presented a value below. All the constructs exhibit a high percentage of variance, between to 43% and 83%.

Table 7. The identification of the latent constructs: exploratory factorial analysis

Dimensions	Statements	Loading* (EFA)	Eigenvalues/Rotation Sums Squared Loadings	Variance (%)	Bartlett's test (sig.)	Kaiser-Meyer-Olkin Measure of Sampling Adequacy
Sincerity	Original	0.825	4.747	43.153	362.011 (<0.001)	0.709
	Real	0.747				
	Down to Earth	0.738				
	Cheerful	0.736				
	Sincere	0.724				
	Wholesome	0.709				
	Honest	0.684				
	Family oriented	0.564				
	Small Town	0.504				
Excitement	Exiting	0.821	4.969	49.689	311.877 (<0.001)	0.768
	Young	0.787				
	Trendy	0.779				
	Spirited	0.760				
	Cool	0.742				
	Imaginative	0.702				
	Up to Date	0.664				
	Independent	0.594				
	Daring	0.584				
	Contemporary	0.559				
Competence	Leader	0.799	4.633	51.480	252.679 (<0.001)	0.863
	Corporate	0.796				
	30. Confident	0.789				
	Hard-Working	0.786				
	Intellegent	0.771				
	Successful	0.75				
	Technical	0.593				
	Reliable	0.564				
	Secure	0.542				
Sophistication	Glamorous	0.883	3.988	66.473	222.830 (<0.001)	0.835
	Charming	0.876				
	Good looking	0.85				
	Upper Class	0.836				
	Smooth	0.725				
	Femine	0.703				

Continued on following page

Table 7. Continued

Dimensions	Statements	Loading* (EFA)	Eigenvalues/Rotation Sums Squared Loadings	Variance (%)	Bartlett's test (sig.)	Kaiser-Meyer-Olkin Measure of Sampling Adequacy
Ruggedness	Western	0.951	4.130	82.610	322.128 (<0.001)	0.816
	Rugged	0.934				
	Masculine	0.896				
	Thought	0.881				
	Outdoorsy	0.880				

Note: *Extraction Method: Principal Component Analysis. Rotation Method: Varimax with Kaiser Normalization;

Confirmatory Factor Analysis

Confirmatory factor analysis was then carried out. A confirmatory analysis is presented in Table 5, and it is evident that the measurement model provides a good fit to the data ($X2/df = 314,000$, $df = 98$; $X2/df = 3.321$; RMSEA = 0.051; CFI = 0.953; TLI = 0.961 and IFI = 0.973) (Hair et al., 2018). The average variance extracted (AVE) and construct reliability (CR) are presented in the following table to determine convergent validity. The results for both CR and AVE are higher than the suggested level (Fornell & Larcker, 1981). Composite reliability (CR) (> 0,6) and average variance extracted (AVE) (> 0,5) values show that the psychometric qualities of the measurement components utilised in model estimate are good (Fornell & Larcker, 1981).

Table 8. Confirmatory factor analysis (CFA)

Dimensions	Statements	Loading* (CFA)	CR	AVE	Cronbach's α
Sincerity	Original	0.876	0.910	0.536	0.853
	Real	0.873			
	Down to Earth	0.743			
	Cheerful	0.762			
	Sincere	0.733			
	Wholesome	0.722			
	Honest	0.683			
	Family oriented	0.601			
	Small Town	0.523			
Excitement	Exiting	0.810	0.915	0.522	0.883
	Young	0.803			
	Trendy	0.783			
	Spirited	0.789			
	Cool	0.756			
	Imaginative	0.743			
	Up to Date	0.712			
	Independent	0.601			
	Daring	0.598			
	Contemporary	0.573			
Competence	Leader	0.809	0.916	0.552	0.869
	Corporate	0.816			
	Confident	0.819			
	Hard-Working	0.806			
	Intellegent	0.791			
	Successful	0.78			
	Technical	0.643			
	Reliable	0.604			
	Secure	0.562			
Sophistication	Glamorous	0.884	0.925	0.675	0.892
	Charming	0.879			
	Good looking	0.862			
	Upper Class	0.842			
	Smooth	0.732			
	Femine	0.714			

Continued on following page

Table 8. Continued

Dimensions	Statements	Loading* (CFA)	CR	AVE	Cronbach's α
Ruggedness	Western	0.955	0.962	0.835	0.946
	Rugged	0.948			
	Masculine	0.895			
	Thought	0.886			
	Outdoorsy	0.881			

Goodness-of-fit X^2/df = 314,000, df = 98; X^2/df = 3.321; RMSEA = 0.051; CFI = 0.953; TLI = 0.961 and IFI = 0.973)

5. DISCUSSION AND CONCLUSIONS

One of the seven brand approaches within the context of brand management is brand personality, which has attracted the interest of numerous academics and researchers over the past 25 years. There are not many research that apply brand personality metrics to the hotel industry, despite the fact that many studies apply these measurements to various brands around the world. Brands get distinct personalities from their consumers (Aaker, 1997). Using the constructs of the Brand Personality Scale (Sincerity, Excitement, Competence, Sophistication, and Ruggedness) as outlined by Aaker (1997). Which of the five Aaker aspects is reproducible in a Kosovan context? was our initial research question, which we answered based on this construction. The dimensions of Sincerity, Competence, Excitement, and Sophistication were determined to be highly representative of Hotel Garden. However, the degree of ruggedness was not mentioned by participants as a characteristic of the Hotel Garden. By using confirmatory analysis, we were able to determine the answer to the second study question, which asked whether these dimensions are repeatable in a Kosovan setting. Based on the Brand Personality Scale, we can infer that Hotel Garden in Prishtina has a strong personality, which answers the third study question. Based on the application of both quantitative and qualitative approaches, Hotel Garden Pristina has a distinct and powerful identity. In terms of Sincerity, Excitement, Competence, and Sophistication, Hotel Grand scored higher.

Regarding the fourth question, we have already determined that the Brand Personality scale's five dimensions—Sincerity, Excitement, Competence, Sophistication, and Robustness—are a helpful tool for learning how consumers view a hotel brand. We next examine how the traits linked to the brand personality may affect the function, productivity, and retention of employees in response to the fourth question (What is the role of employees in the hotel's brand personality?), as well as potential management consequences. In the Sincerity context, employees are supposed to connect with consumers in a genuine and open manner. Authenticity is a major factor in increasing brand trust. Regarding Excitement, the group needs to be able to generate thrilling moments by being animated and passionate. This excitement may have a favourable effect on how the brand is perceived by consumers. Employee competence is essential since they must exhibit the knowledge, abilities, and productivity required for their positions. The perceived competency of the team is inextricably tied to consumer trust in the brand. Employees that embody sophistication in their work must also display professionalism, grace, and refinement to enhance the brand's perceived sophistication. The final measure on the scale, robustness, suggests that staff members need to be resilient, able to handle difficulties and give clients a sense of security.

The team's strength gives people more reason to believe in the stability of the brand. When it comes to associating employee performance with trust in the brand, it is essential to consider the dimensions of the Brand Personality Scale in performance evaluations. It is possible to reinforce related traits with targeted training, and it is necessary to develop an organisational culture that values and supports the intended brand personality.

A key factor in employee retention is paying attention to the aspects of the Brand Personality Scale, in addition to how customers perceive the brand. An environment at work that fosters engagement and satisfaction is produced by coordinating brand expectations and values with workers' day-to-day experiences. Employee loyalty and retention are higher when they identify with the brand personality because they are more likely to feel appreciated and linked to the organization's mission (Michael et al., 2023).

It is recommended that future measures involve investing in specialized training that is in line with the scale's characteristics. This will boost the brand's representation while also enhancing the competencies and abilities of the workforce. This methodology not only fosters the professional growth of staff members but also upholds the significance of their function in communicating the essence of the brand. The incorporation of these components enhances employee happiness and sense of belonging, two critical components for retaining talent, in addition to increasing consumer trust.

The relationship between brand, visitor happiness, and employee retention becomes critical to take into account as hotels strategize for the future. Establishing a work atmosphere that not only embodies the brand's personality but also places a high priority on employees' continuous development creates a win-win situation for the team's stability and the brand's reputation. In addition to strengthening consumer confidence in the brand, this integrated strategy lays the groundwork for long-term expansion and operational excellence.

This study has also its own limitations. First practical reasons, the sample size of this study was not so large. This can lead us to have a non-representative sample for all the guest that Hotel Garden in Prishtina has. Another limitation is related to the possibility of evaluating other dimensions of the brand (social responsibility, engagement, satisfaction, among others) and not only evaluating it from the perspective of customers but also employees. Notwithstanding the aforementioned limitations, this study—which combines qualitative and quantitative analysis—is the first of its kind in Kosovo and establishes a connection between the personality of the brand and the function of hotel employees.

REFERENCES

Aaker, J. (2009). The problems of brand definition. *Sustainable Management and Marketing. Australian and New Zealand Marketing Academy Conference 2009*, 1–10.

Aaker, J., & Fournier, S. (1995). Brand as a character, a partner and a person: Three perspectives on the question of brand personality. *Advances in Consumer Research. Association for Consumer Research (U. S.)*, 22, 391–395.

Aaker, J. L. (1997). Dimensions of Brand Personality. *JMR, Journal of Marketing Research*, 34(3), 347–356. doi:10.1177/002224379703400304

Aitken, P. P., Leathar, D. S., O'Hagan, F. J., & Squair, S. I. (1987). Children's awareness of cigarette advertisements and brand imagery. *British Journal of Addiction*, 82(6), 615–622. doi:10.1111/j.1360-0443.1987.tb01523.x PMID:3475100

Arora, R., & Stoner, C. (2009). A mixed method approach to understanding brand personality. *Journal of Product and Brand Management, 18*(4), 272–283. doi:10.1108/10610420910972792

Blackston, M. (1993). Beyond brand personality: Building brand relationships. In D. A. Aaker & A. L. Biel (Eds.), *Brand equity and advertising: Advertising's role in building strong brands* (pp. 113–124). Lawrence Erlbaum and Associates.

Boksberger, P., Dolnicar, S., Laesser, C., & Randle, M. (2011). Self-congruity theory: To what extent does it hold in tourism? *Journal of Travel Research, 50*(4), 454–464. doi:10.1177/0047287510368164

Bowen, D., & Schneider, B. (1985). Boundary-spanning-role employees and the service encounter: Some guidelines for management and research. In J. A. Czepiel, M. R. Solomon, & C. Surprenant (Eds.), *The service encounter* (pp. 127–147). D. C. Heath.

Brown, T. J. (1998). Corporate Associations in Marketing: Antecedents and Consequences. *Corporate Reputation Review, 1*(3), 215–233. doi:10.1057/palgrave.crr.1540045

Calderón-Fajardo, V., Molinillo, S., Anaya-Sánchez, R., & Ekinci, Y. (2023). Brand personality: Current insights and future research directions. *Journal of Business Research, 166*, 114062. doi:10.1016/j.jbusres.2023.114062

Chen, K. P., Chen, H., & Wang, Y. (2024). The moderating effect of safety image on guests' perceived risk and revisit intentions in luxury hotels. *International Journal of Tourism Research, 26*(1), e2614. doi:10.1002/jtr.2614

De Chernatony, L., & Dall'Olmo Riley, F. (1998). Defining a "brand": Beyond the literature with experts' interpretations. *Journal of Marketing Management, 14*(5), 417–443. doi:10.1362/026725798784867798

Ekinci, Y., & Hosany, S. (2006). Destination Personality: An Application of Brand Personality to Tourism Destinations. *Journal of Travel Research, 45*(2), 127–139. doi:10.1177/0047287506291603

Fornell, C., & Larcker, D. F. (1981). Evaluating Structural Equation Models with Unobservable Variables and Measurement Error. *JMR, Journal of Marketing Research, 18*(1), 39–50. doi:10.1177/002224378101800104

Fournier, S. (1998). Consumers and their brands: Developing relationship theory in consumer research. *The Journal of Consumer Research, 24*(4), 343–373. doi:10.1086/209515

Green, M. S. (2008). The Significance of Self-Expression. *Self-Expression*, 1–20. doi:10.1093/acprof:oso/9780199283781.003.0001

Guan, J., Wang, W., Guo, Z., Chan, J. H., & Qi, X. (2021). Customer experience and brand loyalty in the full-service hotel sector: The role of brand affect. *International Journal of Contemporary Hospitality Management, 33*(5), 1620–1645. doi:10.1108/IJCHM-10-2020-1177

Gulati, C., Mathur, G., & Upadhyay, Y. (2023). Internal Branding: Connecting Links to Establish Employees' Brand Behaviour in Hospitality Sector. *FIIB Business Review*. Advance online publication. doi:10.1177/23197145221143831

Hair, J. F., Black, W. C., Anderson, R. E., & Babin, B. J. (2018). *Multivariate Data Analysis*. Cengage.

Hankinson, G. (2001). Brand orientation in the hotel industry. *International Journal of Contemporary Hospitality Management*, *13*(5), 204–214.

Hillen, J. (2021). Psychological pricing in online food retail. *British Food Journal*, *123*(11), 3522–3535. doi:10.1108/BFJ-09-2020-0847

Kapferer, J. N. (2008). *The New Strategic Brand Management: Advanced Insights and Strategic Thinking*. Kogan Page.

Khairy, H. A., Agina, M. F., Aliane, N., & Hashad, M. E. (2023). Internal Branding in Hotels: Interaction Effects of Employee Engagement, Workplace Friendship, and Organizational Citizenship Behavior. *Sustainability (Basel)*, *15*(5), 4530. doi:10.3390/su15054530

Levy, S. J. (1959). Symbols for sale. *Harvard Business Review*, *37*(4), 117–124.

Li, X., Yen, C.-L. A., & Liu, T. (2020). Hotel brand personality and brand loyalty: An affective, conative and behavioral perspective. *Journal of Hospitality Marketing & Management*, *29*(5), 550–570. doi:10.1080/19368623.2019.1654961

Malär, L., Krohmer, H., Hoyer, W. D., & Nyffenegger, B. (2011). Emotional brand attachment and brand personality: The relative importance of the actual and the ideal self. *Journal of Marketing*, *75*(4), 35–52. doi:10.1509/jmkg.75.4.35

Michael, N., Michael, I., & Fotiadis, A. K. (2023). The role of human resources practices and branding in the hotel industry in Dubai. *Journal of Human Resources in Hospitality & Tourism*, *22*(1), 1–25. doi:10.1080/15332845.2023.2126927

Morgan, N., Pritchard, A., & Pride, R. (2011). Destination branding and the role of the stakeholders: The case of New Zealand. *Journal of Vacation Marketing*, *17*(3), 205–217.

Ngo, L. V., Nguyen, N. P., Huynh, K. T., Gregory, G., & Cuong, P. H. (2020). Converting internal brand knowledge into employee performance. *Journal of Product and Brand Management*, *29*(3), 273–287. doi:10.1108/JPBM-10-2018-2068

Plummer, J. T. (1985). *Brand personality: A strategic concept for multinational advertising*. Paper presented at the Marketing Educator's Conference, New York.

Radler, V. M. (2018). 20 Years of brand personality: A bibliometric review and research agenda. *Journal of Brand Management*, *25*(4), 370–383. doi:10.1057/s41262-017-0083-z

Rahimian, S., ShamiZanjani, M., Manian, A., & Esfidani, M. R. (2021). A framework of customer experience management for hotel industry. *International Journal of Contemporary Hospitality Management*, *33*(5), 1413–1436. doi:10.1108/IJCHM-06-2020-0522

Šerić, M., & Mikulić, J. (2020). Building brand equity through communication consistency in luxury hotels: An impact-asymmetry analysis. *Journal of Hospitality and Tourism Insights*, *3*(4), 451–468. doi:10.1108/JHTI-11-2019-0119

Sop, S. A., & Kozak, N. (2019). Effects of brand personality, self-congruity and functional congruity on hotel brand loyalty. *Journal of Hospitality Marketing & Management*, *28*(8), 1–31. doi:10.1080/19368623.2019.1577202

Su, N., & Reynolds, D. (2017). Effects of brand personality dimensions on consumers' perceived self-image congruity and functional congruity with hotel brands. *International Journal of Hospitality Management, 66*, 1–12. doi:10.1016/j.ijhm.2017.06.006

Su, N., & Reynolds, D. (2019). Categorical differences of hotel brand personality: Identifying competition across hotel categories. *International Journal of Contemporary Hospitality Management, 31*(4), 1801–1818. Advance online publication. doi:10.1108/IJCHM-05-2018-0354

Unurlu, C., & Uca, S. (2017). The effect of culture on brand loyalty through brand performance and brand personality. *International Journal of Tourism Research, 19*(6), 672–681. doi:10.1002/jtr.2139

Wang, X., Cheng, M., Wong, I. K. A., Teah, M., & Lee, S. (2021). Big-five personality traits in P2P accommodation platforms: Similar or different to hotel brands? *Current Issues in Tourism, 24*(23), 3407–3419. doi:10.1080/13683500.2021.1884205

Zhang, X., Yang, H., & Huang, Q. (2019). Examining the impacts of hotel employees' compensation fairness on turnover intention. *International Journal of Contemporary Hospitality Management, 31*(2), 947–965.

Chapter 4
Captivating Talent Through Eco-Friendly Practices:
How Does Signalling Theory Resonate in Green Talent Management?

Yasemin Bal
Yildiz Technical University, Turkey

Nazli Ece Bulgur
https://orcid.org/0000-0001-6164-772X
Yildiz Technical University, Turkey

ABSTRACT

Human resources management has an important role in organizations. This importance comes from the fact that HRM plays an active role in all other functions of the organization. At this point, although it is an important competitive tool for organizations, it has gained importance in organizations in practices that will shape competition. While green talent management, which is one of the most important green HRM functions, comes to the fore, various changes have begun to be seen in the functions due to the fact that the competition is human-oriented. In this regard, organizations have not only developed business strategies for talented individuals, but have begun to develop environmental awareness and business strategies for talented individuals who can take environmental initiatives. In this regard, the aim of the study is to analyze green talent management and how organizations captivate through eco-friendly practices.

1. INTRODUCTION

The fact that the concept of talent is used in other disciplines and is explained with similar concepts and the same content enriches the definitions of the concept of talent. In particular, the integration of the concept of talent into business life has led to an expansion in the scope of the concept. First of all, understanding what the concept we consider as talent means and proceeding in this direction and explain-

DOI: 10.4018/979-8-3693-1938-3.ch004

ing it with the concept of management is important in terms of adding depth to the subject. The element mentioned as talent is individuals. It is a concept that emerges when individuals are described as human resources. Human beings are described as a resource because the capacity of human resources can be improved, they have unlimited abilities and are numerous. The fact that it expresses human resources in its talent shows that it is human capital with its knowledge, skills and abilities. Therefore, talents, which are described as resources for organizations, are of primary importance in ensuring the existence of the organization. In this regard, talent management is primarily expressed as the management of human resources directed within certain goals and objectives. These are the business strategies that organizations put forward and implement in order to retain talented employees.

Business strategies and talent management exist. The most important reason for this is that in talent management, the concept is approached from this perspective in terms of operating an analytical process, making long-term plans and serving the organizations' sustainable competitive advantage. Thus, approaching talent management from a strategic perspective is important for the health of the organization so that the organization can continue its life, meet its mission requirements and maintain its sustainable competitive advantage. Today, due to changing conjunctural reasons, changes have occurred in the evaluation of talent management. Changes in the external environment have brought about changes in the evaluation of human capital by taking into account the changes in the ecosystem of organizations. It has become especially important for organizations that make changes at the core of their business strategies by taking the ecosystem into consideration to include individuals who have high awareness of nature and can minimize the impact of changes in the ecosystem.

In this case, the concept of talent management evolved into the concept of green talent management. What is meant by green talent management is that there are individuals who have a high awareness of nature, who are nature conscious, and who can implement the initiatives they undertake to protect nature both in their individual life and business life, and that these expressions also shape their business strategies. The features mentioned above are of great importance in terms of serving the goals and objectives of organizations. The green talent management practices of organizations and the business strategies they create to retain employees also vary. It is seen that there are differences between talent management and green talent management, and certain differences are created in shaping business strategies. They are similar in that they are both human-oriented, but the strategies they use to increase awareness, the existence of information about nature, the existence of practices that raise awareness among employees about nature, differ. Therefore, in green talent management, practices are created in the processes and activities related to talent management within the framework of nature-oriented policies. The differentiation of green talent practices across organizations paves the way for deepening knowledge about the applicability of the concept. Therefore, providing organizations with information about what types of applications exist allows the expansion of the areas where the concept can be practiced. By doing this, the various green talent management practices that will be included in the study are important in terms of providing information about how they are implemented in which institutions. Another factor that will make the study important is the conceptual evaluation of green talent management within the scope of signaling theory. In this regard, green talent management, which is examined within the scope of signalling theory, is important in terms of providing information about the inputs and outputs of employees and managers and how it has differences from the others theories which had been used in other academics papers.

Establishing a general conceptual framework and then addressing the basic issues regarding talent management are among the primary issues to be addressed in the study. In the later stages of the study, in addition to the elements of the main subject whose conceptual framework has been explained, it will be evaluated within a theoretical framework, and it is aimed to enrich the study by approaching it from a theoretical perspective. Thus, at the end of the study, it is thought that it will be useful both in providing theoretical information and in guiding institutions on how it can be applied in practice.

2. GREEN HUMAN RESOURCES MANAGEMENT

In addition to the economic benefits of human resources management and strategic human resources management for organizations, it also provides benefits in terms of increasing organizational efficiency and effectiveness. Today, considering environmental issues within the scope of management practices has paved the way for positive organizational and individual outcomes. Accordingly, the changes in the business environment have brought about changes in the plans that constitute the steps that organizations will take regarding the environment. Thus, businesses have begun to create plans that will help develop their corporate strategies as well as turning their focus to environmental issues. Therefore, organizations have taken into account being environmentally focused within their corporate systems (Bahuguna et al., 2023).

The issue of environmental management has gained increasing importance in management studies over the years. Especially in organizational management studies, with the inclusion of environmental management, this issue has become visible in various functions of organizational structures. The decrease in the importance of the traditional organizational management approach over time has led to the inclusion of other issues. In particular, organizations' inclusion and consideration of environmental issues in various work plans and raising environmental awareness paves the way for organizations to have more say in modern management areas and to strengthen their dominance in new areas. Thus, environmental planning or environmental management has taken its place in creating a certain vision in the institutional systems of organizations. In this regard, the combination of procedures involved in human resources management and environmental management elements has become accepted by organizations. As a result, the combination and unification of two disciplines, environmental management and human resources management, has paved the way for the emergence of a field called Green Human Resources Management. The definitions of green human resources management based on the established foundations have led to the formation of conceptualizations of what the concept is. In this regard, definitions are included in different studies on green human resources management. These;

- "Green human resources management; It is the combination of environmental management and human resources management practices" (Opatha,
- "These are green practices that are included in the management areas of organizations to achieve their environmental goals"(Masri,
- "It is the simultaneous execution of human resources management and environmental management practices in order to help create positive environmental outcomes" (Renwick et al., 2008; Shah, 2019; Shen et al., 2018; Zaid et al., 2018; Kramar, 2014).

When the main purpose of the combination of environmental management and human resources management functions is to be expressed in summary (Aftab, 2023)

- "Organizations have a vision to achieve environmental goals,"
- "Aiming to be more selfless regarding environmental issues,"
- "Aiming to direct organizations towards sustainability,"
- "The desire of organizations to include sustainability practices within organizations,"
- "Having the aim of improving organizational sustainability,"
- "Having the idea of minimizing the negative aspects of environmental impacts,"
- "It is the desire to have sustainability parameters embodied in human resources practices."

The implementation of green policies as a basis in green human resources management functions shows that environmental management has become an important issue in these functions. Expanding the conceptual scope of environmental management functions by including human resources functions also affects the frequency of implementation of green policies. In particular, the fact that green policies are implemented, a certain organizational performance is achieved and the employees have positive outcomes, reveals the idea that green policies provide a competitive advantage. For this reason, explaining what the functions of green human resources management mean will provide a conceptual understanding of the subject (Table 1).

Table 1. Definitions regarding green human resources functions

Functions	Explanations
Green Business Design	*"It is used to indicate a number of duties and responsibilities related to environmental protection. It also indicates the characteristics that a green business should have."* (Mwita, 2019)
Green Personnel Selection and Placement	*"It involves evaluating candidates based on questions related to the environment. It involves selecting individuals who are environmentally aware and have characteristics that support environmental initiatives."* (Zubahir ve Khan, 2019
Green Training and Development	*"It covers the foundations that enable employees to learn about the environment and link organizational practices with green practices."* (Bhutton, Auranzeb, 2016)
Green Performance Management and Performance Evaluation	*"Green performance management includes issues related to the organization's policies and environmental responsibilities."* (Banwal, Tiwari, 2015).
Green Compensation and Reward Management	*"Green compensation and reward management includes rewarding employees for their green performance in order to contribute to employees and increase their performance, and in addition, creating a green wage structure."* (Limsuwan, Jirawuttinunt, 2019).
Green Employee Relations	*"Green employee relations include staff involvement and empowerment procedures. These procedures include the existence and implementation of green policies."* (Mashala, 2018)
Green Occupational Health and Safety	*"It is a function that aims to provide a green workplace environment for every employee."* (Aruljarah et al., 2015)

Source: This table made by the authors

In this case, it has become an important issue for organizations to focus on green resource management practices to ensure their development at internal service points. It seems that the main purpose is to help nurture external service practices based on internal service practices. Thus, organizations aim to maintain their sustainable competitive advantages, ensure the steps to be taken regarding the creation of a green workforce, and implement green initiatives in organizational environments.

3. TALENT MANAGEMENT

The concept of talent and talent management has become one of the management tools given importance by organizations today. Talent and talent management constitute a specific implementation process and implementation ability and implementation capacity of organizations. The use of talent in the process requires organizations to coincide with the ability to use their talents. Today, distinguishing talented individuals among the individuals working in institutions and shaping programs accordingly constitute the basis for organizations to survive and gain competitive advantage (Beechler & Woodward,2009). Therefore, talent and the ability to manage talent within the organization are important for organizations (Cheese et al, 2023). Before explaining the concept of talent management, it is thought that focusing on the meanings of the concept of management will add a more comprehensive meaning to the subject. Management is the concept that refers to determining goals and objectives within an institution, using resources effectively and efficiently, and benefiting from management functions while ensuring this use. The concept of talent in itself refers to an individual's capacity to understand and interpret anything. According to some studies, talent is conceptualized as a personal skill and a developmental/improvable structure, as well as representing an innate existential structure (Thunnissen et al, 2013). Talent management means creating various business strategies that ensure the retention of employees within the organization. Talent management is not a concept that can be explained with just one explanation or is easy to understand. In various sources, talent management refers to the representation of outstanding employees within a certain business group. At the same time, they are individuals who contribute to the performance of the organization with the knowledge, skills and behavior of the individual and engage in activities that support their success. Accordingly, in another study, it is the capacity of individuals to use the knowledge, skills and behaviors they have (Stahl et al, 2007).

Table 2. Conceptualization of talent and talent management

Talent
"It is the capacity to perform anything, especially a work-related situation, when expressed within the context of organizational individuals."
"It is the state of being able to understand and fulfill anything."
"It is the ability of individuals to reveal that they have processed anything in a mental process."
"It is the embodiment of the parameters of competence, commitment and contribution specific to individuals through the actions taken by individuals."
"They are various internal skills that are also innate. It includes both innate and developable features."
"It can also be expressed as the sum of the inherent skills and learning skills that individuals have."
Management
"Enables organizations to achieve their goals and objectives,"
"Ensuring the effective and efficient use of resources to achieve goals and objectives,"
"It refers to a process used in management functions while trying to achieve both individual goals and organizational goals."
Talent Management
"They are business strategies put forward to attract and retain talented employees in the business."
"It is a management practice in which talented employees who belong to certain elite business groups are represented."
"Talent management refers to various business strategies that will help talented individuals develop and use their knowledge, skills and behaviors."

Source: This table made by the authors

It is a frequently encountered conceptualization in studies that the concept of talent is defined as a concept that emerges as a result of the sum or combination of five components. These are "Triumph", "Ability", "Leadership", "Easiness", "Newfangled" and "Time". The concept of "Triumph" can be defined as the inner power that transforms a certain knowledge from abstract to concrete. "Ability" is the use of this information. "Leadership" can be expressed as the capacity or potential of an individual to direct the individuals around him by having a certain ability. Although "newfangled" encompasses a certain "easiness", it is included in the components of the concept of talent because it includes work motivation, openness to experience and creative abilities. "Time" refers to a process that ensures the fulfillment of previous components within a certain planning (Tansley et al, 2006). It can be seen that all the components put forward constitute the concept of talent. In a way, this can be seen as a collection of components that clarify which elements the concept of talent includes. In particular, as can be understood from the definitions of the concept of talent, it can be seen that all elements are sub-components whose presence can reveal talent. For this reason, when the components that make up the concept of talent are examined, it actually becomes an issue that explains what the elements that make up the subsystems of talent are.

Expressing the various dimensions of talent management is important in terms of providing a comprehensive perspective on the subject. There are many dimensions that make up talent management. It is considered important that the use of these dimensions be organizationally focused rather than individually focused. Because these dimensions describe a process that will enable organizations to retain their employees. It primarily consists of five basic dimensions: creating strategy, attracting and retaining talent, motivating and developing talent, distributing and managing, connecting and activating talent in Table 3. Creating a strategy means developing long-term strategies in order to use talent. Attracting and retaining talent means including individuals with relevant knowledge and skills within the institution. Motivating and developing motivated and talented individuals involves a separate process. It is a dimension that expresses at what points in this process the talent is open to development or in what aspects talented individuals should be given new talents. The connect and enable dimension aims to ensure that individuals are included in elite business groups, make them open to collaboration, and ensure the continuity of their progress within teams (Waheed et al, 2012; Ulrich, 2007)

Table 3. Five dimensions of talent management

Creating strategy	"It refers to business strategies put forward to retain talented potential employees or to retain talented employees."
Attracting and retaining talent	"It refers to the plans put forward to retain talented existing employees and attract talented potential employees to the institution."
Motivating and developing talent	"It includes various steps taken to ensure superior performance of elite business groups consisting of talented employees and to contribute positively to the performance and success of the institution. These are plans in which various development stages are created to focus on the basic points where talented employees are lacking and to compensate for these."
Distributing and managing,	"It includes the distribution of information to be presented to talented employees and the issues that will help these talented individuals achieve both individual goals and organizational goals within the management functions."
Connecting and activating talent	"It is the stage where individuals in talented work groups develop information about the development of interpersonal communication networks and the activation of talent."

Source: This table made by the authors

The five dimensions that constitute talent management in organizations mentioned above are important in shaping talent management systems. First of all, paying attention to these five dimensions in order to implement talent management within the organization lays the foundation for organizations to create talent management systems. In this regard, when the comprehensive evaluation of the five dimensions is taken into consideration, the applicability of the five dimensions becomes evident. At this stage, talent management systems that can lead to its implementation into practice have been tried to be developed. In general, talent and talent management have their place in current management approaches. Talent management, which means evaluating talents or using them effectively and efficiently, is important for an organization to survive, ensure organizational growth and development, and provide competitive advantages.

4. GREEN TALENT MANAGEMENT

Talent management, as previously defined, refers to specific business strategies that involve the retention of talented employees within the organization. It is a management function built on the important thing in talent management to retain or include existing employees and potential employees in the organization. For this reason, it is important that planning, organization, execution, control and coordination are designed to manage talented individuals. The fact that its importance is felt to this extent has paved the way for it to change the scope of talent management. Various human resources functions have also undergone certain changes, especially with the inclusion of sustainability in the management field. If we want to emphasize that this change is in talent management within the scope of the subject, it can be seen that the scope of talent management has been expanded and the concept of green talent management has emerged (Bui, Chang, 2018)

The concept of green talent management is becoming a newly emerging concept today. Being a newly developing concept, it has been inevitable for organizations to begin their practices in this field and for this field to attract attention in the academy. With the awareness that organizations can become healthier organizations, it has become a priority for organizations to give more importance to sustainability issues and for employees and organizations to try to create employees who take the environment into account within certain management functions. In this regard, green talent management exists differently from other management approaches. The background of this existence is the importance that employees attach to the environment and at the same time the environmental awareness of talented individuals who are included in elite business groups. The presence of talented individuals who take the environment into consideration also affects the formation of business strategies. For this reason, it is not enough for the individual to be talented; it is important to have talented individuals with high awareness of the environment (Gardas et al, 2019).

It is not enough to explain green talent management in terms of individual-oriented approaches. It has benefits for the organization as well as for the individual. This has paved the way for green talent management to be evaluated with an organization-oriented approach. Green talent management is a management that affects the internal and external organizational images created by organizations. We can say that green practices have gained importance within the scope of this management. In this regard, it is important to adapt green sustainable practices to the organization in order to create a positive image of the organization. It is important because it is the beginning of a process that positively supports both internal perception and external perception. At the same time, it paves the way for sustainable performance to be positive for both the organization and the individual. Likewise, it is an issue that should not be forgotten at this point that organizations focus their internal service resources on green management in the sectors in which they operate and external service resources are also employed. In addition to ensuring that organizations are healthy organizations, such green practices are very important for organizations in terms of ensuring their growth and development, survival and gaining competitive advantage. Based on this, it can be said that the most important elements that positively support organizational success and the accompanying survival of organizations are organizations where green practices are embodied (Odugbesan et al, 2023; Tosun et al, 2022)

Green talent management is primarily expressed as specific business strategies that try to ensure that individuals working within the organization have high environmental awareness. With the reflection of the concept of sustainability on organizations, this management style has attracted attention and gained importance day by day. In this direction, practical dimensions of green talent management have emerged over time. When you want to express these dimensions, they can be explained as follows. The first is soft green talent management, and the second is hard green talent management. While it can be stated that soft green talent management is individual-oriented, it can be said that hard green talent management adopts an organization-oriented perspective. Soft green talent management emphasizes that it introduces various well-being practices in order to activate employees in ecological initiatives and environmental sustainability areas, that leadership practices are at the forefront and that effective and efficient communication channels are open. Hard green talent management, on the other hand, states that in order to make employees active in ecological initiatives and environmental sustainability, there are practices with mechanistic features, goal orientation, more rigid performance management mechanisms, practices are tried to be carried out in a hierarchical culture, and bureaucratic structures within the organization are operated effectively. (Gardas et al., 2019; John et al., 2009; Berraies et al., 2020; Bui and Chang, 2018; Lee et al., 2017; Adeosun and Ohiani, 2020).

Green talent management has become a notable practice for organizations in general. The fact that this practice is individual-oriented and at the same time has organization-oriented approaches is an element that enriches the content of this management function. The preference of green talent management by organizations paves the way for talented individuals who pay attention to ecological issues and environmental sustainability to be included in elite groups within the organization. Therefore, it is seen that the environmental awareness of talented employees, who are considered among the elite groups within the organization, is a factor that shows that the organization has stepped into a different area in the field of green management. Increasing applicability over time paves the way for organizations to provide competitive advantage both in terms of the organization and in terms of human resources. Ensuring that such green-oriented practices are concretized within the organization ensures that the organization exists in many different areas and becomes a healthy organization. At the same time, it supports the corporate image and is very important in terms of making positive contributions to the growth and development of the organization.

Today, talent management has become one of the most important human resources management functions in organizations. Gaining increasing importance has become the acquisition of talented human resources and the retention of talented employees among the elements in which organizations can compete. The rapidly increasing intensity of competition has required more planning regarding the inclusion of talented human resources within the organization. This has caused management functions to focus on how to better evaluate increasingly talented employees. For this reason, focusing on skilled human resources management has necessitated explanations from both theoretical and practical perspectives. Likewise, today, environmental initiatives being at the forefront and environmental sustainability gaining importance for organizations have significantly changed the focus points in human resources functions. In particular, green talent management has become a function that has gained importance over this time. As a result of organizations focusing on environmental issues, the environmental consciousness and awareness of talented employees has attracted attention. In this regard, the orientation towards elite business groups who are both talented and have high environmental awareness has gained importance within organizations.

In this regard, it is thought that examining studies on green talent management will be beneficial in providing more information about this human resources function that organizations attach importance to. (Table 4)

Table 4. Studies of green talent management

Author/s	Main Findings of Studies
Ogbeibu et al (2021)	*"Findings show that green hard and soft TM and Leader STARA competence (LSC) positively predict turnover intention. "While LSC strengthens the negative effect of green soft TM on turnover intention, LSC and digital task interdependence (DTI) attenuate the positive effect of green hard TM on turnover intention."*
Umair et al (2023).	*"Green hard and soft talent management (TM) both have direct and positive links with employees' IWB and GP. The moderating role of transformational leadership exerts a significant moderating influence between green hard TM and IWB. However, the moderating role of transformational leadership between green soft TM and IWB and the moderating role of transformational leadership between GTM and employee's GP proves insignificant."*
Song and Xie (2020)	*"Findings Employees' education level, per capita material capital, green labor participation rate and green jobs promote China's economic growth."*
Ma et al (2023)	*"This is the first study that explores a moderated mediation model to explain when and how tourism service firms can promote ER through inculcating GTM strategies. The findings indicate that service firms in the tourism industry must develop and retain green talent to exploit pro-environmental strategies. employee retention."*

Source: This table made by the authors

5. EVALUATING THE THEORIES IN THE FRAMEWORK GREEN HUMAN RESOURCES MANAGEMENT AND THEORY SUGGESTION FOR GREEN TALENT MANAGEMENT

In general, green human resources management is explained within the scope of many different theories. The fact that human resources management can be explained theoretically expands the development areas of the discipline within the information provided by different theories. At the same time, seeing the use of theories as embodied in the discipline of human resources management creates a structure that can strengthen the foundations of theories. In this regard, it is thought that it would be useful to touch upon the theories used in green human resources management. It has been determined in the studies that there are a total of eight theories used to explain green human resources management. These theories are included in the literature as institutional theory, systems theory, resource-based theory, process theory, motivation theory, social exchange theory, social identity theory and stakeholder theory (Table 5). The theories used are not only used to help explain green human resources management, but also to help explain the subjects of management science and organizational behavior disciplines. The center of the eight theories expressed is focused on the concretization of human resources management and especially green human resources management practices within the organizational environment. It is focused on strengthening the theoretical infrastructure of green human resources management, which is evaluated within the scope of theories, and making it applicable within the organizational environment. Accordingly, it is appropriate to present information about the theories at this point (Arulrajah et al., 2015; Lewis, 2019; Ababbreh, 2021; Ahmad, 2015; Anwar et al., 2020; Fawehinmi et al., 2020; Aboramadan, 2020; Parida et al., 2021; Chaudhray, 2020)

Table 5. Theories in the framework green human resources management

Theory/ies	Explanation of the Theory/ies
Institutional Theory	*"Institutional theories are theories shaped by the idea of how an organization can have a better management system. By including the field of environmental management in its scope, views on how more environmentally friendly practices can be implemented in corporate systems have emerged. In this regard, it is a theory used to help reveal the basic principles that exist within organizations and concern green human resources management practices."*
Systems Theory	*"The focus is on a theory shaped by the idea of how green human resources management, evaluated within the scope of systems theory, can be made more effective and efficient. In this regard, it offers a theoretical framework for attracting, selecting and retaining individuals with high green awareness and consciousness in the organization."*
Resources-based Theory	*"The resource-based approach, on the other hand, creates a theoretical framework for the subject with the emphasis that organizational management and environmental management disciplines place on how resources can be protected in order to support a sustainable environment."*
Process Theory	*"Process theory, on the other hand, creates a theoretical framework for revealing various steps that can be reflected in green human resources management and organizational culture."*
AMO Theory	*"This theory, which is one of the motivation theories, has a content that guides employees to show green behavior within the scope of how they should be motivated. Thus, it provides a theoretical explanation of how motivated individuals may have the ability to display green behavior."*
Social Exchange Theory	*"Although it is a social theory, it seems that the basis of the theory is based on reciprocity. Social changes taking place in a social interaction environment lead to various outcomes for employees and organizations. When it comes to evaluating these outputs within the scope of green human resources management, there is a theory that explains that organizations will be more willing to adopt green behaviors in their employees if their valuable contributions are reflected on the employee side.*
Social Identity Theory	*"The focus of social identity theory is on employees' desire to belong to a certain group and to adopt the identity of the group. In this respect, it is a theory that clarifies the issue of how green human resources management affects the beliefs of employees and what kind of green behavior employees are at the point of adopting."*
Stakeholder Theory	*"According to the stakeholder theory, it continues to be important in the discipline as it is a theory that reveals the focus on how green human resources management is introduced and for whom green human resources management will exist."*

Source: This table made by the authors

The theories used in today's studies continue to take their place in the academic literature as theories that are still up to date. The eight currently shared theories have common points. Generally, when viewed from the perspective of employees in all theories, it is seen that they focus on the development of employees' green behaviors and skills. From an organizational perspective, attention has been drawn to ensuring organizational sustainability and ensuring the competitive advantage of the organization by taking environmental initiatives. However, some theories other than these theories that will form the basis of green human resources management may be used. It can also benefit from a variety of other theories that will help explain green human resources management. For example, signaling theory can be put forward as a theory that may be suitable to explain green human resources management. According to the basis of this theory, we can see a certain relationship network reflected in a model. It can be stated that in this relationship network, there is primarily a network that gives the signal, the sign, the receiver of the sign, and the effect that occurs after the signal is received. The representation of the relational network as a model can be shown as follows (Figure 1).

Figure 1. Signalling theory for green talent management (Authors)

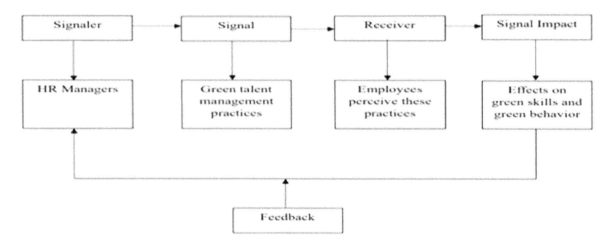

According to signaling theory, a comprehensive explanation can be given to the applicability stages of green talent management. According to the theory, the presence of the person or organization sending the signal constitutes the primary stage. The secondary stage shows the point at which information about what the sign is is revealed. In the secondary stage, this sign draws attention to the existence of practices that will include green talent management. In the third stage, this stage can be expressed as the stage of understanding that employees receive these signs and what these signs mean to them. In the last stage, in the fourth part, it is stated that the signs are passed through a certain cognitive filtering by the employees and that, within the scope of the green talent management practices to be implemented, they support the development of green skills on the part of the employee and guide the employees to show green behavior.

The issue of green talent management can be explained by theories other than the eight theories mentioned above. The main reason why the issue of green talent management is examined within the scope of signaling theory is that it is a theory that can help explain the application of green practices, the fact that these green practices create a certain effect on employees, and their mutual relationship within a cyclical environment. It is suggested that the subject can also be explained within the scope of this theory. One of the shortcomings of other theories in explaining the subject is that such practices do not fully reveal a mutual relationship through feedback within a certain cyclical system. In summary, these theories show that green talent management exists in a cyclical system in that it focuses only on answering certain questions and the signaling theory also explains the existing relational network.

CONCLUSION

Nowadays, the effects of daily activities on the environment and the fact that they are at the stage of being noticed have led individuals and institutions to focus on the green issue. Giving importance to the green issue has created a certain pressure on institutions and required the adaptation of environmentally friendly green practices to institutions. The increasing agenda of environmental management and the increase in studies on the subject have also revealed the necessity for institutions to adopt green practices

(Menta, Chugan, 2015;Mwita, 2019). Human resources management plays a leading role in organizations in focusing corporate policies on green. With the inclusion of green policies in human resources management, it has had a significant impact on reflecting an environmentally sustainable culture within the organization (Benevene, Buonomo, 2020; Bangval, Tiwari, 2015). It has been emphasized in various studies that there are changes in the green performance of organizations with the existence of a green culture (Bangval, Tiwari, 2015). For this reason, it is stated in studies that including green corporate policies within organizational structures plays an important role in both the organization's ability to provide a certain green performance and the development of individuals' green behaviors (Mafrachi et al., 2020). Human resources departments play an important role in implementing green policies and ensuring the continuity of the sustainable culture of the organization. The practices offered by green policies help to achieve green organizational goals and green individual goals, covering the human resources management process from the recruitment of the individual to the time he leaves the job. Thus, human resources management functions also appear to focus on achieving specific green goals. Even though we do not see that all human resources functions have green policies, we can see that green policies are put into effect in certain functions. These green functions are generally green job design, green personnel selection and placement, green training and development, green performance management, green compensation and green occupational health and safety (Bangwal and Tiwari, 2015).

Even though green policies are seen to be implemented in the basic functions of human resources management, we see that green policies are just beginning to be implemented in some functions. For example, talent management is one of the basic functions of human resources management. However, in most studies, it is seen that there are not enough studies focusing on greening talent management. First of all, the concept of talent management refers to a group that includes the knowledge, skills and therefore job performance and task performance within the organization being above a certain standard. The concept of talent management refers to the arrangement of talented employees who have these abilities or are in certain elite groups, according to certain business strategies put forward by the organization. The fact that the scope of the knowledge and skills possessed by talented employees is green-oriented changes the scope of the issue somewhat. In this regard, it would be an accurate definition to state that the scope of green talent management covers an area where the environmental knowledge and environmental behaviors of talented individuals are managed in accordance with certain green business strategies. At this point, it can be said that certain management functions come into play, taking into account not only superior business-related knowledge, skills and performance, but also environmental awareness and the tendency to be involved in environmental initiatives. At this point, it becomes important to conduct studies in this direction in a way that can enable the development of green skills, help the acquisition of green knowledge, and also help increase the frequency of displaying green behaviors. Because the green issue has gained importance and organizations not only support their organizational performance but also gain competitive advantage from human resources is among the important goals of today's organizations.

Nowadays, it is seen that trends in green issues are progressing through green human resources management in organizational studies. However, it is very important for other functions to gain importance on this basis in terms of enriching their perspectives on the subject. In addition to the limited research conducted, it also appears that there is little diversity in the theories used to form a basis for a specific literature on green human resources management. At this point, there is a certain theoretical limitation and efforts to diversify it constitute the main purpose of this study. It has been determined that the theories used progress within a certain limit, and basically institutional theory, systems theory, resource-based theory, process theory, motivation theory, social exchange theory, social identity theory and stakeholder theory are examined by these theories. The basic features of these theories have revealed the need to use other theories on the grounds that they do not have a richness in terms of covering certain functions in green human resources management. The mentioned theories have generally made progress in explaining certain functions of human resources management. In this study, examining green talent management, which is a function of green human resources management, by signaling theory is important because it brings richness to the subject.

The main reason why green talent management is examined within the scope of signaling theory is that it wants to reveal the existence of a cyclical relationship network that does not exist in other theories. The theory generally emphasizes that the areas implemented by certain human resources managers are passed through a certain cognitive process by employees and an effect occurs accordingly. It can be stated that not only human resources practices are evaluated within a specific ecosystem but can be examined in different subjects within the scope of this theory. However, when evaluated within the scope of this issue, it can be explained that there is a system that states that human resources managers communicate the regulations regarding green talent management practices or the corporate policies created regarding green talent management to employees, and that green behaviors are revealed by employees and forms the basis for the development of green skills. Unlike other theories, this horizontal relationship shows that the employees provide certain feedback and that the system operates cyclically. In this regard, it can be stated that he stands out with his emphasis on the possibility of a green talent management that is open to change and transformation. Therefore, it is thought that academic research will show that the stages of implementation of green policies can be established more clearly in studies based on this theory. It is thought that there is a theory that can be put forward by making a model about which applications are communicated by whom to whom within the system and what effect they will have. It is thought that the studies to be carried out within the scope of signaling theory will contribute both to enriching the theoretical infrastructure of green human resources management and to the theoretical enrichment of the subject of green talent management.

Since there are very few conceptual and theoretical studies in the literature on the subject of green talent management, which is included in the field of green human resources management, it is hoped that it will contribute to the relevant literature and shed light on future researchers. Although the scope of the study can be expanded in future studies, it can also be addressed with different theories and contribute to the literature with more comprehensive research.

REFERENCES

Ababneh, O. M. A. (2021). How do green HRM practices affect employees' green behaviors? The role of employee engagement and personality attributes. *Journal of Environmental Planning and Management*, *64*(7), 1204–1226. doi:10.1080/09640568.2020.1814708

Aboramadan, M. (2020). The effect of green HRM on employee green behaviors in higher education: The mediating mechanism of green work engagement. *The International Journal of Organizational Analysis*, *30*(1), 7–23. doi:10.1108/IJOA-05-2020-2190

Adeosun, O. T., & Ohiani, A. S. (2020). Attracting and recruiting quality talent: Firm perspectives. *Rajagiri Management Journal*, *14*(2), 107–120. doi:10.1108/RAMJ-05-2020-0016

Aftab, J., Abid, N., Cucari, N., & Savastano, M. (2023). Green human resource management and environmental performance: The role of green innovation and environmental strategy in a developing country. *Business Strategy and the Environment, 32*(4), 1782–1798. doi:10.1002/bse.3219

Ahmad, S. (2015). Green human resource management: Policies and practices. *Cogent Business & Management, 2*(1), 1030817. doi:10.1080/23311975.2015.1030817

Anwar, N., Mahmood, N. H. N., Yusliza, M. Y., Ramayah, T., Faezah, J. N., & Khalid, W. (2020). Green human resource management for organisational citizenship behaviour towards the environment and environmental performance on a university campus. *Journal of Cleaner Production, 256*, 120401. doi:10.1016/j.jclepro.2020.120401

Arulrajah, A. A., & Opatha, H. H. D. N. P. (2016). Analytical and Theoretical Perspectives on Green Human Resource Management: A Simplified Underpinning. *International Business Research, 9*(12), 153. doi:10.5539/ibr.v9n12p153

Arulrajah, A. A., Opatha, H. H. D. N. P., & Nawaratne, N. N. J. (2015). Green human resource management practices: A review. *Sri Lankan Journal of Human Resource Management, 5*(1), 1–16. doi:10.4038/sljhrm.v5i1.5624

Bahuguna, P. C., Srivastava, R., & Tiwari, S. (2023). Two-decade journey of green human resource management research: A bibliometric analysis. *Benchmarking, 30*(2), 585–602. doi:10.1108/BIJ-10-2021-0619

Bangwal, D., & Tiwari, P. (2015). Green HRM – A way to greening the environment. *IOSR Journal of Business and Management, 17*(12), 43–53.

Beechler, S., & Woodward, I. (2009). The Global War for Talent. *Journal of International Management, 15*(3), 273–285. doi:10.1016/j.intman.2009.01.002

Benevene, P., & Buonomo, I. (2020). Green Human Resource Management: An EvidenceBased Systematic Literature Review. *Sustainability (Basel), 12*(15), 1–25. doi:10.3390/su12155974

Berraies, S., Lajili, R., & Chtioui, R. (2020). Social capital, employees' well-being and knowledge sharing: Does enterprise social networks use matter? Case of Tunisian knowledge-intensive firms. *Journal of Intellectual Capital, 21*(6), 1153–1183. doi:10.1108/JIC-01-2020-0012

Bhutto, S., & Auranzeb. (2016). Effects of Green Human Resources Management on Firm Performance: An Empirical Study on Pakistani Firms. *European Journal of Business and Management, 8*(16), 119–125.

Bui, L. T. T., & Chang, Y. (2018). Talent management and turnover intention: Focus on Danang city government in Vietnam. *International Review of Public Administration, 23*(4), 219–236. doi:10.1080/12294659.2018.1552403

Chaudhary, R. (2020). Green human resource management and employee green behavior: An empirical analysis. *Corporate Social Responsibility and Environmental Management, 27*(2), 630–641. doi:10.1002/csr.1827

Cheese, P., Thomas, R. T., & Craig, E. (2008). *The talent powered organization: Strategies for globalization, talent management and high performance.* Kogan Page.

Faisal, S. (2023). Green human resource management—A synthesis. *Sustainability (Basel)*, *15*(3), 2259. doi:10.3390/su15032259

Fawehinmi, O., Yusliza, M. Y., Mohamad, Z., Faezah, J. N., & Muhammad, Z. (2020). Assessing the green behaviour of academics: The role of green human resource management and environmental knowledge. *International Journal of Manpower*, *41*(7), 879–900. doi:10.1108/IJM-07-2019-0347

Gardas, B. B., Mangla, S. K., Raut, R. D., Narkhede, B., & Luthra, S. (2019). Green talent management to unlock sustainability in the oil and gas sector. *Journal of Cleaner Production*, *229*, 850–862. doi:10.1016/j.jclepro.2019.05.018

Glen, J., Hilson, C., & Lowitt, E. (2009). The emergence of green talent. *Business Strategy Review*, *20*(4), 52–56. doi:10.1111/j.1467-8616.2009.00631.x

Jabbour, C. J. C. (2013). Environmental training in organisations: From a literature review to a framework for future research. *Resources, Conservation and Recycling*, *74*, 144–155. doi:10.1016/j.resconrec.2012.12.017

Jirawuttinunt, S., & Limsuwan, K. (2019). The Effect of Green Human Resource Management on Performance of Certified ISO 14000 Businesses in Thailand. *UTCC International Journal of Business and Economics*, *11*(1), 168–185.

Kramar, R. (2014). Beyond strategic human resource management: Is sustainable human resource management the next approach? *International Journal of Human Resource Management*, *25*(8), 1069–1089. doi:10.1080/09585192.2013.816863

Lee, I., Lin, C., & Lin, T. (2017). The creation of national intellectual capital from the perspective of Hofstede's national culture. *Journal of Intellectual Capital*, *18*(4), 807–831. doi:10.1108/JIC-11-2016-0117

Lewis, L. (2019). Organizational Change. In Origins and Traditions of Organizational Communication. Academic Press.

Ma, X., Bashir, H., & Ayub, A. (2023). Cultivating green workforce: The roles of green shared vision and green organizational identity. *Frontiers in Psychology*, *14*, 1041654. doi:10.3389/fpsyg.2023.1041654 PMID:37008862

Mafrachi, A. M., Abed, H., & Mohammed, M. (2020). Assessing the Role of Green Human Resources Management and Environmental Cooperation: A Case Study on Food Industries Sector in Iraq. *"Ovidius" University Annals. Economic Sciences Series*, *20*(1), 14–23.

Malik, S. Y., Cao, Y., Mughal, Y. H., Kundi, G. M., Mughal, M. H., & Ramayah, T. (2020). Pathways towards sustainability in organizations: Empirical evidence on the role of green human resource management practices and green intellectual capital. *Sustainability (Basel)*, *12*(8), 3228. doi:10.3390/su12083228

Mashala, Y. L. (2018). Green Human Resource Management and Environmental Sustainability in Tanzania: A Review and Research Agenda. *International Journal of Academic Multidisciplinary Research*, *2*(12), 60–68.

Masri, H. A., & Jaaron, A. A. (2017). Assessing green human resources management practices in Palestinian manufacturing context: An empirical study. *Journal of Cleaner Production, 143*, 474–489. doi:10.1016/j.jclepro.2016.12.087

Mehta, K., & Chugan, K. P. (2015). Green HRM in Pursuit of Environmentally Sustainable Business. *Universal Journal of Industrial and Business Management, 3*(3), 74–81. doi:10.13189/ujibm.2015.030302

Mwita, M. K. (2019). Conceptual Review of Green Human Resource Management Practices. *East African Journal of Social and Applied Sciences, 1*(2), 13–20.

Odugbesan, J. A., Aghazadeh, S., Al Qaralleh, R. E., & Sogeke, O. S. (2023). Green talent management and employees' innovative work behavior: The roles of artificial intelligence and transformational leadership. *Journal of Knowledge Management, 27*(3), 696–716. doi:10.1108/JKM-08-2021-0601

Opatha, H. H. D. N. P. (2013). Green human resource management: A simplified introduction. *Proc. HR Dialogue, 1*, 11–21.

Opatha, H. H. P., & Arulrajah, A. A. (2014). Green human resource management: Simplified general reflections. *International Business Research, 7*(8), 101–112. doi:10.5539/ibr.v7n8p101

Parida, S., Ananthram, S., Chan, C., & Brown, K. (2021). Green office buildings and sustainability: Does green human resource management elicit green behaviors? *Journal of Cleaner Production, 329*, 129764. doi:10.1016/j.jclepro.2021.129764

Renwick, D., Redman, T., & Maguire, S. (2008). Green HRM: A review, process model, and research agenda. *University of Sheffield Management School Discussion Paper, 1*(1), 1-46.

Shah, M. (2019). Green human resource management: Development of a valid measurement scale. *Business Strategy and the Environment, 28*(5), 771–785. doi:10.1002/bse.2279

Shah, P., Singh Dubey, R., Rai, S., Renwick, D. W., & Misra, S. (2023). Green human resource management: A comprehensive investigation using bibliometric analysis. *Corporate Social Responsibility and Environmental Management*.

Shen, J., Dumont, J., & Deng, X. (2018). Employees' Perceptions of Green HRM and Non-Green Employee Work Outcomes: The Social Identity and Stakeholder Perspectives. *Group & Organization Management, 43*(4), 594–622. doi:10.1177/1059601116664610

Song, M., & Xie, Q. (2020). How does green talent influence China's economic growth? *International Journal of Manpower, 41*(7), 1119–1134. doi:10.1108/IJM-08-2019-0378

Stahl, G. K., Björkman, I., Farndale, E., Morris, S. P. J., & Stiles, P. (2007). *Global talent management: How leading multinationals build and sustain their talent pipeline.* INSEAD Faculty and Research Papers.

Tanova, C., & Bayighomog, S. W. (2022). Green human resource management in service industries: The construct, antecedents, consequences, and outlook. *Service Industries Journal, 42*(5–6), 412–452. doi:10.1080/02642069.2022.2045279

Tansley, C., Harris, L., Stewart, J., & Turner, P. (2006). *Talent Management: Understanding the Dimensios.* CIPD.

Thunnissen, M., Boselie, P., & Fruytier, B. (2013). A review of talent management: 'infancy or adolescence?'. *International Journal of Human Resource Management, 24*(9), 1744–1761. doi:10.1080/095 85192.2013.777543

Tosun, C., Parvez, M. O., Bilim, Y., & Yu, L. (2022). Effects of green transformational leadership on green performance of employees via the mediating role of corporate social responsibility: Reflection from North Cyprus. *International Journal of Hospitality Management, 103*, 103218. doi:10.1016/j. ijhm.2022.103218

Ulrich, D. (2007). *The Talent Trifecta*. Workforce Management.

Umair, S., Waqas, U., Mrugalska, B., & Al Shamsi, I. R. (2023). Environmental Corporate Social Responsibility, Green Talent Management, and Organization's Sustainable Performance in the Banking Sector of Oman: The Role of Innovative Work Behavior and Green Performance. *Sustainability (Basel), 15*(19), 14303. doi:10.3390/su151914303

Waheed, S., Zaim, A., & Zaim, H. (2012). Talent Management in Four Stages. The USV Annals of Economics and Public Administration, 130-137.

Zaid, A. A., Bon, A. T., & Jaaron, A. A. (2018). Green human resource management bundle practices and manufacturing organizations for performance optimization: a conceptual model. *International Journal of Engineering & Technology, 7*(3.20), 87-91.

Zubair, S. S., & Khan, A. M. (2019). Sustainable development: The role of green HRM. *International Journal of Research in Human Resource Management, 1*(2), 1-6.

Chapter 5
Decoding the Alchemy of Employee Retention:
A Case of the Manufacturing Sector of the National Capital Region, India

Deepti Sinha
https://orcid.org/0000-0001-9931-6563
Christ University, India

Sachin Sinha
Christ University, India

Shreya Jain
Kotak Life Insurance, India

ABSTRACT

The ability of a company to retain its staff is referred to as employee retention. It may also be referred to as a decrease in employee attrition or employee turnover rate. Employee retention is one such mechanism which ensures that the human capital stays with the organisation for a longer duration. The study focusses on identifying the drivers of employee retention in the manufacturing industry with respect to certain factors such as mentoring, career development, work environment, job autonomy, and compensation. This research has used the descriptive research design with some elements of exploratory research design. The sample size for the study was 122. Primary data has been collected with the help of a pre-validated questionnaire with multiple-choice closed-ended questions on a five-point Likert scale. The collected data was analysed using Excel and SPSS with statistical tools like T-test, ANOVA, multiple linear regression, etc. A direct positive relation has been found between mentoring, work environment and compensation, and the employees' intention to stay.

DOI: 10.4018/979-8-3693-1938-3.ch005

1. INTRODUCTION

The ability of a business to reduce employee turnover, or the number of workers who leave their jobs either freely or involuntarily within a specific time frame, is known as employee retention. Retention of employees has a direct impact on a business's performance and profitability. Businesses need to retain their best employees if they want to flourish. The goal of employee retention is to do this. Businesses struggle in the current climate to manage and retain employees. Employee retention is the endeavour undertaken by a business to keep its employees on board. It is also known as a decline in the rate of staff turnover or attrition. One such strategy that makes sure the organization's human capital—its employees—stays with it for a longer period of time is employee retention.

Employers have the ultimate duty for retaining the best human capital; if they don't, the firm will lose its top performers. Increasing employee loyalty or organizational commitment is the ultimate goal of staff retention in order to preserve the organization's sustainability. An entity's productivity is subsequently increased, raising its success rate. Workers are regarded as an organization's most precious resource. Thus, it becomes imperative for an organization to hold onto its talented and skilled staff. In the fast-paced world of today, organizations can gain a competitive advantage by holding onto their competent workforce. They can assist manufacturers in preserving production levels, raising customer happiness levels, and improving the quality of their goods and services. This will therefore promote a happy workplace, which will raise staff morale and increase job satisfaction. In addition, firms can gain a competitive edge through employee retention by holding onto talented and skilled people who can support the growth and success of the business. One of the most important factors in the expansion of manufacturing businesses in the NCR region is staff retention. Elevated employee attrition rates may lead to increased expenses for recruiting and onboarding new staff, reduced output, subpar output, and decreased client contentment.

Employers have always struggled with the issue of low retention (Mathimaran & Kumar, 2017). Mukherjee et al. (2020) investigated the factors that precede employee retention in Indian PSUs, including job security, autonomy, career advancement, organizational culture, and climate. In the current environment, businesses are increasingly concerned about employee retention. Skilled workers frequently leave their current employers in search of better offers. A competitive salary, accommodating work hours, enhanced workplace culture, and opportunities for career growth are among the elements that drive an employee to hunt for employment elsewhere. It is the duty of management and HR staff to intervene when a capable worker indicates that he wishes to quit and to find out the real reasons for the decision. Every firm needs dedicated, knowledgeable workers with the ability to think creatively and outside the box in order to deliver fresh, original work. If an organization's top employees depart, it cannot thrive. Maintaining the people who have made significant contributions to the organization's success is essential to it. What counts is the employee's passion, commitment, and willingness to put in time by fully committing to their task. When developing a long-term retention plan, firms and employers should start by taking the environment into consideration. Employers need to understand the variables that affect a worker's decision to join, stay with, or leave a company. Comparable to a three-legged stool, the join, stay, and leave paradigm means that organizations cannot create an effective retention strategy without understanding all three.

Employee's willingness to join the organisation - A company's ability to offer appealing jobs often attracts employees. Workers seek opportunities for advancement, equitable remuneration, a nurturing work atmosphere, and alignment between their individual principles and the company's ethos. What motivates them is the chance to have a big impact, a sense of purpose, and career advancement. People ultimately want to work for a company that aligns with their goals and values.

Employee's willingness to remain with the organisation - It is important to understand the motivations behind both employees' decisions to leave and stay with a company. Employees build a network of contacts and relationships as they get more involved in their work lives. People are encouraged by these relationships to either leave their employment or work longer hours. Employee retention is higher when they have a stronger sense of belonging to the company. Furthermore, people are less likely to look for work elsewhere if they feel more at ease in their current positions. Employers might interview high performers to find out why they stay on the job.

Employee's willingness to leave the organisation - By better accommodating their current staff, organizations can also attempt to identify the variables that may contribute to employee attrition. Poor dedication and pleasure sometimes set off the withdrawal process, which includes thoughts of quitting in search of more enticing possibilities. If done correctly, exit interviews can provide important insights into the reasons behind employees' departures. The most common reasons for quitting a job are better chances, more hours worked, and more pay. Employers who arrange for an impartial third-party organisation to conduct the interview can obtain more accurate and quantitative data.

1.1 Outcomes of Employee Retention

Retaining staff members benefits the company well beyond just lowering the expense of rehiring them. A longer employee retention period is a sign of a strong organisational culture, value system, and staff dedication to the company. Advantages of employee retention are:

- **Cost Reduction**- organizations incur huge costs associated with hiring of new employees include recruiting, screening, and interviewing. Training and managerial oversight are additional onboarding costs. Other concerns that increase the cost of turnover include reduced productivity, poorer engagement, poor customer service, etc.
- **Motivation** - Companies with effective retention strategies may boost employee morale, facilitate better engagement and connection, and spread contagious positive feelings throughout the organization.
- **Experienced Workforce** - The success of an organization is greatly impacted by keeping senior or experienced staff members on board, since they are more likely to have a deeper understanding of the business and, as a result, be better able to tackle complex challenges on their own. They are also in charge of maintaining and governing organizational culture.
- **Internal Recruitment**- Employees must be trained after being successfully recruited, onboarded, and hired by a firm. However, the expense of training and reskilling the person would be greatly reduced if they were hired from within the company.
- **Rise in Productivity Levels**- Effective employee retention can prevent productivity losses for a company. Workplaces with high retention rates typically have more engaged employees who produce more work. Customer are likely to be better engaged and retained with the organization, productive relationships exist with the vendors and suppliers, stakeholders are able to put more trust and faith in the organization. All these together help in increasing the overall productivity of the organisation.

- **Enhanced Employee Experience-** Organisations may create a better employee experience, which in turn increases retention, by focusing on what employees want and keeping more of their finest talent on staff.
- **Increased Employee Engagement -** Implementing the strategies, techniques, and procedures necessary to keep their finest and brightest employees takes a lot of work, senior oversight, and targeted investment, but it pays off for firms that do so. Businesses that don't prioritise employee retention and turnover reduction can suffer serious setbacks, including lost productivity and knowledge, negative effects on customer and employee experiences, lower morale, and a weaker corporate culture, additionally, the direct costs linked with finding, recruiting, on-boarding, and training replacements will also increase.

While the total cost of employee turnover can reach up to 2000% of their compensation, the expense of replacing an employee could account for as much as 50–60% of their annual revenue. These costs to the business include missed revenue, diminished morale, application views, new hire training, recruiter remuneration, separation processes, and a host of other expenditures. Therefore, in order to manage staff retention before the costs of employee turnover overwhelm the firm, a proactive approach is needed. Businesses that are able to retain their most talented employees are more productive and efficient; if they are unable to do so, their success may suffer. Because of attrition, it is challenging to keep an organization's work culture constant. Employee retention can help a company hold on to skilled and knowledgeable workers, which will boost output, customer satisfaction, employee happiness, and, eventually, profit.

Employers have historically had difficulty keeping their best employees. Following the COVID-19 epidemic, this problem gained even greater urgency. The "Great Resignation," which started in early 2020 and was a worldwide economic trend in which people were observed leaving their positions willingly in large numbers, made the problem of employee turnover much worse and resulted in a severe labour shortage across a variety of industries. As a result, this problem requires quick attention, and this area need increased concentration. The purpose of this chapter is to investigate how demographic factors affect employee retention. It also focuses on how work environments, job autonomy, career development opportunities, mentoring, and pay affect employee retention. Ultimately, the goal is to identify the key factors that contribute to employee attrition and develop improved retention tactics.

2. LITERATURE REVIEW

Employee retention is the ability of an organisation to keep its workers. It is also known as a procedure that motivates staff members to work for a company for a long time in order to secure the organisation's sustainability. Ensuring the satisfaction of all parties involved, including employers and employees, is the ultimate goal of employee retention. It is easier for committed workers to stay with the company for a comparatively longer amount of time, which benefits both parties (Gorde, 2019). Since every firm wants to keep its talent pool, the rise in employee turnover has led to a "talent war" (Kumar et al., 2021). This is causing challenges for enterprises. In the current environment, the company must come up with creative ways to satisfy the demands of its employees and retain them for a longer period of time. Examining the causes of staff retention becomes crucial (Oprea et al., 2022).

The following elements have been determined to be the drivers of employee retention on the basis of literature review:

Mentoring: Mentoring is a crucial tool for both the mutual benefit of employees and businesses (Munde, 2010). In general, mentoring entails a two-way relationship between the mentor and the mentee; the mentee provides the mentee with information and skills, an understanding of their duties, and advice, and the mentor provides the mentee with knowledge and skills, understanding of their roles, and guidance. A consultative kind of approach, such as mentoring, encourages greater levels of engagement. In the past, mentoring only addressed one method of instructional direction, delayed feedback, and mentoring that was senior level specific. Various aspects of mentoring exist in the context of today's workforce, including inclusive coaching style (Lowe et al., 2008), immediate feedback (Sujansky, 2002), quality supervisory relationships (Raman et al., 2011), constant affirmation and praise (Crumpacker & Crumpacker, 2007), and reverse mentoring (Koster, 2013). It is the obligation of superiors to provide employees with the proper guidance, encouragement, and support through an inclusive coaching method. Young workers nowadays desire little oversight in exchange for greater independence and autonomy. According to studies, today's workforce values quick feedback, a solid rapport with superiors, and a cooperative working environment (Cennamo & Gardner, 2008; Weyland, 2011). Therefore, mutual respect and good rapport will help the workforce of today to have higher levels of job engagement. Employees anticipate regular acknowledgement from their supervisor of the work they have done (Crumpacker & Crumpacker, 2007; Raman et al., 2011). If the manager respects them and gives them regular performance feedback, the staff will be more productive (Jones et al., 2005). Reverse mentoring is a form of mentoring procedure in which junior employees teach elders how to use technology, and in return, the seniors offer advice on how to choose work roles and career paths. Reverse mentoring improves peaceful interactions between staff and managers (Koster, 2013). As a result, these mentoring programmes promote greater workplace engagement (Abhilasha & Pathak, 2014).

H1: There is significant influence of mentoring on employee retention

Career Development: Career progression or development is a process of providing opportunities to the employees for their profession growth in the organization. It is a key strategy for improving employee involvement is for organisations (Kovarik, 2008). In the past, career advancement required professional advancement, formal education with step-by-step instructions, and decades of waiting for promotion (Gutner, 2002; Tulgan, 2000; Cherri Ho, 2010). However, today's workforce has different demands and expectations, including supportive management (Solnet & Hood, 2008), the possibility of rapid advancement (Pooley, 2005), mobility in early careers (Cennamo & Gardner, 2008), training and development (Price Waterhouse Coopers, 2008; Dolezalek, 2007), and personal and professional growth (Eisner, 2005; Martin, 2005). Only when a company's values align with the employee's own will they become involved and familiar with the job (Ohlrich, 2011). The company should serve as a helpful environment for employees' lifelong learning and self-improvement (Martin & Tulgan, 2001). The knowledge of their proficiency in their area may influence, employees to aim for swift advancement in their jobs and rapidly move on to other organisations also for the same (Pooley, 2005; Weyland, 2011). Younger employees desire growth rather quickly, hence they switch occupations more than six times in their lifetimes (Burmeister, 2009; Dolezalek, 2007). The management's duty of keeping them on board and motivating them to work harder is therefore onerous. Millennials aspire to advance their careers through constant learning (Eisner, 2005). Long lectures bore employees, so they require engaging, hands-on training instead (Sheahan, 2005). Employees seek out real-world activities and viewpoints in training (Partridge & Hallam, 2006). They prefer multimedia training and e-learning that would enable them to enhance their talents in a multi-directional career system laterally and vertically (Shaw, 2008). Employees, now, favour fast-track leadership programmes and formalised training (Huntley, 2006 &

Sayers, 2007). Learning and growth should therefore foster their individuality and exposure to new experiences (Weyland, 2011). A career should offer workers both professional happiness and freedom in their personal lives (Sayers, 2007). As long as the company offers self-development, employees are loyal (Kerslake, 2005; Logan, 2008). If the company is unable to offer professional training, the workers become less interested and may even leave their positions (Martin, 2005). For their professional development and to advance their growth, millennials favour work-based and vocational skills (Terjesen, Vinnicombe & Freeman, 2007). The process of helping someone succeed professionally by identifying a suitable position to support the organization's objectives is known as career development (Long et al., 2014). Employees are found to become more devoted to their current organisations when presented with multiple options for professional growth and advancement inside the company (Duffield et al., 2014). Having a better understanding about the requirements and scope of their job further results into employee retention (Yarbrough et al., 2017). Millennials have been found to be more driven by growth opportunities within the organization (Islam et al., 2022; Jena and Nayak, 2023) which is a significant source of motivation that fosters retention.

H2: There is significant effect of career development on employee retention

Work Environment: The congenial environment at work is a fundamental requirement that an organization must offer to its employees in order to encourage improved engagement. The workplace is a setting where the employees are impacted by the overall situation, people, and events. Today's employees, in contrast to the other cohorts, have greater preferences for workplaces with flexible and unconventional work environments, common spaces for collaboration, relaxation activities, technological connections and social media, and friendly co-workers (Lowe et al., 2008; Reed, 2010; Raman et al., 2011). The working environment is where people interact, learn, and collaborate (Rai, 2012). Employees need for their workspace include interactive features, comfort, and flexibility (Raman et al., 2011; Rai, 2012). Additionally, they are reenergized at work by leisure and amusement activities (Raman et al., 2012s). The variety of settings, including break-out areas, creative spaces, and even sleeping quarters, can help employees feel comfortable at work (Weyland, 2011). According to Lyons (2003), congenial co-workers and an enjoyable work atmosphere encourage teamwork and idea exchange. The work environment has an impact on employees' decisions to remain with the company as well (Zeytinoglu & Denton, 2005). It has been observed that a tidy, clean, and comfortable work atmosphere motivates employees to stay with the company and ensures dedication in addition to encouraging employees to perform their work properly (Kundu and Lata, 2017; Mangi et al., 2011). Alshurideh (2019) advocated that retaining competent employees has significant influence on retaining customers and enhancing the operational cost efficiency of organizations. It can be concluded that the workplace environment is a crucial instrument for motivating today's workers and thereby enabling them to continue to work with the same employer.

H3: There is significant influence of work environment on employee retention

Job Autonomy: Job autonomy refers to an employee's choice to use their own working methods to complete a task. Self-engagement requires autonomy and independence. Job autonomy in the context of today's workforce includes information on requesting independence and flexibility (Martin, 2005), accepting accountability for their jobs and work (Gravett & Throckmorton, 2007), being creative and receiving value for their ideas (Lowe, Levitt & Wilson, 2008). Today's workforce desires independence and flexibility, wanting to do tasks on their own with minimum supervision (Martin, 2005; Tapscott, 2009; & Weyland, 2011). They don't let other people's opinions guide their judgments. Managers must encourage millennials' creative work as they come up with fresh ideas (Zemke et al., 2000). Workers demand that their views be respected and given consideration by the organization. Employees today look for workplaces with more autonomy because they are self-assured, autonomous, and capable of voicing their ideas.

H4: There is significant influence of job autonomy on employee retention

Compensation: Compensation is cash and non-monetary recompense supplied by the employer for services delivered. It is described as the form of pay that goes to employees in return for the work owing to their employment (Dessler, 2007) and it is an HR function of paramount significance. Bibi et al., (2018) discovered a strong correlation between pay and employee retention. Maintaining the organisation's compensation system while implementing the best initiatives and providing both financial and non-financial benefits is crucial for employee retention. In terms of reducing turnover and raising retention, compensation plays a significant role. Paying employees well encourages them to take responsibility for the assigned responsibilities and fosters a long-term relationship with the company (Moncarz et al., 2009). The basis for thanking and praising the employee for their contributions to the accomplishment of the organisational goals is also communicated through this instrument. Financial advantages including salary, merit pay, bonuses, stock options, and non-financial benefits like training and deputations to the client's location for technology or knowledge transfer, allowances, medical insurance, and group insurance are included in the components. The talent may be gathered under one roof over an extended duration with this organised pay system, which reduces turnover (Kriss at office, 2021). According to the studies (Deckop et al., 2006; Moncarz et al., 2009), a strategized remuneration system significantly boosted employee performance. This is the cornerstone for corporate culture to be respected throughout the company. This beneficial circumstance will benefit everyone involved, including the organisation as a whole, the teams and departments involved, and each individual contributing positively to the growth of the organisation.

H4: There is significant influence of compensation on employee retention

RESEARCH METHODOLOGY

The methical approach that researchers take when conducting research projects is referred to as research methodology. It entails a set of actions used to gather and evaluate data in order to find answers to research questions or validate hypotheses.

The research methodology is crucial in ensuring that the research study is conducted in a valid and reliable manner, and that the findings can be used to draw meaningful conclusions and make informed decisions. The methodology outlines the research design, data collection and analysis methods, and the procedures used to ensure the quality and reliability of the data.

Research Type: Descriptive research is a type of research that focuses on outlining the features of the population or issue under study. This form of research's primary objective is to describe the characteristics of the subject being studied. Exploratory research is one such technique that explores research questions that haven't been thoroughly examined before. The goal of exploratory research design is the formulation of an issue for more focused research or the operational development of the working hypothesis. The development of concepts and insights is the primary goal of these research endeavours. The purpose of this specific mix of research methods is to examine the various factors that influence employee retention in the workplace.

Sampling Frame: The sampling frame is any element of a population that has been accurately recognized and is available for selection at any point during the sampling process. Employees from the manufacturing sector made up the sampling frame for this study in Delhi NCR.

Sampling Technique: The precise method used to choose the sample's units is known as a sampling technique. The probability sampling technique known as "simple random sampling" chooses a number of sample units from a population so that each unit has an equal chance of being chosen. The purpose of this particular sampling approach was to collect viewpoints from as many different sources in the manufacturing sector as feasible. As a result, the outcome was a representation of the entire population under research.

Sampling Size: A sample size is a portion of the population that is taken into account for research purposes. In the case of this study it was 122.

Nature of Data: Primary data is the information that is gathered from first-hand sources. The term "secondary data" refers to information that has already been gathered and is easily accessible from other sources. The study made use of both primary data and secondary data in combination. Secondary data assisted in comprehending the organisational analysis, while primary data aided in gaining insights directly from personnel in manufacturing industry in Delhi NCR Region.

i.   Data Collection Methods:
   ◦   A questionnaire method was used to gather the primary data. A written list of questions is called a questionnaire and it used to collect information from respondents. A questionnaire was developed as a research tool because of its flexibility, scalability, and cost-saving features.
   ◦   A range of sources, including the internet, books, journals, and any other published materials, were used to gather secondary data.

ii. **Data Collection Instrument**: A structured, multiple choice, close ended questionnaire was used for the data collection. It was divided into two parts. Part A catered to the demographic profile of the respondents while part B contained the items related to measurement of the identified constructs.

iii. **Scaling Technique**: Scaling is the process of measuring and allocating numbers to items in accordance with predetermined criteria. The itemized rating scale is an ordinal scale that assigns each category in accordance with scale locations a brief description or a number. Likert scale is an example of itemised rating scale. In a 5-point Likert, the respondents were given a set number of items and asked to indicate how much they agree or disagree with each statement. This scale was selected in order to effectively quantify employee behaviour.

iv. **Data Analysis**: Data analysis is the methodical application of logical and/or statistical approaches to describe and demonstrate, summarise and assess data. The following tools were deployed for data analysis:
   ◦   Descriptive statistics.
   ◦   Statistical techniques such as t-test, ANOVA and Regression using SPSS 22.

3. DATA ANALYSIS

Table 1. Reliability analysis

Cronbach's Alpha	N of items
0.9	12

The survey's internal consistency or reliability is gauged by Cronbach's alpha. A value closer to 1 denotes a higher level of reliability. This statistic has a range of 0 to 1. Since the calculated alpha (0.900) is greater than 0.7, it is regarded as satisfactory and shows that the test or survey items are assessing the same concept and are consistent with one another. This implies that the dataset has a very high level of reliability.

Table 2. Demographic profile of respondents

Variable	Categories	Count	%
Gender	Female	45	36.9
	Male	77	63.1
Age	Less than 30	33	27
	30 – 40 years	49	40.2
	40 – 50 years	31	25.4
	50+ years	9	7.4
Income per annum	Less than 5 lacs	25	20.5
	5 – 10 lacs	52	42.6
	10 – 15 lacs	40	32.8
	15 lac and above	5	4.1
Years of service	< 1 year	23	18.9
	1 – 5 years	38	31.1
	5 – 10 years	42	34.4
	10+ years	19	15.6
Marital Status	Single	84	68.9
	Married	38	31.1
Level of Designation	Top Management	19	15.6
	Middle Level Management	71	58.2
	Lower-Level Management	32	26.2

The table 3, above shows the counts and percentages for different categories within a certain population. The data shows that 45 out of the total sample are female, representing 36.9% of the sample, while

77 are male, representing 63.1% of the sample. It is also evident that the largest age group in the sample is the 30 – 40 years category, with 49 individuals representing 40.2% of the sample, followed by the 40 – 50 years category with 31 individuals representing 25.4% of the sample. It can further be concluded that the most common income range in the sample is 5 – 10 lacs, with 52 individuals representing 42.6% of the sample while the most common length of service in the sample is 5 – 10 years, with 42 individuals representing 34.4% of the sample. Many of the participants in the study are single, making up 84 participants, or 68.9% of the sample. Middle Level Management makes up the majority of the sample, with 71 participants, or 58.2% of the sample.

Table 3. Descriptive statistics

	N	Minimum	Maximum	Mean	Std. Deviation
Mentoring	122	3	15	11.082	3.2387
Career Development	122	3	15	10.83	3.161
Work Environment	122	3	15	10.967	3.2927
Job Autonomy	122	4	15	10.69	3.293
Compensation	122	4	15	10.705	3.1588

Table 4 shows that the mean for the mentioned enablers, namely mentoring, career development, work environment, job autonomy, and compensation, is moderately to highly inclined towards agreeableness pertaining to being major factors contributing to employee retention in an organization.

Influence of Demographic Variables on Employees' Intention to Stay

H1: There is no significant influence of demographic variables like gender, marital status, age, income, years of service and designation on employee retention

Table 4(a). Gender vs employee retention (t-test)

	Gender	N	Mean	Std. Deviation	Std. Error Mean
Employee_Retention	**Female**	45	11.02	3.347	.499
	Male	77	10.99	3.291	.375

Table 4(b). Gender vs employee retention (t-test)

	Equality of Variances		t-test for Equality of Means							
	F	Sig	t	df	Sig. (2-tailed)	Mean Difference	Std Error Difference	Interval of the		
Employee Retention	**0**	**0.996**							Lower	Upper
Equal variance assumed			0.57	120	0.955	0.035	0.621		-1.195	1.266
Equal Variance not assumed			0.056	90.945	0.955	0.035	0.624		-1.205	1.275

It can be inferred from the table above that since the p value (.996) > 0.05, hence it is statistically insignificant as per Levene's test for equality of variances. Therefore, we do not reject the null hypothesis, and consider that there is equality in variance.

Also, it is evident that the p value = .955 >0.05, t calculated .057 < critical value 1.660 and there is a zero between the upper and lower limits, hence we do not reject the null hypothesis. This implies that gender has no statistically significant impact on employee retention.

Table 5(a). Marital status vs employee retention (t-test)

	Marital_status	N	Mean	Std. Deviation	Std. Error Mean
Employee_Retention	**Single**	38	9.63	3.258	.529
	Married	84	11.62	3.143	.343

Table 5(b). Marital status vs employee retention (t-test)

	Equality of Variances		t-test for Equality of Means							
	F	Sig	t	df	Sig. (2-tailed)	Mean Difference	Std Error Difference	Interval of the		
Employee Retention	**0.873**	**0.352**							Lower	Upper
Equal variance assumed			-3.198	120	0.002	-1.987	0.621		-3.218	-0.757
Equal Variance not assumed			-3.154	69.23	0.002	-1.987	0.63		-3.244	-0.731

Here the p value (.352) >0.05, hence it is statistically insignificant as per Levene's test for equality of variances. Therefore, we do not reject the null hypothesis that there is equality of variances. Moreover, from the above table it is evident that the p value = .002<0.05, tabulated t -3.198 >critical value 1.660 hence we reject the null hypothesis. This implies that marital status has statistically significant impact on employee retention.

Table 6. ANOVA (demographic variables vs employee retention)

		Sum of Squares	df	Mean Square	F	Sig.
Age	**Between Groups**	17.037	12	1.420	1.914	.040
	Within Groups	80.865	109	.742		
	Total	97.902	121			
Income	**Between Groups**	14.225	12	1.185	1.968	.034
	Within Groups	65.652	109	.602		
	Total	79.877	121			
Years_of_service	**Between Groups**	32.008	12	2.667	3.530	.000
	Within Groups	82.361	109	.756		
	Total	114.369	121			
Designation	**Between Groups**	6.503	12	.542	1.370	.191
	Within Groups	43.112	109	.396		
	Total	49.615	121			

The above ANOVA Table 6 indicates that the employee retention is influenced by age since p = .040 <0.05 and F value 1.914 > Critical value (tabulated value) 1.83; annual income p = .034<0.05 and F value 1.968 > Critical value (tabulated value) 1.83; years of service p = .000<0.05 and F value 3.530 > Critical value (tabulated value) 1.83. Hence, we can infer that people from different age brackets, or annual income or years of service may have different intentions to stay in the organization. On the other hand, designation with p = .191> 0.05 and F value 1.370 < Critical value (tabulated value) 1.83, doesn't have significant influence on employee retention.

Overall, it can be interpreted that in terms of demographic variables some variables like marital status, age, years of service and annual income have significant influence on employees' intention to stay in the organization, but such statistical significance was not found in case of gender and designation of the employees.

REGRESSION ANALYSIS

Table 7. Multiple linear regression model summary

Model	R	R Square	Adjusted R Square	Std. Error of the Estimate
1	.912[a]	.832	.825	1.381

a. Predictors: (Constant), Compensation, Work_Environment, Mentoring, Job_Autonomy, Career_Development

On the basis of model fit (Table 7), it can be inferred that the predictors namely compensation, work environment, mentoring, career development and job autonomy can influence 83.2% variance in employee retention. It also signifies that the remaining 16.8% of influence could be caused by some other factors.

Table 8. ANOVA

	Model	Sum of Squares	df	Mean Square		Sig.
	Regression	1094.833	5	218.967	114.846	.000[b]
1	Residual	221.167	116	1.907		
	Total	1316.000	121			

The ANOVA table (Table 8) depicts that the model is statistically significant, indicating that the employee retention is influenced by mentioned enablers (M Square=218.967), F (5,116) =114.846, p = .000<0.05 and F value 218.967 > Critical value (tabulated value) 2.29 hence we reject the null hypothesis. This indicates that enablers are statistically significant in employee retention.

Table 9. Multiple linear regression coefficients (enablers)

Model		Unstandardized Coefficients		Standardized Coefficients	t	Sig.
		B	Std. Error	Beta		
	Mentoring	.296	.095	.291	3.119	.002
	Career_Development	.224	.119	.215	1.887	.042
	Work_Environment	.210	.089	.210	2.355	.020
	Job_Autonomy	-.015	.108	-.015	-.134	.894
	Compensation	.281	.085	.269	3.306	.001

The above table (Table 9) implies that variables like mentoring, career development, work environment and compensation have significant influence on employee retention ($p<.05$) but surprisingly, statistical significance of job-autonomy on employee retention could not be established ($p=.894$)

The above analysis can be summarized as, according to the descriptive statistics, the mean for the enablers—mentoring, career development, work environment, job autonomy, and compensation—is moderately to highly inclined towards agreeableness pertaining to being a factor contributing to employee retention in an organisation.

Gender and marital status effects on employee retention were assessed using an independent sample t test. In terms of gender, it was shown to be statistically insignificant, but in terms of married status, it was significant.

ANOVA test between the demographic variables and employee retention revealed that age, income per annum and years of service have a great influence on an employee's intention to stay in a company as they were found to be statistically significant. However, it was not significant in the case of level of designation.

Mentoring, work environment, career development, and compensation are statistically significant factors in employee retention, implying that focusing on these areas while formulating and implementing employee retention strategies would lead to higher organisational commitment and loyalty among the employees, which would further influence the employees' intention to stay with the organisation for a longer duration.

Job autonomy has been found to be statistically insignificant factors in employee retention. As per the data analysis, it does not drive employee retention and has very little influence on an employee's intention to stay with the organisation when measured individually.

The overall regression for the enablers was found to statistically significant meaning that employee retention is influenced by the mentioned factors collectively in an organization to a great extent.

4. CONCLUSION AND SUGGESTIONS

The primary cause of employee attrition may vary depending on the company and industry, but common causes include a lack of opportunities for professional advancement. Employees want to believe that their careers are developing and progressing. If they don't think there are any options for advancement, they might look for other jobs. Poor leadership and terrible managers can cause a hostile work environment, a lack of support, and poor communication. This could lead to disengagement, a sense of being undervalued, and ultimately, employee departure from the company. If employees believe they are not receiving fair compensation or if their benefits package is not online with that of competing companies, they may decide to leave. Inadequate pay and perks and poor work-life balance can lead to stress and burnout, which can lead to workers quitting the company. Employee retention is influenced by the corporate culture. If there is a toxic, unsupportive, or incompatible culture, workers can search for another place to work. Businesses need to identify the primary causes of employee attrition and take proactive steps to address them if they want to see an increase in retention rates.

Creating a welcoming and supportive work environment that caters to employees' needs is one of the principal factors in employee retention. Workers want to feel as though their careers are moving forward and that they have the chance to pick up new skills. An environment that is friendly and encouraging can help employees stay on the job longer. A work environment can be made positive by fostering a culture that values communication, teamwork, and a good work-life balance. Workers require supportive management and leadership that is strong. Workers want to feel appreciated and recognised for their work, therefore awards and recognition are important. A recognition and incentive program can lead to higher employee satisfaction and retention rates. Retention rates can be raised, and stress levels reduced by providing employees with flexible work hours and a healthy work-life balance. Establishing a positive, encouraging work environment that meets employees' needs can help companies increase staff retention rates and reduce the costs associated with employee turnover.

To sum up, the retention of employees plays a critical role in determining the prosperity and expansion of a company. The purpose of this thesis was to investigate the main reasons behind employee attrition, the advantages of staff retention, and the tactics that companies may use to keep their workforces. The results of the research revealed that, among other potentially important elements, remuneration, work environment, and mentoring are statistically significant drivers of employee retention in a firm. Lack of opportunity for career advancement, incompetent management, inadequate pay and benefits, and an unfavourable work environment are the main causes of employee attrition.

Furthermore, employee retention strategies such as competitive compensation and benefits, career development opportunities, positive work environment, employee engagement, work-life balance, recognition and rewards, and strong leadership and management were identified as effective measures to retain employees. The advantages of keeping current employees were also emphasized, including lower rates of staff turnover, higher profitability, more productivity, and improved employee satisfaction. It is advised that businesses use proactive approaches to keep their staff members by putting in place efficient employee retention plans. This will improve an organization's ability to draw in and keep top personnel, increase its marketability, and lead to long-term success and growth.

5. IMPLICATIONS FOR THE INDUSTRY

The foundation of the national economy is the manufacturing sector. Its workforce plays a major role in the enormous amount of work that is done in this industry. In this industry, employee retention becomes a major worry. By providing competitive wage and benefits, it is crucial that enterprises make sure that workers are treated fairly and have access to perks that are on par with those provided by other companies in the industry. It is imperative to provide employees with opportunities for career advancement and development in order to equip them for the future.

Fostering a culture of cooperation, open communication, and appreciation will also help in establishing a happy and encouraging workplace. To demonstrate that the company values employee input and opinions, employee engagement initiatives like employee surveys, focus groups, and feedback systems should be initiated. Employees should be provided flexibility and a healthy work-life balance by allowing them to telecommute, set their own hours, or participate in job sharing programmes. Appreciation and recognition work wonders in developing employee commitment. A platform should be created where employees can be publicly recognised for their efforts. And finally, to establish trust and a trustworthy workplace, open communication and transparency at all organisational levels should be ensured. Employers may raise worker satisfaction, lower employee turnover rates, and keep their best employees by putting these employee retention tactics into practise.

6. SCOPE FOR FUTURE RESEARCH

Retaining employees is a constant source of worry and critical success for all types of organizations. Regarding sample size and statistical analysis soundness, the study has certain drawbacks. Furthermore, its applicability was restricted to workers in the manufacturing industry alone, which reduced its generalizability. In the future, a far more thorough cross-sectional comparative analysis of various sectors might be carried out, utilizing more variables to analyze the employees' intention to stay, more powerful statistical techniques like the structural equation model, mediators, and moderators, and so forth.

REFERENCES

Abhilasha & Pathak, S. (2014). Managing multigenerational workforce: An Indian perspective. *Asian Journal of Research in Business Economics and Management, 4,* 29-37.

Alshurideh, D. M. (2019). Do electronic loyalty programs still drive customer choice and repeat purchase behavior? *International Journal of Electronic Customer Relationship Management, 12*(1), 40–57. doi:10.1504/IJECRM.2019.098980

Bibi, P., Ahmad, A., & Majid, A. H. A. (2018). HRM Practices and Employee Retention: The Moderating Effect of Work Environment. In Applying Partial Least Squares in Tourism and Hospitality Research. Emerald Publishing Limited. doi:10.1108/978-1-78756-699-620181007

Burmeister, M. (2009). It's all about me becomes a cross generational conversation. *Training & Development, 63*(5), 92–93.

Cennamo, L., & Gardner, D. (2008). Generational differences in work values, outcomes and person organization values fit. *Journal of Managerial Psychology, 23*(8), 891–906. doi:10.1108/02683940810904385

Cherri Ho, C. Y. (2010). Intergenerational learning between generation x and y families – a narrative inquiry. *International Education Studies, 3*(4), 60–61.

Crumpacker, M., & Crumpacker, J. D. (2007). Succession planning and generational stereotypes: Should HR consider age-based values and attitudes- a relevant factor or a passing fad? *Public Personnel Management, 36*(4), 349–369. doi:10.1177/009102600703600405

Deckop, J. R., Merriman, K. K., & Gupta, S. (2006). The Effects of CEO Pay Structure on Corporate Social Performance. *Journal of Management, 32*(3), 329–342. doi:10.1177/0149206305280113

Dessler, G. (2007). *Human resource management.* Prentice Hall of India Private Limited.

Dolezalek, H. (2007). X-Y Vision - Generation X is all grown up, and Generation Y is coming into its own. What does this mean for companies' training efforts today and tomorrow? *Training: The Magazine of Manpower and Management Development, 44*(6), 22–29.

Duffield, C., Baldwin, R., Roche, M., & Wise, S. (2014). Job enrichment: Creating meaningful career development opportunities for nurses. *Journal of Nursing Management, 22*(6), 697–706. doi:10.1111/jonm.12049 PMID:23463905

Eisner, S. P. (2005). Managing generation Y. *S.A.M. Advanced Management Journal, 70*(4), 4–15.

Ferri-Reed, J. (2010). The keys to engaging millennials. *Journal for Quality and Participation, 33*(1), 1–33.

Gorde, S. (2019). A Study of Employee Retention. *Journal of Emerging Technologies and Innovative Research, 6*(6), 331–337.

Gravett, L., & Throckmorton, R. (2007). *Bridging the generation gap.* Career Press.

Gutner, T. (2002). A Balancing Act for Gen X Women. *Business Week, 3766,* 82. Retrieved from: https://erualfamilies.uwagec.org/ERFLibrary/Readings/ABalancingActForGenXWomen.pdf

Huntley, R. (2006). *The world according to Y: Inside the new adult generation.* Allen and Unwin.

Islam, M.A., Hack-Polay, D., Rahman, M., Hosen, M., Hunt, A., & Shafique, S. (2022). Work environment, HR practices and millennial employee retention in hospitality and tourism in Bangladesh. *International Journal of Emerging Markets.* . doi:10.1108/IJOEM-06-2021-0859

Jena, L., & Nayak, U. (2023). Organizational career development and retention of millennial employees: The role of job engagement and organizational engagement. *Asia-Pacific Journal of Business Administration.* Advance online publication. doi:10.1108/APJBA-07-2022-0323

Jones, B., Brown, S. P., Zoltners, A. A., & Weits, B. A. (2005). The changing environment of selling and sales management. *Journal of Personal Selling & Sales Management, 25*(2), 105–111.

Kerslake, P. (2005). Words from the Ys. *New Zealand Management, 52*(4), 44–46.

Koster, K. (2013). *Communication and engagement.* Employee Benefit News. https://www.highbeam.com/ publications/employee-benefit-news-p4839/april-2013

Kovarik, M. (2008). How to engage Gen Y. *Inside Supply Management,* 10-12.

Kriss, M., Te, H. S., Elizabeth, C., VanWagner, L. B., Scott, F. I., & Lai, J. C. (2021). National Early Career Transplant Hepatologist Survey: Compensation, Burnout, and Job Satisfaction. *Hepatology Communications, 5*(4), 701–712. doi:10.1002/hep4.1666 PMID:33860127

Kumar, K. K., Mishra, S. K., & Budhwar, P. (2021). Employee turnover in India: insights from the public–private debate. In D. G. Allen & J. M. Vardaman (Eds.), *Global Talent Retention: Understanding Employee Turnover Around the World* (pp. 213–238). Emerald Publishing. doi:10.1108/978-1-83909-293-020211011

Kundu, S. C., & Lata, K. (2017). Effects of supportive work environment on employee retention: Mediating role of organizational engagement. *The International Journal of Organizational Analysis, 25*(4), 703–722. doi:10.1108/IJOA-12-2016-1100

Logan, G. (2008). Anatomy of a Gen Y- er. *Personnel Today,* 24-25.

Long, C. S., Xuan, S. S., Wan Ismail, W. K., Abd Rasid, S. Z., & Kowang, T. O. (2014). An analysis on academicians' job satisfaction in the perspective of HRD practices. *International Education Studies, 7*(7), 85–95. doi:10.5539/ies.v7n7p85

Lowe, D., Levitt, K., & Wilson, T. (2008). Solutions for retaining generation Y employees in the workplace. *Business Renaissance Quarterly, 3*(3), 43–57.

Lyons, S. T. (2003). *An exploration of generational values in life and at work* [PhD Thesis]. Carleton University.

Mangi, R. A., Soomro, H. J., Ghumro, I., Abidi, A. R., & Jalbani, A. A. (2011). A study of job satisfaction among non-PhD faculty in universities. *Australian Journal of Business and Management Research, 1*(7), 83–90. doi:10.52283/NSWRCA.AJBMR.20110107A09

Martin, C. A. (2005). From High Maintenance to High Productivity: What Managers Need to Know about Generation Y. *Industrial and Commercial Training, 37*(1), 39–44. doi:10.1108/00197850510699965

Mathimaran, K. B., & Kumar, A. A. (2017). Employee retention strategies: An empirical research. *Global Journal of Management and Business Research, 17*(1), 17–19.

Moncarz, E., Zhao, J., & Kay, C. (2009). An exploratory study of US lodging properties' organizational practices on employee turnover and retention. *International Journal of Contemporary Hospitality Management, 21*(4), 437–458. doi:10.1108/09596110910955695

Mukherjee, B., Chandra, B., & Singh, S. (2020). Talent retention in Indian public sector units (PSUs): An empirical investigation. *Kybernetes, 49*(6), 1783–1810. doi:10.1108/K-03-2019-0165

Munde, G. (2010). Considerations for managing an increasingly intergenerational workforce in libraries. *Library Trends, 59*(1/2), 89. doi:10.1353/lib.2010.a407808

Ohlrich, K. (2011). *Analyzing Corporate Social Responsibility's Impact on Employee Attraction and Retention with a Focus on Generation Y*. Fielding Graduate University.

Oprea, B., Păduraru, L., & Iliescu, D. (2022). Job crafting and intent to leave: The mediating role of meaningful work and engagement. *Journal of Career Development, 49*(1), 188–201. doi:10.1177/0894845320918666

Pooley, E. (2005). Kids these days. *Canadian Business, 78*(12), 67–68.

Price Waterhouse Coopers. (2008). *Managing tomorrow's people: millennials at work – perspectives from a new generation*. Retrieved from www.pwc.com/managingpeople2020

Raman, G., Ramendran, C., Beleya, P., Nodeson, S., & Arokiasamy, L. (2011). Generation Y in institution of higher learning. *International Journal of Economics and Business Modelling, 2*(2), 142–148.

Sayers, R. (2007). The right staff from X to Y. *Library Management, 28*(8/9), 474–487. doi:10.1108/01435120710837765

Sheahan, P. (2005). *Generation Y: thriving and surviving with Generation Y at work*. Hardie Gran Books.

Solnet, D., & Hood, A. (2008). Generation Y as hospitality employees: Framing a research agenda. *Journal of Hospitality and Tourism Management, 15*(1), 59–68. doi:10.1375/jhtm.15.1.59

Sujansky, (2002). The critical care and feeding of generation Y. *Workforce, 81*(5), 15.

Tapscott, D. (2009). *Grown up digital: how the net generation is changing your world*. McGraw Hill.

Terjesen, S., Vinnicombe, S., & Freeman, C. (2007). Attracting generation Y graduates. *Career Development International, 12*(6), 504–522. doi:10.1108/13620430710821994

Tulgan, B. (2000). *Managing generation X: how to bring out the best in young talent.* W. W. Norton & Company.

Weyland, A. (2011). Engagement and talent management of Gen Y. *Industrial and Commercial Training, 43*(7), 439–445. doi:10.1108/00197851111171863

Wikimedia Foundation. (2022, October 25). *Employee retention.* Wikipedia. Retrieved February 6, 2023, from https://en.wikipedia.org/wiki/Employee_retention

Yarbrough, S., Martin, P., Alfred, D., & McNeill, C. (2017). Professional values, job satisfaction, career development, and intent to stay. *Nursing Ethics, 24*(6), 675–685. doi:10.1177/0969733015623098 PMID:26811397

Zemke, R., Raines, C., & Filipczak, B. (2000). *Generations at work: managing the clash of veterans, boomers, xers, and nexters in your workplace.* AMACOM.

Zeytinoglu, I. U., & Denton, M. (2005). Satisfied workers, retained workers: Effects of work and work environment on homecare workers' job satisfaction, stress, physical health, and retention. Canadian Health Services Research Foundation (CHSRF).

Chapter 6
Diverse Minds, Infinite Potential:
Navigating Neurodiversity in Today's Workplace

Fehmina Khalique
https://orcid.org/0000-0002-2519-3174
Lloyd Business School, India

Nusrat Khan
https://orcid.org/0000-0003-0788-7786
GD Goenka University, India

Shilpi Sarna
https://orcid.org/0000-0001-8505-4750
Lloyd Business School, India

Kartikay Saini
GD Goenka University, India

ABSTRACT

Emergence of the concept of neurodiversity has challenged the conventional perceptions of neurological differences by encapsulating the diversity of neurological variations such as autism spectrum disorders (ASD), attention deficit/hyperactivity disorder (ADHD), sensory stimuli disorders, etc. The neurodiversity concept asserts that these are natural variations in the human brain, each with its own set of strengths and perspectives. This concept advocates for a shift in societal attitudes, to accept and accommodate neurodivergent individuals, transcending a mere acknowledgment of differences. Perception revolving around and support to individuals with neurological differences, striving for a world that appreciates the richness of cognitive diversity is necessary. Embracing inclusivity is not just a moral imperative; it is a strategic business decision that positively impacts employee satisfaction, innovation, talent acquisition and customer relations, ultimately contributing to the overall success and sustainability of a business.

DOI: 10.4018/979-8-3693-1938-3.ch006

1. INTRODUCTION

Over the past few decades, the number of psychiatric disorders has shown an increase. In the first edition of The Diagnostic and Statistical Manual of Mental Disorders, published by The American Psychiatric Association in 1952, listed a number of 128 disease categories, their number had already reached 541 in 2013 (Blashfield et al., 2014).

Neurodiversity as a concept was first introduced by the Australian Sociologist Judy Singer, who laid attention on the diverse personalities of people who were either introverted or extroverted, dyslexic or even autistic, however, they form an integral part of the human race. Taking this aspect into account and considering the fact that approximately 10% of the population is neurodivergent in a way, employers cannot disregard this category of persons, as neurodiversity is beginning to gradually be part of the vocabulary used by the Human Resources department (Faragher, 2018).

Neurodiversity encompasses a range of key definitions that collectively contribute to a comprehensive understanding of the concept. One key definition emphasizes neurodivergence, a term used to describe individuals whose neurological development and functioning differ from what is considered typical (Milton, 2014). This includes conditions such as autism, ADHD, dyslexia and more. Neurodiversity also underscores the notion of neurotypicality, representing individuals whose neurological development aligns with societal expectations.

Disability of any kind related to either mental or learning, can be considered as a lack of ability to function according to the norms. As per the 'medical model of disability', this kind of lacking is caused by health challenges in people; these challenges can be overcome by applying medical treatments. Whereas, the social model of disability focuses on people with disabilities when they view the world. Here the disability is actually because of the way the society is organized, rather than actual challenges of an individual. Barriers can be physical or they can be caused by people's attitudes towards these challenges. Social model, therefore, helps in identifying these barriers effecting the life of people with disabilities and focuses on the ways in which these can be avoided. At the other end, the medical model identifies what is "wrong" with the respective person and not what they need, leading to loss of independence and reduction of control over their own lives (Haegele and Hodge, 2016) (Figure 1).

Figure 1. The medical social model of disability vs. the social model of disability (Haegele & Hodge, 2016)

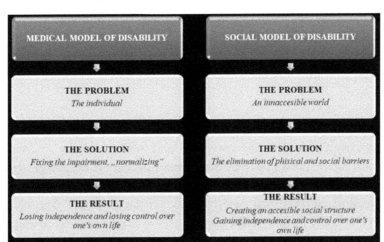

1.1 Forms of Neurodiversity

The notion of neurodiversity was first used to describe and protect people with autism, it has since then expanded to comprise today, apart from the persons with autism-spectrum disorders, persons with other learning and behavioral disabilities, such as dyslexia, dyspraxia, ADHD, dyscalculia and Tourette syndrome.

❖ *Autism-Spectrum-Disorders (ASD)* includes disabilities also known as Autism, Asperger Syndrome and Pervasive Development Disorder. ASD are neurodiverse conditions that impact the social interaction and communication of people. Such people are often characterized by rigid thinking, restrictive and repetitive behaviours, and have a set routine, extremely susceptible to environmental changes, sensitive to sensory organs like lights/noises/smells/tastes etc.

❖ *Dyslexia* is a form of neurodiversity wherein the person has difficulty in reading, writing and spelling. Also, these people can have short-term memory, lack of concentration and ineffective time management and organizing skills.

❖ *Dyspraxia* is also known as Developmental Co-ordination Disorder (DCD). People with dyspraxia experience difficulties with large and/or small movements which may affect balance, fatigue levels, hand-eye coordination, rhythm, hand movements or manipulation skills; reading and writing difficulties; over sensitive to taste, light, touch or noise; poor sense of time, speed, distance, weight, or sense of direction; organizational or planning difficulties; difficulties with accuracy, concentration or following instruction; slowly adaptation to new or unpredictable situations (Barr, 2019).

❖ *Attention-Deficit-Hyperactivity-Disorder (ADHD)* is a different kind of neurodevelopmental disorder. ADHS is related to that part of the brain that controls different functions, self-regulation and inhibition. Due to this dysfunction occurs at different levels like cognitive, social and emotional levels. This leads to inattention or hyperactivity and impulsivity amongst individuals. Poor concentration may lead people with ADHD to become absent-minded, easily distracted and easily bored or having poor organizational skills (Centers for Disease Control and Prevention, 2019).

- *Dyscalculia* is a condition related to brain neurons where the person can have difficulty in dealing with numbers and problems with disciplines like with mathematics where sizing, ordering, and reading and writing numbers is involved (British Dyslexia Association).
- *Tourette syndrome* is also called Tic Disorder that is associated with the involuntary, repetitive movements and vocalizations known as tics. Individuals with Tourette Syndrome (TS) have had at least two motor tics (ex: blinking, eye rolling, grimacing, shoulder shrugging, jumping etc.) and at least one vocal/ phonic tic (whistling, coughing, tongue clicking, animal sounds, saying random words and phrases, swearing (NHS, 2018) in some combination (Tourette Association of America).

Neurodiversity covers a vast spectrum of human brain and neurocognitive functioning, recognizing, and accepting the diversity within both 'neurotypical' and 'neurodivergent' individuals (Bewley and George, 2016). Neurodivergent individuals may experience one or more neurological conditions, sharing common features that manifest in unique approaches to learning and processing information.

All these neurodiversity traits are usually referred to as "On the spectrum." The word spectrum is more generically used than it actually means. While this may seem to be a societal advantage to generalize a larger population with neuro-diverse issues, it also is a disadvantage to those neuro-diverse individuals who are high-functional and "near normal" but because of the tag of "on the spectrum" may tend to get a workplace stigma from co-workers.

1.2 Characteristics of Neuro-Diverse Persons

Studies have suggested that persons with neuro-diversities are: -

- Highly naturally talented in certain areas e.g., graphics, music, calculations, memory, art, sport, etc. They excel in desk jobs, back-office jobs, precision and patience-related jobs, procedural tasks, process-oriented jobs etc.
- Usually lack or are slower in areas that require strategic decisions, forward planning, complex matrix planning, intensive thinking, decisions that have an emotional quotient, direct interactive customer relationship roles, etc.
- Neuro-diverse persons can almost always be trusted for their honesty, punctuality, work and target oriented dedication, respecting time and timelines, following instructions to the hilt, following procedures, obeying company rules, loyalty at work and long sustenance in the company, etc.
- These individuals, due to their neurodiversity, do sometimes showcase impatience, hyperactivity, cannot adapt to quick changing instructions, take time in processing questions and answering, are usually quiet and reserved, which need to be kept in mind before defining their work responsibility.

Therefore, neuro-diverse persons at the workplace will usually be an asset if employed gainfully where these characteristics are identified, and the right work profile is created. They would usually be better than most. Let us delve into the significance of having workforce in organizations which is neurodiverse and how managers can utilize them and increase their worth for better productivity and inclusivity.

2. NEURODIVERSITY IN THE WORKPLACE

Applying the concept of neurodiversity in the workplace can lead to competitive advantage for the organisations. The neurological differences if highlighted can help garner the best out of the employees, therefore such employees should be adequately appreciated and harnessed by employers.

A series of studies conducted has identified an association of dyslexia to the speed of recognizing impossible figures, which suggests dyslexia is associated to a type of enhanced ability to process the visual-spatial information globally (holistically) rather than locally (part by part) (Von Károlyi et al., 2003); this ability can prove quite beneficial for workplaces requiring three-dimensional thinking, such as astrophysics, molecular biology, genetics and engineering (Armstrong, 2015). The global head of human resources for retail banking and wealth management at HSBC points out that the abilities that companies need are evolving fast, with an accent laid more and more now on empathy, creative thinking, innovative problem-solving and the possibility to communicate and build relationships in more networks, all these representing fields in which dyslexics thrive (Taylor, 2019).

Often it is found that people with ADHD learn new opportunities and are professional in handling multiple tasks as a given times, work best under stress and are creative and, given the right incentive, they can "hyperfocus". People with ASD are prominent in the field of Information technology using computer systems effectively with mathematical and programming. On the other hand, Autistic people with Asperger are inclined towards music, as they are more oriented towards detail and they also have enhanced visual-spatial skills. According to a data analyst of the SAP Success Factors Company, diagnosed with autism, people on the autism spectrum have a various set of skills and they prove to be very skilled in a whole range of fields (Elias, 2017), apart from all these, turning out to be punctual, dedicated and loyal employees. The benefits from hiring an autistic person can be among the most varied, going from the possibility to cover some jobs that are hard to fill in among the neurotypicals (such as software testing, customer support); they register less products and services' flaws rate and their corporate communication is more direct and more effective, taking account of the fact that the neuroatypicals do not understand heavy, nuanced language and complicated speech (Kişescu, 2017) (Figure 2).

Figure 2. Neurodiversity in the workplace
(CIPD, 2018)

Auticon an IT consulting company is known for hiring people from ASD as it strongly believes that such adults often have astonishing cognitive skills. Such skills are valuable to the company in the long run to lead towards growth. However, many of these individuals have trouble finding or holding on to a normal job. This policy of the company to hire neurodiverse people has led to growth not only in revenue and profit margins, but also, of the work force, setting a major recruitment action in Great Britain (Munn, 2019).

The HR practices like recruitment, hiring, training and development should be well aligned with neurodivergent persons. It becomes therefore imperative for the HR managers to realize the actual potential of such individuals and should utilize their abilities in a different way. Once these potentials are matched to the job profile further accommodations to the workplace may be needed and may also be initiated by the managers.

Past studies on good practices of companies involving hiring of neurodivergent persons show that there are several ways in which organisations can be supportive and create inclusive work environment for them:

2.1 Recruitment Practices

When recruiting, companies ensure descriptions as clear and concise as possible of the roles to fulfil, ensuring a clear demarcation between skills and experience the applicant should possess or would be preferable to possess, and facilitating easy identification of the basic competences the job requires from the applicant (CIPD, 2018). Conventional face-to-face job for assessing incumbent may not be useful for neurodivergent persons, making them face issues in exhibiting their skills, and this may lead to excluding them from the roles they could have been selected for. An eloquent example of this situation is the fact that candidates with Asperger can have difficulties looking the interviewer in the eye, and numerous autistic persons have an unusual tone of voice or peculiar cadence as compared to the rest of the world and all these things can be misinterpreted (Morgan, 2018; Love, 2019).

Organizations have used a number of altered recruitment strategies to reach to the talent that is neurodivergent (Patton et.al, 2019). There should be specific targeted strategies for the recruitment stage. The research in divergent literatures shows that only 11% of employers have recruiting strategy specific to attracting people with disabilities. There are several repeated statements about the actual desire to hire more people from this group, but the numbers vary.

In order to support organization's diversity and inclusivity with respect to neurodivergent incumbents, strategic changes can result in attracting more neurodivergent applicants. Organizations often include tests in their hiring process based on reading comprehension and mathematical skills. For applicants with learning disabilities, this can present a number of obstacles that have nothing to do with the strengths (e.g., intelligence or abilities in comprehension or mathematics) that they are going to contribute to the organization (Sumner & Brown, 2015). For neurodivergent applicants, Burnett and Trerise (2019) suggest altering these traditional hiring processes and let the applicant have space and time to analyze the questions, even being able to return their response on another day.

2.2 Compensation and Benefits

For neurodivergent employees, there are a number of deliberations around compensation and benefits; the HR must restructure these to strengthen diversity and inclusion. Specifically, reports show that individuals with Asperger's (the highest level of functioning autism) have an unemployment rate of 80% to 85% (Richards, 2012; National Autistic Society, 2016). Therefore, it becomes imperative for the organizations to build diverse pool including the contribution of neurodivergent individuals. The organizations can utilize the unique strengths of neurodivergent employees and compensate them with deserving benefits and pay. This exercise will promote diversity and inclusion by strengthening the association between rewards and performance.

2.3 Employee Relations

Research on autism shows that having supportive senior managers and direct supervisors is related to having a work environment that is accepting of accommodations (Austin & Pisano, 2017; Patton et.al,

2019; Wright, 2016). One example provided by Faragher (2018) describes how a director at an organization signed his emails with the following statement: 'excuse the typos, I'm dyslexic.'

Management and leadership roles in the organization can help build a culture that can help neurodiversity-related efforts to be more inclusive. That is, transformational leadership often is not an effective leadership style for employees who are neurodivergent because the visionary aspects to transformational leadership are too abstract to provide guidance to employees that think in more specific ways (Hurley-Hanson & Giannantonio, 2017; Parr et al., 2013). However, a number of researchers have suggested that authentic leadership (Boekhorst, 2015; Dwertmann & Boehm, 2016; Hurley-Hanson & Giannantonio, 2017; Parr & Hunter, 2014) is a leadership style that is inclusive of neurodiversity. In order to support neurodiversity, organizations should foster employee relations with the fact that effective management and leadership can exert a considerable impact on the experiences of neurodivergent employees.

2.4 Occupational Health and Safety

Discrimination is an important aspect of occupational health and safety with regard to diverse climate; often neurodivergent employees report that diversity climates in their organizations is ineffective when it comes to occupational health and safety of such employees. Research supports this, as employees with neurodivergent conditions are shown to face discrimination in the workplace around hiring practices, treatment on the job, and others' resistance to their workplace accommodations (Richards, 2012).

2.5 Training and Development

Companies have had success with self-paced tutorials or on-the-job training as compared to classroom training or training that takes place on a computer (Patton et.al, 2019; Sumner & Brown, 2015) in order to strengthen diversity climate. It is easy to see how traditional classroom-type trainings may be ineffective for employees with dyslexia, for example, as they are expected to process large amounts of reading or text through training exercises, the training presentations, after-training quizzes, etc. (Sumner & Brown, 2015). Research shows that neurodivergent employees are often overlooked and not selected for important career-building trainings (Patton et.al, 2019; Sumner & Brown, 2015). Across the board, employees say that they want more training and development opportunities.

2.6 Talent Management and Performance

Organizations should foster talent management and performance management in order to promote diversity and inclusion especially in the case of neurodivergent workforce by introducing programs like mentoring and coaching. It is important to consider the working environment which may have contributed to the performance/non-performance of a neurodivergent employee. Moreover, while providing performance feedback to an employee who is neurodivergent, it is relevant to include the working environment which may have contributed to his or her performance or non-performance both. For example, if an employee with dyslexia received excellent performance ratings but was reprimanded during their annual evaluation and then marked down for failure to complete trainings required by HR, it may in fact be unfair that such a demand was expected of them (Sumner & Brown, 2015). Organizations have a role in correcting these wrongs by creating a work environment which would help individuals from the neurominority group.

It is important for all including employees and stakeholders to understand that an acknowledgement for the strengths exists and it will also be supported by the organization in different endeavors.

2.7 Job Design

Job design is an important aspect when it comes to diverse climate especially in the case of neurodivergent employees; it also plays a significant role in building an inclusive culture that support neurodiversity. The accommodation process needs to be strengthened to bring out better results. So many researchers and practitioners have emphasized that accommodations are not as expensive or disruptive as many organizational decision-makers assume them to be (Ovaska-Few, 2018). For example, finding quiet workspaces or low-traffic locations for employees who are neurodivergent are accommodations that researchers (Association for Talent Development, 2018; Austin & Pisano, 2017; Johnson & Joshi, 2016; Wright, 2022) and organizations such as EY suggests as impactful accommodations that do not cost anything (Schur et al., 2014). If anyone in the workforce can request accommodations around scheduling, policy changes, lighting, workspace, and other environmental factors (within reason), it bolsters an inclusion climate for everyone (Patton et.al, 2019; Schur et al., 2014).

2.8 Retention

Presence of neurodivergent employees in the workforce in an organization can help facilitate better understanding of neurodiversity and increase the acceptance of such employees amongst their peers. As an example, Kapp et al. (2019) point out that autistic adults may understand one another better than nonautistic people understand a person with autism (Gernsbacher et al., 2017; Gillespie-Lynch et al., 2017; Komeda, 2015; Milton, 2014). In a study of autistic boys, researchers noted that the boys bonded with each other and recognized the similarities that existed amongst them (i.e., their similar experiences and traits) (Burnham and Muskat, 2017). Moreover, to support diversity and inclusion climate for the neurodivergent employee's retention is crucial. Companies like SAP have created support circles that include people in the workplace (i.e., a manager, a team buddy, a job coach, a mentor, and someone from HR) and also people in the employee's nonwork life (Austin & Pisano, 2017). HPE uses a 'pod' system in which neurodivergent employees' work with four other employees overseen by a manager and neurodiversity consultant (Austin & Pisano, 2017). In practice, this entails organizations supporting employees as they participate in identity and community building events (e.g., Autistic Pride Day), join identity and community-building organizations (e.g., Autism Network International), sport identity and community- building artifacts (T-shirts, stimming toys,), and use vocabulary that is identity and community- building (e.g., Aspie) (Angulo-Jiménez & DeThorne, 2019; Bagatell, 2010; Donaldson et al., 2017).

3. CONCLUSION

Many neurodivergent individuals exhibit a high level of attention to detail, precision, and accuracy. This can be particularly beneficial in roles that require thoroughness and a focus on specific tasks, (Scott, et. al., 2015). The combination of attention to detail and creativity can result in neurodivergent individuals contributing to projects with both precision and innovative thinking, offering a unique blend of skills (Scott, et. al., 2015). Neurodiverse individuals often excel in analytical thinking and problem-solving.

Therefore, organizations must focus on neurodiverse workforce and emphasize on the following tactics to achieve inclusivity and diversity.

3.1 Increasing Awareness on Neurodiversity

Employers should be proactive, providing information about neurodiversity to both employees with neurological conditions and those without such conditions (Morgan, 2018). Managers and senior professionals needs to be given a training to understand the support, help and accommodation that would be required for the neurodivergent employees. Such training sessions will help the managers to understand the need for such neurodivergent employees to help and facilitate them to achieve greater individual productivity. Also, such training sessions, various campaigns and workshops, as well as internal communication in the company may be of help to employees as well, making them better understand what to expect from new colleagues, in terms of differentiation or need to make workplace accommodations, thus leading to finding new ways to support and better work with them (Austin and Pisano, 2017).

3.2 Customizing the Opportunities for Career Development

Neurodivergent employees may feel that promotions are denied to them or that they are underestimated when it comes to undertaking greater responsibilities (Burnett, 2021). Such employees should be promised a long-term career path and organizations should support equal development opportunities in the workplace for all the employees. Continuous development through training programs or mentoring and coaching by managers should be promoted for neurodivergent employees in particular so that they can ride the ladder of professional success.

3.3 Ensuring a Supportive Environment and Workplace Adjustments

Employers are bound by law to provide reasonable adjustments in the workplace to people with disabilities; however, having regard to the fact that the key to success for any company is securing a flexible workplace to enable each employee to assert their strengths, we can say that these adjustments need to be ensured to all employees, regardless of disability or neurodiversity status (Munn, 2019). The needs of neurodivergent employees should be taken into consideration with regard to accommodations. For example, attention should be focused to employees' sensory environments like open-space offices, background noise, lighting and congestion. Moreover, provisions must be made with regard to quiet spaces to work and flexibility in working hours.

Hewlett Packard Enterprise adopts a different approach, the company having developed the Dandelion program, in which they place new neurodivergent employees into groups of approximately 15 persons each, where they work alongside neurotypical colleagues in an approximate percent, while two managers and a consultant are tasked with addressing neurodiversity-related issues (Austin and Pisano, 2017).

Neurodiverse individuals possess a wide range of skills and talents that can greatly contribute to the workplace. It's important to recognize that neurodiversity is not a one-size-fits-all category, and individuals within the neurodiverse spectrum have diverse strengths. Understanding these strengths and skills, various companies have started engaging these people, although the numbers are still very low. Some of the relevant examples which could be cited are: Hotels front office as well as housekeeping, digital marketing companies for graphics and design, Factories in quality assurance and process-oriented jobs, NGOs in art and craft work, data processing companies, even fashion and modelling companies where the right personal portfolio matches, music companies, all companies which require the skill sets mentioned above.

REFERENCES

Angulo-Jiménez, H., & DeThorne, L. (2019). Narratives about autism: An analysis of YouTube videos by individuals who self-identify as autistic. *American Journal of Speech-Language Pathology, 28*(2), 569–590. doi:10.1044/2018_AJSLP-18-0045 PMID:30995116

Armstrong, T. (2015). The myth of the normal brain: Embracing neurodiversity. *AMA Journal of Ethics, 17*(4), 348–352. doi:10.1001/journalofethics.2015.17.4.msoc1-1504 PMID:25901703

Austin, R. D., & Pisano, G. P. (2017). Neurodiversity as a competitive advantage. *Harvard Business Review, 95*(3), 96–103.

Bagatell, N. (2010). From cure to community: Transforming notions of autism. *Ethos, 38*(1), 33-55. Burnett, E. R. (2021). 'Different, not less': pastoral care of autistic adults within Christian churches. *Practical Theology, 14*(3), 211–223.

Barr, D. A. (2019). *Health disparities in the United States: Social class, race, ethnicity, and the social determinants of health.* JHU Press. doi:10.56021/9781421432571

Bewley, H., & George, A. (2016). *Neurodiversity at work.* National Institute of Social and Economic Research.

Blashfield, R. K., Keeley, J. W., Flanagan, E, H., & Miles, S. R. (2014). The cycle of classification: DSM-I through DSM-5. *Annual Review of Clinical Psychology, 10*(1), 25–51. doi:10.1146/annurev-clinpsy-032813-153639 PMID:24679178

Boekhorst, J. A. (2015). The role of authentic leadership in fostering workplace inclusion: A social information processing perspective. *Human Resource Management, 54*(2), 241–264. doi:10.1002/hrm.21669

Burnett, K., & Trerise, M. (2019). Embracing neurodiversity in the workplace. *Train. J*, 28-29.

Burnham Riosa, P., Greenblatt, A., & Muskat, B. (2017). An online ASD learning module for pediatric health care professionals. *Advances in Autism, 3*(3), 154–162. doi:10.1108/AIA-03-2017-0007

Centers for Disease Control and Prevention. (2019). *Attention-Deficit / Hyperactivity Disorder (ADHD).* Retrieved at https://www.cdc.gov/ncbddd/adhd/facts.html

Donaldson, A. L., Krejcha, K., & McMillin, A. (2017). A strengths-based approach to autism: Neurodiversity and partnering with the autism community. *Perspectives of the ASHA Special Interest Groups, 2*(1), 56–68. doi:10.1044/persp2.SIG1.56

Dwertmann, D. J., & Boehm, S. A. (2016). Status matters: The asymmetric effects of supervisor–subordinate disability incongruence and climate for inclusion. *Academy of Management Journal, 59*(1), 44–64. doi:10.5465/amj.2014.0093

Elias, R., & White, S. W. (2018). Autism goes to college: Understanding the needs of a student population on the rise. *Journal of Autism and Developmental Disorders, 48*(3), 732–746. doi:10.1007/s10803-017-3075-7 PMID:28255760

Faragher, J. (2018). Are employers losing out on skills of people with autism? *Occupational Health & Wellbeing, 70*(5), 16–17.

Gernsbacher, M. A., Stevenson, J. L., & Dern, S. (2017). Specificity, contexts, and reference groups matter when assessing autistic traits. *PLoS One, 12*(2), e0171931. doi:10.1371/journal.pone.0171931 PMID:28192464

Gillespie-Lynch, K., Kapp, S. K., Brooks, P. J., Pickens, J., & Schwartzman, B. (2017). Whose expertise is it? Evidence for autistic adults as critical autism experts. *Frontiers in Psychology, 8*, 438. doi:10.3389/fpsyg.2017.00438 PMID:28400742

Haegele, J. A., & Hodge, S. (2016). Disability discourse: Overview and critiques of the medical and social models. *Quest, 68*(2), 193–206. doi:10.1080/00336297.2016.1143849

Hurley-Hanson, A. E., & Giannantonio, C. M. (2017). *LMX and autism: Effective working relationships.* Academic Press.

Hurley-Hanson, A. E., Giannantonio, C. M., Griffiths, A. J., Hurley-Hanson, A. E., Giannantonio, C. M., & Griffiths, A. J. (2020). Leadership and Autism. *Autism in the Workplace: Creating Positive Employment and Career Outcomes for Generation A*, 215-236.

Johnson, T. D., & Joshi, A. (2016). Dark clouds or silver linings? A stigma threat perspective on the implications of an autism diagnosis for workplace well-being. *The Journal of Applied Psychology, 101*(3), 430–449. doi:10.1037/apl0000058 PMID:26595753

Kapp, S. K., Steward, R., Crane, L., Elliott, D., Elphick, C., Pellicano, E., & Russell, G. (2019). 'People should be allowed to do what they like': Autistic adults' views and experiences of stimming. *Autism, 23*(7), 1782–1792. doi:10.1177/1362361319829628 PMID:30818970

Kişescu, R. (2017). *Autism, big data and innovation. About neurodiversity at work.* Retrieved at https://ralucakisescu.ro/autismul-big-data-si-inovatia-despre-neurodiversitate-locul-de-munca-0

Komeda, H. (2015). Similarity hypothesis: Understanding of others with autism spectrum disorders by individuals with autism spectrum disorders. *Frontiers in Human Neuroscience, 9*, 124. doi:10.3389/fnhum.2015.00124 PMID:25852514

Lombardo, M. V., Lai, M. C., & Baron-Cohen, S. (2019). Big data approaches to decomposing heterogeneity across the autism spectrum. *Molecular Psychiatry, 24*(10), 1435–1450. doi:10.1038/s41380-018-0321-0 PMID:30617272

Love, S. (2019). *Offices are a hell for people whose brains work differently.* Retrieved at https://www.vice.com/ro/article/wjvd9q/de-ce-e-sanatos-sa-lucrezi-de-acasa

Milton, D. E. (2014). Autistic expertise: A critical reflection on the production of knowledge in autism studies. *Autism, 18*(7), 794–802. doi:10.1177/1362361314525281 PMID:24637428

Morgan, M. (2018). *Four ways employers can support neurodiversity at work*. Retrieved at https://www.personneltoday.com/hr/four-ways-employers-can-support-neurodiversity-at-work/

Munn, G. (2019). *Thinking diversity*. Retrieved at https://thewellbeingpulse.com/neurodiversity-atwork/.

Munyon, T. P., Summers, J. K., Thompson, K. M., & Ferris, G. R. (2015). Political skill and work outcomes: A theoretical extension, meta-analytic investigation, and agenda for the future. *Personnel Psychology*, *68*(1), 143–184. doi:10.1111/peps.12066

Ovaska-Few, S. (2018). Promoting neurodiversity. *Journal of Accountancy*, *225*(1), 46–49.

Parr, A. D., & Hunter, S. T. (2014). Enhancing work outcomes of employees with autism spectrum disorder through leadership: Leadership for employees with autism spectrum disorder. *Autism*, *18*(5), 545–554. doi:10.1177/1362361313483020 PMID:23886575

Parr, A. D., Hunter, S. T., & Ligon, G. S. (2013). Questioning universal applicability of transformational leadership: Examining employees with autism spectrum disorder. *The Leadership Quarterly*, *24*(4), 608–622. doi:10.1016/j.leaqua.2013.04.003

Patton, D., Johnston, J., Gamble, K., Milham, L., Townsend, L., Riddle, D., & Phillips, H. (2019). Training for readiness and resilience. In *Advances in Human Error, Reliability, Resilience, and Performance: Proceedings of the AHFE 2018 International Conference on Human Error, Reliability, Resilience, and Performance, July 21-25, 2018, Loews Sapphire Falls Resort at Universal Studios, Orlando, Florida, USA 9* (pp. 292-302). Springer International Publishing.

Richards, J. (2012). Examining the exclusion of employees with Asperger syndrome from the workplace. *Personnel Review*, *41*(5), 630–646. doi:10.1108/00483481211249148

SAP. (n.d.). *SAP's Autism at Work Program Provides Meaningful Employment for People on the Autism Spectrum*. Retrieved at http://www.accessibleemployers.ca/wpcontent/uploads/2017/10/SAP-Case-Study-FINAL.pdf

Schur, L., Nishii, L., Adya, M., Kruse, D., Bruyère, S. M., & Blanck, P. (2014). Accommodating employees with and without disabilities. *Human Resource Management*, *53*(4), 593–621. doi:10.1002/hrm.21607

Scott, M., Falkmer, M., Girdler, S., & Falkmer, T. (2015). Viewpoints on factors for successful employment for adults with autism spectrum disorder. *PLoS One*, *10*(10), e0139281. doi:10.1371/journal.pone.0139281 PMID:26462234

Smith, P. A., & Cockburn, T. (2016). *Developing and Leading Emergence Teams: A new approach for identifying and resolving complex business problems*. Routledge. doi:10.4324/9781315576800

Sumner, K. E., & Brown, T. J. (2015). Neurodiversity and human resource management: Employer challenges for applicants and employees with learning disabilities. *The Psychologist Manager Journal*, *18*(2), 77–85. doi:10.1037/mgr0000031

Taylor, C. (2019). *A third of the world's female entrepreneurs face gender bias from investors, HSBC claims*. Academic Press.

Von Karolyi, C., Winner, E., Gray, W., & Sherman, G. F. (2003). Dyslexia linked to talent: Global visual-spatial ability. *Brain and Language*, *85*(3), 427–431. doi:10.1016/S0093-934X(03)00052-X PMID:12744954

Walumbwa, F. O., Avolio, B. J., Gardner, W. L., Wernsing, T. S., & Peterson, S. J. (2008). Authentic leadership: Development and validation of a theory-based measure. *Journal of Management*, *34*(1), 89–126. doi:10.1177/0149206307308913

Wright, A. J. (2022). Deliberate context-driven conceptualization in psychological assessment. *Journal of Personality Assessment*, *104*(5), 700–709. doi:10.1080/00223891.2021.1942024 PMID:34227917

Chapter 7
Diversity and Inclusion:
An Imperative in Global Talent Management

Neeta Baporikar

https://orcid.org/0000-0003-0676-9913

Namibia University of Science and Technology, Namibia & SP Pune University, India

ABSTRACT

Today, no country can claim that its business can be local or national due to the effects of globalization. The world of business has become international. In this new millennium, few economies can afford to ignore global business opportunities. The globalizing wind has broadened the mindsets of executives, extended the geographical reach of firms, and nudged international business into some new trajectories. One such new trajectory is global talent management, which has a tremendous impact on the subject matter of diversity and inclusion. Effective talent management is essential for a competitive edge and survival. Moreover, a volatile economic context makes talent management more crucial to organizational success. Similarly attracting, developing, and retaining talent particularly managerial, professional, and technical sustainably is a herculean task indeed. Hence, this chapter, through grounded research and in-depth literature review, intends to discuss how and why diversity and inclusion have become an imperative in global talent management.

INTRODUCTION

Today, no country can claim that its business can be local or national due to the effects of globalization. The world of business has become international. In this new millennium, few economies can afford to ignore global business opportunities. The globalizing wind has broadened the mindsets of executives, extended the geographical reach of firms, and nudged international business into some new trajectories (Baporikar, 2017a). One such new trajectory is global talent management, which has a tremendous impact on the subject matter of diversity and inclusion. Effective talent management is essential for a competitive edge and survival. Moreover, a volatile economic context makes talent management more crucial to organizational success. Similarly attracting, developing, and retaining talent particularly managerial,

DOI: 10.4018/979-8-3693-1938-3.ch007

professional, and technical in a sustainable way is a herculean task indeed (Baporikar, 2017b). With a growing problem of limited specialist and technical skills in the labor market there is definitely going to be an escalated 'war for talent', both male and female leadership talent might be warranted for organizational success and economic development. There is also a considerable body of research suggesting a link between diversity and inclusion and how a diverse inclusive workforce and leadership – get things done in organizations (Baporikar, 2020; Jain & Lobao, 2012).

Diversity and inclusion are critical to win in the flat world. As global corporations begin operations from offshore locations and cater to global clients, they begin to recognize the value of a diverse talent pool. This is all the more true post pandemic with new work modes and methods (Baporikar, 2021). Workplaces that explicitly celebrate differences encourage employees to draw fully on their individual potential contributing to organizational success (SHRM, 2009). An example is Infosys an Indian firm consistently augmenting the cultural competency and intelligence of their workforce. With operations in 32 countries and employees belonging to 89 nationalities, the company strives to be an equal-opportunity employer by leveraging on differences. Today, diversity and inclusion have become a business imperative to excel in the changing environment, optimize operational efficiency, and maximize benefits.

Hence, this chapter, through grounded research and in-depth literature review intends to discuss how and why diversity and inclusion have become imperative in global talent management. It is hoped that the chapter contributes and adds to the talent management knowledge base and global human resource management paradigm.

LITERATURE REVIEW

Talented employees are considered to be talents because of their knowledge and ability to affect the culture of the organization they work for and by being more than just an employee (Park, 2014). An important element to define "talent" is that it concerns authentic staff members who not only have the right skills and knowledge. They are also able not just to "play" a role, but to be able to stay close to themselves and from that notion provide naturally good service.

Talent management in an organization is an ongoing process of analyzing, developing and effectively utilizing talent to improve business value and to achieve the organizational goals. Everything done to recruit, retain, develop, reward, and make the employees perform forms the process of talent management.

When the economy is opening, so are the job opportunities for talented executives. How to attract them and retain them has become a challenging task for any organization. Talent Management describes the process through which employers of all kinds anticipate their human capital needs and set about meeting them. Getting the right people with the right skills into the right jobs, a common definition of talent management is the basic people management challenge in organizations. Talent management is a professional term that gained maximum exposure in the late 1990s. It basically deals with sourcing talent, integration and aligning talent, developing talent, engaging, and rewarding talent, strategically developing talent and it leads to strategic goals. The idea of developing new talent is not a new concept in any business. Despite intense competition being the key to market development and success, organizations have failed to identify some of the major reasons which highlight why 'good performers' leave (Scullion & Collings, 2011). Past Studies clearly state that one major reason why people leave their organization is because of the organization's failure to bring about a correlation between pay and performance. Human

Resource experts in the industry believe matching the right blend of talent with the right job profile can lead to superior performance. Talent Management broadly have the following components:

- Recruitment
- On Boarding / Induction
- Training and Development
- Performance Management.
- Succession Planning
- Employee Retention initiatives
- Employee Separation

In some of these components, technology including AI and DBMS are playing a crucial role. Most of the organizations are utilizing some form of other technological tools be it training, recruitment or performance management. However, a word of caution is that technology can only facilitate but can replace competencies and human intelligence in effective decision-making. After all, HR function essentially focuses on talent acquisition, management and retaining the talent for the overall good of the organization. Leaders have to be nurtured at each stage by giving them challenging opportunities which help them to grow within the organization and also through proper mentoring and handholding. In the case of talent management, the younger the employees, the more powerful are their aspirations to move up in the ladder. Hence more focus needs to be given to enable them to meet their aspirations. Otherwise, they are bound to leave for greener pastures. Hence, the top management needs to pay attention to four levers to recharge and re-engage these layers. Four levers could be taken into consideration:

1. Enrich the roles: The organization must review and take measures to make the role exciting and to motivate the executives. Make the roles exciting by increasing the responsibilities, enriching the roles and reducing the control to the optimum level.
2. Empower the executives: A feeling of disempowerment at this level could act as a major dampener of new initiatives.
3. Enable the person: The middle managers must lead officers and the non-officers to drive performance. However, they have not been explicitly trained in leadership skills. The aim is to nurture future leaders who cannot use classroom training but rather on-the-job learning, involving a variety of interventions such as special projects, personal coaching, peer assist programs and a customized job rotation program.
4. Engage the employee: Engaging the senior and middle management to create complete ownership of the organization. The working environment in the organization could be such that the employee feels a sense of belonging and ownership of the organization. He realizes that the growth of the organization essentially creates more opportunities for him or her to grow also. The realization is that one's commitment towards the organization is such that he feels constantly doing something to improve the organization.

Talent Concept

What is Talent? According to McKinsey, talent is … "the sum of a person's abilities… his or her intrinsic gifts, skills, knowledge, experience, intelligence, judgment, attitude, character, and drive. It also includes his or her ability to learn and grow". For McKinsey, talent refers to "the best and the brightest" and many organizations adopted the term to refer to their "A Level" employees who rank in the top 10 to 20%. In contrast to the definitions above, talent has become a synonym for the entire workforce in many organizations and a large number of companies do not even know how to define talent. Ulrich (1996) takes a holistic view with his definition: talent = competence + commitment + contribution.

Where:

- Competence means that individuals have the knowledge, skills and values that are required for today and tomorrow. Thus, competence deals with the head (being able), commitment with the hands and feet (being there), and contribution with the heart (simply being).
- Commitment means that employees work hard, put the time in to do what they are asked to do, giving their discretionary energy to the firm's success.
- Contribution means that they are making a real contribution through their work – finding meaning and purpose in their work.

The talent war represents the drive to find, develop, and retain individuals, wherever they are located in the world, which have the competencies and commitment needed for their jobs and who can find meaning and purpose in their work. Despite these competing definitions of talent, the "star" approach, championed by McKinsey, has been the most pervasive. However, recent research shows that the nearly single-minded focus on star individuals that is endemic to companies' strategies for fighting the talent war often backfires and reduces, rather than enhances individuals, teams, and organizations:

The McKinsey concept depends upon three critical assumptions: individual ability is largely fixed and invariant - there are better and worse people; people can be reliably sorted on their abilities and competence; and organizational performance is, in many instances, the simple aggregation of individual performances (Collings, McDonnell, & McMackin, 2017). Although the best (e.g., the top 10%) are much better performers than the rest, the best predictor of future performance is not past performance but general mental ability. IQ is the most powerful predictor of job performance In addition, performance varies over time so, depending on when you look, A players could look like B players and vice versa. The assumption that talent is fixed is dangerous because theories of performance and ability become self-fulfilling prophecies. When people believe they are born with natural and unchangeable intelligence, it causes them to learn less over time; they become too focused on being smart and looking smart, rather than on challenging themselves, expanding their skills and becoming smarter; they don't expend the effort to learn new things or improve old skills and even when they do try, they don't enjoy it. On the other hand, people who believe that intelligence is malleable keep getting smarter and more skilled at what they already can do and are willing to learn new things that they do badly at first. In their research of high-flying CEOs, researchers, and software developers, as well as leading professionals in advertising, investment banking and the law, the researchers found that when a company hires a star, the star's performance plunges and there is a sharp decline in the functioning of the group the person works with and the company's market value falls. Many current responses in talent management have been driven by a scarcity state of mind and action. These approaches include: aggressive and cyclical hiring; 'star' acquisition; obsessive and exclusive' top talent focuses. Creative solutions require a global mindset for people and organizations; professional development that encompasses not only "top talent" but a wider range of employees, as well as the capacity to leverage diversity.

Understanding Talent Management

Talent management refers to the process of attracting, selecting, and training, developing, and promoting employees through an organization (Tansley, 2011). Managers who focus on developing talent in-house ensure their employees have the tools and resources they need to perform well, receive proper compensation and transition to leadership roles. Internally developed leaders are valuable assets because over time they have developed the necessary core competencies and internalized company values. Talent management is about getting the right people in the right jobs doing the right things. This requires predicting how employees will act in the future and getting them to act differently from how they acted in the past. Talent management implies that companies are strategic and deliberate in how they source, attract, select, train, develop, retain, promote, and move employees through the organization. Thus, talent management is the science of using strategic human resource planning to improve business value and to make it possible for companies and organizations to reach their goals. Everything done to recruit, retain, develop, reward and make people perform forms a part of talent management as well as strategic workforce planning (Tansley, 2011). A talent management strategy needs to link to business strategy to make sense. Thus, it is clear that there is a resounding theme on the following being integral to talent management and its function;

- People with ability to perform
- People with ability to learn
- People who need to be retained to benefit from their ability and have a return on their learning and investments made in them

Talent management will always speak to a company's strategic goals otherwise it would have lost its premise, talent should assist the organization achieve or surpass its targets. There is however no universal definition of talent that is applicable in all organizations. In general, those who are regarded as 'talent' provide a firm with a competitive advantage. It is their abilities, skills and commitment that determine the long-term success of their organizations. However, organizations recognize the fact that every employee cannot be talented. Talent is sometimes used as if it is synonymous with hot or scarce skills. In other instances, it refers to leadership capability and yet in others it connotes knowledge workers.

Having understood and acknowledged that companies do not have a single definition for talent management there certainly is a common chord on its expectations; repeated and growing performance. Another common denominator is that individuals who have talent have technical capability and leadership 'potential' to contribute significantly to the effectiveness of their organizations. The Towers Perrin survey (2006) considered the following groups to be 'talent': Senior leadership; mid-level employees with leadership potential; key contributors or technical experts; entry-level employees with leadership potential (Elegbe; et al).

Research done on the value of talent management consistently uncovers benefits in these critical economic areas: revenue, customer satisfaction, quality, productivity, cost, cycle time, and market capitalization. The mindset of this more personal human resources approach seeks not only to hire the most qualified and valuable employees but also to put a strong emphasis on retention. Accordingly, talent has virtues that speak to certain outputs as outlined below;

1. Talent is a reflection of competence; the acquired and practiced knowledge and ability to deliver against challenging objectives
2. Talent is a projection of ambition and or aspiration; the determined and resolute desire / will to achieve greater heights. This is coupled with an openness and agility to learn or explore new knowledge and practices
3. Talent is a tested case of performance; evidence of fulfilling predetermined output
4. Talent is an epitome of character; it is an assurance of an acquired set of values that build legacy and fortitude.

Talent is safeguarded because it is always relevant today and tomorrow especially in a world that has discerning customers and limited resources it is important for companies to have human capital that is malleable, ductile and progressive. It goes without saying that such talented human capital cannot be found in abundance either locally, regionally, or globally. The world's most active economies and industrious countries today greatly grapple with resourcing talent (Baporikar, 2016). Workspan, a magazine of WorldatWork, corroborated this view by stating that finding talent during the years ahead would continue to be difficult particularly in highly specialized areas such as finance and accounting. It noted that a worldwide survey conducted by Deloitte with the Economic Intelligence Unit revealed that 67% of respondents from the Asia-Pacific region claimed that the current supply of finance talent was either limited or inadequate. The challenge is global and has been compounded by the fact that companies are currently facing the departure of baby boomers from the workforce. High rates of turnover attest to the challenge in retaining talent in various occupations.

Talent Management Process

Most talent management strategies focus on five areas: attracting, selecting, engaging, developing, and retaining high quality employees. According to the Society for Human Resource Management (SHRM), talent management is broadly defined as "the implementation of integrated strategies or systems designed to increase workplace productivity by developing improved processes for attracting, developing, retaining and utilizing people with the required skills and aptitude to meet current and future business needs". Organizations are made up of people: people creating value through proven business processes, innovation, customer service, sales, and many other important activities. As an organization strives to meet its business goals, it must make sure that it has a continuous and technologically integrated process for recruiting, training, managing, supporting, and compensating these people. Figure 1 presents the talent management process.

Figure 1. Talent management process (Self-Developed)

A brief description of the above talent management process is given below.

1. Workforce Planning: Integrated with the business plan, this process establishes workforce plans, hiring plans, compensation budgets, and hiring targets for the year.
2. Recruiting: Through an integrated process of recruiting, assessment, evaluation, and hiring the business brings people into the organization.
3. On-boarding: The organization must train and enable employees to become productive and integrated into the company more quickly.
4. Performance Management: by using the business plan, the organization establishes processes to measure and manage employees.
5. Training and Performance Support: Of course, this is a critically important function. Learning and development programs provide support to all levels of the organization. This is where training and development institutions and initiatives play a critical role.
6. Succession Planning: as the organization evolves and changes, there is a continuous need to move people into new positions. Succession planning, a very important function, enables managers and individuals to identify the right candidates for a position. This function also must be aligned with the business plan to understand and meet requirements for key positions 3-5 years out. While this is often a process reserved for managers and executives, it is more commonly applied across the organization.
7. Compensation and Benefits: clearly this is an integral part of people management. Here organizations try to tie the compensation plan directly to performance management so that compensation, incentives, and benefits align with business goals and business execution.
8. Critical Skills Gap Analysis: this is a process which is very important, but often an overlooked function in many organizations. While often done on a project basis, it can be "business critical." For example, today organizations in IT sector face huge numbers of people that might exit/retire. How to identify the roles, individuals, and competencies which are leaving? What should be done

to fill these gaps? This is called "critical talent management" and many organizations are going through this now.

Evolution of Strategic Human Resource Management to Talent Management

Over the period of time and realization that human resource is one of critical strategic resource the domain of strategic HR moved and evolved into talent management in organizations. This was because a mere human resource without the requisite talent may not really be an asset for any organization. For one strategic HR is reactive while Talent Management is pro-active and forward-looking. HR must now take into account the great uncertainty businesses face today and focus on: adopting competency-based recruitment' develop managers and leaders to reinforce culture, instill values, and create a sustainable leadership pipeline; identify competency gaps and fill these gaps through training and e-learning, or use these gaps to hire the right people; manage people in a consistent and measurable way and identify high-performance managers and successors to key positions throughout the organization to make sure there is a highly flexible, responsive organization (Baporikar, 2020).

Two other developments adversely affected long-term talent management. First, the constant re-structuring and realignment of business operations rearranged job and promotion ladders, in most cases severely disrupting them. A candidate might be anticipating promotion to the head of his area, but then businesses would be consolidated, and the position eliminated. Constant Mergers and acquisitions have further aggravated this situation. By 2000, these changes became so frequent and so significant that it was no longer possible for the existing career structures to function even with frequent adjustments. It was essentially impossible to forecast talent requirements with any accuracy. The second development coincided with the general trend in corporate restructuring to downsize and flatten operations, especially financial services firms. The resulting new structures removed many steps from the remaining job lad-ders and further eroded clarity about career advancement.

Traditionally, talent management referred exclusively to the development and replacement of top executives. Nowadays, there is recognition that attracting and retaining talented employees should take place on all levels within the organization. This idea leads to a shift from the idea of one single ladder (i.e. one talent pipeline focused only on (potential) leaders) towards the idea of multiple talent-ladders or pipelines (i.e. talent pipelines for different kinds of people in the organization, not exclusively leaders). At its heart, talent management is simply a matter of anticipating the need for human capital and then setting out a plan to meet it. But today Talent Management has not only to manage organizational objectives but also cater to employee expectations. Given the realities of today's complex business environment, it is no longer possible to satisfy a workforce with one broad, standard approach to managing talent. New research shows that when it comes to managing talent, one size no longer fits all. To be competitive as the economy regains its footing and to maximize the performance of a workforce,

Evolution of Talent Management to Diverse Inclusive Talent Management Strategy

Organizations need to understand and respond to the diverse needs of individual employees. Not only has technology finally advanced enough to make the customization of employment practices possible for the first time. People are now expecting - even demanding - an individualized experience at work based on their own encounters with customization as consumers; this is especially true of Millennials (people born from roughly the late - 1970s to the early 2000s), who have never known anything different. For their part, organizations are facing their most diverse workforce yet - not only in terms of age, gender, and ethnicity but in terms of life pursuits, cultural norms and key values as well. The same forces are having a similar impact on the makeup of senior management teams. But in an era of growing diversity, more complex knowledge work in which jobs are increasingly difficult to standardize, a shortage of qualified workers and talent driven competitive advantages, traditional people practices have been quickly rendered obsolete - and increasingly detrimental to the bottom line (Baporikar, 2013). Great companies are built by high-performing employees who are driven by a passion and a vision that resonates with their own inner calling.

Dynamics in Talent Management

The dynamics in talent management are because of the various changes that occurred and that too dramatic ones. But they are a reality that many employers have not yet grasped. The workforce is in the midst of an unstoppable and radical transformation (Vaiman, Cascio, Collings, & Swider, (2021). Salient changes that organizations face today are:

1. Emergence of both the knowledge society and economy. Today, organizational success is more and more based on the acquisition and use of knowledge. Furthermore, in the knowledge economy, knowledge represents the major resource for economic life and growth. It can be argued that not only (potential) leaders have important knowledge, but other employees at all levels and in all departments of the organization own it as well. For this reason, a shift towards multiple pipelines is growing in interest.
2. Change of employment relations. Whereas in the past, the employment relation used to be based on lifelong employment, nowadays, (young) employees are demanding challenging work, as well as substantive rewards and opportunities to grow and learn. There seems to be a more individualistic look on employment. Furthermore, career mobility is no longer only considered within the hierarchy of the organization one currently works for. With regard to talent management, this means that organizations must take into consideration several groups of talent that are becoming more and more demanding and that value their own development.
3. Globalization pressures. The world is becoming more international, and this severely influences the way business is conducted. This has caused an increase in complexity and uncertainty. As organizations have come to realize, international business depends on the quality of top talent. This talent, however, is becoming more mobile and the management of these talents has to be coordinated globally. A dilemma that needs to be taken into consideration is the global/local debate. Hence, organizations will need a global template for talent management, ensuring consistency across the different subsidiaries of the organization. At the same time, this template should allow local subsidiaries to adapt to their specific circumstances. It can be argued that this requires talent management that is applicable around the world but should also focus on different kinds of talent that are necessary in today's globalised world.
4. Increased diversity of the workforce. Because of the ageing population, a shortage in labor supply will occur, which forces organizations to make full use of all talent available. Therefore, they are becoming more diverse in terms of workforce composition. The dominant group, on which talent management used to focus, is changing and organizations must consider more groups in order to

achieve organizational success. For e.g., in the GCC there is a focus on increased recruitment of nationals including women.

5. External demands by all involved stakeholders. They must focus on the responsibility they have towards society and reputation is perceived as key by all organizations. Reputation can help to differentiate and legitimize the organization. Therefore, corporate social responsibility has to become a strategic issue and organizations have to develop an employee value proposition that shows that talent is valued and will be further developed. Linking this to talent management, organizations cannot ignore the pressures of involved stakeholders to create a positive image that will contribute to the attraction and retention of talents.

SOLUTIONS AND RECOMMENDATIONS

Any credible response to optimizing talent management would first require a principled approach to talent, understanding, practice and progression (Ansar & Baloch, 2018). The understanding has to be certainly that talent management is a journey and not a standpoint; it is a progressive line that will journey on as long as there is strategic and political will of management to achieve incremental results gaining new ground and retaining already conquered fields. Most conversations on the subject seem to agree on a similar pattern and the relevant questions which emerge are:

*   How can we make recruiting process more efficient and effective by using "competency and technology based" recruiting instead of sorting through resumes, one at a time?
*   How can we better develop managers and leaders to reinforce culture, instill values, and create a sustainable "leadership pipeline?"
*   How do we quickly identify competency gaps so we can deliver online training, e-learning, or distance learning development programs to fill these gaps?
*   How do we manage people in a consistent and measurable way so that everyone is aligned, held accountable, and paid fairly?
*   How do we identify high performers and successors to key positions throughout the organization to make sure we have a highly flexible, responsive organization?
*   How do we provide learning that is relevant, flexible, convenient, and timely?

The above questions support the assertion that talent management is closely if not totally dependent on what the company wants to achieve through its human capital. The journey is never ending, it remains a going concern though with an expectation that individuals will join and leave as it progresses. Most scholars perceive it to take this pattern of attraction; recruitment and selection; talent development and talent retention. Figure 2 provides the proposed blueprint that is more diverse, inclusive and prudent for global talent management.

Figure 2. Proposed blueprint for diverse and inclusive global talent management (Self-Developed)

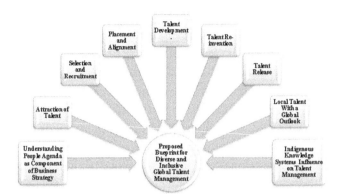

The above proposed blueprint is more inclusive and prudent for global talent management and is discussed below.

1. *Understanding the people agenda as a component of business strategy:* Talent is managed for a predetermined purpose. It is imperative for the company to have a clear understanding of its strategic objectives and to what extent it will require human capital. What type of human capital, at what level of management, technical expertise, gender and perceived professional lifespan. This forms a large part of workforce planning to avoid understaffing and or overstaffing of strategic and critical roles.

2. *Attraction of talent:* Once there is an understanding of talent demographics are required to fulfill business objectives, a natural progression is to package the business in a way that is appealing to the desired audience. Some of the world's leading employers thrive because they attract people who are already ascribing to the culture, values, and business ethos. Companies more than ever are getting involved in company branding not on the basis of products/services they offer but rather the enabling environment that exists for employees to both explore and develop their talents. The premise is to attract and for as long as possible retain talent on cultural, emotional, and sentimental connections.

3. *Selection and recruitment:* There are a notion that 'talent should be obvious at the doorstep' easier said than done. The use of conventional recruitment methods has no place in a world where we are recruiting and selecting talent. The best way, as witnessed by some banks that recruit for critical management roles from early careers or fresh graduates is the use of assessments clinics. Candidates are taken through a whole myriad of assessments comprising; psychometric tests, simulations, face to face interactions and influence measures after which scores are averaged and the best fit is identified and picked. The beauty of talent selection and recruitment is that it can be done both internally and externally. Having discussed external recruitment, a tested method internally is the use of talent reviews and employment of the 9 Box Matrixes. The matrix helps to plot talent and is a function past performance and potential for the future. Depending on where an individual is plotted there is an indication of who is top talent, strong contributor, most promising for future leadership roles and who may still require further incubation to feed succession lines (Mattone and Xavier, 2013).

4. *Placement and alignment:* Although the previously discussed recruitment method is greatly involving and attained at a premium it ensures that the right candidate is picked for the right role to be a perfect match. Many times, banks do recruit talent but end up misplacing it within the organization and ultimately lose to mediocrity or underperformance. Talent should be placed well and if found to be misplaced should be re-aligned. A robust talent management system should allow for periodic talent conversations that seek to identify performance gaps and or career aspirations. A point worth further noting within placement is appropriate and competitive remuneration and reward as per company policy to treat the same. If it is to help retention, talent needs to be placed above market premiums for differentiation and an assurance of appreciation.

5. *Talent development:* It can only be once that talent is aligned or rightly placed that talent conversations can inform the most appropriate development paths to be pursued and invested in. Lest this is a prerequisite, efforts around talent development and succession planning can be greatly compromised and the companies' aspirations be jeopardized. Although the focus of talent development is normally biased towards refining the talent and gaining exponential growth, it has become apparent that it should have a balance with the right culture and values. Many people with talent make it to the limelight, but the ones who have neglected to develop strong character rarely stay there long. Absence of strong character eventually topples talent (Maxwell, 2007). In an industry where talent deals with astronomical sums of money and there is ever-growing pressure to perform, character development is essential to avoid scandals and ensure better governance.

6. *Talent re-invention:* One of the reasons why talent can eventually get lost or disengaged is because of boredom or stagnation. Technical experts who work in highly specialized roles run the greatest risk of this. It is important to note when talent has plateau and requires to be re-invented by setting on a new course or career path. Though it is considered virtuous to be an absolute guru in a field of discipline it is also a threat to talent retention if talented human capital is not allowed to explore new avenues within the same business. The biggest question to ask here is 'having achieved all, what is your real/unexplored passion within this company?' who would leave given such an opportunity and support to fulfill it!

7. *Talent release:* A conversation that line managers often shy from is talent release and or the acceptance to release talent when the time has come. So important is this step as it allows for new talent to discover itself as it graduates from the talent pipeline. If there is a succession pipeline there needs first to be a release. Companies probably must be more creative in the space of talent release and develop more options for the releases in the form of either absorption in greater markets where there is a footprint, graduation into a faculty of executive coaches that may concentrate on coaching and mentoring new generation experts and managers or greasy handshakes into retirement. Whatever is found to be a reasonable cause of action, there must be an understanding and practice of releasing talent to allow for an emergence of new talent. E.g., Michael Jordan a celebrated basketball player for the most of his sportsman life, switched sports after having won many titles and having received endorsements from company such as Nike. To date his silhouette figure is the trademark of Nike's Air Jordan sporting range for basketball. At the point of talent release which should be predetermined, planned and supported he switched to baseball and although he did not match the fame and acclaim of his basketball heydays he excelled at baseball and had a fair share of the glory and fulfillment. Michael was accomplished and even more important he was creating space for new talent. Similar is the Padukone Badminton Academy in India, set up by 1981 World Champion Badminton Player.

8. *Local talent with a global outlook:* Some if not all the world's economies pride themselves in having a competitive edge developed over years of indigenous knowledge systems with a global outlook. Toyota's swift management and production is largely based on ancient practices that have been refined over the years with a clear view of not only satisfying the local market but excelling on a global scale as well. Africans have been very successful at adopting western cultures and in some instances surpassing even the pioneers themselves. A classic example is football; many an African player now plights a living as a professional player in Europe and America. The demand for the African flare, power, speed, boldness, and dexterity of the footballers is insatiable. In the past decade the number of African football players who play in European teams has increased immensely from all sides of Africa; South Africa, Botswana, Ghana, Cameroon, Nigeria, Zimbabwe the list goes on. Africans have become so specialized at playing football that European countries have even embarked on granting them citizenship to play for their national teams in the World Cup and other national games. The true ascension of talent management is to produce talent that is relevant and vibrant for its market before any other. So, no industry or organizations can be different from African footballers.

9. *Indigenous knowledge systems to influence talent management:* When Japanese scholars studying in America first came across Business Process Re-engineering in the 70's, they saw a perfect system to help them further advance the mega industrialized economy. They did not employ management science without first adapting it to their local culture that already resonated with excellence and language as well, ultimately giving birth to the much revered Kaizen. Kaizen is today understood as a Japanese invention though they learnt it from somewhere and owned it and made it work in their turf. The same results have been witnessed repeatedly even in India in different fields such as music, painting, architecture with the prominence of musicians, painters, and leaders like. Nelson Mandela who employed legal and political to traditional governance as a chief to ultimately lead the cause black freedom and influence the international quotient of true leadership.

Hence, in the globalized scenario and the mobility, flow and movement of talent is expected a growing agility and ability that over time will and should release greater output by way of leadership, enhanced performance, and greater spread from talent. The pronouncement to include diversity and inclusion in the approach to manage talent is a call for the cycle to be complete and bear dividends, talent should always bear dividends if allowed to flow and ascend to greater heights in an environment that is both monitored and protected.

FUTURE RESEARCH DIRECTIONS

Though experts provide clear guidance on how to design and implement initiatives that will truly connect and engage diverse individuals in the workplace, talent management is evolving and dynamic. For it to become effective in the global world there is need for industrial and organizational psychologists, organizational scientists and practitioners, human resources professionals, technolgy professionals, managers, executives, and those interested in organizational behavior and performance to undertake further studies, do research, and investigate on how to focus on talent management practice, but grounded in science. Design and develop frameworks of how to translate organizational science of talent management, diversity, and inclusion into practice by generating guidelines, principles, and lessons learned that can shape and guide practice. Investigate and showcase the application of global talent management approaches inclusivity and diversity to solve industrial and organizational problems. Research to document and demonstrate best talent management practices in different industries, sectors and regional organizations is also critical and crucial for benchmarking against best global practices.

CONCLUSION

Talent management strategies that extend beyond rewards and remuneration and are based on other factors such as learning and development opportunities, creating an innovative and attractive work environment, and clear succession planning, diversity, and inclusive approaches among others. Organizations everywhere are grappling with the challenge of attracting, engaging, and retaining talent. Surveys suggest that today's pressure for skills can be won by proper planning and with creative talent management strategies. Companies with clearly defined three to five-year workforce plans that quantifies volumes per critical roles, identifies the market supply potential in the region and globally, and measures the time to proficiency per critical role, among many other such parameters, are on the way to winning the talent war.

REFERENCES

Ansar, N., & Baloch, A. (2018). Talent and talent management: definition and issues. *IBT Journal of Business Studies (JBS), 1*(2).

Baporikar, N. (2013). Understanding Talent Management in Borderless World. *Management Today, 3*(4), 10–16. doi:10.11127/gmt.2013.12.02

Baporikar, N. (2016). Talent Management Integrated Approach for Organizational Development. In Strategic Labor Relations Management in Modern Organizations (pp. 22-48). IGI Global. doi:10.4018/978-1-5225-0356-9.ch002

Baporikar, N. (2017a). Global perspective on talent management: The South African experience. In *Effective talent management strategies for organizational success* (pp. 283–300). IGI Global. doi:10.4018/978-1-5225-1961-4.ch018

Baporikar, N. (2017b). Sustainable framework to attract, develop, and retain global talent. In Driving multinational enterprises through effective global talent management (pp. 50-74). IGI Global. doi:10.4018/978-1-5225-2557-8.ch003

Baporikar, N. (2020). Human Resource Management for Managing Cultural Diversity. *International Journal of Applied Management Sciences and Engineering, 7*(1), 74–99. doi:10.4018/IJAMSE.2020010104

Baporikar, N. (2021). Post-Pandemic Restorative Talent Management Strategy for SME Development. In *Cases on Small Business Economics and Development During Economic Crises* (pp. 80–96). IGI Global. doi:10.4018/978-1-7998-7657-1.ch004

Collings, D. G., McDonnell, A., & McMackin, J. (2017). *Talent management. A Research agenda for human resource management.* Academic Press.

Jain, S., & Lobo, R. (2012). Diversity and inclusion: a business imperative in global professional services. *Globalization of Professional Services: Innovative Strategies, Successful Processes, Inspired Talent Management, and First-Hand Experiences*, 181-187.

Mattone, J., & Xavier, L. F. (2013). *Talent leadership: A proven method for identifying and developing high-potential employees*. Amacom.

Maxwell, J. C. (2007). *Talent is never enough: Discover the choices that will take you beyond your talent*. HarperCollins Leadership.

Park, J. (2014). *Retaining talented employees in the hotel industry in Stavanger: An interview-based qualitative research* (Master's dissertation). Norwegian School of Hotel Management, University of Stavanger.

Scullion, H., & Collings, D. G. (2011). Global talent management: Introduction. In *Global talent management* (pp. 19–32). Routledge. doi:10.4324/9780203865682

SHRM. (2009). *Global diversity and inclusion: Perceptions, practices and attitudes*. Report for the Economic Intelligence Unit – The Economist. Society for Human Resource Management.

Tansley, C. (2011). What do we mean by the term "talent" in talent management? *Industrial and Commercial Training, 43*(5), 266–274. doi:10.1108/00197851111145853

Ulrich, D. (1996). *Human resource champions: The next agenda for adding value and delivering results*. Harvard Business Press.

Vaiman, V., Cascio, W. F., Collings, D. G., & Swider, B. W. (2021). The shifting boundaries of talent management. *Human Resource Management, 60*(2), 253–257. doi:10.1002/hrm.22050

ADDITIONAL READING

Collings, D. G., Mellahi, K., & Cascio, W. F. (Eds.). (2017). *The Oxford handbook of talent management*. Oxford University Press. doi:10.1093/oxfordhb/9780198758273.001.0001

Davis, T., Cutt, M., Flynn, N., & Mowl, P. (2016). *Talent assessment: A new strategy for talent management*. Routledge. doi:10.4324/9781315611815

Elegbe, J. A. (2016). *Talent management in the developing world: Adopting a global perspective*. Routledge. doi:10.4324/9781315611822

Goldsmith, M., & Carter, L. (2009). *Best practices in talent management: how the world's leading corporations manage, develop, and retain top talent*. John Wiley & Sons.

Kim, S., & McLean, G. N. (2012). Global talent management: Necessity, challenges, and the roles of HRD. *Advances in Developing Human Resources, 14*(4), 566–585. doi:10.1177/1523422312455610

Machado, C. (Ed.). (2017). *Competencies and (global) talent management*. Springer. doi:10.1007/978-3-319-53400-8

Schiemann, W. A. (2009). *Reinventing talent management: How to maximize performance in the new marketplace*. John Wiley & Sons.

Shet, S. V. (2020). Strategic talent management–contemporary issues in international context. *Human Resource Development International, 23*(1), 98–102. doi:10.1080/13678868.2019.1650324

Silzer, R., & Dowell, B. E. (Eds.). (2009). *Strategy-driven talent management: A leadership imperative* (Vol. 28). John wiley & sons.

Taylor, S. (2018). *Resourcing and talent management*. Kogan Page Publishers.

Vaiman, V., & Vance, C. (Eds.). (2010). *Smart talent management: building knowledge assets for competitive advantage*. Edward Elgar Publishing.

KEY TERMS AND DEFINITIONS

Borderless World: A borderless world is a global economy in the age of the internet that is thought to have removed all the previous barriers to international trade.

Challenges: Something that by its nature or character serves as a call to make special effort, a demand to explain, justify, or difficulty in a undertaking that is stimulating to one engaged in it.

Competence: Refers to the capacity of individuals/ employees to act in a wide variety of situations. It's their education, skills, experience, energy and their attitudes that will make or break the relationships with the customers and the products or services that are provided.

Competitive Advantage: An advantage that firms has over its competitors, allowing it to generate greater sales or margins and/or retain more customers than its competition. There can be many types of competitive advantages including the knowledge, skills, structure, product offerings, distribution network and support.

Core Competences: Knowledge based technical and human abilities and skills.

Development: Means 'steady progress' and stresses effective assisting in hastening a process or bringing about a desired end, a significant consequence or event, the act or process of growing, progressing, or developing.

Globalization: Globalization is the tendency of businesses, technologies, or philosophies to spread throughout the world, or the process of making this happen. Worldwide integration and development, the process enabling financial and investment markets to operate internationally, largely as a result of deregulation and improved communications.

Knowledge Management and Individual: The individual as the initial point of knowledge management have been neglected, especially as knowledge management has become a topic important in the business world. Most companies at first relied on technology-based knowledge management, which has mostly led to the implementation of databases.

Strategies: Method chosen and plans made to bring about a desired future, achievement of a goals or solutions to a problem. Strategies are a result of choices made. It is that set of managerial decisions and actions that determine the long term performance of a business enterprise.

Training: Organized activity aimed at imparting information and/or instructions to improve the recipient's performance or to help him or her attain a required level of knowledge or skill.

Transformation: The act or process of transforming, change in form, appearance, nature, or character or alteration, especially a radical one. A change in position or direction of the reference axes in a coordinate system without an alteration in their relative angle.

Chapter 8
Effective Talent Management Practices Implemented in the Hospitality Sector

Amrik Singh
https://orcid.org/0000-0003-3598-8787
Lovely Professional University, India

Sanjeev Kumar
https://orcid.org/0000-0002-7375-7341
Lovely Professional University, India

ABSTRACT

The hospitality industry is one of the significant contributors to financial development and survivability. As the biggest segment in the lodging business, the neighborliness business satisfies a substantial capacity to provide food for the necessities and needs of travelers. Hotels are transforming their business operations to stay ahead of this disruption. The hospitality industry is looking for skilled and talented people to fulfill the expectations of the industry. The management's prime duty is to allocate the right task to the right person to achieve the desired results and goals. This study proves the importance of talent management practices and the time to work together with academia and industry to fulfill the industry's expectations. The findings prove that T.M. is measured by talent attraction, talent development, and talent retention.

1. INTRODUCTION

The study's overarching goal is to learn how Talent Management (T.M.) practices in the hospitality industry affect employees' professional growth. This study focuses on the overlap between T.M. and professional development. Because of this, T.M. in the hospitality industry must consider the professional growth of its staff as a whole ((Panda & Sahoo, 2015) 2015) This study is grounded in theory drawn from the fields of management and careers research. In Chapters 2 and 3, we will look at the

DOI: 10.4018/979-8-3693-1938-3.ch008

ideas of ((Payambarpour & Hooi, 2015), Social Cognitive Career Theory (SCCT) (Lindley, 2005), and (Higgins, 1998) 1998. This thesis, however, would argue that a better understanding of how employees' careers are evolving could provide a way to improve T.M. practices for everyone's benefit, as opposed to the current situation where management and career theories operate independently of one another. The literature on T.M. and careers has not given sporadic thought to combining the two fields. Common wisdom holds that T.M. can help businesses achieve recruitment, development, and retention objectives by fostering a more engaged and committed workforce (Stahl & Unkelbach, 2009). However, employees join an organization to help it achieve its goals and satisfy their desires for professional growth (Panda & Sahoo, 2015). As a management tool, T.M. puts the Company's needs ahead of its employees. "(Bratton & Watson, 2018), the emphasis of empirical research has shifted in recent years from talent management practices to aspirations, needs, and career preferences. (Thunnissen et al., 2013). These authors have paved the way for the researcher to adopt and advance this inquiry. The researcher contends that the focus should shift from H.R. practices to something that considers each individual's unique wants, needs, and aspirations in the hospitality industry. To find and cultivate employees with high potential to make a positive impact, companies engage in talent management (T.M.), as defined by (King, 2015). The development of T.M. strategies tailored to the needs and organizational structure of a company and its industry has made this practice an integral part of HRM. Five reoccurring themes are particularly relevant to hospitality organizations when considering a strategic talent management approach. These include economic and day-to-day operational pressures that impede the development of a strategic approach and the importance of the management; a new innovative approach requires and changes the style of working to achieve the desired goal in a limited time with different strategies. The hospitality industry must put the customer first when attracting new customers and keeping existing ones. (Reilly, 2018) examines the potential of T.M. as a tool for fostering a customer-focused mindset in the hospitality industry. Talent management policy and practice are discussed in this paper as a means by which organizations can adapt to the changes brought on by the "experience economy," specifically by attracting and cultivating the right kind of employees. Francis (Baum, 2007) discusses developments in the hospitality industry's H.R. department, highlighting the tensions and conflicts inherent in the field's transition from "operational" to "strategic" talent management. For example, case studies related to T.M. issues (Bratton & Watson, 2018) describe the talent development process at a Scottish National Health Service conference center. As these results show, organizations' long-term environmental sustainability can benefit significantly from an inclusive approach to talent development, which is crucial in fostering a pro-environmental culture. Also, in Scotland, Bratton (Bratton & Watson, 2018) examines the part played by line managers in the country's hospitality sector, arguing that talent management must be tied to the organization's overall goals to be effective. In today's society, talent management is recognized as a vital process. Attracting and retaining top talent and remaining competitive globally require businesses to be flexible enough to respond to shifting demographics and evolving workplace expectations. Human resource management (HRM) is responsible for attracting, selecting, developing, and retaining employees (Singh & Kumar, 2021) who are essential to an organization's success through a variety of leadership styles (Collings & Isichei, 2017)

1.1 The Rationale for the Research

According to studies, the hospitality industry has always struggled to find and keep highly motivated, talented, and qualified workers. (Baum, 2007) The hospitality industry may have a negative reputation as a place to find long-term employment because of its reputation for low pay, unsociable hours, and menial tasks (Barron, 2008), (Saad & Mayouf, 2018), (Baum, 2008). Therefore, TM plays a vital role in the field of hospitality sectors because talented (Saad & Mayouf, 2018) (Preece et al., 2011) employees are "key determinants of service quality, customer satisfaction and loyalty, competitive advantage, and organizational performance" (Saad & Mayouf, 2018). The difficulties hospitality managers face from a human resource management standpoint are discussed below, highlighting the difficulty of T.M. in this industry. Finding, training, and keeping talented employees are the first obstacles to overcome. These problems have long been recognized as severe obstacles in the hospitality sector. It is because of how labor-intensive the industry is, especially in settings with high expectations for customer service (Preece et al., 2011). Topics of interest in the hospitality literature include organizational strategies for attracting, developing, and keeping talented employees (Cappelli & Keller, 2014); investment in T.M. practices aids in retaining top-tier specialists and creating a pipeline of new talent for management roles, demonstrating the value hotels place on their intellectual capital. The second issue is frequent employee departures (Barron, 2008). Long hours, high stress, and low job satisfaction are commonplace in the hospitality industry, leading to high employee turnover that is both expensive and inconvenient for businesses (Hammadi & Noor, 2020); in addition, it could be argued that the time and money required to find and train new workers could reduce productivity while they are absent. Most of these studies focus on employee tenure and organizational engagement (Gurusinghe et al., 2021). Successful businesses understand the importance of keeping their best employees on board. They are the organization's greatest asset in the hospitality industry. They make a noticeable and positive impact on the business by boosting efficiency and revenue. In addition, hotels understand that human capital is a strategic asset that must be managed for optimal performance. It has been argued that a company's talent level is the most important factor in determining its success or failure (Kichuk et al., 2019). The third difficulty is supply and demand (Tarique & Schuler, 2010); in the hospitality industry, demand for top-notch workers greatly exceeds supply (CIPD 2015). Knowledge-based economies like the one we have today required workers with extensive skill sets, and it is getting harder to find people who meet these requirements. According to (Tarique & Schuler, 2010), it is becoming increasingly difficult for hospitality organizations to find enough workers to meet their needs. (Gurusinghe et al., 2021) agrees, stating that a shortage of 18 million highly skilled workers is expected by 2020. Workers who can think on their feet and adapt to changing circumstances are in high demand. As things stand economically, decisive action is required to close skill gaps. The success of any field is directly tied to the quality of its leadership. However, leadership strength and deep talent pools are proving to be a significant business challenge in the hospitality industry, necessitating game-changing innovation. However, history shows that many businesses still have trouble filling key positions, severely limiting their expansion possibilities. A lack of a talent strategy may be to blame for this shortfall, as it prevents essential management and leadership skills from developing in the workforce. In recent years, the hospitality industry has prioritized investments and management training. Therefore, the hospitality sector must implement cutting-edge T.M. practices and human resource systems to educate and retain competent managers who drive productivity and revenue growth. There are five facets to the study's significance. The study's potential application to H.R. managers' ability to make educated judgments about finding the best, attracting, developing, and keeping a highly skilled hospitality workforce is an overarching goal. As a result, human resource managers may gain a deeper appreciation for T.M.'s potential influence on professional growth. As a result, H.R. professionals in the hospitality industry should have a clearer picture of how to develop successful T.M. practices based on each employee's unique preferences, needs, and career goals. Therefore, the study has implications for hotel workers who could gain from enhanced T.M. recruitment, training, and retention strategies. Therefore, employees should have a crystal-clear path of expectations and growth to provide first-rate service. The result should be less employee turnover, higher levels of employee engagement, productivity, and quality of customer service. The result should be an agile, competitive organization where workers and management are on the same page, meritocracy is practiced, and employees have access to a well-defined path to advancement. Educators can also benefit from this study because it will shed light on employees' experiences, perspectives, and hopes regarding career advancement in the hospitality industry. Researchers can also benefit from this study's findings. According to (Wanous & Lawler, 1972), for a study to be considered successful, it must do two things: (1) mention in the study the existing body of knowledge in the research field, and (2) improve how practitioners understand organizations and implement their findings. The study also proves to contribute to a more holistic framework that takes into account the experiences of individual employees and emphasizes the role of T.M. practices for personal career development in the hotel sector, shifting the focus from a narrow one on H.R. practices to one on people's needs, preferences, and expectations from work. The study also has implications for applying novel research strategies in the hospitality industry. This study uses narrative inquiry to examine hotel workers' seven unique perspectives to understand better how T.M. practices have affected their professional growth. It is the first-time narrative interviewing has been used in this way. This methodology allows for a unique and insightful look into the working lives and professional trajectories of those in the industry.

1.2 Introduction to Talent Management

Hotels and the hospitality industry have long been intertwined in T.M.'s long and storied past. The term "war for talent" was popularized by McKinsey and Company in their report of the same name (Michaels et al., 2001). New human resource management methods were developed as this idea gained traction. (Glenn, 2012), defines T.M. as "the method by which a company helps a new hire adjust to the work environment and become productive members of the team." Companies' most valuable resources are educated, astute businesspeople who are also technologically savvy, mobile, and open to new opportunities (Preece et al., 2011). In addition, McKinsey & Company asserts that organizations can only win the talent war by making it an urgent business priority. (Langenegger et al., 2011) McKinsey & Company outlined the primary difficulties for businesses in attracting and retaining top talent in a 2001 report (Michaels et al., 2001). In addition, McKinsey enlightened businesses worldwide and introduced novel concepts to HRM. Research on T.M. in the hospitality industry can be traced back to an American human resource expert (Collings & Isichei, 2017). He predicted that H.R. departments would be evaluated shortly based on how effectively they boosted their companies' competitive advantages. More recent studies of T.M. in the hospitality industry have focused on staffing shortages, employee turnover, and skill development (Bambacas & Kulik, 2013). T.M. research in the hospitality industry has been criticized for focusing on T.M. issues in US-based hospitality organizations (Vaiman et al., 2012). Mainly, U.S. researchers raised an essential question on the fundamental meaning of T.M. for the hospitality industry. In the U.K., the first T.M. study in hospitality can be traced to (Langenegger et al., 2011), where the issues and challenges that the U.K. hospitality industry faces are explored. In the same vein, (Barron, 2008) identifies the dynamic nature of the hospitality industry and the subsequent consequences that were presented for T.M. strategies. Later on, (Bratton Watson, 2018)primarily evaluates literature that addressed the development of the hospitality industry, as this is a significant component of T.M. The latest research on T.M. in hospitality (Boonbumroongsuk Rungruang, 2022)examines employee retention through strategies such as maintaining work-life balance using Deer's(Schoon Parsons, 2002)framework for improving employee retention rates. Therefore, this research, which aims to understand the experience of individual employees within the hotel sector and the role of T.M. practices in personal career development, is the most recent in the U.K.'s hospitality industry. Talent has always been necessary but now needs to become an inseparable part of business strategy on a par with technology and finance (Cobb et al., 2015). The place has commercial interest for the ten significant hotel groups. Talent generates high performance and revenues and attracts new talent to an organization (Davies Davies, 2010). Furthermore, it is argued that hospitality talent drives productivity, quality, and innovation improvements. Hotels must respond quickly to these trends with novel ways of working, recruiting, monitoring performance, rewarding, and managing to attract and retain vital talent. Therefore, large and small hotel brands fully attract, develop, and retain top skills.

2. LITERATURE REVIEW

The literature review chapters will combine two domains: human resource management (HRM) and career development. The objective is to comprehend the career development of individual hotel employees, which may offer a means to inform and enhance Talent Management (T.M.) practices for mutual gain. This Chapter reviews the literature on HRM, and T.M. HRM focuses on people management within the employer-employee relationship (Johnson et al., 2021). It adds value by designing and implementing employee motivating HRM policies and practices. The subtopics of HRM include work-life balance, job satisfaction, motivation and system of rewards and evaluations, and employee turnover. As this research focuses on humans, the emphasis is on the latter. The human guide focuses on managing the relationship between employer and employee. The TM section examines the foundations of the T.M. concept. It defines the limits of the talent phenomenon, contributing to an in-depth understanding of what constitutes T.M. and laying the groundwork for the T.M. argument. Second, it describes the etymology of talent and the dual conceptualization of talent found in HRM literature. The concept of the talent pool will be explained, which allows an understanding of the relationship between the organization and the employee, which can be beneficial for exploring hotel employees' experiences. Thirdly, it examines the issues and debates in T.M. literature.

2.1 Human Resource Management

With a comprehensive understanding of HRM, examining the broader management concept is necessary. The five management fundamentals always help achieve organizational objectives (Ford, 2017). Consequently, it is evident that by utilizing physical and financial resources through H.R., management should "achieve predetermined goals and objectives" (Wilton, 2019). It demonstrates the significance of human resources in the management process. HRM is a subset of management & it applies different concepts, principles, and techniques to the management of an organization's human resources (Ford, 2017); according to research, HRM terminology originated in the United States after the human relations movements (Meyers et al., 2013) According to (Kaufman, 2022), textbook literature in the mid-1960s, specifically about the specialist function that was interchangeably known as human resources or personnel. In the 1980s, interest in HRM grew in the United Kingdom, both among academics and practitioners (Abdullahi et al., 2022). Four distinct traditions are identified by utilizing (Decramer et al., 2013) and investigating their classification. The predominant approach in the literature stems from personnel management and examining the most effective tools and techniques for practitioner use. According to U.S. literature, its underlying values were fundamentally Unitarian, presuming that employees and employers could collaborate to achieve mutual objectives. It is beneficial to comprehend how organizations operate.

I.   **Industrial relations:** According to this tradition, HRM is "part of a system of employment regulations in which internal and external influences shape the management of the employment relationship" (Prowse & Prowse, 2010). The tradition contributes a pluralistic perspective to HRM, emphasizing the collective aspects of the employment relationship.

II. **Organizational psychology:** Despite being widespread in the United States, the contribution of this tradition became significant when U.K. scholars examined HRM issues.

2.2 Work-Life Balance and Job Satisfaction

As per the study conducted by (WLB) (Fagnani & Letablier, 2004), this remains a concern for human resource management (HRM) because it is difficult for management to track and control. The concept of WLB is challenging to define due to the various definitions of "work," "life," and "balance." In recent years, obtaining a WLB has received considerable attention in the hospitality literature (Deery & Jago, 2015); the findings of (Young et al., 2013) focus on WLB and job satisfaction among workers of different generations. Many authors have mentioned that managers are essential in ensuring employees maintain a healthy work-life balance. According to (Cardon et al., 2009), there is a strong correlation between WLB and employee job satisfaction; therefore, organizations should implement HRM policies and programs for employees to meet their unique needs and preferences. According to (Gregory & Milner, 2009), employees exhibit greater job satisfaction and commitment when various organizational programs support WLB. According to (Chen & Choi, 2008), in the past, businesses utilized a bureaucratic approach in which employees were viewed as nothing more than a resource to achieve organizational objectives. However, significant changes have occurred over the past few years. Major brands such as Accor, Hyatt, Intercontinental, Hilton, and Ritz-Carlton recognize the significance of human capital to the performance of an organization. Practical strategies and policies regarding work-life balance were implemented to manage a diverse workforce. According to (Chen & Choi, 2008), employees of the same generation have some shared values and attitudes toward the work. Therefore, sometimes, the argument that this calls into question the value of multigenerational employees (Kumar et al., 2024), who may have different work attitudes and levels of job satisfaction and commitment. (Abdullahi et al., 2022), Studies prove a substantial gap between Generation X and Generation Y, the most prevalent generations in today's workforce. According to (Wey Smola & Sutton, 2002), generation X, or the Xers, who were born between 1965 and 1977, have been affected by recession, high unemployment, and family instability. They were characterized by (Wong et al., 2008) as being realistic, self-reliant, and independent, seeking work-life balance.

Table 1. Main features of generation X and Y

Generation X	Generation Y
Were born and raised in poverty	Raised by active parents
Society is unfriendly to children	Family values are in the centre
Time of economic downturn	Time of revaluation of the values and cultural wars
Independence stressed	High expectations of self
Self-reliant, cynical, highly independent	Highly optimistic, confident, savvy
Work to earn money for leisure	Work-life balance is the key
Employment is perceived as a job	Thrive on challenging and complicated tasks
Learning opportunity to increase career growth	Sceptical to organisational loyalty, want to make impact immediately
Flexible and eager to adapt to new working environment	Expect very fast promotion and development, impossible to adapt and difficult to fit in
Normally shared leadership and team involvement	Require constant feedback and recognition, have high career aspirations and expectation from job roles
Expect friendly, casual work relations with colleagues	Prefer structure and direction rather than casual work relations

Source: Adapted from Chen and Choi (2008)

(Chen Choi, 2008) mentioned in his study that different generations have different characteristics in the workforce, which can be beneficial to organizations in terms of diversity

Table 2. Reasons for job satisfaction of generation X and Y

Generation X	Generation Y
Job Security – 70%	Job Security – 70%
Benefits – 60%	Benefits – 62%
Opportunities to use skills/abilities – 58%	Opportunities to use skills/abilities – 58%
The work itself – 56%	The work itself – 55%
Organisation's financial stability – 54%	Organisation's financial stability – 54%

Source: Adapted from Shekhar and Narzaru (2012)

Table 2.2 shows that both X and Y list job security as one of the reasons related to job, and the results show that 60% of Generation X and 62% of Generation Y, respectively. Skills are equally crucial for both generations. Work occupies 56% of Generation X and 55% of Generation Y, respectively, which is valuable for TM.

2.3 Motivation and Rewards

Today's great competition is going on in the market, and it is tough for organizations to motivate and reward their employees. As per the study conducted by (Stumpf et al., 2013), rewards are the motivational factor for any employee, in terms of pay bands, promotions, welfare facilities, or perks motivating employees. Rewarded employees also give their 100% to the organization to achieve its objectives, and the study also says that those who are not rewarded or neglected become dissatisfied and demotivate.

Figure 1. Effectiveness of appraisals (Lawler III, 2010)
Source: Adapted from Lawler III (2010)

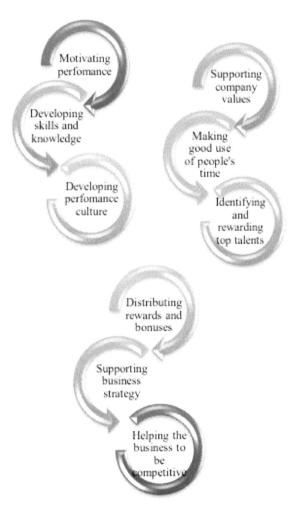

It is evident from Figure 1 that performance reviews motivate talented employees and cultivate the skills and knowledge necessary to propel a company forward. Overall, a performance culture is fostered, which contributes to the competitiveness and success of an organization. Increased salaries, bonuses, and other incentives strengthen employee and employer relationships. In addition, they increase the likelihood that talented employees will remain with the same Company over time. Talented employees feel highly valued and motivated to support the Company's business strategy, and (Bambacas & Kulik, 2013) contend that organizational appraisals provide opportunities for feedback, a positive attitude, and communication. According to (Holgersson et al., 2008), movement to a more prestigious position within an organization, or promotion, is also considered a reward. The promotion recognizes exceptional performance and allows talented employees to feel valued and invested in the organization's growth. Possibilities for more extraordinary advancement foster job satisfaction and long-term dedication. According to (Armstrong, 2006), a reward-promotion system enables management to recruit the most qualified candidates for senior positions.

Figure 2. Interrelations between performance appraisals and rewards (Bambacas and Kulik, 2013)
Source: Adapted from Bambacas and Kulik (2013)

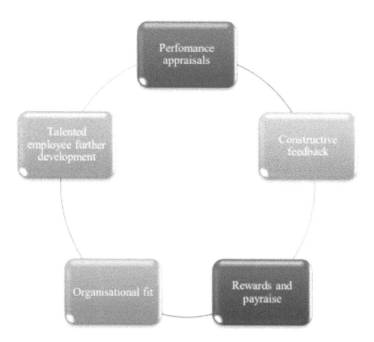

2.4 Employee Turnover

A significant problem for any hospitality business is employee turnover (Robinson et al., 2014); loss of institutional knowledge, disruption of operations, and the expense of replacing departing employees are just some of the direct and indirect costs associated with employee turnover (Tracey & Hinkin, 2008). The Chartered Institute of Personnel and Development (CIPD) found that throughout a 40-year career, an employee in a large company might hold various positions, such as sales assistant, sales manager, operations director, and chief executive officer. As a result, turnover can be seen as a barometer for the security and precariousness of a company's employment climate. The term turnover "refers to the ratio of the number of people" that left an organization during the period under consideration, divided by the average number of people in that organization during the period, and can be traced back to the extensive research of Price. Other theories also prove positive (Daileyl & Kirk, 1992), examining various factors affecting hospitality turnover, including social integration, pay, career development opportunities, and training. According to (Trevor & Nyberg, 2008), high turnover in the hospitality industry can average between 200 and 300 percent per year due to factors such as low skill, low-paying work, unsocial hours, and a lack of career development opportunities (Mohsin et al., 2013). Several articles discussed the potential influence of recruitment and selection practices, workplace discrimination, and professional development opportunities on employee turnover (Mimoun & Gruen, 2021)

Table 3. Reasons for turnover

Dissatisfaction with work	Alternatives
Wages-amount , wages-equity	Returning to university, military service for men, government service, starting own business
Benefits, hours of shift	Similar job: the same industry, other industry
Working conditions	Voluntary early retirement transfer to subsidiary
Supervision-technical, supervision-personal	New position in another organisation
Relationship with co-workers	Location and better earning

External factors	Organisation initiated
Housing, transportation, child care	Resignation in lieu of dismissal
Health care facilities	Violation of policy, unsatisfactory probation period
Working conditions	Attendance, performance, layoff: downgrade
Leisure activities, physical environment, social environment, educational opportunities	End of temporary employment
Personal factors	Other
Spouse transferred , to be married, illness or death in the family, personal injury	Transfer, leave or absence, on loan to
Personal illness, maternity leave	Retirement, death

Source: Adapted from Bonn and Forbringer (1992)

Iverson and (Deery Jago, 2015) conducted more research focused on "employee turnover in the hospitality industry." The most defining feature of this culture is its normalization of employee departures.

Organizational and job-related factors are examples of structural variables that (Deery & Jago, 2015) found to have an indirect effect on the decision to leave an organization. Personality characteristics and affective states, both positive and negative, are examples of pre-entry variables. Employee orientations address job satisfaction and organizational commitment issues, environmental variables relate to extracurricular activities, and union variables include union loyalty and intention to leave (Kumar et al., 2019). The following diagram illustrates the philosophy of high turnover in the hospitality industry.

Figure 3. Turnover culture philosophy of the hospitality industry (Iverson and Deery, 1997)
Source: Adapted from Iverson and Deery (1997)

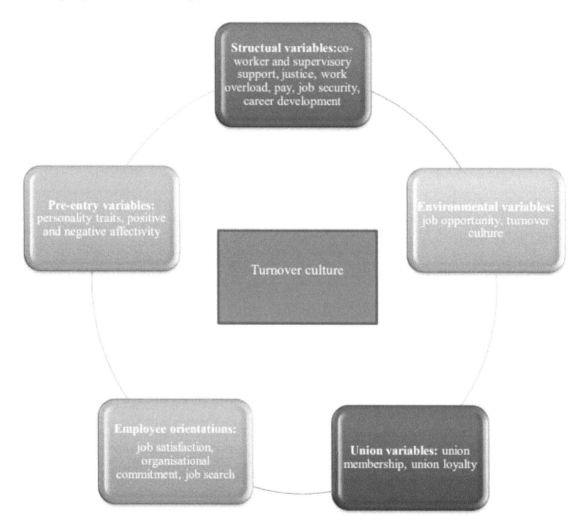

Finally, (Mohsin et al., 2013) study conducted on the "influence of employees' intention" who left the origination for various reasons, which could be "job-related factors and organizational factors."

In this figure shows the dichotomy factors.

Figure 4. A conceptual framework of talent management career development

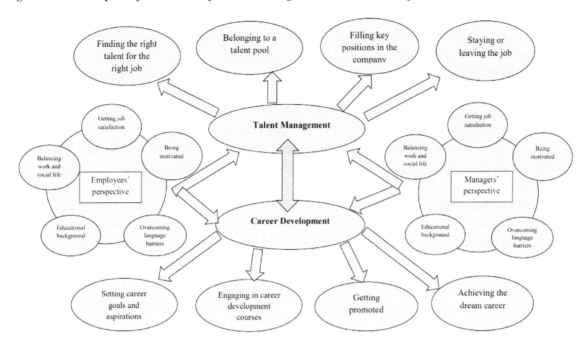

2.5 Effective Talent Management Practices Implemented in the Hospitality Sector

Talent management in the hospitality sector is crucial for ensuring high-quality service delivery, guest satisfaction, and overall business success.

I.   **Comprehensive Recruitment Strategies:** Implementing targeted recruitment strategies to attract talent with the right skills, experience, and cultural fit for the organization. This may include utilizing online job boards, career fairs, and partnerships with hospitality schools.

II. **Robust Training and Development Programs:** Providing comprehensive training programs to equip employees with the necessary skills and knowledge required for their roles. This could include technical training (e.g., customer service, food safety) as well as soft skills development (e.g., communication, problem-solving).

III. **Career Path Planning:** Offering clear career paths and advancement opportunities to motivate employees and foster long-term commitment. This involves identifying and developing high-potential employees for leadership positions through mentoring, coaching, and succession planning initiatives.

IV. **Performance Management Systems:** Implementing performance management systems to set clear performance expectations, provide regular feedback, and recognize and reward high performers. This could involve regular performance evaluations, goal-setting processes, and incentive programs.

V.   **Employee Engagement Initiatives:** Creating a positive work environment and fostering employee engagement through various initiatives such as employee recognition programs, team-building activities, and open communication channels.

VI. **Workforce Diversity and Inclusion:** Promoting diversity and inclusion within the workforce to leverage different perspectives and create a more inclusive workplace culture. This may involve implementing diversity hiring initiatives, providing diversity training, and fostering an inclusive environment where all employees feel valued and respected.

VII. **Work-Life Balance:** Recognizing the importance of work-life balance and implementing policies and practices that support employee well-being. This could include flexible work arrangements, employee assistance programs, and wellness initiatives.

VIII. **Employee Feedback Mechanisms:** Establishing channels for employees to provide feedback and voice their concerns or suggestions. This could involve regular employee surveys, suggestion boxes, and open-door policies to encourage two-way communication between management and staff.

IX. **Continuous Improvement and Adaptation:** Regularly reviewing and refining talent management strategies based on feedback, industry trends, and organizational needs to ensure they remain effective and aligned with business objectives. By implementing these talent management practices effectively, hospitality organizations can attract, develop, and retain top talent, ultimately enhancing guest satisfaction and driving business success.

3. CONCLUSION

Today, TM is recognized as a crucial activity. One of the most significant challenges for organizations is adapting to shifting demographics and work expectations to attract and retain the best talent and compete sustainably globally. On the other hand, Human Resource Management (HRM) is expected to create new forms of leadership for employees through talent attraction, selection, development, and retention, which are essential for organizational success (Collings & Isichei, 2017). Various literature reviews over the past two decades (1997-2017) using the Web of Science database. Therefore, the research objectives are identifying problems, trends, and practices related to hospitality industry talent management and conducting a literature review. The hospitality industry's difficulties are discussed, including hotel employees' precariousness and poor working conditions. The literature review indicates that it is the responsibility of organizations to recognize the need for practices that engage employees in trusting relationships.

Therefore, organizations should prioritize talent management in this sector, attempting to instill a vision that people are the organization's most valuable asset and deserve the best treatment and respect, which may result in higher motivation and, consequently, successful employee retention. This study concludes, consistent with the findings, that T.M., measured by talent attraction, talent development, and talent retention, significantly affects the indicators of discretionary work behavior. Talent is essential to human resource management, especially when a position needs to be filled, but it continues beyond there. Different study findings prove that "discretionary work behavior can be encouraged in the hospitality industry" by implementing talent management. This study suggests that human resource professionals and organizational leaders should implement talent management to increase discretionary work behavior in their respective organizations. Through the discretionary work behavior of talent in the hospitality industry, the results of this study confirm the value of talent management in enhancing hospitality business performance and sustainability. This study implies that leaders of hospitality organizations, such as top and middle management, should identify the talent of the employees, and based on that, they should get some extra rewards from the direction; on the other hand, management should provide annually or quarterly training to newly hired employees when-ever changes see in the technologies. Finally, talent should be rewarded in various modes to encourage employee morale. However, on the other hand, it was also observed that some compensation policies discourage the employees and, finally, keep them from leaving the organization. In addition, the research may have been limited by the absence of moderation or contextual factors. Therefore, future research should include a moderating variable to determine whether the results would be the same. A further limitation of this study is the number of incorrectly completed questionnaires by the participants.

4. RECOMMENDATIONS FOR FURTHER RESEARCH

Since talent management research is still developing, many important questions remain, so several implications for future research have been identified. This study's conceptual framework suggests future research. First, learning how those excluded from the talent pool view company career opportunities would be interesting (Dhiraj & Kumar, 2023a). This understanding should improve T.M. practices and allow managers to create a successful T.M. strategy that acknowledges all employees. Second, this study's findings could be applied to hotels in emerging market economies, where T.M. practices are poorly understood, with sensitivity to cultural contexts (Vaiman et al., 2012). Thus, theory-building, effective T.M. practices, and personal career development are needed to understand the experiences of hotel employees in emerging market economies. Finally, understanding individual employees' experiences and the role of T.M. practices followed in the various other service industries like banking, construction, and real estate may inform or extend research on T.M. practices in multiple settings. This study will also help to build further research on T.M. practices as the author mentioned in the survey, banking (Lopamudra & Acharya, 2015), construction (FMI 2007; Agency central report 2014; (Baum, 2008), real estate ((Mesthrige Jayantha & Sze Man, 2013); Right et al. group report 2014), and retail and Associates. The findings could also improve practice standards in several disciplines, but more research is needed. A comparative study would help us understand hospitality and its workers.

REFERENCES

Abdullahi, M. S., Raman, K., & Solarin, S. A. (2022). Talent management practices on employee performance among academic staff of Malaysian private universities: Employee engagement as a mediator. *Journal of Applied Research in Higher Education*, *14*(1), 135–158. doi:10.1108/JARHE-08-2020-0283

Armstrong, M. (2006). *A handbook of human resource management practice* (10th ed.). Kogan Page.

Bambacas, M., & Kulik, T. C. (2013). Job embeddedness in China: How HR practices impact turnover intentions. *International Journal of Human Resource Management*, *24*(10), 1933–1952. doi:10.1080/0 9585192.2012.725074

Barron, P. (2008). Education and talent management: Implications for the hospitality industry. *International Journal of Contemporary Hospitality Management*, *20*(7), 730–742. doi:10.1108/09596110810897583

Baum, T. (2007). Skills, training and development within an insular labour market: The changing role of catering managers in the healthcare environment. *Journal of Management Development, 26*(2), 132–147. doi:10.1108/02621710710726044

Baum, T. (2008). Implications of hospitality and tourism labour markets for talent management strategies. *International Journal of Contemporary Hospitality Management, 20*(7), 720–729. doi:10.1108/09596110810897574

Boonbumroongsuk, B., & Rungruang, P. (2022). Employee perception of talent management practices and turnover intentions: A multiple mediator model. *Employee Relations, 44*(2), 461–476. doi:10.1108/ER-04-2021-0163

Bratton, J., & Watson, S. (2018). Talent management, emotional labour and the role of line managers in the Scottish hospitality industry: A roundtable discussion. *Worldwide Hospitality and Tourism Themes, 10*(1), 57–68. doi:10.1108/WHATT-10-2017-0063

Cappelli, P., & Keller, J. (2014). Talent Management: Conceptual Approaches and Practical Challenges. *Annual Review of Organizational Psychology and Organizational Behavior, 1*(1), 305–331. doi:10.1146/annurev-orgpsych-031413-091314

Cardon, M. S., Wincent, J., Singh, J., & Drnovsek, M. (2009). The nature and experience of entrepreneurial passion. *Academy of Management Review, 34*(3), 511–532. doi:10.5465/amr.2009.40633190

Chen, P., & Choi, Y. (2008). Generational differences in work values: A study of hospitality management. *International Journal of Contemporary Hospitality Management, 20*(6), 595–615. doi:10.1108/09596110810892182

Cobb, M., Branson, N., McGreevy, P., Lill, A., & Bennett, P. (2015). The advent of canine performance science: Offering a sustainable future for working dogs. *Behavioural Processes, 110*, 96–104. doi:10.1016/j.beproc.2014.10.012 PMID:25444772

Collings, D. G., & Isichei, M. (2017). Global talent management: What does it mean for expatriates? In Research Handbook of Expatriates (pp. 148–159). Edward Elgar Publishing. doi:10.4337/9781784718183.00016

Daileyl, R. C., & Kirk, D. J. (1992). Distributive and Procedural Justice as Antecedents of Job Dissatisfaction and Intent to Turnover. *Human Relations, 45*(3), 305–317. doi:10.1177/001872679204500306

Davies, B., & Davies, B. J. (2010). Talent management in academies. *International Journal of Educational Management, 24*(5), 418–426. doi:10.1108/09513541011055983

Decramer, A., Smolders, C., & Vanderstraeten, A. (2013). Employee performance management culture and system features in higher education: Relationship with employee performance management satisfaction. *International Journal of Human Resource Management, 24*(2), 352–371. doi:10.1080/09585192.2012.680602

Deery, M., & Jago, L. (2015). Revisiting talent management, work-life balance and retention strategies. *International Journal of Contemporary Hospitality Management, 27*(3), 453–472. doi:10.1108/IJCHM-12-2013-0538

Dhiraj, A., & Kumar, P. D. S. (2023). Impact of E-learning on the Higher Education Sector during the COVID-19 pandemic through Pedagogy tools: An observational Study. *Revista de Educación y Derecho*, *27*(27). Advance online publication. doi:10.1344/REYD2023.27.40935

Fagnani, J., & Letablier, M.-T. (2004). Work and Family Life Balance: The Impact of the 35-Hour laws in France. *Work, Employment and Society*, *18*(3), 551–572. doi:10.1177/0950017004045550

Ford, D. G. (2017). Talent Management and Its Relationship to Successful Veteran Transition Into the Civilian Workplace: Practical Integration Strategies for the HRD Professional. *Advances in Developing Human Resources*, *19*(1), 36–53. doi:10.1177/1523422316682736

Glenn, T. (2012). The state of talent management in Canada's public sector: Talent Management in Canada's Public Sector. *Canadian Public Administration*, *55*(1), 25–51. doi:10.1111/j.1754-7121.2012.00204.x

Gregory, A., & Milner, S. (2009). Editorial: Work-life Balance: A Matter of Choice? *Gender, Work and Organization*, *16*(1), 1–13. doi:10.1111/j.1468-0432.2008.00429.x

Gurusinghe, R. N., Arachchige, B. J. H., & Dayarathna, D. (2021). Predictive HR analytics and talent management: A conceptual framework. *Journal of Management Analytics*, *8*(2), 195–221. doi:10.1080/23270012.2021.1899857

Hammadi, H. A. A., & Noor, M. A. B. M. (2020). The Role of Leadership in the Talent Management and Employee Retention of Education in Abu Dhabi. *European Journal of Multidisciplinary Studies*, *5*(1), 68. doi:10.26417/301nxi33o

Higgins, E. T. (1998). Promotion and Prevention: Regulatory Focus as A Motivational Principle. In Advances in Experimental Social Psychology. Elsevier. doi:10.1016/S0065-2601(08)60381-0

Holgersson, S., Gottschalk, P., & Dean, G. (2008). Knowledge Management in Law Enforcement: Knowledge Views for Patrolling Police Officers. *International Journal of Police Science & Management*, *10*(1), 76–88. doi:10.1350/ijps.2008.10.1.76

Johnson, R. D., Stone, D. L., & Lukaszewski, K. M. (2021). The benefits of eHRM and AI for talent acquisition. *Journal of Tourism Futures*, *7*(1), 40–52. doi:10.1108/JTF-02-2020-0013

Kaufman, B. E. (2022). The academic-practitioner gap: Past time to bring in the practitioner perspective. *Human Resource Management Review*, *32*(2), 100895. doi:10.1016/j.hrmr.2022.100895

Kichuk, A., Brown, L., & Ladkin, A. (2019). Talent pool exclusion: The hotel employee perspective. *International Journal of Contemporary Hospitality Management*, *31*(10), 3970–3991. doi:10.1108/IJCHM-10-2018-0814

King, K. A. (2015). Global talent management: Introducing a strategic framework and multiple-actors model. *Journal of Global Mobility*, *3*(3), 273–288. doi:10.1108/JGM-02-2015-0002

Kumar, S., Kapoor, B., & Shah, M. A. (2024). Contemporary Issues and Challenges Facing the Hospitality Industry. In N. Kumar, K. Sood, E. Özen, & S. Grima (Eds.), *The Framework for Resilient Industry: A Holistic Approach for Developing Economies* (pp. 55–64). Emerald Publishing Limited. doi:10.1108/978-1-83753-734-120241004

Kumar, S., Tiwari, P., & Zymbler, M. (2019). Internet of Things is a revolutionary approach for future technology enhancement: A review. *Journal of Big Data, 6*(1), 1–21. doi:10.1186/s40537-019-0268-2

Langenegger, P. B., Mahler, P., & Staffelbach, B. (2011). Effectiveness of talent management strategies. *European Journal of International Management, 5*(5), 524. doi:10.1504/EJIM.2011.042177

Lindley, L. D. (2005). Perceived Barriers to Career Development in the Context of Social Cognitive Career Theory. *Journal of Career Assessment, 13*(3), 271–287. doi:10.1177/1069072705274953

Lopamudra & Acharya, S. K. (2015). Case Study on Culture of Recruiting Rewarding and Retaining Strategy for Talent Management. *Adarsh Journal of Management Research, 8*(2), 42. doi:10.21095/ajmr/2015/v8/i2/88214

Mesthrige Jayantha, W., & Sze Man, W. (2013). Effect of green labelling on residential property price: A case study in Hong Kong. *Journal of Facilities Management, 11*(1), 31–51. doi:10.1108/14725961311301457

Meyers, M. C., van Woerkom, M., & Dries, N. (2013). Talent — Innate or acquired? Theoretical considerations and their implications for talent management. *Human Resource Management Review, 23*(4), 305–321. doi:10.1016/j.hrmr.2013.05.003

Michaels, E., Handfield-Jones, H., & Axelrod, B. (2001). *The war for talent*. Harvard Business School Press.

Mimoun, L., & Gruen, A. (2021). Customer Work Practices and the Productive Third Place. *Journal of Service Research, 24*(4), 563–581. doi:10.1177/10946705211014278

Mohsin, A., Lengler, J., & Kumar, B. (2013). Exploring the antecedents of intentions to leave the job: The case of luxury hotel staff. *International Journal of Hospitality Management, 35*, 48–58. doi:10.1016/j.ijhm.2013.05.002

Panda, S., & Sahoo, C. K. (2015). Strategic talent development interventions: An analysis. *Industrial and Commercial Training, 47*(1), 15–22. doi:10.1108/ICT-05-2014-0031

Payambarpour, S. A., & Hooi, L. W. (2015). The impact of talent management and employee engagement on organisational performance. *International Journal of Management Practice, 8*(4), 311. doi:10.1504/IJMP.2015.073483

Preece, D., Iles, P., & Chuai, X. (2011). Talent management and management fashion in Chinese enterprises: Exploring case studies in Beijing. *International Journal of Human Resource Management, 22*(16), 3413–3428. doi:10.1080/09585192.2011.586870

Prowse, P., & Prowse, J. (2010). Whatever happened to human resource management performance? *International Journal of Productivity and Performance Management, 59*(2), 145–162. doi:10.1108/17410401011014230

Reilly, P. (2018). Building customer centricity in the hospitality sector: The role of talent management. *Worldwide Hospitality and Tourism Themes, 10*(1), 42–56. doi:10.1108/WHATT-10-2017-0068

Robinson, R. N. S., Solnet, D. J., & Breakey, N. (2014). A phenomenological approach to hospitality management research: Chefs' occupational commitment. *International Journal of Hospitality Management, 43*, 65–75. doi:10.1016/j.ijhm.2014.08.004

Saad, H., & Mayouf, M. (2018). Talent Management Strategies and Practices in Five Star Hotels: An Exploratory Study. *International Journal of Heritage. Tourism and Hospitality, 12*(2), 32–49. doi:10.21608/ijhth.2019.31649

Schoon, I., & Parsons, S. (2002). Teenage Aspirations for Future Careers and Occupational Outcomes. *Journal of Vocational Behavior, 60*(2), 262–288. doi:10.1006/jvbe.2001.1867

Singh, A., & Kumar, S. (2021). Identifying Innovations in Human Resources: Academia and Industry Perspectives. In A. Pathak & S. Rana (Eds.), Advances in Human Resources Management and Organizational Development. IGI Global. doi:10.4018/978-1-7998-4180-7.ch006

Stahl, C., & Unkelbach, C. (2009). Evaluative learning with single versus multiple unconditioned stimuli: The role of contingency awareness. *Journal of Experimental Psychology. Animal Behavior Processes, 35*(2), 286–291. doi:10.1037/a0013255 PMID:19364238

Stumpf, S. A., Tymon, W. G. Jr, & van Dam, N. H. M. (2013). Felt and behavioral engagement in workgroups of professionals. *Journal of Vocational Behavior, 83*(3), 255–264. doi:10.1016/j.jvb.2013.05.006

Tarique, I., & Schuler, R. S. (2010). Global talent management: Literature review, integrative framework, and suggestions for further research. *Journal of World Business, 45*(2), 122–133. doi:10.1016/j.jwb.2009.09.019

Thunnissen, M., Boselie, P., & Fruytier, B. (2013). Talent management and the relevance of context: Towards a pluralistic approach. *Human Resource Management Review, 23*(4), 326–336. doi:10.1016/j.hrmr.2013.05.004

Tracey, J. B., & Hinkin, T. R. (2008). Contextual Factors and Cost Profiles Associated with Employee Turnover. *Cornell Hospitality Quarterly, 49*(1), 12–27. doi:10.1177/0010880407310191

Trevor, C. O., & Nyberg, A. J. (2008). Keeping Your Headcount When All About You Are Losing Theirs: Downsizing, Voluntary Turnover Rates, and The Moderating Role of HR Practices. *Academy of Management Journal, 51*(2), 259–276. doi:10.5465/amj.2008.31767250

Vaiman, V., Scullion, H., & Collings, D. (2012). Talent management decision making. *Management Decision, 50*(5), 925–941. doi:10.1108/00251741211227663

Wanous, J. P., & Lawler, E. E. (1972). Measurement and meaning of job satisfaction. *The Journal of Applied Psychology, 56*(2), 95–105. doi:10.1037/h0032664

Wey Smola, K., & Sutton, C. D. (2002). Generational differences: Revisiting generational work values for the new millennium. *Journal of Organizational Behavior, 23*(4), 363–382. doi:10.1002/job.147

Wilton, N. (2019). *An introduction to human resource management* (4th ed.). SAGE.

Wong, M., Gardiner, E., Lang, W., & Coulon, L. (2008). Generational differences in personality and motivation: Do they exist and what are the implications for the workplace? *Journal of Managerial Psychology, 23*(8), 878–890. doi:10.1108/02683940810904376

Young, S. J., Sturts, J. R., Ross, C. M., & Kim, K. T. (2013). Generational differences and job satisfaction in leisure services. *Managing Leisure, 18*(2), 152–170. doi:10.1080/13606719.2013.752213

Chapter 9
Employee Retention Strategies Through Predictive Data Analytics and AI

P. Bhanumathi

(iD) https://orcid.org/0000-0001-8670-8250

M.S. Ramaiah Institute of Management, India

M. Anjali Naidu

In2IT Enterprise Business Services Pvt. Ltd., India

B. Sathish Babu

RV College of Engineering, India

ABSTRACT

One of the main challenges today's organizations face is retaining talented and competent employees. Managing and keeping employees has become a concern in the increased competition and changing market demand. The human resource management team should always be ready to meet such threats from the competitor's talent poaching attitudes and to retain their well-performing employees. It is strategically necessary to develop plans to identify the potential employees who may submit the papers due to short-term benefits and initiate preventive actions to stop them from leaving the organization. The conventional techniques of identifying such employees have often proven error-prone and ineffective due to delays in arriving at conclusions. There is a great opportunity available to management decision-makers to use digital assets, such as employee-centric data, to predict the chances of employees leaving the organization soon and create retention strategies around the outcome of data analysis.

DOI: 10.4018/979-8-3693-1938-3.ch009

INTRODUCTION

One of the main challenges today's organizations face is retaining talented and competent employees. Managing and keeping employees has become a concern due to the increased competition and changing market demand. The human resource management team should always be ready to meet such threats from the competitor's talent poaching attitudes and to retain their well-performing employees. It is strategically necessary to develop plans to identify the potential employees who may submit the papers due to short-term benefits and initiate preventive actions to stop them from leaving the organization.

The conventional techniques of identifying such employees have often proven error-prone and ineffective due to delays in arriving at conclusions. There is a great opportunity available to management decision-makers to use digital assets, such as employee-centric data, to predict the chances of employees leaving the organization soon and create retention strategies around the outcome of data analysis. This method of understanding employee sentiments leads to creating customized retention strategies that may be specific to an employee or a group.

The chapter presents employee retention and its impact on organizational growth and performance, the criticality of employee attrition, and an emphasis on the various conventional retention strategies. The chapter provides an overall idea of employee poaching, ethics etiquette, and classical techniques. Also, the analytical tools to identify the less committed employee or an employee planning to exit to create /finetune the various retention strategies. (Kim, J. H,2014).

Overview of Employee Retention and its Impact on the Organization's Growth and Performance

Employee retention is the organization's capacity to prevent employee turnover or where employees prefer to stay on with their present company and don't actively look for any other job prospects. Employee retention is more than just keeping the employees on board; it is also about creating an atmosphere in which employees are motivated, engaged, safe, and satisfied with their work, which helps the firm's overall success. It is essential to human resource management and organizational performance (Deshwal, 2015).

Organizations must focus on the retention rate and the reason behind the high attrition. *Employee Retention Rate= (Total Number of remaining employees / Total Number of employees) *100*

Impact of Employee Retention on Organizational Performance

Employee retention makes employees stay in the company longer, which ensures higher productivity and active engagement levels, ultimately increasing revenue. The main aim of the company retention strategy is to reduce the turnover as low as possible by improving the work conditions and providing good work experience. The impact of employee retention on organizational performance is as follows: Figure 1.

1.   Cost Reduction

In every organization, employee turnover is expensive. A lot of time, effort, and resources go into sourcing, recruiting, onboarding, and training the new ones. Organizations can reduce costs associated with the process by efficiently utilizing the available resources and retaining people.

2. Experienced Employees

Working and experiencing in the same organization for many years will gain valuable knowledge and competence. This expertise will help address complex issues and challenges, maintain high-quality standards, and contribute to the firm's growth.

3. Increased Productivity

Employees with many years of experience in the same setup are more productive since they are familiar with the business processes, can operate more effectively and efficiently, contribute more productively, and achieve better results.

4. Relationships with Customers

Employees working in the organization for many years develop strong and cordial relationships with all employees and better bonding with customers. Better understanding and relationships lead to consumer loyalty, and a higher chance of doing repeated business is critical for long-term success.

5. Involvement of employees

Higher attrition leads to low morale and the disengagement of employees. Employees' active engagement is possible when motivated, recognized, appreciated, and secure, further enhancing the organization's productivity and overall corporate culture.

6. Knowledge Transfer

Retaining personnel allows for more effective mentoring and training of new hires. The smooth transfer of information guarantees that the organization's best practices and standards are supported.

7. Reputation of the Brand

Organizations with a high staff turnover rate may find attracting top personnel and clients difficult. As a result of high employee retention, the organization's brand can benefit.

Figure 1. Impact of employee retention on organizational performance

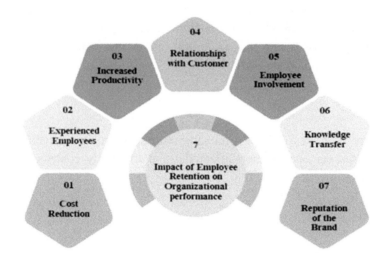

List critical reasons for employee attrition and emphasize the conventional/traditional retention strategies (Howe et al. 2023).

Employee attrition is the term used to describe the voluntary or involuntary departure of employees from the organization due to various circumstances, such as retirement, resignation, termination, or death. Remarkably, when a person who has worked for several years leaves on time, it is an occasion to celebrate. However, when a valuable and productive worker departs the company, it creates a culture of uncertainty and anxiety among the management. For companies of all kinds, high employee turnover rates are a significant problem since they lead to higher expenses, lesser productivity, and low employee morale among the organization's existing employees. These are the reasons that employees are thinking about moving on:

- **Lack of motivation and reduced job satisfaction**

Motivation will play a significant role in improving the performance of the individual and the organization. Employees who lack motivation and are dissatisfied with their jobs will not perform well, and their contribution to the organization is comparatively less.

There are several reasons for low motivation, namely:

1. Unfair treatment among employees
2. There is a lot of gender discrimination in the workspace
3. Employees find the job less challenging or exciting.

- **No Work-life balance**

Pre- and post-COVID scenarios, employees look for a proper work-life balance, which is evident. Work-life balance has changed the workspace's strict 9-to-5 hours to increased remote work. It has a broader meaning; employees think holistically about a healthy working environment that helps them manage their personal and professional lives.

- **Lesser flexibility option**

During the COVID-19 pandemic, the traditional office culture changed to remote work options, and employees were open to flexibility. At the same time, post-COVID, not all organizations are embracing flexibility, but organizations that did stand out to job seekers. Employees were happy, satisfied, and comfortable when the work-from-home option was available because they used to get a lot of time for intermittent exercise, increased food choices and mealtimes, and improved work-life balance. The scenario has changed now that, in post-pandemic, more than half of employees globally would quit their jobs without flexibility.

• **Change in attitudes on the road to career**

In earlier days, people used to join companies as young and gracefully retired after attaining the age of 58 and passed the baton to the next generation to lead their lives happily. Employee loyalty and commitment towards a single company was high; they used to work for 20 to 25 years and used to have stable careers.

Now, the shift in attitude and career aspect because of the following

1. Freelance or contract work is on the rise.
2. There's more focus on personal growth and continuous learning.

• **Lack of appreciation and underappreciation among employees**

Most employees in any organizational setup like to hear appreciation from their employers for their efforts and contributions. The employees like to hear "thank you" for their daily work and interactions: managers must regularly recognize, congratulate, and appreciate their staff. Otherwise, retaining employees will be a significant issue.

Retention Strategies

Employee turnover occurs when employees quit their positions for alternative opportunities or causes. Retaining current employees is the ability of an organization to minimize employee turnover. A company's ability to achieve its objectives is directly impacted by its ability to retain a large enough workforce, leading to increased employee retention. Two ways to improve employee retention are lower turnover and managing and achieving the company objectives, which lead to success. Typically, it starts with selecting the best candidate for the job, and the other strategies are as follows:

• **Apply comprehensive hiring practices.**

One of the best strategies to retain employees is following the best hiring process. The process should identify the right candidate for the right job at the right time. It starts with hiring the right person for the organization; the best way is to ensure the company hires the right candidate.

The hiring process should not be heavy as the attention and retention span of the candidates is less, and it may send the candidates elsewhere to look out for the job. A well-designed interview process helps the organization better understand the candidate's potential for a specific role or will be able to develop on the job.

• **Conducive and supportive working environment.**

A better workspace makes employees feel comfortable and contribute more to the organization, and it is the mantra to retain employees for a long time. Therefore, organizations must strive to create a good working environment for employees to perform and flourish at their best potential by providing on-the-job training, open and transparent communication, and offering employees the best package and perks.

- **Designing proper recognition programs.**

Every employee feels that their contributions are recognized and valued. In this regard, organizations should design and implement reward or peer reward programs to appreciate, encourage, and motivate employees and help create a positive workspace. Organizations must show employees that they value talented and potential employees. Companies use software to recognize the contribution of employees' work, offer rewards, and scale up this program quickly to reach out to many.

- **Offer a fair salary package or compensation.**

Attrition is a primary concern in any workspace, as employees feel underpaid for their unwavering dedication, commitment, and contribution to the organization. Therefore, the best way to retain employees is to ensure fair compensation with allowances, promotions, and salary hikes, changing the nature of the employee's work, and adding responsibilities based on experience and expertise.

- **Provide regular performance reviews to employees.**

Employees' career growth and contribution to the organization are possible only when they know about their work through proper feedback mechanisms. They'll know areas of high performance and specific skills that need improvement.

This feedback shows employees you care about their performance and how it affects the company. When feedback is actionable, you show that you care about their development and aren't just instructing them to do better with no additional advice.

If feedback is not communicated immediately, employees will be unsure about the work and their performance, and it may not be possible for them to get proper guidance.

- **Instil and promote proper work-life balance.**

If employees feel they are expected to work 24/7, they will be stressed and most likely develop a burnout feeling. Employees may leave the job and look for other alternatives elsewhere. Instead, the organization should focus on supporting the employees to have a proper work-life balance and set boundaries. For example, set rules and guidelines for work, breaks, programs on appropriate work-life balance, and other recreation activities.

- **Exercise change management.**

All workplaces have to deal with change, which can sometimes be unexpected. The COVID-19 pandemic is an excellent example of practicing effective change management. Millions of people worldwide were suddenly expected to pivot to different working styles, and change management was necessary to prepare workers for these changes and create a smooth transition.

Being able to reassure employees when changes are happening, both big and small, can help assuage any fears and anxieties they may have about doing their jobs. Without this, employees may feel left behind and seek opportunities elsewhere.

Employee Poaching, Ethics, and Etiquette of Employee Poaching

Employee poaching is also employee raiding, which involves recruiting employees to work at competing companies. Job poachers are the companies that look for workers with a specific skill set in competitive job markets. It is proactive. Instead of waiting for job seekers to apply, companies actively seek out individuals already employed elsewhere. For this strategy to be used, companies should have a thorough understanding of the talent landscape and the ability to identify potential value-adding employees. Every organization will look for great talent to drive the company in a better way through recruitment. This recruitment would get good employees through interviews, advertisements, and cold calling. The newly hired employees are to be trained, which would add cost to the company. If the recruitment doesn't yield good results, the only option is to poach an employee from a competitor. Companies are facing heavy cutthroat competition in the market. To survive in the market, they pull out competent employees from competitor companies; hence, employee poaching is common and aggressively practiced worldwide. For instance, tech giants like Apple, Google, and Facebook have been known to poach talent from their main competitors. These companies recognize the importance of acquiring top talent to maintain their competitive edge and drive innovation. It is widely practiced in industries where specialized skill sets are required and employees are unavailable.

In earlier days, it was difficult to identify a person with competency and talent and hire them for the company after thoroughly understanding such employees per the organizational requirements. With technological advancements and social media platforms like LinkedIn or Career Builder, it has become easier to identify the best candidate for the organization. Job poachers think that employees already proven in the present company can benefit new companies with the same expertise and skill set.

Kumar, 2015 studied Indian employees' attitudes towards poaching. The study observed that the reasons for an employee to get poached are business-minded and have less moral. Usually, the companies participating in poaching will be perceived more negatively than those not. The primary purposes of being poached are job status, salary, and the prevailing social environment.

Li, M., 2023 studied the impact of employee poaching on productivity and their employer responses. The study found that the constructive reactions of the organization towards poaching enhanced productivity. The response would be to offer the best package, provide a good working environment, and give many opportunities for professional development. Also, the study emphasizes that retaliatory responses from the organization will negate employee productivity. Alternatively, the company should focus more on defensive modes like legal protections and non-compete agreements to safeguard employees. The organization should focus on developing agility by providing flexibility, supporting innovation, and adopting a culture. (Pivateau, 2011).

Employee Poaching has both positives and negatives. Some of the advantages of employee poaching are

- Whenever organizations decide on employee poaching, they look for a win-win condition. Employee poaching benefits the company, which acts as a poacher, and the employee being poached benefits the company.
- Poaching leads to knowledge transfer from experienced and competent employees to a rising company. It helps share the company's load with a highly qualified employee who has been poached.
- In today's scenario, every organization faces intense competition in the market, and they need to poach skilled employees to be competitive enough. The main intention is for a less-performing company to contribute better in the market. Further, the company will get improved sales and services and product productivity (Li et al., 2023).
- Poaching helps organizations to allocate resources effectively and efficiently.
- It can disrupt competitors and weaken their day-to-day operations. Any company that successfully lures energetic employees away from a rival gains valuable talent and weakens the competition. Further, it shifts market dynamics and gives the poaching company a competitive advantage.
- Poaching can help companies to fill critical positions quickly. Poaching is a viable solution to address talent gaps (Pivateau, 2011).

The main consequences of employee poaching are as follows (Amankwah-Amoah, 2015):

- In any organizational setup, intellectual capital is lost because of employee poaching. Organizations have tried hard to train employees for specific roles, and they don't want to leave such employees.
- High risk of spreading insider information: Employees might end up sharing confidential and sensitive data, which helps the new company.
- Loss of competitive advantage: Competitive job poachers encash creativity and innovation into their business without much effort.
- Employee domino effect: Job poachers might not stop taking only one employee. It is a chain reaction, and they will attract and influence more employees through good salary packages, benefits, and conducive work culture. Also, a poacher encourages the new hire to spread the message among old colleagues to join them, which means they inspire others to join the company for their betterment. The employee domino effect led to trust issues with the existing company and greatly impacted morale.
- Financial Consequences: When an employee leaves, there's a cost. The associated costs are training, recruitment, and potential business loss with the poached employee's departure.
- Change in the market dynamics of poached company.

A question arises in everyone's mind: Is employee poaching ethical? (Gardner.2010)

- Legal complications exist if employees break the organizations' signed contracts or disclose trade secrets with other employers.
- Sometimes, lateral hiring can cross the limitations. Theft or hiring someone solely to harm a company is considered unethical and illegal (Nandin et al.,2020).

There are no poaching laws to prevent employees from switching jobs. They are not employers' property and can freely move from one to another unless they have signed a written contract.

The following ways can minimize employee poaching: The section discusses how to poach-proof the organizational employees. (Weber, 2004)

- By focusing on employee engagement and improving the quality of work and its culture.
- Providing fair pay and proper incentivization to employees
- Helping employees envision their future
- Understanding and meeting the employees' needs.
- Implementing No poach agreements. (Norlander,2023).
- By supporting employees in having a proper work-life balance.
- A longevity bonus must be introduced, which acts as a retention strategy in an organization.
- One-on-one interactions with employees.
- Organizations must conduct exit interviews.
- Organizations must listen to employee concerns.
- Implementing non-compete agreements ensures poaching employees should not work for competing companies. The agreements protect trade secrets and confidential information of the former company. (Lafontaine et al.2023)

Khare et al.'s 2014 study opined that employee poaching should not be done but should still be used to get the capable, competent, and experienced. The study interpreted that poaching can be dismissed by non-disclosure, work-for-hire, incentive compensation agreements, and, most importantly, employment manuals that discuss the employee code of conduct. Poaching is a solution to get experienced employees for the organization, but it is a problem that capable employees could get poached.

Poaching is to meet the immediate organizational requirements. The study showed that poached candidates require a longer time to adjust to the new culture, and sometimes, they might damage the organizational culture of the new company. The poachers should give proper training to these poached employees. Poaching will lead to internal equity issues where achieving equilibrium is a significant concern. It was pragmatic that the employee poached would soon be the target of another company. If this poaching is frequent, there is a risk of having an image of a disloyal employee or lacking professionalism. Poaching was quite common among IT companies. (Nimaish,2019)

Etiquettes of employee poaching: Employee poaching is usually controversial, but there are ways to approach it ethically and responsibly.

Consideration of employee poaching: the key points to be well-thought-out while employee poaching responsibly is as follows: (Li et al 2023)

- Always ensure that the company maintains professionalism and respect when poaching new employees. Companies should avoid aggressive mode or false promises to entice individuals to be on board. They should communicate the opportunities and benefits the poacher gets after joining the company.
- Maintain confidentiality throughout the process. Contact potential candidates privately, using appropriate channels such as professional networks or discreet emails.
- HR manager can inspire candidates to change jobs by explaining the career progression they can provide within the organization and how they can become a fit. Poachers should avoid misleading information. The intention of employee poaching should be apparent to the poached employee.
- Review the non-compete agreements that the employee may have with the current employer so that poachers can avoid legal repercussions that prevail in the future.
- Organizations must offer a higher salary and benefits than the existing employer. It also covers a conducive working environment and better opportunities for career progression.

Employee Poaching Legalities

Employees must sign non-compete and non-solicitation agreements during employment (Harrison et al.,2023). The signed contracts restrict the employees' mobility or choice of getting hired for a year or more after they leave the job (Martins et al.,2023). These clauses or agreements restrict employee behavior during and after employment so as not to hamper business growth. The legal aspects related to employee poaching are deliberated below.

Non-compete agreement: A legal agreement or a clause in an employee contract that talks about not entering into any competition with the employer after leaving the job or the employment term is over. This agreement forbids an employee from close-fitting confidential information and trade secrets to other parties throughout the tenure. The employers expect current and former employees to sign this non-compete agreement. The employee should not work with the competitors for a specific duration regardless of whether the employee is terminated or resigned (Martins et al.2022). Companies have agreements to protect trade secrets, procedures, and processes used to manufacture products and services, as well as intellectual property and proprietary information, to have a competitive advantage.

The agreement should be in place to prevent employees from sharing the information and starting their unit based on the expertise sought by the former company. This non-compete agreement suits media, manufacturing firms, and IT fields. In most jurisdictions, this would be considered a reasonable cause to sign a non-compete agreement.

Non-compete agreements differ from non-disclosure agreements (NDAs), which usually won't stop employees from working for a competitor. NDAs stop the employee from close-fitting information the employer considers confidential or original, like client lists, applied technology, product design, and other development details (Pelczarski,2013).

The various components of a non-compete agreement are as follows:

Duration: It covers specific time frames, six months or one year.

Geography: Geographical location barring an ex-employee from working in particular areas for a specified duration.

Scope: Agreements should specify the nature of the work or services that a poached employee cannot work.

Competitors: The company should specify the industry and types of businesses the employee decides not to work in.

Damages: Employers should specify the damages to which the employee is entitled if they break the contract or agreement. (Garrison,2015)

Non-Solicitation Agreements: Non-solicitation is one such clause that favours every employer. An agreement between an employer and the employee prohibits them from utilizing the contact numbers of clients and customers for personal use after leaving the company. Usually, the non-solicitation is valid for 24 months (Polden, 2023).

The various components in the agreement are as follows (Scott,2023):

Contract: The necessary information about the parties involved, like the party's name, address, date of agreement, and signature.

Tenure: It is for a specific period, usually months or years, depending on the nature of the company.

Definitions: Defining the legal jargon to simplify the contract is essential.

Exclusions: The contract should cover all exclusions and mention the restricted behavior of employees.

Covered employees: Covered employees embrace confidential data and information. Those employees protected from being poached by an ex-employee are called covered employees, one of this agreement's most essential terms.

Severability: It is necessary to ensure the non-solicitation agreement does not fall flat simply because any other contract provision becomes unenforceable.

Transition provisions: The company hires an agency temporarily to complete the exact work. Contractors might work with their competitors once the job is completed. Therefore, in such conditions, particulars about the transition period.

Trade Secrets and Confidential Information: Companies will have legal protection for their trade secrets and organization's confidential information. Poaching employees must be cautious not to unlawfully disclose any information or practice companies' trade secrets from their previous employers, which may be upshot in legal penalties, i.e., trade secret misappropriation claims. (Jerrold, 2018).

It is crucial for every employee and employer engaging in employee poaching to refer legal professionals to understand the specific rules and regulations governing poaching activities within their jurisdiction. In addition to the above, following ethical practices and respecting contractual obligations can lessen legal risks and maintain positive professional relationships.

Classical Techniques for Employee Poaching and Their Identifications

Employee poaching can be either internal or external. Internal employee poaching is identifying the best talent within the organization and onboarding them based on the organizational needs and requirements. If an internal candidate is not competent in handling the work, they look for a competitor's company, i.e., external employee poaching (Kumar, etal.2020)

Internal Employee Poaching: The various nuances of internal poaching are as follows:

- Company culture:

The company follows different cultures while handling the various departmental tasks. There will be a lot of competition between the departments and their managers. Few companies have extreme control over employees in shifting careers within the organization, making it impossible for employees to work on their progression. On the other hand, few companies encourage career progression, cross-training, and transfers within and across departments. It is believed that if the company supports and assists employees in broadening their careers and skill sets, they tend to remain loyal and work long-term.

So, internal poachers need to understand the type of culture prevailing in the organization and act accordingly. A kind of transfer-friendly culture that supports and benefits all in the long run.

- Trusted relationship:

Suppose a company has an open culture that allows employees to expand their horizons in different domains or departments to uplift their careers; the managers may not leave the top performers. If the relationship with other department managers is good, the poacher department can recognize and get the transfer of those competent employees, and the internal employee poaching becomes smooth.

- Protocols of the organization:

Employee poaching from other departments is considered unethical and underhanded. Protocols will be a significant concern if it is not done systematically following specific protocols. Transferring employees from one department to another could be either a stop-gap arrangement for project completion or permanently. However, there generally is a period during which the employee still maintains some of the duties of their original department. As mentioned above, this gives the user department manager time to recruit or train another employee to assume the departing employee's responsibilities. In all cases, it is a suitable protocol for the managers of both departments to work out the logistics first. Following the protocol enables internal employee poaching to be effective.

- Employee engagement and empathy make the difference.

Transfer of employees from one department to other results in furthering their career goals and aspirations; at the same time, managers will get benefits in terms of required expertise for the department. However, the process can be challenging to accept for managers who lose talent. So, managers need to maintain a cordial relationship with other department managers to understand the requirements and ill effects of poaching. Poaching could benefit the organization when all the managers engage and empathize well in the organizational process (Kumar et al., 2020).

External Poaching or Talent Poaching

There are various methods to encourage competitors' employees to join new organizations, as follows (Shi et al.,2023):

Developing Poaching strategy: Santahosh's 2020 study emphasizes formulating a poaching strategy to attract the best talent from the competing company, resulting in employee career development and organizational growth.

Also, they suggested that the company should not force poaching employees; instead, the poacher should provide the right message through job descriptions and convince them that they will be given a better place to work with a good package and benefits in the long run. If the poacher is looking for a senior-level post, they need to be considerate and realistic as much as possible. The poacher should be friendly in introducing themselves and giving employees scope to voice their opinions about their willingness to join (Battiston et al.,2021).

- Hire a Third-Party Recruiter

The benefit of hiring a third-party recruiter is approaching the best potential candidate for the organization. The third-party recruiter will not disclose the company name until the candidates are screened for interviews. The recruiter will identify the suitability of the job and gauge the candidate's interest in the job without disclosing too much information about the company.

- Creating a positive approach

High performers and potential candidates from other companies will be looking for higher-level jobs with designation based on career opportunities. Be respectful of candidates and willing to create long-term relationships with them. Professional networking platforms like LinkedIn and other employment network sites will give information about the prospective candidate. This search will enable the poacher to understand and choose the candidate beforehand within the available time.

- Professional Networking

Poachers must attend industry conferences, seminars, or events to meet potential candidates. They leverage networking platforms like LinkedIn to identify suitable candidates and connect with the best talent. It will enable poachers to showcase company culture and available job opportunities. Engage with prospective or potential candidates through targeted advertising and regular updates on your company's social media channels.

- Online Job Platforms

Use social media platforms, reputable job boards, and websites to create awareness about the job openings. Engage with passive candidates by promoting the company culture and values on these platforms.

- Referral Programs

They encourage existing employees to refer suitable candidates from their professional networks. The referral scheme becomes effective if it is incentivized.

- Company Branding

Poachers will have to build a strong brand by showcasing a positive work environment, success stories of employees, and available growth opportunities. Also, the management can create the company's online presence through social media platforms and websites.

- Targeted Direct Outreach

Poachers should identify the best talents and reach out to these candidates directly. They are personalizing the communication to highlight why the candidates would be an excellent fit for the organization based on their skills and career goals (Japheth,2023).

Data Science Approaches for Identifying the Less Committed Employee and Employee Retention

Data science deals with unearthing the patterns in the data, and data analytics deals with understanding these patterns to help strategic decision-making. In the case of classical techniques for identifying the less committed employee, the decisions are based on the manager's abilities, which may sometimes lead to improper and inaccurate decision-making. Data science techniques depend exclusively on applying statistical measures to the data collected.

The human resource management function produces a lot of employee data, including personal data, skill sets, professional data, service data, etc. These data items are helpful for career planning, promotions, performance evaluation, assigning roles, changing roles, etc. They may fail to identify the implicit nature of an employee regarding their commitments toward organizational goals and mission. The failure to recognize employee commitment may lead to many operational inefficiencies due to the sudden leaving of an employee, not finding timely replacements, no opportunity for employee counseling, knowledge drain toward competitors, loss of intellectual properties, etc.,

The data science approach for this scenario is advantageous for an organization to reduce these losses. Suggested methodologies (data set) for employee retention are given in Table 1.

Table 1. Dataset for the analytics on employee retention (Alshehhi et al., 2021)

Sl. No.	Type of Dataset	Purpose of the Dataset
1	Employee Engagement Dataset	This dataset covers the quantitative and qualitative data items collected on employee job satisfaction, job roles and responsibilities, how good the employee is in team dynamics, and the leadership capabilities of an employee. Etc.,
2	Turnover trends Dataset	This dataset, created by a parent company and similar companies, comprises the number of employees leaving the organizations and the possible reasons. This dataset helps identify the risks in advance.
3	Dataset on employee performance	The detailed dataset on employee performance attributes can identify declining job satisfaction and poor workplace engagement levels.
4	Attendance and Time management dataset	The dataset collected on these factors helps to analyze an employee's poor punctuality and commitment toward meeting deadlines.
5	The dataset collected on employee and manager interactions	The collected dataset is vital to understanding the employees' work cohesion with the managers and higher-ups. This data will help discover the presence of unconscious human bias in employee-manager work relations. (Hendrick, 2011)

Data Preprocessing (Yadav et al., 2018)

Table 2. Types of data preprocessing

SL. No.	Type of Data Preprocessing	Purpose of Data Preprocessing in the Employee Retention Dataset
1	Data Cleaning	There is always a possibility that employees will not answer all the survey questions, which they think are profound and private. The data scientist is responsible for filling these values by using other secondary resources of the data collected over the employee over time.
2	Data Transformation	Data transformation will be crucial for transforming the data collected into machine-understandable logical formats. The data transformation in the employee retention dataset is helpful when employees express their opinions verbally or in writing. Encoding these into some numerical forms is required for analysis purposes. Sometimes, the majority of the data collected looks skewed to specific issues, which you think need to be considered and addressed immediately, which favor employee retention if it is of serious type or maybe neglected over the priority.
3	Data Reduction	The data reduction stage makes us focus on the essentials of the collected datasets. This process involves reducing dataset scope and dimension by limiting it to only essential features for analysis. Data reduction comes primarily in employee retention datasets while identifying the features attributing to increased employee turnover trends. This reduction process helps to do better analytics by only focusing on the essential features to build the model instead of considering all the data collected, which may be unnecessary from the analysis point of view.
4	Data Integration	Usually, employee retention data will have to be collected from various sources. It is not possible to have a single comprehensive dataset indicating all the values and attributes. Data analytics should fuse these datasets from different sources over some concepts for analyzing employee retention status and types.
5	Data Formatting	Finalizing the data attributes, like type, range, precision, uncertainty factors, etc., becomes crucial for building models that sustain the history of events or transactions. Sometimes, decisions are made regarding the data format while developing the models. Data should be available for analysis and subjected to specific format changes instead of rigid form.
6	Treating Imbalanced data	Dataset spread and reach will decide the quality of the data collected. The primary importance is to ensure the data collected is a real-world representation of the phenomenon. The periodicity used for sampling and the amount of data collected may sometimes lead to over and under-sampling scenarios. These scenarios may not fetch the actual insight. We may encounter heterogeneity of employee classes we address in employee retention datasets, and their volume differs. If we keep analyzing over-sampled cases, we may lose a talented and competent employee, and trying to satisfy a talented technical employee, we may lose an essential batch that may not be critical but difficult to replace within a short period.
7	Dealing with Text data	Natural language expressions by employees are the primary and critical data for analysis. The challenge may be going through the big corpus and coming out of inferences.

Data Visualization

Data visualization is an industry-accepted tool for visualizing the data for better understanding. Visualization can happen in many ways, and an effective visualization method is crucial in any data science project. In the present model, building and visualizing the dataset of employees to understand the trends and symptoms will be an excellent input for human resource managers to make any strategic decisions in advance. Data scientists may use tools to create visualizations such as scatter plots, charts, tree maps, heat maps, tables, Gantt charts, dashboards, etc. Table 3 illustrates the purpose of these tools for employee retention datasets.

Table 3. Tools for employee retention datasets

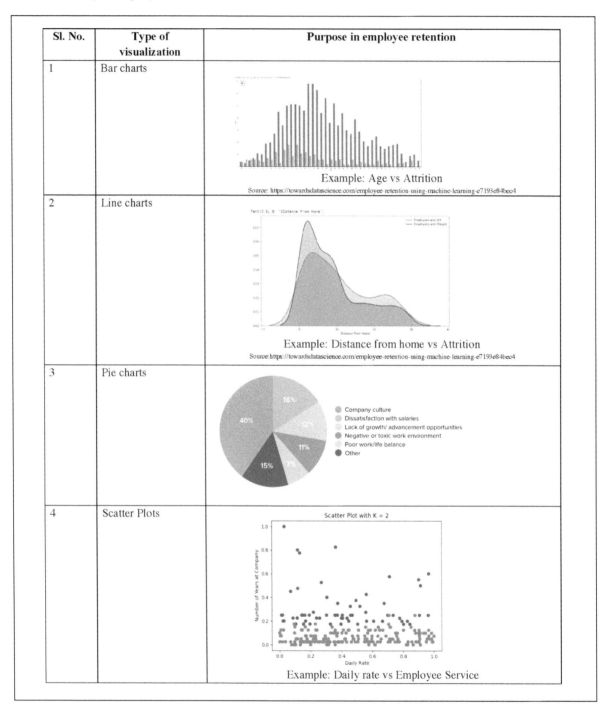

Sl. No.	Type of visualization	Purpose in employee retention
1	Bar charts	Example: Age vs Attrition Source: https://towardsdatascience.com/employee-retention-using-machine-learning-e7193e84beo4
2	Line charts	Example: Distance from home vs Attrition Source:https://towardsdatascience.com/employee-retention-using-machine-learning-e7193e84beo4
3	Pie charts	Company culture Dissatisfaction with salaries Lack of growth/ advancement opportunities Negative or toxic work environment Poor work/life balance Other
4	Scatter Plots	Example: Daily rate vs Employee Service

Continued on following page

Table 3. Continued

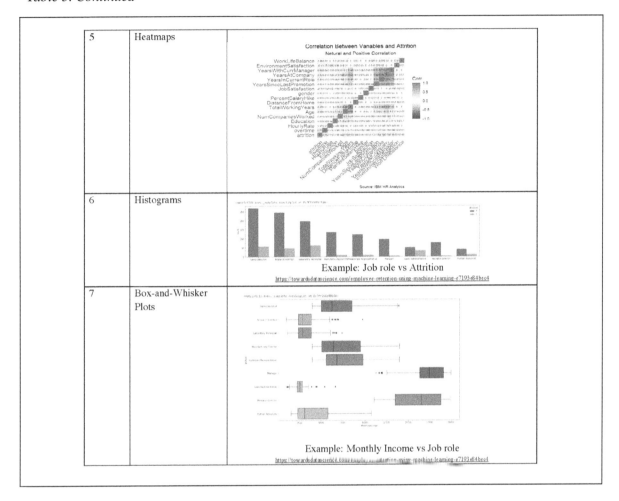

5	Heatmaps	
6	Histograms	Example: Job role vs Attrition https://towardsdatascience.com/employee-retention-using-machine-learning-e7193e84bec4
7	Box-and-Whisker Plots	Example: Monthly Income vs Job role https://towardsdatascience.com/employee-attrition-using-machine-learning-e7193e84bec4

Creation of a Business Dashboard for Tracking Employee Retention

An efficient system for employee retention monitoring uses data collected at various stages of the employee work lifecycle. When the organization's size grows, and the number of employees reaches thousands, monitoring the data is overwhelming and challenging. One of the solutions is creating an employee retention dashboard.

Businesses must identify key performance indicators (KPIs) relevant to employee retention practices in the dashboard. These KPIs will vary depending on the industry and the business's needs; typical examples include attrition rates versus age, job location, job type, job level, department, etc.

The data from various sources can be sourced into the employee retention dashboard to provide stakeholders with real-time updates on employee retention trends. In addition to providing real-time updates, the dashboard can also provide tools for data analysis, such as filters and drill-down capabilities. These tools allow stakeholders to analyze the data and identify patterns and trends to improve employee performance and job satisfaction. For instance, stakeholders can analyze the data to determine the root cause of employees leaving the organization. Furthermore, these dashboards can help businesses improve employee management by monitoring work satisfaction levels in real time (Dubey,2018).

The steps involved in the creation of such a dashboard can be summarized as follows:

Figure 2. Steps for creating dashboards

Step 1: Identify Key Performance Indicators (KPIs): The first step in creating a dashboard is identifying the KPIs relevant to the employee management system. These KPIs can vary based on the business's needs but may include employee-related metrics.

Step 2: Collect Data: Once the KPIs have been identified, the next step is to collect data from the various sources available throughout the organization. Data can be sourced on various aspects of employee management, such as performance, satisfaction, job commitment levels, and quality control metrics, and stored in a centralized database for analysis.

Step 3: Visualize Data: Once the data has been sourced, it can be envisaged on the business dashboard. The dashboard can provide real-time updates on the KPIs identified earlier, allowing stakeholders to assess employee work performance and turnover trends quickly. The data can be visualized as charts, graphs, and tables, giving stakeholders clear and concise views.

Step 4: Analyze Data: The dashboard can also provide tools for data analysis, such as filters and drill-down capabilities. These tools allow stakeholders to analyze the data and identify patterns and trends, helping them make informed decisions to improve the workspace quality and reduce employee turnover rates.

Step 5: Act: Based on the insights gained from the dashboard, stakeholders can take action to improve the performance. For example, if the attrition rates are high, stakeholders can investigate the root cause of the issue and implement corrective actions. Similarly, if the job satisfaction levels are low, stakeholders can adjust the production plan to ensure that job satisfaction levels are maintained at the desired level.

Sample Employee Retention Dashboards

Figure 4. Fluctuation report (https://www.tableau.com/solutions/human-resources-analytics/dashboards)

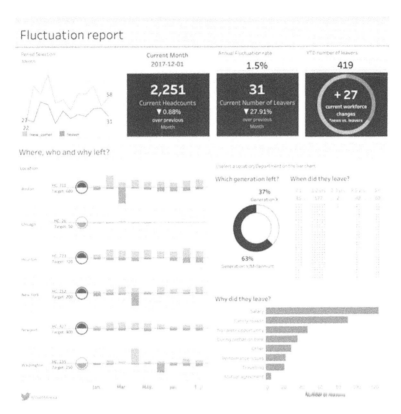

Figure 3. Employee retention dashboard (https://www.slidegeeks.com/)

Role of AI in Employee Retention

Artificial intelligence has entered various business functions, including human resource management. AI's ability to perform classifications, predictions, and generations of new content has made businesses leverage the potential of AI in conducting business functions effectively. The basic notion of AI is to build a model based on machine learning or deep learning to train an algorithm to make decisions without human intervention. AI model essentially depends on the given dataset for development; therefore, it is the responsibility of the data analyst to provide the correct dataset for training the model. As mentioned above, various data sources and attributes have gone through the data analysis pipeline, and we will be ready with model training and validation. Table 4 shows multiple applications of AI in employee retention (Salunkhe, 2018).

Table 4. AI in employee retention

Sl. No.	AI Model	Purpose of the Model in Employee Retention
1	Predictive Analytics	Predicts the employees who have a high chance of leaving the organization
2	Sentiment Analytics	Used to identify the negative sentiments in employees towards the organization's goals
3	Employee engagement Guide	Used to create personalized career progression plans for employees
4	Retention Risks Evaluator	Used to classify the employee based on the chance of leaving the organization. He may be a potential candidate for employee poachers.
5	Wellness supporting system	Integrating fitness and AI into employees' lives will enable managers to learn about their stress levels and provide them with free air.
6	Chat Services	NLP-based chatting, both formal and casual, will help to improve employee engagement levels in the workplace.
7	Leadership sourcing	AI-based solutions can identify the second line of leaders, who can take up the responsibilities if the key employee leaves the organization abruptly.
8	Generative AI	Generative AI models can be used to create personalized channels for communication with employees. Many works performed by human in-built skills can be taken over by generative AI, like conducting surveys, providing feedback, analyzing feedback, making personalized recommendations, etc. Adding training technologies in the employee duty cycle may make employees more accountable and responsible for their jobs.
9	AI-based personalized mentoring system	Mentoring is one of the critical ways to retain the employee from exit. Identifying the right time for mentoring and the right approach for personalized mentoring through AI can be achieved over time.
10	AI-based onboarding systems with Metaverse	These systems will create various onboarding options digitally available to different workforce classes. Onboarding is considered one of the essential and primary activities when newly hired staff members are connected to the organization's work culture. An additional technology that can be leveraged here is Metaverse, which will give employees an immersion experience to understand the workplace and ecosystem.

Examples of AI Applications Which Contribute to Employee Retention Strategies

IBM: The company has developed an AI-powered retention tool called **IBM Watson Talent**. The tool will enable the company to analyze the various data points on employee performance metrics, sentiments, and engagement levels in an organization to identify the probability and risk of leaving the job. Based on the data, the company formulates employee retention strategies.

Google: The company uses AI-powered feedback and recognition tool **"gThanks"** to improve employee retention. This platform ensures proper feedback, especially real-time feedback, and recognizes and communicates employee contributions. A culture of appreciation and recognition drives employee morale and job satisfaction and further helps improve retention rates.

Unilever: The Company uses AI-powered talent analytics (**Unilever's Talent Data Insights**) for employee retention. The analytics discusses employee performance reviews and the factors influencing job satisfaction and turnover. This data-driven approach enables Unilever to develop targeted retention strategies.

Accenture: The company uses an AI-driven workforce planning tool (**Accenture's Workforce Planning Optimization Tool**) to optimize employee retention. The tool enables Accenture to identify potential talent gaps and retention strategies based on trends and business forecasts.

Microsoft: Microsoft employs AI-driven diversity and inclusion analytics (**Microsoft's Diversity and Inclusion Analytics Tool**) to reduce attrition based on feedback and analysis of the diverse workforce. A data-driven approach helps retain diverse talent and creates a more equitable workplace, increasing employee satisfaction and retention.

CONCLUSION

This chapter on employee retention strategies using predictive data analytics and AI discusses the meaning of employee retention, followed by classical and modern approaches used by competitor companies for employee poaching, and also provides an ethical angle for the same. The discussion continues by providing the data science and analytics angle to increase employee retention by predicting the data generated directly or indirectly on the employee. The chapter also highlights various strategies for integrating modern data analytics solutions with existing businesses. The chapter suggests that a good business dashboard for employee retention is a value addition for companies to understand their workforce better and plan remedies.

REFERENCES

Alshehhi, K., Zawbaa, S. B., Abonamah, A. A., & Tariq, M. U. (2021). Employee retention prediction in corporate organizations using machine learning methods. *Academy of Entrepreneurship Journal, 27*, 1–23.

Amankwah-Amoah, J. (2015). An integrative review of the antecedents and consequences of lateral hiring. *Journal of Management Development, 34*(7), 754–772. doi:10.1108/JMD-01-2014-0007

Boeri, T., Garnero, A., & Luisetto, L. G. (2023). *Non-compete agreements in a rigid labor market: The case of Italy*. Academic Press.

Callaci, B., Gibson, M., Pinto, S., Steinbaum, M., & Walsh, M. (2023). *The Effect of Franchise No-poaching Restrictions on Worker Earnings*. Working Paper.

Deshwal, S. (2015). Employee retention-perspective of employees. *International Journal of Applied Research, 1*(6), 344–345.

Dubey, A., Maheshwari, I., & Mishra, A. (2018). Predict Employee Retention Using Data Science. *Journal of Diversity Management (JDM), 5.*

FerrésD.KankanhalliG.MuthukrishnanP. (2023). Anti-Poaching Agreements, Innovation, and Corporate Value: Evidence from the Technology Industry. Available at SSRN 4552393. doi:10.2139/ssrn.4552393

Gardner, T. M., Stansbury, J., & Hart, D. (2010). The ethics of lateral hiring. *Business Ethics Quarterly, 20*(3), 341–369. doi:10.5840/beq201020326

Garrison, M. J., & Wendt, J. T. (2015). Employee Non-competes and Consideration: A Proposed Good Faith Standard for the Afterthought Agreement. *U. Kan. L. Rev., 64*, 409.

Harrison, J. S., Boivie, S., & Withers, M. C. (2023). Executives' prior employment ties to interlocking directors and interfirm mobility. *Organization Science*, *34*(4), 1602–1625. doi:10.1287/orsc.2022.1638

Hendrick, R. Z., & Raspiller, E. E. (2011). Predicting employee retention through pre-employment assessment. *Community College Journal of Research and Practice*, *35*(11), 895–908. doi:10.1080/10668920802421561

Howe, A. S., Lo, J., Jaiswal, S., Bani-Fatemi, A., Chattu, V. K., & Nowrouzi-Kia, B. (2023). Engaging Employers in Apprentice Training: Focus Group Insights from Small-to-Medium-Sized Employers in Ontario, Canada. *International Journal of Environmental Research and Public Health*, *20*(3), 2527. doi:10.3390/ijerph20032527 PMID:36767893

Japheth, O., Rahab, M., & Albert, K. (2023). The Efficacy of Talent Selection Approaches on the Competitiveness among Five Star Hotels in Nairobi City County, Kenya. *Journal of Human Resource and Sustainability Studies*, *11*(3), 736–758. doi:10.4236/jhrss.2023.113041

Jerrold, L. (2018). Poaching employees. *American Journal of Orthodontics and Dentofacial Orthopedics*, *153*(5), 755–756. doi:10.1016/j.ajodo.2018.02.003 PMID:29706224

Khare, K., Singhal, S., Singhal, S., & Singh, D. Rajendra, Employee Poaching - Why? & Whom? (November 3, 2014). IJRSS, Vol. 4, Issue 4, November 2014, Available at SSRN: https://ssrn.com/abstract=2956777

Kim, J. H. (2014). Employee poaching: Why it can be predatory. *MDE. Managerial and Decision Economics*, *35*(5), 309–317. doi:10.1002/mde.2637

Kumar, R. S., & Peter, H. (2020). A study on talent stalk with the support of employee poaching in automobile sector with particular reference to Krishnagiri District, Tamilnadu, India. *Editorial Board*, *9*(4), 29.

Kumar, S., Savani, K., Sanghai, A., Pochkhanawalla, S., Dhar, S., Ramaswami, A., & Rose Markus, H. (2015). Indian employees' attitudes toward poaching. *Business Perspectives and Research*, *3*(2), 81–94. doi:10.1177/2278533715578553

Lafontaine, F., & Slade, M. (2023). *No-Poaching Clauses in Franchise Contracts, Anticompetitive or Efficiency Enhancing?* Anticompetitive or Efficiency Enhancing. doi:10.2139/ssrn.4404155

Li, M., Malik, M. S., Ijaz, M., & Irfan, M. (2023). Employer Responses to Poaching on Employee Productivity: The Mediating Role of Organizational Agility in Technology Companies. *Sustainability (Basel)*, *15*(6), 5369. doi:10.3390/su15065369

MartinsP. S.ThomasJ. (2022). Training, Worker Mobility, and Employer Coordination. Battiston, D., Espinosa, M., & Liu, S. (2021). Talent poaching and job rotation. Available at SSRN 3778068.

Martins, P. S., & Thomas, J. P. (2018). Employer collusion and employee training. *New York Times*, 2.

Martins, P. S., & Thomas, J. (2023). *Employers' associations, worker mobility, and training*. Nova SBE Working Paper Series, (653).

Nimisha, N. (2019). Employee Poaching and Career Advancement: A study on CUSAT Alumni. *International Journal of Scientific Research and Review*, *8*(2), 235–243.

Norlander, P. (2023). *New Evidence on Employee Non-compete, No-Poach, and No Hire Agreements in the Franchise Sector.* Academic Press.

Pelczarski, K. (2013). Dealing with non-compete agreements. *Tribology & Lubrication Technology, 69*(11), 98.

Pivateau, G. T. (2011). Preserving Human Capital: Using the Non-compete Agreement to Achieve Competitive Advantage. The Journal of Business. *Entrepreneurship & the Law, 4*(2), 3.

Polden, D. J. (2023). *Restrictions on Worker Mobility and the Need for Stronger Policies on Anticompetitive Employment Contract Provisions.* Academic Press.

Salunkhe, T. P. (2018). *Improving employee retention by predicting employee attrition using machine learning techniques* (Doctoral dissertation, Dublin Business School).

Scott, C., Sackmaster, S., Schembre, D., Rice, G. M., & Vicari, J. (2023). *Best practice recommendation: advanced practice providers contract terms and negotiations.* iGIE.

Shi, J., Wang, J., Kang, L., & Sun, J. (2023). How to poach the talents? Role of social capital and contextual knowledge base. *Technological Forecasting and Social Change, 197,* 122905. doi:10.1016/j.techfore.2023.122905

Weber, C. (2004). Breaking the circle: How do you say goodbye to a partnership and reinvent a practice? *Residential Architect, 8*(9), 39–45.

Yadav, S., Jain, A., & Singh, D. (2018, December). Early prediction of employee attrition using data mining techniques. In *2018 IEEE 8th International Advance Computing Conference (IACC)* (pp. 349-354). IEEE. 10.1109/IADCC.2018.8692137

Chapter 10
Employee Well–Being and Mental Health:
Critical Role in Retention Strategies

P. Bhanumathi

https://orcid.org/0000-0001-8670-8250

M.S. Ramaiah Institute of Management, India

P. Keerthi Chandrika

Deloitte, India

B. Sathish Babu

RV College of Engineering, India

ABSTRACT

Due to increased work pressure and organizational performance expectations, employees struggle to maintain their mental health and peace, leading to decreased motivation and employee attrition. Adding to the work pressure, maintaining a work-life balance has become crucial for building a successful career for any employee. Today's Generation X and Generation Y (millennials) employees have varied preferences and priorities, and their expectations from the organization have changed a lot. The organization is responsible for creating strategies and policies tailor-made for heterogeneous work groups by identifying the critical concerns of employee well-being and mental health and developing mechanisms to address them effectively to retain the talented workforce.

INTRODUCTION

Overview of Well-Being

Well-being at the workplace significantly impacts employee health, which further impacts the organization's overall productivity. The individual's lifestyle, demographics, and financial stability often

DOI: 10.4018/979-8-3693-1938-3.ch010

progress to well-being. A well-established work environment can enhance well-being and productivity while encouraging a contributed workplace environment. To establish a relationship between employee well-being and productivity, we must analyze the factors driving the individual to achieve productivity. Workplace well-being has been an essential factor that potentially impacts the individual's overall performance. Analyzing and assessing this factor helps the organization enhance its overall productivity.

Factors for the Positive Well-Being of an Individual

Good communication between the individuals in the organization should establish greater coordination among the employees. Positive relations among peers play an important role in building a supportive environment, ensuring employee engagement while fostering job satisfaction. When assisted with requirements by his peers or from the organization, the individual helps him solve the paradoxes at the workplace while enhancing his productivity. In such environments, the individual feels safe and confident in attaining job satisfaction. After achieving job satisfaction, the individual can work in favorable conditions while excelling (Dutraj et al., 2022) (Ilies et al., 2024)

Greater job satisfaction tends to increase the level of well-being at the workplace. By analyzing each role played by the individual in the aspect of interpersonal roles, support, and job satisfaction, the firms can enhance these aspects of the analysis. The better the outcomes these aspects are proven to be, the better the well-being of individuals is prone to be(Supardi et al.,2023)

Consequences of Positive Well-Being

Individual well-being is directly proportional to the support received from the organization, along with balanced work-life dynamics. Employees who experience good mental status and health are more flexible and contribute more, further minimizing the risk associated. Better well-being leads to job satisfaction, employee engagement, and increased productivity (Schmitt et al.2014)

When the well-being benefits are not up to the mark, there is a negative impact on employees' perspective of the work-life while reducing the productivity of the individual and altering the absenteeism rate. A positive work environment can be created through transparency and mutual understanding while enhancing the work culture. Individuals who feel that their well-being benefits them tend to perform collectively as a group, restricting insecurities among the groups through open communication. In contrast to positive well-being, there are specific barriers individuals might encounter across their path, such as workplace stressors, which might alter the workplace relationships among peers, resulting in ineffective communication while portraying the differences among them (Yoon et al. 2022). The antecedents and consequences of well-being are shown below in Table 1.

Table 1. Well-being antecedents and consequences

Well-Being Antecedents	Well-Being Consequences
Psychosocial and workplace relationships (Interpersonal relationships, Social Support, Job Satisfaction)	Holistic Wellness and professional Connections (Physical Health, Work Productivity, Interpersonal Relationships)
Individual Flourishing and Growth (Healthy Lifestyle, Education, Financial Stability)	Emotional Resilience and Life Fulfilment (Mental Health, Longevity, Happiness) (Dikshit et al. 2024)
Environment and Social Justice (Safe Environment, Health Access, Social Justice)	Community Involvement (Social Participation, Quality of life, Life Satisfaction)

Here are several reasons highlighting the importance of employee well-being:

- *Employee Performance and Productivity*: Mentally and physically healthy and happy employees are more likely to be engaged and motivated, increasing productivity. Well-being is linked to better cognitive function, creativity, and problem-solving skills, contributing to higher job performance (Bella,2023).
- *Retention and Loyalty*: Workers who feel they are getting support and are more valued are more likely to stay in the organization longer, reducing turnover costs. A positive work environment that prioritizes well-being fosters loyalty and commitment among employees(Gelencsér et al., 2023)
- *Health and Safety*: Promoting well-being contributes to a healthier workforce, reducing illness-related absenteeism. Focusing on employee well-being can also enhance workplace safety awareness, reducing accidents and injuries.
- *Morale and Job Satisfaction*: A workplace that values well-being creates a positive atmosphere, leading to higher morale and job satisfaction. Satisfied employees are more likely to approach their tasks enthusiastically and positively.
- *Proper Work-Life Balance*: Supporting well-being programs involves acknowledging the importance of work and personal life and reducing stress and burnout. Organizations that respect and facilitate a healthy balance create a more sustainable and fulfilling work experience.
- *Employee Engagement*: Well-being initiatives can enhance employee engagement by fostering belongingness. Engaged employees are likely to contribute ideas, collaborate with colleagues, and go the extra mile for the organization (Willett et al .2023).
- *Corporate Image and Reputation*: Organizations prioritizing employee well-being are seen as socially responsible and caring, enhancing their reputation. A positive corporate image can attract top talent and improve relationships with customers and clients.
- *Less cost*: Well-planned well-being programs lead to savings in the long run. It will further reduce healthcare expenses and employee turnover and increase productivity.
- *Legal and Ethical Considerations*: Governments and regulatory bodies may emphasize employee well-being through laws and regulations, making it essential for organizations to comply with ethical and legal standards.
- *Adaptability and Resilience*: Employees who are physically and mentally well are better equipped to handle challenges and changes in the workplace. A resilient workforce is crucial for adapting to evolving business environments.

In summary, prioritizing employee well-being is a moral responsibility and a strategic business decision. It positively impacts individual employees and the sustainable organization's overall contribution (Vanhala et al.2006)

Overview of Mental Health

"Health is a state of complete physical, mental, and social well-being and not merely the absence of disease or infirmity." An important implication of this definition is that mental health is more than just the absence of mental disorders or disabilities. In mental health, employees realize their abilities, manage everyday organization and personal stresses, perform productively, and contribute to their community.

Mental health is how humans think, emote, interact with each other, earn a living, and enjoy life. On this basis, promoting, protecting, and restoring mental health can be regarded as a vital concern of individuals, communities, and societies worldwide. The difference between mental health and well-being is shown below in Table 2.

Table 2. Difference between mental wealth and well-being

Mental Health	Well-Being
Focuses on psychological and emotional well-being	It covers physical and mental health, social connections, financial stability, environmental factors, and personal fulfillment.
Individual experiences and challenges related to mental well-being	It extends beyond the individual and includes multiple aspects of life, such as physical health, relationships, work-life balance, financial stability, and community involvement
Diagnoses mental disorders and assesses mental resilience and coping mechanisms	Evaluate overall life satisfaction, happiness, and a sense of purpose (Rurkkhum, 2023)
Address the specific mental health conditions and provide proper therapies, medications, and interventions.	It enhances various aspects of life and promotes self-care, positive emotions, and meaningful relationships.

Effect of Mental Health and Employee Well-Being on Organizational Productivity

Mental health is a state where an employee or an individual can embellish to the maximum extent of their potential, cope effectively with the everyday stresses of life, and positively contribute to their community and the world at large, as defined in a report by WHO in 2014. This report has proven a significant relationship between employee mental health, well-being, and productivity. The individual's mental health and well-being must be prioritized to increase productivity. The employees who were well-being and had good mental health exceeded their performance, while individuals dealing with mental well-being issues were not up to the mark (Ling, 2023).

The unalignment of mental health and employee well-being can significantly impact individuals' productivity at the workplace and in their personal lives. When an individual tries to balance both personal and professional life, there are certain obstacles each comes across to establish a good work-life balance. In their journey of attaining work-life balance, there are scenarios where the individual.

When mental health conditions are not satisfactory, employees tend to exhibit instability in the workplace. Sometimes, they might be ineffective as their performance at the workplace does not align with the predefined standards. These individuals are likely to be less focused at the workplace, thus reducing their engagement. This depletes the organization's overall performance. They tend to postpone their work while poorly managing their time and the organization's. This stability also might lead to differences among the peers, thus reducing their coordination (Ling, 2023).

When employees deal with continued stresses, these stressors can affect the performance of the individuals over a chronic period. This might lead to reduced employee morale, causing a lack of employee trust. Stressors cannot be predetermined as such scenarios, too. How employers and employees address these stressors can have a long-lasting impact on the performance and productivity of the individuals. Individuals dealing with many stressors can disrupt the workplace, reducing productivity (Bubonya, 2017).

From a psychological perspective, work stressors affect the individual's psychological state at work. The performance of the individual is affected by the efforts one tries to put into the workplace. The optimistic view states that there is a significant impact on these stressors and employee performance, proving that stressors can be a motivating factor that helps employees to thrive better at the workplace while enhancing their efficiency. In contrast, another view states that stress negatively impacts the individual's performance, showing that employees spend more of their time and energy dealing with these stressors, further increasing the burden of these individuals while showing a deficiency in productivity. When the stressors are moderate, employees will try to perform at their best. The researcher's view proposes that there is no considerable relationship between the mental health of individuals and productivity. Work stressors can neither motivate the individuals nor show a deficiency in productivity.

Factors Affecting the Productivity of Employees, Employee Well-Being, and Mental Health

In the absence of work-life balance, individuality, and DEI, certain practices may significantly affect employee mental health, well-being, and performance at the workplace. Certain factors can affect mental health and well-being in the workplace.

Employees who cope with their scheduled timelines exhibit greater work satisfaction while meeting the established performance standards. The pressure an individual endures at the workplace is directly proportional to the individual's stressors. When executing job rotation strategies that help the individual cope with job dissatisfaction, a few organizations can experience a difference in their routine. While this adds value for experience, this process also increases the individuals' stressors. This further affects the motivation levels of the individuals to perform at the workplace (Mustika et al., 2023).

Keeping a work-life balance: Working all day can also drain the individual's energy. They initially find it challenging to establish a bridge between work life and personal life. It was pragmatic that employees with excellent work-life balance could succeed. On the other hand, individuals who were poor at managing work-life balance resulted in poor productivity compared to their moderate stages. Individuals who are good at managing time are good with their work-life balance. It is always essential to look for procedures that enhance work-life balance. Individuals who do not try to prioritize their mental health harm their peers around them. Employees must analyze and understand the essential factors affecting their mental health for better adoption (Yusuf et al., 2022).

After-hours work: If the individual is prone to get into a routine of working after hours, it may somehow affect their mental health. Overworking may exhaust the individuals, which leads to a distortion of work-life balance. Occasionally, overtime is considerable as they meet their deadlines, but it should not only be a routine of overworking as it decreases employee motivation. Managing time is also an essential practice for the individual to avoid stressors. Employees' confidence will increase when they can meet their deadlines, which shows a positive result.

Workplace toxicity and internal politics: Peace and harmony in the organization directly impact employee well-being and productivity. Unfortunately, workplace toxicity and internal politics are inevitable. Coworkers who gossip, backbite, or refuse to take responsibility for their mistakes can force you to retaliate or relent. The resulting ethical dilemmas are stressful and prime factors affecting mental health. The stressors are likely to be amplified. Organizations have implemented a zero-tolerance policy to resist differences and internal politics, which states that all legal enforcement is applicable completely but not partially. Individuals who violate established procedures are punished according to standard operating procedures, including termination, to solve organizational politics and toxicity in the workplace.

Lack of recognition: When individuals are unrecognized for what they do, this leads to decreased motivation. Not being recognized or appraised is the reason why there is an increased turnover rate of the individuals. High employee turnover will increase the costs the organization invests in its employees either in the short term or in the future. Appraisal and recognition also enhance healthy employee competition, increasing the individual's self-driven trait while influencing coworkers in the work environment(Yusuf et al., 2022).

Leaders analyze that recognizing the employees' contributions is vital in fostering a healthy work culture. Studies show that employees give importance to recognition as much as to salary. According to the surveys, most employees feel highly motivated to function when recognized and praised for their work.

Workplace challenges: A challenge stimulates the intellect and forces people out of their comfort zones. Good leadership constantly appreciates the staff and often sets a challenge for them. When employees can deal with problems at work, their self-esteem rises, and they start to take more initiative and do more work. If organizations don't challenge employees, they are not challenged and do not achieve their full potential. Although it does not seem like a problem, unfortunately, a lack of challenges at work factors mental health.

Consequently, they develop self-doubt and might consider looking for a job where they are challenged more often or are provided with opportunities. That's why it's critical to regularly challenge workers' knowledge and skills. As a result, your employees will have better mental and professional health and be happier at work.

Micromanagement: Micromanagement in any space troubles the mindset of an employee. There is no trust, improper communication, and no active employee engagement. This micromanagement indicates no employee empowerment and a lack of autonomy. Employees without self-reliance and confidence often think they can't perform well and occasionally solve the issues.

Critical Reasons for Employee Attrition, Focusing on Work-Life Balance and Professional Competition

Employee attrition is when an employee leaves an organization for some reason and is not replaced for a long time. The consequences involve decreasing the size of an organization's or department's workforce because positions become vacant. Attrition can occur throughout an entire company or in specific departments or divisions. Attrition occurs as a result of automation or new technologies replacing employees. There are different types of employee attrition, as given in Table 3.

Table 3. Types of attrition

VOLUNTARY ATTRITION	Voluntary attrition occurs when employees choose to leave the organization voluntarily for various reasons like selecting a new organization or leaving due to personal issues, health issues, domain change, or abroad opportunities.
INVOLUNTARY ATTRITION	Involuntary attrition takes place when the company eliminates the employees. This occurs during layoffs or eliminating the positions, NO BUDGET, PROJECTS, and behavior of employees.

Work-Life Balance

THE PURSUIT OF HEALTHY WORK is work-life balance. It is the ability to balance the professional and personal responsibilities. Work-life balance is crucial in building employees' productivity and indirectly impacts the organization's performance. Managing the workloads, relationships, stress, and balancing the work is critical. Stress weakens the immune system, leading to many health issues, from colds to backaches to heart disease. According to recent research, chronic stress can double the risk of having a heart attack. The best way to balance work at the organization is by setting priorities, having realistic goals, taking enough breaks, being efficient at work, networking, and communicating effectively. The best way to balance personal responsibilities is to stay active and prioritize health and family (Borowiec et al., 2022).

Impact of Work-Life Balance on Employee Attrition

The new technological era has brought many changes in the expectations of employees. People choose the organization with two main criteria: work-life balance and organizational culture. Organizations with good people management are booming. Work-life balance plays a vital role in the employee attrition rate. It is a huge loss for an organization, a loss of knowledge, and an increase in the cost of an organization.

As per the focus group discussion, the main reasons employees leave the organization include work pressure, no increments, no work-life balance, unhappiness with shift timings, office politics, personal reasons like weddings, and family issues.

Impact of Professional Competition on Employee Attrition

Professional competition involves the dynamic interaction between individuals or organizations. Professional competition in terms of market share, ethical environment, innovation, and quality of service between organizations impacts the employees and guides them in choosing new opportunities. The reasons employees switch organizations include no personal development, no career growth, work culture, unethical environment, no increments, no realistic goals, rewards and recognition, brand, salary & benefits, succession planning, promotion, and top management based on the focus group discussion.

Employee Retention

When employees tend to leave the organization, the turnover rate increases, increasing the organization's cost of investing in the other employees. Hence, an organization must identify employee retention factors and strategies. It includes determinants like career opportunities, work design and rewards, and existing employee relationships. The employee retention factors are compensation, employee development opportunities, work-life balance, conducive working environment, proper management/leadership, employee work autonomy, training and development opportunities, social support, etc. (Le et al., 2023)

Development Opportunities: Many studies indicate that employees, irrespective of any generational gap, tend to stay longer in organizations that provide great developmental opportunities for their career growth in this technological era.

Leadership: Leadership has become the decision factor for employees to stay in an organization. According to studies, the indirect effect of transformational leadership on the attrition of the baby boomer generation is more robust than that for Gen X and Y. Management styles directly affect employees, and their impact leads to the success or loss of a company.

Autonomy in Job: Organisations design job autonomy for their employees, which is a crucial factor to be considered for retention. Some factors to be protected to retain Gen Y employees include job opportunities, Self-managing tasks, and constant and regular feedback from peer groups and colleagues.

Work Environment: The management mainly focuses on the work culture to retain employees. The work environment includes the organization's locations, employees engaged in work-related activities and employment conditions. It is where employees perform their jobs, setting their social and physical conditions.

Compensation: There is a positive correlation between compensation and employee retention. It was observed in many organizations where proper and timely remuneration heavily impacts Gen Y employees' retention. Employee recognition is also a significant element in retaining Gen Y employees.

Identification of employees who have mental health issues and considering them positively to counsel, help, and improve their mental states rather than sidelining them. Organizations must take initiatives to enhance employee's psychological well-being by reducing the stress related to work and self and making the environment more conducive. Employee health programs should be designed to reduce and eliminate the stigma. The organization regularly must conduct an assessment survey of the mental health-pressure jobs and find ways to overcome them (Le et al.2023). The organization's Human Resources must formulate and develop strategies to create a healthy and less stressful environment in the workplace and identify the areas for improvement. Capacity-building programs must be designed and executed to enhance psychological well-being, and well-trained managers use techniques to make the workplace less stressful. Managers should emphasize providing employees with a productive and stress-free working environment to ensure job satisfaction, work engagement, and a healthy work/life balance.

Various Strategies Followed by Companies for Employee Well-Being and mental Health for Gen. X and Gen. Y Employees

Organizations are experiencing a crisis regarding talent as employee turnover rates are very high, especially in Gen X and Y. The turnover rate of Gen Y is comparatively high when compared to X. The marketplace combines Generation X, Y, and Z. Organizations need to analyze and understand the composition of their workforce and professional traits to establish a better working environment while retaining talent. By analyzing their professional characteristics, organizations can plan, and design suitable retention strategies based on the priorities of the individuals. As per the scenario, the workplace traits should be analyzed thoroughly to meet the dynamics of the existing workforce and to forecast the required essentials and strategies for future generations. The shift in the workforce dynamics implies that organizations must analyze the traits of each generation by comparing them with other generations (Badri et al., 2023).

The traits of Gen X and Y can be defined by the expectations of their requirements along with their preferred work styles.

Coming to the workstyles of Gen X, they establish more significant goals to fulfill their needs. They do not actively seek a job change but don't back out if a better opportunity awaits them. They prefer workstyles with more flexibility. Most of the Gen X are multi-taskers in nature. They try to be more independent and are poor at micro-managing things while techno driven. Most of the individuals of this generation try to work independently to accomplish the assigned tasks.

On the other hand, generation Y seeks technologically driven workplaces as most are prone to depend on technology for better and more accurate outcomes. They mainly seek quality if they want to pursue a professional career. Gen Y doesn't depend on their superiors as they feel they can learn independently and find ways to get information about their roles and responsibilities. Most of the individuals of this generation tend to function in teams as they seek support from each other while attaining better benefits at the workplace (Badri et al., 2023).

Generation X requires autonomy as their expectations for a job. They seek development at the workplace and expect flexibility in time. They tend to perform better in an independent environment as they don't like to depend on others, and they see them as hurdles to their functioning. They believe they can perform independently, thus taking care of themselves. These are job expectations that the X generation looks out for when pursuing professional life.

While coming to Gen Y, they primarily depend on the need for growth and advancement in their careers while seeking better opportunities and finding a sense of satisfaction in their jobs. They work in a healthy environment where communication is one of the vital aspects that help them function effectively. They most likely work in groups and help each other overcome certain hurdles. So, Generation Y prefers a workplace that promotes harmony and collectivity.

Strategies for Gen X Employees Are as Follows

By offering a Flexible Work Environment: Companies that provide flexible work options can enhance employees' work-life balance needs.

Opportunities for Professional Development: Companies must provide a platform for continuous learning, skill development, and career growth to engage and motivate employees.

Health and Wellness Programs: Companies must conduct wellness programs focusing on the employees' physical health, stress management, and preventive care.

Financial Well-being Support: Companies must conduct financial wellness programs, for example, retirement planning and counseling about finance, and to address the unique concerns, if any (Fishman, 2016).

Company Mentorship Programs: Companies must take the initiative to mentor employees through experienced leaders for better guidance and support.

Strategies for Gen Y (Millennial) Employees Are as Follows

Work-Life Integration: Recognizing and supporting the desire for work-life integration by offering flexible work hours, remote work options, and unlimited vacation policies.

Technology and Digital Platforms: Leveraging technology and digital platforms to facilitate communication, collaboration, and learning, aligning with the preferences of tech-savvy Millennials.

Social Impact Initiatives: Engaging in corporate social responsibility (CSR) and sustainability initiatives, as Millennials often value working for socially responsible and environmentally conscious organizations.

Employee Resource Groups (ERGs): Establishing Employee Resource Groups that focus on diversity, equity, and inclusion, creating a sense of belonging and community for Millennials.

Mental Health Support: Offering mental health support through Employee Assistance Programs (EAPs), counseling services, and stress management workshops (Askari, 2023) will improve performance.

Feedback and Recognition: Providing regular feedback and recognition to Millennials, who often value continuous feedback and seek meaningful work experiences.

Strategies for Both Generations X and Y

Positive Work Culture: A positive and inclusive working culture promotes employee collaboration, open communication, and a sense of belonging to the organization.

Employee Assistance Programs (EAPs): Programs shall provide counseling and support services for employees to deal with professional and personal challenges.

Transparency and Open Communication: Open communication and transparency build employee trust and reduce work uncertainty about organizational goals and performance expectations.

Recognition and Rewards Programs: Companies must introduce recognition and reward programs for employees to acknowledge and appreciate Gen X and Y's contributions.

Promoting Work-Life Balance: Encouraging a healthy work-life balance by setting realistic expectations, promoting time off, and discouraging a culture of overwork.

In summary, strategies create a workplace environment that supports the well-being and mental health of Gen X and Y employees.

Tools to Track Employee Well-Being and Motivational Levels

Many organizations use conventional methods to track employees' mental status and well-being. The most common traditional methods are both quantitative and qualitative. The various internal and external factors that contribute to the well-being of an employee are a Safe workplace, job security, employee autonomy, skill development opportunities, positive relationships with peers and other officials, recognition and reward for the contribution, career development opportunities, reasonable workload, less job stress, time flexibility, inclusive culture by the organization, transparency in work, open communication, etc., The above factors will significantly impact employee job satisfaction and productivity and further help retain the employees for a longer tenure.

Some of the popular conventional methods to track the employee well-being and motivational levels are as follows:

- *Periodic surveys*: Organisations conduct surveys at regular intervals by developing and administering them, which cover various factors, namely mental and physical health, job satisfaction, career advancement, job security, working environment, etc.

- *FGDs (Focus group discussions)*: FGDs are to be conducted to know the specific aspects of an employee's well-being and to get deeper insights. Employees are believed to be more vocal and share their views and opinions with the management.
- *Wellness programs*: These programs help the organization monitor the employee's physical well-being by checking their cholesterol levels, BP levels, etc.,
- *Performance evaluation*: Performance evaluation of employees regularly helps to know the pluses and minuses of an employee towards the work and self. Managers can address the concerns, if any.
- *Monitoring the employee leaves*: The organization should monitor the attendance status and the reasons for leave of absence. The extended leave will indirectly indicate the well-being of an individual.
- *Feedback session*: The organization should conduct one-on-one meetings with employees and allow all to express their views and opinions about the work and self, further enhancing the relationships and belongingness towards the organization.
- *Exit interviews*: The organization conducts interviews to learn about the employees' opinions towards the work, their challenges during the job, and suggestions to minimize problems.

The above methods are combined to have a detailed understanding of the status of employee well-being, concerns, and how to improve employees' mental and physical well-being.

Some of the challenges faced in the traditional method of tracking employee well-being are as follows:

- Employees may not share accurately due to fear and negative repercussions.
- Some employees may be reluctant to share the data as it is a matter of privacy.
- Traditional methods are subjective, and bias occurs due to manual reporting.
- It is periodic, and real-time and continuous data will go unnoticed.
- Unable to capture the remote workspace data
- It will help assess specific well-being and doesn't cover an employee's comprehensive or holistic view.
- Collecting, storing, and managing employee well-being data by the organization has increased concerns about data security and compliance with privacy regulations. Employers must take measures to safeguard such data as per the laws.
- Sometimes, addressing the issues by taking proper action may not be possible.

Some of the popular conventional methods to track employee motivational levels are as follows:

- *Performance evaluation*: The organization should review the employee performance regularly to know the work contribution, status of employee motivation, and engagement levels.
- *Performance check-ins*: The organization continuously checks and monitors employee performance to discuss individual goals, aspirations, and challenges encountered and suggest ways to overcome them.
- *Exit interviews*: In this interview, the organization will learn about the reason for leaving the job and how they can improve the working space to keep employees motivated and engaged.
- *Job rotation*: Job rotation will help the employee learn about the various jobs, and at the same time, it will motivate and actively engage them.

By regularly checking, assessing, monitoring, and addressing employee motivation levels, organizations require a combination of the above methods tailored to the unique employee's needs. Organizations must create a conducive working space that fosters motivation through intrinsic and extrinsic factors.

Some of the challenges faced while tracking the motivational levels of an employee are as follows:

- Assessment can sometimes be subjective by managers as they follow different criteria for evaluation, which leads to biased interpretation.
- Tracking employee motivation levels may inadvertently lead to demotivation, especially when employees perceive it as intrusive, micromanaging, or lacking transparency.
- Employee resistance to formal evaluation is one of the significant challenges.
- Conventional assessments may lack the context to understand the factors influencing an employee's motivation. It will result in a surface-level understanding without addressing the root cause of it.
- Focus only on either external or internal motivation indicators.

Tracking employee well-being and motivational levels is crucial for maintaining a healthy and productive working environment and organizational success and enhancing employee satisfaction.

Several tools and platforms are used to track employee well-being and motivational levels for various reasons and are as follows:

- It helps identify the potential issues related to the employee's well-being and required motivation. The data will help in proactively addressing the problems.
- Monitoring motivation levels gives the employer how and at what level employees are engaged.
- By tracking well-being and motivation levels, the employer can formulate strategies to retain competent and talented employees for a longer tenure.
- Tracking highlights work-life balance; the company uses data to develop policies and procedures to reduce stress and employee burnout.
- Regularly tracking well-being and motivational levels enhances job satisfaction.

Several industry tools and platforms are available to help organizations monitor and enhance employee well-being. Some of the popular tools used by the organization are surveys.

Employee Survey Forms: The Monkey Survey is a widely used platform to collect data through employee feedback. TINY pulse: platform measures based on continuous and real-time data related to happiness, trends over time, and employee engagement with the organization.15Five: The tool will ensure regular and faster check-ins (Continuous performance), facilitating continuous employee feedback.

Employee wellness apps: The app helps in tracking employee wellness. Virgin Pulse: This tool focuses on wellness and well-being programs to encourage employees to have a healthy lifestyle. Wellable: This focuses on improving the employee experience and health with a suitable wellness program that promotes healthy employee behaviors, further enhances company culture, and increases productivity(Monteiro et al.,2023).

Performance Management System: A system that tracks and monitors the employee's goal setting, feedback, rewards, and performance. BambooHR: This is for SMEs to help in the hiring process and throughout the employee life cycle. Also, review the employee performance. Workhuman Conversations: it gives a holistic view of an employee in terms of work progress, feedback on the work carried out, and review of the same.15Five: It offers a pulse survey and helps set and track the employee's goals to optimize employee performance. Perform yard: It allows employees' annual reviews by setting quarterly employee goals and providing consistent feedback.

Communication Platforms: The platform helps the organization communicate easily and quickly with employees and supports the employees' well-being(Qin et al., 2023). Tools like Slack and Nextiva are adopted for internal communication to share information with a particular department, office, etc. Some popular communication tools are Google Meet, Zoom, GoTo Meeting, and Microsoft Teams.

Employee Assistant Programs: The ModernHealth tool provides personalized treatment plans, behavioral coaching, sessions, and the required therapy per the employees clinically validated self-assessment. TELUS: Provides 24-hour counseling and wellness information for employees and their families. Optum: This offers a solution for employee well-being concerns and counseling services.

Employee Recognition and Rewards Platforms: Nectar is a 360 recognition and reward platform that recognizes and helps team members feel more valued and engaged. Bonusly: It helps managers run quick surveys to identify and measure satisfaction levels of employees, gather onboarding/exit insights, and discover work environment priorities. WorkTango: This simple and easy-to-use recognition platform helps companies create highly engaged teams and workspaces where everyone feels inspired and happy.

Learning and Development Platforms: Udemy for any Business provides a platform for employees to acquire new skills and knowledge to perform and contribute to the organization's growth. Moodle is an open-source platform that offers robust learning and development tools for corporations and educational institutions. LinkedIn Learning: This platform provides several courses to support employee development and motivation.

In summary, the organization can use various tools based on the need and urgency, which adds value; upholding open communication, nurturing a positive work culture, and addressing issues on time are equally vital for employee well-being and motivation. Organizations must select tools that align with the existing process, goals, and their specific culture,

Data Science Approaches for Employee Well-Being and Mental Health

Data science deals with unearthing the patterns in the data, and data analytics deals with understanding these patterns to help strategic decision-making. In the case of classical techniques for creating schemes for employee well-being, the decisions are based on the manager's abilities and company policies. This may sometimes lead to improper and inaccurate decision-making, affecting employee retention due to poor privileges and schemes available. Data science techniques depend solely on applying statistical measures to the data collected from various sources to create effective and mostly personalized schemes for employee well-being and mental status monitoring.

The human resource management function produces a lot of workforce data, including personal data, skills, professional data, service data, etc., and the officials who develop policies for employee well-being look for suitable solutions that may sometimes fit all employees. The amalgamation of data from various sources should be retrieved scientifically to develop employee well-being and mental health schemes. Any failure to identify the mental status would lead to employee turnover, which is a high cost to the company and also influences the company's overall outcome.

The data science approach for employee well-being and mental health monitoring is an advantage for an organization to reduce these costs and take the right approach to manage the workforce with the highest level of motivation. The following are the suggested methodologies for this;

Dataset for the Analytics for Employee Well-Being

The data set that can help in identifying employee well-being is in Table 4 below (Lathabhavan, 2023):

Table 4. Dataset for the analytics for employee well-being

Type of Dataset	Purpose of the Dataset
Employee regularity and commitment levels (Meyer et al., 2010).	This dataset includes the employee's regularity in the work. It reflects the time punctuality and the employee's commitment to an organization regarding the tangible outcomes produced. It also measures employee motivation towards the assigned work and the level of satisfaction the employee enjoys in the role.
Employee feedback dataset	This dataset is sourced by conducting various surveys, including pulse surveys, to understand the employees' sentiment towards the organizational vision, mission, goal, targets, etc. These data would serve the purpose of gauging the employees' job satisfaction levels and interpersonal and interprofessional skills.
Dataset from employee monitoring	Real-time work monitoring gives many insights about the employees, like their work habits, co-working nature, happiness index, disturbance motivation, casual attitude, laziness, engagement levels, etc.
Secondary sources of data	Govt. and private organizations' data, magazines, industry reports, past successful industry well-being programs, etc., ensure the creation of a data set that would establish the required Employee well-being programs.
Dataset on employee medical history	This dataset, constructed out of other related sources from healthcare and organizations linked to healthcare, provides valuable insights into the employees' physical condition, and helps predict the retention duration. Sometimes, these parameters also create personalized health plans for employees, which is an added attraction.

Data Preprocessing

The type and purpose of data processing are as follows in Table 5.

Table 5. Data preprocessing

Type of Data Preprocessing	Purpose of Data Preprocessing in the Employee Well-Being and Mental Health Dataset
Data Cleaning	There is always a possibility that applicants may fail to answer some of the critical questions, which they think would affect their privacy. The data scientist is responsible for filling in these values using other secondary resources of the employee's data or making predictions on these missing values. It is also essential to remove the noise in the data, which may occur due to casual responses from the employee. Outliers will affect to a greater extent while doing the analysis; treating outliers properly and establishing data normalization is necessary.
Data Transformation	Data transformation will transform the collected data into machine-understandable logical formats. The data transformation in the employee well-being datasets is beneficial when employees express their opinions verbally or in writing. Encoding these into some numerical forms is required for analysis purposes. Sometimes, most of the data collected looks similar and redundant, which needs a preprocessing stage to pick the valuable data to initiate decisions. If carried out properly, this stage would establish the salient features of the employee's mental health status.
Data Reduction	The data reduction stage makes us focus on the essentials of the collected datasets. This process involves reducing dataset scope and dimension by limiting it to only essential features for analysis. Data reduction comes primarily in well-being datasets while identifying the features that quantify the employee mental status in the company compared to others. This reduction process helps to do better analytics by only focusing on the essential features to build the model instead of considering all the data collected, which may be unnecessary from the analysis point of view.
Data Integration	Applicant data are collected from various sources. The data comes in multiple forms, sometimes structured and sometimes unstructured. A data analyst has to look to derive a pattern from these datasets, which predicts the very nature of the applicant and classifies the employee's mental status into various levels, which helps create well-being plans.
Data Formatting	Finalizing the data attributes, like type, range, precision, uncertainty factors, etc., becomes crucial for building models that sustain the history of events or transactions. Sometimes, the data formats will be decided while building the models. Data should be available for analysis, which can be subjected to specific format changes instead of rigid form.
Treating Imbalanced data	Dataset spread and reach will decide the quality of the data collected. The primary importance is to ensure the data collected is a real-world representation of the phenomenon. The periodicity used for sampling, and the amount of data collected may sometimes lead to over and under-sampling scenarios. These scenarios may not fetch the actual insight. We may encounter heterogeneity in employee mental health in datasets, and their volume differs. If we keep analyzing over-sampled cases, we may lose out a critical employee, and trying to satisfy a talented employee, we may lose a batch that is essential and may not be critical but challenging to replace within a short period.
Dealing with Text data	Natural language expressions by employees and employers are the major and critical data for analysis. The challenge may be going through the extensive data corpus and coming out of inferences to make well-being strategies.

Data Visualization

Data visualization is an industry-accepted tool for visualizing the data for better understanding. Visualization can happen in many ways, and an effective visualization method is crucial in any data science project. In the present model, building for visualizing the dataset of employees to understand the trends and symptoms will be an excellent input for human resource managers to make any strategic decisions in advance. Data scientists may use tools to create visualizations such as scatter plots, charts, tree maps, heat maps, tables, Gantt charts, dashboards, etc. The following section illustrates the purpose of these tools to understand the employees' mental health status and work commitment.

Employee Mental Health Tools

Figure 1. Level of agreement vs. mental health parameter (https://researchgate.net)

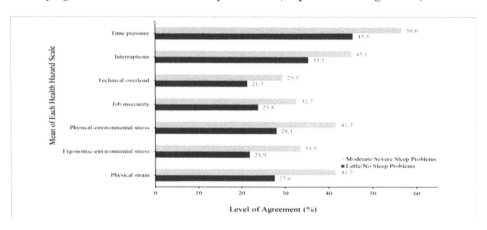

Figure 2. Top reasons (https://www.linkedin.com/posts/joshcyphers_are-you-experienc ing-burnout-heres-how-activity-6887107406430658560-LXb8/)

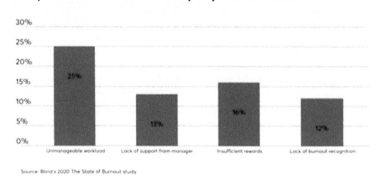

Figure 3. Various disorder levels (https://www.nejm.org/doi/full/10.1056/NEJMp1315214)

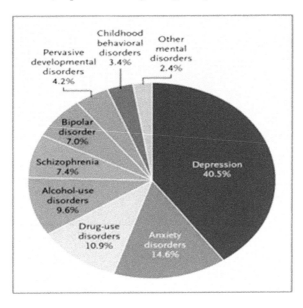

Figure 4. Employee mental health attitude (https://journeytods.wp.imt.fr/2022/12/14/identifying-the-ris k-factors-for-mental-health-issues-in-the-tech-industry/)

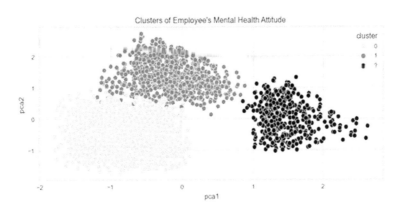

Figure 5. Density plots (https://journeytods.wp.imt.fr/2022/12/14/identifying-the-ris k-factors-for-mental-health-issues-in-the-tech-industry/)

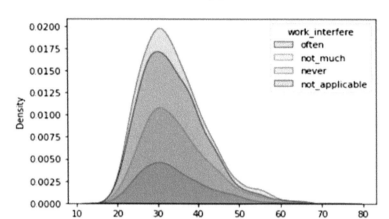

Figure 6. Distribution of mental health disorders in the workplace (https://nidhi729.github.io/DataVis-Mental-Health/)

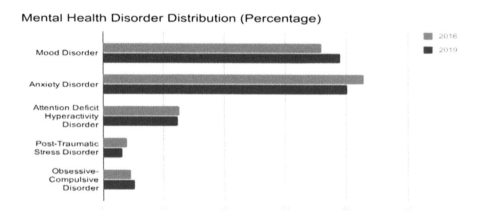

Creation of a Dashboard for Tracking Employee Mental Health Status

An efficient system for developing employee well-being policies can be developed by periodically tracking the employee's mental health status. When the organization's size grows and the number of employees reaches thousands, manually monitoring the mental health data is overwhelming and challenging. One of the solutions is creating a mental-health monitoring dashboard.

Dashboard creation involves the identification of key performance indicators (KPIs) relevant to employee well-being practices and effectiveness in any organization. These KPIs will vary depending on the industry and the business's needs; typical examples include the happiness index, mental health reasons, distribution percentages, etc.

Sourced data can be unified into the dashboard to give stakeholders real-time updates on employees' mental health status. In addition to providing real-time updates, the dashboard can also provide tools for data analysis, such as filters and drill-down capabilities. These tools allow stakeholders to analyze the data and identify patterns and trends that can be used to improve mental health status. For instance, stakeholders can analyze the data to determine the root cause of the poor happiness index. Furthermore, these dashboards can help businesses improve their work-life balance by monitoring various quality indicators of the employees' well-being plans in real-time.

The steps involved in the creation of such a dashboard can be summarized as follows:

Step 1: Identify Key Performance Indicators (KPIs): The first step in creating a dashboard is identifying the KPIs relevant to the employee well-being plans. These KPIs can vary based on the business's needs but may include employee-related metrics.

Step 2: Collect Data: Once the KPIs have been identified, the next step is to collect data on the employee's mental health status from the various data points available through primary and secondary sources. Data collection techniques can gather information such as performance, satisfaction, job commitment levels, and quality control metrics. The collected data can be stored in a centralized database for analysis.

Step 3: Visualize Data: Once the data has been collected, it can be visualized on the business dashboard. The dashboard can provide real-time updates on the KPIs identified earlier, allowing stakeholders to quickly assess employee mental health status. The data can be visualized as charts, graphs, and tables, giving stakeholders clear and concise views.

Step 4: Analyze Data: The dashboard can also provide tools for data analysis, such as filters and drill-down capabilities. These tools allow stakeholders to analyze the data and identify patterns and trends, helping them make informed decisions to improve the effectiveness of existing policies on employee well-being or introduce alternate policies.

Step 5: Act: Based on the insights gained from the dashboard, stakeholders can take action to improve their mental health status. For example, if the work pressure is high in specific departments, stakeholders can investigate the root cause of the issue and implement corrective actions. Similarly, if the work-life balance is low, stakeholders can adjust the work schedule to ensure that employees' work-life balance is maintained at the desired level.

Figure 7. Sample employee mental-health/employee well-being dashboards (https://www.businesswire. com/news/home/20191107005265/en/New-Fidelity%C2%AE-Total-Well-Being-Solution-Provides-Employers-With-Greater-Insight-on-Employee-Needs-to-Help-Drive-Benefits-Utilization)

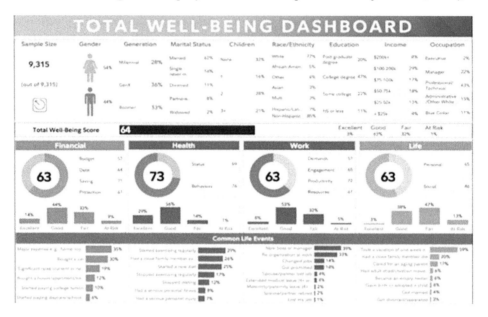

VII Role of AI in Employee Well-being and Mental Health Monitoring

Artificial intelligence has entered various business functions, including human resource management. AI's ability to perform classifications, predictions, and generations of new content has made businesses leverage the potential of AI in conducting business functions effectively. The basic notion of AI is to build a model based on Machine learning or Deep learning to train an algorithm to decide without human intervention. AI model essentially depends on the given dataset for development; therefore, it is the responsibility of the data analyst to provide the correct dataset for training the model. As mentioned above, various data sources and attributes have gone through the data analysis pipeline, and we will be ready with model training and validation. Table 6 gives multiple applications of AI in employee well-being and mental health status monitoring.

Table 6. Applications of AI in employee well-being and mental health status monitoring

AI Model	Purpose of the Model in Employee Well-Being and Mental Status Monitoring
Predictive Analytics	Used to predict; • Employee Stress levels • Employee burnout levels • Mental health levels • Emotion levels • Regularity • Work commitment levels, etc. (Guest,2017)
Sentiment Analytics	Used to identify the sentiments of employees' like; • Motivation level • Social presence and communications • Apply natural language processing to understand employees' informal communications and impact.
Chatbots	Conversational chatbots can be used as career counselors and also for mentoring.
Fitness data analytics	Data collected over the physical parameters and vitals, sleep patterns, etc., can be used to assess employees' fitness levels.
AI-based flexible work schedules	AI-based work schedulers can be used to create duty shift plans for employees. These plans will address mental health status and provide schedules to restore motivational levels. The flexible work schedules attract Gen-Y employees.
Generative AI.	Generative AI models can create personalized or cluster employee well-being plans in conversation with employees.
AI-based personalized mobile apps	Since Gen-Y employees are more accustomed to using mobile-based applications, it is beneficial to have customized apps designed for mental status monitoring and feedback/counseling.
AI-based collaborative workspace	Promoting cross-cultural teams and cross-functional collaboration through proper mix-and-match using AI would benefit the employee by killing the monotony and opening up new avenues for performance.

CONCLUSION

This chapter on employee well-being and mental status using predictive data analytics and AI discusses the meaning of employee well-being and purpose, followed by classical and modern approaches used for employee mental status monitoring, and also provides an overview of various challenges faced during creating well-being policies. The discussion continues by providing the data science and analytics angle to increase the effectiveness of well-being policies by predicting the data generated directly or indirectly on the employees' mental health status data. The chapter also highlights various AI-based strategies for integrating modern data analytics solutions with existing business processes specific to employee mental health status monitoring. The chapter suggests that a good business dashboard for monitoring employee mental health status is an advantage for effective HRM.

REFERENCES

Askari, M. R. (2023). *Retention Strategies for Managers of Generation Y Employees* (Doctoral dissertation, Walden University).

Badri, S. K. Z., Yung, C. T. M., Wan Mohd Yunus, W. M. A., & Seman, N. A. A. (2023). The perceived effects of spirituality, work-life integration and mediating role of work passion to millennial or gen Y employees' mental health. *Management Research Review, 46*(9), 1278–1295. doi:10.1108/MRR-04-2021-0275

Bella, K. M. J. (2023). The power of employee well-being: A catalyst for organizational success. *International Journal of Scientific Research in Modern Science and Technology, 2*(4), 20–26.

Borowiec, A. A., & Drygas, W. (2022). Work–Life Balance and Mental and Physical Health among Warsaw Specialists, Managers and Entrepreneurs. *International Journal of Environmental Research and Public Health, 20*(1), 492. doi:10.3390/ijerph20010492 PMID:36612813

Bubonya, M., Cobb-Clark, D. A., & Wooden, M. (2017). Mental health and productivity at work: Does what you do matter? *Labour Economics, 46*, 150–165. doi:10.1016/j.labeco.2017.05.001

De Silva, K. D., Punsith, H., Damayanthi, H. N. P., Perera, R., Chandrasiri, S., & De Silva, H. (2023). Promoting Remote Employee Well-being: Role of Emotion Detection, Social Media Analysis, Mental Health Monitoring, and Performance Tracking. *International Research Journal of Innovations in Engineering and Technology, 7*(10), 42.

Dikshit, S., Grover, Y., Shukla, P., Mishra, A., Sahu, Y., Kumar, C., & Gupta, M. (2024). Empowering Employee Wellness and Building Resilience in Demanding Work Settings Through Predictive Analytics. *EAI Endorsed Transactions on Internet of Things, 10*.

Dutraj, R., & Sengupta, P. R. (2022). Employee Well-Being and Influences of its various Factors. *Asian Journal of Management, 13*(4), 335–344. doi:10.52711/2321-5763.2022.00055

Fishman, A. A. (2016). How generational differences will impact America's aging workforce: Strategies for dealing with aging Millennials, Generation X, and Baby Boomers. *Strategic HR Review, 15*(6), 250–257. doi:10.1108/SHR-08-2016-0068

Gelencsér, M., & Szabó-Szentgróti, G. (2023, June). Analysis of the determinants of employee well-being and retention through a sample of Hungarian employees. In *Proceedings of FEB Zagreb International Odyssey Conference on Economics and Business* (Vol. 5, No. 1, pp. 178-192). University of Zagreb, Faculty of Economics and Business.

Guest, D. E. (2017). Human resource management and employee well-being: Towards a new analytic framework. *Human Resource Management Journal, 27*(1), 22–38. doi:10.1111/1748-8583.12139

Ilies, R., Bono, J. E., & Bakker, A. B. (2024). Crafting Well-Being: Employees Can Enhance Their Own Well-Being by Savoring, Reflecting upon, and Capitalizing on Positive Work Experiences. *Annual Review of Organizational Psychology and Organizational Behavior, 11*(1), 63–91. doi:10.1146/annurev-orgpsych-110721-045931

Lathabhavan, R. (2023). Mental well-being through HR analytics: Investigating an employee supportive framework. *Personnel Review*. Advance online publication. doi:10.1108/PR-11-2022-0836

Le, D. A., Le-Hoai, L., Le, V. H., & Dang, C. N. (2022, September). Factors Affecting Employee Retention in Construction: Empirical Study in the Mekong Delta Region. In *ICSCEA 2021: Proceedings of the Second International Conference on Sustainable Civil Engineering and Architecture* (pp. 263-277). Singapore: Springer Nature Singapore.

Ling, L. M. (2023). Prevalence Of Mental Health and Its Impact on Employee Productivity. *Reviews of Contemporary Business Analytics*, *6*(1), 1–13.

Meyer, J. P., & Maltin, E. R. (2010). Employee commitment and well-being: A critical review, theoretical framework and research agenda. *Journal of Vocational Behavior*, *77*(2), 323–337. doi:10.1016/j.jvb.2010.04.007

Monteiro, E., & Joseph, J. (2023). A Review on the Impact of Workplace Culture on Employee Mental Health and Well-Being. *International Journal of Case Studies in Business IT and Education*, *7*(2), 291–317.

Mustika, M. I., & Martdianty, F. (2023). Factors Influencing Employee's Well-Being and Job Performance: The Perspective of State-Owned Enterprise Employee. *IJHCM*, *7*(1), 86–103. doi:10.21009/IJHCM.07.01.7

Nabawanuka, H., & Ekmekcioglu, E. B. (2022). Millennials in the workplace: Perceived supervisor support, work–life balance and employee well–being. *Industrial and Commercial Training*, *54*(1), 123–144. doi:10.1108/ICT-05-2021-0041

Qin, Y. S., & Men, L. R. (2023). Exploring the impact of internal communication on employee psychological well-being during the COVID-19 pandemic: The mediating role of employee organizational trust. *International Journal of Business Communication*, *60*(4), 1197–1219. doi:10.1177/23294884221081838

Rurkkhum, S. (2023). A bundle of human resource practices and employee resilience: The role of employee well-being. *Asia Pacific Journal of Business Administration*. Advance online publication. doi:10.1108/APJBA-01-2022-0050

Schmitt, M. T., Branscombe, N. R., Postmes, T., & Garcia, A. (2014). The consequences of perceived discrimination for psychological well-being: A meta-analytic review. *Psychological Bulletin*, *140*(4), 921–948. doi:10.1037/a0035754 PMID:24547896

Supardi, A. M., Salehah, M., & Komalasari, S. (2023, March). The Role of Workplace Well-Being on Employee Work Satisfaction. In Conference of Psychology and Flourishing Humanity (PFH 2022) (pp. 318-327). Atlantis Press. doi:10.2991/978-2-38476-032-9_33

Vanhala, S., & Tuomi, K. (2006). HRM, company performance and employee well-being. *Management Revue*, 241-255.

Willett, J. F., LaGree, D., Shin, H., Houston, J. B., & Duffy, M. (2023). The role of leader communication in fostering respectful workplace culture and increasing employee engagement and well-being. *International Journal of Business Communication*. doi:10.1177/23294884231195614

Yoon, D. J., Bono, J. E., Yang, T., Lee, K., Glomb, T. M., & Duffy, M. K. (2022). The balance between positive and negative affect in employee well-being. *Journal of Organizational Behavior*, *43*(4), 763–782. doi:10.1002/job.2580

Yusuf, J. E. W., Saitgalina, M., & Chapman, D. W. (2022). Work-life balance and well-being of graduate students. In *Work-Life Balance in Higher Education* (pp. 63–88). Routledge. doi:10.4324/9781003314868-8

Chapter 11
Employer Branding and Its Significance in Today's World

Rohit Shaji
PES University, India

Zidan Kachhi
ⓘD https://orcid.org/0000-0002-8317-6356
PES University, India

ABSTRACT

In today's globally interconnected world, the concept of employer branding has come up as an important strategy that is used by organizations to attract and retain high-calibre talent. This chapter will cover the significance of employer branding in the modern organizational scene and will also extensively cover strategies, drawbacks, and its relationship with other similar concepts. Another related concept that is included in the chapter is the concept of internal marketing and the different strategies associated with it. Employer branding is a very important element of not only retaining employees and attracting future employees; it is also concerned with differentiating the organisation from its competitors in terms of employee experience.

INTRODUCTION

Employer Branding is a process that is concerned with developing and enhancing an organization's image as an employer to its current and future workforce. This process encompasses varied aspects such as the organization's culture, values, benefits and the overall employee experience. The overall objective of employer branding is to establish the organization as a favoured employer and thus, to attract and retain (Ambler & Barrow, 1996).

In the modern organizational landscape, where there is intense competition for skilled and talented professionals, the significance of employer branding is not emphasized enough. Organizations also have to face the challenges of distinguishing themselves and developing a positive employer image to navigate the process of talent acquisition and retention successfully. Employer branding works as a tool that is

DOI: 10.4018/979-8-3693-1938-3.ch011

used to actively shape the awareness and perceptions of current employees, potential employees, and stakeholders toward a specific organization.

The advantages of a strong employer brand extend across various dimensions, yielding significant benefits for organizations. Lower recruitment costs, improved employee relations, heightened retention rates and the ability to offer competitive salaries compared to companies with weaker employer brands, all of which contribute to the continued growth and viability of an organization This highlights the importance of employer branding alongside corporate branding with parallels in the organizational context.

Emphasizing key organizational aspects such as culture, brand name, reward system, career development opportunities, and employee capabilities, employer branding carefully paints an attractive image to potential employers These strategic competencies are not as simple as they will not only attract top talent that is critical to the success of the organization but also the loyalty of existing employees. Integrity is also a factor in increasing performance and fostering a positive organizational culture, as highlighted by Leekha Chhabra and Sharma (2014).

Essentially, the varied nature of employer branding contributes to its main role in addressing the complex challenges of talent management. As organizations navigate today's challenging workforce environment, strategically cultivating a positive employer brand is emerging as an essential process for continued success and growth.

Here are a few examples of a few organisations using employer branding strategies effectively:

1. McDonald's felt the need to change the negative perception associated with working at the organisation to a more positive image. They used surveys along with focus groups placed internally and externally to understand the perceptions of potential employees and they launched a rebranding campaign through press and in store advertisements.

2. Barclays Bank wanted to challenge the reputation it had of being bureaucratic and faceless, and not a good place to work at. By focusing on employer branding, they upgraded their overall image by working on advertising as an employer, and used different internal marketing techniques to promote themselves as an employer. The bank later on managed to The Top 20 Big Companies to Work For by the Sunday Times.

3. Fujitsu Services recruited 45 employees a week on an average. They felt the need to make sure that their employees are fully aware of the brand's values and that the same values were instilled in the new recruits. They conducted surveys on the staff and they recognised that their "honest and straightforward" values were felt the most. They recruited managers and made use of various other tactics to improve upon and promote their reputation as an honest and straightforward brand.

4. London & Quadrant Housing Group made use of employer branding to increase the attractiveness of the organization as a career option. By focusing on different areas under employee attraction and retention, they managed to make huge gaps on charts that ranked the best companies to work for at that time.

These examples clearly show how certain organizations have made use of employer branding strategies to improve their perception as an employer to their working employees and future recruits (Leekha Chhabra & Sharma, 2014).

The influence of employer brand is not only limited towards developing employee attitudes but it also influences the formation of a service brand and customer experience. Research shows that perceived employer branding strongly influences the shaping of employee attitudes, that includes employee satisfaction and corporate engagement and the research underlines the importance of having a strong employer brand to effectively influence (Schlager et al., 2011).

Research suggests that there exists a connection between employer branding and employee attitudes, especially in service brands. Employer Branding plays an important role in service management, affecting employee satisfaction, and engagement with the company and at the end, affects overall customer experience too. A good Employer Brand will not only provide the workforce with a more positive work environment but also will encourage employees to provide certain facilities to organizations. Perceived Employer Brand also seems to be a major factor that affects employee behaviour. The motives behind the perception of the organization's employer brand are economic value, diversity value, social value, brand value and promotional value. These motives contribute heavily to developing employee satisfaction and also create a sense of belonging (Schlager et al., 2011).

A strong employer brand nurtures a positive attitude among employees which ultimately affects customer experiences. Content employees would be more likely to go above and beyond for customers, encouraging positive interactions and building strong enduring customer relationships. A strong employee brand also builds a strong sense of the employee's identification with the company and it stills a sense of pride and ownership, ultimately motivating to them actively contribute to the company's overall success.

To effectively enhance and current employees, the organisation should focus on strengthening the company's development value, social value and diversity value. Development value includes providing training opportunities developing creativity and offering mentorship to facilitate professional growth. social value is concerned with cultivating a work environment that is supportive and inclusive, encouraging friendly relationships among colleagues and embracing a "people first" attitude. Strengthening diversity value involves being more inclusive, fostering a sense of belonging, and appreciating diverse perspectives. When we discuss essential elements of an employer brand important for attracting potential employees, two primary values come to the forefront, Social value and Reputation value. Social value places an important role in attracting employees, encouraging a positive work environment, and it helps in building stronger interpersonal connections. Organisations that prioritize a supportive and inclusive culture naturally become more appealing to potential employees. Reputation value, which is another crucial element in attracting potential employees, refers to the organization's overall recognition from the general public from the perspective of a job seeker. A company's reputation may include factors such as "well-known products", "good brand to have on one's résumé" and "good reputation of the company among friends". Research has indicated that current employees perceive merits in working with an organization that has a good reputation (Schlager et al., 2011).

To help in the creation of a strong employee brand, it is obvious that, a combination of strategies that aim at employee satisfaction and employee identification must be considered. For example, a research study suggests a strong relationship of social value with favourable employee satisfaction and identification. So, it would be reasonable for organizations to focus on expanding this dimension. The study also suggests that companies should also focus on development value and reputation value when creating their employer brand. It is not easy, but finding the right proportion of focus on these values will help the organization with the outcome they want to acheive (Schlager et al., 2011). It is crucial to note that these factors are not mutually exclusive, and companies should strive to create a comprehensive employer brand that encompasses both social value and reputation value. By doing so, companies can effectively attract and retain high-potential employees who are poised to contribute to the company's future success (Schlager et al., 2011).

Ensuring employee contentment holds a key position in shaping the employer brand's overall impact, delivering value to employees across various aspects. Schlager et al. (2011) highlight the significance of strategically focusing on specific value dimensions, namely development value, social value, and diversity value, as effective means to significantly boost employee satisfaction and identification. Taking proactive steps to influence employee satisfaction involves actions like providing training opportunities, nurturing creativity, offering mentorship, fostering a social culture that promotes friendly relationships among colleagues, and adopting a "people-first" approach.

The research emphasizes the substantial impact of a company's reputation on employee satisfaction. Companies with a positive reputation or well-known products are more likely to attract and retain satisfied employees. This underscores the crucial role of investing in building and sustaining a positive reputation to elevate overall employee satisfaction (Schlager et al., 2011).

With relevance to communicating their employer brand, the case of Cadbury employs a very unique strategic approach. According to Prasenjith Bhattacharya, Founder of the Great Place to Work Institute, organizations use many different ways to communicate their employer brand, and Cadbury stands out in this aspect with a distinctive method.

Cadbury reinforces its company values, mission, objectives as an employer, essentially their employer brand, with the help of an anthem they made inspired by 'chale chalo', a very popular Hindi song from the movie Lagaan. The anthem is used by Cadbury to capture the core of their work culture, having employees from all levels and departments in the video to show an inclusive image that stresses on unity and solidarity among different levels of the organization.

A point to focus on is that the process of creating the anthem involved an in-house team consisting of employees from various departments. This cooperative effort ensures that the anthem not only represents the current workforce but also reflects on the organization's evolving culture. As new employees join the workforce, the anthem is updated and refreshed annually to include these additions making it an excellent expression of the organization's image and values.

The strategy behind using the anthem goes beyond just using it to display internal workings. Cadbury plays the anthem at the end of all their conferences and meetings, thus reinforcing the organization's beliefs and values. This helps create an impactful and consistent experience for employees. By using this creative and appealing approach, Cadbury manages to not only communicate its employer brand but also reinforce it, making it a very important aspect of the organization's culture.

This example underlines the importance of using innovative and inclusive methods to effectively communicate the employer brand. Cadbury's strategy shows us that an anthem, used to represent the shared spirit of their employees, can be used as an excellent tool in communicating and reinforcing a positive employer brand. Strategies such as this help not only in strengthening internal cohesion but also helps to the external perception of the organization. This makes it a persuasive example of the relevance and impact of employer branding in today's corporate world (Kapoor, 2010).

A study by Schuler et al highlights the importance of a strong employer brand in the field of global talent management. For global companies, a strong employer brand is very important for helping in dealing with talent shortages and surpluses. It not only attracts high-calibre talent from all around the world but also makes it easier to place and relocate individuals into key roles. Adding more to this, a positive employer brand plays an important role in retaining the best employees by offering more career development opportunities and by encouraging a favourable work environment.

The approaches used to develop and promote the employer brand must align the employer brand with the overall values and strategies of the organization. Constant communication must be maintained and they should continuously asses and monitor the employee experience. Through these concerted efforts, multinational corporations can boost their ability to attract, retain, and nurture top-tier talent, ultimately strengthening their success in the global marketplace (Schuler et al., 2011).

Dimensions of Employer Branding

As mentioned in the previous sections, Employer Branding works as a strategic framework to help organizations attract and retain employees. In today's highly competitive job market, it is advantageous for an organization to be concerned with these strategies that might help them attract and retain high-calibre talent. To understand the conceptual framework of employer branding better, A study identified several dimensions of employer branding with respect to multiple research studies (Junça Silva & Dias, 2022). These are some the dimensions that were identified:

In the model given by Ambler and Barrow (1996), there are three dimensions (or benefits as mentioned in the study) concerned with employer branding:

Functional Benefits: Functional Benefits in this model concern the various responsibilities, programs and activities that are offered to employees to help foster their development. Employee benefits and opportunities for the professional development of employees are benefits that attract a candidate applying for a job. Organizations that provide these benefits are seen by candidates as places where they can work in roles with satisfactory employee benefits, and where they can develop their skills and continuously grow as an individual. Functional benefits also might include initiatives such as promoting work-life balance, flexible working hours and perks such as recreational facilities and daycare show that the the organiation is committed to the growth of the employee

Economic Benefits: Economic Benefits is concerned with material and monetary gains provided by the organization. This is a very crucial part of employer branding, obviously. Competitive salaries, bonuses and financial incentives highly influence an organization's attractiveness to an employee or a candidate. Candidates tend to gravitate towards organizations that not only recognize the effort they put into their work but also compensate them with monetary or material rewards that reflect their value as an employee.

Psychological Benefits: Psychological Benefits are concerned with the employee's feelings of purpose, direction and fulfilment at work. It also includes the employee's feelings of belongingness to the organization. Organizations that provide positive work environments, value employee engagement and employee satisfaction are seen as workplaces that offer high psychological benefits. Such organizations are attractive for employees that seek more than just employment but also fulfilling and meaningful experiences at work, where they are able to find personal and professional fulfillment.

Berthan et al (2005) expanded on the above model in their study, which expanded the three dimensions to five dimensions. The following are the dimensions of Berthan et al (2005) model:

Interest Value: is concerned with whether an organization's appeal is influenced by the creativity shown by employees, innovational practices at work, producing better products and creating a positive work environment. Basically this dimension is concerned with how attractive an organization is to it's potential employees (this aspect is derived from the dimension of psychological benefits as mentioned in Ambler and Barrow (1996)).

Social Value: looks into the role of interpersonal relationships and a healthy work environment in determining the attractiveness of an organization (this aspect is also derived from the dimension of psychological benefits as mentioned in Ambler and Barrow (1996)).

Economic Value: is concerned with the effect of job security, competitive salaries, and career growth opportunities on the attractiveness of a company to its potential employees (this aspect is derived from the dimension of economic benefits as mentioned in Ambler and Barrow (1996)).

Development Value: examines the role of professional career growth and recognition from the employer, that paves the way for future job oppurtunities, on the company's attractiveness (this aspect is derived from the dimension of functional benefits as mentioned in Ambler and Barrow (1996)).

Application Value: explores whether a company's attractiveness is influenced by the opportunities the employee has to share and apply their knowledge in a customer focused setting and opportunities they have to engage in altruistic actions (this aspect is also derived from the dimension of functional benefits as mentioned in Ambler and Barrow (1996)).

A thorough understanding and usage of these employer branding elements are crucial for organizations to attract potential employees in a highly competitive job market. With the strategic inclusion of psychological, economical and functional benefits into the process of developing their employer brand, organizations can be seen as places where high-calibre talent can find purpose, thrive and contribute meaningfully.

Strategies Associated With Creating a Positive Employer Brand

Creating a positive employer brand is a complex task that involves using a bunch of diverse strategies to attract and retain great talent. These strategies that are going to be mentioned below involve a spectrum of organizational practices and initiatives (Ahmed et al., 2022).

1.Offering Competitive Compensation and Benefits

Any employee looks for a job that's most beneficial to them and in a market full of competition, so providing employees with the most appealing benefits is very important for strengthening the employer brand.(Chhabra and Sharma, 2014) And this obviously goes beyond salaries and includes flexible benefits and oppurtunities for continuous growth and development. For example, Work-Life balance initiatives, flexible working hours, additional perks like daycare facilities or gym memberships can play a huge role in creating an attractive compensation package, showcasing the extensive commitment the organiation has, for the well-being and professional development of its employees.

2. Fostering a Positive Work Environment

One of the most important aspects of keeping an employee interested is to create a very positive and inclusive workspace. Cultivating a culture where employees feel valued, respected and supported can be hugely beneficial. There are a lot of ways companies can do this, a few of the most efficient ways is to promote teamwork, this could be done using activities that build team motivation and collaborative interests, also recognizing and rewarding employee achievements can go a long way. And as mentioned before, prioritizing employee well-being and satisfaction is also something that does a lot to contribute positively to employee branding (Deepa and Baral, 2019).

3. Communicating Organizational Values and Purpose

One major part of a job satisfaction is whether or not the employees values match the values of the organization. And it's found that effectively communicating the organization's mission, values and goals helps build employed branding in a lot of ways. For example, being transparent in conveying the company's culture and principles helps potential candidates understand its ethics and this attracts candidates aligned with these values and also promotes a sense of purpose and connection among existing employees. The organization can use various communication channels such as company websites, social media platforms, employee testimonials to properly articulate their values and purposes.

4. Implementing Effective Talent Management Practices

Vigorous talent management practices including, but not limited to spanning recruitment, onboarding, training and career development, demonstrates just how much the organization is committed to invest in its employees growth and success. This, no doubt contributes to a positive employer brand by attracting and retaining top talent (Minchington, 2010). A well structured process is like the first sign employees look in a company to assure themselves that this organization is dedicated to support their professional journey and is thus, one other main element.

5. Implementing Job Design Initiatives

The way jobs are structured is a key factor in influencing just how much an employee is likely to stay engaged. The way a job is set up is usually expelled through aspects like having certain skills. Clear task identity, meaningful tasks, autonomy and feedback. These are actually part of the job characteristics model (Hackman and Oldham, 1975). Although there might be studies that support the argument that job design has motivational aspects, there isnt enough proff that shows it directly leads to employee branding. However researchers have started considering it as a factor that influences both employee engagement and employer branding (Ashraf et al., 2018).

6. Building a Strong Corporate Reputation

A positive corporate reputation is very closely linked to employer branding. So, maintaining a good reputation by delivering promises, providing excellent customer services, and engaging in corporate social responsibility initiatives serves great. A strong corporate reputation not only enhances the organization's attractiveness to customers but also positively impacts the reputation of the employee outside which increases employer brand and is also likely to remain associated with the employer in the long run.

7. Tailoring Employer Branding to Target Audiences

Recognizing that there is a large diversity in preferences and priorities among different demographic groups is very important. Organizations should try to understand the specific needs and expectations of their target audience and they should construct their employer branding strategies in a way to cater to the right audience. This might include knowing what specific benefits and values to put in the spotlight, so that these features can resonate with the desired talent. The organizations should also try to make sure the employer brand is able to appeal to a diverse range of candidates.

Integrating all these strategies together contributes a lot to developing a strong positive employer brand. This makes the organization more efficient in attracting, engaging and retaining high-calibre talent.

Certain Challenges Associated With Employer Branding

The global market for jobs is a space that is dynamic and intricate, the space is also filled with built-in information imbalances. There is a lack of complete knowledge that exists between both potential employees and employers about each other's capabilities and qualities that only reveal itself after the start of the employment relationship. This lack of knowledge can cause a lot of significant challenges, especially in the form of adverse selection. Both employees and employers feel a need to find ways of addressing this information gap to benefit each other, given the lasting implications of employment contracts.

From the potential employee's perspective, the imbalance of information comes from the hidden or unobservable characteristics. This includes factors such as work climate, career development opportunities and overall employee satisfaction. Understanding that these indiscernible factors are very important to their employment experience, potential employees seek insights of their potential employers through various sources such as social media platforms, company websites, word-of-mouth and reviews from current employees.

Incomplete information or misconceptions about an organization can lead to potential employees associating more risks with the organization, which prompts them to explore alternate employer choices as less risky. On the other hand, actively managing the organization's employer brand becomes crucial, ensuring that it is accurate in mirroring the organization's positive qualities and is aligned with the expectations of the desired potential talent.

Recognizing the negative role that the imbalance of information can cause, employers are prompted to promote their competencies and qualities to the job market, with the employer brand playing a very important role in shaping potential employee perceptions. A strong employer brand would effectively communicate the organization's work culture, values, and commitment towards it's workforce, helping in the process of attracting and retaining desired talent by portraying a clearer and more authentic image of the organization

While most of the focus of employer branding centres on attracting potential employees, it is important to recognize that existing employees also perceive signals from the organization about its suitability as an employer. Brand signals can impact the attitudes and commitment of existing employees towards the employer. Dell et al. (2001) stress that the employer brand shapes the identity of the firm as an employer, encapsulating values, systems, policies, and behaviors directed at attracting, motivating, and retaining the workforce.

The purposeful design of an employer brand helps organizations in steering uncertainties and avoiding risks experienced by both future and existing employees. A strong employer brand not only attracts and retains high calibre talent but also helps in reducing turnover costs and is also helpful in enhancing employee productivity. Other than this, a positive employer brand adds to the organization's reputation and thus gaining positive attention from the media, which helps in promoting their appeal as an employer to future employees.

Employer brand equity, a concept that is increasingly being recognized by financial markets as a crucial factor that contributes towards the overall market value of an organization, is the area which is directly influenced by initiatives of employer branding on talent attraction and retention. In the employee context, brand equity refers to the effectiveness of brand knowledge on existing and potential employees in terms of their perception towards the organization or the job (Backhaus & Tikoo, 2004). This emphasises the increasingly important role of human resources in ascertaining the organization's success and overall value, underlining the strategic need of cultivating a positive and appealing employer image in the competitive job market.

Psychological Contract and Internal Marketing

In the area of employer branding, the concept of the psychological contract is considered to be very important for shaping an organization's unique employer brand and ensuring employee satisfaction. This contract involves the expectations and beliefs employees or future employees have regarding their agreement with the organization, including both explicitly written terms and implicit factors that influence the employee experience.

Employer branding depends heavily on the psychological contract as potential employees form expectations based on the organization's promoted brand. This includes various promises, goals and information that are conveyed through the organization's branding efforts. The fulfilment of these expectations is crucial to shaping the work experience for the organization's current employees.

The content of the psychological contract covers all of the organization's promises and the employee's expectations and helps develop the unique nature of the employment relationship within the organization. It has a significant role in making the organization's employment brand stand out and shaping the perception of the employee in terms of the organization's identity, values and principles.

Effectively trying to integrate the psychological contract into the employer brand requires the organizations to make sure that their branding efforts present the organization's values, cultures and employment offerings authentically. This involves genuinely representing the organization's core characteristics to both current and potential employees. Furthermore, organizations should prioritize the creation of a supportive employment experience, ensuring impartial reward distribution and fair treatment to enhance employee alignment with the employer brand.

Using the psychological contract as a framework equips organizations to manage and understand employee experiences and expectations. Associating the employer brand with the psychological contract enables the creation of an attractive and positive work experience that appeals to both potential recruits and existing employees.

Internal Marketing (IM) has become a highly relevant strategy in the service industry, closely related to employer branding. It recognizes the necessary role of employees in delivering excellent service consistently. IM includes treating employees as internal customers to promote satisfaction, ultimately moving towards a more market-oriented, sales-focused and customer-conscious environment.

The roots of IM can be traced all the way back over to two decades ago when it was initially proposed to guarantee the consistent delivery of high-quality service. Over time, it has developed into a strategic tool that is not only meant to meet but also surpass customer expectations. Various research scholars like Varey and Lewis, Mudie, Papasolomou-Doukakis, and Lings have made influential contributions to the literature, underlining the growing importance of IM in molding organizational dynamics. This development underlines the shift towards the viewing of employees as integral to achieving and exceeding customer satisfaction.

Different interpretations of Internal Marketing (IM) have come into view, all of them revolving around the central idea of treating employees as internal customers. One definition suggests that IM helps as a mechanism to inspire employees towards a service-oriented mindset along with customer-focused behaviours, using an active, marketing-like approach. Another definition explains IM as an organizational marketing activity that guides the employee's attention towards internal changes that would ultimately lead to improving external marketplace performance. A more comprehensive definition defines IM as a planned effort that uses a marketing-like strategy to overcome aversion to organizational change, aiming to coordinate, motivate and align employees for the effective application of functional and corporate strategies. This enables customer satisfaction to grow through the development of motivated and customer-oriented employees.

At the heart of IM is the concept of regarding employees as "internal customers". This perspective is rooted in the belief that by meeting the needs of internal customers, and the employees, a company is better equipped to provide the desired quality to external customers. This reasoning implies that the idea of meeting employee needs increases their motivation and retention, ultimately contributing to higher levels of employee satisfaction, an important factor in achieving external customer satisfaction and retention.

The main goal of IM is to establish a workspace that motivates and inspires employees to be customer-focused and service-oriented. We can do this by executing internal activities that are similar to marketing strategies. Through a calculated and intentional approach, IM foceses on internal processes that need to adjust to improve the company's overall performance in the external marketplace.

IM focuses mainly on three key areas: social, development and diversity value. Development value is concerned with the area of fostering creativity, offering training and providing opportunities as well as mentorships to support the employee's professional growth. Social value highlights the importance of building inclusive and friendly work environments that foster positive interpersonal relationships among employees. Diversity value deals with promoting inclusivity, fostering a sense of belonging and integrating diverse perspectives.

According to Papasolomou & Vrontis, an effective IM approach plays an important role in satisfying and motivating employees, and this in turn contributes to the development of interactive marketing and corporate branding. This relation is particularly important in the service industry, where the quality of employee-customer interaction significantly influences the delivery of high-quality services and customer satisfaction.

In the context of service transactions, positive results depend on the quality of interactions between the service deliverers and customers. Effective buyer-seller interaction is a key factor for achieving satisfactory service transactions. When the interaction is effective, it contributes to the customer being satisfied with the transaction which also helps retain the customers.

Research suggests that successful service organizations have a competitive advantage with their customers, partly due to the competitive edge they have with their employees. These organizations strategically invest in their employees' success on the job, prioritizing satisfaction and motivation through IM to create a positive work environment that fosters a strong relationship between the employees and the employer.

Investing in employees' on-the-job success includes various factors, such as mentorship opportunities, training programs, and developing a work culture that values and recognizes employees. When employees feel valued and supported, they are more likely to use a customer-centric approach in their interactions. This customer-centric approach plays a key role in creating a competitive advantage in the service industry (Papasolomou & Vrontis, 2006).

Internal Marketing has become an integral part of the service industry, focusing on the importance of treating employees as internal customers. This strategy aims to create a work environment that is not only concerned with the needs of the internal workforce but is also concerned with aligning them with the organization's goals, ultimately leading to better customer satisfaction and retention. As organizations increasingly recognize the importance of IM, it continues to develop as an integral part of modern service management (Papasolomou & Vrontis, 2006).

Internal Marketing Strategies

Effectively making use of Internal Marketing principles in organizational practices is important for increasing employee satisfaction and optimizing overall performance. The following are a few IM strategies through which a few key managerial inferences can be made (Rafiq & Ahmed, 2000):

Strategic communication: Managers must prioritize clearly and frequently conveying organizational and marketing strategies to ensure that employees understand their roles in implementing strategies and achieving objectives. Supportive senior management is important for IM initiatives, recognizing their significance and fostering inter-functional coordination (Zeithaml et al., 1988).

Job Design and Satisfaction: Treating jobs as products would also involve designing them with features that future or current employees will value. Focusing on job satisfaction is also important for attracting and retaining top talent. Marketing and human resource managers should collaboratively design detailed job specifications, especially for roles that would include customer interactions.

Recruitment Practices and Training: Recruitment practices should aim at attracting individuals who have the right attitudes and are aligned with the organization's customer-oriented and sales-minded focus. Investing in training is also essential to equip employees with the skill necessary to effectively meet organizational and customer needs. Research suggests that training based on specific job requirements reduces role ambiguity and increases job satisfaction.

Managing Customer-Employee Interactions: In service marketing, managing customer-contact employees and moments of truth during interactions is crucial for the smoother functioning of the sales transaction. This involves training employees to be more customer-oriented and sales-minded. Also adopting a participative style of management and allowing a level of discretion to frontline employees is needed to meet customer expectations while maintaining flexibility.

Inculcating Customer Orientation Throughout the Organization: Customer Orientation should extend throughout all levels of the organization, especially among customer-contact employees. This kind of approach is beneficial towards achieving customer satisfaction and the goals of the organization. Customer orientation is a skill that should be embodied in even part-time marketers and those involved in relationship marketing along with those involved in delivering products or services.

Marketing- Like Approach to Motivation: It is encouraged for managers to adopt a marketing like approach to developing employee motivation and inter-functional coordination. Human Resource strategies that are traditionally used may fall short on this context. Organizations, by integarting marketing techniques, can better associate internal practices with the external market scene. It is essential though to adapt and assess these techniques carefully to the market.

It is essential for managers to create a workplace culture that mirrors the external market scene that helps promote employee satisfaction and ultimately the organization's success by prioritizing the above-mentioned aspects and recognizing the need for a marketing-like approach to strategies used internally (Rafiq & Ahmed, 2000).

The Effect of Employee Attitudes on Brand Differentiation

Present research has consistently shown that having satisfied and engaged employees is important to make sure that there is a consistently positive service experience, especially in markets where service quality is usually lacking. While a positive service attitude is definitely a key factor, there is an important question that arises: does the impact of employees on brand differentiation go beyond being just positive? There is a lot of strong evidence that suggests that employees are very important in establishing a more long-lasting service brand image, that reaches into the emotional values connected with a unique service style.

The general agreement is that it is harder for competitors to replicate the abstract aspects of a brand, which includes emotional values that are tied to a unique service style, compared to the operational characteristics of a service brand experience. Even though operational differentiation is still very important for gaining a competitive edge, the time used by competitors to replicate the aspects which make a brand distinct has become shorter. For example, Innovative operating models, like EasyJet in the airline business, eventually will face competition from other rival airlines like Ryan Air too.

A thorough study of successful service brands shows that they consistently focus on the role of their employees in providing a distinct brand experience. Major service brands highlight the importance of their employees creating a memorable and unique brand experience. A good example of this would be Starbucks, where the effort put in by Starbucks employees is considered to be important in encouraging an emotional bond that loyal customers develop. The study on the 'Starbucks Experience' by Joseph Michelli focuses on the complex details and emotional connections that contribute to customer loyalty, and also acknowledges the personal investment made by Starbuck employees.

This emphasis on the pivotal role of employees is not unique to Starbucks. Howard Schultz, Starbucks' founder, consistently emphasizes that the most crucial component of their brand is the employee—the individuals contributing to creating the magic and the overall experience. Similar instances of the indispensable role of employees in brand creation are evident in various case studies, as reported in 'Corporate Religion,' 'Living the Brand,' and 'Uncommon Practice.' Together, these examples underscore that employees not only play a central role in delivering positive service but also in shaping the emotional values and distinctive style that set successful service brands apart in the marketplace (Mosley, 2007).

The Importance of the Employer's Symbolic Image

There has been a lot of new research in the field that highlights just how crucial an employee's symbolic brand image is, in shaping the organization's identity and influencing the employee's perceptions. This concept which is rooted in Aaker's model of brand personality includes dimensions like sincerity, ruggedness, competence, excitement, and sophistication. Historically resembling brand personality scales which are used in consumer branding, measurements of the symbolic brand image that the employer creates have evolved to focus on two primary domains: organizational warmth and competence.

The warmth domain covers qualities such as trustworthiness, honesty, friendliness, ethics and social responsibility. And on the other hand, the competence domain covers traits like reliability, flourishment, and achievement orientation. Studies also reveal diverse perceptions of organizational warmth and competence, challenging the usual thinking that is associated with non profit organizations with more warmth but less competence, whereas business organizations are usually viewed as competent but less warm.

A thorough study done by Davies et al. in 2008 delves into the connection between how employers are perceived symbolically and how satisfied and engaged employees feel. The study shows that an employer's symbolic image significantly influences employee engagement through satisfaction, emphasizing the crucial role of this mediating factor. Additionally, this impact even expands to various other outcomes for organizations that include emotional connections, differentiation and return on investment within other indirect effects (Davies, 2008).

The study also highlights how important the symbolic image of an employer is, especially when companies try to stand out and keep their employees. In cases where things like pay and job security does not provide a lot of distinction, an employer's brand image becomes a really important tool that helps shape perceptions and promotes engagement. The warmth and competence aspects not only helps attract employees but it also predicts their satisfaction. Highlighting the need for organizations to efficiently balance these qualities.

So all in all, the symbolic image of an employer is a very important part of an organization's success and differentiation in a competitive environment. And this goes beyond traditional metrics and offers a detailed understanding of how warmth and competence helps create a unique identity. And as organizations struggle to find and retain talented employees, the strategy of managing their symbolic image becomes a major factor in promoting a positive environment that influences employees attitudes that at the end of the day, contribute to the overall success of the organization (Wisker, 2022).

Challenges Faced

Employer branding comes with a lot of challenges that needs to be very carefully navigated by organizations so they can successfully attract and retain their top tier talent. And these challenges can be widely classified into three primary areas: differentiation, authenticity and communication.

Standing Out (Differentiation)

In today's super competitive job market, there's a major challenge for employer branding and it is, organization's need to be different from their competitors. And to attract top talent, companies don't have to just stand out but also offer something unique. Now clearly expressing the organization's culture, values and work experience is very important but many organizations struggle to effectively convey their special strengths to potential recruits. And without a clearly defined strategy in this regard, organizations run the risk of blending in with other employers and end up missing opportunities to attract the most fitting candidates that they need.

So to overcome this challenge of differentiation, organizations should carry out a detailed analysis of their external and internal environment. And this requires a deep understanding of the organization's culture, values and work experience. And this should be done while also assessing the very competitive market and while properly understanding potential recruits' expectations. Pinpointing what sets the organization apart can help create a very strong employer brand that highlights their unique qualities which then attracts candidates who actually resonate with the organization's culture and values (Gilani & Cunningham, 2017).

Authenticity

Making sure of an authentic portrayal of the organization's work experience is one other super important challenge in employer branding. In the age where future employees are paying more attention to general marketing messages, the demand for genuinity and transparency in employer branding has risen. Any sort of misalignment between the actual experience of an employee and the employer brand can lead to dissatisfaction and that could potentially damage the entire reputation of the organization.

So to address this authenticity challenge, organizations need to make sure that their employer brand genuinely reflects the actual reality of the employment experience. And this again requires a good understanding of the organization's values, cultures and practices. And it's better when its paired with ongoing monitoring of the experience of current employees. Organizations should focus on creating a positive work environment that actually aligns with what the employer branding promises. Also regular communication and feedback from the employees are very helpful to identify and address the gaps between the branding and the experience, and this helps make necessary adjustments to maintain said authenticity. (Gilani & Cunningham, 2017).

Effective Communication

Effective communication plays a huge role in successful employer branding but the problem is reaching and engaging with the target audience. Organizations should plan a very comprehensive strategy to convey their employer brand in an effective way through multiple channels like social media, job advertisements, career websites and employee testimonials. Crafting powerful and consistent messages that resonates with potential recruits, is a challenge that has been persistent everywhere. To add to that, there are big difficulties in reaching the target audience and standing out in the market too.

To overcome these communication challenges, organizations should make strategic investments in research and market analysis to gain a deeper understanding of their target audience. Tailoring communication strategies accordingly and leveraging technology and social media can prove instrumental in helping organizations reach a broader audience. Consistently communicating the employer brand and showcasing unique attributes will enable organizations to effectively attract and engage top talent (Gilani & Cunningham, 2017).

In a study by Mosley (2007), it was noted that a common flaw in Internal Marketing (IM), internal branding, and more recently, employer branding lies in overemphasizing the communication of brand promises, neglecting the effective management of the long-term employee experience. To tackle this issue, organizations are now adopting a similar approach seen in managing the customer brand experience. The understanding is that ensuring a consistent on-brand service experience goes beyond managing communication channels; it involves overseeing every significant operational and interpersonal interaction with the customer.

Understanding that being an employee is more complicated than just being a customer, more and more companies are realizing the importance of taking a thorough approach to how they manage their employees. Managing employees involves a bunch of different processes and things provided by HR, like training sessions, meetings, and feedback sessions – we call these "employee touchpoints."

Think of it like walking through a hallway with different doors representing each of these touchpoints. These touch-points happen at different times, from when someone first applies for a job, to when they start working, to when they receive feedback on their performance.

And just like how companies have a path for customers to follow, they also have a path for employees – we call this the "employee journey." This journey includes everything from how people are hired and trained, to how they're supported by departments like HR and facilities management, to how they're recognized and developed in their roles. Additionally, some certain values and skills guide how employees and managers interact every day. These are like the unwritten rules of the company, helping everyone know what's expected of them and how they should act.

So, in simpler terms, companies are realizing they need to treat their employees well by having organized processes in place and making sure everyone knows what they should be doing and how they should be doing it.

Employer Attractiveness Scale (EmpAt)

Due to the nature of today's competitive corporate landscape, Companies have recognized that human resources have developed way beyond their traditional role and one such area where there are changes seen is the aspect of creating and maintaining the employer brand. The organization's image is influenced by factors like company culture, work environment, values and career advancement opportunities. Companies now find themselves with the need to understand what makes them attractive to employees to gain a competitive edge in the global market. The Employer Attractiveness (EmpAt) scale is an efficient tool for this. This scale helps measure the following aspects:

Work-Life Balance: Organizations, recognizing the importance placed by the employees on the balance between their work and personal life, can stand out from the other companies by promoting flexibility and a positive work-life culture

Company Culture and Values: The company values and work culture matter a lot, as the alignment between the employee's values and the organization's values develops a sense of belonging and engagement.

Company Reputation: A good reputation based on the brand's recognizability, the company's standing in the industry, and ethical practices will develop the organization's appeal to potential employees.

Compensation and Benefits: Competitive salary packages and other such benefits play a key role in attracting and retaining employees.

Career Development Opportunities: To retain ambitious high-calibre employees, providing opportunities for professional growth, training and development in job-related skills.

Tools like EmpAt provide organizations with valuable insights to refine and strengthen their employer branding strategies (Berthon et al., 2005). In a world where attracting and retaining talent is a race, understanding these dimensions is key to staying ahead of the competition.

REFERENCES

Ahmed, R. R., Azam, M., Qureshi, J. A., & Hashem, E. (2022). The Relationship Between Internal Employer Branding and Talent Retention: A Theoretical Investigation for the Development of a Conceptual Framework. *Frontiers in Psychology*, *13*, 859614. doi:10.3389/fpsyg.2022.859614 PMID:35369242

Ambler, T., & Barrow, S. (1996, December). The employer brand. *Journal of Brand Management*, *4*(3), 185–206. doi:10.1057/bm.1996.42

Backhaus, K., & Tikoo, S. (2004, August). Conceptualizing and researching employer branding. *Career Development International*, *9*(5), 501–517. doi:10.1108/13620430410550754

Berthon, P., Ewing, M., & Hah, L. L. (2005, January). Captivating company: Dimensions of attractiveness in employer branding. *International Journal of Advertising, 24*(2), 151–172. doi:10.1080/026504 87.2005.11072912

Davies, G. (2008, May 30). Employer branding and its influence on managers. *European Journal of Marketing, 42*(5/6), 667–681. doi:10.1108/03090560810862570

Dell, D., Ainspan, N., Bodenberg, T., Troy, K., & Hickey, J. (2001). *Engaging employees through your brand* (Research Report 1288-01-RR). New York: The Conference Board.

Edwards, M. R. (2009). An integrative review of employer branding and OB theory. *Personnel Review, 39*(1), 5–23. doi:10.1108/00483481011012809

Gilani, H., & Cunningham, L. (2017). Employer branding and its influence on employee retention: A literature review. *The Marketing Review, 17*(2), 239–256. doi:10.1362/146934717X14909733966209

Kapoor, V. (2010). Employer Branding: A Study of Its Relevance in India. *IUP Journal of Brand Management, 7.*

Leekha Chhabra, N., & Sharma, S. (2014, March 4). Employer branding: Strategy for improving employer attractiveness. *The International Journal of Organizational Analysis, 22*(1), 48–60. doi:10.1108/ IJOA-09-2011-0513

Mosley, R. W. (2007, October 9). Customer experience, organisational culture and the employer brand. *Journal of Brand Management, 15*(2), 123–134. doi:10.1057/palgrave.bm.2550124

Papasolomou, I., & Vrontis, D. (2006, September). Using internal marketing to ignite the corporate brand: The case of the UK retail bank industry. *Journal of Brand Management, 14*(1–2), 177–195. doi:10.1057/palgrave.bm.2550059

Rafiq, M., & Ahmed, P. K. (2000, November 1). Advances in the internal marketing concept: Definition, synthesis and extension. *Journal of Services Marketing, 14*(6), 449–462. doi:10.1108/08876040010347589

Schlager, T., Bodderas, M., Maas, P., & Luc Cachelin, J. (2011, October 11). The influence of the employer brand on employee attitudes relevant for service branding: An empirical investigation. *Journal of Services Marketing, 25*(7), 497–508. doi:10.1108/08876041111173624

Schuler, R. S., Jackson, S. E., & Tarique, I. (2011, October). Global talent management and global talent challenges: Strategic opportunities for IHRM. *Journal of World Business, 46*(4), 506–516. doi:10.1016/j. jwb.2010.10.011

Silva, A. J., & Dias, H. (2022). The relationship between employer branding, corporate reputation and intention to apply to a job offer. *The International Journal of Organizational Analysis, 31*(8), 1–16. doi:10.1108/IJOA-01-2022-3129

Turban, D. B., Forret, M. L., & Hendrickson, C. L. (1998, February). Applicant Attraction to Firms: Influences of Organization Reputation, Job and Organizational Attributes, and Recruiter Behaviors. *Journal of Vocational Behavior, 52*(1), 24–44. doi:10.1006/jvbe.1996.1555

Wells, C., Malik, R. F., & Edmondson, V. C. (2021). The Influence of Diversity Climate on Employer Branding: 2020 and Beyond. *IUP Journal of Brand Management, 18*(1).

Wisker, Z. L. (2022, November 25). Managing Employee-Based Brand Equity and Firm Performance in the Hospitality Industry: The Role of an Employer's Symbolic Brand Image and Work Environment. *Proceedings: 2021 ITP Research Symposium.* 10.34074/proc.2205019

Zeithaml, V. A., Rajan Varadarajan, P., & Zeithaml, C. P. (1988, July 1). The Contingency Approach: Its Foundations and Relevance to Theory Building and Research in Marketing. *European Journal of Marketing, 22*(7), 37–64. doi:10.1108/EUM0000000005291

Chapter 12
Fostering Diversity and Inclusion for Global Talent Acquisition and Retention

Surjit Singha

https://orcid.org/0000-0002-5730-8677

Kristu Jayanti College (Autonomous), India

ABSTRACT

This chapter explores the vital significance of attracting and keeping global talent, emphasizing the critical role of diversity and inclusion. It looks at various approaches for creating an inclusive workplace, implementing efficient diversity training initiatives, and using technology to improve talent management procedures. The ability to draw in and hold on to global talent is essential for organizational success in the intensely competitive business market. Businesses can attract and retain people from diversified backgrounds by putting a high priority on diversity and inclusion. Teams must adopt these ideas as core beliefs to promote creativity and long-term success. Remaining competitive requires leveraging technology innovations and adjusting to changing labour market conditions. Creating inclusive work environments and leveraging technology to encourage diversity and personal development will be essential for drawing and retaining talent in the future. Businesses can thrive globally by putting these principles first and using innovative strategies.

INTRODUCTION

Organizations increasingly recognize the critical importance of talent acquisition and retention for their overall achievement amidst the ever-changing business environment characterized by globalization, technological progress, and shifting consumer inclinations. As the global community becomes more interconnected, organizations are increasingly obligated to hire a more comprehensive range of candidates, regardless of their origin, ethnicity, gender, or other demographic characteristics, to secure the most talented and intelligent individuals. Promoting diversity and inclusion has become a critical strategic requirement for organizations aiming to succeed in the highly competitive marketplace of the

DOI: 10.4018/979-8-3693-1938-3.ch012

twenty-first century (Coles, 2021). The present chapter explores the significant sub-theme of diversity and inclusion in the context of global talent management. This study investigates how organizations can leverage diversity to stimulate innovation, cultivate creativity, and promote an inclusive culture that attracts and retains highly skilled individuals worldwide. By analyzing paradigm shifts and concrete instances from the real world, we aim to illuminate the critical need for organizations to seamlessly incorporate diversity and inclusion into their talent strategies. The business rationale for diversity and inclusion has grown substantially in prominence recently. Research consistently indicates that diverse teams are more profitable, innovative, and equipped to solve complex problems. Furthermore, given the continuous expansion of the global marketplace, organizations must maintain a workforce that mirrors the diversity of their clientele to gain a competitive advantage and bolster their brand image. In addition to financial factors, organizations have a moral responsibility to foster inclusive environments that respect, appreciate, and enable all members to share their distinct viewpoints and abilities (Morley, 2018).

More than simply employing personnel from various backgrounds is required to achieve genuine diversity and inclusion. Dismantling systemic barriers, confronting unconscious biases, and fostering an environment that provides equal opportunities for development and advancement necessitate a collective endeavour. A dedication to diversity and inclusion should permeate each stage of the talent management lifecycle, including hiring and recruitment procedures, employee development, and leadership training (Harris & Foster, 2010). This chapter explores how organizations can adopt various initiatives and strategies to promote diversity and inclusion at each phase of the employee lifecycle. There are numerous strategies that organizations can employ to foster a more inclusive workplace culture, including the establishment of affinity groups, the implementation of inclusive recruitment practices, the provision of cultural competency training, and the promotion of diverse leadership representation. By advocating for diversity and inclusion as fundamental principles and integrating them into the structure of their corporate identity, businesses can attract highly skilled individuals and maximize their staff's capabilities. In the contemporary era of globalization, achieving successful talent procurement and retention requires an unwavering commitment to diversity and inclusion. Organizations can enhance their prospects for sustained success in an ever more interconnected and diverse global landscape by cultivating an inclusive culture that recognizes and appreciates the value of each individual and views diversity as a valuable asset. Using cooperative endeavours and an unwavering dedication to ongoing enhancement, it is possible to establish work environments conducive to diversity, innovation, and realizing individuals' utmost capabilities.

The contemporary corporate environment, characterized by globalization and technical progress, has made talent acquisition and retention vital to company success. The global community's interconnectedness puts more and more pressure on enterprises to diversify their workforce to access a wider talent pool. Diversity and inclusion have become strategic imperatives for an organization to stay innovative and competitive.

The study's theoretical framework includes ideas related to organizational behaviour, talent acquisition, and diversity management. Critical theories include the Resource-Based View, which emphasizes the strategic significance of human capital in organizational success, and Social Identity Theory, which clarifies how people identify with and relate to social groups.

The main ideas of the conceptual framework are organizational performance, talent management, diversity, and inclusion. It considers how corporate culture, practices, and policies affect diversity and inclusion initiatives, which in turn affect the results of hiring and retaining talent. This study aims to investigate the value of diversity and inclusion in international talent management and methods for using diversity to promote inclusive workplace environments, innovation, and creativity.

This study's main topic is the role of inclusion and diversity in talent management in a global setting. It looks at different programs and tactics businesses use to support inclusion and diversity at every hiring, training, and leadership stage.

This study's primary research question is: How can businesses successfully include diversity and inclusion into their talent management plans to attract and keep highly qualified workers in the global economy? This investigation focuses on four main objectives. In the first place, it seeks to examine the importance of diversity and inclusion in the context of global talent management, realizing that these factors are critical to the competitiveness and success of organizations in today's linked world. Second, it probes into companies' many tactics to promote inclusion and diversity at various phases of the employee lifecycle, such as hiring, training, and leadership. Thirdly, the study aims to assess the concrete effects of diversity and inclusion programs on employee satisfaction and organizational performance measures, offering insights into how well these initiatives work to promote beneficial results. Finally, it summarises best practices and provides valuable advice for businesses looking to strengthen their efforts to promote diversity and inclusion in talent management procedures. This will help to foster inclusive workplace cultures that foster creativity, expansion, and long-term success.

UNDERSTANDING DIVERSITY AND INCLUSION

Diversity and inclusion are intricate notions that transcend the simple act of representing various demographic groups within an organizational setting. They comprise an extensive range of viewpoints, life experiences, and social identities, all contributing to developing a dynamic and culturally diverse workplace. Fundamentally, diversity pertains to variations among persons, including age, disability, race, ethnicity, gender, sexual orientation, and socioeconomic status. On the contrary, inclusion relates to the degree to which every member of the organization, irrespective of their personal history or identity, is esteemed, treated with regard, and granted the authority to engage deeply in the prevailing culture (Garelnabi et al., 2022). Diversity comprises the entire spectrum of human distinctions, including both apparent and imperceptible qualities that influence the identities and experiences of individuals. Race, ethnicity, gender, sexual orientation, age, disability, religion, nationality, socioeconomic status, educational background, and other such variables are among those that may contribute to these distinctions. In contrast, inclusion involves establishing a setting where each person is valued, respected, and recognized as an asset due to their unique contributions. The process entails cultivating a feeling of inclusion and empowerment for every individual within the institution, irrespective of their personal history or sense of self (Swartz et al., 2019).

The advantages of diversity and inclusion for organizations transcend ethical considerations and manifest in measurable improvements to organizational performance, creativity, innovation, and problem-solving. Organizations can access a more excellent reservoir of ideas and insights—and consequently, generate more innovative solutions and improve their decision-making processes—by convening individuals who possess a variety of experiences, perspectives, and areas of expertise. Furthermore, diverse teams with an enhanced capacity to comprehend and address the requirements of a wide range of clientele increase customer loyalty and contentment (Judd & McKinnon, 2021). Furthermore, the promotion of an inclusive culture has the potential to enhance employee engagement, morale, and productivity. Employees are more inclined to exhibit high work engagement and dedication to the organization's objectives when they perceive themselves as being esteemed and acknowledged for being true to themselves. Inclusive environments encourage trust and collaboration among team members, leading to increased innovation and cooperation (Swartz et al., 2019). Organizations with diverse leadership teams are more effectively positioned to comprehend and address the requirements of various markets; this results in enhanced market share and competitiveness.

Furthermore, organizations that commit to social responsibility and inclusiveness should embrace diversity and inclusion initiatives to strengthen customer loyalty and brand reputation (Gürlek et al., 2017). Organizations must comprehensively comprehend diversity and inclusion to flourish in today's globalized and intricate environment. Organizations can achieve sustainable success and maximize the capabilities of their workforce by cultivating inclusive environments that affirm the worth and agency of every individual and recognizing diversity as a valuable asset.

GLOBAL BEST PRACTICES IN TALENT ACQUISITION

In the contemporary era of globalization, talent acquisition necessitates a strategic methodology that surpasses conventional recruitment techniques. It is imperative for organizations to proactively pursue a wide range of candidates and enforce employment procedures that are inclusive and devoid of prejudice. It undertakes an examination of international standards for acquiring talent, with a particular emphasis on strategies for recruiting for diversity, conducting inclusive interviews and selection procedures, and mitigating biases during the employment process (Coles, 2021). Organizations must implement proactive recruitment strategies that reach a large population of candidates from various demographics and backgrounds to construct diverse teams. It may involve leveraging technology to get candidates from underrepresented groups, forming partnerships with diversity-focused organizations and institutions, and conducting targeted outreach to diverse communities. Organizations may also establish metrics and objectives for diversity to monitor their progress and ensure they hold themselves accountable for constructing inclusive workforces (Rosales et al., 2022). Establishing an interviewing and selection procedure that includes affording every candidate an equitable chance to demonstrate their qualifications and skills is critical. It entails training recruiting managers and interviewers on techniques to recognize and mitigate unconscious bias, implementing structured interview formats that utilize standardized questions, and forming diverse interview panels to diminish the impact of personal biases. Furthermore, to concentrate exclusively on qualifications and experience, organizations may employ blind resume screening methods that eliminate identifying details, including names, genders, and ethnicities, during the preliminary phases of the screening process.

Unconscious biases can potentially impact recruiting decisions, thereby contributing to the maintenance of organizational homogeneity. To surmount recruiting biases, organizations must initially recognize their presence and proactively strive to alleviate their consequences. It may incorporate integrating objective criteria and assessments into decision-making processes, conducting routine audits of recruiting processes to detect and rectify bias hotspots, and implementing diversity training programs for hiring managers and employees. Furthermore, to mitigate the influence of personal biases and promote impartial results, organizations may choose to implement collaborative decision-making processes and establish hiring committees that reflect diversity (Bendick & Nunes, 2012). Organizations can cultivate inclusive and diverse teams that mirror the multifaceted array of human experiences and viewpoints by adopting these worldwide standards in talent acquisition. Organizations can enhance their workforce's capabilities and achieve long-term success in the current competitive environment by recognizing diversity as a valuable asset and cultivating inclusive work environments that respect and value every individual.

BUILDING AN INCLUSIVE WORKPLACE CULTURE

It is critical for nurturing diversity, encouraging employee engagement, and propelling organizational success to establish an inclusive workplace culture. Fostering an atmosphere that recognizes, appreciates, and enables members to share their distinct abilities and perspectives necessitates a collaborative effort from leadership, management, and staff across all hierarchical levels. It examines approaches to establishing an all-encompassing organizational climate, such as fostering a sense of community and belonging, advocating for inclusive approaches to leadership and management, and capitalizing on employee resource groups and affinity networks (Tagliaro et al., 2023). A culture of belonging is distinguished by an atmosphere where everyone is esteemed, accepted, and welcomed for uniqueness. Promoting open communication, empathy, and reciprocal respect among its workforce nurtures a sense of belonging within an organization. It may entail adopting inclusive policies and practices that cater to diverse groups' concerns and requirements, providing platforms for employees to exchange their insights and experiences, and recognizing and appreciating the distinctive contributions made by individuals from various backgrounds. In addition, organizations can cultivate a sense of community and belonging by providing opportunities for employees to develop relationships in person and virtually (Barnes et al., 2023).

It is vital to have inclusive leadership to foster an environment where diversity and inclusion flourish. Leaders and managers are critical in establishing the organization's atmosphere, exemplifying inclusive conduct, and advocating for diversity. It requires employers to provide feedback, actively listen to diverse viewpoints, and take proactive measures to rectify systemic obstacles and prejudices (Fujimoto & Uddin, 2021). In addition to prioritizing diversity and inclusion in decision-making, inclusive leaders ensure that every voice is acknowledged and considered. By establishing a culture that promotes respect and inclusion and as a model for others to emulate, leaders can cultivate an atmosphere of collaboration and fairness among staff members (Barnes et al., 2023). Employee affinity networks and employee resource groups (ERGs) are grassroots initiatives that unite personnel who share commonalities regarding identity, experiences, or interests. The purpose of these groups is to provide mutual support, advocate for organizational change, and foster diversity and inclusion. ERGs furnish a forum wherein personnel can establish connections, exchange experiences, and cooperate regarding endeavours that tackle the issues and requirements of heterogeneous groups.

Additionally, they provide leadership and management with a valuable resource to obtain insights into the experiences and perspectives of various employee populations. Organizations exhibit their dedication to diversity and inclusion and enable employees to effectuate constructive transformations in the work environment by endorsing ERGs and affinity networks (Byrd, 2022). Establishing an inclusive work environment necessitates deliberate endeavour and dedication from every institution member. Organizations can cultivate an atmosphere conducive to diversity, innovation, and individual growth by establishing a sense of community, advocating for inclusive leadership and management approaches, and utilizing employee resource groups and affinity networks. By fostering collaboration and a mutual dedication to ongoing enhancement, it is possible to establish work environments that are inclusive, empowering, and welcoming to all.

DIVERSITY AND INCLUSION TRAINING AND DEVELOPMENT

Implementing successful diversity and inclusion training and development programs is of the utmost importance to increase organizational awareness, cultivate comprehension, and encourage behaviour modification. Organizations can develop a fair and hospitable work environment by equipping leaders and employees with the knowledge, abilities, and resources to navigate diverse environments and promote inclusive practices effectively (Judd & McKinnon, 2021). It examines fundamental elements of training and development about diversity and inclusion. These elements include mentorship and sponsorship initiatives, inclusive leadership development programs, and diversity training programs. The primary objectives of diversity training programs are to foster inclusive behaviours, challenge biases, and heighten employees' consciousness regarding diversity-related matters across all organizational levels (Kuknor & Kumar, 2023; Roberson et al., 2013). These programs may address fostering inclusive work environments, implicit bias, cultural competence, and power and privilege dynamics. In addition to increasing participants' awareness, effective diversity training equips them with practical abilities and resources to identify and address bias, encourage candid discussions, and advocate for diversity and inclusion in their day-to-day engagements. Organizations can enhance employee inclusivity and foster a more progressive work environment by implementing continuous and comprehensive diversity training programs (Cox, 2022). In all of this, one of the most important things to keep in mind is stress. It has been discovered that stress, resilience, and healthy cognitive performance are all related (Singha, 2024). While analyzing key aspects of training and development associated with diversity and inclusion, it is of the utmost importance to consider the influence that stress and resilience have on the proper functioning of the cognitive system. The levels of stress that an individual is experiencing have been shown to correlate with their cognitive function, with increased stress levels frequently resulting in poorer cognitive capacities. Consequently, in the context of diversity training programs that are designed to encourage inclusive behaviours and challenge biases, it is absolutely necessary for businesses to address the possible stressors linked with these activities. Organizations can increase the success of diversity training programs by implementing methods that reduce stress and promote resilience among participants. These tactics include the provision of suitable support networks, the promotion of self-care practices, and the cultivation of a culture that emphasizes psychological safety. This holistic approach not only provides workers with the practical skills necessary to combat bias and promote inclusion, but it also guarantees that they can do so with mental clarity and optimal cognitive functioning, which ultimately contributes to the development of a workplace that is more progressive and welcoming to people of all backgrounds.

Implementing inclusive leadership development programs is crucial to give managers and leaders the knowledge, abilities, and standards necessary to promote diversity and inclusion in their organizations and teams. Inclusive leadership development programs may emphasize aspects such as fostering psychologically secure work environments, active listening, empathy, and inclusive communication. In addition, the program may incorporate interactive discussions, self-reflection exercises, and case studies to assist leaders in examining their prejudices and formulating approaches to foster diversity and inclusion in their leadership endeavours. Organizations can foster a culture that appreciates and respects all members by empowering leaders to champion diversity initiatives, lead by example, and invest in inclusive leadership development (Najmaei & Sadeghinejad, 2019). Mentorship and sponsorship initiatives are highly beneficial instruments for fostering the professional growth and progress of underrepresented personnel in establishments. Mentors give mentees direction, counsel, and assistance, assisting them in navigating the complexities of an organization, acquiring new competencies, and attaining their professional objectives.

In contrast, sponsors proactively champion the progress of their protégés, grant them entry into advantageous circumstances, and leverage their way to ensure their triumph. Sponsorship and mentoring initiatives can significantly assist underrepresented groups in overcoming advancement barriers by granting them access to networks, visibility, and growth opportunities. Organizations can establish a conducive environment for developing and achieving diverse talent by cultivating a mentoring and sponsorship culture (Kuknor & Kumar, 2023). Training and development initiatives about diversity and inclusion that are successful are critical for increasing organizational awareness, nurturing comprehension, and encouraging behaviour modification. Organizations can foster a fair and inclusive workplace environment conducive to every individual's success and growth by implementing mentorship and sponsorship schemes, comprehensive diversity training programs, and initiatives for inclusive leadership development. Constructing inclusive, empowering, and hospitable institutions through cooperative endeavours and a mutual dedication to ongoing education and enhancement is possible.

MEASURING AND EVALUATING DIVERSITY AND INCLUSION EFFORTS

Measuring and evaluating diversity and inclusion initiatives is essential to identify improvement areas, gauge progress, and hold organizations accountable for their diversity and inclusion commitments. Organizations can enhance their understanding of the efficacy of their diversity and inclusion endeavours and drive substantial transformation through data-driven decision-making by implementing feedback mechanisms and surveys, establishing key performance indicators (KPIs), and benchmarking against industry standards (Barbu et al., 2021). It examines these measurement and evaluation strategies in greater depth. Organizations can use key performance indicators (KPIs) to monitor their progress toward diversity and inclusion objectives via quantifiable metrics. Key Performance Indicators (KPIs) may exhibit variability contingent upon the organization's goals and priorities. However, they frequently encompass metrics such as underrepresented employee retention rates, employee engagement and satisfaction scores among diverse groups, and hiring and promotion rates that promote diversity. Setting clear and measurable key performance indicators (KPIs) that allow organizations to track progress, celebrate successes, and solve problems is a consistent way to improve their diversity and inclusion efforts (Swartz et al., 2019).

Using industry standards as a benchmark, businesses can compare their diversity and inclusion efforts to those of their rivals and peers. Engaging in benchmarking surveys and studies, analyzing industry-wide data and benchmarks, and searching out best practices and case studies from other organizations are all potential approaches to this end. By benchmarking against industry standards, organizations can ascertain their relative performance relative to their competitors and pinpoint any areas in which they may be lagging or succeeding excessively. Organizations can use this data to inform strategic decision-making and establish attainable objectives and targets for diversity and inclusion endeavours (Kasprowicz et al., 2023). Feedback mechanisms and surveys serve as valuable instruments for collecting input from stakeholders and employees regarding their encounters with diversity and inclusion initiatives implemented within the institution. It may encompass the implementation of employee engagement surveys, diversity climate surveys, and pulse surveys to gauge opinions regarding fairness, belonging, and inclusivity.

Furthermore, organizations may employ feedback mechanisms such as focus groups, town hall meetings, and one-on-one conversations to acquire qualitative insights regarding the efficacy of their diversity and inclusion initiatives. Through proactive solicitation of employee feedback, organizations can discern areas that require enhancement, attend to apprehensions, and exhibit a dedication to openness and responsibility concerning diversity and inclusion (Davies et al., 2021). It is critical to assess and analyze diversity and inclusion initiatives to facilitate substantial transformation and establish work environments that are fair and inclusive for all. Organizations can optimize the efficacy of their diversity and inclusion endeavours by utilizing feedback mechanisms and surveys, establishing key performance indicators, and benchmarking against industry standards. It enables them to make data-driven decisions that foster ongoing enhancements. By consistently conducting assessments and evaluations, organizations can foster inclusive environments that promote diversity and success, ensuring everyone has an equal opportunity to prosper.

CHALLENGES AND SOLUTIONS IN GLOBAL TALENT RETENTION

Retaining global talent poses distinct obstacles for businesses operating in dynamic and diverse environments. Crucial components of talent retention strategies include mitigating turnover and attrition, promoting employee engagement and satisfaction, and retaining a diverse talent pool. It probes into the challenges above and analyzes prospective resolutions to surmount them. Increased attrition and turnover rates can result in substantial ramifications for organizations, such as heightened expenses associated with recruitment, depletion of institutional knowledge, and diminished morale among the remaining workforce. Before addressing attrition and turnover, organizations must determine the fundamental factors that motivate employees to depart. Potential steps in this process include performing exit interviews, examining attrition statistics, and soliciting input from present and former staff members (Gupta et al., 2022). After identifying the fundamental factors contributing to employee attrition, organizations can devise and execute focused strategies to mitigate those factors. It may incorporate the provision of competitive remuneration and benefits packages, avenues for professional growth and progression, enhancements to initiatives that promote work-life balance, and cultivating a favourable organizational culture that appreciates and acknowledges employee contributions. Further, organizations can ensure managers have the necessary competencies and resources to support and retain their teams by investing in leadership development programs (Allen et al., 2010).

Retaining diverse talent necessitates deliberate endeavours to establish an inclusive work environment characterized by feelings of worth, esteem, and empowerment for every individual. To assist underrepresented employees in advancing their careers, organizations may implement mentorship and sponsorship programs, employee resource groups, and diversity training initiatives, among other strategies. In addition, organizations can ensure that promotion and advancement opportunities are accessible and equitable for all, provide opportunities for employees to engage in meaningful work that aligns with their values and interests, and offer flexibility and accommodations to meet the needs of a diverse workforce (Judd & McKinnon, 2021). Employee satisfaction and engagement are pivotal factors in retaining top talent. There is a positive correlation between employee engagement and motivation, productivity, and organizational loyalty; consequently, engaged personnel exhibit more excellent retention and lower turnover rates. To cultivate employee engagement and fulfilment, organizations may establish avenues for employees to offer input and engage in decision-making procedures, acknowledge and incentivize employee contributions, and advocate for a culture that values transparent communication (Moore & Hanson, 2022). In addition, organizations can cultivate a sense of community and belonging among their staff, provide support for work-life balance, and offer professional development and advancement opportunities. Critical challenges in global talent retention include addressing turnover and attrition, retaining diverse talent, and nurturing employee engagement and satisfaction. Organizations can foster an inclusive work environment where employees are esteemed, assisted, and motivated to achieve excellence by adopting focused approaches to tackle these obstacles (Pincus, 2022). Organizations can foster long-lasting success in the competitive business environment by constructing resilient and high-performing teams via proactive measures to retain and support their personnel.

THE FUTURE OF GLOBAL TALENT ACQUISITION AND RETENTION

In the face of a progressively intricate and competitive international environment, organizations must anticipate the impact of emerging trends in diversity and inclusion, the ongoing development of talent management technology, and the necessity to equip themselves for the future workforce on talent acquisition and retention. It examines these essential trends within this segment and deliberates on approaches to maintaining a competitive edge in the swiftly evolving talent environment. In talent procurement and retention, there will be an increasing recognition of the critical nature of diversity and inclusion as fundamental business objectives. Organizations must expand their perspectives beyond conventional metrics to foster diversity and adopt more comprehensive definitions such as diversity of thought, heritage, and experience. Addressing systemic barriers and biases within organizations, in addition to implementing proactive measures like blind recruitment techniques and diverse interview panels, will be necessary to achieve this goal. Additionally, a greater priority will be cultivating a culture of belonging in which employees feel valued, respected, and empowered to contribute their distinct perspectives and abilities. It may entail the execution of tactics such as inclusive leadership development initiatives, employee resource groups, and allyship programs, all aimed at fostering diverse environments that facilitate individuals' optimal growth and development.

Technology will persist in its pivotal position within talent management, facilitating the streamlining of recruitment procedures, identifying exceptional personnel, and improving employee engagement and growth. Artificial intelligence (AI) and machine learning algorithms will increasingly analyze massive datasets and identify trends and patterns in talent procurement and retention. Furthermore, utilizing digital platforms and tools will empower organizations to provide employees with individualized learning and development prospects, irrespective of their geographical location or personal history. As remote and hybrid work arrangements become more prevalent, organizations must modify their talent management strategies to facilitate virtual collaboration and distributed team operations. Swift technological progressions, demographic transformations, and evolving perspectives regarding employment and labour will distinguish the forthcoming labour force. Organizations must modify their talent acquisition and retention approaches to effectively draw in and retain skilled individuals in this dynamic environment.

It may entail a reevaluation of conventional concepts of labour and employment, as well as the adoption of alternative talent models like freelancing and contract work, in addition to flexible work arrangements. Additionally, to prepare their workforce for the jobs of the future, organizations will need to invest in reskilling and upskilling initiatives, especially in emerging disciplines like artificial intelligence, data science, and cybersecurity. Furthermore, organizations must establish diversity, equity, and inclusion as foundational tenets that inform their approaches to acquiring and retaining talent. Organizations can foster innovation and long-term success by cultivating diverse and resilient teams and establishing environments that foster a sense of worth, respect, and empowerment for every individual. Emergent trends in diversity and inclusion, ongoing technological advancements in talent management, and the imperative to equip oneself for the future workforce will influence the trajectory of global talent acquisition and retention in the coming years. In an ever more competitive and dynamic global marketplace, organizations can position themselves for success by embracing these emerging trends and implementing forward-thinking strategies.

DISCUSSION

The conversation surrounding acquiring and retaining talent from around the world is complex. It involves various topics, including organizational culture, talent management techniques, and the crucial role diversity and inclusion play. Many firms realize that diversity and inclusion are essential to successful strategies for acquiring and retaining talent. A diverse workforce brings together a wide range of perspectives, life experiences, and abilities, which helps to cultivate an atmosphere that encourages creative thinking and creativity within the firm. Workplaces that are inclusive and foster a sense of value and respect for all employees contribute not only to the attraction of top talent but also to increased levels of engagement and happiness among staff members.

A key component of talent acquisition is locating and luring qualified individuals to fill open positions within a business. In today's increasingly globalized climate, companies must cast a wide net to find talented individuals from various cultural and ethnic backgrounds. Utilizing technology improvements such as data analytics and online recruitment platforms can help optimize talent acquisition procedures and identify individuals who are the best fit for the firm's requirements.

Once acquired, retaining talent becomes crucial. The primary goal of retention tactics is to create a working environment that fosters employee contentment, encourages intellectual development, and makes it easier for employees to advance in their careers. Implementing measures such as building a healthy workplace culture, providing opportunities for professional growth, and delivering competitive remuneration and benefits packages should be considered. In addition, organizations must modify their strategies to fit the many regulatory frameworks and cultural nuances worldwide when participating in global talent acquisition and retention initiatives. It is necessary to tailor recruitment and retention strategies so that they are in line with the varied needs and preferences of heterogeneous workforces all over the world.

Businesses prioritizing diversity and inclusion and implementing effective talent management methods gain a competitive edge in the market. They develop employee-driven cultures that encourage outstanding performance, foster innovation, attract top talent, and lead to extraordinary success. By continuously refining their talent acquisition and retention strategies, organizations can position themselves for long-term success in an increasingly linked and dynamic world.

CONCLUSION

In conclusion, in today's interconnected and intensely competitive business climate, the acquisition and retention of global talent are as crucial as linchpins for the success of an organization. Firms must prioritize diversity and inclusion within their people management strategies to recognize the urgency of attracting and retaining top-tier personnel from various backgrounds. Our in-depth investigation into acquiring and retaining talent globally has highlighted the crucial significance of cultivating inclusive work cultures, implementing targeted diversity training efforts, and utilizing technology to speed talent management procedures.

As we look to the future, businesses must make diversity and inclusion fundamental principles that guide their efforts to acquire and keep talented employees. Organizations can ignite innovation, spur creativity, and pave the way for sustained prosperity by cultivating diverse teams that perform exceptionally well. In this regard, it is of the utmost importance to embrace workplace cultures that are inclusive and that allow for the development of a sense of value, respect, and empowerment for all people.

Furthermore, as technology innovations continue to transform the work landscape, firms must modify their approaches to talent management to meet the changing dynamics of the workforce and embrace flexible work arrangements. Enterprises can maintain a competitive edge in the evolving talent market by leveraging technology to enhance recruitment processes, identify exceptional talent, and offer personalized opportunities for learning and advancement.

Fundamentally, the future of international talent acquisition and retention depends on the successful application of technical breakthroughs that foster conditions conducive to every individual's flourishing while promoting diversity and inclusiveness. Businesses can cultivate resilient and high-performing teams positioned for sustainable success in the contemporary, interconnected global landscape by prioritizing these principles and adopting forward-thinking methods.

REFERENCES

Allen, D. G., Bryant, P. C., & Vardaman, J. M. (2010). Retaining talent: Replacing misconceptions with evidence-based strategies. *The Academy of Management Perspectives*, *24*(2), 48–64. https://www.jstor.org/stable/25682398

Barbu, S. J., McDonald, K. A., Brazil-Cruz, L., Sullivan, L., & Bisson, L. F. (2021). Data-driven decision-making. In Springer eBooks (pp. 47–59). doi:10.1007/978-3-030-85668-7_3

Barnes, J., Hall, J. B., & Grubb, B. (2023). Cultural humility and inclusion: Transformation to a culture of belonging. In Building Leadership Bridges (pp. 25–38). doi:10.1108/S2058-880120230000009003

Bendick, M. Jr, & Nunes, A. P. (2012). Developing the research basis for controlling bias in hiring. *The Journal of Social Issues*, *68*(2), 238–262. doi:10.1111/j.1540-4560.2012.01747.x

Byrd, M. Y. (2022). Employee resource groups: Enabling developmental relationships to support socially just and morally inclusive organizations. In Springer eBooks (pp. 219–237). doi:10.1007/978-3-030-85033-3_10

Coles, A. (2021). Diversity and inclusion in talent acquisition. In Springer eBooks (pp. 171–183). doi:10.1007/978-3-030-60060-0_12

Cox, W. T. L. (2022). Developing scientifically validated bias and diversity training that work: Empowering agents of change to reduce bias, create inclusion, and promote equity. *Management Decision*, *61*(4), 1038–1061. doi:10.1108/MD-06-2021-0839 PMID:37090785

Davies, S. W., Putnam, H. M., Ainsworth, T. D., Baum, J. K., Bove, C. B., Crosby, S. C., Côté, I. M., Duplouy, A., Fulweiler, R. W., Griffin, A., Hanley, T. C., Hill, T. M., Humanes, A., Mangubhai, S., Metaxas, A., Parker, L. M., Rivera, H. E., Silbiger, N. J., Smith, N. S., ... Bates, A. E. (2021). Promoting inclusive metrics of success and impact to dismantle a discriminatory reward system in science. *PLoS Biology*, *19*(6), e3001282. doi:10.1371/journal.pbio.3001282 PMID:34129646

Fujimoto, Y., & Uddin, M. J. (2021). Inclusive leadership for reduced inequality: Economic–social–economic cycle of inclusion. *Journal of Business Ethics*, *181*(3), 563–582. doi:10.1007/s10551-021-04920-2

Garelnabi, M., Cowdin, M. A., Fang, Y., Shrestha, B., Ushio–Fukai, M., Aikawa, E., Graham, G., Molema, G., Yanagisawa, H., & Aikawa, M. (2022). Embracing diversity, equity, and inclusion in the scientific community—Viewpoints of the North American vascular biology organization's diversity, equity, and inclusion committee. *Frontiers in Cardiovascular Medicine*, *9*. Advance online publication. doi:10.3389/fcvm.2022.863256 PMID:35463765

Gupta, S. K., Bhatia, N., & Bhagat, M. (2022). A review of employee turnover models and their role in the evolution of turnover literature. *The Indian Journal of Labour Economics : the Quarterly Journal of the Indian Society of Labour Economics*, *65*(1), 185–214. doi:10.1007/s41027-022-00366-w

Gürlek, M., Düzgün, E., & Uygur, S. M. (2017). How does corporate social responsibility create customer loyalty? The role of corporate image. *Social Responsibility Journal*, *13*(3), 409–427. doi:10.1108/SRJ-10-2016-0177

Harrisr, L., & Foster, C. (2010). Aligning talent management with approaches to equality and diversity. *Equality, Diversity and Inclusion*, *29*(5), 422–435. doi:10.1108/02610151011052753

Judd, K., & McKinnon, M. (2021). A systematic map of inclusion, equity and diversity in science communication research: Do we practice what we preach? *Frontiers in Communication*, *6*, 744365. Advance online publication. doi:10.3389/fcomm.2021.744365

Kasprowicz, V., Waddilove, K. D., Chopera, D., Khumalo, S. B., Harilall, S., Wong, E., Karita, E., Sanders, E. J., Kilembe, W., Gaseitsiwe, S., & Ndung'u, T. (2023). Developing a diversity, equity and inclusion compass to guide African scientific capacity-strengthening efforts. *PLOS Global Public Health*, *3*(12), e0002339. doi:10.1371/journal.pgph.0002339 PMID:38117812

Kuknor, S., & Kumar, V. (2023). Impact of training and development interventions for diversity & inclusion: Proposing an organizational schema. *Development and Learning in Organizations*, *38*(1), 16–19. doi:10.1108/DLO-11-2022-0233

Moore, J., & Hanson, W. R. (2022). Improving leader effectiveness: Impact on employee engagement and retention. *Journal of Management Development*, *41*(7/8), 450–468. doi:10.1108/JMD-02-2021-0041

Morley, T. (2018). Making the business case for diversity and inclusion. *Strategic HR Review*, *17*(1), 58–60. doi:10.1108/SHR-10-2017-0068

Najmaei, A., & Sadeghinejad, Z. (2019). Inclusive leadership: A scientometric assessment of an emerging field. In Advanced series in management (pp. 221–245). doi:10.1108/S1877-636120190000022012

Pincus, J. D. (2022). Employee engagement as human motivation: Implications for theory, methods, and practice. *Integrative Psychological & Behavioral Science*, *57*(4), 1223–1255. doi:10.1007/s12124-022-09737-w PMID:36577907

Roberson, L., Kulik, C. T., & Tan, R. Y. (2013). Effective diversity training. In Oxford University Press eBooks (pp. 341–365). doi:10.1093/oxfordhb/9780199736355.013.0019

Rosales, R., León, I. A., & León-Fuentes, A. L. (2022). Recommendations for recruiting and retaining a diverse workforce: A report from the field. *Behavior Analysis in Practice*, *16*(1), 346–361. doi:10.1007/s40617-022-00747-z PMID:36212634

Singha, R. (2024). Stress, Resilience, and brain performance. In S. Saluja, J. Kukreja, & S. Sharma (Eds.), *Building Organizational Resilience With Neuroleadership* (Vol. 1, pp. 14–29). IGI Global., doi:10.4018/979-8-3693-1785-3.ch002

Swartz, T. H., Palermo, A. S., Masur, S. K., & Aberg, J. A. (2019). The science and value of diversity: Closing the gaps in our understanding of inclusion and diversity. *The Journal of Infectious Diseases*, *220*(Supplement_2), S33–S41. doi:10.1093/infdis/jiz174 PMID:31430380

Tagliaro, C., Migliore, A., Mosca, E. I., & Capolongo, S. (2023). Room for diversity: A review of research and industry approaches to inclusive workplaces. *Journal of Corporate Real Estate*. Advance online publication. doi:10.1108/JCRE-04-2023-0017

KEY TERMS AND DEFINTIONS

Competitive Advantage: The unique attributes or strategies that set an organization apart from its competitors and enable it to outperform them in the marketplace, leading to sustainable success.

Diversity: Refers to the presence of various backgrounds, perspectives, and characteristics within a group or organization, encompassing differences in race, ethnicity, gender, age, etc.

Global Practices: Refers to the strategies, policies, and procedures that organizations implement globally to address challenges and capitalize on opportunities in diverse international markets.

Inclusion: Creating an environment where all individuals feel valued, respected, and empowered to contribute their unique perspectives and talents, regardless of their background or identity.

Retention: The ability of an organization to retain its employees over time, involving strategies to ensure that employees remain engaged, satisfied, and committed to the organization.

Talent Acquisition: The process of identifying, attracting, and recruiting qualified individuals to fill vacant positions within an organization to meet current and future talent needs.

Workplace Culture: The shared values, beliefs, behaviours, and norms that characterize the work environment within an organization, influencing how employees interact and work together.

Chapter 13
Gender-Based Microaggressions, Impostor Phenomenon, and Turnover Intention Among Women IT Employees

Sharon Elizabeth Jacob
Christ University, India

P. Lijeesh
Christ University, India

Mary Rani Thomas
https://orcid.org/0000-0003-1372-3032
Christ University, India

ABSTRACT

Microaggressions are everyday verbal, behavioural, or environmental slights that signal hostility towards marginalised groups. Such microaggressions when extended towards women in a workplace can lead to a lasting impact on the health and well-being of the women employees. The professional growth and development also would be hampered, deterring women from climbing ladders of professional success. The present study aims to understand the impact of gender-based microaggressions on women and questions whether such microaggressions can be linked to impostor phenomenon and turnover intention in them. Primary data was collected from 129 women IT employees employed in Bangalore's informational technology sector in four different job positions. Descriptive statistics, correlation analysis, and Kruskal-Wallis Test were used for data analysis. The results show that there are significant and positive relationships between gender-based microaggressions and impostor phenomenon and turnover intention among women IT employees.

DOI: 10.4018/979-8-3693-1938-3.ch013

INTRODUCTION

Women's presence in the corporate world has been steadily on the rise and overt discrimination against them is becoming uncommon. But covert discrimination in the form of gender-based microaggressions are still prevalent in workplaces, harming both the organisation and women employees alike. Continued instances of this subtle form of sexism leads to female employees' productivity and self-esteem being lowered and causes increased self-doubt and intention to turnover. A rise in impostor phenomenon in the employees, a belief in an individual that their success can be attributed to only luck or accidents and not their skills or capabilities, may also be observed due to chronically being subjected to such microaggressions. Thus, as an indirect result of the presence of gender-based microaggressions in the workplace, the professional advancement of women employees is questioned.

Companies that prioritise diversity and inclusion outperform their less diverse counterparts in terms of performance, talent acquisition, employee engagement, and employee retention (Dixon-Fyle et al., 2019). According to Deloitte Global, big global technology organisations will, on average, have about 33% of women working there in 2022, slightly up by 2 percentage points from 2019. According to the Ministry of Electronics & Information Technology 2017–2018, more women have gotten employed in the IT (information technology) field during the past ten years, making up 34% of the sector's overall employment (Gupta, 2021). Even intensive programmes to find, hire, keep, and promote women were proven to work slowly. Although this development is positive, IT businesses may need to put in even more effort in the future to raise these figures (Hupfer et al., 2021). The highly male dominated work environment could be one among the many plausible reasons behind the gender disparity. Studying the presence of gender-based microaggressions from the perspective of women employees in the information technology sector may give further insight into why women lag behind in assuming higher positions and leadership roles in the corporate field.

This paper aims to study gender based microaggressions in the workplace affecting women and further connect the presence of the aforesaid microaggressions to impostor phenomenon and turnover intention.

Gender Discrimination

Women have historically struggled to obtain academic reputation and success because they have been denied access, opportunities, and inclusion. They also have poor professional visibility and standing (Hinton, 2001). According to the Gender Gap Report from the World Economic Forum, "no country in the world has yet managed to eliminate the gender gap" (Hausmann et al., 2006). In the areas evaluated by Women, Business and the Law, women still only have about three-quarters of the economic rights that men do, and about 2.4 billion women of working age reside in nations where they do not have the same economic freedoms as men. Access to childcare and law enforcement also continue to be challenges (Women, Business and the Law, 2022). Although there are many factors contributing to these ongoing gender disparities, it is obvious that conventional gender preconceptions and ideas (gender prejudice) have a significant impact. Boys and girls are taught how to act, what activities they should engage in, and which toys or clothes they should favour very early in life (Eccles et al., 2000).

Over the years, the genesis, persistence, and change of gender discrimination have all been thoroughly examined in research on gender and organisations. Organisations become gendered through supposedly gender-neutral (but typically masculine) practices and policies. Organisations become environments where one gender is routinely viewed as inferior (Kelan, 2008). Open acts of discrimination, sexist stereotypes, and discrimination motivated by sexist views are becoming less prevalent in society today (Swim et al., 1995). Similarly, a person cannot be openly discriminated against in the workplace too because of a number of protected characteristics, such as race, disability, including gender (King and Cortina 2010). Although the prevalence of overt sexism is declining, it may still be seen in both subtle and explicit forms (Basford et al., 2013). In the workplace, in academia, and in sports, women experience microaggressions causing them to feel inferior (Kaskan & Ho, 2014), sexually objectified, and constrained by traditional gender norms (Ross-Sheriff, 2012). Thus, more subtle types of discrimination known as "microaggressions" need to be contrasted with traditional, overt forms of bias, or overt discrimination (Jones et al., 2016).

Microaggressions

Microaggressions are everyday verbal, behavioural, or environmental slights that signal hostility, denigration, or negative views toward stigmatised or culturally marginalised groups. They can be deliberate or inadvertent (Sue, 2010). The perpetrators of microaggressions may have good intentions generally and be oblivious to the effects of what they say (Paludi, 2012). According to Kanter et al., even though they may seem innocuous to onlookers, microaggressions are a form of covert racism or everyday discrimination (2017). When questioned by a member of the minority group or a bystander, those who engaged in the microaggression will frequently claim that it was an innocent mistake, a joke, or something trivial that shouldn't be given too much attention (Love, 2009).

The term "microaggressions" was coined by Chester M. Pierce, a psychiatrist at Harvard University, to characterise the slurs and rejections that he frequently saw non-black Americans inflict on African Americans (Sue, 2010). Today, the term is used to encapsulate the persistent and ongoing experiences of marginalised groups in our society (Brondolo et al., 2008). Microaggressions undermine the receivers' sense of worth (Clark et al., 1999), cause resentment and irritation (Franklin, 1999), drain mental energy (King, 2005), lower perceptions of subjective well-being and self-worth (Noh & Kaspar, 2003), cause physical health issues (Smedley & Smedley, 2005), reduce life expectancy, and deny minority communities equitable access to and opportunity in areas such as education (Sue et al., 2008), work (Wei et al., 2008), and health care (Williams et al., 2003).

Gender-based Microaggressions

Well-meaning males who support gender equality and would never purposefully discriminate against women unintentionally engage in actions that disadvantage women, stereotype them, or treat them in a way that prevents them from having equal access to opportunities (Swim et al., 1995). Women claim that gender microaggressions commonly happen and that they hinder their effectiveness in social, educational, and professional settings by undervaluing their contributions, objectifying them as sex objects, and discrediting their achievements (Banaji & Greenwald, 1995; Morrison & Morrison, 2002).

Microassaults, microinsults, and microinvalidations are the three main subtypes of microaggressions (Sue et al., 2007). Microassaults are deliberate, overt acts of discrimination (verbal, nonverbal, or environmental) that are intended to cause pain to the victim. They mimic so-called traditional forms of racism or sexism, such as calling women "bitches" or making sexist jokes. Microinsults, which denigrate a person's gender identity, are frequently unintentional messages or behaviours that "convey stereotypes, rudeness, and insensitivity". Communications that discredit or exclude the ideas, emotions, or lived experiences of a marginalised person are known as microinvalidations. This category includes gender blindness and the denial of personal prejudice (Sue, 2010).

Impact of Microaggressions

Covert discrimination may be much more detrimental than overt discrimination. Members of marginalised groups often fail to determine whether harmful behaviours are brought on by their marginalised status or by any other factors. The accumulation of seemingly trivial microaggressions can also have a significant long-term impact on the target due to its chronic nature, compared to overt discrimination (Jones et al., 2016). The presence of microaggressions have been linked to higher instances of depression, anxiety, post-traumatic stress disorder and impaired psychological well-being (M. T. Williams et al., 2021). Such subtle microaggressions are also associated with hypertension (Din-Dzietham et al., 2004) and higher body mass index (Brody et al., 2018).

Gender-based workplace microaggressions can have costly repercussions for both the organisations and female employees alike (Diehl et al., 2020). It has been proven that gender microaggressions negatively affect work performance (Cortina et al., 2001; Chan et al., 2008), employee commitment (Lim and Cortina, 2005; Brondolo et al., 2008), self-efficacy (Oswald et al., 2019), self-esteem (Dardenne et al., 2007; Jones et al., 2016), and job satisfaction (Glick and Fiske, 2001). According to Nadal and Haynes, gender microaggressions are also claimed to impede women's professional advancement because they keep them from realising their full professional potential and advancing to leadership roles (2012).

Impostor Phenomenon

Discrimination in the workplace can negatively impact the recipient's sense of self. For instance, the damaged self-image of those subjected to discrimination in employment has been linked to as the "impostor phenomenon" or the belief that a person's achievement is the consequence of luck or accident (Clance & Imes, 1978). People who experience this phenomenon also devalue praise, are very critical of themselves, and think their accomplishments are the result of luck, hard effort, or interpersonal skills rather than inherent talent, intellect, or competence (Matthews and Clance, 1985). In the sample chosen by Clance and Imes (1978), women professionals reported feeling over-evaluated by administrators and peers, which is a possible result of them suffering from impostor phenomenon. Instead of being caused by exposure to situations that invalidate people, such as microaggressions, the impostor phenomenon is frequently explained as the result of a flawed personality (King, 2022).

According to Deshmukh et al. (2022), Impostor phenomenon is not a "symptom" that has to be "cured", but rather, for certain people, it may actually serve as a motivating factor for greater achievement. Others, however, may experience negative effects on their health and job advancement due to the impostor phenomenon. High IP personnel are more likely to have unfavourable psychological effects that might affect their ability to grow in their careers and stay with their current employers. They also commonly doubt their professional validity. (Bravata et al., 2020). Impostor phenomenon has been linked to tension, worry, and depression, according to a study by Leach et al. (2019).

Studies may indicate that specialised groups like veterinarians or nurses experience IP more frequently as IP is studied in such specialised groups more than others. More generalised employee samples have been studied recently, and this promotes further research into larger employee groups to permit comparisons across demographics (Bravata et al., 2020).

Turnover Intention

A conscious and intentional desire to quit an organisation is known as turnover intention. It is regarded as the final in a series of withdrawal cognitions, a group to which intention to look for other employment and quitting thoughts also belong (TETT & MEYER, 2006). As found by Mobley (1977), an employee goes through three distinct stages before leaving the organisation they work for. The first stage is thinking of quitting the organisation. The second stage is actually looking for other job opportunities and the final stage is the actual intention to quit the organisation. According to Griffeth et al. (2000) turnover intention and turnover actually have a positive correlation.

There was also a significant correlation between turnover intention and the occurrence of microaggressions based on gender (King et al., 2010). A strong presence of a male culture in an organisation, where instances of gender-based microaggressions would be high, has a positive correlation with women employees' intention to quit. (Diehl et al., 2020). Presence of workplace incivility (which is any easily overlooked rude behaviour that persists in the workplace for a long period which has low intensity but is damaging to individuals, such as microaggressions) also has strong positive correlations with turnover intention (Namin et al., 2021).

Research Gap

Gender-based microaggressions have been studied in the western world, primarily in social and academic contexts. Several scales such as The Racial and Ethnic Minority Scale (REMS) (2011) and The Gendered Racial Microaggressions scale (GRMS) (2015) have also been developed to measure its presence. Attempts have also been made to study such microaggressions in the workplace and develop scales for workplaces specifically. In the present paper, an attempt has been made to study gender-based microaggressions in the context of Indian workplaces. The paper also tries to connect the presence of gender-based microaggressions to impostor phenomenon and turnover intention in women. Thus, there exists the research gap.

Research Questions

- Is there a link between the presence of gender-based microaggressions and impostor phenomenon in women working in the IT sector?
- Is positive turnover intention linked to the presence of gender-based microaggressions in women working in the IT sector?
- Are impostor phenomenon and turnover intention positively correlated?

Research Methodology

The research is a primary quantitative. Data was collected through three structured questionnaires from women employees working in India's southwest region's Informational Technology sector. Gender-based microaggressions in the workplace were measured using Microinsults and Microinvalidations - 16 Scale was developed by Mona Algner and Timo Lorenz in 2022 to measure microaggressions against women in the workplace. Respondents were required to rate 16 items on a scale from 1 (I do not agree at all) to 6 (I fully agree). Impostor phenomenon was measured using the Clance Impostor Phenomenon Scale

(CIPS) developed by Clance in 1985. CIPS was developed to measure the idea that people are success-ful by external standards but believe they are incompetent on the inside. There are 20 self-report items in it, and respondents are asked to rate their responses on a 5-point Likert scale. Turnover intention was measured using the Turnover Intention Scale (TIS-6) developed by G Roodt in 2004 measuring the extent to which respondents intended to stay in the organisation they were employed in. Respondents were required to rate items on a 5-point Likert scale where 1 = "Always" and 5 = "Never". Convenience sampling was employed to collect data. The sample size of the study was 129 respondents. Respondents were encouraged to give their genuine and authentic responses and confidentiality was assured. The data was not normally distributed and thus non-parametric tests were employed for data analysis. Data was analysed using Descriptive Statistics, Kruskal Wallis and Correlation Analysis.

RESULTS AND DISCUSSION

Descriptive Statistics

Table 1. Descriptive statistics

Demographic Characteristics	Frequency	Percentage (%)
Age		
18-25 years	63	48.84
25-35 years	57	44.19
35-50 years	6	4.65
Above 50 years	3	2.33
Total	129	100
Income		
Below Rs. 5 lakhs per annum	45	34.88
Rs. 5-10 lakhs per annum	36	27.91
Rs. 10-25 lakhs per annum	39	30.23
Above Rs. 25 lakhs per annum	9	6.98
Total	129	100
Job Position		
Developer	27	20.93
Engineer	36	27.91
Analyst	39	30.23
Manager	27	20.93
Total	129	100

Table 2. Descriptive statistics

	Mean	Standard Deviation
Gender-Based Microaggressions	2.93	1.02
Impostor Phenomenon	3.2	0.88
Turnover Intention	2.85	0.73

Hypothesis Testing

The results of the study are based on the five hypotheses which were formed for the purpose of the study.

Figure 1. Hypothesis 1

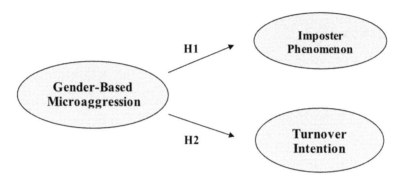

There is no significant relationship between gender based microaggressions and impostor phenomenon among the women employees in the IT sector.

Table 3. Correlation between gender-based microaggressions and impostor phenomenon

		Microaggressions	**Impostor Phenomenon**
Microaggressions	Spearman's rho	1	0.202
	Sig. (2-tailed)		0.02*
	N	129	129

* Correlation is significant at the 0.05 level (2-tailed).

The study expected no significant relationship between gender-based microaggressions and impostor phenomenon. But, as the significance value is less than 0.05, the null hypothesis is rejected. There is a significant and positive relationship between gender based microaggressions and impostor phenomenon among the employees.

Hypothesis 2

There is no significant relationship between gender based microaggressions and turnover intention among the women employees in the IT sector.

Table 4. Correlation between gender-based microaggressions and turnover intention

		Microaggressions	**Turnover Intention**
Microaggressions	Spearman's rho	1	0.178
	Sig. (2-tailed)		0.04*
	N	129	129

* Correlation is significant at the 0.05 level (2-tailed).

The study expected no significant relationship between gender-based microaggressions and turnover intention. But, as the significance value is less than 0.05, the null hypothesis is rejected. There is a significant and positive relationship between gender based microaggressions and turnover intention among the employees.

Hypothesis 3

There is no significant difference between the presence of gender based microaggressions among the women employees in the IT sector belonging to different age groups.

Table 5. Kruskal-Wallis test statistics

	Microaggressions
Kruskal-Wallis H	9.023
Df	3
Asymp. Sig	0.029

As the significance value is less than 0.05, the null hypothesis is rejected. There is a significant difference between the presence of gender based microaggressions among employees belonging to different age groups.

Hypothesis 4

There is no significant difference between the presence of gender based microaggressions among the women employees in the IT sector holding different job positions.

Table 6. Kruskal-Wallis test statistics

	Microaggressions
Kruskal-Wallis H	4.872
Df	3
Asymp. Sig	0.181

As the significance value is more than 0.05, the null hypothesis is accepted. There is no significant difference between the presence of gender based microaggressions among employees holding different job positions.

Hypothesis 5

There is no significant relationship between the presence of impostor syndrome and turnover intention among the women employees in the IT sector.

Table 7. Correlation between impostor phenomenon and turnover intention

		Impostor Phenomenon	Turnover Intention
Impostor Phenomenon	Spearman's rho	1	0.170
	Sig. (2-tailed)		0.054
	N	129	129

As the significance value is more than 0.05, the null hypothesis is accepted. There is no significant relationship between the presence of impostor syndrome and turnover intention among the employees.

Implication to Stakeholders

HR Management and Strategic Policymakers in Organisations

The results of the present study show that there are positive and significant relationships between gender-based microaggressions and impostor phenomenon and gender-based microaggressions and turnover intention in women in IT. There are numerous repercussions for these findings. Impostor phenomenon in its employees and employees with positive turnover intentions are both detrimental to the health of an organisation and can prove to be very costly. As organisations would like to keep their turnover low at all times, much effort must be expended by the organisations to reduce the instances of microaggressions. When women are subjected to subtle forms of sexism every day, it affects the way they perceive themselves and their achievements, such as in the case of impostor phenomenon, impeding their professional advancement and growth.

Organisations should recognise and acknowledge the presence of microaggressions in the workplace as they stand to gain many benefits in curbing such practices. Creating and providing a safe and equal workplace for all the employees will ensure that the maximum benefits, in terms of both productivity and employee well-being, can be reaped. The first step to the creation of a safe workplace is for organisations and policymakers to be aware of the presence of microaggressions and its negative effects. Awareness should be followed by policies and measures intending to control and reduce the presence of these microaggressions. There are multiple policies that can be adopted by organisations, including but not limited to – drafting a "microaggressions policy" for the organisation, encouraging the creation of employee resource groups (ERGs) to discuss and study the presence of microaggressions and ways to deal with it, penalties for being found exhibiting microaggressions towards any marginalised group, etc. Such policies will ensure that the organisation encourages a diverse, safe, and productive workplace for all employees.

Managers or Leaders

Although microaggressions frequently occur on an individual basis, managers should not tolerate any form of excluding or discriminatory language directed at any employee. Leaders, on becoming aware that such offences have occurred, have a duty to correct individuals to ensure that it is not repeated (Washington, 2022). If tolerated, microaggressions can contribute to a hostile work atmosphere that reduces the authenticity of people from marginalised socioeconomic groups (Fattoracci & King, 2022). Thus, the role that can be played by managers in curbing and uprooting microaggressions is huge.

Women

Multitude of women may be negatively impacted by gender-based microaggressions in their workplaces daily without even being aware of what they are subjected to. Thus, the major implication of this paper is making women aware that the everyday slights that come their way carry a lot more weight than what they would think. Women may suffer from both mental and physical health problems when the seemingly small microaggressions accumulate over time. Being aware of the presence of gender-based microaggressions can enable them to take the necessary steps to reduce its negative effects on them. They may report to higher officials of such instances which may lead to policies being drafted that can stop such practices in the workplace. They may also, being fully aware of microaggressions, stand up to the perpetrators and ask them to rethink their ways.

Limitations and Future Research

The limitations of the study include the time factor and the limited sample size of the study. Owing to the limited sample size, the data was found to be not normally distributed and thus non-parametric tests were employed. Results cannot be applied to all employees in the IT sector as the data collection was limited to the city of Bangalore. The study being restricted to the IT sector alone is another limitation. Also, the demographic factors considered for the study were only three – age, income bracket and job position.

Thus, there is future scope for the study to be conducted in various other regions of the country taking into consideration various other sectors. The sample size can also be increased, and data can be collected over a longer reference period. Various other demographic factors can also be studied in relation to gender-microaggressions. Specialised scales can also be developed for various job positions across industries to measure microaggressions, as the scale used in the present study is a generalised scale for all workplaces. Gender-based microaggressions were linked to only impostor phenomenon and turnover intention in this study and there are various other variables that can be further studied in relation to workplace gender-based microaggressions such as stress, anxiety, depression, job satisfaction etc.

CONCLUSION

Overt discrimination seems to be on the decline in the past few decades with women playing increasingly important roles in all domains, whether professional or personal. But covert discrimination still exists, one form of which is gender-based microaggressions. These subtle forms of sexism can have deep and lasting impact on the victims while the perpetrators may not even be aware of the damage they are causing. Negative effects include depression, anxiety and low self-esteem in the victims leading to lasting impact on their quality of life. In a professional setting women may end up feeling like "impostors" or that they don't deserve the recognition and appreciation they very well deserve. Prolonged exposure to such settings may also lead women to quit the organisation, hampering their professional growth and development. The present study also proves the same. There is a significant and positive relationship between such microaggressions, impostor phenomenon and turnover intention. Age also seems to play a role in how women employees perceive these microaggressions. It is important that we further study the presence and the negative effects of these microaggressions in the workplace. Awareness may subsequently lead to measures in reducing and tackling such microaggressions, leading to a positive environment for women at work.

REFERENCES

Algner, M., & Lorenz, T. (2022). You're Prettier When You Smile: Construction and Validation of a Questionnaire to Assess Microaggressions Against Women in the Workplace. *Frontiers in Psychology*, *13*, 809862. Advance online publication. doi:10.3389/fpsyg.2022.809862 PMID:35369207

Arshadi, N., & Damiri, H. (2013). The Relationship of Job Stress with Turnover Intention and Job Performance: Moderating Role of OBSE. *Procedia: Social and Behavioral Sciences*, *84*, 706–710. doi:10.1016/j.sbspro.2013.06.631

Banaji, M. R., & Greenwald, A. G. (1995). Implicit gender stereotyping in judgments of fame. *Journal of Personality and Social Psychology*, *68*(2), 181–198. doi:10.1037/0022-3514.68.2.181 PMID:7877095

Basford, T. E., Offermann, L. R., & Behrend, T. S. (2013). Do You See What I See? Perceptions of Gender Microaggressions in the Workplace. *Psychology of Women Quarterly*, *38*(3), 340–349. doi:10.1177/0361684313511420

Bravata, D. M., Watts, S. A., Keefer, A. L., Madhusudhan, D. K., Taylor, K. H., Clark, D., Nelson, R., Cokley, K., & Hagg, H. (2020). Prevalence, Predictors, and Treatment of Impostor Syndrome: A Systematic Review. *Journal of General Internal Medicine*, *35*(4), 1252–1275. doi:10.1007/s11606-019-05364-1 PMID:31848865

Brody, G. H., Yu, T., Chen, E., Ehrlich, K. B., & Miller, G. E. (2018). Racial discrimination, body mass index, and insulin resistance: A longitudinal analysis. *Health Psychology*, *37*(12), 1107–1114. doi:10.1037/hea0000674 PMID:30307274

Brondolo, E., Beatty, D. L., Cubbin, C., Pencille, M., Saegert, S., Wellington, R., Tobin, J., Cassells, A., & Schwartz, J. (2009). Sociodemographic Variations in Self-Reported Racism in a Community Sample of Blacks and Latino(a)s. *Journal of Applied Social Psychology*, *39*(2), 407–429. doi:10.1111/j.1559-1816.2008.00444.x

Brondolo, E., Brady, N., Thompson, S., Tobin, J. N., Cassells, A., Sweeney, M., McFarlane, D. J., & Contrada, R. J. (2008). Perceived Racism and Negative Affect: Analyses of Trait and State Measures of Affect in a Community Sample. *Journal of Social and Clinical Psychology*, *27*(2), 150–173. doi:10.1521/jscp.2008.27.2.150 PMID:19079772

Chan, D. K., Lam, C. B. I., Chow, S. Y., & Cheung, S. F. (2008). Examining The Job-Related, Psychological, and Physical Outcomes of Workplace Sexual Harassment: A Meta-Analytic Review. *Psychology of Women Quarterly*, *32*(4), 362–376. doi:10.1111/j.1471-6402.2008.00451.x

Clance, P. R., & Imes, S. A. (1978). The impostor phenomenon in high achieving women: Dynamics and therapeutic intervention. *Psychotherapy: Theory, Research &Amp. Practice*, *15*(3), 241–247. doi:10.1037/h0086006

Clark, R., Anderson, N. B., Clark, V. R., & Williams, D. R. (1999). Racism as a stressor for African Americans: A biopsychosocial model. *The American Psychologist*, *54*(10), 805–816. doi:10.1037/0003-066X.54.10.805 PMID:10540593

Cortina, L. M., Magley, V. J., Williams, J. M., & Langhout, R. D. (2001). Incivility in the workplace: Incidence and impact. *Journal of Occupational Health Psychology*, *6*(1), 64–80. doi:10.1037/1076-8998.6.1.64 PMID:11199258

Dardenne, B., Dumont, M., & Bollier, T. (2007). Insidious dangers of benevolent sexism: Consequences for women's performance. *Journal of Personality and Social Psychology*, *93*(5), 764–779. doi:10.1037/0022-3514.93.5.764 PMID:17983299

Deshmukh, S., Shmelev, K., Vassilades, L., Kurumety, S., Agarwal, G., & Horowitz, J. M. (2022). Impostor phenomenon in radiology: Incidence, intervention, and impact on wellness. *Clinical Imaging*, *82*, 94–99. doi:10.1016/j.clinimag.2021.11.009 PMID:34801842

Diehl, A. B., Stephenson, A. L., Dzubinski, L. M., & Wang, D. (2020). Measuring the invisible: Development and multi-industry validation of the Gender Bias Scale for Women Leaders. *Human Resource Development Quarterly*, *31*(3), 249–280. doi:10.1002/hrdq.21389

Din-Dzietham, R., Nembhard, W. N., Collins, R., & Davis, S. K. (2004). Perceived stress following race-based discrimination at work is associated with hypertension in African–Americans. The metro Atlanta heart disease study, 1999–2001. *Social Science & Medicine*, *58*(3), 449–461. doi:10.1016/S0277-9536(03)00211-9 PMID:14652043

Dixon-Fyle, S., Dolan, K., Hunt, D. V., & Prince, S. (2019). Diversity wins: How inclusion matters. In *McKinsey & Company*. Retrieved December 29, 2022, from https://www.mckinsey.com/featured-insights/diversity-and-inclusion/diversity-wins-how-inclusion-matters

Dwivedi, S. (2015). Turnover Intentions: Scale Construction & Validation. *Indian Journal of Industrial Relations*, *50*(3), 452.

Fattoracci, E. S. M., & King, D. D. (2022). The Need for Understanding and Addressing Microaggressions in the Workplace. *Perspectives on Psychological Science*. Advance online publication. doi:10.1177/17456916221133825 PMID:36379041

Franklin, A. J. (1999). Invisibility Syndrome and Racial Identity Development in Psychotherapy and Counseling African American Men. *The Counseling Psychologist*, *27*(6), 761–793. doi:10.1177/0011000099276002

Glick, P., & Fiske, S. T. (2001). An ambivalent alliance: Hostile and benevolent sexism as complementary justifications for gender inequality. *The American Psychologist, 56*(2), 109–118. doi:10.1037/0003-066X.56.2.109 PMID:11279804

Griffeth, R. W., Hom, P. W., & Gaertner, S. (2000). A Meta-Analysis of Antecedents and Correlates of Employee Turnover: Update, Moderator Tests, and Research Implications for the Next Millennium. *Journal of Management, 26*(3), 463–488. doi:10.1177/014920630002600305

Gupta, P. (2021, December 27). *[Year in Review 2021] Times are changing as women in tech reach new heights.* YourStory.com. https://yourstory.com/herstory/2021/12/women-technology-leader-gender-diversity

Hausmann, R., Tyson, L. D., & Zahidi, S. (2006). The global gender gap report 2006. *World Economic Forum.*

Hinton, K. G. (2001). *The experiences of African American women administrators at predominantly white institutions of higher education* [Unpublished PhD dissertation]. Indiana University, Bloomington, IN.

Holmes, T. H., & Rahe, R. H. (1967). The social readjustment rating scale. *Journal of Psychosomatic Research, 11*(2), 213–218. doi:10.1016/0022-3999(67)90010-4 PMID:6059863

Hupfer, S., Mazumder, S., Bucaille, A., & Crossan, G. (2021, November 30). *Women in the tech industry: Gaining ground, but facing new headwinds.* Deloitte Insights. https://www2.deloitte.com/us/en/insights/industry/technology/technology-media-and-telecom-predictions/2022/statistics-show-women-in-technology-are-facing-new-headwinds.html.html.html

Jones, K. P., Peddie, C. I., Gilrane, V. L., King, E. B., & Gray, A. L. (2016). Not So Subtle. *Journal of Management, 42*(6), 1588–1613. doi:10.1177/0149206313506466

Kanter, J. W., Williams, M. T., Kuczynski, A. M., Manbeck, K. E., Debreaux, M., & Rosen, D. C. (2017). A Preliminary Report on the Relationship Between Microaggressions Against Black People and Racism Among White College Students. *Race and Social Problems, 9*(4), 291–299. doi:10.1007/s12552-017-9214-0

Kaskan, E. R., & Ho, I. K. (2014). Microaggressions and Female Athletes. *Sex Roles, 74*(7–8), 275–287. doi:10.1007/s11199-014-0425-1

Kaushik, N., Sharma, A., & Kumar Kaushik, V. (2014). Equality in the workplace: A study of gender issues in Indian organisations. *Journal of Management Development, 33*(2), 90–106. doi:10.1108/JMD-11-2013-0140

Kelan, E. K. (2008). Gender fatigue — Camouflaging gender discrimination in organizations. *Proceedings - Academy of Management, 2008*(1), 1–6. doi:10.5465/ambpp.2008.33645060

King, E. B., & Cortina, J. M. (2010). The Social and Economic Imperative of Lesbian, Gay, Bisexual, and Transgendered Supportive Organizational Policies. *Industrial and Organizational Psychology: Perspectives on Science and Practice, 3*(1), 69–78. doi:10.1111/j.1754-9434.2009.01201.x

King, E. B., Hebl, M. R., George, J. M., & Matusik, S. F. (2010). Understanding Tokenism: Antecedents and Consequences of a Psychological Climate of Gender Inequity. *Journal of Management, 36*(2), 482–510. doi:10.1177/0149206308328508

King, K. R. (2005). Why Is Discrimination Stressful? The Mediating Role of Cognitive Appraisal. *Cultural Diversity & Ethnic Minority Psychology, 11*(3), 202–212. doi:10.1037/1099-9809.11.3.202 PMID:16117588

King, R. (2022). *Microaggressions, Impostor Phenomenon, and People of Color: A Quantitative Analysis* (Order No. 29258450). Available from ProQuest Dissertations & Theses Global. (2705775654). https://christuniversity.knimbus.com/loginAndLaunch?docUrl=?url=https://www.proquest.com/dissertations-theses/microaggressions-impostor-phenomenon-people-color/docview/2705775654/se-2

Koch, J. L., Tung, R., Gmelch, W., & Swent, B. (1982). Job stress among school administrators: Factorial dimensions and differential effects. *The Journal of Applied Psychology, 67*(4), 493–499. doi:10.1037/0021-9010.67.4.493 PMID:7130071

Leach, P. K., Nygaard, R. M., Chipman, J. G., Brunsvold, M. E., & Marek, A. P. (2019). Impostor Phenomenon and Burnout in General Surgeons and General Surgery Residents. *Journal of Surgical Education, 76*(1), 99–106. doi:10.1016/j.jsurg.2018.06.025 PMID:30122638

Lewis, J. A., & Neville, H. A. (2015). Construction and initial validation of the Gendered Racial Microaggressions Scale for Black women. *Journal of Counseling Psychology, 62*(2), 289–302. doi:10.1037/cou0000062 PMID:25867696

Lim, S., & Cortina, L. M. (2005). Interpersonal Mistreatment in the Workplace: The Interface and Impact of General Incivility and Sexual Harassment. *The Journal of Applied Psychology, 90*(3), 483–496. doi:10.1037/0021-9010.90.3.483 PMID:15910144

Love, K. L. (2009). An emancipatory study with African -American women in predominantly White nursing schools. *Dissertation Abstracts International.*

Mastari, L., Spruyt, B., & Siongers, J. (2019). Benevolent and Hostile Sexism in Social Spheres: The Impact of Parents, School and Romance on Belgian Adolescents' Sexist Attitudes. *Frontiers in Sociology, 4*, 47. Advance online publication. doi:10.3389/fsoc.2019.00047 PMID:33869370

Matthews, G., & Clance, P. R. (1985). Treatment of the impostor phenomenon in psychotherapy clients. *Psychotherapy in Private Practice, 3*(1), 71–81. doi:10.1300/J294v03n01_09

Mobley, W. C. (1977). Intermediate linkages in the relationship between job satisfaction and employee turnover. *The Journal of Applied Psychology, 62*(2), 237–240. doi:10.1037/0021-9010.62.2.237

Morrison, T. G., & Morrison, T. G. (2003). Development and Validation of a Scale Measuring Modern Prejudice Toward Gay Men and Lesbian Women. *Journal of Homosexuality, 43*(2), 15–37. doi:10.1300/J082v43n02_02 PMID:12739696

Nadal, K. L. (2011). The Racial and Ethnic Microaggressions Scale (REMS): Construction, reliability, and validity. *Journal of Counseling Psychology, 58*(4), 470–480. doi:10.1037/a0025193 PMID:21875180

Nadal, K. L., & Haynes, K. (2012). *The effects of sexism, gender microaggressions, and other forms of discrimination on women's mental health and development.* Women and Mental Disorder.

Namin, B. H., Øgaard, T., & Røislien, J. (2021). Workplace Incivility and Turnover Intention in Organizations: A Meta-Analytic Review. *International Journal of Environmental Research and Public Health*, *19*(1), 25. doi:10.3390/ijerph19010025 PMID:35010292

Ngo-Henha, P. E. (2018). A Review of Existing Turnover Intention Theories. Zenodo *(CERN European Organization for Nuclear Research)*. doi:10.5281/zenodo.1316263

Noh, S., & Kaspar, V. (2003). Perceived Discrimination and Depression: Moderating Effects of Coping, Acculturation, and Ethnic Support. *American Journal of Public Health*, *93*(2), 232–238. doi:10.2105/AJPH.93.2.232 PMID:12554575

Oswald, D. L., Baalbaki, M., & Kirkman, M. S. (2019). Experiences with Benevolent Sexism: Scale Development and Associations with Women's Well-Being. *Sex Roles*, *80*(5–6), 362–380. doi:10.1007/s11199-018-0933-5

Paludi, M. (2012). Managing Diversity in Today's Workplace: Strategies for Employees and Employers [4 volumes] (Women and Careers in Management). Praeger.

Ross-Sheriff, F. (2012). Microaggression, Women, and Social Work. *Affilia*, *27*(3), 233–236. doi:10.1177/0886109912454366

Saks, A. M. (2006). Antecedents and consequences of employee engagement. *Journal of Managerial Psychology*, *21*(7), 600–619. doi:10.1108/02683940610690169

Schaufeli, W. B., & Bakker, A. B. (2004). Job demands, job resources, and their relationship with burnout and engagement: A multi-sample study. *Journal of Organizational Behavior*, *25*(3), 293–315. doi:10.1002/job.248

Seppälä, P., Mauno, S., Feldt, T., Hakanen, J., Kinnunen, U., Tolvanen, A., & Schaufeli, W. (2008). The Construct Validity of the Utrecht Work Engagement Scale: Multisample and Longitudinal Evidence. *Journal of Happiness Studies*, *10*(4), 459–481. doi:10.1007/s10902-008-9100-y

Shukla, A., & Srivastava, R. (2016). Development of short questionnaire to measure an extended set of role expectation conflict, coworker support and work-life balance: The new job stress scale. *Cogent Business &Amp. Management*, *3*(1), 1. doi:10.1080/23311975.2015.1134034

Smedley, A., & Smedley, B. D. (2005). Race as biology is fiction, racism as a social problem is real: Anthropological and historical perspectives on the social construction of race. *The American Psychologist*, *60*(1), 16–26. doi:10.1037/0003-066X.60.1.16 PMID:15641918

Solorzano, D. G., Ceja, M., & Yosso, T. J. (2000). Critical Race Theory, Racial Microaggressions, and Campus Racial Climate: The Experiences of African American College Students. *The Journal of Negro Education*, *69*, 60–73.

Sue, D. W. (2010). *Microaggressions in Everyday Life: Race, Gender, and Sexual Orientation* (1st ed.). Wiley.

Sue, D. W., Capodilupo, C. M., & Holder, A. M. B. (2008). Racial microaggressions in the life experience of Black Americans. *Professional Psychology, Research and Practice*, *39*(3), 329–336. doi:10.1037/0735-7028.39.3.329

Sue, D. W., Capodilupo, C. M., Torino, G. C., Bucceri, J. M., Holder, A. M. B., Nadal, K. L., & Esquilin, M. (2007). Racial microaggressions in everyday life: Implications for clinical practice. *The American Psychologist*, *62*(4), 271–286. doi:10.1037/0003-066X.62.4.271 PMID:17516773

Swim, J. K., Aikin, K. J., Hall, W. S., & Hunter, B. A. (1995). Sexism and racism: Old-fashioned and modern prejudices. *Journal of Personality and Social Psychology*, *68*(2), 199–214. doi:10.1037/0022-3514.68.2.199

Tett, R. P., & Meyer, J. P. (2006). Job satisfaction, organizational commitment, turnover intention, and turnover: Path analyses based on meta-analytic findings. *Personnel Psychology*, *46*(2), 259–293. doi:10.1111/j.1744-6570.1993.tb00874.x

Washington, E. F. (2022, May 10). Recognizing and Responding to Microaggressions at Work. *Harvard Business Review*. https://hbr.org/2022/05/recognizing-and-responding-to-microaggressions-at-work

Wei, M., Ku, T. Y., Russell, D. W., Mallinckrodt, B., & Liao, K. Y. H. (2008). Moderating effects of three coping strategies and self-esteem on perceived discrimination and depressive symptoms: A minority stress model for Asian international students. *Journal of Counseling Psychology*, *55*(4), 451–462. doi:10.1037/a0012511 PMID:22017552

Williams, D. R., Neighbors, H. W., & Jackson, J. S. (2003). Racial/Ethnic Discrimination and Health: Findings From Community Studies. *American Journal of Public Health*, *93*(2), 200–208. doi:10.2105/AJPH.93.2.200 PMID:12554570

Williams, M. T., Skinta, M. D., & Martin-Willett, R. (2021). After Pierce and Sue: A Revised Racial Microaggressions Taxonomy. *Perspectives on Psychological Science*, *16*(5), 991–1007. doi:10.1177/1745691621994247 PMID:34498518

Women, Business, and the Law. (2022). International Bank for Reconstruction and Development. doi:10.1596/978-1-4648-1817-2

Wong, Y. N. (2012). World Development Report 2012: Gender equality and development. *Forum for Development Studies*, *39*(3), 435–444. doi:10.1080/08039410.2012.722769

Chapter 14
Innovative Recruitment Channels:
Leveraging Social Media and Virtual Job Fairs for Talent Acquisition

Surjit Singha
ⓘ https://orcid.org/0000-0002-5730-8677
Kristu Jayanti College (Autonomous), India

V. Muthu Ruben
ⓘ https://orcid.org/0009-0006-7723-8596
Christ University, India

Ranjit Singha
ⓘ https://orcid.org/0000-0002-3541-8752
Christ University, India

Alphonsa Diana Haokip
ⓘ https://orcid.org/0000-0003-2578-0114
Christ King High School, India

Melita Stephen Natal
ⓘ https://orcid.org/0009-0004-1240-7817
Amity University, Noida, India

ABSTRACT

Amidst the dynamic realm of talent acquisition, organizations are increasingly adopting inventive approaches propelled by technological progressions and shifts in candidate conduct. Employing social media platforms has evolved into a crucial strategy for engaging, retaining, and attracting top talent. Ethical considerations, data-driven insights, and compliance are critical factors that significantly influence recruitment practices. Emerging virtual job marketplaces provide employers with novel opportunities to network with prospective employees. By embracing digital transformation, leveraging emerging technologies, and prioritizing candidate experience, organizations can remain competitive in attracting and retaining talent in today's dynamic job market.

DOI: 10.4018/979-8-3693-1938-3.ch014

INTRODUCTION

Amidst the ever-evolving realm of modern business, the procurement and maintenance of skilled personnel represent critical obstacles for enterprises on an international scale. The exponential growth of technology and the widespread adoption of digital platforms are causing a significant paradigm shift in conventional recruitment approaches. This chapter explores novel recruitment channels, focusing on effectively utilizing social media platforms and virtual job fairs as talent procurement tools. Recruitment is no longer limited to physical employment fairs and classified advertisements. In the present era, social media platforms have developed into dynamic environments where professionals can exhibit their expertise, personal growth, and ambitions. Social media platforms provide unparalleled access to a wide-ranging pool of prospective candidates, ranging from professional networking opportunities on LinkedIn to real-time engagement on Twitter. Furthermore, the platforms' interactive characteristics facilitate recruiters' ability to establish personal connections with candidates, encouraging genuine exchanges and significant connections (Landers & Schmidt, 2016).

Virtual job fairs have significantly transformed the recruitment industry by overcoming geographical limitations and logistical complexities. Organizations can effectively engage candidates worldwide by organizing immersive and interactive recruitment events through virtual platforms. In addition to providing an identical experience to conventional job fairs, these virtual environments permit candidates to participate from the solace of their residences, thereby enhancing convenience and accessibility (Vik et al., 2018). In the current digital transformation era, organizations must adopt inventive recruitment strategies that correspond with the inclinations and conduct of the contemporary workforce. Through virtual job fairs and social media platforms, organizations can broaden their scope of influence, interact with exceptional candidates, and ultimately foster long-term expansion and prosperity. It explores the intricacies of these nascent recruitment channels, revealing pragmatic insights and optimal strategies for proficient talent acquisition in the era of digitalization

Organizations seeking to secure top talent and obtain a competitive edge have elevated talent acquisition to a strategic priority in the current labour market, which is highly competitive. The rapid evolution of conventional recruitment methods is attributable to technological advances, changes in candidate preferences, and alterations in behaviour. To effectively attract, engage, and retain top-tier candidates, organizations must comprehend these transformations and adjust their recruitment strategies accordingly (Adeosun & Ohiani, 2020). A comprehensive theoretical framework incorporating principles and concepts from diverse academic disciplines, including marketing, human resource management, and psychology, forms the foundation of prominent talent acquisition strategies. To promote organizational success, human capital theory, for instance, emphasizes investing in employee capabilities and skills. Social exchange theory delineates the symbiotic association between employers and employees, emphasizing the criticality of trust and reciprocal advantages. In addition, marketing theories, including segmentation and branding, provide insights into developing employer brand strategies and efficiently targeting candidates.

Key components of the conceptual framework for talent acquisition include technology, candidate experience, employer branding, and recruitment channels. Employer branding entails moulding the organization's public perception and hiring decisions to establish itself as an employer of preference. The candidate experience comprises all engagements between the organization and the candidates during the recruitment process, and it impacts the candidates' level of contentment and probability of accepting job offers. To engage and attract candidates, recruitment channels comprise a variety of platforms and methods, including established channels such as job boards and nascent channels like social media and virtual job fairs. The utilization of technology is essential for optimizing strategies and outcomes, streamlining recruitment processes, and augmenting efficiency through the application of data-driven insights. Organizations may harmonize these components within an all-encompassing conceptual framework to cultivate comprehensive and efficacious talent acquisition strategies.

THE EVOLUTION OF RECRUITMENT IN THE DIGITAL AGE

The historical lineage of conventional recruitment practices is extensive, encompassing several centuries, and serves as a testament to the progression of societies and economies. During the Roman Empire and ancient China, the leading recruitment methods utilized were interpersonal connections, word-of-mouth recommendations, and local networks. Organizations utilize social connections, personal recommendations, community networks, and familial connections to identify prospective employees with the intended credentials and capabilities (Rynes-Weller et al., 2013). During the medieval and Renaissance periods, guilds and apprenticeship systems became significant channels for acquiring talent as societies advanced. Craftsmen and artisans instructed apprentices through structured apprenticeship programs, facilitating the intergenerational transmission of knowledge and expertise. Guilds were early manifestations of labour unions and professional associations, significantly influencing apprenticeships and regulating professions (De Munck, 2020). The Industrial Revolution ushered in a substantial shift in recruitment methodologies, as the proliferation of factories, manufacturing facilities, and urban areas generated an enormous demand for labour. Employment agencies and labour exchanges aim to facilitate the connection between employers and job applicants by acting as intermediaries during the recruitment process. Classified advertisements in newspapers and trade publications became a popular means of advertising job openings, allowing employers to reach a broader audience of potential candidates (Ivaldi et al., 2021).

Conventional approaches to recruitment underwent modifications over the 20th century, influenced by shifting technological developments, economic circumstances, and societal patterns. The emergence of job fairs, campus recruiting events, and in-person interviews as customary methods for candidate identification and selection occurred. On the other hand, networking events and professional associations served as platforms for employers to connect with individuals with expertise in particular sectors or occupations (Rynes-Weller et al., 2013). Despite the emergence of online recruitment platforms and digital technology, traditional recruitment methods have incorporated digital channels and technologies to remain relevant and practical. Personal referrals, networking, and direct outreach play a critical role in talent acquisition, underscoring the enduring significance of interpersonal relationships and human connections in recruitment (Griffeth et al., 2013). Numerous factors have contributed to the transition towards digital recruitment, fundamentally altering conventional approaches to talent acquisition. The globalization of commerce has expanded the population of prospective candidates beyond regional and national borders. Digital recruitment platforms allow organizations to access various skills and experiences from a global talent pool (McCartney & Fu, 2022). Rapid technological progress, most notably the proliferation of mobile devices and the Internet, has fundamentally transformed how individuals establish connections and exchange information. By utilizing these technological advancements, digital recruitment platforms streamline interactions between employers and candidates, thereby increasing the accessibility and efficiency of the recruitment process (Nikolaou, 2021). A growing proportion of technologically proficient individuals in the workforce, specifically millennials and Generation Z, prefer online interactions and digital communication channels. These demographic groups receive digital recruitment platforms because they facilitate job searches and establish connections with prospective employers effortlessly and conveniently (Silva & Machado, 2023). Digital recruitment platforms frequently provide more economical alternatives when compared to conventional methods of recruitment, such as in-person job fairs or print advertisements. Employers can save on printing materials, venue rentals, and travel costs by utilizing online platforms for job postings, candidate screening, and interviews (Rodrigues & Martinez, 2020).

Digital recruitment platforms optimize the recruitment process by utilizing data analytics and insights. Organizations can monitor and analyze various performance indicators, including applicant engagement, conversion rates, and time-to-fill positions, to optimize recruitment strategies and achieve more favourable results (Signore et al., 2023). The increased prevalence of flexible employment arrangements and remote work has heightened the need for digital recruitment solutions that facilitate the sourcing and employment of qualified candidates by organizations, irrespective of their physical location. Digital recruitment practices have incorporated virtual interviews, online assessments, and remote induction procedures as essential components (Silva & Machado, 2023). Organizations must employ innovative recruitment strategies to attract and retain top talent in a competitive labour market. Digital recruitment platforms confer a competitive edge upon organizations by providing a streamlined and captivating candidate experience, the exhibition of employer branding, and the differentiation of said platforms from their rivals (Fernandes & Machado, 2022). Prominent factors such as competitive pressures, technological advancements, demographic shifts, cost-effectiveness, data analytics, and the prevalence of remote work have all contributed to the extensive adoption of digital recruitment platforms as indispensable instruments for contemporary talent acquisition strategies.

The digital transformation of talent procurement has been characterized by several significant milestones, each of which has considerably advanced how organizations engage, recruit, and retain talent. The Development of Online Job Boards: Online employment boards such as Monster.com, CareerBuilder.com, and Indeed.com significantly transformed recruiting during the late 1990s and early 2000s. These platforms enabled job candidates to search for opportunities and employers to post job openings in a centralized location, substantially expanding the recruitment process's reach and accessibility (Silva & Machado, 2023). Since their inception in the 1980s, applicant tracking systems have increased throughout the 2000s, revolutionizing how businesses expedite and administer recruitment. Automating communication, applicant screening, resume parsing, interview scheduling, and ATS software increases efficiency and enhances the candidate experience (Jansen et al., 2005). The emergence of social media platforms such as LinkedIn, Facebook, and Twitter provided recruiters with additional avenues to locate and interact with candidates. LinkedIn has emerged as a potent instrument for talent acquisition and professional networking, allowing recruiters to proactively explore candidates, construct talent pipelines, and exhibit employer branding (Chen, 2022). Artificial intelligence and machine learning technologies have grown into recruitment procedures to automate tedious duties, discern exceptional candidates, and mitigate bias. By conducting preliminary screening interviews, predicting candidate suitability, and analyzing resumes, AI-powered tools allow recruiters to allocate their time and resources towards more valuable endeavours (Ujlayan et al., 2024). Businesses recognize the importance of employer branding and recruitment marketing in attracting and retaining top talent. By utilizing digital platforms; employers can exhibit their organization's values, culture, and distinctive selling points to prospective employees via captivating content, videos, and testimonials; this enables the development of an employer brand that strongly connects with potential recruits (Poljarić & Došen, 2023). Online recruiting events and virtual job fairs have become increasingly prevalent instead of conventional in-person career expos and job fairs. Employers can connect with candidates in real time, irrespective of location, through virtual networking platforms and video conferencing at these events (Vik et al., 2018). This provides a cost-effective and practical method of reaching and engaging with potential employees. The COVID-19 pandemic expedited the implementation of remote recruitment practices, such as online assessments, virtual interviews, and remote induction procedures. Organizations expeditiously implemented virtual hiring and remote work, thereby showcasing the adaptability and durability of digital recruitment strategies in surmounting unanticipated obstacles (Balconi et al., 2022). The aforementioned significant achievements in the digital transformation of talent acquisition exemplify the continuous development of recruitment methodologies in light of technological progress, evolving market conditions, and candidate demands. As organizations adopt digital innovations, talent acquisition is poised to become a more streamlined process that prioritizes candidates and relies on data.

SIGNIFICANCE OF EMBRACING DIGITAL CHANNELS FOR TALENT ACQUISITION

By utilizing digital recruitment channels, businesses can access a broader and more heterogeneous applicant pool than conventional approaches. Recruiters can establish connections with potential employees globally via social media and the Internet, thereby gaining access to a vast applicant pool that may be inaccessible via regional or local channels alone (Signore et al., 2023). In this digital era, virtually everyone can access the Internet and digital devices. Digital recruitment channels offer convenience and accessibility to the recruiting process, enabling candidates and recruiters to participate from any location and at any time. The study by Signore et al. (2023) demonstrates how accessibility enhances the effectiveness and convenience of recruitment endeavours for all participants. Digital recruitment channels frequently present a more economically viable alternative when compared to conventional approaches like in-person events or print advertising. Organizations of all scales can consider online job postings, social media campaigns, and virtual recruitment events a cost-effective alternative due to their higher returns and reduced investment requirements (Fernandes & Machado, 2022). By streamlining the hiring process, digital recruitment channels decrease the time required to complete positions and increase overall productivity. By utilizing automated systems, such as applicant tracking software and online assessments, recruiters can expedite the screening and evaluation of candidates. As a result, recruiters can make hiring decisions more rapidly and complete administrative duties in less time (Gilch & Sieweke, 2020). By providing organizations with valuable data and analytics, digital recruitment channels enable them to optimize recruitment strategies and make more informed decisions. The efficacy of various channels and strategies can be assessed through metrics such as conversion rates, applicant engagement, and source efficacy.

This knowledge empowers recruiters to enhance their methods to achieve superior outcomes. Digital recruitment channels offer candidates a streamlined and interactive experience, augmenting their overall evaluation of the organization and its employer brand. Practical strategies for attracting and retaining high-calibre personnel include implementing mobile-friendly application processes, fostering interactive recruitment events, and implementing personalized communication channels (Bahri-Ammari et al., 2022). In a time characterized by the proliferation of digital nomadism, remote labour, and globalization, digital recruitment channels are crucial for businesses to adapt and prosper. Recruiters can source, interview, and enrol candidates irrespective of their geographical location through these channels (Bahri-Ammari et al., 2022). As a result, they are indispensable for constructing diverse and dispersed teams in the ever-changing modern workplace. In contemporary times, digital recruitment channels have assumed a critical role owing to their capacity to engage a more extensive demographic, their affordability and ease of use, their effectiveness and velocity, their facilitation of data-driven decision-making, their contribution to an improved candidate experience, and their capability to accommodate evolving work patterns. Organizations can maintain a competitive edge in the digital era and efficiently attract and retain high-calibre personnel by adopting digital recruitment channels.

Digital approaches to talent procurement offer many benefits that substantially enhance the recruitment process's efficiency, scope, and efficacy in contrast to conventional methods. Digital strategies enable organizations to transcend geographical limitations and engage with a worldwide audience. By utilizing online job forums, social media platforms, and virtual recruitment events, employers can effectively distribute job opportunities to a wide-ranging and global pool of candidates, gaining entry to a more extensive repertoire of skills and experiences (Fernandes & Machado, 2022).

In many cases, digital methods are more economical than their traditional counterparts. Generally speaking, posting job openings online is less expensive than print advertising. Moreover, online assessments and virtual recruitment events eliminate the necessity for tangible facilities and travel, yielding financial benefits for employers and applicants (Fernandes & Machado, 2022). Using digital recruitment processes dramatically diminishes the duration required for candidate identification, screening, and hiring. ATS streamlines the evaluation process by automating resume screening and correspondence, whereas online assessments and video interviews accelerate the assessment process. Ensuring this efficiency level is paramount to retaining competitive advantage and attracting high-calibre personnel (Signore et al., 2023). By granting recruiters access to voluminous data and analytics, digital strategies enable them to make well-informed decisions. The tracking and analysis metrics, including candidate engagement, source effectiveness, and application conversion rates, enable data-driven optimizations of recruitment strategies and the ongoing enhancement of results (Nocker & Sena, 2019). Digital methodologies enhance the overall candidate experience. Personalized communication via email or messaging platforms, mobile-friendly application processes, and virtual interactions contribute to a more streamlined and captivating experience for potential candidates. Establishing a favourable employer brand and recruiting high-calibre personnel are contingent upon this positive experience (Bahri-Ammari et al., 2022). Digital recruitment methods provide candidates and recruiters with increased accessibility and flexibility. Recruiters can conduct virtual interviews, further streamlining and accommodating the application process for job seekers with varying schedules and preferences (Gilch & Sieweke, 2020).

Digital methodologies enable the implementation of inventive recruitment tactics, including gamified assessments, social media recruiting, and virtual job fairs. (Bower et al., 2014) These tactics attract the interest of technologically proficient applicants and demonstrate the organization's dedication to remaining up-to-date and fostering innovative interactions with candidates. The rise of remote work has led to the seamless integration of digital approaches into remote recruitment processes. With the increasing prevalence of remote and flexible work arrangements, organizations can effectively recruit talented individuals from any location by implementing remote induction procedures, online assessments, and virtual interviews (Aczél et al., 2021). Social media platforms facilitate ongoing interaction with prospective candidates. Recruiters amass and sustain talent pipelines proactively, engage with dormant candidates, and impart knowledge about the organizational culture. Continuous interaction between organizations and potential recruits maintains the relevance of the former for both parties (Trunfio & Rossi, 2021).

Digital methodologies aid in promoting environmental sustainability by reducing dependence on paper-centric procedures and tangible resources. Digital documentation, online communication, and virtual events mitigate the ecological repercussions of conventional recruitment approaches (Pierli et al., 2023).

Modern recruitment strategies must incorporate digital approaches to talent acquisition due to their numerous benefits, which include global reach, cost-effectiveness, efficiency, data-driven decision-making, improved candidate experience, flexibility, innovation, adaptation to remote work trends, continuous engagement, and sustainability. By adopting digital strategies, businesses are better equipped to effectively navigate the ever-changing talent acquisition landscape (Ramesh & Das, 2022). The advent of remote work and globalization have significantly influenced recruitment strategies, compelling organizations to modify and advance their methods of acquiring talent. By extending the talent pool beyond national and local borders, globalization has enabled organizations to gain access to a broad range of skills and experiences from around the world. Recruitment strategies place a premium on engaging and connecting with candidates globally via digital channels, including social media platforms, online employment boards, and virtual recruitment events (Ariss, 2014).

A greater understanding of the significance of diversity and inclusion in the workplace has resulted from globalization. A growing emphasis is being placed on procuring candidates from underrepresented groups and diverse backgrounds to cultivate a more inclusive workforce. Organizations can facilitate diversity initiatives by hiring personnel based on their qualifications and skill sets rather than geographical proximity (Chaudhry et al., 2021). Conversely, the proliferation of remote work has generated fresh prospects for employers and applicants. Organizations can attract high-calibre personnel irrespective of their physical location by providing remote or flexible work arrangements and expanding their talent pool. To attract candidates in search of flexibility and work-life balance, recruitment strategies emphasize remote work opportunities and the advantages of a casual work environment (Aczél et al., 2021). Organizations have implemented virtual recruitment processes to facilitate remote employment in response to the rise of remote work. Virtual interviews, online assessments, and remote induction procedures have evolved into essential recruitment strategies, allowing establishments to evaluate and integrate candidates irrespective of their geographical location. Virtual processes offer several benefits to both employers and candidates, including increased efficiency, decreased costs, and scheduling flexibility (Fernandes & Machado, 2022).

In terms of recruitment, globalization and remote work have introduced distinct obstacles, including logistical constraints, communication barriers, and cultural variations. Recruiting strategies currently integrate various measures to tackle these challenges. These include providing recruiters with cross-cultural training, utilizing multilingual communication tools, and offering flexible scheduling options for virtual interviews. In pursuit of developing immersive and captivating virtual recruitment experiences, organizations allocate resources towards technological advancements, including virtual reality simulations and collaboration platforms (Aczél et al., 2021). As the advent of remote work diminishes the distinction between physical locations, organizations place greater emphasis on employer branding and corporate culture as a means to draw in and retain skilled personnel. Recruitment strategies employ various digital platforms, social media interactions, and virtual events to communicate the organization's values, mission, and culture effectively. Prospects for remote work candidates are searching for opportunities that reflect their values and provide a welcoming and tolerant atmosphere; thus, employer branding emerges as a pivotal component of recruitment tactics (Poljarić & Došen, 2023). Globalization and the rise of remote work have reshaped recruitment strategies, including access to global talent, diversity and inclusion initiatives, remote work opportunities, virtual recruitment processes, adaptation to remote recruiting challenges, and an emphasis on employer branding and culture. Organizations that successfully utilize digital channels and adopt remote work practices in their recruitment strategies have an advantageous position in the current globalized and remote-friendly work environment to attract, engage, and retain high-calibre personnel.

STRATEGIES FOR EFFECTIVE RECRUITMENT THROUGH SOCIAL MEDIA

Building a strong employer brand on social media platforms is paramount for organizations aiming to attract top talent and cultivate a positive perception among potential candidates. It involves defining the organization's values, mission, and culture while ensuring alignment across all social media channels. By developing a unique employer brand identity that resonates with the target audience, organizations can set themselves apart from competitors and showcase what makes them an attractive place to work. Sharing authentic content that provides insights into the company culture, values, and employee experiences humanizes the brand and fosters a deeper connection with potential candidates. Engaging with the audience through two-way communication, responding promptly to inquiries and feedback, and encouraging employee advocacy strengthen the employer brand's credibility and authenticity. Providing value-added content, highlighting employee benefits and perks, and actively managing the organization's online reputation are essential components of an effective employer branding strategy on social media. Through these efforts, organizations can effectively attract top talent, showcase their employer brand, and maintain a positive online reputation in today's competitive job market (Carbajal-Cribillero et al., 2022).

Targeted job postings and advertising techniques are indispensable strategies for organizations to reach and attract qualified candidates on social media platforms effectively. By identifying the specific demographics, interests, and qualifications of target candidates, organizations can tailor their messaging and targeting criteria to ensure maximum relevance. Leveraging targeted advertising features offered by platforms like Facebook, LinkedIn, and Twitter allows organizations to create custom audience segments based on job title, industry, interests, and location, thus ensuring that job postings reach the most relevant candidates. Crafting compelling job descriptions, accompanied by visually appealing images and videos, further enhances engagement and captures the attention of potential candidates scrolling through their social media feeds. Implementing A/B testing enables organizations to experiment with different variations of job postings and optimize them for maximum effectiveness. Sharing job postings across multiple channels and encouraging employee referrals amplifies the reach of job opportunities to a broader audience. By tracking and measuring performance metrics such as impressions, clicks, and conversions, organizations can assess the effectiveness of their targeting strategies and refine their approach over time. Ultimately, targeted job postings and advertising techniques on social media platforms contribute to attracting qualified candidates, increasing engagement, and improving the quality of hires for organizations (Nayak & Budhwar, 2023).

Engaging with passive candidates through social networking involves a strategic approach to acquiring talent, focusing on building relationships with individuals who possess desirable skills and experience but may not actively seek new job opportunities. This process begins with identifying passive candidates through advanced search filters and techniques on professional networking platforms like LinkedIn while also paying attention to indicators of potential interest in new opportunities. Personalized outreach messages tailored to the individual's background and career aspirations help demonstrate genuine interest and relevance, fostering a meaningful connection. Providing value-added content, participating in industry groups and discussions, and nurturing long-term relationships are essential for maintaining engagement and building trust with passive candidates over time. Leveraging employee referrals and tracking interactions for follow-up are additional strategies to effectively engage with passive candidates and cultivate a pipeline of potential hires for current and future job opportunities (Adeosun & Ohiani, 2020). Through these efforts, organizations can expand their talent pool, access high-quality candidates, and strengthen their recruitment efforts on social networking platforms.

CASE STUDIES SHOWCASING SUCCESSFUL RECRUITMENT CAMPAIGNS VIA SOCIAL MEDIA

Starbucks launched the #ToBeAPartner campaign on social media platforms, inviting potential candidates to share their stories and experiences working at Starbucks using the hashtag. The campaign highlighted the company's inclusive culture, opportunities for career growth, and commitment to community engagement. The campaign generated widespread engagement and social media participation from current employees and potential candidates. Starbucks received thousands of user-generated content submissions, showcasing employees' positive experiences and reinforcing the company's employer brand. The #ToBeAPartner campaign helped Starbucks attract diverse talent and strengthen its employer brand on social media platforms. The campaign's focus on employee stories and community impact resonated with audiences and contributed to a positive perception of Starbucks as an employer of choice. Starbucks' #ToBeAPartner campaign demonstrates the power of leveraging user-generated content and storytelling to engage with potential candidates on social media. By highlighting employees' experiences and showcasing the company culture, Starbucks effectively attracted top talent and reinforced its employer brand values.

Deloitte launched the #LifeAtDeloitte campaign on social media platforms to showcase the company's workplace culture, diversity initiatives, and career development opportunities. The campaign featured employee testimonials, behind-the-scenes glimpses, and interactive content to engage with potential candidates. The #LifeAtDeloitte campaign generated significant traction and engagement across social media platforms, with employees sharing their experiences and insights using the hashtag. Deloitte's recruitment team actively monitored and responded to user-generated content, fostering conversations and building relationships with potential candidates. The #LifeAtDeloitte campaign helped Deloitte strengthen its employer brand and attract top talent in a competitive market. The campaign's focus on authenticity, transparency, and employee advocacy resonated with candidates, positioning Deloitte as an employer of choice for diverse talent. Deloitte's #LifeAtDeloitte campaign highlights the importance of authenticity and employee advocacy in social media recruitment initiatives. Deloitte successfully showcased its workplace culture and values by empowering employees to share their experiences and engage with potential candidates, ultimately driving recruitment success.

Airbnb launched the #WeAccept campaign on social media platforms in response to global events, reaffirming the company's commitment to diversity, inclusion, and belonging. The campaign featured user-generated content, community stories, and initiatives to support marginalized groups. The #WeAccept campaign received widespread attention and engagement on social media, with users sharing their support and solidarity with Airbnb's message of inclusivity. The campaign sparked conversations around diversity and social impact, attracting positive attention to Airbnb's employer brand. The #WeAccept campaign helped Airbnb strengthen its reputation as a socially responsible company and attract like-minded candidates who align with its values. The campaign's emphasis on inclusivity and community resonated with potential employees, contributing to recruitment success. Airbnb's #WeAccept campaign demonstrates the importance of aligning recruitment efforts with company values and social impact initiatives. By leveraging social media to amplify its message of inclusivity and belonging, Airbnb attracted candidates who shared its commitment to diversity and social responsibility.

These case studies illustrate how companies leverage social media for talent acquisition, analyze the results and outcomes of their recruitment campaigns, and derive key takeaways and lessons learned from successful initiatives. By focusing on authenticity, employee advocacy, and alignment with company values, organizations can effectively engage with potential candidates on social media platforms and attract top talent to support their recruitment objectives.

STRATEGIES FOR EFFECTIVE SOCIAL MEDIA RECRUITMENT

Crafting an engaging employer brand on social platforms is crucial for organizations striving to attract top talent and differentiate themselves in today's competitive job market. It involves defining the organization's values, mission, and culture and ensuring alignment across all social media platforms to develop a unique employer brand identity that resonates with the target audience. By showcasing company culture and values through authentic and engaging content, including employee testimonials and behind-the-scenes glimpses, organizations can humanize their brand and provide potential candidates with insights into what it is like to work there. Furthermore, fostering two-way communication with the audience, encouraging employee advocacy, and providing value-added content demonstrate transparency, responsiveness, and a commitment to employee satisfaction, enhancing the employer's brand's credibility and appeal. Highlighting employee benefits, perks, and opportunities and actively managing the organization's online reputation further attract top talent and maintain a positive perception among potential candidates. Through these strategies, organizations can effectively build and cultivate an engaging employer brand on social platforms, ultimately attracting top talent and fostering a solid employer-employee relationship (Kaoud & ElBolok, 2022).

Targeted job postings and advertisement tactics play a crucial role in the success of a social media recruitment strategy. By identifying the ideal target audience based on job roles, industry, skills, and location, organizations can tailor their messaging to resonate with potential candidates effectively. Leveraging the advanced targeting features offered by social media platforms enables organizations to reach specific demographics, interests, and job titles, ensuring that the most relevant candidates see job postings. Crafting compelling job postings with precise descriptions and eye-catching visuals helps capture the attention of potential candidates as they scroll through their social media feeds. Experimenting with different ad formats and conducting A/B testing allows organizations to optimize ad performance and refine their messaging strategies. Moreover, promoting job openings across multiple channels through paid advertising and organic reach maximizes visibility and engagement with potential candidates. By implementing targeted job postings and advertisement tactics on social media platforms, organizations can attract qualified candidates and enhance the quality of hires (Demir & Günaydın, 2022).

Leveraging employee advocacy and referral programs is a powerful strategy for enhancing social media recruitment efforts. Organizations can empower employees as brand ambassadors by encouraging active participation in promoting the organization's employer brand on social media platforms and providing training and resources to communicate the organization's values and culture effectively. Fostering a culture of employee engagement and advocacy and regular communication about the organization's goals and achievements encourages employees to share their positive experiences on social media, amplifying the employer's brand. Implementing a structured referral program incentivizes employees to refer qualified candidates, with rewards for successful hires, boosting employee engagement and expanding the organization's talent pool. Recognizing and rewarding employees for successful referrals further encourages participation in the referral program and enhances morale. Tracking and measuring referral performance allows organizations to assess the effectiveness of their efforts and make necessary adjustments. Encouraging employees to share job postings and company updates on their personal social media profiles and providing training on social media best practices ensures a consistent representation of the organization's brand (Lee & Kim, 2020). By leveraging employee advocacy and referral programs, organizations can tap into their employees' networks, attract top talent, and build a strong employer brand presence online.

NAVIGATING THE SOCIAL MEDIA LANDSCAPE FOR TALENT ACQUISITION

Selecting the right social media platforms for talent acquisition is a strategic process that involves understanding the target audience, researching platform features, and aligning platform capabilities with recruitment objectives. By identifying the key demographics and behaviours of ideal candidates, organizations can tailor their approach to match the preferences of each platform. From LinkedIn's professional networking to Instagram's visual appeal, evaluating content preferences and competitor presence further refines the selection process. Setting clear objectives and metrics ensures focused efforts while testing and iteration allow long-term optimization. By following these steps, organizations can effectively leverage social media to reach and engage with potential candidates, achieving their recruitment goals precisely and efficiently (Frampton et al., 2020).

Understanding and adapting to platform-specific recruitment dynamics is paramount for organizations aiming to maximize the effectiveness of their talent acquisition efforts on social media. By thoroughly researching platform features and understanding audience behaviour, organizations can tailor their content and messaging to resonate with users' preferences on each platform, whether it is LinkedIn, Facebook, Twitter, or Instagram. Leveraging platform-specific tools and features like job postings and targeted advertising allows organizations to enhance recruitment efforts and engage with candidates more effectively. Additionally, experimenting with different content formats and posting times and proactively engaging with candidates fosters meaningful connections and boosts engagement. Continuous monitoring and analysis of performance metrics enable organizations to assess the effectiveness of their strategies and make data-driven adjustments as needed while staying updated on platform changes and trends, ensuring they remain competitive and adaptive in their approach. By incorporating these strategies, organizations can optimize their social media recruitment efforts and achieve their talent acquisition goals with precision and success (Khatri et al., 2015).

Compliance and ethical considerations are paramount in social media recruitment, ensuring fair and responsible practices when engaging with candidates. Organizations must adhere to equal opportunity employment laws, preventing discrimination based on race, gender, age, religion, or disability. Respect for candidates' privacy rights and following regulations such as GDPR and CCPA are crucial, requiring obtaining consent for data usage and ensuring secure data handling. Transparency and authenticity are key, necessitating accurate information in job postings and interactions to build trust. Deceptive tactics must be avoided, with job postings accurately representing roles and responsibilities. Candidate preferences regarding communication channels and frequency should be respected, and professionalism should be maintained in all interactions. Feedback on recruitment practices should be monitored and addressed promptly, and staff should receive training on compliance and ethical considerations (Hunkenschroer & Luetge, 2022). Upholding these principles demonstrates a commitment to fair hiring practices, fosters positive candidate relationships, and safeguards the organization's reputation in the competitive talent market.

MEASURING SUCCESS: METRICS AND ANALYTICS IN SOCIAL MEDIA RECRUITMENT

Key Performance Indicators (KPIs) serve as vital benchmarks for assessing the effectiveness and success of social media recruitment endeavours. These metrics provide valuable insights into various aspects of the recruitment process, from candidate engagement to cost-effectiveness and the overall impact on organizational success. Metrics like application conversion, engagement, and click-through rates indicate candidate interest and interaction with job postings. Cost per application helps evaluate recruitment campaigns' efficiency while hiring quality measures and recruiting candidates' performance and fit. Time to fill provides insights into recruitment process efficiency, while candidate satisfaction gauges the experience of potential hires throughout the process. Finally, social media reach, and impressions quantify the visibility and exposure of recruitment efforts. By diligently monitoring and analyzing these KPIs, organizations can pinpoint strengths and weaknesses in their recruitment strategies, enabling them to make informed decisions and optimize their approaches for tremendous success (Heijnen et al., 2013).

Numerous tools and technologies are available to aid in tracking and analyzing recruitment campaigns on social media platforms. Social media analytics platforms like Sprout Social, Hootsuite, and Buffer offer comprehensive dashboards to monitor key metrics like engagement, reach, clicks, and conversions across various channels. Google Analytics provides insights into website traffic from social media, while applicant tracking systems like Lever and Greenhouse help track candidate interactions and sources. Social media advertising platforms, including Facebook Ads Manager and LinkedIn Ads, offer robust tracking capabilities for monitoring ad performance and conversions. URL tracking tools like Bitly and Google URL Builder provide insights into click-through rates and referral sources.

In contrast, social listening tools like Brandwatch and Mention offer valuable insights into brand sentiment and candidate feedback. Additionally, heatmap and session recording tools like Hotjar and Crazy Egg visualize user interactions on the organization's website, aiding in identifying areas for optimization. By leveraging these tools, recruiters can optimize their social media recruitment strategies based on data-driven insights and achieve better results in attracting and engaging top talent (Smith et al., 2023). Continuous improvement through data-driven insights is paramount for optimizing social media recruitment strategies. Organizations can achieve better results by regularly analyzing key performance indicators (KPIs) like application conversion rate, engagement rate, click-through rate, and cost per application to pinpoint areas of strength and areas for enhancement. A/B testing enables experimentation with various job posting formats, visuals, and messaging to identify what resonates best with the target audience. Tracking the candidate journey helps identify friction points and streamline recruitment while optimizing targeting and segmentation to reach the most relevant candidates. Experimentation with ad formats and platforms helps allocate resources effectively while soliciting candidate feedback, which provides valuable insights for refining recruitment approaches. Staying updated on industry trends and best practices ensures adaptability and relevance, ultimately leading to more successful recruitment outcomes aligned with organizational objectives. This iterative approach fosters agility and effectiveness in social media recruitment strategies.

UNLOCKING THE POTENTIAL OF VIRTUAL JOB FAIRS

Virtual job fairs offer a modern solution to traditional recruitment events, providing accessibility, convenience, cost-effectiveness, and sustainability benefits. Organizers and participants alike can leverage these advantages to streamline the recruitment process and maximize opportunities for engagement. Organizers should select user-friendly platforms to ensure successful virtual job fairs, employ diverse marketing strategies, offer training and support, develop engaging content, and facilitate meaningful networking opportunities. By adhering to these best practices, virtual job fairs can connect employers with job seekers in today's digital landscape, fostering valuable connections and driving recruitment success (Chen, 2021). Preparing for a virtual job fair requires careful planning and execution to ensure a successful outcome. Design your virtual booth by customizing it with compelling branding materials, company information, and multimedia content to attract and engage job seekers effectively. Make sure your booth is visually appealing and easy to navigate. Be proactive and responsive during the event by initiating conversations in chat rooms, promptly responding to inquiries, and scheduling one-on-one meetings or interviews with interested candidates. This proactive approach demonstrates your commitment to engaging with potential hires. Use the virtual job fair to showcase your employer's brand and company culture. Share employee testimonials, success stories, and videos highlighting what sets your organization apart and makes it an attractive workplace. Provide clear and detailed job descriptions for each position you are looking to fill. Clearly outline job responsibilities, qualifications, and application instructions to make it easy for job seekers to understand the requirements and apply directly through the virtual job fair platform. Remember to follow up with qualified candidates after the event. Take advantage of the leads and connections generated during the job fair by scheduling interviews, providing additional information about job opportunities, and maintaining communication throughout the hiring process. Following these best practices, organizations can create engaging and productive virtual job fairs. At the same time, participants can effectively showcase their employer's brand and connect with top talent in a virtual environment.

INTEGRATING INNOVATION INTO RECRUITMENT STRATEGIES

Innovation is pivotal in enhancing talent acquisition and retention by introducing new approaches, technologies, and strategies that streamline processes, improve efficiency, and create a more engaging employee experience. Innovative technologies such as applicant tracking systems (ATS), AI-powered resume screening tools, and automated scheduling platforms help recruiters streamline recruitment. By automating routine tasks and leveraging data analytics, organizations can identify top talent more efficiently, reduce time-to-hire, and provide a more seamless experience for candidates (Hunkenschroer & Luetge, 2022). Innovation in recruitment enables organizations to provide candidates with a more personalized and engaging experience. Features such as chatbots for instant support, virtual reality (VR) simulations for job previews, and video interviews for remote assessments create a more interactive and immersive recruitment journey, leading to higher candidate satisfaction and engagement (Jatobá et al., 2022). Innovative recruitment tools and analytics platforms allow organizations to collect and analyze vast amounts of data to gain insights into candidate behaviour, preferences, and performance. By leveraging data-driven insights, recruiters can make informed decisions, optimize recruitment strategies, and identify the best-fit candidates more effectively, leading to better hiring outcomes and retention rates. Adopting innovative technologies and remote work solutions has transformed how organizations approach talent acquisition and retention. Organizations can attract a wider pool of candidates, improve work-life balance, and enhance employee satisfaction and retention by offering flexible work arrangements, such as remote work options, flexible hours, and telecommuting opportunities.

Innovation in learning and development initiatives enables organizations to provide employees with opportunities for continuous skill development and career advancement. Online learning platforms, microlearning modules, and AI-powered training tools offer personalized and adaptive learning experiences tailored to individual needs, fostering employee growth, engagement, and retention. Employee Engagement and Recognition: Innovative employee engagement platforms and recognition programs help organizations create a positive work environment and foster a sense of belonging and loyalty among employees. Features such as peer-to-peer recognition, gamification elements, and social recognition tools encourage collaboration, boost morale, and increase employee retention rates. Innovation enhances talent acquisition and retention by empowering organizations to adapt to changing market dynamics, attract top talent, and create a positive employee experience. By embracing innovative technologies and strategies, organizations can stay competitive in the talent market and achieve long-term success in attracting, developing, and retaining their workforce (Lemmetty & Billet, 2023).

Emerging technologies are reshaping the recruitment landscape, revolutionizing traditional processes, and enabling organizations to attract, identify, and engage with top talent more effectively. Artificial intelligence (AI) and machine learning-powered recruitment tools use machine learning algorithms to automate various aspects of the recruitment process, such as resume screening, candidate matching, and predictive analytics. These technologies help recruiters quickly identify the most qualified candidates, reduce bias, and make data-driven decisions. Chatbots and virtual assistants provide instant support and assistance to candidates throughout recruitment. They can answer frequently asked questions, schedule interviews, provide updates on application status, and offer personalized recommendations, enhancing the candidate experience and improving engagement. Video interviewing platforms enable organizations to conduct remote interviews with candidates from anywhere. These platforms provide features such as live interviews, pre-recorded interviews, video assessments, and AI-driven video analysis, allowing recruiters to assess candidates' communication skills, personality traits, and cultural fit more effectively. Gamification and assessment tools use game-like elements and interactive simulations to evaluate candidates' skills, competencies, and job-related knowledge. These tools engage candidates in immersive experiences, provide real-time feedback, and help recruiters identify top performers and cultural fits more accurately (Philip, 2021).

Predictive analytics and big data tools analyze large datasets to identify trends, patterns, and correlations related to recruitment and workforce management. These tools help organizations forecast future hiring needs, optimize recruitment strategies, and improve decision-making based on actionable insights derived from data analysis. Augmented reality (AR) and virtual reality (VR) technologies offer immersive experiences that simulate real-world environments and scenarios, making them valuable tools for job previews, training simulations, and onboarding programs. These technologies enable candidates to explore job roles, environments, and company cultures virtually, leading to more informed decisions and higher retention rates (Jain & Maitri, 2018). Talent Relationship Management (TRM) systems provide a centralized platform for managing relationships with candidates, alums, and passive talent pools. These systems offer features such as candidate relationship management (CRM), talent community building, and automated communication workflows, helping organizations nurture relationships, build talent pipelines, and engage with candidates proactively (Trost, 2014). By leveraging these emerging technologies and tools, organizations can transform their recruitment processes, gain a competitive edge in talent acquisition, and build a strong employer brand that attracts and retains top talent in today's dynamic and competitive job market.

DISCUSSION

The emergence of virtual job fairs represents a significant shift in the recruitment landscape, offering employers and job seekers a more accessible and convenient way to connect. This discussion explores the implications of virtual job fairs and their potential impact on recruitment strategies and practices.

One key aspect of virtual job fairs is their ability to overcome geographical barriers. Traditional job fairs often require participants to travel to a specific location, limiting access for individuals who cannot attend due to distance or travel constraints. Virtual job fairs eliminate this limitation by providing an online platform where job seekers can engage with employers anywhere. This expanded reach opens up new opportunities for employers, who can tap into a larger talent pool, and job seekers, who have access to more job opportunities regardless of location.

Moreover, virtual job fairs offer more convenience and flexibility than traditional in-person events. Participants can access the job fair from any internet-enabled device, allowing them to attend from the comfort of their own homes or offices. This convenience is particularly beneficial for individuals with busy schedules or mobility limitations who may need help attending in-person events. Additionally, virtual job fairs often provide features such as chat rooms, video conferencing, and searchable job listings, enhancing the overall experience for both candidates and recruiters.

Furthermore, virtual job fairs are cost-effective for both employers and job seekers. Employers can save on renting venues, travel, and accommodation expenses, while job seekers can attend the event for free, avoiding transportation and lodging expenses. This cost-effectiveness makes virtual job fairs attractive for organizations looking to maximize their recruitment budget while reaching a wider audience of potential candidates.

However, despite the many benefits of virtual job fairs, there are also some challenges and considerations to be aware of. For example, the virtual format may require more personal interaction and networking opportunities, often a highlight of in-person events. Additionally, technical issues such as internet connectivity problems or platform glitches can sometimes disrupt the smooth running of virtual job fairs.

Virtual job fairs represent a modern and efficient approach to recruitment, offering accessibility, convenience, cost-effectiveness, and sustainability. While they may partially replace traditional in-person events, virtual job fairs provide an effective alternative for connecting job seekers with employers in today's digital age. As technology evolves, virtual job fairs will likely become an increasingly integral part of recruitment strategies, helping organizations attract and hire top talent worldwide.

Incorporating social media and virtual job fairs has fundamentally transformed the execution of talent procurement strategies. Nevertheless, as institutions adopt these novel communication platforms, it is crucial to thoroughly examine the ethical and legal implications that are intrinsic to their implementation.

Using social media platforms for candidate recruitment raises ethical concerns about privacy infringements and unjust hiring practices. Recruiters must delicately balance obtaining public information while upholding candidates' privacy rights. Furthermore, the risk of prejudice stemming from data obtained from social media profiles highlights the criticality of implementing anti-discrimination policies and fostering an environment of diversity and inclusion during the hiring procedure.

Organizations are legally obligated to guarantee adherence to data protection regulations, including the General Data Protection Regulation (GDPR) within the European Union. Adhering strictly to data privacy laws is essential to protecting candidates' rights when collecting, storing, and using personal information obtained from social media profiles. Furthermore, implementing AI algorithms for candidate screening brings forth intricacies about accountability, transparency, and bias reduction; thus, meticulous examination of the legal ramifications is imperative.

Given the ethical and legal complexities involved, evaluating the cost-effectiveness of virtual job fairs and social media is imperative to making well-informed decisions. Although these channels offer benefits such as access to a broader range of candidates and a shorter hiring process, they also entail costs associated with advertising, platform subscriptions, and personnel resources. Implementing these novel recruitment channels can lead to potential cost reductions, including decreased travel expenditures and enhanced resource allocation, underscoring their economic benefits.

Social media recruitment strategies do, however, have certain constraints. Recruiters face obstacles, including restricted accessibility to specific demographic groups, excessive content availability, and spreading false information. In addition, amid the vast digital landscape, sustaining a positive employer brand and authenticating candidate profiles necessitates a cautious approach to avoiding potential pitfalls.

Understanding the complexities of social media recruitment in each sector is critical to tailoring approaches that align with industry standards and efficiently reach the desired talent pools. Various industries, including technology, healthcare, finance, and retail, offer distinct prospects and obstacles when utilizing social media platforms to acquire talent. Organizations can hone their recruitment strategies and bolster their competitive edge by analyzing sector-specific trends and optimal methodologies for attracting high-calibre personnel.

Although social media and virtual job fairs provide unparalleled prospects for securing qualified candidates, navigating their ethical, legal, and practical implications is critical to maximizing their efficacy and guaranteeing adherence to regulatory frameworks. By effectively managing these obstacles and capitalizing on industry-specific knowledge, businesses can maximize the effectiveness of novel recruitment methods to entice, capture, and retain exceptional personnel in a fiercely competitive worldwide environment.

The results obtained from these investigations collectively emphasize the changing significance of social media in recruitment in diverse settings. To begin with, the research conducted by Benedict et al. (2019) emphasizes the efficacy and efficiency of social media recruitment, specifically in its capacity to involve young adult and adolescent cancer survivors in scientific investigations. The substantial rise in student enrollment and decrease in the need for study resources provide concrete evidence of the advantages associated with implementing social media platforms. Nevertheless, contingent on the recruitment source, the study reveals substantial differences in patient-reported outcomes and participant characteristics. These issues give rise to apprehensions concerning the potential introduction of biases into the results and the restricted applicability of outcomes derived exclusively from social media recruitment techniques.

Aggerholm and Andersen (2018) conducted a study investigating the profound effects that Web 3.0 strategies have on the realm of recruitment communication. Employing an "open source recruitment strategy" signifies a fundamental change in approach, shifting the focus of employee involvement from their profession to their spheres. This deviation challenges conventional notions about the balance between work and personal life, as well as the inner workings of an organization. Furthermore, the research emphasizes the intricacies that are intrinsic in the execution of recruitment strategies for Web 3.0, underscoring the importance of strategic forethought and instruction in order to successfully navigate challenges related to managerial oversight, power relations, and interaction. Koch et al. (2018) underscore the increasing importance of social media platforms, specifically LinkedIn, within South Africa's employment context. The research findings, based on worldwide patterns, indicate a reduced application of alternative social media platforms for recruitment within the specific context of South Africa. This highlights the significance of customized approaches and sufficient instruction to leverage social media tools' capabilities for recruitment.

The studies above strengthen the argument that social media recruitment is a complex endeavour, highlighting the necessity for a nuanced strategy considering the particular setting, intended recipients, and possible prejudices introduced by various recruitment techniques. To optimize the advantages of social media in recruitment, ongoing training, strategic planning, and targeted messaging are essential for ensuring its successful implementation.

CONCLUSION

The talent acquisition landscape continuously evolves, driven by technological advancements, candidate behaviour changes, and shifting industry dynamics. From traditional methods to innovative strategies, organizations are exploring new avenues to attract, engage, and retain top talent. Digital channels, mainly social media, have become indispensable tools for reaching candidates, building employer brands, and facilitating recruitment efforts.

By leveraging social media platforms effectively, organizations can showcase their employer brand, engage with passive candidates, and target specific demographics with tailored job postings and advertisements. Compliance and ethical considerations are paramount to maintaining fair and responsible recruitment practices and ensuring equal opportunities for all candidates.

Metrics and analytics play a crucial role in measuring the success of recruitment campaigns, providing valuable insights for optimization and continuous improvement. Through data-driven insights, organizations can refine their strategies, enhance candidate experiences, and achieve better outcomes in talent acquisition.

Furthermore, the emergence of virtual job fairs presents exciting opportunities for connecting employers with candidates in a virtual environment, offering convenience, accessibility, and efficiency in the recruitment process.

Organizations must stay agile, adaptable, and innovative as we navigate the evolving talent acquisition landscape. Organizations can attract and retain top talent in today's competitive job market by embracing digital transformation, leveraging emerging technologies, and prioritizing candidate experience and engagement.

REFERENCES

Aczél, B., Kovács, M., Van Der Lippe, T., & Szászi, B. (2021). Researchers working from home: Benefits and challenges. *PLoS One*, *16*(3), e0249127. doi:10.1371/journal.pone.0249127 PMID:33765047

Adeosun, O. T., & Ohiani, A. S. (2020). Attracting and recruiting quality talent: Firm perspectives. *Rajagiri Management Journal*, *14*(2), 107–120. doi:10.1108/RAMJ-05-2020-0016

Aggerholm, H. K., & Andersen, S. E. (2018). Social Media Recruitment 3.0. *Journal of Communication Management (London)*, *22*(2), 122–137. doi:10.1108/JCOM-11-2017-0131

Ariss, A. A. (2014). Global talent management: An introduction and a review. In Management for Professionals (pp. 3–13). doi:10.1007/978-3-319-05125-3_1

Bahri-Ammari, N., Soliman, M., & Salah, O. B. (2022). The impact of employer brand on job seekers' attitudes and intentions: The moderating role of value congruence and social media. *Corporate Reputation Review*. Advance online publication. doi:10.1057/s41299-022-00154-8

Balconi, M., Fronda, G., Cassioli, F., & Crivelli, D. (2022). Face-to-face vs. remote digital settings in job assessment interviews: A multilevel hyperscanning protocol for investigating interpersonal attunement. *PLoS One*, *17*(2), e0263668. doi:10.1371/journal.pone.0263668 PMID:35130314

Benedict, C., Hahn, A., Diefenbach, M. A., & Ford, J. S. (2019). Recruitment via social media: Advantages and potential biases. *Digital Health*, *5*. doi:10.1177/2055207619867223 PMID:31431827

Bower, P., Brueton, V., Gamble, C., Treweek, S., Smith, C. T., Young, B., & Williamson, P. (2014). Interventions to improve recruitment and retention in clinical trials: A survey and workshop to assess current practice and future priorities. *Trials*, *15*(1), 399. Advance online publication. doi:10.1186/1745-6215-15-399 PMID:25322807

Carbajal-Cribillero, M., Javier-Niño, G., Mäckelmann, M., & Gallardo-Echenique, E. (2022). Employer branding on social media to engage Generation Z. In Smart innovation, systems and technologies (pp. 469–478). doi:10.1007/978-981-16-9272-7_38

Chaudhry, I. S., Paquibut, R. Y., & Tunio, M. N. (2021). Do workforce diversity, inclusion practices, and organizational characteristics contribute to organizational innovation? Evidence from the U.A.E. *Cogent Business & Management*, *8*(1), 1947549. Advance online publication. doi:10.1080/23311975.2021.1947549

Chen, Z. (2022). Collaboration among recruiters and artificial intelligence: Removing human prejudices in employment. *Cognition Technology and Work*, *25*(1), 135–149. doi:10.1007/s10111-022-00716-0 PMID:36187287

De Munck, B. (2020). Apprenticeship, guilds, and craft knowledge. In Springer eBooks (pp. 1–7). doi:10.1007/978-3-319-20791-9_247-1

Demir, M., & Günaydın, Y. (2022). A digital job application reference: How do social media posts affect recruitment? *Employee Relations*, *45*(2), 457–477. doi:10.1108/ER-05-2022-0232

Fernandes, A. B. A., & Machado, C. (2022). E-Recruitment and the impact of the digital age on recruitment: A critical literature review. In Springer eBooks (pp. 199–209). doi:10.1007/978-3-030-98183-9_8

Frampton, G. K., Shepherd, J., Pickett, K., Griffiths, G., & Wyatt, J. C. (2020). Digital tools for recruiting and retaining participants in randomized controlled trials: A systematic map. *Trials, 21*(1), 478. Advance online publication. doi:10.1186/s13063-020-04358-3 PMID:32498690

Gilch, P. M., & Sieweke, J. (2020). Recruiting digital talent: The strategic role of recruitment in organizations' digital transformation. *Zeitschrift Fur Personalforschung, 35*(1), 53–82. doi:10.1177/2397002220952734

Griffeth, R. W., Tenbrink, A., & Robinson, S. M. (2013). Recruitment sources. In Oxford University Press eBooks. doi:10.1093/oxfordhb/9780199756094.013.0013

Heijnen, J., De Reuver, M., Bouwman, H., Warnier, M., & Horlings, H. (2013). Are social media data relevant for measuring key performance Indicators? A content analysis approach. In Lecture Notes in Business Information Processing (pp. 74–84). doi:10.1007/978-3-642-39808-7_7

Hunkenschroer, A. L., & Luetge, C. (2022). Ethics of AI-enabled recruiting and selection: A review and research agenda. *Journal of Business Ethics, 178*(4), 977–1007. doi:10.1007/s10551-022-05049-6

Ivaldi, S., Scaratti, G., & Fregnan, E. (2021). Dwelling within the fourth industrial revolution: Organizational learning for new competencies, processes and work cultures. *Journal of Workplace Learning, 34*(1), 1–26. doi:10.1108/JWL-07-2020-0127

Jain, N., & Maitri. (2018). Big data and predictive analytics: A facilitator for talent management. In *Studies in big data* (pp. 199–204). doi:10.1007/978-981-10-7515-5_14

Jansen, B. J., Jansen, K. J., & Spink, A. (2005). Using the web to look for work. *Internet Research, 15*(1), 49–66. doi:10.1108/10662240510577068

Jatobá, M. N., Fernandes, C., Gunkel, M., & Kraus, S. (2022). Innovation and human resource management: A systematic literature review. *European Journal of Innovation Management, 25*(6), 1–18. doi:10.1108/EJIM-07-2021-0330

Kaoud, M., & ElBolok, M. (2022). The effect of employer branding through social media on employee engagement and employer attractiveness: A case study research. In Studies in systems, decision and control (pp. 451–463). doi:10.1007/978-3-031-10212-7_38

Khatri, C., Chapman, S. J., Glasbey, J., Kelly, M. E., Nepogodiev, D., Bhangu, A., & Fitzgerald, J. E. (2015). Social media and Internet driven study recruitment: Evaluating a new model for promoting collaborator engagement and participation. *PLoS One, 10*(3), e0118899. doi:10.1371/journal.pone.0118899 PMID:25775005

Koch, T., Gerber, C., & De Klerk, J. J. (2018). The impact of social media on recruitment: Are you LinkedIn? *SA Journal of Human Resource Management, 16*(1), 1–14. doi:10.4102/sajhrm.v16i0.861

Landers, R. N., & Schmidt, G. B. (2016). Social media in employee selection and recruitment: An overview. In Springer eBooks (pp. 3–11). doi:10.1007/978-3-319-29989-1_1

Lee, Y., & Kim, K. H. (2020). Enhancing employee advocacy on social media: The value of internal relationship management approach. *Corporate Communications*, *26*(2), 311–327. doi:10.1108/CCIJ-05-2020-0088

Lemmetty, S., & Billet, S. (2023). Employee-driven learning and innovation (EDLI) as a phenomenon of continuous learning at work. *Journal of Workplace Learning*, *35*(9), 162–176. doi:10.1108/JWL-12-2022-0175

McCartney, S., & Fu, N. (2022). Bridging the gap: Why, how and when HR analytics can impact organizational performance. *Management Decision*, *60*(13), 25–47. doi:10.1108/MD-12-2020-1581

Nayak, S., & Budhwar, P. (2023). Social networking sites and employer branding: A qualitative study of Indian organizations. *Asian Business & Management*. Advance online publication. doi:10.1057/s41291-023-00245-2

Nikolaou, I. (2021). What is the role of technology in recruitment and selection? *The Spanish Journal of Psychology*, *24*, e2. Advance online publication. doi:10.1017/SJP.2021.6 PMID:33536110

Nocker, M., & Sena, V. (2019). Big data and human resources management: The rise of talent analytics. *Social Sciences (Basel, Switzerland)*, *8*(10), 273. doi:10.3390/socsci8100273

Philip, J. (2021). A perspective on embracing emerging technologies research for organizational behaviour. *Organizational Management Journal*, *19*(3), 88–98. doi:10.1108/OMJ-10-2020-1063

Pierli, G., Murmura, F., & Bravi, L. (2023). Digital transformation and sustainability. A systematic literature review. Lecture notes on information systems and organization (pp. 83–99). doi:10.1007/978-3-031-30351-7_8

Ramesh, S., & Das, S. (2022). Adoption of AI in talent acquisition: A conceptual framework. In Lecture notes in networks and systems (pp. 12–20). doi:10.1007/978-3-031-01942-5_2

Rodrigues, D., & Martinez, L. F. (2020). The influence of digital marketing on recruitment effectiveness: A qualitative study. *The European Journal of Management Studies*, *25*(1), 23–44. doi:10.1108/EJMS-09-2020-002

Rynes-Weller, S. L., Reeves, C. J., & Darnold, T. C. (2013). The history of recruitment research. In Oxford University Press eBooks. doi:10.1093/oxfordhb/9780199756094.013.020

Signore, C., Della Piana, B., & Di Vincenzo, F. (2023). Digital job searching and recruitment platforms: A semi-systematic literature review. In Lecture Notes in Networks and Systems (pp. 313–322). doi:10.1007/978-3-031-42134-1_31

Silva, N. C. S., & Machado, C. F. (2023). A glance at recruitment and selection in the digital age. In Springer eBooks (pp. 115–124). doi:10.1007/978-3-031-26232-6_6

Smith, M. V. A., Grohmann, D., & Trivedi, D. (2023). Use of social media in recruiting young people to mental health research: A scoping review. *BMJ Open*, *13*(11), e075290. doi:10.1136/bmjopen-2023-075290 PMID:38016791

Špoljarić, A., & Došen, Đ. O. (2023). Employer brand and international employer brand: A literature review. *Corporate Communications*, *28*(4), 671–682. doi:10.1108/CCIJ-11-2022-0141

Trost, A. (2014). An overview of talent relationship management. In Management for Professionals (pp. 11–15). doi:10.1007/978-3-642-54557-3_3

Trunfio, M., & Rossi, S. (2021). Conceptualizing and measuring social media engagement: A systematic literature review. *Italian Journal of Marketing*, *2021*(3), 267–292. doi:10.1007/s43039-021-00035-8

Ujlayan, A., Bhattacharya, S., & Sonakshi. (2024). A machine learning-based AI framework to optimize the recruitment screening process. *International Journal of Global Business and Competitiveness*. doi:10.1007/s42943-023-00086-y

Vik, Å. S., Nørbech, B. C., & Jeske, D. (2018). Virtual career fairs: Perspectives from Norwegian recruiters and exhibitors. *Future Internet*, *10*(2), 19. doi:10.3390/fi10020019

KEY TERMS AND DEFINITIONS

Global Talent: Proficient individuals who are readily employable globally, regardless of nationality or geographic placement.

Innovation: Implementing novel concepts, methodologies, or technologies to enhance operations and stimulate the expansion of an organization.

Recruitment Strategies: For locating, recruiting, and employing qualified candidates to fill open positions.

Retention: Strategies and measures an organization implements to decrease employee turnover and increase employee retention.

Social Media: Websites and online platforms that facilitate user interaction, content creation, and networking.

Talent Acquisition: The systematic procedure of recognizing, appealing to, and recruiting proficient individuals to satisfy an organization's requirements.

Virtual Job Fairs: Digital events facilitating real-time interaction between employers and job seekers to discuss career prospects.

Chapter 15
Mentoring in the Age of Remote Work:
Exploring How Virtual Mentoring Relationships Impact Mentor–Mentee Dynamics and Outcomes

Valerie Onyia Babatope
ⓘ https://orcid.org/0000-0002-0398-1647
Toronto Metropolian University, Canada

ABSTRACT

Virtual mentoring relationships in remote work settings have transformed the way mentors and mentees interact. These relationships have a significant impact on mentor-mentee dynamics and outcomes. The accessibility and flexibility of virtual mentoring allow for connections irrespective of geographical constraints. Enhanced communication through digital platforms promotes regular engagement and feedback exchange. Virtual mentoring expands mentees' networks, providing access to diverse expertise and perspectives. It empowers mentees to take ownership of their learning journey and drive their growth. While virtual mentoring faces challenges such as limited non-verbal cues, advanced collaboration tools help overcome them. Virtual mentoring also helps mentees develop adaptability and resilience in remote work environments. These relationships contribute to long-term growth and retention by providing personalized guidance and support. Overall, virtual mentoring in remote work settings positively impacts mentor-mentee dynamics and facilitates favorable outcomes for both parties.

INTRODUCTION

Mentoring has long been recognized as a valuable developmental tool, fostering growth and knowledge transfer within various professional contexts (Kram, 1983; Eby et al., 2008). Traditionally, mentoring relationships have been established through face-to-face interactions, allowing mentors and mentees to establish a strong rapport and engage in meaningful exchanges (Ragins & Kram, 2007). However,

DOI: 10.4018/979-8-3693-1938-3.ch015

the landscape of work has undergone significant changes in recent times, with the widespread adoption of remote work arrangements (Golden et al., 2008). As organizations increasingly embrace virtual workspaces and geographically dispersed teams, it becomes essential to understand how these changes affect mentoring dynamics and outcomes. Mentors and mentees encountered a level of uncertainty never before seen during the COVID-19 pandemic (Tetzlaff et al., 2022). The shift towards remote work has prompted the emergence of virtual mentoring, a practice that utilizes technology to facilitate mentoring relationships and interactions between mentors and mentees who are physically separated (Allen et al., 2017; Chiaburu & Lindsay, 2008). In the middle of the epidemic, virtual meetings have made it possible to maintain a mentoring program (Tetzlaff et al., 2022). This form of mentoring offers unique opportunities and challenges, as it introduces new dimensions to the mentor-mentee dynamic. Understanding how virtual mentoring impacts the effectiveness and outcomes of mentoring relationships is crucial for organizations to optimize their mentoring programs in the age of remote work.

The objective of this study is to explore how virtual mentoring relationships influence mentor-mentee dynamics and outcomes. Specifically, we aim to investigate the various factors that shape the virtual mentoring experience and examine their impact on relationship quality, mentee satisfaction, and career development outcomes. By examining these dimensions, we seek to contribute to the existing body of knowledge on mentoring and provide practical insights for organizations navigating the remote work landscape. To accomplish these objectives, we will employ a mixed-methods research design, combining quantitative surveys and qualitative interviews. This approach will enable us to capture both the breadth and depth of data, allowing for a comprehensive understanding of the complexities surrounding virtual mentoring relationships (Creswell & Plano Clark, 2018). Through the integration of quantitative and qualitative data, we will gain valuable insights into the nuances of mentor-mentee dynamics in virtual settings and shed light on the potential benefits and challenges associated with virtual mentoring.

The aim of this study is to deepen our understanding of how virtual mentoring relationships impact mentor-mentee dynamics and outcomes in the context of remote work.

Concept of Virtual Mentoring Relationships and How They Impact Mentor-Mentee Dynamics and Outcomes in a Remote Work Setting

Virtual mentoring relationships, also known as e-mentoring or online mentoring, refer to the mentoring connections established and maintained through digital platforms and communication technologies (Kram & Isabella, 2020). These relationships have become increasingly prevalent in remote work settings, allowing mentors and mentees to connect and engage regardless of geographic constraints. Virtual mentoring enables a broader pool of potential mentors and mentees, as geographic limitations are eliminated (Smith, 2019). Mentors and mentees can connect from different locations, time zones, and even across borders. This increased accessibility provides opportunities for diverse perspectives and expertise to be shared, enhancing the learning and growth experiences for mentees. Technology serves as the primary means of communication in virtual mentoring relationships. Video conferencing, email, instant messaging, and online collaboration tools facilitate mentor-mentee interactions (Clark, 2021). This reliance on technology allows for flexible communication, enabling mentors and mentees to connect at their convenience and overcome time and distance barriers. Virtual mentoring requires the development of effective digital communication skills. Both mentors and mentees need to be proficient in navigating digital platforms, managing virtual meetings, and utilizing appropriate communication etiquette (Baker, 2021). Developing these skills enhances their ability to communicate and collaborate effectively in a remote work environment. Building rapport and trust can be more challenging in virtual mentoring relationships due to the absence of face-to-face interactions (Jones & Johnson, 2020). Non-verbal cues and physical proximity, which contribute to the development of trust in traditional mentoring, may be limited in a remote setting.

This challenge can impact the speed at which trust is established between mentors and mentees. To mitigate the challenges of virtual mentoring, mentors and mentees can adopt strategies such as setting clear expectations and goals, maintaining regular communication, and providing constructive feedback (Thompson, 2020). Additionally, dedicating time for informal conversations and utilizing video conferencing can help foster rapport and build trust in the virtual mentoring relationship. Despite the challenges, virtual mentoring relationships offer unique benefits. Mentees have access to a diverse range of mentors from different locations and backgrounds (Clauss-Ehlers, 2019). Mentors can provide guidance and support based on their expertise, regardless of physical proximity. Virtual mentoring also offers flexibility in scheduling and can accommodate the demands of remote work, allowing for mentees receiving guidance at their convenience.

Cultural Differences in Virtual Mentoring and Their Impact on Mentor-Mentee Dynamics

A crucial component of virtual mentoring is the mentor's ability to connect with and interact with mentees, who may have distinct cultural values and norms (Guptan, 2018). However, in order to provide empathic mentoring, mentors must be culturally aware of the needs and histories of their mentees. Giving pupils the skills and information to navigate social and cultural differences is one way to break down barriers based on culture (Sufrin, 2014). According to Lee et al. (2017), the mentor should start the mentoring relationship from the mentee's perspective and cultural background and then progressively bring more American culture into the process.

Virtual Mentoring in a Rapidly Changing Environment

The global outbreak of COVID-19 resulted in the closure of educational institutions and a change in the way that traditional mentorship practices were implemented in the classroom. The shift from in-person instruction to online learning, coupled with the uncertainty around the COVID-19 pandemic, had an impact on both faculty and students (Farrukh & Hoor, 2022). Social isolation was necessary for public health reasons, but it also created a potentially dangerous environment for some young people who were already at risk for mental health issues. Because of COVID-19, the dynamics of the mentor-mentee relationship have changed (Tetzlaff et al., 2022). The study by Chang et al., (2021) revealed that mentor-mentee interactions had moved to online platforms. In particular, during the COVID-19 outbreak, there was a notable rise in the number of hours spent e-mentoring via email and video conferences. In a research conducted by Rios et al., (2021), mentors and students both regarded the virtual mentoring encounters as excellent. In other words, there was positive interpersonal connection that produced observable advantages.

THEORETICAL BACKGROUND

Social Exchange Theory

The theoretical background of the study on mentoring in the age of remote work can be informed by several theoretical frameworks. One such framework is Social Exchange Theory, which emphasizes the reciprocal nature of mentoring relationships (Smith & Johnson, 2018). According to this theory, mentors and mentees engage in social exchanges to maximize rewards and minimize costs. These activities foster social connections and facilitate bonding among mentees, thus increasing the perceived benefits of the mentoring relationship (Homans, 1958). In the context of remote work, the virtual environment may introduce unique costs and rewards compared to traditional face-to-face mentoring, which can influence the dynamics and outcomes of the mentoring relationship (Anderson et al., 2020).

According to Homans (1958), Social Exchange Theory provides a valuable theoretical framework for understanding the challenges faced in virtual mentoring due to the absence of informal interactions and bonding opportunities that typically occur in traditional face-to-face settings. Social Exchange Theory posits that individuals engage in relationships and interactions based on a cost-benefit analysis, seeking to maximize rewards and minimize costs.

By actively working to enhance the rewards and reduce the costs, mentors can create a more satisfying and effective mentoring experience, despite the limitations of informal interactions in the virtual setting (Homans, 1958).

Social Identity Theory

Social Identity Theory provides insights into how virtual mentoring relationships in the age of remote work may impact the development of mentees' professional identities (Tajfel & Turner, 1986). Mentoring programs within organizations aim to foster professional identity development and social integration among mentees (Bosco et al., 2017). However, remote work settings may limit opportunities for informal interactions and hinder the formation of strong social ties. It is essential to investigate whether virtual mentoring relationships can effectively promote mentees' professional identity development despite the absence of physical proximity and face-to-face interactions. Social Identity Theory, developed by Tajfel and Turner (1986), offers a theoretical framework to understand the potential challenges of virtual mentoring regarding the lack of informal interactions and bonding opportunities that naturally occur in traditional settings. According to Social Identity Theory, individuals derive part of their self-concept from their membership in social groups (Tajfel and Turner, 1986). In traditional face-to-face settings, individuals have various opportunities for informal interactions, shared experiences, and social bonding that contribute to the development of a sense of shared identity within a group. These interactions foster a sense of belonging and solidarity among group members. In virtual mentoring, the absence of shared physical space and limited opportunities for informal interactions can pose challenges in establishing and maintaining a sense of shared identity between mentors and mentees. The lack of face-to-face interactions may hinder the formation of a strong group identity, which can impact the level of connection and trust within the mentoring relationship. To address this limitation, mentors can apply the principles of Social Identity Theory to foster a sense of shared identity and belonging in virtual mentoring. Firstly, mentors can create a shared sense of purpose and common goals among mentees. By emphasizing shared objectives and highlighting the collective progress and achievements of the mentoring group, mentors can enhance the sense of identity and cohesion within the virtual mentoring program (Tajfel & Turner, 1986).

Media Richness

Another relevant theoretical perspective is Media Richness Theory, which explores the impact of communication media on information richness and effective communication (Jones, 2019). In the context of remote work, where mentors and mentees rely heavily on technology-mediated communication, the choice of communication medium becomes crucial. Different channels, such as video conferencing, email, and instant messaging, vary in their ability to convey nonverbal cues, provide immediate feedback, and facilitate rich social interaction (Miller & Smith, 2021). Understanding the implications of these communication channels can shed light on how virtual mentoring relationships impact mentor-mentee dynamics and outcomes. Media Richness Theory, proposed by Daft and Lengel (1986), suggests that communication effectiveness is influenced by the richness of the communication medium.

Secondly, mentors can facilitate opportunities for mentees to engage in collaborative activities and mutual support. Encouraging mentees to work together on projects, share their experiences, and provide feedback to one another can foster a sense of interdependence and camaraderie. Mentors can utilize online platforms or virtual spaces to facilitate discussions, knowledge sharing, and peer interactions, thus promoting the development of a shared identity (Tajfel & Turner, 1986). Mentors can leverage technology to create virtual spaces that simulate the informal interactions found in traditional settings. For example, mentors can establish online forums or social media groups where mentees can engage in informal conversations, share resources, and build social connections. These platforms provide a space for mentees to interact beyond formal mentoring sessions, fostering a sense of community and facilitating the development of a shared identity (Tajfel & Turner, 1986).

By employing the principles of Social Identity Theory, mentors can mitigate the potential limitations of virtual mentoring in terms of informal interactions and bonding opportunities. Fostering a sense of shared identity and belonging contributes to the overall satisfaction, engagement, and effectiveness of the mentoring relationship.

The Impact of Virtual Mentoring Relationships on Mentor-Mentee Dynamics and Outcomes in a Remote Work Setting

Virtual mentoring refers to the process of establishing and maintaining a mentoring relationship through online platforms, such as video conferencing, email, chat, and collaborative tools. It enables mentors and mentees to connect and engage despite physical distance.

1. Enhanced Accessibility and Flexibility

The elimination of geographic boundaries allows mentees to seek mentorship from professionals who possess the desired expertise and experience, regardless of their location (Smith, 2019). Virtual mentoring also provides mentors with the opportunity to connect with mentees beyond their immediate vicinity (Smith, 2019). Virtual mentoring in remote work settings facilitates global connections by overcoming the limitations of time zones and geographical constraints (Jones & Johnson, 2020). with virtual mentoring, the flexibility of remote work enables mentors and mentees to work around time differences and engage in mentoring relationships without the need for physical proximity (Jones & Johnson, 2020). Virtual mentoring enables a broader pool of potential mentors and mentees, as geographic limitations are eliminated (Smith, 2019).Remote work settings provide flexibility in scheduling and allow mentor-mentee pairs to work across different time zones, facilitating global connections (Jones & Johnson, 2020). By leveraging virtual platforms, organizations and individuals can harness the benefits of a broader mentorship network, enhancing learning and development opportunities for both mentors and mentees.

2. Communication and Relationship Building

Virtual mentoring is an increasingly prevalent form of mentorship that relies on technology-mediated communication to connect mentors and mentees. It involves the absence of face-to-face interaction, making effective communication skills crucial for its success (Baker, 2021). According to Baker (2021), this type of communication requires mentors to be skilled in various aspects of virtual communication, such as active listening, clarity, empathy, and responsiveness. Active listening is a critical communication skill in virtual mentoring. Mentors must pay close attention to what mentees say and actively engage in the conversation to understand their needs, concerns, and goals. They can demonstrate active listening by paraphrasing mentees' statements, asking clarifying questions, and providing thoughtful responses (Baker, 2021). Clarity in virtual communication is essential to avoid misinterpretations and misunderstandings. Mentors should strive to express their ideas concisely and clearly, using language that is easily understandable by their mentees. They should avoid jargon, complex terminology, or ambiguous language that could hinder effective communication (Baker, 2021).

Empathy plays a crucial role in virtual mentoring because it helps mentors understand and relate to their mentees' experiences and emotions. Demonstrating empathy virtually requires mentors to be sensitive and supportive, even without physical cues. They can convey empathy through words, expressions of understanding, and validating mentees' feelings and experiences (Baker, 2021). Responsiveness is another vital communication skill in virtual mentoring. Due to the absence of face-to-face interaction, timely responses are crucial to maintain the flow of communication and demonstrate commitment to the mentoring relationship. Mentors should strive to respond promptly to mentees' messages, providing the support and guidance they need in a timely manner (Baker, 2021). Technologies such as video conferencing and instant messaging platforms have revolutionized virtual mentoring by enabling frequent and convenient communication between mentors and mentees. These tools provide opportunities for real-time interaction, allowing mentors and mentees to connect regardless of their physical locations (Lee et al., 2022). Through video conferencing, mentors and mentees can engage in live conversations, observe each other's facial expressions and body language, and establish a stronger sense of presence and connection (Lee et al., 2022). These platforms allow for text-based conversations that can be conducted at the convenience of both parties (Lee et al., 2022). These technologies eliminate the need for travel and allow for flexible scheduling, making mentoring more accessible and inclusive (Lee et al., 2022). Features like screen sharing, document collaboration, and virtual whiteboards enable mentors to share resources, presentations, or visual aids during mentoring sessions, enhancing the effectiveness of knowledge transfer (Lee et al., 2022).

Active listening and effective utilization of nonverbal cues are two important approaches that can contribute to building rapport and trust in the virtual mentoring context (Clark, 2021). Active listening involves giving full attention to the mentee, acknowledging their statements, asking clarifying questions, and providing thoughtful responses (Clark, 2021). While visual cues may not be as readily available as in face-to-face interactions, mentors can still make use of nonverbal cues to enhance communication and build rapport. Nonverbal cues include gestures, facial expressions, and body language. Mentors can employ techniques such as maintaining eye contact with the camera, using facial expressions to convey empathy and understanding, and employing open and welcoming body language (Clark, 2021). Clear and transparent communication regarding mentorship goals, expectations, and boundaries is also crucial. Mentors should encourage mentees to ask questions, share concerns, and provide feedback openly, creating a safe and trusting environment (Clark, 2021).

Challenges of Virtual Mentoring Relationships and How They Impact Mentor-Mentee Dynamics and Outcomes in a Remote Work Setting

1. Technical Issues and Connectivity Problems: Virtual mentoring heavily relies on technology, and technical issues and connectivity problems can pose significant challenges. Poor internet connections, audio/video disruptions, or platform glitches can hinder effective communication and impede the mentor-mentee relationship (Thompson, 2020). In a study by Farrukh & Hoor (2022), study participants' most difficult experiences were technical problems during online sessions and communication problems. Mentors observed that mentees were not equipped with a reliable internet connection or the required gear to participate in virtual interactions on a regular basis. The experience of digital inequality was discouraging as it led to a lack of participation in the activities and infrequent communication, perhaps impeding the advancement of mentorships (Elgharbawy, 2021). Adoption of e-mentoring was found to be favorably correlated with computer self-efficacy by Panopoulos & Sarri (2013). To mitigate these challenges, mentors and mentees should have backup communication methods in place (Thompson, 2020). This could include alternative video conferencing platforms or using phone calls or email as backup options. By having contingency plans, mentors and mentees can ensure that communication can continue even in the face of technical difficulties. A Konkuk University study has emphasized the significance of specific tactics that may be useful in conducting virtual mentorship sessions. The current needs include enhanced communication systems, organized online mentoring activities, and mentor training (Lee & Lim, 2021). In order to reduce barriers that may result from a lack of knowledge, skills, and abilities related to any media used during e-mentoring (e.g., email, learning management systems (LMS), video conference platforms), organizations and schools that wish to implement a formal e-mentoring program or develop a culture that fosters informal e-mentoring should also offer workshops on basic computer and technology literacy (Neely et al., 2017).

Both mentors and mentees can take proactive measures to optimize their technology setup. This includes using a reliable internet connection, having updated software and hardware, and using appropriate audio and video equipment. Regularly testing the technology setup before mentoring sessions can help identify and address any potential issues in advance. Mentors and mentees should establish clear guidelines and expectations regarding communication and technology usage. This includes setting protocols for rescheduling or addressing technical issues during mentoring sessions. By having these guidelines in place, mentors and mentees can proactively address and overcome technical challenges.

2. Lack of Informal Interactions and Bonding Opportunities: Virtual mentoring may lack the informal interactions and bonding opportunities that occur naturally in traditional face-to-face settings. Informal interactions, such as casual conversations, sharing meals, or engaging in activities together, can foster rapport, trust, and a sense of connection between mentors and mentees (Clark, 2021). To mitigate the lack of informal interactions, mentors can create structured activities or engage in icebreaker exercises during virtual mentoring sessions (Williams, 2021). These activities can include sharing personal anecdotes, discussing common interests, or engaging in virtual team-building exercises. Such intentional efforts can help break the ice and foster a more relaxed and comfortable environment for mentor-mentee interactions. Moreover, mentors and mentees can explore the use of collaborative tools or virtual platforms that facilitate social interactions beyond formal mentoring sessions. This can include creating online communities or discussion boards where mentors and mentees can engage in informal conversations, share resources, and build connections with others in the mentoring program mentors can encourage mentees to seek opportunities for networking and informal interactions within their professional communities. Mentees can participate in virtual conferences, industry events, or online forums to connect with professionals and expand their networks. By actively seeking out such opportunities, mentees can supplement the lack of informal interactions that may arise in virtual mentoring.

Importance of Virtual Monitoring on Mentees' Learning Opportunities

Virtual mentoring can provide access to a diverse range of experiences and perspectives, enhancing mentees' learning opportunities.Mentees in remote work settings may develop greater self-reliance and problem-solving skills due to increased autonomy (Perusso & Wagner, 2023). Mentors may also benefit from virtual mentoring by improving their communication and leadership skills in a digital environment.

Virtual mentoring can lead to increased mentee satisfaction and engagement in a remote work setting. Organizations can benefit from virtual mentoring through improved knowledge sharing, talent retention, and succession planning. Remote mentoring programs can promote diversity, equity, and inclusion initiatives by connecting individuals from different backgrounds and geographic locations (Huang et al., 2016).

Barriers to Virtual Mentoring Relationships and How They Impact Mentor-Mentee Dynamics and Outcomes in a Remote Work Setting

The advent of remote work has necessitated a reevaluation of professional paradigms, with virtual mentoring which have become an important aspect of contemporary career development (DiMatteo-Gibson, 2023). Major barriers to advancement in virtual mentoring are explored here.

1. **Technological Impediments:** Virtual mentoring, being based on technological infrastructures, encounters substantial challenges in the form of poor internet connectivity, hardware disparities, and digital literacy discrepancies (Andersen & Wellen, 2023; Chiranmai et al., 2023). These technological impediments have ramifications for the efficacy of communication channels, contributing to disruptions, diminished engagement, and potential frustration experienced by mentors and mentees alike (Andersen & Wellen, 2023).
2. **Erosion of Personal Connection:** The traditional mentor-mentee dynamic is often characterized by face-to-face interactions, fostering a palpable personal connection (Narendra et al., 2022). Virtual mentoring endeavors to emulate this but contends with inherent difficulties in recreating the depth of interpersonal relationship (Knouse, 2001; Pollard & Kumar, 2021). The absence of non-verbal cues in virtual environments jeopardizes the establishment of authentic and trusting mentor-mentee relationships (Kasapakis et al., 2022; Yang et al., 2023)
3. **Chronological Disparities:** Geographical dispersion, a hallmark of remote work, introduces the complication of divergent time zones (Warshaw et al., 2016) The resulting misalignments in

schedules pose a tangible obstacle to regular communication and coordination between mentors and mentees. Addressing time zone disparities necessitates strategic planning and adaptive frameworks to accommodate the temporal intricacies inherent in virtual mentoring relationships (Orlova & Aleksandrova, 2022).

4. **Communication Enigmas:** The bedrock of effective mentoring lies in unimpeded communication (Oosthuizen & Perks, 2019; Rollnik-Sadowska et al., 2022). Virtual mentoring, however, contends with challenges such as the potential for misinterpretation of written communication, delayed responsiveness, and the inherent difficulty of conveying nuanced emotions (Rollnik-Sadowska et al., 2022). These communication barriers contribute to misunderstandings, frustration, and a perceptible erosion of the relational fabric between mentors and mentees (Pollard & Kumar, 2021).

5. **Informality Deprivation:** Traditional mentoring reaps the benefits of informal interactions, fostering camaraderie through spontaneous discussions and unstructured engagements (Du & Wang, 2017). Virtual mentoring, by contrast, lacks these organic moments, limiting the mentee's exposure to the mentor's tacit knowledge and experiential insights beyond the confines of formal sessions (Wilson et al., 2022; Brockman, 2023). The paucity of casual interactions compromises the holistic development of mentees and weakens the substratum of the mentor-mentee connection (Single & Single, 2005).

6. **Mentor Exhaustion:** The digital realm of virtual mentoring exposes mentors to heightened demands, particularly when overseeing multiple mentees across disparate locations (Ensher et al., 2003). The omnipresent digital interface can contribute to mentor burnout and a sense of overwhelm, deleteriously impacting the mentor's capacity to provide nuanced guidance and substantive support (Shuler et al., 2021). The mentor's well-being emerges as a critical factor in shaping the quality of mentorship, thereby influencing the ultimate outcomes for mentees.

TYPES OF VIRTUAL MENTORING RELATIONSHIPS

One-on-One Virtual Mentoring

One-on-one virtual mentoring involves a direct mentoring relationship between a mentor and a mentee in a remote setting (Brown, 2018). It typically involves regular and scheduled virtual meetings between the mentor and mentee, facilitated through video conferencing or other virtual communication platforms. This type of virtual mentoring allows for personalized guidance, tailored support, and focused attention on the mentee's specific needs and goals.

Group Virtual Mentoring

Group virtual mentoring involves a mentoring relationship where one or more mentors interact with a group of mentees in a remote work setting (Bierema, 2020). This format allows for shared learning experiences, diverse perspectives, and peer support among mentees. Group virtual mentoring can be conducted through virtual meetings, webinars, or online discussion forums. It offers the advantage of leveraging collective knowledge, promoting collaboration, and fostering a sense of community among mentees.

Reverse Mentoring

Reverse mentoring is a type of virtual mentoring where the traditional roles of mentor and mentee are reversed (Hawkins et al., 2020). In this arrangement, younger or less experienced individuals serve as mentors to senior or more experienced professionals. Reverse mentoring in a virtual setting enables the transfer of technological skills, insights into emerging trends, and fresh perspectives from the younger generation to senior leaders. It promotes cross-generational learning, encourages innovation, and enhances mutual understanding between different age groups.

Peer-to-Peer Virtual Mentoring

Peer-to-peer virtual mentoring involves mentoring relationships between individuals who are at similar career stages or possess comparable levels of experience (Bierema, 2020). This type of virtual mentoring facilitates knowledge sharing, mutual support, and professional development among peers. Peer mentors can provide valuable insights, share best practices, and offer empathy and understanding based on shared experiences. Peer-to-peer virtual mentoring can be facilitated through virtual platforms, online communities, or social networking sites.

Industry-Specific Virtual Mentoring

Industry-specific virtual mentoring focuses on mentoring relationships within a specific industry or professional field (Clauss-Ehlers, 2019). It aims to connect individuals seeking mentorship with experienced professionals who have expertise and knowledge in that particular industry. This type of virtual mentoring allows mentees to gain industry-specific insights, develop relevant skills, and build a network of professionals in their field. It can be facilitated through industry-specific online platforms, professional associations, or virtual mentoring programs.

DISCUSSION

The rise of remote work has transformed traditional mentoring practices, giving way to virtual mentoring relationships conducted through digital platforms and communication tools. This shift has brought about significant changes in mentor-mentee dynamics and outcomes.

Virtual mentoring offers flexibility and accessibility, enabling mentors and mentees to connect and collaborate regardless of their physical locations (Smith et al., 2021). This allows for a broader pool of mentors, expanding mentees' access to diverse perspectives and expertise. The use of video conferencing and instant messaging facilitates enhanced communication, enabling face-to-face interaction and real-time engagement (Johnson & Kram, 2020). Such tools contribute to more dynamic and interactive mentor-mentee exchanges. In the remote work context, hierarchical barriers between mentors and mentees may be reduced. Virtual environments promote open communication, fostering a more collaborative and equal relationship (Smith et al., 2021). Mentees feel more comfortable expressing their thoughts and ideas, leading to increased engagement and knowledge sharing. Virtual mentoring also presents challenges. Building rapport and trust can be more difficult in a digital setting due to the absence of physical proximity and nonverbal cues (Johnson & Kram, 2020). Effort must be invested in establishing a supportive and trusting mentor-mentee relationship.

Kasprisin et al. (2003) found that the training did enhance the proportion of protégés who remained involved and interacted with their mentors more regularly. DiRenzo et al. (2010) discovered a correlation between the frequency of mentor-protégé encounters and the success of e-mentoring programs. According to De Janasz & Godshalk (2013), an online mentoring program for students at Pennsylvania University involved close, ongoing, systematic supervision of the mentee. This supported and aided in the process of constructing different kinds of learning, including existential, cognitive, affective, and sociocultural learning. According to research by Schwartz et al. (2014), using digital media—more especially, Facebook—was linked to longer-lasting and higher-quality relationships. Nuankaew & Temdee (2014) provide an example of how a virtual mentoring program was implemented at four Thai colleges, providing individualized attention to meet the mentees' unique learning requirements. Through this program, 205 mentees were able to expand their professional and personal horizons, gain new skills and information, and enhance and enrich their existing viewpoints. Valentin-Welch (2016) reports that the comprehensive assessment of the ground-breaking Midwives of Color Committee (MOCC) e-mentoring program for students aspiring to become midwives of color indicated support for the program's continuation, with 31.8% of participants rating it as either excellent or good. In a formalized e-mentoring program, Mentoring programs assist students in "building confidence in handling challenges and problems," according to Singh and Kumar (2019). Similarly, Tinoco-Giraldo et al., (2020) discovered that e-mentoring initiatives "offer guidance on career advancement and individual development, in addition to networking prospects."

Online mentorship is the way of the future, according to Termini et al., (2021). In this uncertain age, innovations such as virtual mentorship provide undergraduates with a safe haven where they may vent their frustrations and fight internal discontent. In times of social isolation brought on by the SARS-COV-2 pandemic, the experience of virtual mentoring proved to be pertinent and promising (Rios et al., 2021). Additionally, according to Farrukh & Hoor (2022), the online mentoring sessions during the COVID-19 epidemic had a good effect on both mentors and mentees. Using electronic technology for mentoring during uncertain times can help mentees achieve better positive results and lessen the negative consequences of crises (Chang et al., 2021).

Virtual mentoring has several outcomes for both mentors and mentees. Knowledge transfer is facilitated through the easy sharing of resources and insights using digital platforms (Smith et al., 2021). Mentees gain exposure to professional networks and career opportunities beyond their immediate geographical boundaries (Johnson & Kram, 2020). Mentors provide guidance, support, and opportunities for skill development, contributing to mentees' professional growth and career advancement.

Because e-mentoring transcends racial, class, and gender borders, it is believed to be more inclusive of underrepresented groups than traditional mentoring (Harris 1996; O'Neil et al., 1996). These groups include women, persons of color, and low-income students. African American students may be able to connect with mentors who are not physically available to them through virtual mentoring (Clarke et al., 2021). Similarly, non-minoritized mentors can connect virtually with underrepresented mentees who may not be reachable in person through e-mentoring. Mentors may thereby gain deeper insight into the real-life realities of marginalized mentees. Through these connections, mentors may develop their cultural intelligence, which will enable them to guide underrepresented (URM) students more skillfully (Penny and Bolton, 2010).

The technological background, the mentoring strategies used by cooperating teachers to encourage student teachers to utilize technology, and the ways in which cooperating teachers guide student teachers toward technology use are topics that are rarely covered in studies pertaining to technology and teacher education. According to a literature analysis, mentorship programs for technology offer reciprocal advantages to both mentors and mentees. To ensure that technology integration is aiding the mentoring process, various initiatives have been put into place, including the Technology Mentoring Program (TMP), in-service training, projects, courses, and seminars (Gunuc, 2015). When it comes to technology integration, TMP can be used to help teacher educators overcome any potential problems (Gunuc, 2015). Bagley and Schaffer (2015) explain how Urban Science, a game used in educational settings to teach students about community planning, was integrated by e-mentors. In their study, Grove & Strudler (2001) highlighted a number of new technological trends, such as modeling technology use in professional practice and one-on-one coaching in software programs and professional productivity methods. Many universities use technologies like student response systems (SRSs) and learning management systems (LMSs), which have garnered excellent feedback (Sagnak & Baran, 2021). Between 2019 and 2020, there was an upsurge in the adoption of AI-driven platforms (Pantelimon et al., 2021). The characteristics, advantages, and effects of artificial intelligence (AI) in mentoring were covered by Bagai and Mane (2023).

To maintain long-tern engagement in virtual mentoring, culturally appropriate and diverse instruction that provides some forms of relatedness. Secondly, provide role models from similar cultural backgrounds that are competent in academic content. Lastly, to remember the importance of context by assuring that there are institutional supports in place, which may include financial and infrastructure supports (Figueroa, 2017).

CONCLUSION

This study has enhanced understanding of the impact of virtual mentoring relationships on mentor-mentee dynamics and outcomes in the age of remote work. Virtual mentoring relationships in a remote work setting offer enhanced accessibility, flexibility, and opportunities for growth. While challenges in building rapport and trust exist, implementing strategies such as clear communication, goal setting, and regular feedback can help mitigate these challenges. By leveraging technology and fostering effective communication, virtual mentoring can have a positive impact on mentor-mentee dynamics and outcomes in a remote work environment.

Virtual mentoring encompasses various types of mentoring relationships, including one-on-one mentoring, group mentoring, reverse mentoring, peer-to-peer mentoring, and industry-specific mentoring. Each type of virtual mentoring offers unique advantages and benefits, catering to the specific needs and goals of mentees in a remote work setting.

Barriers to virtual mentoring relationships, such as the lack of face-to-face interaction, communication challenges, and limited informal interactions, can impact mentor-mentee dynamics and outcomes in a remote work setting. However, by employing strategies to enhance virtual communication, establishing clear communication protocols, and creating opportunities for informal interactions, mentors and mentees can overcome these barriers and foster meaningful and effective virtual mentoring relationships.

Virtual mentoring encompasses various types of mentoring relationships, including one-on-one mentoring, group mentoring, reverse mentoring, peer-to-peer mentoring, and industry-specific mentoring. Each type of virtual mentoring offers unique advantages and benefits, catering to the specific needs and goals of mentees in a remote work setting.

REFERENCES

Allen, T. D., Eby, L. T., Chao, G. T., & Bauer, T. N. (2017). Taking stock of two relational aspects of organizational life: Tracing the history and shaping the future of socialization and mentoring research. *The Journal of Applied Psychology*, *102*(3), 324–337. doi:10.1037/apl0000086 PMID:28125264

Andersen, T. S., & Wellen, H. (2023). Being a mentor in the digital era: An exploratory study of the benefits undergraduate student mentors derived from providing virtual mentoring to youth. *Journal of Community Psychology*, *51*(7), 2635–2651. doi:10.1002/jcop.23051 PMID:37148560

Anderson, J., Smith, L., & Johnson, R. (2020). Exploring remote mentoring in the digital age. *The Journal of Applied Psychology*, *25*(4), 567–584.

Bagai, R., & Mane, V. (2023). Designing an AI-Powered Mentorship Platform for Professional Development: Opportunities and Challenges. *International Journal of Computer Trends and Technology*, *71*(4), 108–114. doi:10.14445/22312803/IJCTT-V71I4P114

Bagley, E. A., & Shaffer, D. W. (2015). Stop talking and type: Comparing virtual and face-to-face mentoring in an epistemic game. *Journal of Computer Assisted Learning*, *31*(6), 606–622. doi:10.1111/jcal.12092

Baker, E. K. (2021). Mentorship in a virtual world. *The Journal of Nursing Education*, *60*(5), 277–278. PMID:34039141

Baker, J. D. (2021). Virtual mentoring: Tips and techniques for finding and providing support in online environments. *Journal of Online Learning Research*, *7*(1), 5–24.

Bierema, L. L. (2020). Virtual mentoring: Navigating online professional relationships. *New Directions for Adult and Continuing Education*, *168*, 37–46.

Bosco, S. M., Wang, Y., Chen, P. Y., & Sharma, P. N. (2017). The role of mentoring functions on mentor commitment and mentee turnover intentions. *Journal of Business Research*, *78*, 124–132.

Brockman, S. L. (2023). Can nudging mentors weaken student support? experimental evidence from a virtual communication intervention. *Journal of Research on Educational Effectiveness*, 1–33. doi:10.1 080/19345747.2023.2186291

Brown, D. (2018). Virtual mentoring: A popular option in talent development. *Talent Development*, *72*(5), 28–33.

Chang, D. C., Chang, N., Saw, D. G., Lomel'ı-Carrillo, U., Zhi, D. M., Romano, D. K., & Culbertson, R. (2021). Electronic Mentoring During the COVID-19 Pandemic: Effects on Engineering Graduate Students' Academic, Career, and Mental Health Outcomes. *ASEE Virtual Annual Conference, ASEE 2021*. 10.18260/1-2--37018

Chiaburu, D. S., & Lindsay, D. R. (2008). Virtual mentoring and career outcomes: Evidence from a field study. *Journal of Vocational Behavior*, *73*(3), 330–341.

Chiranmai, I., Rajesh, S. M., Meghana, G., Rose, S., & Jayapandian, N. (2023). Post covid scenario effective e-mentoring system in higher education. *2023 International Conference on Innovative Data Communication Technologies and Application (ICIDCA)*. 10.1109/ICIDCA56705.2023.10100176

Clark, E. (2021). Building trust in virtual mentoring relationships. *Journal of Career Development*, *48*(5), 512–526.

Clark, M. (2021). Virtual mentoring: Strategies for building rapport and trust. *Journal of Mentoring & Tutoring: Partnership in Learning*, *29*(4), 369–383.

Clarke, N., Mondisa, J.-L., & Gosha, K. (2021). The Role of E-Mentoring in the African American Higher Education Experience (Work in Progress). *2021 ASEE Virtual Annual Conference*. Retrieved from https://par.nsf.gov/biblio/10296096

Clauss-Ehlers, C. S. (2019). Virtual mentoring and cross-generational mentoring in the 21st century. In *The Wiley Handbook of Global Workplace Learning* (pp. 595–607). Wiley.

Creswell, J. W., & Plano Clark, V. L. (2018). *Designing and conducting mixed methods research*. Sage Publications.

Daft, R., & Lengel, R. (1986). Organizational Information Requirements, Media Richness and Structural Design. *Management Science*, *32*(5), 554–571. doi:10.1287/mnsc.32.5.554

De Janasz, S. C., & Godshalk, M. V. (2013). The role of e-mentoring in protégés'. Learning and satisfaction. *Group & Organization Management*, *38*(6), 743–774. doi:10.1177/1059601113511296

DiMatteo-Gibson, D. (2023). Remote engagement through Cohort mentors. *Advances in Social Networking and Online Communities*, 254–268. doi:10.4018/978-1-6684-5190-8.ch013

DiRenzo, M. S., Linnehan, F., Shao, P., & Rosenberg, W. L. (2010). A moderated mediation model of e-mentoring. *Journal of Vocational Behavior*, *76*(2), 292–305. doi:10.1016/j.jvb.2009.10.003

Du, F., & Wang, Q. (2017). New teachers' perspectives of informal mentoring: Quality of mentoring and contributors. *Mentoring & Tutoring*. *Mentoring & Tutoring*, *25*(3), 309–328. doi:10.1080/13611267.2017.1364841

Eby, L. T., Allen, T. D., Evans, S. C., Ng, T., & DuBois, D. L. (2008). Does mentoring matter? A multidisciplinary meta-analysis comparing mentored and non-mentored individuals. *Journal of Vocational Behavior*, *72*(2), 254–267. doi:10.1016/j.jvb.2007.04.005 PMID:19343074

Elgharbawy, H. (2021). *Understanding Mentoring Relationships during and after COVID-19 Restrictions from the Perspective of Mentors: A Community-Engaged Participatory Approach*. Master of Science Thesis. University of Victoria, Canada.

Ensher, E. A., Heun, C., & Blanchard, A. (2003). Online mentoring and computer-mediated communication: New directions in research. *Journal of Vocational Behavior*, *63*(2), 264–288. doi:10.1016/S0001-8791(03)00044-7

Farrukh, K., & Hoor, T. (2022). Online mentoring session during COVID-19: Experiences of mentees and mentors -A phenomenology. *The Professional Medical Journal*, *29*(12), 1886–1891. doi:10.29309/TPMJ/2022.29.12.7126

Figueroa, O. (2017). Virtual Mentoring: Practitioner Strategies for Students Underrepresented in Industry. *Journal of Management and Sustainability*, *7*(2), 2. doi:10.5539/jms.v7n2p144

Golden, T., Veiga, J., & Dino, R. (2008). The Impact of Professional Isolation on Teleworker Job Performance and Turnover Intentions: Does Time Spent Teleworking, Interacting Face-to-Face, or Having Access to Communication-Enhancing Technology Matter? *The Journal of Applied Psychology, 93*(6), 1412–1421. doi:10.1037/a0012722 PMID:19025257

Grove, K., & Strudler, N. (2001). 1 Cooperating Teacher Practice in Mentoring Student Teachers Toward Technology Use. *Journal of Research on Technology in Education, 37*.

Gunuc, S. (2015). Implementation and Evaluation of Technology Mentoring Program Developed for Teacher Educators: A 6M-Framework. *Qualitative Research in Education, 4*(2), 164–191. doi:10.17583/qre.2015.1305

Guptan, S. U. (2018). *Mentoring 2.0: A Practitioner's Guide to Changing Lives.* SAGE Publishing India.

Harris, M. (1996). Aggressive Experiences and Aggressiveness: Relationship to Ethnicity, Gender, and Age. *Journal of Applied Social Psychology, 26*(10), 843–870. doi:10.1111/j.1559-1816.1996.tb01114.x

Hawkins, A. H., Ouellette, J. A., & Hadley, W. S. (2020). Reverse mentoring as an intergenerational exchange: A review and practical implications. *Human Resource Development Review, 19*(4), 455–480.

Homans, G. C. (1958). Social behavior as exchange. *American Journal of Sociology, 63*(6), 597–606. doi:10.1086/222355

Huang, C.-Y., Weng, R.-H., & Chen, Y.-T. (2016). Investigating the relationship among transformational leadership, interpersonal interaction and mentoring functions. *Journal of Clinical Nursing, 25*(15-16), 2144–2155. doi:10.1111/jocn.13153 PMID:27108764

Johnson, W. B., & Kram, K. E. (2020). Mentoring in the digital age. The Oxford Handbook of Workplace Mentoring, 295-314.

Jones, M. R. (2019). *Communication in the digital age: Understanding the impact of technology on human interaction.* Routledge.

Jones, S. M., & Johnson, M. A. (2020). The future of mentoring: How remote work is reshaping mentorship. *Catalyst : Feminism, Theory, Technoscience, 32*(3), 55–59.

Kasapakis, V., Dzardanova, E., Nikolakopoulou, V., & Vosinakis, S. (2022). Evaluation of a virtual reality learning enviroment testbed and non-verbal cue integration. *2022 International Conference on Interactive Media, Smart Systems and Emerging Technologies (IMET).* 10.1109/IMET54801.2022.9929618

Kasprisin, C. A., Single, P. B., Single, R. M., & Muller, C. B. (2003). Building a better bridge: Testing e-training to improve e-mentoring programmes in higher education. *Mentoring & Tutoring, 11*(1), 67–78. doi:10.1080/1361126032000054817

Knouse, S. B. (2001). Virtual mentors: Mentoring on the internet. *Journal of Employment Counseling, 38*(4), 162–169. doi:10.1002/j.2161-1920.2001.tb00498.x

Kram, K. E. (1983). Phases of the mentor relationship. *Academy of Management Journal, 26*(4), 608–625. doi:10.2307/255910

Kram, K. E., & Isabella, L. A. (2020). Virtual mentoring: The state of the art. *Journal of Management*, *46*(8), 1228–1254.

Lee, J. J., Bell, L. F., & Shaulskiy, S. L. (2017). Exploring mentors' perceptions of mentees and the mentoring relationship in a multicultural service-learning context. *Active Learning in Higher Education*, *18*(3), 243–256. doi:10.1177/1469787417715203

Lee, S., Kim, S., Lee, K., & Choi, Y. (2022). The role of digital technologies in online mentoring: An analysis of mentoring platforms and applications. *Interactive Learning Environments*, *30*(2), 235–250.

Lee, Y., & Lim, K. (2021). A Case Study on the University Freshman Adaptation Program Using an Online Mentoring Program during the COVID-19 Pandemic. *Korean J Gen Edu*, *15*(4), 217–231. doi:10.46392/kjge.2021.15.4.217

Madore, M. R., & Byrd, D. (2022). Optimizing mentoring relationships with persons from historically marginalized communities through the use of difficult dialogues. *Journal of Clinical and Experimental Neuropsychology*, *44*(5–6), 441–449. doi:10.1080/13803395.2022.2108770 PMID:35924945

Miller, A. J., & Smith, K. L. (2021). *Communicating in a digital world: Principles, practices, and perspectives*. Oxford University Press.

Narendra, U. P., Jain, R. R., Rao, N. S., Shreesha, H. R., Udith, D., & Prashanth, S. (2022). An intelligent ubiquitous online application for mentoring system. *International Journal of Multidisciplinary Research and Analysis*, *05*(06). Advance online publication. doi:10.47191/ijmra/v5-i6-30

Neely, A. R., Cotton, J., & Neely, A. D. (2017). E-mentoring: A Model and Review of the Literature. *AIS Transactions on Human-Computer Interaction*, *9*(3), 220–242.

Nuankaew, P., & Temdee, P. (2014). Determining of compatible different attributes for online mentoring model. In *Information Theory and Aerospace & Electronics Systems (VITAE)*. IEEE. doi:10.1109/VITAE.2014.6934434

O'Neill, D. K., Wagner, R., & Gomez, L. M. (1996). Online Mentors: Experimenting in science class. *Educational Leadership*, *54*(3), 39–42.

Oosthuizen, N., & Perks, S. (2019). The enabling conditions necessary for effective online mentoring: A proposed model. *International Journal of Academic Research in Business & Social Sciences*, *9*(6). Advance online publication. doi:10.6007/IJARBSS/v9-i6/5975

Orlova, M. V., & Aleksandrova, I. Yu. (2022). Distributed teams: Challenges and opportunities. *Vestnik Universiteta*, (2), 33–40. doi:10.26425/1816-4277-2022-2-33-40

Panopoulos, A., & Sarri, K. (2013). E-mentoring: The adoption process and innovation challenge. *International Journal of Information Management*, *33*(1), 217–226. doi:10.1016/j.ijinfomgt.2012.10.003

Pantelimon, F.-V., Bologa, R., Toma, A., & Posedaru, B.-S. (2021). The Evolution of AI-Driven Educational Systems during the COVID-19 Pandemic. *Sustainability (Basel)*, *13*(23), 13501. doi:10.3390/su132313501

Penny, C., & Bolton, D. (2010). Evaluating the outcomes of an eMentoring program. *Journal of Educational Technology Systems*, *39*(1), 17–30. doi:10.2190/ET.39.1.c

Perusso, A., & Wagenaar, R. (2023). Electronic work-based learning (eWBL): A framework for trainers in companies and higher education. *Studies in Higher Education*, 1–17. Advance online publication. doi:10.1080/03075079.2023.2280193

Pollard, R., & Kumar, S. (2021). Mentoring graduate students online: Strategies and challenges. *International Review of Research in Open and Distance Learning*, *22*(2), 267–284. doi:10.19173/irrodl.v22i2.5093

Ragins, B., & Kram, K. (2007). The Handbook of Mentoring at Work. Academic Press.

Rios, I. C., de Medeiros, M. E. Jr, de Almeida Fernandes, M. T., & Zombini, E. V. (2021). Virtual mentoring for medical students in the Covid-19 times. *Revista Brasileira de Educação Médica*, *45*(3), e170. doi:10.1590/1981-5271v45.3-20200419.ing

Rollnik-Sadowska, E., Glińska, E., & Ryciuk, U. (2022). Model of communication effectiveness in the mentoring process. *WSEAS Transactions on Business and Economics*, *19*, 1–12. doi:10.37394/23207.2022.19.1

Sagnak, H., & Baran, E. (2021). Faculty members' planned technology integration behaviour in the context of a faculty technology mentoring programme. *Australasian Journal of Educational Technology*, 1–21. doi:10.14742/ajet.5912

Schwartz, S. E. O., Rhodes, J. E., Liang, B., Sánchez, B., Spencer, R., Kremer, S., & Kanchewa, S. (2014). Mentoring in the digital age: Social media use in adult-youth relationships. *Children and Youth Services Review*, *47*, 205–213. doi:10.1016/j.childyouth.2014.09.004

Shuler, H., Cazares, V., Marshall, A., Garza-Lopez, E., Hultman, R., Francis, T.-K., Rolle, T., Byndloss, M. X., Starbird, C. A., Hicsasmaz, I., AshShareef, S., Neikirk, K., Johnson, P. E. C., Vue, Z., Beasley, H. K., Williams, A., & Hinton, A. Jr. (2021). Intentional mentoring: Maximizing the impact of underrepresented future scientists in the 21st Century. *Pathogens and Disease*, *79*(6), ftab038. Advance online publication. doi:10.1093/femspd/ftab038 PMID:34283236

Singh, P., & Kumar, K. (2019). E-mentoring Alternative Paradigm for Entrepreneurial Aptitude Development. *Academy of Entrepreneurship Journal*, *25*, 1–12.

Single, P. B., & Single, R. M. (2005). E-mentoring for social equity: Review of research to inform program development. *Mentoring & Tutoring. Mentoring & Tutoring*, *13*(2), 301–320. doi:10.1080/13611260500107481

Smith, E. (2019). Virtual mentoring: Mentoring across the digital divide. *Journal of Community Practice*, *27*(1-2), 5–26.

Smith, J., & Johnson, M. (2018). Social Exchange Theory: Its Structure and Influence in the Social Sciences. In D. Byrne & J. M. Ragin (Eds.), *The SAGE Handbook of Case-Based Methods* (pp. 255–270). Sage.

Smith, J., Roberts, D., & Petrie, N. (2021). Virtual mentoring in the remote workplace: A systematic review and research agenda. *Journal of Career Development*, *48*(2), 116–133.

Smith, J. A. (2019). Virtual mentoring: Expanding the boundaries of traditional mentoring relationships. *Journal of Leadership & Organizational Studies*, *26*(2), 261–273.

Sufrin, R. L. (2014). *The role of multicultural competence, privilege, attributions, and team support in predicting positive youth mentor outcomes.* Master's Thesis. DePaul University, USA.

Tajfel, H., & Turner, J. C. (1986). The social identity theory of intergroup behavior. In S. Worchel, & W. G. Austin (Eds.), Psychology of Intergroup Relations (pp. 7-24). Nelson-Hall.

Tetzlaff, J., Lomberk, G., Smith, H. M., Agrawal, H., Siegel, D. H., & Apps, J. N. (2022). Adapting Mentoring in Times of Crisis: What We Learned from COVID-19. *Academic Psychiatry*, *46*(6), 774–779. doi:10.1007/s40596-022-01589-1 PMID:35217939

Thompson, G. L. (2020). Technology and virtual mentoring: Challenges and opportunities. *Journal of Human Behavior in the Social Environment*, *30*(8), 988–1003.

Tinoco-Giraldo, H., Torrecilla Sánchez, E. M., & García-Peñalvo, F. J. (2020). E-Mentoring in Higher Education: A Structured Literature Review and Implications for Future Research. *Sustainability (Basel)*, *12*(11), 4344. doi:10.3390/su12114344

Valentin-Welch, M. (2016). Evaluation of a National E-Mentoring Program for Ethnically Diverse Student Nurse-Midwives and Student Midwives. *Journal of Midwifery & Women's Health*, *61*(6), 759–767. doi:10.1111/jmwh.12547 PMID:27926807

Warshaw, J., Whittaker, S., Matthews, T., & Smith, B. A. (2016). When distance doesn't really matter. *Proceedings of the 19th ACM Conference on Computer-Supported Cooperative Work & Social Computing.* 10.1145/2818048.2835237

Williams, L. M. (2021). Creating connections: The role of structured activities in virtual mentoring. *Journal of Youth Development*, *16*(3), 79–93.

Yang, C.-L., Matsumoto, K., Yu, S., Sawada, L., Arakawa, K., Yamada, D., & Kuzuoka, H. (2023). Understanding the effect of a virtual moderator on people's perception in remote discussion using social VR. *Frontiers in Virtual Reality*, *4*, 1198024. Advance online publication. doi:10.3389/frvir.2023.1198024

Chapter 16
Methods to Attract and Retain Talented Employees in Romanian Organizations:
A Compared Approach Between X, Y, and Z Generations

Nicoleta Valentina Florea
https://orcid.org/0000-0002-1154-7744
Valahia University of Targoviste, Romania

Gabriel Croitoru
https://orcid.org/0000-0002-8327-3455
Valahia University of Targoviste, Romania

Valentina Ofelia Robescu
https://orcid.org/0000-0002-2356-6854
Valahia University of Targoviste, Romania

Daria Florea
Valahia University of Targoviste, Romania

Mihai Bogdan Croitoru
Valahia University of Targoviste, Romania

ABSTRACT

Companies to achieve their objectives need talented employees with unique skills and competencies to obtain competitive advantage. The chapter's goal is to analyze the influence of attracting and retaining talents on organizational performance in Romanian companies. There were also investigated the characteristics of the three generations of talents, perceived through these human resources (HR) processes. Using PLS-SEM 4.0, it was determined that all the attraction and retention proposed variables had a positive and direct influence on organizational performance. The most important influential attraction factors are brand and nondiscrimination (4.63), salary and work conditions (4.60), and as retaining factors the offered training programs and good communication (4.73) and working atmosphere (4.70). The three generations were analysed according to attraction and retention variables, and because their scores were different, HR department could build a future guide based on their specificities in order to attract the best talents and to keep them to achieve long run performance.

DOI: 10.4018/979-8-3693-1938-3.ch016

INTRODUCTION

It is very difficult to find talented employees, especially in this challenging environment, where change is every step, where social, political, economic, and technological factors are constantly and continuously influencing companies environment. In this talent of war environment, through the best in- class attracting and retaining practices, companies are trying to realize their visions and to succeed through talented employees, and perceived them as an important asset, investing continuously in their development. Employees are perceived now as being the core competencies for companies and to attract, retain, and engage talents is very important in order to obtain sustainable performance (Yildiz et al., 2020). Important for companies is to perceive the talented employees with the adequate skills, knowledge and attitudes as employees who are commercially savvy and smart enough to obtain performance in a dynamic and challenging environment (Mofokeng, 2018). It is important not only to attract the talented employees, but especially to invest in them, retain them and recognize their value (Bostjancic & Slana, 2018).

Talent management is the answer of companies to the challenges braught by the present economy (Stuss, 2020). Talent is an important and strategic resource not only for local development but also for regional economic and social development (Shi et al., 2022). In this global environment, it is evaluated the mobility of talented employees, thus, talent is perceived as a vital resource necessary to achieve sustainable development for any country, and attracting and retaining these talented employees all over the world became the strategic way to increase the country's talent reverse (Wang & Shi, 2023). The term „war of talent" was proposed for the first time by McKinsey in 1998, and since then the specialists analysed it in many studies, theoretical or practical (Liu & Tan, 2022). This known phenomenon about „war of talent" became a key element for organizations as long as they want to be competitive (Luna-Arocas & Danvila-del-Valle, 2022), and the talent assets must be also quantitaive and qualitative (Howaniec et al., 2022). In order to survive and thrive, the companies must base on talents as it became a critical function in the war of talent period (Park et al., 2022). Exceptional talent is not about the person, is about the journey the employee makes through development, innovation, creativity, becoming the best in order to obtain individual and organizational performance, and moving from today into a new tomorrow, by self-orietation, and success (Dinnen & Alder, 2017).

One of the most important factors that require a special attention are talented people who are working in the organization (Sims R.R., 2002). Competitive advantage belongs to those organizations that know how to attract, select, retain and develop talented employees (Bohlander & Snell, 2007). In the XXI century, human resources are the major source through which competitive advantage is obtained and perhaps an important determinant in achieving the organization's long-term performance. Thus, the success of the organization depends on attracting and retaining well-trained people who can respond to changes in the external environment.

Organizations have realized that their success depends on their ability to attract, develop and retain talented staff (Reich R., 2002). People want to make sure they are valued by their employer and learn from these value for themselves. When are valued, people are more confident and will have potential that will lead them to organizational success (Holbeche & Mayo, 2012).

People are that essential resource that leads to achieving organizational goals and achieving performance (Sims R.R., 2002). In the 1980s the strategy was developed based on the analysis of the link between strategy and the external environment, and the link between strategy and resources and skills held by the organization being neglected; in this current period we will present the vital importance of talented employees in achieving sustainable performance. The analysis of the link between resources and performance has received the term "resource-based vision of the organization" (Faulkner, 2002).

From a theoretical point of view, this chapter is contributing to the existing studies in the field of attracting and retaining talented staff, and, also, evoking the specific features of the two important HR processes with real impact on organizational performance. The goal of this chapter is to demonstrate that adequate attraction and retention HR techniques will have positive and direct impact on organizational performance. This chapter has as novelty element the development of the right attracting techniques and retaining techniques in Romanian organizations, especially in this challenging era, where the talented employees are important to obtain individual and organizational sustainable performance, in this present war of talents. Another novelty is that the authors developed a questionnaire necessary to analyse these two talent techniques, based on using modelling through the use of PLS-SEM 4.0.

The chapter is structured as follows: starting from the literature in the field, the first section analyse each proposed variable from attraction and retention talent techniques with influence on organizational performance and also develops the research hypotheses and the development of analysis model related to attraction and retaining talented employees and their particularities. The second section is dedicated to the research methodology, specifically, data collection and analysis and the third section presents the results obtained from the research. In the final part of the chapter are presented the discussions and the conclusions to which are added the theoretical and managerial contributions of the paper together with its limits and future directions.

1. BACKGROUND

Literature Review and Research Hypothesis

Talented staff are the lifeline of any company and has an important contribution to the company's success (Eger et al. 2019).

1.1. Attraction of the Talented Employees and Performance

To attract talented employees is an objective for every commpany who want performance on long term. In this sub-section is presented the literature in the field of attraction talented staff and also were developed research hypothesis according to the literature found in the field.

- **Attraction techniques and organizational performance**

Attracting the most valuable talent was becoming a real need in this challenging environment (Shikweni et al., 2019) and one of the key roles of modern human resource management (Coculova & Tomcikova, 2021). Attracting skilled and talented employees is the answer to obtain competitive advantage (Pandiya et al., 2023). Searching and attracting talented staff became the objective of companies in this "race of talents" (Dauth et al., 2023). When the supply of labor is scarce, advertisements should also have the quality of attracting potential candidates, not just informing them about the main characteristics of the job in question (Cole, 2000). But ads must also be able to attract candidates when the job offer is sufficient, because: "... Both in times of extremely high unemployment and when it remains extremely low, advertisers may be surprised by a very poor response rate: it would seem that people would rather live off state aid than risk another layoff, and those who have work ... They sit quietly in their place, unless the announced post offers extraordinary possibilities... „. Thus, according to this ideea, we may develop the following research hypothesis: ***H1-Attracting the right talented employees will have positive influence on organization performance.***

• Brand and performance

Brand is helping organizations to obtain a powerful position in the chellenging work world by creating a clear, positive, and reputation-based image used to attract talented employees for vacant jobs and retain them to grow together (Rana et al., 2021). Brand is used now by the companies as a tool to attract, select, and retain the adequate talented staff (Ada et al., 2023; Tarique, 2022). Attraction of talented workforce is a challenge for organization; attraction based on branding was a challenge too, especially during COVID-19 crisis, when branding was a strong HR practice (Diba, 2023). Candidates are attracted to the working conditions offered by a brand, which means a name, a sign, a symbol or design, or a combination of these elements that seek to identify and differentiate a product or organization (Ormeno M., 2007). A very used tool for talented candidates attraction was creation of branding and the promotion of organization image on the labor market (Sarkiunaite & Sciukauske, 2021).

In the mind of the future employee is important the name of the company. A study among 277 employees revealed on a fiction name if they attracted or not by it, resulting high rates (McChesney, 2022). A name is important in being chosen as a company to be employeed, so the company is chosen based on its name or brand, according to the 3R: easy to be render, recognized, and reminded (Stevens R.E. et al., 2013). In the current period, people react more and more to the name of the organization and its reputation and to rumors or information provided by acquaintances (Kapferer, 2008). Knowledge and innovation are very important in obtaining performance and knowledge is found at the talented employees; attracting these talented employees through the brand organization became an important HR technique (Gourova & Gourova, 2017). Studies indicated that the higher the brand is, the higher moving between the companies is especially for talented and elite employees (Antons et al., 2023).

The success of recruiting and attracting talented candidates depends largely on the effectiveness of the recruitment message and the presentation of the brand (Pandiya et al., 2023) or the name of the company to which the job belongs (Compton et al., 2009) in which the name of the organization and its object of activity must be presented in the form of concise references (Karkhanis et al., 2023), because it is a way of indirect advertising, and the company can make itself known, and companies that have a good reputation will attract valuable candidates (Pânişoară & Panişoară, 2007). Thus, we may develop the next hypothesis, as ***H1a- Brand has a positive influence on organization performance.***

• Department presentation and performance

Many organizations have gained experience by presenting the department in which they will work (Schultz et al., 2005). Identity through branding, position, department, product has expanded to persons and even symbols (Schroeder et al., 2006). Using the presentation of the department in the organization, means to use its employees as a brand. They become ambassadors of the organization and contribute to attracting talent as much as the organization. Candidates are attracted to the organization's brand, through employees, departments, mission, vision and values of the organization. Thus, the brand comes to life (de St Aubin & Carlsen, 2008). So, we propose as hypothesis: ***H1b- Clear presentation of department has a positive influence on organization performance.***

• Presentation of the job title and performance

Is important to know for talented peolpe the job title and tasksto reduce any discrepancy and to increase the motivation of the involved parts (Dai & Si, 2023). It should be noted that, no matter where they are displayed, ambiguous ads are not appropriate because they will encourage too many people to apply for a job, without providing details about the job title (Armstrong, 2006). A job title may attract the talents from competition, which is called "poaching", being the first and the most visible public source of information about knowledge and key roles of the future employee (Zunino et al., 2023). A clear recruitment add will provoque the candidate to subscribe its CV or not and also could see, acoording to its tasks presentation, if are many, the future implication, exhaustion, stress, burnout, or emotional health (Mijakoski et al., 2023). Thus, they will avoid some of the overloads in the recruitment process and will reduce the area of inconvenience caused by this process, both to candidates and to the organization (Pânişoară G., Pânişoară I.-O., 2007). Thus, we developed the hypothesis: ***H1c- Clear presentation of the job title has a positive influence on organization performance.***

• Notdiscrimination and performance

It should be remembered that the advertisement must not discriminate, except for jobs whose duties can only be performed by a certain sex. Ad details should be brief but comprehensive. The form of the advertisement varies according to the importance of the organization, the value and number of employees and must avoid discrimination (Lakhdar et al., 2001). Racial discrimination must be avoided so that the organization does not have problems with the law against discrimination (Armstrong M., 2006). The construction of these ads is a decisive factor contributing to the efficiency of recruitment and attracting talented staff (Pânişoara G., Pânişoara I.-O., 2007). Other recommendations would be that the recruitment ad should not contain discriminatory aspects based on age, sex, physical appearance, etc., or should not have specificity, meaning to be concrete and fair with what is offered, so the candidate will be disappointed and other people will find out.

Specialized studies have shown that the image that the company transmits through recruitment ads is very important in attracting the desired candidates. This has a much greater impact than the way the vacancy is described (Byars & Rue, 1987). In addition to information about the organization, position and salary, the simplest and most obvious approach is to write the job title in bold letters and not to use discrimination. A study was conducted using official data drawn from the 2017 Eurobarometer in which they showed the importance of non-discrimination by gender, indicating that women played an important role in the Olympic Games in all activities carried out (Scharfenkamp et al., 2023). Discrimination must be avoided in recrutment add in order to ensure the ideal number of talented employees no matter their gender or age (Lee et al., 2022). So, we proposed the following hypothesis as: ***H1d- Notdiscrimination in the recruitment add has a positive influence on organization performance.***

• Presentation of the salary and performance

The announcement should arouse the reader's desire and seize the opportunity (Martin M., Jackson T., 2008), and the message should be written in such a way as not only to catch the eye but also to encourage them to read it to the end (Armstrong, 2006). Candidates will be suspicious if the advertisement says that "salary will be according to seniority and level of experience" or "negotiable salary". This means either that the salary is so low that the organization wants not to disclose it, or the pay policies are not so consistent that the organization has no idea how much to offer until the candidate asks for a certain amount. In astudies made among 169 employees from South Africa (Schlechter et al., 2014) or among Romanian students was found that between attracting and keeping talented employees and remunaration system used by the company there is a direct relation (Turnea et al., 2020). In one study it was found that the salary, national, cultural, and gender differences are important in attracting and retaining best talents (Eger et al., 2019), especially to gain competitive advantage. Recruitment is a vital activity for companies, and using key criteria to attract the right talent is very important, such as the salary and job requirements (Aggarwal et al., 2023). Thus, we developed as hypothesis: ***H1e- Clear presentation of the salary has a positive influence on organization performance.***

• Benefits and work ensurance and performance

Benefits are challenging for attracting talents (Komarraju et al., 2023), and due to these, the organization will receive a sufficient number of applications from talented candidates (Martin & Jackson, 2008), such as a work laptop or car, which proved to be the most attractive, therefore they must be expressly mentioned (Armstrong, 2006). Advertising through a recruitment advertisement must be designed in such a way as to attract attention, to create and maintain interest, to stimulate action on the part of those interested, which can be achieved by offering health, education or unemployment insurance (Zorlenţan et al., 1996) or by offering opportunities to invest in private pension packages or purchase shares (Peterson, 2023). So, based on this material, we proposed the hypothesis: ***H1f- Presentation of the benefits and work ensurence has a positive influence on organization performance.***

• Career management and promotion plans and performance

A study made among employees from National Science Foundation, USA, indicated that a good career management and clear promotion plans for employees will attract more talented employees for a job (Hur & Koh, 2023), and they will obtain performance. Another studies showed that, among 181 workers and managers or in South-Africa in water sector (Theys & Barkhuizen, 2022), a development plan as attraction tool is having influence on organizational performance (Sakka et al., 2022). The following hypothesis was proposed: ***H1g- Presentation of career management and promotion plans has a positive influence on organization performance.***

• Work conditions and performance

Work conditions must be clearly presented. Not only the physical work conditions must be presented, but also the psychological ones, especially in special environment (police force for example), where job satisfaction, organizational behavior, and health are very important in attracting talents (Annell et al., 2018). For example, if there are more difficult noise, dust, or dangerous conditions in the workplace, they must be mentioned in the recruitment announcement to attract exactly the candidates who have worked in such conditions before, creating interest in the job, but should not be under- or overvalued (Armstrong M., 2006). The companies who are working under pressure are using specific expressions to show that are hard working conditions for exploitative companies and to be attracted by them (Min, 2023). Presenting the conditions of the future work environment are vital, especially for workers with disability conditions or health related problems (Suomi et al., 2022).

The organization has the obligation to ensure ergonomic working conditions, regarding the level of pollutants, ventilation, lighting and protective equipment. The classification is not limited to the simple formal act of completing and signing the employment contract, it also involves the integration into the community of the newcomers, their accommodation and adaptation with work colleagues, with direct managers, with the complex technical-social-economic environment, consisting in a broad sense in adapting the parts to the whole. This process can be faster or longer, depending on a number of factors, but once accomplished, its essence consists in establishing a two-way harmony between the employee and the work community in which he was assigned (Cornescu et al., 2001). Thus, it was proposed the following hypothesis, as: ***H1h- Presentation of work conditions has a positive influence on organization performance.***

• Job tasks and qualifications and performance

To ensure diversity and engagement of future employees, the prezentations of qualifications is vital (Hammond et al., 2022). To attract the right employees, the company must use the two omportant criteria as core skills and essential knowledge and qualifications (Ge et al., 2023). The first part of the announcement contains information on the job duties and the second part on the candidates' profile (Sutter P.-E., 2007). At the heart of any job advertisement are personnel specifications and job duties (Cole, 2000; Bogathy, 2004). In the recruitment notice it is important to provide sufficient details on the essential characteristics of the job, which will help potential candidates identify the extent to which it suits their interests. The qualifications and experience required must be established as truthfully as possible (Panisoara & Panisoara, 2007). So, the hypothesis was developed, as: ***H1i- Job tasks and qualifications presentation has a positive influence on organization performance.***

• HR specialists name, email, and phone number and performance

The content of the advertisement in order to attract suitable and talented candidates must meet the following criteria in addition to describing the organization, the job and its tasks as clearly as possible, the application procedure and deadline (Armstrong, 2006), the reference to the organization's website and even providing the email for the contact person designated by the company (Marinas, 2006; Cole, 2000). The deadlines offered in the recruitment notice must be fixed, clear and not very long (de Falco, 2011). Recruitment ad must be clear and based on the 5 w- who to recruit, why, for what, wheter to recruit, and when to recruit, so data about the term necessary to subscribe de resume is very important (Humphrey, 2014). Thus, contact data are very important for talents attraction, no matter if the recruitment ad is traditional or virtual (Guo et al., 2021). Therefore, the following research hypothesis was established: ***H1j- Offering in recruitment ad of HR specialists name, email, and phone number has a positive influence on organization performance.***

1.2. Retention of Talented Employees and Performance

To retain the best and the talented employees became an objective for companies who want sustainable performance. In this sub-section we presented the literature in the field of retention process and established research hypothesis according to this literature.

• **Retention techniques and organizational performance**

Retention techniques have an important role in obtaining performance for organizations (Dana et al., 2023). Keeping talented employees led organizations to reduced costs, achieving objectives, obtaining social responsibility, and economic growth (Parlinska & Stawicka, 2018). If the companies do not have adequate retention strategies, its results, organizational performance and sustainable growth, will suffer (Ghani et al., 2022). To achieve succes based on using talent management organizations must find the right techniques for keeping the right talented individuals in order to obtain performance, using work flexibility, strong leadership, adequate work environment, attractive work conditions, strong culture of the company, or financial and non-financial benefits (Savov et al., 2022). To achieve performance and to develop successful HR processes, the compoanies must develop adequate retention techniques of talented employees and more important to use their potential (Tej et al., 2022). Thus, we may develop the following research hypothesis, as: ***H2- Retention of the right talented employees will have positive influence on organization performance.***

• Enjoyable work environment and performance

Employees who work in a safe and healthy work environment, where employees are insured and protected from various accidents (Sakka et al., 2022), where the management of employment relationships, administration of human resources procedures and policies, operationalization of human resources information systems are constant and continuous processes (Armstrong M., 2006), and employees will have a higher performance and will be retained for a longer period (Manolescu A., 2006). In some studies, the respondents being asked about how is described a pleasant work environment, they answered: a positive and enjoyable environment (Polyakova-Norwood et al., 2023), fun, enjoyment, and social activities with their families (Abdelmotaleb, 2023), and during COVID-19 period for an enjoyable virtual environment without stress and anxiety (Bodet-Contentin et al., 2023). So, we may develop the hypothesis, as: ***H2a- An enjoyable work environment has a positive influence on organization performance.***

• Productive work environment and performance

Environmental factors (temperature, noise, light, etc.) and appropriate relationships of employees with colleagues and managers can lead to increased productivity and improved social climate; Psychological phenomena that occur in small groups, such as "leadership", "networking and communication with stakeholders" or "change management" can increase productivity, while those based on tension can diminish (Radu et al., 2004). The involvement of talented employees in various tasks (Stahl &; Bjorkman, 2006) and ethical behavior (Deckop, 2006) can also lead to increased production. Working in teams with talented employees, not those with lower performance, will lead to increased production and productivity (Price, 2000). There has been demonstrated that a productive work environment had positive influence on performance (Feng et al., 2022), and another study made on 254 employees demonstrated the same thing through the use of engagement and organizational factors (Abdelwahed & Al Doghan, 2023). Thus, we can claim that: ***H2b- A productive work environment has a positive influence on organization performance.***

• Communication and performance

Akay (2006) compares the organization to a tower, in which the four pillars of support are represented by the organization, management, communication, and production, and the foundation is represented by the effectiveness of its policies and procedures. Communication skills will make employees better decisionmakers, more analytical, technical and interpresonal, developing also the emotional intelligence (Ellahi et al., 2024). Communication is one of the five important factors with real influence on supply chain, where actually the war is begining to win on the market (Xiao & Khan, 2024). Communication skills determine the relationship with colleagues and organization, obtaining performance (Kang et al., 2023). It was demonstrated that internal communication represents a key practice area for employees engaged in obtaining performance (Arif et al., 2023). In a recent survey of 703 people, 61% said their most recent job was through acquaintances (Cassidy & Kreitner, 2010). The message is simple: employees in organizations talk about their jobs to their friends and families. They will encourage those people who want to apply for a vacancy in their organization if they think well about the organization, about the bosses and about the job. ensuring an appropriate communication system between management and other employees, as well as between various departments and functions of the organization; providing the necessary mechanisms to enable the organization to cope with the human consequences of change (Cole, 2000). Thus, in order to attract talented candidates, the organization must start from within the organization, which means that the brand must not only be a smart and appealing advertisement developed by the company's marketing department, but must ensure that what it looks like on the outside, so it is on the inside (by St. Aubin & Carlsen, 2008), and these are achieved through a two-way communication process (Sakka et al., 2022). Thus, we may conclude, that ***H2c- A good communication at work has a positive influence on organization performance.***

• Trust and commitment and performance

An organization performance is depending on its ability to attract and retain a talented employees. A research made among 218 respondents, indicated that between the company recruitment behaviour and employee commitment there was a direct influence among young employees using PLS-SEM (Buitek et al., 2023). In order to become a reference employer, organizations must improve their ability to attract and retain employees and candidates (Chaminade, 2010). The longer employees remain loyal to the organization, the more the organization will invest in them. Trusting in the compnay and identifying with it will led to increased performance (Glavas et al., 2023). We may develop the following hypothesis, as: ***H2d- Trust and commitmentat work has a positive influence on organization performance.***

- Teamwork and performance

When such an information about working in teams is presented by the company to retain talents, employees will think of the many benefits they can obtain: resilience (Jiang et al., 2024), better communication, collabortaion, gaining new knowledge and experiences (Samudra et al., 2024), innovation, sustainability, better opportunities for transitions to new work conditions (Scarbrough et al., 2024), cooperation, complementarity, increased team production (Fischer et al., 2023), acquire external knowledge, creativity, new capabilities, new solutions for problem-solving (Venkataramani; Tang, 2023), social integration, increased cognitive process (Aggarwal et al., 2022), or interdisciplinary work between departments and internal funding opportunities (Jaskyte et al., 2023). The combination of human resources and marketing will enable the organization to excel in attracting talent and customers (Gitman & McDaniel, 2009). Organizations need to attract employees in the same way they attract customers. In order to be a true "magnet" among candidates, the organization must know how to attract, and once the relationship between them is established, it must hire and retain them (Schumann & Sartain, 2009). Teamwork is a marketing tool that ensures the necessary number of employees. Usually, people inquire about this aspect when looking for aspects related to the efficiency of teamwork or who leads the work team, so teamwork becomes an easy and familiar way to compare jobs (Schultz et al., 2005). So, the following hypothesis was proposed, as: ***H2e- A workteam environment has a positive influence on organization performance.***

- Empowerment at work and performance

Empowerment and implication reprezents a mean to improve performance and retain talented staff, no matter the sex, or the age. Empowerment to take decision, even for women is important to ensure performance, and even psychological not only physical (Yu et al., 2023). Through these processes, employees are motivated and encouraged to intensify efforts and acquire new skills so that the organization can achieve its goals and meet its own needs (Armstrong, 2006). Engagement refers to identifying employees with the goals and values of the organization and striving for it (Manolescu, 2006). Employees represent the organization, and the organization involves people and depends on their effort. Many people tend to regard the organization as their own and its successes as their own, while the organization's failures are felt as personal failures. Organizations are involved in people's daily lives and represent a part of their daily existence, the place where they consume most of their time (Manolescu, 2006). There are associations which offer to employees in need or women affected by violence, empowerment programs such as: financial literacy education, vocational training, and employment opportunities (Corple, 2023) or psychological empowerment for adult employees who will retire or who will become voluteers (Drazic et al., 2023). Thus, we developed the following hypothesis: ***H2f- Empowerment at work has a positive influence on organization performance.***

- Payed training programs and performance

Thus, organizations will adopt specific procedures, practices for employee involvement (eg volunteering, in order to maintain the health of employees and organizations, based on sustainable development principles) (Manolescu, 2006), will use better strategies and techniques for personnel, attraction and retention, development and training (eg offering an insurance package and a higher salary in employee retention, providing health services, development and training programs offered free of charge by the organization (Schuller & Jackson S., 2007). Training programs promised by the company in recruotment ad will bring, if they are made, a lot of benefit as: improved performance (Miller-Kuhlmann et al., 2024), safety training programs in hard working conditions using virtual programs (Al-Khiami & Jaeger, 2023), So, we proposed the following hypothesis: ***H2g- Payed training programs has a positive influence on organization performance.***

• Flexible and a good experience work environment and performance

The organizational culture, due to the relevant values promoted, positively influences the desire to recruit and hire candidates (Manolescu, 2006). Large organizations are adopting more sophisticated and socially responsible HR management activities because of the costs involved and because they are under pressure to gain legitimacy (Schuller & Jackson, 2007). Flexibility at work bring job satisfaction and less burnout (Lee & Chang, 2022), freedom to work with tasks (Kincaid &Reynolds, 2023), succes of employees at work (Yimsai et al., 2022) or reduce conflicts between personal and professional life (Rose, 2015). So, it was proposed the following hypothesis: ***H2h- A flexibile and a good experience environment has a positive influence on organization performance.***

• Challenging tasks and performance

Task management will allow employees to detect, develop, and manage information on tasks across their professional and personal contexts (Williams et al., 2023). Between offering a work environment based on offering challenging tasks and performance there is a strong and positive relationships even when was turbulent conditions like COVID-19 crisis, these chellenging tasks were perceived as good HR techniques (Saleem et al., 2023). Talented employees need skills in mobilizing their own resources - knowledge, professional knowledge, behavioral characteristics, motivations, in order to perform challenging actions and tasks and expect expected results (Hosdey, 2010). Thus, a talented individual will be able to mobilize his personal capabilities, use environmental resources efficiently and be able to combine the two qualities in a creative manner. The war of talent must be silent, because it does not announce a very large number of people, but must reach only those people with rare skills necessary to carry out certain activities. So, "it's not easy to attract real talent!" (Dejoux & Thevenet, 2010). So, the research hypothesis was developed: ***H2i- Challenging tasks has a positive influence on organization performance.***

• Good work atmosphere and performance

An organization if is offering work authenticity, good relationship and a good working athmosphere based on coworking, a good performance will be obtained (Tang et al., 2022).

Professional integration aims at familiarizing with the new place and working conditions, facilitating the accommodation of the new employee with the work group, creating an atmosphere of safety, confidentiality and belonging, so that the new employee acquires confidence in his own ability to fulfill the tasks of the job (Omer, 2003), increasing his interests and aspirations, the pace of progress, reactions to different stimuli, job satisfaction, team spirit and participation in achieving the organization's objectives (Tracy, 2008). A good working atmosphere is considered when is based on team atmosphere, work control (Wagner & Koob, 2022), chat, cooperation, communication, collaboration, lightning of the work space, colors, flavour, fragrance (Ishikawa & Yamazaki, 2021); COVID-19 transformed work environment into a more intimate space, the one from home, called teleworking, and all these processing of collaboration, chatting, team work and control are missing. Thus, the following hypothesis was developed: ***H2j- A good work atmosphere has a positive influence on organization performance.***

2. RESEARCH METHODOLOGY

2.1. Conceptual Model

Based on the literature review on attraction (AlQudah et al., 2023; Ludviga et al., 2016; Jimoh & Kee, 2022; Rafique et al., 2023) and retention (Gelencser et al., 2023; Kalia et al., 2023; Ramirez-Asis et al., 2023; El-Sherbeeny et al., 2023; Han et al., 2023) using PLS-SEM of talented employees theory, we proposed the conceptual model in which attracting variables (AV which has 10 sub-variables AV1-AV10) and retaining variables (RV which has ten sub-variables RV1-RV10) of talented staff directly influences organizational performance variables (PV which has three sub-variables PV1-PV3).

2.2. Research Goal, Model Used, Sample

The chapter goal is to analyse the influence of attracting and retaining practices of talented employees on organizational performance.

The study is made on employees from Dambovita county, Romania, showing the importance could have attracting and retaining talented staff on organizational performance. The study took place from November to Dcember 2023. The questionnaire was sent to 500 respondents, but replies were received from 470 respondents, this being the reason of selecting an equal number for the three categories of analysed categories of ages (450 respondents), meaning that we obtained a return rate of 90.0%. The authors randomly selected employees from the Dambovita county, Romania, but 150 from each analysed category. In Table 1 is presented the socio-demographical data of the respondents. As we may observe, from the 450 respondents, 285 were female (63.3%), from 16-24 years (generation Z) are 150 respondets, from generation Y (25-39 years) 150 respondents, and from generation X (40-55 years) 150 respondents. From urban area were 267 (59.3%), with bachelo's studies were 74 respondents (16.4%), with master's studies 312 respondents (69.3%) and with PhD studies were 64 respondents (14.2%). The authors have chosen different fileds of activities for the employeees analysed, ensuring a work environment based on notdiscrimination and diversification. Thus, there were 98 respondents from production sector (21.8%), 65 from construction sectir (14,4%), 78 from banking system (17.3%), 58 from education (12.9%), 70 from IT sector (15.6%), 28 from health sector (6.2%), 24 from transportation (5.3%) and 29 from sales sector (6.4%).

Table 1. Demographic characteristics of respondents

Gender	Frequency	Percent	Age	Frequency	Percent
Male	165	36.7	16-24 years (generation Z)	150	33.3
Female	285	63.3	25-39 years (generation Y)	150	33.3
			40-55 years (generation X)	150	33.3
Residence	Frequency	Percent	**Field of activity**	Frequency	Percent
Urban	267	59.3	Production	98	21.8
Rural	183	40.7	Construction	65	14.4
			Banking	78	17.3
Studies	Frequency	Percent	Education	58	12.9
Bachelor's level	74	16.4	IT sector	70	15.6
Master level	312	69.3	Health	28	6.2
PhD level	64	14.2	Transportation	24	5.3
			Sales sector	29	6.4

2.3. Questionnaire and Confirmatory Factor Analysis

The questionnaire (Table 2) was developed using a five-point Likert scale (1- total disagreement and 5- total agreement), and the sample of the study was formed by 450 employees with work contracts made in Romania, Dambovita county.

Table 2. Confirmatory factor analysis and descriptive statistics

Construct	Item	Measure	Mean	Mean for gen Z	Mean for gen Y	Mean for gen X	VIF	Loading (St.Est.)	Chro alpha	AVE	CR
1. Attraction variables									0,834	0,781	0,897
	AV1	It is presented the brand/name of the organzation	4.63	4.80	4.60	4.50	1.59	0.855			
	AV2	It is presented the department where the vacancy is	4.33	4.10	4.30	4.60	3.45	0.723			
	AV3	It is presented the title of the job	4.17	3.90	4.10	4.50	3.44	0.753			
	AV4	It is not used discrimination in the recruitment ad	4.63	4.80	4.60	4.50	1.62	0.873			
	AV5	It is presented the level of salary	4.60	5.00	4.50	4.30	2.47	0.777			
	AV6	Are presented the benefits and the work ensurence	4.37	4.70	4.30	4.10	2.28	0.816			
	AV7	Career management and promotion plans	4.57	4.90	4.50	4.30	1.36	0.844			
	AV8	Are presented the work conditions	4.60	4.80	4.50	4.50	1.95	0.770			
	AV9	Are clearly presented the job tasks and the requested qualifications	4.37	4.20	4.30	4.60	1.69	0,780			
	AV10	Are presented the name of the HR specialist, the due time, the phone number and the e-mail for contact	4.33	4.50	4.20	4.30	1.65	0,739			
2. Retention variables									0,867	0,843	0,888
	RV1	An enjoyable work environment	4.67	4.90	4.60	4.50	1.49	0.943			
	RV2	A productive work environment	4.13	3.60	4.30	4.50	2.34	0.773			
	RV3	A work environment based on good communication	4.73	4.90	4.60	4.70	1.68	0.878			
	RV4	Trust and commitment	4.17	3.20	4.50	4.80	2.84	0.790			
	RV5	Team work environment	4.6	4.50	4.70	4.60	2.37	0.736			
	RV6	Empowerment to work	4.3	3.50	4.60	4.80	2.40	0.868			

Continued on following page

291

Table 2. Continued

Construct	Item	Measure	Mean	Mean for gen Z	Mean for gen Y	Mean for gen X	VIF	Loading (St.Est.)	Chro alpha	AVE	CR
	RV7	Payed training programs	4.73	4.90	4.70	4.60	3.04	0.752			
	RV8	Flexible and good experience environment	4.4	4.80	4.30	4.10	1.66	0.712			
	RV9	Challenging tasks	4.3	4.70	4.30	3.90	1.86	0.827			
	RV10	A good working atmosphere	4.7	4.80	4.60	4.70	2.28	0.715			
3. Performance variables									0,833	0,750	0,836
	PV1	The company invests more in their talented employees	4.10	4.50	4.10	3.70	2.26	0.882			
	PV2	The company perceives the employees as an asset, not as a cost	4.35	4.55	4.10	4.40	1.61	0.832			
	PV3	The company develops compensation techniques based on talent of the employees	3.77	4.30	3.80	3.20	2.41	0.882			

In table above, was calculated the Mean for the entire sample, but also the Mean for each analysed group of ages (generation Z, Y, and X).

The model was based on using partial least squares-based structural equation modeling in SmartPLS 4.0.

The obtained results are indicating that there is an internal consistency of the model (Table 1) because all item loadings are over 0.7 (Hair et al., 2010); Cronbach alpha's exceeding 0.7 (Henseler & Sarstedt, 2013); and CR (composite reliability) values are also over 0.7 (Nemteanu et al., 2022). According to the Fornell-Larcker (1981) procedure, for each latent variable AVE's value is higher than the correlation coefficient between the competent and all distinct variables (Table 3).

Table 3. Discriminant validity – Fornell – Larcker criterion

	Attracting Talented Employees	Organisational Performance	Retain Talented Employees
Attracting talented employees	1		
Organisational performance	0.623	1	
Retain talented employees	0.735	0.752	1

3. RESULTS

The analysis made was developed to assess the relationship between the latent variables. Based on t-statistics, all the hypotheses were accepted (Table 4).

Attracting talented employees had a positive and significant influence on organizational performance ($\beta = 0.453$; T-value $= 4.08$; $p < 0.001$), therefore better and more efficient attraction techniques of talented employees will lead to an increased organizational performance; thus, *H1* is accepted.

Each from all ten variables proposed as attracting effectively the talented staff were positively influenced the organizational performance (β between 0.723 and 0.873, T between 4.374 and 34.045, $p < 0.001$), thus *H1a-H1j* were all accepted.

Table 4. The path coefficients of the structural equation model

Paths	Path Coeff (P) or (β)	Sample Mean (M)	Standard Deviation (STDEV)	T Statistics (|P/STDEV|)	P Values (* $p < 0.1$; ** $p < 0.01$; *** $p < 0.001$)	Hypothesis
ATE -> OP (H1)	0.453	0.157	0.037	4.08	0.000	H1-supported
ATE (AV1) -> OP (H1a)	0.855	0.251	0.058	4.374	0.000	H1a – supported
ATE (AV2) -> OP (H1b)	0.723	0.567	0.044	13.004	0.000	H1b – supported
ATE (AV3) -> OP (H1c)	0.753	0.447	0.046	9.944	0.000	H1c – supported
ATE (AV4) -> OP (H1d)	0.873	0.57	0.05	11.537	0.000	H1d – supported
ATE (AV5) -> OP (H1e)	0.777	0.772	0.043	18.059	0.000	H1e – supported
ATE (AV6) -> OP (H1f)	0.816	0.609	0.059	10.110	0.000	H1f – supported
ATE (AV7) -> OP (H1g)	0.844	0.542	0.05	10.85	0.000	H1g – supported
ATE (AV8) -> OP (H1h)	0.770	0.77	0.023	34.045	0.000	H1h – supported
ATE (AV9) -> OP (H1i)	0.780	0.677	0.038	17.699	0.000	H1i – supported
ATE (AV10) -> OP (H1j)	0.739	0.742	0.023	31.801	0.000	H1j – supported
RTE -> OP (H2)	0.640	0.641	0.033	19.341	0.000	H2-supported
RTE (RV1) -> OP (H2a)	0.943	0.541	0.039	13.841	0.000	H2a – supported
RTE (RV2) -> OP (H2b)	0.773	0.671	0.044	15.256	0.000	H2b – supported
RTE (RV3) -> OP (H2c)	0.878	0.477	0.059	8.057	0.000	H2c – supported
RTE (RV4) -> OP (H2d)	0.790	0.787	0.036	21.881	0.000	H2d – supported
RTE (RV5) -> OP (H2e)	0.736	0.634	0.058	11.007	0.000	H2e – supported
RTE (RV6) -> OP (H2f)	0.868	0.666	0.053	12.667	0.000	H2f – supported

Continued on following page

Table 4. Continued

Paths	Path Coeff (P) or (β)	Sample Mean (M)	Standard Deviation (STDEV)	T Statistics (|P/ STDEV|)	P Values (* p < 0.1; ** p < 0.01; *** p < 0.001)	Hypothesis
RTE (RV7) -> OP (H2g)	0.752	0.749	0.042	17.850	0.000	H2g – supported
RTE (RV8) -> OP (H2h)	0.712	0.711	0.035	20.287	0.000	H2h – supported
RTE (RV9) -> OP (H2i)	0.827	0.630	0.029	21.544	0.000	H2i – supported
RTE (RV10) -> OP (H2j)	0.715	0.716	0.027	26.208	0.000	H2j – supported

Retaining techniques had also a positive and significant influence on organizational performance (β = 0.640; T-value = 19.341; $p < 0.001$).

The ten retaining developed variables have all positive influence on organizational performance (β between 0.712 and 0.943, T between 8.057 and 26.208, $p < 0.001$), thus *H2a-H2j* were all accepted.

4. DISCUSSION

The influence of attraction techniques of talented employees on organization performance is positive and strong (β = 0.453; T-value = 4.08; $p < 0.001$), which has been observed by many researchers who argue that employees' attraction has become a practical concern, and a study indicated that intrinsic and extrinsic factors influenced employees to choose a company (Vogel & Satzher, 2023). A study made in Bosnia and Herzegovina determined that talent management through attracting talented employees, has a direct and positive influence on company performance (Cizmic & Azmic, 2021).

All the other attracting techniques proposed for the model are influencing positively the organization performance.

As we may observe branding has a positive influence (β = 0.855; T-value = 4.374; $p < 0.001$) on organization performance. Studies indicated that employer branding is used to put the organisation in the minds of present or future employees by using a combination of different benefits; this study was made using over 35,000 platform reviews to analyse and interpret the perceptions of employees (Karkhanis et al., 2023). A few studies made among 197 respondents from India and among 300 students fron Latvia and Turkey determined, that organisational talent management is strongly and positively related to organization branding (Maurya & Agarwal, 2018; Alniacik et al., 2014). Using PLS-SEM it was demonstrated that among 322 employees from hospitality will obtain performance (economic and environmental) if they perceive green HRM and a strong brand and reputation (Umrani et al., 2022).

The presentation of department in recruitment ad dis also influencing positively the organization performance (β = 0.723; T-value = 13.004; $p < 0.001$). Studies indicated that the ad should be composed in such a way as to keep the candidate's interest awake (Martin & Jackson, 2008) and to read the whole message, to communicate in an interesting and attractive way about the department and organization without exaggerating (Armstrong M., 2006). Presenting the name of the company, the internal culture and the fit with the job will attract more the employee (Abraham et al., 2023).

Presenting clearly the title job is also have a positive impact on organization performance ($\beta = 0.753$; T-value $= 9.944$; $p < 0.001$). Studies have shown that because there are other employers on the labor market looking for well-trained candidates, the ad must capture the attention of the target audience. The advertisement must contain information about the post and its title in order to attract the appropriate number of candidates (Panisoara & Panisoara, 2007); thus. An irresistible title that presents the attributions of the job (Ahamad et al., 2023), but also along with the required employment conditions and qualifications, not being exaggerated (Armstrong, 2006) will attract the right talented candidates to achieve performance.

Eliminating discrimination in recruitment add this thing may attract talented employees in such a positive work environment ($\beta = 0.873$; T-value $= 11.537$; $p < 0.001$). To attract a talented employee is important for company to use specific tools to reduce discrimination and increase diversity necessary tools to increase workforce homogeneity and attract new talented employees (Brymer & Rocha, 2023). Using social media, the company wants to ensure fairness. In a study, using LinkedIn for recruitment, it was shown that among 401 candidates, there was no evidence of discrimination amongst women or people of colour (Henderson & Welsh, 2023).

Presenting salary in the recruitment ad, could attract the best talented employees, sometimes being the only reason to leave the old company ($\beta = 0.777$; T-value $= 18.059$; $p < 0.001$). A study made among employees from metallurgy and mechanics segment indicated that if they are not motivated using good salaries, their productivity will suffer, will appear frustration, distrust and distancing from their job (Fernandes et al., 2023). A good salary is on the first place (Hand & Reid, 2022) to be attracted a talented employee, who play a vital role in obtaining performance (Kondaiah & Varshney, 2022), by an ad recruitment, and than is the size of the company (Lei, 2022).

Benefits and work insurance granted by the employer could be an important variable to attract talented people ($\beta = 0.816$; T-value $= 10.413$; $p < 0.001$). According to a study based on employer attractiveness, was revealed that the candidates are attracted to benefits (Hand & Reid, 2022) and to work-life balance benefits and recommendations (Ahamad et al., 2023). Besides known benefits the organization may offer a package for investing in private pensions or buying stocks and bonds (Peterson, 2023), becoming a real factor used to attract talented employees.

Another important variable who can attract talented employees is career management and promotion plans offered by the company ($\beta = 0.844$; T-value $= 10.85$; $p < 0.001$). A study made among 135 workers and 64 managers indicated that clear development plans is an important technique for attraction and has positive impact on performance (Sakka et al., 2022). Another study made in China among employees from IT Industry indicated that employees are attracted by the company who use teambuilding activities (Lei, 2022), and another in South Africa among women from mining industry determined that the efficient plan for career awareness is on the first place as retention HR policy (Mashada & Botha, 2023).

Work conditions offered by the companies are efficient attracting ways of talents ($\beta = 0.770$; T-value $= 34.045$; $p < 0.001$). To capture talented employees organizations are using attraction techniques as flexible work arrangements (Smit & Lawson, 2023), positive climate work conditions (Maier et al., 2022) or offering job satisfaction and promoting employee wellbeing (Dancza et al., 2022, location or working hours per week (Lei, 2022). As non-monetary attraction policies was found in a study as being supportive work environment and recognition of work (Kondaiah & Varshney, 2022).

Job tasks and qualifications are important in attracting the righr talented candidates ($\beta = 0.780$; T-value $= 17.699$; $p < 0.001$). If the job is well balanced, between professional and personal life, than an employee will be happy with his work and will choose a company to work there for a long time. For example, in a study made among 1446 teachers from Australia, revealed that heavy workloads, health and wellbeing concerns for teachers and the status of the profession are the most important issues in leaving the institution (Heffernan et al., 2022). Candidates to be attracted by a recruitment ad, it must contain clear information about the profile of the candidate (Sutter P.-E., 2007) and its qualifications and also the job tasks (Bogathy, 2004).

In an efficient recruitment add are important to be presented the due time, name of HR specialists, email and phone number ($\beta = 0.739$; T-value = 31.801; $p < 0.001$). To attract the right candidate at the right time, moment and for the right job is important to offer at the end of the recruitment add data about the due time (Armstrong, 2006), and is important to not be so long (de Falco, 2011), the phone number of the HR specialist (Marinaş, 2006), and the email (Cole, 2000).

As retaining techniques, we mention that offering an enjoyable work environment is very important to increase organization performance ($\beta = 0.640$; T-value = 19.341; $p < 0.001$). Studies indicated that a work environment could also be chosen according to the office design, ergonomy, creative workspace (Maier et al., 2022), positive culture, supervision (Dancza et al., 2022). A study made among 332 nurses from Pakistan indicated that job love and job fit are important retention factors who contribute to organizational performance (Bibi et al., 2022) and another study made among 242 respondents identified as the most wanted retention techniques are work environment and support from managers (Hand & Reid, 2022).

A productive work environment is also important in retaining the talented employees ($\beta = 0.943$; T-value = 13.841; $p < 0.001$). A productive and in the same time a safer work environment is wanted by future employees as an attraction HR process (Uddin et al., 2021). To attract a talented person is important to use HR policies as productive work environment based on business characteristics, working environment, and global opportunities (Ada et al., 2023).

Work environment based on good communication is a good retaining technique ($\beta = 0.773$; T-value = 15.256; $p < 0.001$). Some studies indicated that good communication, mutual respect and friendship (Li, 2023), communication based on employees feedback and reviews, or awards for companies or managers (Zhang et al., 2023) can facilitate attraction of talented employees and obtaining good work capacity. Communication based on CSR is perceived as a good attraction term for new employees (Boehncke, 2023).

Trust and commitment are very influencing techniques in retaining talented staff ($\beta = 0.878$; T-value = 8.057; $p < 0.001$). Employees when send their CV are attracted by the work involvement from the company engagement and commitment (Buitek et al., 2023), and prosocial motivation (Glavas et al., 2023). Trust is very important in obtaining long run performance and improve work capacity (Li, 2023).

Work team offer a positive environment and retain on long run talented employees ($\beta = 0.790$; T-value = 21.881; $p < 0.001$). Engagement in working on teams of employee was demonstrated in India as a good factor of attraction of talented employees. An analysis based on Exploratory factor Analysis and SPSS made among 382 employees demonstrated that engagement is an influential factor on performance in order to attract talents (Durai & Viji, 2022). Another study demonstrated that lack of anxiety, cooperation based on similarities are leading to good work in teams and operate as important factors of attraction of talents (George & Chattopadhyay, 2022).

Empowerment to work is very wanted by challenging and talented employees ($\beta = 0.736$; T-value = 11.007; $p < 0.001$). Studies indicated that empowerment at work is very important as attraction policy, to take actions and decisions (Jayasinghe et al., 2022) as employees and especially as leaders, to have voice, values, and express authenticity (appels, 2023). A research made among 324 respondents revealed the strong relationships between the talent management process and organisational performance with mediating role of job empowerment (Pawar et al., 2022).

Offered paid training programs are important for talented employees who want to remain longer by growing once with the company ($\beta = 0.868$; T-value $= 12.667$; $p < 0.001$).

A study based on using PLS-SEM, made in 2023, demonstrated that offering training programs (Luna-Arocas, 2023) for employees it will be a good retaining technique for talented employees and increase task performance among 302 employees from bank sector in Nigeria (Jimoh & Kee, 2022) or among bank employees from Malaysia, where career plans and well-being are important in keeping talents (Selvanathan et al., 2022). Development is an important factor in being attracted by a company, and knowledge assimilation, sharing and transformation are at the core of attraction process (Latukha et al., 2023).

Flexible and good experience environment are important for present employees, especially for the young ones ($\beta = 0.752$; T-value $= 17.850$; $p < 0.001$). Candidates are attracted by healthy lifestyle and workplace vigor. A study found that between these two characteristics and organizational performance there is a positive relation, so recruiters may use these attraction-policies to attract the talented employees (Yu et al., 2023). Job crafting (employee proactivity and environment for activity) is influencing tha retention of talents. This analysis may be a signal for organizations to adapt their activities according to the forecasting for 2030 when 50% of the jobs will disappear (Cardenas-Munoz & Ramon Campos-Blazquez, 2023).

Challenging tasks are important variables for talented employees in order to be kept longer in organization ($\beta = 0.712$; T-value $= 20.287$; $p < 0.001$). Offering challenging tasks for future and present employee is constituting an attraction technique, and those based on pre- and post- internship experience are very wanted companies as employer (Sekiguchi et al., 2023). Routine tasks are boring for talented employees or managers, that being the reason of being a challenging attraction policy (Bechtold, 2015). Its important that HR specialists to fet the skills of talented candidates with the roles, jobs, and tasks (Weller et al., 2019).

A pleasant atmosphere is requested by talented employees ($\beta = 0.827$; T-value $= 21.544$; $p < 0.001$). A study, using PLS-SEM, made in China revealed among 208 employees, that workplace friendship and well-being are influencing organizational performance (Wang et al., 2023). Another study among 89 employees from internal affairs indicated that a pleasant work environment based on psychological health and socio-psychological adaptation is motivating for performance (Scharfenkamp et al., 2023).

5. CONCLUSIONS, SOLUTIONS, AND IMPLICATIONS

Our study revealed that according to the three analysed generations, the attraction and retaining techniques are having different mean scores, indicating that for specific ages, specific attraction and retaining techniques are wanted. So, policy makers must adopt their HR guides to these groups af ages.

Conclusions and Solutions

Thus, the main conclusions for attracting and retaining talented employees according to the three generations are the following:

- Attraction and retention of generation Z (16-24 years)

For generation Z (16-24 years) the most important attraction techniques are the salary (5.00), the career management plans (4.90), and the brand, eliminating discrimination from recruitment ad, and work conditions (each with a score of 4.80).

A few attraction techniques indicated a significant influence on organizational performance using PLS-SEM, such as: workload and employee engagement among 365 persons from Latvia in public sector (Ludviga et al., 2016); challenging tasks in banking sector from Nigeria among 302 employees (Jimoh & Kee, 2022); empowerment among 346 employees from public sector university (Rafique et al., 2023).

As for retaining techniques the more important for Z generation was an enjoyable environment, good communication and payed training programs (4.90), and then flexible work and good working atmosphere (4.80).

Generation Z (16-24 years) in the workplace provoked a challenge for organizations; they must update their management and policies according to their behavior, values, and beliefs. For example, a study made on 283 young employees from China, determined that illegitimate tasks are leading generation Z to leave their work (Fan et al., 2023). Some studies, one made in Germany on 308 students, has indicated that the talents from Generation Z their top expectations were about: the fun from work, an adequate team atmosphere and relations based-support with colleagues and managers, and aspects as practical issues and work-life balance were not found significant (Lassleben & Hofmann, 2023); the second study made in Saudi Arabia among young employees was found that lack of commitment is a factor without significance (Alanazi, 2022). Another study indicated that in the career profile for generation Z is important to develop the social cognitive process (Lee & Yu, 2023); other study made among first year of university studies from Romania, was demonstrated that the most important factors used in attraction policies were: job itself, brand and firm attributes, salary and benefits, and supportive work environment (Migalca et al., 2022); and other study made by companies among young candidates determined that more attractive to younger generations, is new knowledge, resilience, work-life balance, flexible schedules, recognition of value, and the opportunities for promotion (Metro et al., 2022).

Other studies indicated that talent management has significant impact on retention of employees using PLS-SEM among 183 academics (AlQudah et al., 2023); well-being at work on retention among 406 participants (Gelencser et al., 2023); work participation, health and safe conditions among 365 textile workers from India (Kalia et al., 2023); among 326 service sector employees demonstrated that between goodwill of the company and keeping talented employees there is a strong relationship (Ramirez-Asis et al., 2023); ergonomics and work engagement among Egyptian workers from tourism (El-Sherbeeny et al., 2023); green training and employee satisfaction in the hospitality sector (Han et al., 2023).

• Attraction and retention of generation Y (25-39 years)

For generation Y (25-39 years) the most wanted attraction techniques were the brand and eliminating discrimination (4.60), and the salary, career management plans and work conditions (4.50). For Y generation were important as retaining techniques working in teams and training programs (4.70). As retention techniques the most wanted techniques were team work and paid training programs (4.70), and then enjoyable environment, good communication, empowerment and work atmosphere (4.60).

Generation Y grew with the use of Internet, so, the organization who is based on using brand to attract talents, must use communication strategies based on using website (Micik & Mikudova, 2018). Also on generation Y was made a study among employees from 12 major organizations from Indonesia, indicating that the lack of understanding and correctly managing the talent and low commitment from each department are the more important issues for this generation (Wahyuningtyas & Anggadwita, 2017). A study made among 368 respondents indicated that benefits are very important to attract generation

Y, and then work-life balance more than career advancement; access to learning opportunities were the least important for managers from this generation, as retention technique (Pregnolato et al., 2017).

• Attraction and retention of generation X (40-55 years)

For generation X (40-55 years) the most wanted attraction techniques were the presentation of department where the employee will work and the future tasks and qualifications needed for the job (4.60) and the job presentation, the elimination of discrimination, work conditions (4.50).

As retention techniques, the study revealed that for generation X the most important variables were trust and commitment, empowerment (4.80), and good communication and good working atmosphere (4.70).

Studies indicated that generation Y for any organization is very important since the generation X in minimum ten years will be retired, so important techniques to retain generation Y must be developed (Lim, 2013), but also for generation X.

Other studies revealed that generation X and Y are very interested in training, development, and career advancement, compared to Baby Boomers (Festing & Schafer, 2014).

Implications

The study is based on the fact that attraction and retaining talented employees are leading to increased organizational performance.

The study generate some important implications, for theoretical ground, but also for practical one.

• Theoretical implications

Attraction an retaining talented employees are very influencing factors, so studying these two HR techniques, the organizations will obtain increased performance. The literature in the field described in this chapter will contribute to the research in the area, by analysing the attraction and the retaining of talents.

• Practical implications

• *implications for employees*- employees are unique, so unique attraction and retaining techniques must be developed in this war of talents era. A 1-to-1 relationship is imposed according to the vacancy, to the channels used to make known the recruitment ad, and according to the generation is addressed for. Thus, employees will be attracted more and retained longer if specific talent techniques will be used.

• *implications for HR managers as policy makers*- As we may see, the three generations have a different view on attraction and retaining techniques, so HR department could have the opportunity to build a guide based on the three generations in order to attract the best talents and to keep them in order to achieve long run individual and organizational performance.

• *implications for society*- knowing better the attraction and retaining techniques, the whole society will benefit, having advantages of determining a real analysis of strengths and weaknesses of talents, developing policies based on flexibility, on matching skills and talent with the job, or a strategy based on talents who look for an adequate job or vice versa, according to skills, experience, knowledge and attitude of the three analysed generations.

6. LIMITS AND FUTURE DIRECTIONS

Some limitations were found when performing the research for this study. To carry out the literature review, the most important limitation was related to the reduced number of models implemented for analysing the attraction and retention employer techniques, which led to resulted in developing this model.

Another limitations was the reduced sample proposed for the analysis, which may affect the research findings. But the large number of variables proposed for attraction and retention and the diverse fields proposed for the sample improved this limitation. Having said that, future studies might cover not only employees from the county, but also from regional areas.

The practical experience of the authors in the field of HRM helped improved the analysed variables proposed for analysis. The findings can be used by HR specialists to improve their present talent management processes, and offer opportunities for future research and also for specialists in fields related to this topics, as HR management, psychology, sociology, economics, econometry, modelling, and other areas. An increased transparency in some variables information sharing (for example for salary, benefits, or insurance) should encourage to increase the quality of attraction and retention techniques for organizations and for employees at all levels.

REFERENCES

Abdelmotaleb, M. (2023). Exploring the effect of perceived fun at work on hospitality employees' behaviors in and out of work. *International Journal of Contemporary Hospitality Management*. Advance online publication. doi:10.1108/IJCHM-02-2023-0139

Abdelwahed, N. A. A., & Al Doghan, M. A. (2023). Developing Employee Productivity and Performance through Work Engagement and Organizational Factors in an Educational Society. *Societies (Basel, Switzerland)*, *13*(3), 65. Advance online publication. doi:10.3390/soc13030065

Abraham, M., Kaliannan, M., Avvari, M., & Thomas, S. (2023). Reframing talent acquisition, retention practices for organisational commitment in Malaysian SMEs: A managerial perspective. *Journal of General Management*. Advance online publication. doi:10.1177/03063070231184336

Ada, N., Korolchuk, M., & Yunyk, I. (2023). The Role of Employer Branding Practices on Management of Employee Attraction and Retention. *Economics Ecology Socium*, *7*(1), 46–60. doi:10.31520/2616-7107/2023.7.1-5

Aggarwal, I., Schilpzand, M. C., Martins, L. L., Woolley, A. W., & Molinaro, M. (2022). The Benefits of Cognitive Style Versatility for Collaborative Work. *The Journal of Applied Psychology*, *108*(4), 647–659. doi:10.1037/apl0001035 PMID:35901407

Aggarwal, R., Lee, M., & Midhac, V. (2023). Differential Impact of Content in Online Communication on Heterogeneous Candidates: A Field Study in Technical Recruitment. *Information Systems Research*, *34*(2), 609–628. doi:10.1287/isre.2022.1120

Ahamad, F., Saini, G., & Jawahar, I. M. (2023). Interactive influence of work-life balance benefits, employee recommendation, and job attributes on employer attractiveness and job pursuit intentions: Two experiments. *Asian Business & Management*, *22*(4), 1215–1242. doi:10.1057/s41291-022-00184-4

Akay, V. (2006). Business is the people and people are the business. Humanizing the corporation, iUniverse.

Al-Khiami, M. I., & Jaeger, M. (2023). Safer Working at Heights: Exploring the Usability of Virtual Reality for Construction Safety Training among Blue-Collar Workers in Kuwait. *Safety (Basel, Switzerland)*, *9*(3), 63. Advance online publication. doi:10.3390/safety9030063

Alniacik, E., Alniacik, U., Erat, S., & Akcin, K. (2014). Attracting Talented Employees to the Company: Do We Need Different Employer Branding Strategies in Different Cultures? *10th International Strategic Management Conference*, *150*, 336-344. 10.1016/j.sbspro.2014.09.074

AlQudah, N. F., Anjum, M. A., Naeem, K., Ajloun, M. M. A., Ahmed, A., & Shtnaoui, H. (2023). Examining the antecedents of employee retention among Jordanian private Universities: The moderating role of knowledge sharing. *Cogent Business & Management*, *10*(2), 2208429. Advance online publication. doi:10.1080/23311975.2023.2208429

Annell, S., Lindfors, P., Kecklund, G., & Sverke, M. (2018). Sustainable Recruitment: Individual Characteristics and Psychosocial Working Conditions Among Swedish Police Officers. *Nordic Journal of Working Life Studies*, *8*(4), 3–24.

Antons, D., Piening, E. P., & Salge, T. O. (2023). The Elites-Mutual-Attraction Effect: How Relative Reputation Influences Employee Flows between Organizations. *Journal of Management Studies*. Advance online publication. doi:10.1111/joms.12935

Appels, M. (2023). CEO Sociopolitical Activism as a Signal of Authentic Leadership to Prospective Employees. *Journal of Management*, *49*(8), 2727–2765. doi:10.1177/01492063221110207

Arif, S., Johnston, K. A., Lane, A., & Beatson, A. (2023). A strategic employee attribute scale: Mediating role of internal communication and employee engagement. *Public Relations Review*, *49*(2), 102320. Advance online publication. doi:10.1016/j.pubrev.2023.102320

Armstrong, M. (2006). *A handbook of human resources management practice*. Kogan Page.

Bechtoldt, M. N. (2015). Wanted: Self-doubting employees- Managers scoring positively on impostorism favor insecure employees in task delegation. *Personality and Individual Differences*, *86*, 482–486. doi:10.1016/j.paid.2015.07.002

Bibi, N., Bin Saeed, B., & Afridi, M. A. (2022). An Integrated Approach to Linking Job Love with Contextual Factors and Performance: An Empirical Study from Pakistan. *Journal of Asian FinanceEconomics and Business*, *9*(5), 157–169. doi:10.13106/jafeb.2022.vol9.no5.0157

Bodet-Contentin, L., Letourneur, M., & Ehrmann, S. (2023). Virtual reality during work breaks to reduce fatigue of intensive unit caregivers: A crossover, pilot, randomised trial. *Australian Critical Care*, *36*(3), 345–349. doi:10.1016/j.aucc.2022.01.009 PMID:35246356

Boehncke, G. A. (2023). The role of CSR in high Potential recruiting: Literature review on the communicative expectations of high potentials. *Corporate Communications*, *28*(2), 249–273. doi:10.1108/CCIJ-02-2022-0021

Bogathy, Z., Ilin, C., Virga, D., Palos., R., Erdei. I., Sava, P.A., & Zoborila, C.A. (2004). Manual de psihologia muncii şi organizaţională, Editura Polirom.

Bohlander, G., & Snell, S. (2010). *Managing human resources* (15th ed.). Cengage Learning.

Bostjancic, E., & Slana, Z. (2018). The Role of Talent Management Comparing Medium-Sized and Large Companies - Major Challenges in Attracting and Retaining Talented Employees. *Frontiers in Psychology*, 9, 1750. Advance online publication. doi:10.3389/fpsyg.2018.01750 PMID:30283391

Brymer, R. A., & Rocha, V. (2023). Affiliation-based hiring in startups and the origins of organizational diversity. *Personnel Psychology*. Advance online publication. doi:10.1111/peps.12612

Buitek, E. K., Kaliyeva, S. A., Turginbayeva, A. N., Meldakhanova, M. K., & Shaikh, A. A. (2023). How much does an employer's attractiveness matter to youth employment? Evidence from a developing country. *Asia-Pacific Journal of Business Administration*. Advance online publication. doi:10.1108/APJBA-02-2023-0086

Byars, L. L., & Rue, L. W. (2010). *Human resource management*. McGraw-Hill Higher Education.

Cardenas-Munoz, M., & Ramon Campos-Blazquez, J. (2023). Towards an integrated definition of job crafting. *Intangible Capital*, 19(1), 42–54. doi:10.3926/ic.2107

Cassidy, C., & Kreitner, R. (2010). *Supervision: setting people up for success*. South-Western Cengage Learning.

Chaminade, B. (2010). *Attirer et fidéliser les bonnes competences. Créer votre marque d'employeur*. AFNOR Editions, St. Denis Cedex.

Cizmic, E., & Ahmic, A. (2021). The Influence of Talent Management on Organisational Performance in Bosnia & Herzegovina as a Developing Country. *Management*, 26(1), 129–147. doi:10.30924/mjcmi.26.1.8

Coculova, J., & Tomcikova, L. (2021). Innovative Human Resource Management Practices for the Talent Management Implementation. *Marketing and Management of Innovations*, 4(4), 47–54. doi:10.21272/mmi.2021.4-04

Cole, G. A. (2000). *Personnel management*. Editura CODECS.

Compton, R., Morrissey, W., & Nankervis, A. (2009). Effective recruitment and selection practices, CCH a Wolters, Australia

Cornescu, V., Mihăilescu, I., & Stanciu, S. (2001). *Management general*. Editura Actami.

Corple, D. J. (2023). Empowerment at Work?: Examining Employment-Based Economic Empowerment Initiatives for Survivors of Commercial Sexual Exploitation. *Violence Against Women*. Advance online publication. doi:10.1177/10778012231181047 PMID:37321818

Dai, X., & Si, K. (2023). The Fundamental Recruitment Error: Candidate-Recruiter Discrepancy in Their Relative Valuation of Innate Talent vs. Hard Work. *Organization Science*. Advance online publication. doi:10.1287/orsc.2023.1667

Dana, L. P., Gautam, O., Gupta, A., & Sharma, N. (2023). *Indian SMEs and start-ups*. World Scientific Publishing. doi:10.1142/13239

Dancza, K. M., Choi, Y. M., Amalia, K., Wong, P. S., Hu, J. H., & Yap, L. W. (2022). An Appreciative Inquiry Approach to Understanding What Attracts and Retains Early-Career Therapists to Work in Community Organizations. *The Internet Journal of Allied Health Sciences and Practice, 20*(1). Advance online publication. doi:10.46743/1540-580X/2022.2002

Dauth, T., Schmid, S., Baldermann, S., & Orban, F. (2023). Attracting talent through diversity at the top: The impact of TMT diversity and firms' efforts to promote diversity on employer attractiveness. *European Management Journal, 41*, 9-20. doi:10.1016/j.emj.2021.10.007

de Falco, H. (2011). *Maitriser ses recrutements. 7 etapes clés pour faire le bon choix* (4th ed.). Dunod.

De StAubin, D., & Carlsen, B. J. (2008). *Attract, engage and retain top talent: 50 plus one strategies used by the best.* AuthorHouse.

Deckop, J. R. (2006). *Human resources management ethics.* Information Age Pub.Inc.

Dejoux, C., & Thevenet, M. (2010). *La gestion des talents. La GRH d 'apres- crise.* Dunod.

Diba, H. (2023). Employer Branding: The Impact of COVID-19 on New Employee Hires in IT Companies. *IT Professional, 25*(5), 4–9. doi:10.1109/MITP.2023.3321926

Dinnen, M., & Alder, M. (2017). *Exceptional talent. How to attract, acquire, and retain the very best employees.* Kogan Page.

Drazic, I., Schermuly, C. C., & Buesch, V. (2023). Empowered to Stay Active: Psychological Empowerment, Retirement Timing, and Later Life Work. *Journal of Adult Development.* Advance online publication. doi:10.1007/s10804-023-09453-8 PMID:37361380

Durai, K., & Viji, R. (2022). Impact of Talent Management Practices on Organisational Engagement in Start-Ups in India. *Polish Journal of Management Studies, 25*(2), 138–156. doi:10.17512/pjms.2022.25.2.09

Eger, L., Micik, M., Gangur, M., & Rehor, P. (2019). Employer Branding: Exploring Attractiveness Dimensions in a Multicultural Context. *Technological and Economic Development of Economy, 25*(3), 519–541. doi:10.3846/tede.2019.9387

El-Sherbeeny, A. M., Al-Romeedy, B. S., Abd Elhady, M. H., Sheikhelsouk, S., Alsetoohy, O., Liu, S., & Khairy, H. A. (2023). How Is Job Performance Affected by Ergonomics in the Tourism and Hospitality Industry? Mediating Roles of Work Engagement and Talent Retention. *Sustainability (Basel), 15*(20), 14947. Advance online publication. doi:10.3390/su152014947

Ellahi, A., Javed, Y., Jan, M. F., & Sultan, Z. (2024). Determining the Effect of Software Project Managers' Skills on Work Performance. *International Journal of Information Technology Project Management, 15*(1), 1–20. doi:10.4018/IJITPM.333620

Fan, P., Zhang, H., Yang, S., Yu, Z., & Guo, M. (2023). Do Illegitimate Tasks Lead to Work Withdrawal Behavior among Generation Z Employees in China? The Role of Perceived Insider Status and Overqualification. *Behavioral Sciences (Basel, Switzerland), 13*(9), 702. Advance online publication. doi:10.3390/bs13090702 PMID:37753980

Faulkner, D. (2002). *Strategy: critical perspectives on business and management.* Routledge.

Fernandes, C.A., Kanan, L.A., Mayer, A.B., & Lopes, F.N.C. (2023). Demotivation for work: the lack of attraction for existing vacancies in industries in the metallurgy and mechanics segment in serra catarinense. *Revista de Gestao e Secretariato- GESEC, 14*(3), 4022-4042. doi:10.7769/gesec.v14i3.1867

Fischer, M., Rilke, R. M., & Yurtoglu, B. B. (2023). When, and why, do teams benefit from self-selection? *Experimental Economics, 26*(4), 749–774. doi:10.1007/s10683-023-09800-2

Ge, C., Shi, H., Jiang, J., & Xu, X. (2023). Investigating the Demand for Blockchain Talents in the Recruitment Market: Evidence from Topic Modeling Analysis on Job Postings. *Information & Management, 59*(7), 103513. Advance online publication. doi:10.1016/j.im.2021.103513

Gelencser, M., Szabo-Szentgroti, G., Komuves, Z. S., & Hollosy-Vadasz, G. (2023). The Holistic Model of Labour Retention: The Impact of Workplace Wellbeing Factors on Employee Retention. *Administrative Sciences, 13*(5), 121. Advance online publication. doi:10.3390/admsci13050121

George, E., & Chattopadhyay, P. (2022). Like Attracts Like? The Effects of Anxiety, Implicit Bias, and Perception of Diversity Culture on Team Attraction. *Makara Hubs- Asia, 26*(2), 114-131. doi:10.7454/hubs.asia.1270622

Gitman, L. J., & McDaniel, C. (2009). *The future of business: the essentials.* South-Western.

Glavas, A., Hahn, T., Jones, D. A., & Willness, C. R. (2023). Predisposed, Exposed, or Both? How Prosocial Motivation and CSR Education Are Related to Prospective Employees' Desire for Social Impact in Work. *Business & Society.* Advance online publication. doi:10.1177/00076503231182665

Gourova, N., & Gourova, E. (2017). Attracting Talents, Book Group Author Assoc Comp Machinery, *Proceedings of the Vikingplop 2017 Conference on Pattern Languages of Program.* 10.1145/3158491.3158497

Hair, J. F., Black, W. C., & Babin, B. J. (2010). *Multivariate Data Analysis: A Global Perspective.* Pearson.

Hammond, J., Davies, N., Morrow, E., Ross, F., Vandrevala, T., & Harris, R. (2022). "Raising the curtain on the equality theatre": A study of recruitment to first healthcare job post-qualification in the UK National Health Service. *Human Resources for Health, 20*(1), 57. Advance online publication. doi:10.1186/s12960-022-00754-9 PMID:35804352

Han, J. W., Kok, S. K., & McClelland, R. (2023). The impact of green training on employee turnover intention and customer satisfaction: An integrated perspective. *Corporate Social Responsibility and Environmental Management, 30*(6), 3006–3019. doi:10.1002/csr.2534

Hand, M. C., & Reid, A. (2022). Men in Nursing Academia Factors Associated with Recruitment and Retention. *Nurse Educator, 47*(4), 246–251. doi:10.1097/NNE.0000000000001150 PMID:35113054

Henderson, K., & Welsh, E. T. (2023). Potential bias when using social media for selection: Differential effects of candidate demographic characteristics, race match, perceived similarity, and profile detail. *International Journal of Selection and Assessment.* Advance online publication. doi:10.1111/ijsa.12454

Henseler, J., & Sarstedt, M. (2013). Goodness-of-fit indices for partial least squares path modeling. *Computational Statistics, 28*(2), 565–580. doi:10.1007/s00180-012-0317-1

Holbeche, L., & Mayo, A. (2012). *Motivating people in Lean organizations.* Butterworth-Heineman.

Hosdey, A. (2010). *Pour des entretiens d'evaluation efficaces*. Edi.Pro.

Howaniec, H., Karyy, O., & Pawliczek, A. (2022). The Role of Universities in Shaping Talents-The Case of the Czech Republic, Poland and Ukraine. *Sustainability, 14*. doi:10.3390/su14095476

Humphrey, S. (2014). Recruiters and applicants: An exchange of words. *Journal of Financial Services Marketing, 19*(2), 94–103. doi:10.1057/fsm.2014.8

Ishikawa, T., & Yamazaki, Y. (2021). Atmosphere Sharing System by Lighting and Fragrance to Enhance Quality of Work in Telework. *2021 IEEE 3rd Global Conference on Life Sciences and Technologies*, 416-418. 10.1109/LifeTech52111.2021.9391858

Jaskyte, K., Hunter, A., & Mell, A. C. (2023). Predictors of Interdisciplinary Team Innovation in Higher Education Institutions. *Innovative Higher Education*. Advance online publication. doi:10.1007/s10755-023-09676-3

Jayasinghe, S., Suraweera, T., & Samarasinghe, D. (2022). Job seeker value proposition conceptualised from the perspective of the job choice theory. *Sri Lanka Journal of Social Sciences, 45*(2), 107–126. doi:10.4038/sljss.v45i2.8341

Jiang, S., Ling, F. Y. Y., & Ma, G. (2024). Fostering Resilience in Project Teams: Adaptive Structuration Perspective. *Journal of Management Engineering, 40*(1), 04023047. Advance online publication. doi:10.1061/JMENEA.MEENG-5615

Jimoh, L. A., & Kee, D. M. H. (2022). Talent management: The way out of poor task performance. *Industrial and Commercial Training, 54*(4), 623–636. doi:10.1108/ICT-03-2022-0016

Kalia, P., Singla, M., & Kaushal, R. (2023). Human resource management practices and employee retention in the Indian textile industry. *International Journal of Productivity and Performance Management, 73*(11), 96–121. Advance online publication. doi:10.1108/IJPPM-01-2022-0057

Kang, M., Lee, E., Kim, Y., & Yang, S. U. (2023). A Test of a Dual Model of Positive and Negative EORs: Dialogic Employee Communication Perceptions Related to Employee-Organization Relationships and Employee Megaphoning Intentions. *Journal of Public Relations Research, 35*(3), 182–208. Advance online publication. doi:10.1080/1062726X.2023.2194025

Kapferer, J.-N. (2008). The new strategic brand management: creating and sustaining brand equity, Les editions d'Organization.

Karkhanis, G. V., Chandnani, S. U., & Chakraborti, S. (2023). Analysis of employee perception of employer brand: A comparative study across business cycles using structural topic modelling. *Journal of Business Analytics, 6*(2), 95–111. doi:10.1080/2573234X.2022.2104663

Kincaid, R., & Reynolds, J. (2023). *Unconventional Work, Conventional Problems: Gig Microtask Work, Inequality, and the Flexibility Mystique*. Soxiological Quarterly. doi:10.1080/00380253.2023.2268679

Kondaiah, B. V., & Varshney, P. K. (2022). A Comparative Study (Engineering) on Employer Branding Practices to Retain Talent in Professional Engineering Colleges in A.P. W.R.T West Godavarir (DT). *International Journal of Early Childhood Speacial Education, 14*(2), 7657–7665. doi:10.9756/INTJECSE/V14I2.875

Lakhdar, S. (2001). *Gestion de ressources humaines*. Universite de Boeck.

Lassleben, H., & Hofmann, L. (2023). Attracting Gen Z talents: Do expectations towards employers vary by gender? *Gender in Management*, *38*(4), 545–560. doi:10.1108/GM-08-2021-0247

Latukha, M., Zhang, Y., Panibratov, A., Arzhanykh, K., & Rysakova, L. (2023). Talent management practices for firms' absorptive capacity in a host country: A study of the Chinese diaspora in Russia. *Critical Perspectives on International Business*, *19*(2), 181–205. doi:10.1108/cpoib-07-2020-0099

Lee, H., Operario, D., Yi, H., Choo, S., Kim, J. H., & Kim, S. S. (2022). Does Discrimination Affect Whether Transgender People Avoid or Delay Healthcare?: A Nationwide Cross-sectional Survey in South Korea. *Journal of Immigrant and Minority Health*, *24*(1), 170–177. doi:10.1007/s10903-021-01193-9 PMID:33881679

Lee, H. F., & Chang, Y.-J. (2022). The Effects of Work Satisfaction and Work Flexibility on Burnout in Nurses. *The Journal of Nursing Research*, *30*(6), e240. Advance online publication. doi:10.1097/jnr.0000000000000522 PMID:36166364

Lee, L., & Yu, H. (2023). Socioeconomic diversity in the hospitality industry: The relationship between social class background, family expectations and career outcomes. *International Journal of Contemporary Hospitality Management*, *35*(11), 3844–3863. Advance online publication. doi:10.1108/IJCHM-11-2022-1356

Lei, N. (2022). Research on Job Preference in China's Internet Industry Through the Conjoint Analysis. *Journal of Industrial Integration and Management-Innovation and Entrepreneurship*, *07*(03), 273–309. doi:10.1142/S2424862222500142

Liu, R., & Tan, J. (2022). A review of talent management research at home and abroad. *Journal of Chinese Human Resource Management*, *13*(1), 39–58. doi:10.47297/wspchrmWSP2040-800502.20221301

Ludviga, I., Sennikova, I., & Kalvina, A. (2016). Turnover of Public Sector Employees and the Mediating Role of Job Satisfaction: An Empirical Study in Latvia. Society, Integration, Education, 4, 364-378. doi:10.17770/sie2016vol4.1577

Luna-Arocas, R. (2023). The key role played by innovation in the talent management and organizational performance relationship. *Employee Relations*, *45*(6), 1347–1370. doi:10.1108/ER-09-2022-0430

Luna-Arocas, R., & Danvila-del-Valle, I. (2022). The impact of talent management on ethical behavior and intention to stay in the organization. *Journal of Management & Organization*, 1–16. Advance online publication. doi:10.1017/jmo.2022.64

Maier, L., Baccarella, C. V., Wagner, T. F., Meinel, M., Eismann, T., & Voigt, K. I. (2022). Saw the office, want the job: The effect of creative workspace design on organizational attractiveness. *Journal of Environmental Psychology*, *80*, 101773. Advance online publication. doi:10.1016/j.jenvp.2022.101773

Manolescu, A. (2006). *Managementul resurselor umane*. Ed. Economica.

Marinaş, C. (2006). *Managementul comparat al resurselor umane*. Teză de doctorat. ASE Bucureşti.

Martin, M., & Jackson, T. (2008). *Practica de personal*. Editura CODECS.

Mashaba, N., & Botha, D. (2023). Factors affecting the attraction of women to technical mining positions in South Africa. *SA Journal of Human Resource Management, 21*(1). Advance online publication. doi:10.4102/sajhrm.v21i0.2227

Maurya, K. K., & Agarwal, M. (2018). Organisational talent management and perceived employer branding. *The International Journal of Organizational Analysis, 26*(2), 312–330. doi:10.1108/IJOA-04-2017-1147

McChesney, J., Campbell, C., Wang, J., & Foster, L. (2022). What is in a name? Effects of game-framing on perceptions of hiring organizations. *International Journal of Selection and Assessment, 30*(1), 182–192. doi:10.1111/ijsa.12370

Metro, K., Bogus, S. M., & Harper, C. (2022). Hiring for the New Age: Job Advertisements and the Transportation Workforce. *Construction Research Congress 2022: Health and Safety, Workforce, and Education,* 501-509. 10.1061/9780784483985.051

Mihalca, L., Mengelkamp, C., Brendea, G., & Metz, D. (2022). Job Attribute Preferences of Incoming University Students and Newly-Hired Employees in the Context of the Romanian Labour Market. *Journal for East European Management Studies, 27*(1), 31–63. doi:10.5771/0949-6181-2022-1-31

Mijakoski, D., Atanasovska, A., Bislimovska, D., Brborovic, H., Brborovic, O., Cvjeanov, K. L., Milosevic, M., Minov, J., Onal, B., & Pranjic, N. (2023). Associations of burnout with job demands/resources during the pandemic in health workers from Southeast European countries. *Frontiers in Psychology, 14,* 1258226. Advance online publication. doi:10.3389/fpsyg.2023.1258226 PMID:37954180

Miller-Kuhlmann, R., Sasnal, M., Gold, C. A., Nassar, A. K., Korndorffer, J. R. Jr, Van Schaik, S., Marmor, A., Williams, S., Blankenburg, R., & Rassbach, C. E. (2024). Tips for developing a coaching program in medical education. *Medical Education Online, 29*(1), 2289262. Advance online publication. doi:10.1080/10872981.2023.2289262 PMID:38051864

Min, J. (2023). A Symbolic Framing of Exploitative Firms: Evidence from Japan. *Journal of Business Ethics.* Advance online publication. doi:10.1007/s10551-023-05404-1

Mofokeng, M. (2018). Future-Proofing Talent for the Bank of the Future: A Study of Employees in a Bank Operating in Africa. *Proceedings of the 6th International Conference on Management, Leadership and Governance,* 453-461.

Nemțeanu, M. S., Dinu, V., Pop, R. A., & Dabija, D. C. (2022). Predicting Job Satisfaction and Work Engagement Behavior in the COVID-19 Pandemic: A Conservation of Resources Theory Approach. *E&M Economics and Management, 25*(2), 23–40. doi:10.15240/tul/001/2022-2-002

Omer, I. (2003). *Psihologia muncii.* F. România de Mâine, Ed.

Ormeno, M. (2007). *Managing corporate brands- a new approach to corporate communication.* GWV Fachverlage GmbH.

Pandiya, B., Tewari, V., & Upadhyay, C. K. (2023). An empirical assessment of antecedents able to attract the prospective talented workforce for information technology industry across borders. *European Journal of International Management, 19*(4), 491–517. doi:10.1504/EJIM.2023.129531

Pânişoară, G., & Pânişoară, I.-O. (2007). *Managementul resurselor umane: ghid practic.* Editura Polirom.

Park, H. M., Patel, P., Varma, A., & Jaiswal, A. (2022). The challenges for macro talent management in the mature emerging market of South Korea: A review and research agenda. *Thunderbird International Business Review*, *64*(5), 393–404. doi:10.1002/tie.22260

Parlinska, A., & Stawicka, E. (2018). Corporate Social Responsibility: Measuring And Reporting the Effectiveness of Community Involvement on the Basis of the LBG Model. Economic Science for Rural Development, 48, 313-320. doi:10.22616/ESRD.2018.100

Pawar, A., Cahyono, B. T., Indrati, K., Siswati, E., & Loupias, H. (2022). Validating the effect of talent management on organisational outcomes with mediating role of job empowerment in business. *International Journal of Learning and Intellectual Capital*, *19*(6), 527–547. doi:10.1504/IJLIC.2022.126297

Peterson, J. R. (2023). Employee bonding and turnover efficiency. *Journal of Economics & Management Strategy*, *32*(1), 223–244. doi:10.1111/jems.12499

Polyakova-Norwood, V., Creed, J., Patterson, B., & Heiney, S. (2023). Making group work gratifying: Implementing and evaluating a three-stage model of group processes in an online nursing course. *Journal of Professional Nursing*, *46*, 13–18. doi:10.1016/j.profnurs.2023.02.004 PMID:37188401

Price, A. (2000). *Priciples of human resources management: an active learning approach*. Blackwell Business.

Radu, E., Tigu, G., & State, O. (2004). *Conducerea resurselor umane*. Editura ASE.

Rafique, M. A., Hou, Y., Chudhery, M. A. Z., Gull, N., & Ahmed, S. J. (2023). The dimensional linkage between public service motivation and innovative behavior in public sector institutions; the mediating role of psychological empowerment. *European Journal of Innovation Management*, *26*(1), 207–229. doi:10.1108/EJIM-02-2021-0098

Rana, G., Agarwal, S., & Ravindra, S. (2021). *Employer branding for competitive advantage*. CRC Press.

Reich, R. (2002). *The company of the future. Fast company 19*, 1998, 124, from Sims R.R. In *Organizational success through effective human resources management*. Greenwood Pub. Inc.Group.

Rose, E. (2015). Temporal Flexibility and its Limits: The Personal Use of ICTs at Work. *Sociology*, *49*(3), 505–520. doi:10.1177/0038038514542121

SakkaF.GhadiM. Y.GoldmanA. (2022). Talent Management and Professional Development of Employees using Digital Technologies. *TEM Journal- Technology Education Management Informatics, 11*(4), 1612-1619. DOI doi:10.18421/TEM114-23

Saleem, I., Qureshi, T. M., & Verma, A. (2023). Task Challenge and Employee Performance: A Moderated Mediation Model of Resilience and Digitalization. *Behavioral Sciences (Basel, Switzerland)*, *13*(2), 119. Advance online publication. doi:10.3390/bs13020119 PMID:36829348

Samudra, S., Walters, C., Williams-Dobosz, D., Shah, A., & Brickman, P. (2024). Try Before You Buy: Are There Benefits to a Random Trial Period before Students Choose Their Collaborative Teams? *CBE Life Sciences Education*, *23*(1), ar2. Advance online publication. doi:10.1187/cbe.23-01-0011 PMID:38085687

Sarkiunaite, I., & Sciukauske, I. (2021). The Assessment of Employer Brand Impact on the Attraction of Employees in International Organization. *Transformations in Business & Economics, 20*(3C), 387–404.

Savov, R., Kozakova, J., & Tluchor, J. (2022). Talent Retention In Slovak Companies: Explorative Study. *E+M. Ekonomie a Management, 25*(1), 77–95. doi:10.15240/tul/001/2022-1-005

Scarbrough, H., Sanfilippo, K. R. M., Ziemann, A., & Stavropoulou, C. (2024). Mobilizing pilot-based evidence for the spread and sustainability of innovations in healthcare: The role of innovation intermediaries. *Social Science & Medicine, 340,* 116394. Advance online publication. doi:10.1016/j.socscimed.2023.116394 PMID:38000177

Scharfenkamp, K., Wicker, P., & Frick, B. (2023). Female representation at the national level and women sport volunteering in European countries. *Nonprofit Management & Leadership, 33*(4), 783–806. doi:10.1002/nml.21550

Schlechter, A., Hung, A., & Bussin, M. (2014). Understanding talent attraction: The influence of financial rewards elements on perceived job attractiveness. *SA Journal of Human Resource Management, 12*(1). Advance online publication. doi:10.4102/sajhrm.v12i1.647

Schroeder, J. E., & Salzer-Morling, M. (2005). Brand culture. In Corporates brand cultures and communities. Routledge.

Schuller, R. S., & Jackson, S. E. (2005). *Strategic human resources management.* Blackwell Pub.

Schultz, M., Antorini, Y. M., & Csaba, F. F. (2005). Corporate branding- an evolving concept, from Corporate branding: purpose, people, process- towards the second wave of corporate branding. Copenhagen Business School Press.

Schumann, M., & Sartain, L. (2009) *Brand for talent.* Wiley.

Sekiguchi, T., Mitate, Y., & Yang, Y. (2023). Internship Experience and Organizational Attractiveness: A Realistic Job Fit Perspective. *Journal of Career Development, 50*(2), 353–371. doi:10.1177/08948453221094311

Shi, X., Chen, Y., Xia, M., & Zhang, Y. (2022). Effects of the Talent War on Urban Innovation in China: A Difference-in-Differences Analysis. *Land (Basel), 11*(9), 1485. Advance online publication. doi:10.3390/land11091485

Shikweni, S., Schurink, W., & van Wyk, R. (2019). Talent management in the South African construction industry. *SA Journal of Human Resource Management, 17.* Advance online publication. doi:10.4102/sajhrm.v17i0.1094

Sims, R. R. (2002). *Organizational success through effective human resources management.* Greenwood Pub. Inc.Group. doi:10.5040/9798400693953

Smit, B. W., & Lawson, K. M. (2023). Growth mindsets increase flexible work arrangement attractiveness: A policy-capturing study. *Personnel Review, 52*(1), 342–362. doi:10.1108/PR-10-2020-0793

Stahl, G. K., & Bjorkman, I. (2006). *Handbook of research in international HRM.* Edward E. Pub.Ltd.

Stevens, R. E., Loudon, D. L., & Cole, H. (2013). *Concise encyclopedia of church and religious organization marketing*. Routledge. doi:10.4324/9780203725443

Strelnikova, Y. Y., & Goncharova, N. A. (2023). Psychological Features of Professional Demand and Motivation of Law-Enforcement Officers. *Psychology and Law, 13*(1), 27–39. doi:10.17759/psylaw.2023130102

Stuss, M. M. (2020). Talent Management - War for Talents. *Proceedings of the 11th Business & Management Conference*, 198-212. 10.20472/BMC.2020.011.013

Suomi, A., Schofield, T., & Butterworth, P. (2022). Does receipt of unemployment benefits change recruiter perceptions of candidates' personality, work relevant skills and employability? *Work (Reading, Mass.), 71*(4), 1029–1041. doi:10.3233/WOR-205048 PMID:35253667

Sutter, P.-E. (2007). *Comment... recruter ou se faire recruter*. Editions de Boeck Universite.

Tarique, I. (2022). *Contemporary talent management. A research companion*. Routledge.

Theys, N. A., & Barkhuizen, E. N. (2022). The development of an employee value proposition framework for the South African water board sector. *SA Journal of Human Resource Management, 20*. Advance online publication. doi:10.4102/sajhrm.v20i0.1944

Tracy, B. (2008). *Cum să angajaţi şi să păstraţi cei mai buni oameni*. Meteor Press.

Turnea, E. S., Prodan, A., Boldureanu, G., Ciulu, R., Arustei, C. C., & Boldureanu, D. (2020). The Importance of Organizational Rewards on Attracting and Retaining Students at Work. *Transformations in Business & Economics, 19*(2B), 923–943.

Uddin, M. A., Azim, M. T., & Haque, M. M. (2021). Does Compliance to the Prescribed Standards in Readymade Garments Sector Predict Employee Turnover Intention? The Mediating Role of Job Satisfaction and Organizational Attraction. *Iim Kozhikode Society & Management Review, 10*(2), 209–221. doi:10.1177/2277975221989109

Umrani, W. A., Channa, N. A., Ahmed, U., Syed, J., Pahi, M. H., & Ramayah, T. (2022). The laws of attraction: Role of green human resources, culture and environmental performance in the hospitality sector. *International Journal of Hospitality Management, 103*, 103222. Advance online publication. doi:10.1016/j.ijhm.2022.103222

Venkataramani, V., & Tang, C. (2023). When Does External Knowledge Benefit Team Creativity? The Role of Internal Team Network Structure and Task Complexity. *Organization Science*. Advance online publication. doi:10.1287/orsc.2023.1661

Vogel, R., & Satzger, M. (2023). What Drives the Attractiveness of Public and Private Employers? Comparative Evidence from an Online Employer Review Platform. *American Review of Public Administration*. Advance online publication. doi:10.1177/02750740231206805

Wagner, B., & Koob, C. (2022). The relationship between leader-member exchange and work engagement in social work: A mediation analysis of job resources. *Heliyon, 8*(1), e08793. Advance online publication. doi:10.1016/j.heliyon.2022.e08793 PMID:35128097

Wang, H., Sha, H., Wang, Y., Cheng, L., Yu, Q., Jia, D., & Lu, L. (2023). How Does Friendship Motivate Frontline Employees to Exhibit Brand Ambassador Behavior: The Important Role of Well-Being and Helping Behavior. *Sustainability (Basel)*, *15*(8), 6859. Advance online publication. doi:10.3390/su15086859

Wang, Y., & Shi, Y. (2023). Evolvement of international mobility of talents: A complex network perspective. *International Journal of Innovation Science*, *15*(2), 317–328. doi:10.1108/IJIS-02-2021-0029

Weller, I., Hymer, C. B., Nyberg, A., & Ebert, J. (2019). How Matching Creates Value: Cogs and Wheels for Human Capital Resources Research. *The Academy of Management Annals*, *13*(1), 188–214. doi:10.5465/annals.2016.0117

Williams, A. C., Iqbal, S., Kiseleva, J., & White, R. W. (2023). Managing Tasks across the Work-Life Boundary: Opportunities, Challenges, and Directions. *ACM Transactions on Computer-Human Interaction*, *30*(3), 1–31. Advance online publication. doi:10.1145/3582429

Xiao, Q., & Khan, M. S. (2024). Exploring factors influencing supply chain performance: Role of supply chain resilience with mixed method approach empirical evidence from the Chinese healthcare Sector. *Cogent Business & Management*, *11*(1), 2287785. Advance online publication. doi:10.1080/23311975.2023.2287785

Yildiz, D., Temur, G. T., Beskese, A., & Bozbura, F. T. (2020). Evaluation of positive employee experience using hesitant fuzzy analytic hierarchy process. *Journal of Intelligent & Fuzzy Systems*, *38*(1), 1043–1058. doi:10.3233/JIFS-179467

Yimsai, T., & Booranapong, N., Nhomuang, P., Boonthaim, H., Wongpinpech, P., & Chunin, M. (2022). Work Flexibility and Self-Regulation Predicting the Success in Work of Private Company Employees. *International Journal of Early Childhood Special Education*, *14*(2), 3028–3035. doi:10.9756/INTJECSE/V14I2.298

Yu, L., Zhong, J., Lam, W., Wang, Y., & Chen, H. (2023). Healthy lifestyle is a signal: How applicants' healthy lifestyle information affects recruiter judgments. *Journal of Business Research*, *167*, 114148. Advance online publication. doi:10.1016/j.jbusres.2023.114148

Yu, R., Gan, Q., Bian, J., Chen, R., Sun, X., & Ling, H. (2023). The mediating role of psychological empowerment in perceptions of decent work and work immersion among Chinese nurses: A cross-sectional study. *International Nursing Review*, inr.12883. Advance online publication. doi:10.1111/inr.12883 PMID:37647225

Zhang, Y. C., Shum, C., & Belarmino, A. (2023). "Best Employers": The Impacts of Employee Reviews and Employer Awards on Job Seekers' Application Intentions. *Cornell Hospitality Quarterly*, *64*(3), 298–306. doi:10.1177/19389655221130741

Zorlenţan, T., Burduş, E., & Căprărescu, G. (1996). *Managementul organizaţiei*. H. Reporter, Ed.

KEY TERMS AND DEFINITIONS

Attraction Techniques: To acquire talented employees is a need for performant organization to enter in the "war of talents" and create a strategic and attractive recruitment ad who must promise exactly with what the company will offer when the candidate become its employee. Thus, the company will ensure it will have a valuable asset in which it can invest, and not to have costs., in order to have a win-win situation, based on trust, commitment, and performance.

Generation X (40-55 Years) Attraction and Retention: This generation is at the core of the company performance; it is based on learning and gaining new knowledge, it is trustworthy, based on commitment, good communication, collaboration face-to-face, communion and because in between 10 and 25 years this generation will be retired, it is necessary the organization to transform some of this staff in coaches or mentors, to help young generations transfer new knowledge and sharing, and developing together.

Generation Y (25-39 years) Attraction and Retention: Is a generation based on physical activities but also on virtual ones. It rely on involvement and empowerment, it needs directions and development to be retained for a long run.

Generation Z (16-24 Years) Attraction and Retention: Is a special generation, and organizations must develop specific techniques to attract and retain talented employees from this generation. It is considered lazy, based on using new technologies and surprising, thus surprising must be the attraction and retention processes used by the organizations who want to stay competitive over time.

Retention Process: Those activities used by the performant organization in order to keep talented employees and gain competitive advantage for long term. These techniques will ensure not only the company survival, but the differentiation, and also the success.

Talented Employees: Those unique employees with unique interests, skills, knowledge, attitudes, experiences which can make the difference between the failure and success of any company.

Chapter 17
Navigating Employer Branding in the Digital Age:
Exploring the Impact of Social Media Networking During the COVID-19 Pandemic

Bhanupriya Khatri
Independent Researcher, India

Nidhi Sharma
https://orcid.org/0000-0002-3014-2312
Chandigarh University, India

Shad Ahmad Khan
https://orcid.org/0000-0001-7593-3487
University of Buraimi, Oman

Girija Nandini
Centurion University of Technology and Management, India

ABSTRACT

The COVID-19 pandemic has transformed the world of work, and social media has emerged as a critical platform for companies to connect with their employees, customers, and stakeholders. As companies navigate the new reality, their ability to adapt to the challenges posed by the pandemic and maintain their employer branding has become more important than ever. Thus, the foremost goal of the study is to examine the impact of social media networking on employer branding during the COVID-19 pandemic. The target audience of the study was HR professionals of private organizations situated in Tri-city (Chandigarh, Panchkula, and Mohali). Findings of the study revealed that social media has a crucial role in employer branding during the COVID-19. Also, the study revealed that performance expectancy (PE), effort expectancy (EE), social influence (SI) significantly influence behavioural intentions (BI); further, facilitating conditions (FC) and BI significantly influence actual use.

DOI: 10.4018/979-8-3693-1938-3.ch017

1. INTRODUCTION

The COVID-19 pandemic has been a defining moment in society, prompting technological advancements and digitalization along with structural transformation (Bocar et al., 2022; Khan & Magd, 2021; Khan et al., 2022; Yadav et al. 2025). As individuals and businesses modified their way of responding to the threat of getting the infection, millions of people mislaid their work or were assigned to "government assistance programs". For almost the same circumstances, millions of other people significantly changed their working style, migrating from workplaces to their residences (Bocar et al., 2022; Khatri et al., 2023). Because of their employment conditions, millions of persons were at an elevated threat of getting COVID-19 (Bocar et al., 2022; Khatri et al., 2023, Khan & Naim, 2023; Zareen & Khan, 2023). In the situation of this pandemic social media played an important role in helping all of us stay connected and many companies have started opting for social media for employer branding (Saleem et al., 2022; Saleem et al., 2023; Magd & Khan, 2022; Magd et al., 2023a; Sharma et al., 2024).

The notion of employer brand has been defined by Ambler and Barrow (Ambler & Barrow, 1996). They emphasized the need to adopt brand management strategies in HRM, defining the employer brand as "the package of functional, economic, and psychological benefits supplied by employment, and associated with the employing organization." There is currently a scarcity of research into employer branding. These few research findings illustrate that various recruitment strategies are leveraged to sell the brand outwardly while also increasing applicant number, excellence, and administrative presentation (Collins & Stevens, 2002; Kamal et al., 2022). Employer branding is a beneficial method for developing a valuable business brand, according to most of the studies (Ambler & Barrow, 1996; Saleem et al., 2022; Khan et al., 2022). As per Berthon et al. (2005), an explanation of what makes an organization appealing to present and probable employees is required. This is a crucial area because if an employer brand is appealing to employees, it can create the necessary results.

With the growth of digital technologies like artificial intelligence (AI), Internet of Things (IoT), Digital Marketing (DM), and Machine Learning (ML), it is expected that social media interactions will become even more prominent and interactive in the future (Naim et al., 2023; Naim et al., 2024a; 2024b; Khan, 2023; Khan et al., 2023; Naim & Khan, 2023; Magd et al., 2023; Karyamsetty, et al., 2023; Magd et al., 2023b; Khan et al., 2024; Masoom et al., 2024). This will inevitably impact employers and individuals alike.

Social media (SM) is "a group of Internet-based applications that build on the ideological and technological foundations of Web 2.0, and that allow the creation and exchange of User Generated Content" (Kaplan & Haenlein, 2010a; Sharma et al., 2023a; 2023b; Saleem et al., 2023). The furthest protruding in the professional context is LinkedIn. LinkedIn is primarily used as a tool for both companies and job seekers in the hiring process (Chiang & Suen, 2015). User can create public accounts on the platform and make their social connections accessible. It's a fantastic way to connect with additional connections and their buddies' stretched networks. For a company, this denotes having contact with a diverse pool of job candidates. Both employers and job seekers benefit from the simplicity and accessibility that social networking sites provide, and these attributes make them a popular source of information throughout the job search (Kissel & Büttgen, 2015). For an employer, this means having access to a diverse pool of active and passive job candidates. SM networks can be a useful medium for promoting and connecting with current and potential employees. As a result, many businesses use their SM sites as a marketing tool, a method of posting job openings on the internet that, according to various studies, has a favorable impact on the organization's image (Theurer et al., 2018; Ligori et al., 2022). For various reasons, today's executives must embrace SM in terms of employer branding. First and foremost, it is less expensive; second, it allows for speedy and engaging engagement with young people; and third, it allows for the learning of real-time information and unfiltered feedback (Dutta, 2010).

The current global employment market has substantially raised the strategic importance of human resources in a firm. For many firms, attracting and maintaining highly qualified staff has become a major concern. Employers adopt a variety of steps to acquire the best employees and discover potential to demonstrate their competitive edge (Kucherov & Zavyalova, 2012). In recent times, the idea that improving a company's reputation as a decent and honest employer can boost employees' loyalty to that organization or their engagement in the activities performed has grown in popularity (Khatri et al., 2024). Empirical research has found a link between a positive employer image and high employee commitment (Dögl & Holtbrügge, 2014). As the overall influence in the work market is easily moving towards workers. If a couple of years prior, it was the workers who needed to apply to organizations in many ventures, today it is an ever-increasing number of often organizations that need to 'apply' to qualified experts and administrators (Baumgartl, 2019).

Past studies have been done on employer branding in different contexts (Grzesiuk & Wawer, 2018) focused on how employer branding can be done through social media. (Nelke, 2021) Explained the impression of COVID-19 on employer branding. (Sivertzen et al., 2013) The study investigated which aspects of employer branding should be prioritized by firms. (Bondarouk et al., 2014) this study tried to look into what the future holds for social media employer branding. However, no study till now has focused on social media, employer branding, and COVID-19 together. So, the research study is an attempt to eradicate this gap by examining the impact of social media on employer branding during COVID-19. The foremost purpose of this study is to explore the impact of social media on employer branding during the COVID-19 pandemic.

The paper is divided into the following sections, such as Section 2 includes review of the literature. The third Section includes research methodology. The fourth section comprises the results of the study. The Fifth Section includes the conclusion followed by implications and at last limitations of research.

2. LITERATURE REVIEW

2.1. Employer Branding (EB)

EB is a notion that has been around for a while. The word was initially introduced to a management audience in the early 1990s, and it is now frequently used in the worldwide management community. According to the CIPD (2007), there are four main reasons for branding to be focused on HRM: (a) The influence of HR procedures on a company, (b) the rising concentration on employee engagement, (c) the struggle for talent, and (d) the power of branding (Biswas & Suar, 2014). Employer branding is defined by marketing concepts, in which brands are the most valuable assets of many businesses (Backhaus & Tikoo, 2004). EB follows the same principles as corporate branding in that it aims to create a prominent, relevant, and distinct brand that sets it apart from its competition. While corporate branding focuses on the positive and negative associations that stakeholders have with the company, employee branding focuses on current and future workers. According to the Conference Board (Backhaus & Tikoo, 2004), successful EB provides a competitive advantage, assists employees in internalizing business values, and aids in employee retention (Zareen & Khan, 2023, Khatri et al., 2023; Gangwar & Khan, 2022).

Ambler & Barrow (1996) described EB as "the package of functional, economic, and psychological benefits supplied by employment, and associated with the employing organization." As per Backhaus & Tikoo (2004) EB, according to a later definition, is "the process of creating a distinctive and unique employer identity, as well as the employer brand as a concept of the organization that distinguishes it from its rivals." Employer branding has been conceived as a technique for organizational sustainability and enhanced profitability from an organizational standpoint (Parment et al., 2017). EB is a sort of human capital that focuses on present and potential workers. It is characterized as a technique of wise investment in human capital (Backhaus & Tikoo, 2004; Ansari & Khan, 2023). Employer branding in today's world takes a more comprehensive approach to branding operations, based on the concept of the "one brand" (Parment et al., 2017). In this perspective, digital technology has blurred the boundaries between internal and external facets of the corporate brand, necessitating that all branding actions be based on a collaborative branding strategy, with cooperation between internal HR and external marketing efforts becoming increasingly crucial to properly building an authentic "one brand" (Parment et al., 2017).

2.2. Social Media (SM)

One of the most popular phrases in recent years has been "social media." Mersey describes SM as a new communication medium with unique qualities, requiring messages to be adapted to the intended audience (Mersey, 2009). (Backhaus & Tikoo, 2004; Bissola & Imperatori, 2014; Janta & Ladkin, 2013) have all expressed curiosity about social media's usage as a new instrument for recruiting. The rising usage of SM sites as well as technological advancements, have transformed the information flows in businesses. The conventional flow of information had a better "command and control" approach (Cornelissen, 2014); however, SM has blurred the lines between content sources and users. While the blurred lines create a barrier to business communications, also they present a chance to develop new methods for a firm to contact and involve its stakeholders more directly. In terms of building the reputation of the company, SM now allows internal stakeholders like workers to directly engage with other stakeholders even without any gatekeeping, significantly diminishing the control of the company upon the information stakeholders have accessibility.

SM is a new social concept that hasn't been thoroughly studied yet (Roth et al., 2016). Rapidly developing technology diversifies corporate processes in general, and branding and marketing management in particular. In today's environment, most of the communication takes place online (Khan & Magd, 2021, Magd et al., 2023, Magd & Khan, 2022). User Generated Content (UGC) became a phenomenon because of technological advancements in Web 2.0 and an accessible ideology (Kaplan & Haenlein, 2010b). The evolution of SM has resulted in a substantial shift in the methods and technologies that businesses employ to communicate with their customers. SM is a collection of internet-based technologies that allow the establishment of matter by allowing persons to transition from content customers to producers (Scott & Jacka, 2011). People with a high level of visibility on SNWs develop links between users of various media that can be very beneficial to organizations. Businesses were enticed to embrace social media because of its high availability, access, and big amount of information about individuals for instance, in recruiting, to find the right individual for a specific job at the lowest imaginable rate and in the straight imaginable time. Surprisingly, social media was never meant for use by businesses (Kluemper & Rosen, 2009).

2.3. Theoretical Background

Several concepts and theories have been used to find out the connection among beliefs, attitudes, and behavioral intentions (BI) to utilize expertise and techniques in recent times. UTAUT (Venkatesh et al., 2003a; Sharma et al., 2023a) was introduced as an extension of the well-known TAM (Venkatesh et al., 2003a). UTAUT model is a method of user acceptance of information technology (Venkatesh et al., 2003a). Performance expectancy (PE), effort expectancy (EE), social influence (SI), and facilitating conditions (FC) are four fundamental factors in UTAUT that determine BI to use of technology (Carlsson et al., 2006; Sharma et al., 2023b). In the UTAUT, PE, SI, and EE are hypothesized to influence BI to use technology, whereas BI and FC influence technology use.

2.4. Hypotheses Development

2.4.1. Performance Expectancy (PE)

PE is a powerful predictor of BI, implying that people will practice expertise if they feel it will result in an optimistic result (Compeau et al., 1999). The desired effect in this scenario could be something like a faster perception of information availability or a faster interaction with other people. It expresses the belief that using social media will enhance daily tasks, not just job productivity, social relationships, and access to information (Curtis et al., 2010a). Many studies have confirmed that PE significantly influences BI (Amaro & Duarte, 2013; San Martín & Herrero, 2012; Al-Somali et al., 2009). So, we hypothesize -
H1: PE significantly influences BI to use social media for employer branding during COVID-19.

2.4.2. Effort Expectancy (EE)

The mark of easiness connected with customers' usage of technology and know-how is referred to as effort expectation. In the social media world, some individuals are more familiar with social media platform technologies, while others are less so. Individuals will become more eager to utilize social media if they perceive it as simple to use, such as if it is available in their native language (Al Omoush et al., 2012). Many studies have confirmed that EE significantly influences BI (Martins et al., 2014; Curtis et al., 2010b; Kang, 2014). So, we hypothesize -
H2: EE significantly influences BI to use social media for employer branding during COVID-19.

2.4.3. Social Influence (SI)

The amount to which customers trust that key people feel they must utilize a specific technique is known as SI (Venkatesh et al., 2003a). It can be interpreted in the setting of the contemporary work as the behavior of using social media while being significant to others, particularly family and colleagues. SI has been discovered to be a key precursor of BI in most of the research in information systems (Tarhini et al., 2013; Venkatesh et al., 2003a; Tarhini et al., 2014). So, we hypothesize –
H3: SI significantly influences BI to use social media for employer branding during COVID-19

2.4.4. Facilitating Conditions (FC)

FC is termed as "Consumers' perceptions of the resources and support available to perform a behavior" (Venkatesh et al., 2003a). By way of it remained proven that the adjacent situation either supports or inhibits the adoption of new technologies, the UTAUT model claimed that the user's understanding of FC strongly affects technology acceptance. Existing research (Alwahaishi & Snásel, 2013; Akour, Iman A and Dwairi, 2011) has shown that FC has a significant influence on AU. So, we hypothesize -

H4: FC significantly influences AU to use social media for employer branding during COVID-19

2.4.5. Behavioral Intentions (BI)

BI is a person's readiness to engage in an exact performance (Ajzen, 1991). Actual behavior is "the manifest, observable response in a given situation concerning a given target" (Ajzen, 1991). In IT acceptance studies, there is substantial evidence of the important effect of Behavioral intention on AU (Venkatesh et al., 2003a; Venkatesh et al., 2012; Tarhini et al., 2013; Venkatesh & Zhang, 2010; Khan & Magd, 2023; Khan et al., 2021; Khan & Magd, 2021). So, we hypothesize -

H5: BI significantly influences AU to use social media for employer branding during COVID-19.

2.4.6. Constructs and Items for the Study

The five constructs mentioned above were further divided into four items to be placed in the measurement model. The details of the same is given in Table 1.

Table 1. Constructs and items for the measurement model

Construct	Code	Items
Performance Expectancy (PE)	PE01	I would find social media useful for HR managers in employer branding during Covid-19.
	PE02	Using social media enables HR managers to do employer branding more quickly during Covid-19.
	PE03	I would find social media useful as it provides the news about how HR managers can do employer branding during Covid-19.
	PE04	I can save time while using social media as a tool for employer branding during Covid-19.
Effort expectancy (EE)	EE01	Learning how to use social media for employer branding during Covid-19 is easy for me.
	EE02	My interaction (working) with others on the social media would be clear and understandable to do employer branding during Covid-19.
	EE03	It would be easy for me to become skilful at using social media as a tool for employer branding during Covid-19.
	EE04	I would find social media easy to use it as a tool for employer branding during Covid-19.
Social Influence (SI)	SI01	People who influence (relatives) my behavior that I should use social media as a tool for employer branding during Covid-19.
	SI02	People who are important (non-relatives) to me influence me that I should use social media as a tool for employer branding during Covid-19.
	SI03	In general, the community encourages me to use social media for employer branding during Covid-19.
	SI04	People who are important to me has been helpful in the use of the social media for employer branding during Covid-19.
Facilitating Conditions (FC)	FC01	Using social media enhances my knowledge about how to do employer branding during Covid-19.
	FC02	I have necessary knowledge to use social media for employer branding during Covid-19.
	FC03	I have necessary resources to use social media for employer branding during Covid-19.
	FC04	All the content of social media for employer branding during covid-19 is easy to read and understand by me.
Behavioral Intention (BI)	BI01	Assuming I had access to social media, l intend to use it as a tool for employer branding during Covid-19.
	BI02	Given that I had access to social media, I predict that I would use it as a tool for employer branding during Covid-19.
	BI03	I plan to use social media as a tool for employer branding during Covid-19.
	BI04	I will suggest others that they should use social media as a tool for employer branding during Covid-19.
Actual Usage (AU)	AU01	I consider myself a regular user of social media for employer branding during Covid-19.
	AU02	I prefer to use social media when available for employer branding during Covid-19.
	AU03	I firmly believe to frequently use social media for employer branding during Covid-19.
	AU04	I do employer branding during Covid-19 mostly by using social media.
	AU05	I confirm that I can use social media as a tool for employer branding during Covid-19.

3. RESEARCH METHODOLOGY

The target audience of the study was HR professionals of private organizations situated in Tri-Cities

(Chandigarh, Panchkula, and Mohali). A simple random method was used for the collection of data through an online questionnaire. All statements of the questionnaire were prepared using a Likert scale (5-point) in which "1 = strongly agree" to "5 =strongly disagree". In this study, the minimum sample size calculated was 159 but the selected sample size for this study was 295. The rationale for selecting a larger size of sample than the minimum size is that the reliability of results will enhance (Charter, 1999) so a sample size of 295 was a preferable choice. Software named G*Power version 3.1.9.7 for calculating the size of the sample to establish the minimum necessary sample size was utilized (Faul et al., 2007, 2009). The collected data was analyzed using SmartPLS Software 3.3.3 version using PLS-SEM.

*Figure 1. G*Power analysis*

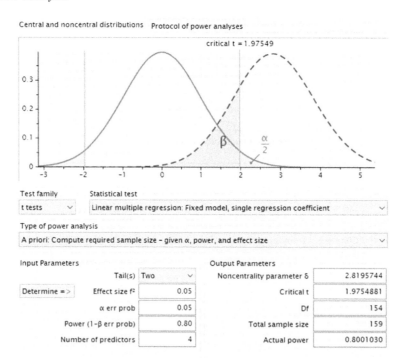

4. RESULTS

4.1. Demographic Information

Table 2 showed that from 295 respondents 67.11% were males and 32.88% were females. The maximum of people fell under the age of 26-35 years at 46.44% while 10.16% fell under 15-25 years with the lowest number. 52.54% of respondents were married while 47.45% were unmarried. Most respondents were postgraduates with 57.28% while 17.62% were graduates and 25.08% had professional qualifications. 48.13% of respondents were at the middle level 35.25% were at the top level and 16.61% were at the junior level.

Table 2. Demographic information of the respondents

Measures	Frequency (n =295)	Percentage (%)
Gender		
Female	97	32.88%
Male	198	67.11%
Age		
15-25 years	30	10.16%
26-35 years	137	46.44%
36-45 years	77	26.10%
45 years and above	51	17.28%
Marital status		
Married	155	52.54%
Unmarried	140	47.45%
Qualification		
Graduation	52	17.62%
Post –Graduation	169	57.28%
Professional	74	25.08%
Designation		
Top Level	104	35.25%
Middle Level	142	48.13%
Junior Level	**49**	**16.61%**

Figure 2. Structural model

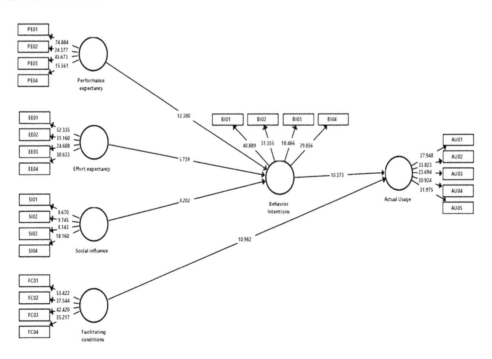

4.2. Measurement Model Results

Measurement model results are shown in Table 3 which includes Factor loadings (FL), Cronbach's Alpha (CA), Henslers' RhoA (Rho_A), Composite reliability (CR), and Average Variance Extracted (AVE). All the values of AVE in result range between 0.506 to 0.665 which meets the requirement of the minimum requirement of 0.5 (Hair et al., 2019). The standards of CA, Rho_A and CR also meet the significant requirement of 0.70 (Hair et al., 2019). The standard of FL is above 0.078 which is the minimum requirement (Hair et al., 2019) except PE04, SI01, SI02, SI03.

Table 3. Results of the measurement model

Constructs	Indicators	FL	CA	Rho_A	CR	AVE
PE	PE01	0.881	0.812	0.886	0.872	0.633
	PE02	0.745				
	PE03	0.872				
	PE04	0.665				
EE	EE01	0.818	0.814	0.886	0.870	0.627
	EE02	0.794				
	EE03	0.756				
	EE04	0.797				
SI	SI01	0.671	0.733	0.917	0.802	0.506
	SI02	0.668				
	SI03	0.655				
	SI04	0.836				
FC	FC01	0.856	0.831	0.835	0.888	0.665
	FC02	0.793				
	FC03	0.815				
	FC04	0.794				
BI	BI01	0.799	0.774	0.782	0.855	0.596
	BI02	0.771				
	BI03	0.725				
	BI04	0.790				
AU	AU01	0.804	0.856	0.861	0.896	0.634
	AU02	0.796				
	AU03	0.736				
	AU04	0.833				
	AU05	**0.809**				

Discriminant validity was examined using Fornell and Lackers' method (1981). As all the values of the variables are different from each other and there is no similarity between them, it meets the criteria of Fornell and Lackers' method. Therefore, there is no such problem of discriminant reliability. Table 4 shows the results.

Table 4. Fornell-Larcker

	AU	BI	EE	FC	PE	SI
AU	0.796					
BI	0.692	0.772				
EE	0.542	0.600	0.792			
FC	0.706	0.427	0.317	0.815		
PE	0.666	0.730	0.517	0.473	0.796	
SI	**0.297**	**0.431**	**0.311**	**0.171**	**0.377**	**0.711**

The next method utilized to check discriminant validity is Heterotrait Monotrait (HTMT) ratio. The value of HTMT should be less than 0.85 (Henseler et al., 2015; Rasoolimanesh et al., 2019; Khan et al., 2021) and all the values of the constructs of this study meet this requirement as shown in Table 5.

Table 5. HTMT

	AU	BI	EE	FC	PE	SI
AU						
BI	0.830					
EE	0.568	0.680				
FC	0.841	0.531	0.340			
PE	0.755	0.847	0.552	0.546		
SI	**0.279**	**0.439**	**0.325**	**0.161**	**0.353**	

The bootstrapping technique was applied even without changing signs to find out the p-values for the relationships described in the study (Hair et al., 2020). The results revealed that PE, EE, and SI are positively related with BI with Std. Beta (β) 0.281, 0.530, and 0.144 respectively, further FC and BI are significantly related with BI with Std. Beta (β) 0.502 and 0.478 respectively. The suggested p-value is 0.05 and all the hypotheses of the study have p-value 0.000. All the constructs have a t-value more than the required value of 1.96. All the results are described in Table 6.

Table 6. Hypotheses testing of relationships

Hypotheses	Relationship	Std. Beta (β)	Std. Error	t-Value	P-Value	Supported
H1	PE -> BI	0.530	0.043	12.380	0.000	Yes
H2	EE -> BI	0.281	0.042	6.739	0.000	Yes
H3	SI -> BI	0.144	0.034	4.202	0.000	Yes
H4	FC -> AU	0.502	0.046	10.982	0.000	Yes
H5	**BI -> AU**	**0.478**	**0.046**	**10.373**	**0.000**	**Yes**

4.3. Overall Fit of the Model

To evaluate goodness of fit while using PLS-SEM, SRMR is used. The suggested SRMR value is less than 0.08 (Hair et al., 2020) and the SRMR value of this study is 0.100 which reveals that the model has very high explanatory power (Hu & Bentler, 1999; Henseler et al., 2016).

4.3.1. Predictive Relevance f²

To examine the predictive relevance the effect size of f2 of the model is used. The suggested limits are 0.02, 0.15, and 0.35 indicating weak, strong, and moderating effect sizes (Cohen, 2013) respectively for studying the change in R2 in respect to independent variable impact on dependent variables. BI with the value of f2 = 0.595 shows a strong effect size on AU. Also, FC with f2=0.656 indicates that it is the most relevant construct of AU. The f2 value of PE is 0.500 showing a strong effect on BI while EE and SI have f2=0.148 and 0.045 respectively revealed a weak effect on BI.

5. CONCLUSION

To examine the predictive relevance the effect size of f2 of the model is used. The suggested limits are 0.02, 0.15, and 0.35 indicating weak, strong, and moderating effect sizes (Cohen, 2013) respectively for studying the change in R2 in respect to independent variable impact on dependent variables. BI with the value of f2 = 0.595 shows a strong effect size on AU. Also, FC with f2=0.656 indicates that it is the most relevant construct of AU. The f2 value of PE is 0.500 showing a strong effect on BI while EE and SI have f2=0.148 and 0.045 respectively revealing a weak effect on BI.

Social media has a huge and diverse impact on employer branding. To sum up, social media platforms are becoming essential resources for developing and promoting an employer brand inside a company. They provide businesses with unmatched chances to present their workplace culture, values, and atmosphere to a worldwide audience. Employers must, however, exercise caution when monitoring their internet presence to make sure it is consistent with their intended brand image.

6. THEORETICAL IMPLICATIONS

From a theoretical perspective, UTAUT, which encompasses the use of SM in EB during COVID-19, confirms the findings of the current study. All the relationships were empirically supported in this research work. All the aspects which affect the behavior of using SM for employer branding were significantly confirmed. The research findings could be considered one of the very first empirical research on using social media for employer branding during COVID-19. Apart from all this PE, EE, and SI had having significant impact on BI.

7. PRACTICAL IMPLICATIONS

The outcomes of the research study promote the creation of marketing strategies and communication approaches by the employer that emphasize on online environments as factors that can more effectively influence employer branding.

8. LIMITATION AND FUTURE SCOPE

This research was conducted in India so it cannot be fully generalizable to other geographical areas, however it gives a good idea about the way social media has been affecting employer branding in the present digital era. So, in future research, researcher can replicate this study in other geographical areas. Secondly, this study did not consider or focused on single social media platforms and it considered the entire social media platforms consequently future research can be done on single social media platform such as LinkedIn. Lastly, UTAUT model is used to examine the impact of SM on employer branding so future research can be done using extended UTAUT or UTAUT 2 with more variables like hedonic motivation and the price value.

REFERENCES

Ajzen, I. (1991). The theory of planned behavior. *Organizational Behavior and Human Decision Processes*, *50*(2), 179–211. doi:10.1016/0749-5978(91)90020-T

Akour, I. A., & Dwairi, M. A. (2011). Testing technology acceptance model in developing countries: The case of Jordan. *International Journal of Business and Social Science, 2*(14).

Al Omoush, K. S., Yaseen, S. G., & Atwah Alma'aitah, M. (2012). The impact of Arab cultural values on online social networking: The case of Facebook. *Computers in Human Behavior*, *28*(6), 2387–2399. doi:10.1016/j.chb.2012.07.010

Al-Somali, S. A., Gholami, R., & Clegg, B. (2009). An investigation into the acceptance of online banking in Saudi Arabia. *Technovation*, *29*(2), 130–141. doi:10.1016/j.technovation.2008.07.004

Alwahaishi, S., & Snásel, V. (2013). Consumers' Acceptance and Use of Information and Communications Technology: A UTAUT and Flow Based Theoretical Model. *Journal of Technology Management & Innovation, 8*(2), 9–10. doi:10.4067/S0718-27242013000200005

Amaro, S., & Duarte, P. (2013). Online travel purchasing: A literature review. *Journal of Travel & Tourism Marketing, 30*(8), 755–785. doi:10.1080/10548408.2013.835227

Ambler, T., & Barrow, S. (1996). The employer brand. *Journal of Brand Management, 4*(3), 185–206. doi:10.1057/bm.1996.42

Ansari, M. S. A., & Khan, S. A. (2023). FDI, disinvestment and growth: An appraisal of Bhutanese economy. *Journal of Chinese Economic and Foreign Trade Studies. Journal of Chinese Economic and Foreign Trade Studies, 16*(1), 64–82. Advance online publication. doi:10.1108/JCEFTS-05-2022-0031

Backhaus, K., & Tikoo, S. (2004). Conceptualizing and researching employer branding. *Career Development International, 9*(5), 501–517. doi:10.1108/13620430410550754

Baumgartl, C. (2019). *Employer brand experience. Theoretical foundations and empirical findings on how employees experience the employer brand.* MERKUR - Writings on Innovative Marketing Management.

Berthon, P., Ewing, M., & Hah, L. L. (2005). Captivating company: Dimensions of attractiveness in employer branding. *International Journal of Advertising, 24*(2), 151–172. doi:10.1080/02650487.2005.11072912

Bissola, R., & Imperatori, B. (2014). Recruiting Gen Yers Through Social Media: Insights from the Italian Labor Market. doi:10.1108/S1877-6361(2013)0000012007

Bocar, A. C., Khan, S. A., & Epoc, F. (2022). COVID-19 Work from Home Stressors and the Degree of its Impact: Employers and Employees Actions. *International Journal of Technology Transfer and Commercialisation, 19*(2), 270–291.

Bondarouk, T., Ruël, H., Axinia, E., & Arama, R. (2014). What Is the Future of Employer Branding Through Social Media? Results of the Delphi Study into the Perceptions of HR Professionals and Academics. doi:10.1108/S1877-6361(2013)0000012006

Carlsson, C., Carlsson, J., Hyvonen, K., Puhakainen, J., & Walden, P. (2006). Adoption of Mobile Devices/Services — Searching for Answers with the UTAUT. *Proceedings of the 39th Annual Hawaii International Conference on System Sciences (HICSS'06)*, 132a–132a. 10.1109/HICSS.2006.38

Chiang, J. K.-H., & Suen, H.-Y. (2015). Self-presentation and hiring recommendations in online communities: Lessons from LinkedIn. *Computers in Human Behavior, 48*, 516–524. doi:10.1016/j.chb.2015.02.017

Cohen, J. (2013). *Statistical Power Analysis for the Behavioral Sciences.* Routledge., doi:10.4324/9780203771587

Collins, C. J., & Stevens, C. K. (2002). The relationship between early recruitment-related activities and the application decisions of new labor-market entrants: A brand equity approach to recruitment. *The Journal of Applied Psychology, 87*(6), 1121–1133. doi:10.1037/0021-9010.87.6.1121 PMID:12558218

Compeau, D., Higgins, C. A., & Huff, S. (1999). Social Cognitive Theory and Individual Reactions to Computing Technology: A Longitudinal Study. *Management Information Systems Quarterly*, *23*(2), 145. doi:10.2307/249749

Curtis, L., Edwards, C., Fraser, K. L., Gudelsky, S., Holmquist, J., Thornton, K., & Sweetser, K. D. (2010). Adoption of social media for public relations by nonprofit organizations. *Public Relations Review*, *36*(1), 90–92. doi:10.1016/j.pubrev.2009.10.003

Dögl, C., & Holtbrügge, D. (2014). Corporate environmental responsibility, employer reputation and employee commitment: An empirical study in developed and emerging economies. *International Journal of Human Resource Management*, *25*(12), 1739–1762. doi:10.1080/09585192.2013.859164

Dutta, S. (2010). What's Your Personal Social Media Strategy? *Harvard Business Review*, *88*(11), 127–130. PMID:21049685

Gangwar, V., & Khan, S. (2022). Analyzing the Role of Micro-Entrepreneurship and Self-Help Groups (SHGs) in Women Empowerment and Development: A Bottom-of-Pyramid Perspective. Driving Factors for Venture Creation and Success in Agricultural Entrepreneurship. In Driving Factors for Venture Creation and Success in Agricultural Entrepreneurship. IGI-Global. doi:10.4018/978-1-6684-2349-3.ch011

Girard, A., Fallery, B., & Rodhain, F. (2014). *Integration of Social Media in Recruitment: A Delphi Study*. doi:10.1108/S1877-6361(2013)0000012009

Gomez Vasquez, L. M., & Soto Velez, I. (2011). *Social Media as a strategic tool for Corporate Communication. Los Medios Sociales como una Herramienta Estratégica para la Comunicación Corporativa*. doi:10.5783/RIRP-2-2011-09-157-174

Grzesiuk, K., & Wawer, M. (2018, September 6). Employer branding through social media: The case of largest polish companies. *10th International Scientific Conference "Business and Management 2018."* 10.3846/bm.2018.42

Hair, J. F. Jr, Howard, M. C., & Nitzl, C. (2020). Assessing measurement model quality in PLS-SEM using confirmatory composite analysis. *Journal of Business Research*, *109*, 101–110. doi:10.1016/j.jbusres.2019.11.069

Hair, J. F., Risher, J. J., Sarstedt, M., & Ringle, C. M. (2019). When to use and how to report the results of PLS-SEM. *European Business Review*, *31*(1), 2–24. doi:10.1108/EBR-11-2018-0203

Henseler, J., Hubona, G., & Ray, P. A. (2016). Using PLS path modeling in new technology research: Updated guidelines. *Industrial Management & Data Systems*, *116*(1), 2–20. doi:10.1108/IMDS-09-2015-0382

Henseler, J., Ringle, C. M., & Sarstedt, M. (2015). A new criterion for assessing discriminant validity in variance-based structural equation modeling. *Journal of the Academy of Marketing Science*, *43*(1), 115–135. doi:10.1007/s11747-014-0403-8

Hew, J.-J., Lee, V.-H., Ooi, K.-B., & Wei, J. (2015). What catalyses mobile apps usage intention: An empirical analysis. *Industrial Management & Data Systems*, *115*(7), 1269–1291. doi:10.1108/IMDS-01-2015-0028

Hu, L., & Bentler, P. M. (1999). Cutoff criteria for fit indexes in covariance structure analysis: Conventional criteria versus new alternatives. *Structural Equation Modeling*, *6*(1), 1–55. doi:10.1080/10705519909540118

Janta, H., & Ladkin, A. (2013). In search of employment: Online technologies and Polish migrants. *New Technology, Work and Employment*, *28*(3), 241–253. doi:10.1111/ntwe.12018

Kamal, S., Naim, A., Magd, H., Khan, S. A., & Khan, F. M. (2022). The Relationship Between E-Service Quality, Ease of Use, and E-CRM Performance Referred by Brand Image. In *Building a Brand Image Through Electronic Customer Relationship Management* (pp. 84–108). IGI Global. doi:10.4018/978-1-6684-5386-5.ch005

Kang, S. (2014). Factors influencing intention of mobile application use. *International Journal of Mobile Communications*, *12*(4), 360. doi:10.1504/IJMC.2014.063653

Kaplan, A. M., & Haenlein, M. (2010). Users of the world, unite! The challenges and opportunities of Social Media. *Business Horizons*, *53*(1), 59–68. doi:10.1016/j.bushor.2009.09.003

Karyamsetty, H. J., Khan, S. A., & Nayyar, A. (2023). Envisioning Towards Modernization of Society 5.0- A Prospective Glimpse on Status, Opportunities, and Challenges With XAI. In F. Al-Turjman, A. Nayyar, M. Naved, A. K. Singh, & M. Bilal (Eds.), *XAI Based Intelligent Systems for Society 5.0* (pp. 223–267). Elsevier. doi:10.1016/B978-0-323-95315-3.00005-X

Khan, S. A. (2023). E-Marketing, E-Commerce, E-Business, and Internet of Things: An Overview of Terms in the Context of Small and Medium Enterprises (SMEs). In A. Naim & V. Devi (Eds.), *Global Applications of the Internet of Things in Digital Marketing* (pp. 332–348). IGI Global. doi:10.4018/978-1-6684-8166-0.ch017

Khan, S.A, Epoc, F., Gangwar, V.P., Ligori T.A.A, & Ansari, Z.A. (2021). Will Online banking sustain in Bhutan post Covid – 19? A quantitative analysis of the customer e-satisfaction and e-loyalty in the Kingdom of Bhutan. *Transnational Marketing Journal*, *9*(3), 607-624. doi:10.33182/tmj.v9i3.1288

Khan, S. A., & Magd, H. (2021). Empirical Examination of MS Teams in Conducting Webinar: Evidence from International Online Program conducted in Oman. *Journal of Content. Community and Communication*, *7*(1), 159–175. doi:10.31620/JCCC.12.21/13

Khan, S. A., & Magd, H. (2023). New Technology Anxiety and Acceptance of Technology: An Appraisal of MS Teams. In *Advances in Distance Learning in Times of Pandemic* (pp. 105–134). CRC Press, Taylor and Francis. doi:10.1201/9781003322252-5

Khan, S. A., Magd, H., Ansari, M. S. A., Sharma, P. P., Tirwa, I. P., & Bhuyan, U. (2022). Analysis of Regional Tourists in Bhutan before Covid-19. *Anusandhan-NDIM's Journal of Business and Management Research*, *4*(1), 39–58. doi:10.56411/anusandhan.2022.v4i1.39-58

Khan, S. A., Magd, H., Bhuyan, U., Jonathan, H., & Naim, A. (2024). Digital Marketing (DM): How are Small Business Enterprises (SBEs) of Bhutan and Sikkim (India) Responding to it? In Digital Influence on Consumer Habits: Marketing Challenges and Opportunities (pp. 135-145). Emerald Publishing Limited. doi:10.1108/978-1-80455-342-820241008

Khan, S. A., Magd, H., & Epoc, F. (2022). Application of Data Management System in Business to Business Electronic Commerce. In Competitive Trends and Technologies in Business Management. (pp. 109-124). Nova Science Publishers.

Khan, S. A., Magd, H., Khatri, B., Arora, S., & Sharma, N. (2023). Critical Success Factors of Internet of Things and Digital Marketing. In A. Naim & V. Devi (Eds.), *Global Applications of the Internet of Things in Digital Marketing* (pp. 233–253). IGI Global. doi:10.4018/978-1-6684-8166-0.ch012

Khan, S. A., & Naim, A. (2023). XAI in Society 5.0 through the lens of Marketing and HRM. In F. Al-Turjman, A. Nayyar, M. Naved, A. K. Singh, & M. Bilal (Eds.), *XAI Based Intelligent Systems for Society 5.0* (pp. 327–363). Elsevier. doi:10.1016/B978-0-323-95315-3.00004-8

Khan, S. A., Narula, S., Kansra, P., Naim, A., & Kalra, D. (2024). Should Marketing and Public Relations be Part of the Institutional Accreditation Criterion of Business Schools? An Appraisal of Accreditation Criterion of Selected Accreditation Agencies. In A. Naim (Ed.), *Accreditation Processes and Frameworks in Higher Education* (pp. 349–375). Nova Science Publishers. doi:10.52305/QUVJ6658

Khatri, B., Shrimali, H., Khan, S. A., & Naim, A. (2023). Role of HR Analytics in Ensuring Psychological Wellbeing and Job Security: Learnings From COVID-19. In R. Yadav, M. Sinha, & J. Kureethara (Eds.), *HR Analytics in an Era of Rapid Automation* (pp. 36–53). IGI Global. doi:10.4018/978-1-6684-8942-0.ch003

Khatri, B., Singh, R. K., Arora, S., Khan, S. A., & Naim, A. (2024). Optimizing Supply Chain Management Indicators for Sustainable Supply Chain Integration and Customer Loyalty: Potential Role of Environmentally Responsible Practices. In Y. Ramakrishna & B. Srivastava (Eds.), *Strategies for Environmentally Responsible Supply Chain and Production Management* (pp. 156–181). IGI Global. doi:10.4018/979-8-3693-0669-7.ch008

Kissel, P., & Büttgen, M. (2015). Using social media to communicate employer brand identity: The impact on corporate image and employer attractiveness. *Journal of Brand Management, 22*(9), 755–777. doi:10.1057/bm.2015.42

Kluemper, D. H., & Rosen, P. A. (2009). Future employment selection methods: Evaluating social networking web sites. *Journal of Managerial Psychology, 24*(6), 567–580. doi:10.1108/02683940910974134

Kucherov, D., & Zavyalova, E. (2012). HRD practices and talent management in the companies with the employer brand. *European Journal of Training and Development, 36*(1), 86–104. doi:10.1108/03090591211192647

Ligori, T. A. A., Suresh, N., Khan, S. A., Rabgay, T., & Yezer, K. (2022). The mediating effect of university image on the relationship between curriculum and student satisfaction: An empirical study of the Royal University of Bhutan. *International Journal of Pluralism and Economics Education, 13*(2), 192–208. doi:10.1504/IJPEE.2022.127218

Luo, X., Li, H., Zhang, J., & Shim, J. P. (2010). Examining multi-dimensional trust and multi-faceted risk in initial acceptance of emerging technologies: An empirical study of mobile banking services. *Decision Support Systems, 49*(2), 222–234. doi:10.1016/j.dss.2010.02.008

Magd, H., Ansari, M. S. A., & Khan, S. A. (2023a). Need for Explainable Artificial Intelligence Ethnic Decision Making in Society 5.0. In F. Al-Turjman, A. Nayyar, M. Naved, A. K. Singh, & M. Bilal (Eds.), *XAI Based Intelligent Systems for Society 5.0* (pp. 103–127). Elsevier. doi:10.1016/B978-0-323-95315-3.00010-3

Magd, H., Jonathan, H., & Khan, S. A. (2023b). Education Situation in Online Education before the Pandemic and in the Time of Pandemic. In Advances in Distance Learning in Times of Pandemic. CRC Press, Taylor and Francis. doi:10.1201/9781003322252-3

Magd, H., & Khan, S. A. (2022). Strategic Framework for Entrepreneurship Education in Promoting Social Entrepreneurship in GCC Countries During and Post COVID-19. In International Perspectives on Value Creation and Sustainability Through Social Entrepreneurship (pp. 61-75). IGI Global.

Magd, H., & Khan, S. A. (2022). Effectiveness of using online teaching platforms as communication tools in higher education institutions in Oman: Stakeholders perspectives. *Journal of Content. Community and Communication*, *16*, 148–160. doi:10.31620/JCCC.12.22/13

Martins, C., Oliveira, T., & Popovič, A. (2014). Understanding the Internet banking adoption: A unified theory of acceptance and use of technology and perceived risk application. *International Journal of Information Management*, *34*(1), 1–13. doi:10.1016/j.ijinfomgt.2013.06.002

Masoom, K., Rastogi, A., & Khan, S. A. (2024). Impact of AI on Knowledge-based Marketing: A Study of B2B Markets. In N. Singh, P. Kansra, & S. L. Gupta (Eds.), *Digital Influence on Consumer Habits: Marketing Challenges and Opportunities* (pp. 147–158). Emerald Publishing Limited. doi:10.1108/978-1-80455-342-820241009

Naim, A., & Khan, S. A. (2023). Impact and Assessment of Electronic Commerce on Consumer Buying Behaviour. In A. Naim & V. Devi (Eds.), *Global Applications of the Internet of Things in Digital Marketing* (pp. 264–289). IGI Global. doi:10.4018/978-1-6684-8166-0.ch014

Naim, A., Khan, S. A., Malik, P. K., Hussain, M. R., & Dildar, M. S. (2023). Internet of things support for Marketing Sports and Fitness Products. *2023 3rd International Conference on Advancement in Electronics & Communication Engineering (AECE)*, 215-219. 10.1109/AECE59614.2023.10428323

Naim, A., Khan, S. A., Mohammed, A. B., & Malik, P. K. (2024a). Applications of High Performance Computing and AI in Green Digital Marketing. In A. Naim (Ed.), *AI Applications for Business, Medical, and Agricultural Sustainability* (pp. 47–67). IGI Global. doi:10.4018/979-8-3693-5266-3.ch003

Naim, A., Mohammed, A. B., Fatima, N., Khan, S. A., Alnfiai, M. M., & Malik, P. K. (2024b). Applications of Artificial Intelligence in Environmental Resource Business Management and Sustainability. In AI Applications for Business, Medical, and Agricultural Sustainability (pp. 1-22). IGI Global. doi:10.4018/979-8-3693-5266-3.ch001

Nelke, A. (2021). Impact of the COVID-19 pandemic on corporate employer branding. *Technium Social Sciences Journal*, *16*, 388–393. doi:10.47577/tssj.v16i1.2436

Ollington, N., Gibb, J., & Harcourt, M. (2013). Online social networks: An emergent recruiter tool for attracting and screening. *Personnel Review*, *42*(3), 248–265. doi:10.1108/00483481311320390

Parment, A., Anna, D., & Lutz. (2017). *Employer branding: Employer branding: how employers build strong brands*. Academic Press.

Pavlou & Fygenson. (2006). Understanding and Predicting Electronic Commerce Adoption: An Extension of the Theory of Planned Behavior. *MIS Quarterly, 30*(1), 115. doi:10.2307/25148720

Rasoolimanesh, S. M., Taheri, B., Gannon, M., Vafaei-Zadeh, A., & Hanifah, H. (2019). Does living in the vicinity of heritage tourism sites influence residents' perceptions and attitudes? *Journal of Sustainable Tourism, 27*(9), 1295–1317. doi:10.1080/09669582.2019.1618863

Roth, P. L., Bobko, P., Van Iddekinge, C. H., & Thatcher, J. B. (2016). Social Media in Employee-Selection-Related Decisions. *Journal of Management, 42*(1), 269–298. doi:10.1177/0149206313503018

Saleem, M., Khan, S. A., Al Shamsi, I. R., & Magd, H. (2023). Digital Marketing Through Social Media Best Practices: A Case Study of HEIs in the GCC Region. In A. Naim & V. Devi (Eds.), *Global Applications of the Internet of Things in Digital Marketing* (pp. 17–30). IGI Global. doi:10.4018/978-1-6684-8166-0.ch002

Saleem, M., Khan, S. A., & Magd, H. (2022). Content Marketing Framework for Building Brand Image: A Case Study of Sohar International School, Oman. In Building a Brand Image Through Electronic Customer Relationship Management (pp. 64-83). IGI Global.

San Martín, H., & Herrero, Á. (2012). Influence of the user's psychological factors on the online purchase intention in rural tourism: Integrating innovativeness to the UTAUT framework. *Tourism Management, 33*(2), 341–350. doi:10.1016/j.tourman.2011.04.003

Scott, P. R., & Jacka, J. M. (2011). *Auditing Social Media: A Governance and Risk Guide*. Willey.

Sharma, N., Khatri, B., & Khan, S. A. (2023b). Do e-WOM Persuade Travelers Destination Visit Intentions? An investigation on how Travelers Adopt the Information from the Social Media Channels. *Journal of Content. Community and Communication, 17*(9), 147–161. doi:10.31620/JCCC.06.23/11

Sharma, N., Khatri, B., & Khan, S. A. (2024). Exploring the Past and Identifying the Future Research Agenda for Social Media and Tourist Behavior: A Bibliometric Analysis. In C. Ramos, T. Costa, F. Severino, & M. Calisto (Eds.), *Social Media Strategies for Tourism Interactivity* (pp. 261–284). IGI Global. doi:10.4018/979-8-3693-0960-5.ch011

Sharma, N., Khatri, B., Khan, S. A., & Shamsi, M. S. (2023a). Extending the UTAUT Model to Examine the Influence of social media on Tourists' Destination Selection. *Indian Journal of Marketing, 53*(4), 47–64. doi:10.17010/ijom/2023/v53/i4/172689

Sivertzen, A.-M., Nilsen, E. R., & Olafsen, A. H. (2013). Employer branding: Employer attractiveness and the use of social media. *Journal of Product and Brand Management, 22*(7), 473–483. doi:10.1108/JPBM-09-2013-0393

Suar, D. (2014). Antecedents and Consequences of Employer Branding. *Journal of Business Ethics*. https://doi.org/ doi:10.1007/s10551-014-2502

Tarhini, A., Hone, K., & Liu, X. (2013). User Acceptance Towards Web-based Learning Systems: Investigating the Role of Social, Organizational and Individual Factors in European Higher Education. *Procedia Computer Science*, *17*, 189–197. doi:10.1016/j.procs.2013.05.026

Tarhini, A., Hone, K., & Liu, X. (2014). The effects of individual differences on e-learning users' behaviour in developing countries: A structural equation model. *Computers in Human Behavior*, *41*, 153–163. doi:10.1016/j.chb.2014.09.020

Theurer, C. P., Tumasjan, A., Welpe, I. M., & Lievens, F. (2018). Employer Branding: A Brand Equity-based Literature Review and Research Agenda. *International Journal of Management Reviews*, *20*(1), 155–179. doi:10.1111/ijmr.12121

Venkatesh, M., Morris, Davis, & Davis. (2003). User Acceptance of Information Technology: Toward a Unified View. *Management Information Systems Quarterly*, *27*(3), 425. doi:10.2307/30036540

Venkatesh, T., Thong, & Xu. (2012). Consumer Acceptance and Use of Information Technology: Extending the Unified Theory of Acceptance and Use of Technology. *Management Information Systems Quarterly*, *36*(1), 157. doi:10.2307/41410412

Venkatesh, V., & Zhang, X. (2010). Unified Theory of Acceptance and Use of Technology: U.S. Vs. China. *Journal of Global Information Technology Management*, *13*(1), 5–27. doi:10.1080/1097198X.2010.10856507

Yadav, U. S., Tripathi, R., Rena, R., Khan, S. A., & Ghosal, I. (2025). Use and Effect of Fintech Awareness in Women for Sustainable Development in Small Industry during COVID-19 Pandemic: An Empirical Analysis with UTUAT model. *International Journal of Electronic Finance*. Advance online publication. doi:10.1504/IJEF.2025.10062118

Zareen, S., & Khan, S. A. (2023). Exploring Dependence of Human Resource Management (HRM) on Internet of Things (IoT) and Digital Marketing in the Digital Era. In A. Naim & V. Devi (Eds.), *Global Applications of the Internet of Things in Digital Marketing* (pp. 51–66). IGI Global. doi:10.4018/978-1-6684-8166-0.ch004

Chapter 18
Neurodiversity at the Workplace:
The New Paradigm of Talent Acquisition and Retention

Sachin Sinha
Christ University, India

Deepti Sinha
🆔 https://orcid.org/0000-0001-9931-6563
Christ University, India

ABSTRACT

The importance of neurodiversity in the workplace has gained popularity in recent years. Companies can access a pool of distinctive skills and viewpoints that can stimulate innovation, creativity, and productivity by embracing neurodiversity in the workplace. This chapter examines the idea of neurodiversity in relation to hiring and retaining talent, emphasizing the advantages for both companies and workers. It covers methods for establishing welcoming environments at work that support neurodiverse workers and help them reach their full potential. It also looks at how corporate culture, HR regulations, and leadership all contribute to creating a welcoming workplace for individuals who are neurodiverse. Companies can promote diversity, equity, and inclusion at the workplace in addition to attracting and retaining neurodiverse employees (NDEs). A conceptual framework has been proposed to demonstrate the influence of various factors like awareness, perceived benefits, accommodation, organizational policy, stigma, and unconscious bias on retention of NDEs.

DOI: 10.4018/979-8-3693-1938-3.ch018

INTRODUCTION

Come to think of it, there is nothing in this world which can be called 'normal'. We all carry our own 'normality' within ourselves. Or, maybe we are all at different points in the continuum of 'normality'. Also, come to think of it, Nature also did not intend its design to be normal. There is no particular default design in Nature. The infinite diversity that exists in the cross-section of Nature bears ample testimony to the fact that there is no 'normal' default design in Nature.

The phenomenon is perhaps as old as the hills, but the nomenclature is new. Neurodiversity is a contemporary concept that has emerged in response to a strong and persistent need of the hour. The need to acknowledge and encourage the inclusion and participation in the workforce of people whose minds are wired differently. Neurodiversity is an official and formal acceptance on the part of society at large and the working world in particular that there exists a wide variety and diversity in the functioning of human brains, although they might biologically consist of the same cells and tissues. In fact, this term can be seen as the neurological counterpart of 'biodiversity' (Walker 2014). Just as there is an immeasurable amount of diversity among flora and fauna and all other life forms dotting the earth, similarly there are innumerable individual differences among minds of people populating the plane. The explicit and manifest affirmation of this reality is what the sum and substance of neurodiversity is all about. But the phenomenon does not end there. Autistic sociologist Judy Singer coined the terms 'neurodiverse' and 'neurodivergent' in the nineties to substitute the discriminatory (and also derogatory) word 'disorder'. The idea was to bring into prominence the salient attributes of autistic individuals like their capabilities of concentration, identification of patterns and retention of facts and figures. A 'neurodivergent' individual is one who lies somewhere on the autism spectrum. Neurodivergent people's brains process things in a manner quite unlike the brains of the majority of people. Neurodivergent individuals may be found to experience and exhibit learning disabilities, attention deficit and anxiety disorders, obsessive-compulsive disorder and Tourette's syndrome. Looked at from a neurodiversity standpoint, these are not 'abnormalities' but just different shades of normality (Singer, 1998; Singer, 1999).

About 15–20% of people worldwide fall under the neurodiverse spectrum. Their general IQ scores are greater than those of the general population, and they are endowed with a unique competency in pattern recognition, memory, and mathematical abilities. Research indicates that teams with a neurodiverse composition tend to be 30% more productive and make fewer mistakes (Montvelisky, 2021). However, because they continue to face the stigma of not being seen as having "neurotypical" qualities, they also have a very poor employment situation. According to mydisabilityjobs.com, their unemployment rate is three times higher than that of those with any other type of disability and eight times higher than that of people without any form of impairment. The justification for the urgent need for increased participation and inclusion.

LITERATURE REVIEW

A wide cross-section of studies have explore and unearthed different aspects and dimensions of the phenomenon of neurodiversity in all its manifestations. Some of these studies have been summarized her.

First of all, the social model of disability had an influence on the formulation of the fundamental concept of "neurodiversity" (Kreck, 2012; Shakespeare & Watson, 1997; Charlton, 1998). This idea's roots can be found in the concept of "biodiversity," which was developed with the goal of preserving the environment and ensuring the long-term viability of a robust ecosystem. Advocates of neurodiversity extended the argument of biodiversity to suggest that society might gain unrealized gains by recognizing and developing the unique strengths resulting from autism or dyslexia (Baker, 2011; Ortega, 2009).

The field of neurodiversity and employment research is still young (Krzeminska et al., 2019; LeFevre-Levy et al., 2023), and not much is known about how to manage organizational neurodiversity for neurodivergent employees' long-term employment. For those who are neurodiverse, a segment of the general population that has historically witnessed unemployment and underemployment rates as high as 85–90%, the last ten years have seen a spectacular opening of new job prospects (Roux et al., 2015). According to Jaarsma and Welin (2012), neurodiversity views neurological advancements that are typically thought of as abnormal or even as diagnosable illnesses, such dyslexia or autism, and instead views them as regular human variation. Many neurodiverse people, according to proponents of this viewpoint, are capable of working effectively in organizations and have valuable talents, but they are not given the opportunity to find employment because they are considered as examples of human variation, "at the edges of the bell curve" (Robison, 2013). This point of view contends that the issue lies not with neurodiverse individuals but rather with recruiting practices that overly define talent, particularly with regard to the use of job interviews, which are prejudiced toward candidates who engage in unusual ways. This approach aligns with the initial critiques of employment attitudes that perceived diversity as "the problem" instead of the issue being improper diversity management (Härtel & Fujimoto, 2000). Ali et al., (2023) provided a pioneering basis for awareness of workplace neurodiversity and the influence of knowing neurodivergent employees and neurodiversity practices followed by organizations on their benefits and challenges.

According to a research titled 'Neurodiversity at Work 2023: Demand, Supply, and a Gap Analysis', which was funded by McDonald's, Sage, and Rolls-Royce, the following four goals should be prioritised for the neurodiversity-in-business movement: 1. Make inclusivity and well-being for all people, including ND employees, a cornerstone of business strategy to capitalize on varied talent. 2. Objectively assess and encourage the efficacy of modifications to determine what works for whom and how to benchmark and communicate quality of service. 3. Emphasise relationships to promote shared accountability, especially psychological safety and line manager confidence. 4. Think about how practices and policies can help people advance their goals and careers from just surviving to thriving (McDowall, Doyle & Kiseleva, 2022).

According to a study by Dunn and colleagues (2023), it is critical that professionals acknowledge and value the variety of social preferences among people with autism. Individual needs and strengths should be taken into account when designing treatments, as opposed to imposing neurotypical standards. This method celebrates diversity as authentic manifestations of neurodiversity, empowering and promoting autonomy. Furthermore, it is imperative that healthcare professionals and educators transition from deficit-based to strengths-based modes of support, fostering inclusive cultures that recognize the intrinsic worth of each individual, irrespective of their neurotype (Frizell et al., 2024). Therefore, accepting neurodiversity in social preferences promotes an inclusive and respectful society, encouraging people to revaluate their preconceptions and prejudices and opening the door to a more compassionate and inclusive comprehension of the social experiences of autistic people.

An article titled 'A rising tide lifts all boats: Creating a better work environment for all by embracing neurodiversity', published in 'Deloitte Insights', talks about opportunities arising when companies embrace and fully utilise the neurodivergent workforce, as they are being forced to revaluate many of their workforce tactics and tried-and-true formulas for success. Nowadays, a large number of US businesses are more eager to hire neurodivergent employees and are prepared to provide the necessary accommodations. Organizations that do not go in this direction run the risk of losing out to other companies that provide professionals a modern and safe work environment, especially considering the advantages these professionals bring in terms of innovation and production. The actions taken by enterprises to foster an inclusive work environment for their neurodivergent workforce may have repercussions for the workforce as a whole. The workforce as a whole can benefit from the lessons managers and leaders gain from addressing the particular demands of neurodivergent workers. While common concerns for neurodivergent professionals may change established HR procedures, they will always improve and make the workplace a safer and more welcoming environment for all employees (Mahto, Hogan & Sniderman, 2022).

Not only are neurodivergent workers a valuable asset to the company, but they also offer a competitive edge. It has been discovered that neurodivergent people have some of the most in-demand talents in the modern workplace. Neurodivergent employees give the business a competitive edge in addition to being a valued asset. It has been shown that among the most sought-after skills in the contemporary workplace are those possessed by neurodivergent individuals. Creativity, risk-taking, high energy, and the urge to multitask are just a few of the symptoms of ADHD that, when used appropriately, in the correct context, may become valuable assets in the workplace. In the meantime, dyslexics often create narrations which can simplify complex tasks or products and see connections that others cannot.

Elevated productivity: "Elevated productivity" refers to a state where an individual, team, or organization achieves a higher level of efficiency and output in their work or activities compared to previous performance or industry standards. This can result from various factors such as improved processes, better time management, enhanced focus, effective delegation, use of technology, motivation, and a conducive work environment. Professionals in JPMorgan Chase's 'Autism at Work project' were 90% to 140% more productive and made less mistakes than their neurotypical counterparts, according to a case study (Neurodiversity in workplace).

Ability to take a different perspective: The ability to take a different perspective, often referred to as 'perspective-taking' is a crucial skill in various aspects of life, including interpersonal relationships, problem-solving, and decision-making. It involves the capacity to understand and empathize with the viewpoints, feelings, and experiences of others, as well as to consider alternative viewpoints beyond one's own. People who are neurodiverse "wired" differently from neurotypical people, which allows them to contribute creative problem-solving and creative ways of thinking to teams and organizations.

Furthermore, putting neurodiversity first at work has a major positive impact on important business KPIs like:

Team productivity and performance: Team productivity and performance refers to the collective efficiency, effectiveness, and output of a group of individuals working together towards a common goal or objectives. It encompasses the ability of a team to achieve desired results within specified timelines while maintaining quality standards and collaboration. Research suggests that teams with neurodivergent professionals in some roles can be 30% more productive than those without them. This is probably due to the distinct skills and cognitive abilities of neurodiverse workers, which enable them to approach jobs and solve issues in a different way than their teammates (Luc, 2024).

Retention: Retention refers to the ability of an organization to retain its employees over a certain period. High retention rates indicate that employees are satisfied with their jobs, feel valued, and are likely to stay with the organization for the long term. Retention is crucial for maintaining stability, preserving institutional knowledge, and avoiding the costs associated with employee turnover. Employee turnover rates among neurodiverse employees are much lower than those of neurotypical employees, perhaps due to the company's supportive and inclusive environment. Four of the biggest U.S. autism employment initiatives are sponsored by EY, SAP, JPMorgan Chase, and Microsoft; together, they have a retention rate of over 90%.

Engagement: Employee engagement refers to the level of commitment, passion, and enthusiasm employees have toward their work and the organization they work for. Engaged employees are more likely to go above and beyond their basic job responsibilities, contribute innovative ideas, and strive for excellence. They are emotionally invested in the success of the organization and are motivated to help achieve its goals. In general, workers who have a strong sense of inclusion and belonging are more engaged at work. Hiring neurodiverse workers can thereby enhance workers' views of DEI and corporate culture, which in turn promotes worker engagement. Neurotypical employees who work in areas of the business that are addressed by neurodiversity programs report that "involvement makes their work more meaningful and their morale higher," according to organizations that have adopted such programs.

Innovation: Innovation refers to the process of introducing new ideas, methods, products, or services that create value and lead to positive change. It involves identifying opportunities for improvement, challenging the status quo, and implementing creative solutions to address existing problems or meet evolving needs. Workers that are neurodiverse might encourage creativity among their teams since their thought processes differ from those of their neurotypical colleagues. In fact, according to SAP, one of their neurodivergent workers created a technological solution that helped the business save an estimated $40 million.

Talent attraction: Talent attraction refers to the process of attracting qualified and skilled individuals to join an organization. It involves various strategies and initiatives aimed at positioning the organization as an attractive employer and enticing talented individuals to apply for open positions. Effective talent attraction strategies are essential for building a talented and capable workforce, driving innovation, and achieving organizational goals. DEI matters for the majority of employees and job seekers across age groups, but it matters more for younger employees, women, and people of color. Prioritizing neurodiversity as a crucial component of diversity is crucial for businesses looking to draw in the next wave of talent. It's practically an untenable talent strategy to not consider the demands of these populations in the company, given that up to 30% of the population is considered neurodivergent. The truth is that doing the right thing is beneficial for the business as well as for the individuals (Luc, 2024).

IMPEDIMENTS IN THE RECRUITMENT AND RETENTION OF NDEs

Acquiring neurodivergent staff is a desirable practice, but it comes with its own set of difficulties. It's an audacious and brave undertaking that necessitates a few things, the most important of which is a supportive environment that can accommodate persons with a wide range of neurological variations. Organizations facing this difficult task may face a wide range of primary issues related to hiring, screening, onboarding, and training. During the recruitment and selection process, neurodivergent individuals might be immediately eliminated if it is determined that they lack basic interpersonal skills. It's possible that recruiters aren't fully aware of the advantages of working with neurodivergent candidates. It's also possible that companies haven't developed tailored interview formats that cater to the unique requirements of candidates who are neurodivergent. Furthermore, there can be a complete lack of specially designed training and induction programs for the unique needs of neurodiverse new hires. Crucially, neurodiverse workers may find the sensory overload to be too much for them. It's possible that the organization's current policies and procedures may not sufficiently accommodate neurodivergent employees. Both overt and covert forms of prejudice may be directed towards the neurodiverse staff. Conflicts pertaining to communication can also frequently occur between peers and between bosses and subordinates. Some other impediments in the acquisition and retention of NDEs are:

Outdated mindset and organizational culture: Many people belonging to older generations or Gen X, may have a more outdated view of what neurodiversity is all about, especially those who lack awareness about what neurodiversity is actually about. They often view neurodiversity inclusion programs as pertaining only to specific jobs rather than being more comprehensive across the organization. Part of the challenge may reside in a basic misunderstanding about the capabilities of neurodiverse individuals. For example, some believe that the inherent characteristics of neurodiverse individuals makes them especially well-suited for certain types of tasks that are repetitive in nature and do not require much social interaction, like coding or administrative functions. By this reasoning, other roles that require spontaneous judgments would preclude neurodiverse individuals.

Unrealistic expectation: Another challenge that permeates many expectations, particularly among the neurotypical, is the "myth of the superhero." Organizations may expect neurodiverse employees to show exceptionality or intelligence gifts before being accepted. Not only can it limit the opportunities for an organization to integrate the skills and talents of neurodiverse professionals, but it can also place an undue burden on the neurodivergent professional to be a superstar in a specific area.

Self-disclosure and lack of trust in the organization: One of the more frequently shared challenges we heard in our interviews was employee hesitancy to self-disclose a neurodiverse condition. If one in five in the general population are neurodivergent, chances are one or more of your colleagues are neurodivergent, but may not be disclosing. Some who don't disclose may not know or have a diagnosis. Others who are neurodivergent may choose not to self-disclose, most often due to a lack of trust in their employer. One study focused on employers with disability programs found that more than 90% encourage employees with a disability to self-identify, but on average, only 3.7% of their employees disclosed their disability.

Organisations can tap the goldmine of the latent talent and potential of neurodiverse employees and engender a healthy spirit of diversity and inclusion in the working arena by focussing their attention and energies on these possible pitfalls.

FACTORS INFLUENCING RETENTION OF NDEs

Employee retention has always been a cause of concern for the organization. It is mainly due to the high cost of attrition due to loss of valuable employees, productivity, break in the workflow and loss of innumerable intangible contributions that an employee makes for the organization. More than the cost of attrition, another higher cost is that of acquiring the right kind of employee. These concerns are all the more significant if an organization is dealing with a special category of employees, especially those who are neurodiverse, since this category of employee requires use of a different selection process, training and onboarding. To retain neurodivergent workers, organizations are mindful to match workers with good fitting roles based on the assessment of individuals' strengths and weaknesses. A proper fit between a person's characteristics and those of the tasks that are performed at work allows neurodivergent individuals to use their strengths and thrive at work, providing them feelings of self-worth. The careful alignment between employees' skills and job requirements helps to improve the retention of neurodivergent employees. Taken together, these efforts allow employees to become socialized into the organization in a psychologically safe way and provide employees with the social support structures needed to become embedded within the organization.

For neurodivergent workers, finding a job is essential, but in order to benefit both individuals and companies, it's also crucial to comprehend the elements influencing their perspectives of neurodiversity and HRM practices at work. A number of studies have been conducted in order to identify the factors that may contribute to the better retention of NDEs:

Neurodiversity awareness: The term neurodiversity awareness refers to employees' perception towards neurodiversity and specific steps taken by the organization to make employees aware of it. Because neurodiverse conditions are often invisible, in contrast to many other forms of diversity, such as gender and race, and are not necessarily disclosed due to fear of stigmatization (Patton, 2022), it is possible that employees may not be fully aware of the extent of neurodiversity in their workplace. Moreover, stigma perpetuates due to lack of knowledge and incorrect information (Jacobs and Quinn, 2022), and thus an efficient way to target stigma is by providing accurate information. For instance, awareness and knowledge campaigns, intended to change negative attitudes and provide accurate information, have been found to be effective in helping understand NDEs. Although personal information provided by workers to the human resources (HR) department is kept private, direct supervisors frequently need access to parts of that data in order to carry out their responsibilities, such as handling requests for accommodations. (Lindsay et al., 2021). Understanding neurodiversity within the context of employment is a relatively new area of research (LeFevre-Levy et al., 2023), with little understanding developed to date about how to manage organizational neurodiversity for sustainable employment of neurodivergents. Moreover, it would not be incorrect to state that such awareness and understanding towards neurodivergent people in the organization would definitely contribute towards inclusivity thereby leading to better retention of NDEs.

Proposition1: Awareness about neurodiversity will have a significant influence in retention of NDEs

Perceived benefits: Perceived benefits about having NDEs in the workforce not only presents a positive image of the organization but also contributes towards the Diversity & Inclusivity (D&I) culture. Aligned with the value-in-diversity perspective (Herring, 2009), in addition to a better understanding of various customer needs and improved decision making due to a wider range of perspectives, neurodivergent individuals often have unique advantages (Szulc et al., 2021). For instance, individuals on the autism spectrum are better at performing repetitive activities, recognizing complex patterns, and processing difficult work through hyper-focus. (Shein, 2020). While those with dyslexia are more likely to have strong planning, attention to detail, and visual thinking abilities, those with ADHD frequently have superior creative problem solving abilities. (Szulc et al., 2021). These unique strengths can be harnessed for organizational productivity if matched to the right jobs (Harris et al., 2020). Thus, neurodiversity is recognized as a possible source of competitive advantage, much like other forms of diversity. This is evident in the trend of changing HR procedures to draw in neurodivergent job seekers. (Rao and Polepeddi, 2019). In order to realize the potential value of neurodiversity, it is important to recognize its associated benefits. Executive and management programs frequently emphasize the advantages of recruiting for diversity because of its ability to impact retail consumers' positive attitudes and behaviors toward the company. This is done in order to increase the programs' commitment to diversity management. Exposure to such information is expected to lead to an improved understanding of the value of neurodiversity in offering advantages to organizations, which is expected to manifest in better adjustment and thereby, reduced attrition of NDEs.

Proposition 2: Perceived benefits associated with neurodiversity will positively result in improved retention of NDEs.

Work Accommodation: Neurodivergent individuals can be overstimulated and distracted from work unless the organization is willing to provide solutions, many of which are simple and cost-effective. Site surveys can help employers who want to implement a neurodiversity employment program understand if their office or online infrastructure is accommodating. While a DEI program that embraces neurodiversity stands to offer real benefits to an organization, employers may also be legally obligated to offer reasonable accommodations to the neurodiverse individuals they employ. Employee accommodation is therefore often a crucial consideration in embracing neurodiversity in the workforce (Tortora & Strohbehn, 2023). Finding employment is only half the battle for NDEs. Unless there is a supportive company culture with proper education and an accommodating environment, neurodivergent employees may face barriers to success. Neurodivergent individuals can be overstimulated and distracted from projects unless the employer is willing to provide solutions, many of which are simple and cost-effective. Several environmental factors are evaluated including lighting, sounds and scents. Special sensory needs, difficulties in modulating sensory responses and over-responsivity (overload) are common symptoms shared by neuro diverse people. Accommodations like screen readers and noise-canceling headphones can be highly helpful in providing comfort to NDEs (Yilmaz, 2023). Physical workplace adjustments, which may benefit neurodiverse workers in regard to work performance and health/well-being, may have wider reaching benefits, such as occupational longevity and systemic inclusion (Doyle & McDowall, 2021; Doyle, 2020).

Proposition 3: Workplace accommodation has a significant positive influence on retention of NDEs

Organizational Policy: Organizations may introduce neurodiversity practices to improve understanding of neurodiversity conditions and mitigate exclusion and discrimination. Since a lot of value is associated with diversity (Cox and Blake, 1991, Herring, 2009), such practices signal that the organization considers neurodivergent employees valuable, shows interest in integrating them, and puts special efforts into supporting them (Kalev et al., 2006). Organizations are increasing their commitment to the neurodivergent population through investments in programs that aim to acquire neurodivergent candidates. Rather than drawing on the commonly used selection criteria like educational attainment or previous professional experience, skill-based hiring emerged as a norm in these programs, which allows individuals to circumvent traditional selection methods that focus more heavily on interpersonal interaction. Additionally, some organizations provide workshops or internships in which individuals have the opportunity to demonstrate their skills rather than having to identify their own strengths. Organizations are increasingly implementing HR policies and procedures to be more inclusive of neurodivergent employees. Many organizations (Hennekam & Follmer, 2024). Attention is also being paid on creating conducive policies related to leaves, working conditions, rewards and incentives, appraisal, promotion, welfare, etc. to address the needs of NDEs. It also signifies the overall concern of the top-management towards the welfare and retention of the NDEs.

Proposition 4: Organizational policy, alongwith awareness, perceived benefits, work accommodation, will significantly strengthen the retention of NDEs.

Stigma: Stigma associated with personal characteristics, discredits an individual's social identity. Stereotypes are generalized views about groups of individuals that are socially communicated and replicated in ways that strengthen the stereotype even when the information is untrue. Stereotypes are frequently the basis for these negative connotations (Jacobs and Quinn, 2022). A very common stigma associated with NDEs is that they are a liability (Patton, 2019), which is one of the major challenges of neurodiversity. Stereotyping, the cognitive process of classifying individuals based on their membership in social groupings, is connected to stigmatization and is subsequently linked to unfavorable attributions (Ragins et al., 2007). By better understanding and learning about the many neurodiversity conditions, stereotypes and negative associations (stigma) of neurodiversity may be lessened. This knowledge can reduce the perception of neurodivergent workers' homogeneity. Therefore, it's possible that the difficulties faced by neurodivergent individuals are less severe than first thought.

Proposition 5: Stigma associated with neurodiversity is significantly impacts the attrition of NDEs

Unconscious Bias: Stereotypes are frequently formed unconsciously to make cognitive processing easier. In other words, people may see themselves as different from other members of their group, but view others as similar to each other. This distinction is likely to be made in situations of lack of knowledge and/or cognitive resources that are needed to process interpersonal differences (Hilton and Von Hippel, 1996). Stigma often leads to conscious and/or unconscious bias, particularly affecting neurodivergents, who are seen as less capable than people with physical disabilities (Scheid, 2005). The key contributing factors to the low employment among neurodivergents are unconscious biases held by hiring managers (Praslova, 2021) like systemic biases in recruitment and selection practices and exacerbated perceptions of high accommodation costs (Buckley et al., 2020). Such associations make NDEs less employable and continued reflection of these biases may result in high attrition of NDEs.

Proposition 6: Unconscious biases adversely affect the retention of NDEs

On the basis of above discussion, following conceptual framework has been proposed

Figure 1. Conceptual framework

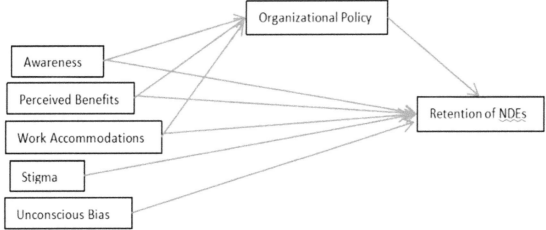

ORGANIZATIONAL PRACTICES

Neurodiversity in the context of work is gaining more and more attention from employers. Neurodiversity constitutes an understudied yet promising topic of inquiry. Review of organizational practices provided insight into how neurodiversity is managed and perceived in the workplace. Most organizations have programs for neurodivergent individuals as a group but some offer condition-specific programs. There is growing awareness about neurodiversity in the workplace and the specific needs that these NDEs have. It has been observed that most of the programs cater to the requirements of autism spectrum disorder while other forms of neuro-cognitive differences tend to receive less attention.

It has also been found that many of the accommodations made for neurodivergent workers may also benefit their neurotypical employees. For instance, setting clear expectations, giving more explicit feedback, and providing consistent communication can improve efficiency and productivity across all employees, without singling out neurodivergent employees. Employers should try to make work more universally accommodating to all employees regardless of their neuro-cognitive differences. When universal design principles are not possible or sufficient, organizations and employees may benefit from job crafting, i.e. bringing changes in the job to balance job demands and job resources with the personal abilities and needs of the individuals. This concept helps in achieving improved person-job fit. For instance, providing employees with more resources (e.g., support, time to complete tasks, flexible arrangements) and reducing demands (e.g., face-to-face interactions, daily stressors, etc.), can improve both personal and work-related outcomes for individuals. Organizations may be able to retain hard-working, capable employees by making changes to the job design and physical workplace arrangements (Weber, 2022), rather than trying to "mold" employees to fit a traditional job structure. In order to promote the participation of neurodivergent workers, an evaluation of current HR policies and practices pertaining to neurodiversity in businesses is required. This will help to identify, share, and build upon beneficial practices (Henekkam and Follmer, 2024).

Neurodivergent employees are often subjected to stigma and discrimination which can impact their ability to obtain and maintain employment. Rather than focusing on differences and how these employees diverge from the neurotypical population, organizations have shifted to using strength-based perspectives in which the focus is on the positive characteristics of neurodiversity. Identifying factors that facilitate successful transitions for neurodivergent individuals can contribute to the development of organizational policies and practices focused on specific life transitions such as first-time employment experiences, job changes, or return to work after absences. Some of the well identified HR related practices that organizations are making use of are mentioned below:

Onboarding, integration and retention: After hiring neurodivergent workers, the onboarding procedure starts. We discovered a variety of organizational procedures designed to facilitate the onboarding and integration of new hires while also raising retention rates. For example, IBM promoted the integration of its neurodivergent workforce by organizing social events and frequent get-togethers, which helped to lower social anxiety and improve teamwork and collaboration. Similarly, in an effort to lessen loneliness, JP Morgan Chase paired up new hires with lunch partners. Ernst and Young gave neurodivergent employees a chance to acquaint themselves with their new work environment, as well as a job coach and office mates who had already undergone neurodiversity training and Microsoft offered incoming neurodivergent employees the option to work with a mentor who is informed on the advantages and resources offered by the company. Additionally, they offered career growth options and identification assistance through expert mentors.

Job design: It is found that organizations have actively created an inclusive environment for neurodivergent individuals through job design practices. Employees are offered multimodal communication options (e.g., video/audio, chat and transcription services) at Ultranauts, so that they can communicate in a way with which they are most comfortable. IBM uses an application called Content Clarifier for simplifying potentially complex instructions which are easy to understand for individuals with autism. Microsoft in collaboration with a non-profit organization provides assistive technology for dyslexic and dysgraphic workers. It has also created an inclusive design toolkit that provides a structure for designing more inclusive products and services. Searching for exclusion, learning from diversity, and 'solving for one extending to many' are among the guiding ideas of this toolkit. Everyone in charge of a team or project has access to this resource.

Flexible work options and remote work: One of the most widely used HR practices to accommodate NDEs is flexible work arrangement. Ultranauts provides desired-time-equivalent work weeks so that individuals can arrange their work schedules as per their needs. It can be full-time, three-quarters-time, or half-time. Salary is calculated on a pro-rata basis. This strategy doesn't try to fit everyone in the same mold and enables NDEs to contribute to their work as per their ability and to suit their lifestyle requirements. Moreover, post COVID, work from home has become quite a common practice. Working in a familiar environment is a lot more conducive for the NDEs. They can work in the comforts of their home and can be their true self. It further reduces their level of stress and anxiety, which NDEs usually face in the formal organizational set up.

Training: In order to accommodate NDEs, it is not only them who require training but training needs to be conducted for neurotypical people. Many organizations offer training programs to generate awareness and acceptance of NDEs. People are sensitized to minimize stigmas and unconscious biases. These training programs are to increase inclusivity in the organization and also to reduce those instances where unknowingly NDEs may get hurt or face unconscious bias due to lack of awareness. At Ultranauts, equitable promotions workshops are provided to create equitable approaches to career growth. Special workshops are organized for NDEs to improve their communication and adapt to the organizational environment. Many organizations conduct training programs for the leaders, so that they can create better organizational policies catering to the needs of NDEs. Dell trains leaders to adopt a more inclusive leadership style which can improve working relationships with neurodivergent individuals. For example, a virtual autism awareness program at Westpac made sure that all team members who work with autistic people have a certain degree of knowledge and comprehension. Through the Dandelion Program at DXC, neurodiversity consultants provide one-on-one training when managers face issues in addition to conducting neurodiversity-awareness training to provide useful skills and techniques to effectively serve neurodivergent colleagues. Moreover, it also had a toolkit called "Supporting a Neurodiverse Workforce: A Mental Health and Well-Being Resource and Training Package", co-designed with individuals with autism, their colleagues, and scholars. This toolkit was used to improve the mental wellbeing of the ASDs. Some organizations provide customized training to other organizations to better manage their NDEs. SAP launched the SAP Autism Inclusion Pledge initiative that helped other organizations become more inclusive of autistic individuals.

Although it is clear that organizations are implementing multiple strategies to increase inclusivity of neurodivergent employees, a lot more needs to be done to make such a huge talent pool become organizationally viable. Lot of effort is still required not only from the organizations or employers but also from all other segments of the society who are directly or indirectly associated with this group of people.

In nutshell, it can be said that the stigma associated with neurodiversity is gradually losing its negative implications. Organizations have started to develop a positive outlook towards this highly capable talent pool. Organizations have started to prepare themselves to face the challenges that they may come across in ensuring neuro inclusivity. A huge shift has been seen in the organizational mindset about work to successfully foster inclusive environments for neurodiverse employees in areas that go beyond hiring and include leading practices in recruitment, training and development, retention, and advancement.

The Road ahead: Practitioners have become more sensitive to neurodiversity in the workplace; hence, it is important that an individual's whole identity is taken into account. This means that organizations shouldn't only pay attention to catering to the needs of NDEs while they are in the organization but also when they are in an external environment also. Also, these individuals shouldn't only be recognized as NDEs, or dyslexic or autistic. They also have their social identity, gender, race, age, etc. based on differentiations and it is the organization's responsibility to assess them in totality. It is becoming important not to be governed by any prejudices and discriminatory practices in order to improve interpersonal relations and for the creation of a more conducive work environment. In fact, the more people connect with each other and accept each other despite differences, the more we will be able to get rid of any kind of stigma or biases. Neurodiversity is not a condition that is either contagious or harmful for the people who are neurotypical. It is simply about having a different connection of neurons in the brain which makes this particular set of people more susceptible to changes in their environment, light and sound setting, heightened consciousness about disruptions in their usual work settings, etc. Acquiring and retaining this talent pool (Harper, 2022) may require modifications to the work environment and creation of processes which are more conducive to their work style like private offices or cubicles for reduced noise, noise canceling headphones, or facility of working from home. Attention has been paid to managing the sensitivity towards light by providing anti-glare filters, fluorescent tube covers, personal visors, and window shades. In order to improve the air quality, air purifiers have been installed and provisions have been made for odor control. Special stress management sessions, in-house counselling, mentoring, etc. have also been initiated by the organizations especially for the NDEs. Special recruitment drives, with well curated selection processes, have also been taken into consideration since entirely different sets of selection processes need to be developed to assess their potential. Neurodivergents are less comfortable in appearing for an interview and rather do much better in those selection processes which tests them through application of their knowledge like work sampling, demonstration, simulations, etc. These people may be different but not lacking in potential.

Now that people have started to pay attention to NDEs, it becomes imperative for the organizations to explore this potential and tap it to the best of their ability. Fostering a neuroinclusive culture and developing the necessary mindset is an ongoing process, not a one-time initiative. Organizations need to start small. There is a need to start with a readiness assessment and prepare target functions and teams who could work with neurodiverse professionals in advance through initial education and training. Organizations need to come out of their old models and should learn from other companies about how they integrate neurodiverse workers and share leading practices with them as well. The more organizations collaborate to exchange best practices and occasionally even candidates, the more success is possible for those who are committed to seizing this chance. Ultimately, everyone in an organization stands to gain from neuroinclusion, the neurodiverse professionals who don't self-disclose, the neurodivergent professionals, and the organization. This is an opportunity that will probably only grow in significance in the future, so now is the best moment to take advantage of it.

REFERENCES:

Ali, M., Grabarski, M. K., & Baker, M. (2023). An exploratory study of benefits and challenges of neurodivergent employees: Roles of knowing neurodivergents and neurodiversity practices. *Equality, Diversity and Inclusion*. Advance online publication. doi:10.1108/EDI-03-2023-0092

Baker, D. L. (2011). *The Politics of Neurodiversity: Why Public Policy Matters*. Lynne Rienner Publishers. doi:10.1515/9781685851224

Buckley, E., Pellicano, E., & Remington, A. (2020). The real thing I struggle with is other people's perceptions: The experiences of autistic performing arts professionals and attitudes of performing arts employers in the UK. *Journal of Autism and Developmental Disorders*, *51*(1), 45–59. doi:10.1007/s10803-020-04517-0 PMID:32356080

Charlton, J. (1998). *Nothing about Us without Us: Disability, Oppression and Empowerment*. University of California Press.

Cox, T. Jr, & Blake, S. (1991). Managing cultural diversity: Implications for organizational competitiveness. *The Academy of Management Executive*, *5*(3), 45–56.

Doyle, N. (2020). Neurodiversity at work: A biopsychosocial model and the impact on working adults. *British Medical Bulletin*, *135*(1), 108–125. doi:10.1093/bmb/ldaa021 PMID:32996572

Doyle, N., & McDowall, A. (2021). Diamond in the rough? An 'empty review' of research into 'neurodiversity' and a road map for developing the inclusion agenda. *Equality, Diversity and Inclusion*, *41*(3), 352–382. doi:10.1108/EDI-06-2020-0172

Dunn, D., de la Garza, J. D., Jones, D. R., & Sasson, N. J. (2023). Awkward but so what: Differences in social trait preferences between autistic and non-autistic adults. *Neurodiversity*, *1*. doi:10.1177/27546330231203833

Harper, T. (2022). *How To Hire And Retain Neurodivergent Employees*. https://www.forbes.com/sites/forbeshumanresourcescouncil/2022/08/22/how-to-hire-and-retain-neurodivergent-employees/?sh=61763be7264e

Harris, C., van der Vloodt, R., & Maddocks, J. (2020). *Championing neurodiversity and emotional intelligence in the workplace*. Available at: https://content.psionline.com/whitepaperchampioning-neurodiversity-and-emotional-intelligence-in-the-workplace

Härtel, C. E. J., & Fujimoto, Y. (2000). Diversity is not the problem – openness to perceived dissimilarity is. *Journal of Management and & Organization*, *6*(1), 14–27. doi:10.1017/S1833367200005484

Hennekam, S., & Follmer, K. (2024). Neurodiversity and HRM: a practice-based review and research agenda. Equality, Diversity and Inclusion. doi:10.1108/EDI-12-2023-0424

Herring, C. (2009). *Does diversity pay? Race, gender, and the business case for diversity*. American. doi:10.1177/000312240907400203

Hilton, J. L., & Von Hippel, W. (1996). Stereotypes. *Annual Review of Psychology*, *47*(1), 237–271. doi:10.1146/annurev.psych.47.1.237 PMID:15012482

Jaarsma, P., & Welin, S. (2012). Autism as a natural human variation: Reflections on the claims of the neurodiversity movement. *Health Care Analysis*, *20*(1), 20–30. doi:10.1007/s10728-011-0169-9 PMID:21311979

Jacobs, S., & Quinn, J. (2022). Cultural reproduction of mental illness stigma and stereotypes. *Social Science & Medicine*, *292*, 114552. doi:10.1016/j.socscimed.2021.114552 PMID:34802779

Kalev, A., Dobbin, F., & Kelly, E. (2006). Best practices or best guesses? Assessing the efficacy of corporate affirmative action and diversity policies. *American Sociological Review*, *71*(4), 589–617. doi:10.1177/000312240607100404

Krcek, T. E. (2012). Deconstructing disability and neurodiversity: Controversial issues for autism and implications for social work. *Journal of Progressive Human Services*, *24*(1), 4–22. doi:10.1080/10428 232.2013.740406

Krzeminska, A., Austin, R. D., Bruyere, S. M., & Hedley, D. (2019). The advantages and challenges of neurodiversity employment in organizations. *Journal of Management & Organization*, *25*(4), 453–463. doi:10.1017/jmo.2019.58

LeFevre-Levy, R., Melson-Silimon, A., Harmata, R., Hulett, A. L., & Carter, N. T. (2023). Neurodiversity in the workplace: Considering neuroatypicality as a form of diversity. *Industrial and Organizational Psychology: Perspectives on Science and Practice*, *16*(1), 1–19. doi:10.1017/iop.2022.86

Lindsay, S., Osten, V., Rezai, M., & Bui, S. (2021). Disclosure and workplace accommodations for people with autism: A systematic review. *Disability and Rehabilitation*, *43*(5), 597–610. doi:10.1080/0 9638288.2019.1635658 PMID:31282214

Luc, K. (2024). *Neurodiversity in the workplace: Why it matters.* https://www.cultureamp.com/blog/neurodiversity-in-the-workplace

Mahto, M., Hogan, S. K., & Sniderman, B. (2022). *A rising tide lifts all boats: Creating a better work environment for all by embracing neurodiversity.* Deloitte Insights.

McDowall, A., Doyle, N. & Kiseleva, M. (2022). *Neurodiversity at Work 2023: Demand, Supply and a Gap Analysis.* Academic Press.

Mellifont, D. (2019). DESerting clients? A study investigating evidence-based measures supporting the long-term employment of neurodiverse Australians. *Management and Labour Studies*, *44*(4), 455–466. doi:10.1177/0258042X19882519

Montvelisky, J. (2021). *Neurodiversity as a Strengthening Point for Your Team and Our Society.* Available https://www.forbes.com/sites/forbestechcouncil/2021/08/13/neurodiversity-as-a-strengthening-point-for-your-team-and-our-society/?sh=4f2b186228f9

Neurodiversity in the workplace. (2023). https://mydisabilityjobs.com/statistics/neurodiversity-in-the-workplace

Ortega, F. (2009). The cerebral subject and the challenge of neurodiversity. *Biosocieties*, *4*(4), 425–446. doi:10.1017/S1745855209990287

Patton, E. (2019). Autism, attributions and accommodations. *Personnel Review*, *48*(4), 915–934. doi:10.1108/PR-04-2018-0116

Patton, E. (2022). To disclose or not disclose a workplace disability to coworkers: Attributions and invisible health conditions in the workplace. *Equality, Diversity and Inclusion, 41*(8), 1154–1180. doi:10.1108/EDI-09-2021-0228

Praslova, L. N. (2021). *Autism Doesn't Hold People Back at Work. Discrimination Does.* Available on: https://hbr.org/2021/12/autism-doesnt-hold-people-back-at-work-discrimination-does

Ragins, B. R., Singh, R., & Cornwell, J. M. (2007). Making the invisible visible: Fear and disclosure of sexual orientation at work. *The Journal of Applied Psychology, 92*(4), 1103–1118. doi:10.1037/0021-9010.92.4.1103 PMID:17638468

Rao, B., & Polepeddi, J. (2019). Neurodiverse workforce: Inclusive employment as an HR strategy. *Strategic HR Review, 18*(5), 204–209. doi:10.1108/SHR-02-2019-0007

Robison, J. E. (2013). What is neurodiversity? *Psychology Today.* https://www.psychologytoday.com/us/blog/my-life-aspergers/201310/what-is-neurodiversity

Roux, A. M., Shattuck, P. T., Rast, J. E., Rava, J. A., & Anderson, K. A. (2015). *National autism indicators report: Transition into young adulthood. Life Course Outcomes Research Program.* AJ Drexel Autism Institute, Drexel University. doi:10.17918/NAIRTransition2015

Scheid, T. L. (2005). Stigma as a barrier to employment: Mental disability and the Americans with Disabilities Act. *International Journal of Law and Psychiatry, 28*(6), 670–690. doi:10.1016/j.ijlp.2005.04.003 PMID:16112732

Shakespeare, T., & Watson, N. (1997). Defending the social model. *Disability & Society, 12*(2), 293–300. doi:10.1080/09687599727380

Shein, E. (2020). Hiring from the autism spectrum. *Communications of the ACM, 63*(6), 17–19. doi:10.1145/3392509

Singer, J. (1998) *Odd People In: The Birth of Community Amongst People on the Autism Spectrum: A personal exploration of a New Social Movement based on Neurological Diversity.* An Honours Thesis presented to the Faculty of Humanities and Social Science, the University of Technology, Sydney.

Singer, J. (1999). Why can't you be normal for once in your life? From a "Problem with No Name" to a new category of disability. Sociological Review, 74(2), 208-224.

Szulc, J. M., Davies, J., Tomczak, M. T., & McGregor, F. L. (2021). AMO perspectives on the well-being of neurodivergent human capital. *Employee Relations, 43*(4), 858–872. doi:10.1108/ER-09-2020-0446

Tortora, E. M., & Strohbehn, X. S. (2023). *Embracing and Accommodating Neurodiversity: Equitable and Legal Considerations for Neurodiverse Employees in the Workplace.* https://www.venable.com/insights/publications/2023/11/embracing-and-accommodating-neurodiversity

Walker, N. (2014). *Neurodiversity: Some basic terms & definitions.* Available on: https://neuroqueer.com/neurodiversity-terms-and-definitions/https://neuroqueer.com/neurodiversity-terms-and-definitions/

Weber, C., Krieger, B., Häne, E., Yarker, J., & McDowall, A. (2022). Physical workplace adjustments to support neurodivergent workers: A systematic review. *Applied Psychology.*

Yilmaz, G. (2023). *Silence and Focus: Noise-Canceling Headphones as Assistive Tools for Cognitive Disabilities.* Available https://blogs.perficient.com/2023/10/05/silence-and-focus-noise-canceling-headphones-as-assistive-tools-for-cognitive-disabilities/

Chapter 19
Nurturing Employee Well-Being and Mental Health:
The Cornerstone of Retention Strategies

Ranjit Singha

https://orcid.org/0000-0002-3541-8752
Christ University, India

Surjit Singha

https://orcid.org/0000-0002-5730-8677
Kristu Jayanti College (Autonomous), India

ABSTRACT

This chapter explores the critical importance of employee mental health and well-being concerning global talent procurement and retention strategies. This study examines the dynamic nature of mental health in the workplace, emphasizing its potential to improve employee retention. Through an analysis of contemporary methodologies, obstacles, and inventive resolutions, this chapter aims to furnish organizations endeavouring to establish healthier and more efficient work environments with valuable insights. Furthermore, the chapter predicts forthcoming developments and trends in this crucial field.

INTRODUCTION

The importance of employee mental health and wellbeing in talent acquisition and retention has increased significantly. Given the dynamic nature of the contemporary business environment and the substantial financial repercussions that can result from employee attrition and skilled professional scarcity, organizations are obligated to give utmost importance to the comprehensive wellbeing of their personnel. The increased recognition of the significant influence that employee wellbeing and mental health have on team dynamics, individual performance, and organizational success has led to this shift in emphasis (Khalid & Syed, 2024; Kundi et al., 2020). Amid the intricate processes of acquiring and retaining talent, organizations face the dual task of attracting exceptional individuals and cultivating a work environment

DOI: 10.4018/979-8-3693-1938-3.ch019

that nurtures their continuous development and involvement. In addition to competitive compensation and benefits packages, organizations must exhibit an authentic dedication to promoting their staff's physical and mental health (Davenport et al., 2016; Khalid & Syed, 2024). The chapter explores the complex interplay among talent retention, mental health, and global employee wellbeing. Through an analysis of exemplary approaches, prevalent obstacles, and inventive resolutions implemented by establishments spanning diverse sectors and geographical areas, our objective is to furnish practical knowledge that can be utilized to improve strategies for acquiring and retaining talent. The crux of this discourse is acknowledging that employees' mental health and wellbeing are strategic investments and ethical obligations. Employees with the confidence, worth, and assistance to prioritize their mental and emotional health are more inclined to demonstrate increased job satisfaction, loyalty, and productivity. As a result of ignoring these factors, organizational performance may suffer, and absenteeism, presenteeism, and attrition may all increase.

This chapter examines various strategies for fostering employees' wellbeing and mental health. These strategies will encompass proactive motions, such as implementing comprehensive wellness programs and flexible work arrangements, and reactive actions, such as providing mental health support services and destigmatization initiatives. Furthermore, we shall analyze the impact of leadership, organizational culture, and workplace policies on establishing a conducive atmosphere that nurtures resilience, work-life balance, and psychological safety. By examining the interconnection between employee wellbeing, mental health, and talent retention, we aim to provide organizations with the understanding and resources necessary to foster a prosperous workforce amidst changing opportunities and challenges. Emphasizing the comprehensive wellbeing of personnel not only fortifies the structure of institutions but also aids in the development of a worldwide labour force that is more resilient, empathetic, and sustainable. Given their significant effects on employee engagement, contentment, and overall organizational performance, employee wellbeing and mental health have become critical considerations for enterprises worldwide. Organizations are putting more effort into creating plans to assist their employees' mental health and overall wellness due to realizing the changing nature of the modern workplace and the growing recognition of the importance of employee wellbeing. The many facets of employee wellbeing are explored in this study, including aspects like physical health, emotional stability, social support, work-life balance, job satisfaction, and a sense of purpose. It recognizes how these factors are interrelated and how much they impact worker productivity and organizational success.

Additionally, the study framework incorporates concepts linked to social support, stress coping mechanisms, organizational justice, and models like the Job Demands-Resources Model by relying upon theories from psychology, organizational behaviour, and human resource management. The main goal is to find practical methods for enhancing employee wellbeing in organizational settings while also looking into the relationship between employee wellbeing, mental health, and organizational outcomes. The purpose of the study is to investigate the several factors that influence the mental and physical health of employees, clarify methods for improving these aspects, and assess the effects of these aspects on performance, productivity, and employee retention within the firm. Examining organizational elements like leadership, culture, and policies—all of which significantly impact employee wellbeing—is at the heart of this investigation. The research aims to offer insights and suggestions that can guide organizational practices and help create a positive, supportive work environment that promotes employee wellbeing and organizational success by thoroughly examining these factors.

This research will use a systematic literature review methodology to study and assess pertinent studies, theories, and empirical evidence regarding employee wellbeing, mental health, and organizational outcomes. Adhering to defined criteria and protocols guarantees the thoroughness and precision of the evaluation procedure. The first stage entails formulating precise research questions based on the study objectives, emphasizing the variables affecting employee wellbeing, practical approaches to fostering wellbeing, the influence of wellbeing on organizational results, and the role organizational factors play in determining employee wellbeing. Then, utilizing keywords associated with the research themes, a thorough search strategy will be created to locate pertinent literature from scholarly databases, journals, conference proceedings, and grey literature sources. To ensure inclusivity, the literature search will include manual searches of reference lists, citation monitoring, and electronic searches across several databases. Retrieved studies will undergo a two-step screening procedure based on predetermined inclusion and exclusion criteria. To guarantee uniformity, data extraction will be done using a consistent format. Methodological rigour will be assessed using known methodologies to determine the quality of the included research. Identifying common themes, patterns, and linkages among research through data synthesis and thematic analysis will result in the clear and organized reporting of findings by predetermined parameters. The ultimate goal of this systematic literature review is to contribute to evidence-based practices for improving organizational performance and employee wellbeing by offering a thorough understanding of employee wellbeing, successful promotion strategies, and their effects on organizational outcomes.

UNDERSTANDING EMPLOYEE WELLBEING AND MENTAL HEALTH

Employee wellbeing comprises the mental, emotional, and physical condition of individuals in the work environment. Wellness encompasses more than the absence of illness or tension; it entails a comprehensive sense of accomplishment, contentment, and success in one's professional and personal lives. Wellbeing is a multifaceted concept that comprises physical health, emotional resilience, social connections, work-life balance, job satisfaction, and a sense of purpose and meaning in one's professional endeavours. Employee wellbeing and professional success are indicators of the quality of life experienced by the workforce (Singh & Gautam, 2023). Mental health in the professional setting pertains to the psychological welfare of staff members, which includes the proper functioning of their emotions, cognition, and behaviour. This concept concerns how employees perceive, handle, and adapt to workplace pressures, obstacles, and stressors. Work-related stress, anxiety, melancholy, and burnout are all mental health conditions that can have a substantial adverse effect on job performance, interpersonal relationships, and overall job satisfaction. It is imperative to prioritize mental health in the workplace to cultivate an atmosphere that is psychologically secure, inclusive, and supportive, wherein employees feel appreciated, comprehended, and empowered to seek assistance when necessary (Cadorette & Agnew, 2017; Kelloway, 2017).

The correlation between mental health and wellbeing underscores the interdependence of wellness's physical, emotional, and psychological dimensions and employees' health. Recognizing that mental health is an essential element of holistic wellness, employee wellbeing offers a more comprehensive structure for comprehending and advocating for mental health in the workplace. On the other hand, it is critical to acknowledge and attend to mental health issues to foster resilience, productivity, and employee engagement and improve overall wellbeing (Nimmi et al., 2022). By recognizing and confronting the convergence of wellbeing and mental health, organizations can formulate all-encompassing approaches that promote the holistic wellness of their personnel and foster an environment of concern, empathy, and assistance in the work setting.

GLOBAL PRACTICES IN PROMOTING EMPLOYEE WELLBEING

Employer-sponsored initiatives known as Employee Assistance Programs (EAPs) aim to assist personnel in navigating personal and professional difficulties that have the potential to affect their health and job performance. Generally, these programs provide confidential counselling, assistance with mental health, referrals to pertinent resources, and legal and financial aid. Employee Assistance Programs (EAPs) vary in scope and implementation among distinct regions and industries. Nevertheless, their fundamental objective remains to furnish practical, confidential, and easily accessible assistance to employees who encounter various challenges (Attridge, 2009; Van Der Voordt & Jensen, 2021). EAPs are extensively utilized and firmly established in North America. In addition to conventional counselling, they frequently provide wellness coaching, legal consultations, and financial planning, among other services. With an expanding focus on work-life balance initiatives and mental health support, EAPs are acquiring traction in Europe. Additionally, EAPs are increasing in prevalence in the Asia-Pacific region, albeit with cultural modifications to combat stigma associated with mental health and cultural norms (Guarino et al., 2016).

The influence of cultural and regional distinctions on developing wellbeing initiatives within organizations is substantial. The definition of wellbeing and the optimal approaches to fostering it can significantly differ due to cultural conventions, societal demands, and regional obstacles. For instance, wellbeing initiatives in collectivist cultures might emphasize interpersonal relationships and community support more. Self-care and personal development, on the other hand, may be given greater weight in individualistic cultures. When operating in various global contexts, organizations must ensure that their wellbeing initiatives align with the cultural norms and preferences of the local communities. Potential strategies to promote inclusivity and acknowledge diverse viewpoints on wellbeing include modifying communication approaches, providing culturally appropriate resources and support services, and cultivating inclusive practices (Maulana & Khawaja, 2022). Globally, technological advancements present promising opportunities for advancing employee wellness and mental health assistance. Digital platforms, mobile applications, and online resources allow employees to access wellness programs, mental health resources, and self-help tools from any location with ease and convenience (Coppens et al., 2023).

Employing virtual counselling services, teletherapy, and online support groups, personnel can conveniently and discreetly obtain mental health assistance, thereby surmounting obstacles, including social disapproval, physical separation, and timetable limitations. Health-tracking applications and wearable technology foster a culture of accountability and self-awareness by enabling employees to monitor and manage their physical and psychological wellbeing proactively. Nevertheless, to optimize their efficacy and reception among heterogeneous employee cohorts, it is critical to guarantee that technological solutions are user-friendly, encompass all demographics, and adhere to privacy and security protocols. By incorporating technological advancements into conventional wellbeing programs, their scope, scalability, and effectiveness can be expanded, thereby assisting organizations in cultivating a well-being-oriented environment that surpasses geographical and cultural barriers.

MENTAL HEALTH STIGMA AND WORKPLACE CULTURE

To effectively combat the stigma associated with mental health in the workplace, proactive measures by organizational executives to dismantle barriers and encourage open dialogue are among the most vital. How leadership influences attitudes and behaviours regarding mental health is crucial in defining the corporate culture (Yang, 2023). Leaders can set an exemplary standard by candidly sharing their struggles with mental health, exhibiting vulnerability, and placing significant emphasis on the necessity of prioritizing one's wellbeing. Leaders can foster a supportive atmosphere for employees to seek assistance without apprehension of criticism or retaliation by normalizing discussions regarding mental health across all organizational tiers, thereby aiding in the reduction of stigma associated with the subject (Brohan & Thornicroft, 2010; Taubman & Parikh, 2023). Furthermore, it is critical to implement training and education programs for leaders and administrators so that they are equipped with the necessary knowledge, abilities, and resources to support the mental health of their employees. It encompasses educating employees on identifying indicators of distress, facilitating empathetic dialogues, and facilitating connections to suitable support services and resources (Genrich et al., 2022). Leaders can champion policies and practices that foster mental health and overall wellbeing. These may include advocating for access to mental health resources, flexible work arrangements, and sufficient time off. Leadership that regards the wellbeing of employees as a strategic imperative can cultivate an environment that promotes psychological stability and resilience, which are advantageous for the organization and its members (Barry, 2012). To eradicate mental health stigma and advance employee wellbeing, it is vital to foster an environment of openness and support. To cultivate such a culture, organizations may adopt various initiatives and practices that place mental health at the forefront and nurture a supportive atmosphere for staff (Loch et al., 2021).

Consistent communication and awareness campaigns can enhance consciousness regarding mental health concerns, dispel misunderstandings, and furnish personnel with pertinent details regarding accessible support services and resources. Employees are empowered to attend to their health and offer assistance to their coworkers through acquiring self-care knowledge and abilities facilitated by mental health literacy training and education (Gaiha et al., 2020). Implementing support networks, including peer support programs and employee resource groups, enables personnel to connect with others undergoing comparable difficulties and seek assistance in a secure and private setting (Anderson et al., 2020). Incorporating mental health considerations into organizational policies and practices, including accommodations for employees facing mental health challenges, return-to-work programs, and performance evaluations, is possible. Through the incorporation of mental health practices throughout the organization, executives can convey that the welfare of individuals is esteemed and backed on every level. A concerted effort is required from leaders, managers, and employees to cultivate a culture of openness and support. Organizations can foster a conducive work environment where mental health is taken seriously, and all employees can flourish by collaborating to dismantle stigma, increase awareness, and establish a supportive atmosphere.

MEASURING THE IMPACT: METRICS AND ASSESSMENT

Assessing the return on investment (ROI) for wellbeing programs is critical to validate their efficacy and maintain organizational stakeholders' backing and financial investment. Although the indirect influence of wellbeing on organizational outcomes and the complexity of wellbeing can make it difficult to quantify the return on investment (ROI) of such initiatives, several metrics and evaluation techniques can assist in determining their effectiveness. An approach to assessing return on investment (ROI) involves analyzing the monetary savings or advantages linked to wellbeing initiatives, including but not limited to diminished healthcare expenditures, reduced employee attrition, enhanced productivity, and improved staff retention. Through a quantitative return on investment (ROI) ratio, which contrasts the investment in wellbeing initiatives with the measurable results obtained, organizations can ascertain the cost-effectiveness of their programs.

Additionally, qualitative evaluations, including interviews, focus groups, and employee surveys, may yield significant knowledge regarding the perceived effects of wellbeing initiatives on work-life balance, employee engagement, job satisfaction, and the organization's overarching culture. By soliciting employee feedback, organizations can gain insights into their requirements, inclinations, and opportunities for development, thereby guiding the development and execution of subsequent programs (Lub, 2015). The evaluation of mental health in the workplace encompasses an examination of multiple determinants that influence the psychological wellbeing of employees. These determinants comprise stress levels, job satisfaction, work-life balance, and availability of support services. Organizations can utilize surveys and questionnaires, such as the WHO-5 Wellbeing Index and the Maslach Burnout Inventory, to evaluate the mental health status of their employees, detect potential risk factors, and monitor temporal developments (Bandyopadhyay, 2017).

Organizations may employ objective indicators, including but not limited to absenteeism rates, attrition rates, disability claims, and performance metrics, to assess the influence of mental health on organizational outcomes in conjunction with self-report measures. By conducting a trend and pattern analysis of these data, it is possible to identify areas of concern and develop targeted interventions that promote employees' mental health and wellbeing (Gelencsér et al., 2023). Consistent mental health evaluations and assessments, coupled with ongoing monitoring and assessment, empower organizations to proactively detect concerns, monitor advancements, and enhance their strategies for fostering employee welfare (Cresswell-Smith et al., 2022). Establishing success benchmarks to monitor progress, set objectives, and compare performance against industry standards and best practices is essential. Benchmarks may exhibit variability contingent upon the particular aspirations and objectives of wellbeing endeavours, in addition to the distinctive requirements and attributes of the institution (Ruggeri et al., 2020).

As standard performance indicators, wellbeing program success indicators include employee engagement score improvements, absenteeism and attrition rate reductions, productivity and performance metric increases, and employee satisfaction and morale enhancements. By establishing precise and quantifiable objectives for these critical performance indicators, organizations can evaluate the efficacy of their wellbeing endeavours and propel ongoing enhancement through data-informed decision-making (De Oliveira et al., 2022). Engaging in benchmarking activities with industry partners and leading organizations can yield significant insights about emerging trends, innovative methodologies, and potential improvement areas. By benchmarking performance against external standards, organizations can discern potential areas for improvement in their wellbeing initiatives, thereby ensuring they retain and attract high-calibre personnel (Wijngaards et al., 2021). To holistically measure the efficacy of wellbeing initiatives, it is critical to quantify the return on investment (ROI) of such programs, evaluate mental health in the workplace, and establish success benchmarks. Organizations can foster positive outcomes for both employees and the organization by showcasing the value of investing in employee wellbeing using quantitative and qualitative metrics.

INNOVATIVE RETENTION STRATEGIES

There is a growing trend in innovative retention strategies to prioritize the wellbeing of their employees. In light of the interconnectedness between wellbeing, job satisfaction, engagement, and retention, organizations are adopting strategies prioritizing their employees' overall health and pleasure. (Elsamani et al., 2023) This integration entails providing conventional benefits and fostering a culture that encourages personal development, mental health support, and work-life balance opportunities. Organizations may establish all-encompassing wellness programs incorporating various components such as work-life balance initiatives, mental health resources, physical fitness, and stress management techniques. Additionally, they might allocate resources towards employee development initiatives, mentoring programs, and coaching sessions to foster professional advancement and satisfaction. By integrating wellbeing into employee retention strategies, businesses promote a satisfying and nurturing workplace atmosphere that encourages and retains exceptional personnel (Gelencsér et al., 2023). Flexible work arrangements have become a fundamental component of inventive approaches to employee retention, providing workers with increased independence and jurisdiction over their work schedules and surroundings. Organizations can cater to a wide range of employees' preferences and requirements through the provision of flexible work arrangements, work hours, and locations; this can also serve to mitigate stress and burnout, as well as improve the equilibrium between work and personal life (Tsen et al., 2021). Flexible work arrangements encompass a variety of manifestations, such as job sharing, telecommuting, flexible hours, and compressed workweeks. According to Boga et al. (2023), these configurations enable personnel to balance their personal and professional obligations more efficiently, increasing job satisfaction, productivity, and employee retention.

Adopting flexible work arrangements positively affects employee morale, absenteeism, recruitment, and retention (Brega et al., 2023). Organizations can sustain productivity and unity while promoting employee wellbeing and flexibility by utilizing technology to enable remote collaboration and communication. The rise in the prevalence of remote work can be attributed to technological advancements, evolving perspectives on work-life balance, and the worldwide transition to digitalization. Although remote work provides several advantages, including flexibility, autonomy, and financial savings, it also poses distinct concerns regarding the welfare of employees that need to be attended to by businesses (Fatima et al., 2022). A difficulty is the erosion of professional and personal boundaries; remote workers may find it difficult to detach from their work and preserve a healthy work-life equilibrium. Organizations can mitigate this challenge by establishing clear expectations regarding working hours, encouraging employees to take frequent breaks, and providing resources for managing stress and exhaustion (Fatima et al., 2022).

An additional obstacle that remote workers encounter is social isolation and disconnection, as they may be deprived of the social interactions and sense of inclusion characteristic of traditional office settings. Organizations can promote connection and solidarity among remote teams by fostering virtual communities, encouraging regular communication and collaboration, and organizing virtual social events (Петитта & Ghezzi, 2023). The potential effects of remote work on employee wellbeing depend on how organizations manage its integration and assistance. Organizations can promote employee wellbeing and satisfaction by emphasizing communication, flexibility, and connection by utilizing remote work as a retention strategy.

MENTAL HEALTH SUPPORT IN TIMES OF CRISIS

Pandemics and other crises can exacerbate stress, anxiety, depression, and other mental health conditions among employees, which can have significant negative impacts on their mental health. Anxieties regarding infection, social isolation, economic instability, and daily routine disruptions are all elements that may contribute to increased levels of psychological distress among employees (Kupcová et al., 2023). Additionally, in periods of crisis, mental health may be adversely affected by the heightened demands of remote work, caregiving obligations, and preoccupations with job stability. In light of the distinct difficulties presented by crises, organizations must give precedence to mental health assistance within their response endeavours. Organizations can promote resilience and coping mechanisms among employees and alleviate the adverse effects of crises on mental health by attending to staff's emotional and psychological requirements (Allden et al., 2009; Li et al., 2021; Troup et al., 2021). Organizations must prioritize strategies that support and enhance employee wellbeing during periods of crisis. These measures encompass the following: cultivating an environment of candid and transparent dialogue, guaranteeing the availability of crucial mental health resources and support services, granting flexible work schedules to accommodate individual requirements, advocating for self-care behaviours among staff members, facilitating initiatives to foster virtual communities and connections, imparting knowledge on mental health awareness and coping mechanisms, and exemplifying leadership support through the display of empathy and comprehension. The significance of these measures has been emphasized by global crises such as the COVID-19 pandemic. Such crises highlight the need for proactive leadership, adaptability, readily available resources, community support, and continuous education as fundamental elements of an efficient crisis response (Wasil et al., 2021). By integrating these insights and approaches, institutions can more efficiently manage crises while ensuring their personnel's psychological wellbeing and adaptability.

ANTICIPATING FUTURE TRENDS

In anticipation of the future, several significant developments and trends will likely influence employee wellbeing. One prediction is a heightened emphasis on holistic wellbeing, including physical health and emotional, social, and financial wellness. Organizations may implement more all-encompassing wellbeing initiatives that encompass these aspects, acknowledging their interdependence and influence on employees' overall satisfaction and productivity (Van Der Voordt & Jensen, 2021). In addition, proactive interventions and a greater focus on preventive measures may be required to safeguard mental health and avert fatigue. One potential strategy is to utilize data analytics and predictive modelling to detect stress in its nascent stages and offer specialized assistance to employees who are at risk before the escalation of problems (Zhang, 2023). Integrating wellbeing principles and practices into organizational culture is an additional development to monitor. Incorporating wellbeing considerations into all facets of the employee experience, including performance management, leadership development, and recruitment and orientation, is an alternative approach organizations may adopt (Joyce et al., 2022).

The potential of technology to significantly improve mental health support in the workplace is substantial. Access to care is revolutionized by virtual counselling platforms, teletherapy services, and mental health applications, making it more affordable and convenient for employees to seek assistance when necessary. Anticipated technological progress will inevitably give rise to additional innovations, such as virtual reality therapy programs, AI-powered mental health assessments, and customized digital interventions that cater to the unique requirements of each individual (Prescott, 2022). Additionally, the utilization of technology can streamline the process of gathering and evaluating data about the welfare of employees, thereby empowering businesses to detect patterns, track advancements, and assess the efficacy of their mental health endeavours. Organizations can utilize a data-driven methodology to facilitate more efficient resource allocation to support employee mental health and promote evidence-based decision-making (Van Der Voordt & Jensen, 2021).

Organizations must proactively foresee and adjust to emergent trends to remain competitive in talent retention. An area of potential advancement lies in the increasing need for purpose-driven labour and significant employment prospects. There is a growing trend among employees to prefer employers that share their values and provide avenues for both personal and professional development, satisfaction, and influence on society. To maintain the services of their most qualified personnel, businesses may need to give precedence to purpose-driven endeavours, programs of corporate social responsibility, and opportunities for employee growth that align with the values and ambitions of their staff (Ott et al., 2018). Moreover, in light of the increasing diversity and globalization of the workforce, organizations must adopt inclusivity and diversity as fundamental tenets of their strategies for retaining talent. It requires the establishment of inclusive organizational cultures, promoting psychological safety and a sense of belonging, and resolving systemic obstacles to advancement and representation (Alburo et al., 2020). In the foreseeable future, employee wellbeing will likely be distinguished by an emphasis on comprehensive wellness, proactive interventions, and incorporating wellbeing principles into the ethos of organizations. The integration of technology will be pivotal in augmenting the provision of mental health support. Concurrently, organizations must prioritize diversity and inclusion initiatives and purpose-driven work to be prepared for the next frontier in talent retention (Tortia et al., 2022). Organizations can position themselves as preferred employers and cultivate resilient, engaged, high-performing workforces for the future by proactively anticipating and responding to these trends.

DISCUSSION

The discussion explores how employee wellbeing is changing, how technology may help with mental health, and how important it is for businesses to foresee future developments in talent retention. It emphasizes the importance of proactive and adaptable methods in the ever-changing workplace. There has been a significant change in perspective from a primarily physical health-focused perspective to one that recognizes the multifaceted character of employee wellbeing. This holistic approach acknowledges the interconnected dimensions of emotional, social, and financial wellness, a crucial aspect of worker satisfaction and productivity. Predicted patterns point to a shift away from oversimplified conceptions of employee requirements and toward an increasing embrace of comprehensive wellbeing programs by businesses.

Technological innovations have the potential to completely transform workplace mental health support by improving convenience, accessibility, and customization. Platforms like mental health apps and teletherapy services empower employees to take charge of their mental health, democratizing access to healthcare. AI and data analytics can provide prospects for predictive modelling and precise interventions, allowing enterprises to address mental health issues proactively. Organizations need to prioritize diversity, inclusiveness, and purpose-driven initiatives to anticipate future trends in talent retention.

Workers seek companies that share their values and provide professional and personal development opportunities. Organizations can attract and hold onto top talent by creating inclusive cultures and purpose-driven workspaces.

Building inclusive and resilient workforces requires a proactive approach to talent retention, mental health, and wellbeing benefits. Combining the systematic literature review data yields valuable insights into the variables influencing worker wellbeing, doable ways to improve it, and the following organizational consequences. The discussion critically analyzes these findings using well-established theoretical frameworks and provides recommendations for organizations and practitioners. Finding new directions for study emphasizes how crucial it is to keep learning about employee wellbeing and mental health. Subsequent research endeavours may investigate the capacity of technology to augment wellbeing initiatives. Creating supportive work environments and long-term organizational performance depends significantly on making employee wellbeing a strategic imperative. Companies need to put their employees' overall health first, use technology wisely, value diversity and inclusion, and look ahead to future developments in talent retention. Organizations can foster cultures where people flourish and contribute to the company's overall success by using evidence-based practices and maintaining flexibility.

CONCLUSION

Organizations must give careful attention to the future of employee wellbeing, the role of technology in supporting mental health, and the need to prepare for the next frontier in talent retention as they navigate the ever-changing workplace environment. As society progresses, it becomes increasingly evident that comprehensive wellbeing strategies, which consider the financial, emotional, physical, and social aspects, will be critical in promoting employee engagement, satisfaction, and performance. Technology will persistently be crucial in democratizing access to mental health support, enabling personalized interventions, and empowering employees to assume responsibility for their wellbeing.

Moreover, to attract and retain top talent, organizations must remain vigilant and proactive in addressing emerging trends such as diversity and inclusion initiatives and purpose-driven work. They must also recognize the growing significance of these elements. Organizations can establish themselves as preferred employers and cultivate resilient, prosperous, and high-performing workforces for the future by capitalizing on employee wellbeing, promoting inclusive cultures, and inviting innovation. The pursuit of establishing a more supportive, inclusive, and fulfilling workplace is perpetual. However, organizations can foster an atmosphere conducive to employee success and growth by being dedicated to these principles.

REFERENCES

Петитта, Л., & Ghezzi, V. (2023). Remote, disconnected, or detached? Examining the effects of psychological disconnectedness and cynicism on employee performance, wellbeing, and work–family interface. *International Journal of Environmental Research and Public Health*, 20(13), 6318. doi:10.3390/ijerph20136318 PMID:37444165

Alburo, J., Bradshaw, A. K., Santiago, A. E., Smith, B. L., & Vinopal, J. (2020). Looking beyond librar-ies for inclusive recruitment and retention practices: Four successful approaches. In Advances in library administration and organization (pp. 85–109). doi:10.1108/S0732-067120200000041009

Allden, K., Jones, L., Weissbecker, I., Wessells, M. G., Bolton, P., Betancourt, T. S., Hijazi, Z., Galappatti, A., Yamout, R., Patel, P., & Sumathipala, A. (2009). Mental health and psychosocial support in crisis and conflict: Report of the mental health working group. *Prehospital and Disaster Medicine*, *24*(S2), s217–s227. doi:10.1017/S1049023X00021622 PMID:19806544

Anderson, G., Di Nota, P. M., Groll, D., & Carleton, R. N. (2020). Peer support and crisis-focused psychological interventions designed to mitigate post-traumatic stress injuries among public safety and frontline healthcare personnel: A systematic review. *International Journal of Environmental Research and Public Health*, *17*(20), 7645. doi:10.3390/ijerph17207645 PMID:33092146

Attridge, M. (2009). Employee assistance programs: A research-based primer. In C. L. Cooper, J. C. Quick, & M. J. Schabracq (Eds.), *International handbook of work and health psychology* (3rd ed., pp. 383–407). Wiley Blackwell. doi:10.1002/9780470682357.ch17

Bandyopadhyay, G. (2017). Determinants of psychological wellbeing and its impact on mental health. In India, studies in business and economics (pp. 53–95). doi:10.1007/978-981-10-6104-2_5

Barry, M. M. (2012). Promoting positive mental health and wellbeing: Practice and policy. In Springer eBooks (pp. 355–384). doi:10.1007/978-94-007-5195-8_16

Brega, C., Briones, S., Javornik, J., León, M., & Yerkes, M. A. (2023). Flexible work arrangements for work-life balance: A cross-national policy evaluation from a capabilities perspective. *The International Journal of Sociology and Social Policy*, *43*(13/14), 278–294. doi:10.1108/IJSSP-03-2023-0077

Brohan, E., & Thornicroft, G. (2010). Stigma and discrimination of mental health problems: Workplace implications. *Occupational Medicine*, *60*(6), 414–415. doi:10.1093/occmed/kqq048 PMID:20719967

Cadorette, M., & Agnew, J. (2017). Mental health in the workplace. *Workplace Health & Safety*, *65*(9), 448. doi:10.1177/2165079917716188 PMID:28703037

Coppens, E., Hogg, B., Greiner, B. A., Paterson, C., De Winter, L., Mathieu, S., Cresswell-Smith, J., Aust, B., Leduc, C., Van Audenhove, C., Pashoja, A. C., Kim, D., Reich, H., Fanaj, N., Dushaj, A., Thomson, K., O'Connor, C., Moreno-Alcázar, A., Amann, B. L., & Arensman, E. (2023). Promoting employee wellbeing and preventing non-clinical mental health problems: A preparatory consultation survey. *Journal of Occupational Medicine and Toxicology (London, England)*, *18*(1), 17. Advance online publication. doi:10.1186/s12995-023-00378-2 PMID:37582790

Cresswell-Smith, J., Kauppinen, T., Laaksoharju, T., Rotko, T., Solin, P., Suvisaari, J., Wahlbeck, K., & Tamminen, N. (2022). Mental health and mental wellbeing impact assessment frameworks—A sys-tematic review. *International Journal of Environmental Research and Public Health*, *19*(21), 13985. doi:10.3390/ijerph192113985 PMID:36360865

Davenport, L. J., Allisey, A., Page, K. M., LaMontagne, A. D., & Reavley, N. (2016). How can organizations help employees thrive? The development of guidelines for promoting positive mental health at work. *International Journal of Workplace Health Management, 9*(4), 411–427. doi:10.1108/IJWHM-01-2016-0001

De Oliveira, C. M., Almeida, C. R. S., & Giacomoni, C. H. (2022). School-based positive psychology interventions that promote wellbeing in children: A systematic review. *Child Indicators Research, 15*(5), 1583–1600. doi:10.1007/s12187-022-09935-3 PMID:35637709

Elsamani, Y., Mejía, C., & Kajikawa, Y. (2023). Employee wellbeing and innovativeness: A multi-level conceptual framework based on citation network analysis and data mining techniques. *PLoS One, 18*(1), e0280005. doi:10.1371/journal.pone.0280005 PMID:36608048

Fatima, F., Oba, P., & Sony, M. (2022). Exploring employee wellbeing during the COVID-19 remote work: Evidence from South Africa. *European Journal of Training and Development, 47*(10), 91–111. doi:10.1108/EJTD-06-2022-0061

Gaiha, S. M., Gulfam, F. R., Siddiqui, I., Kishore, R., & Krishnan, S. (2020). Pilot community mental health awareness campaign improves service coverage in India. *Community Mental Health Journal, 57*(5), 814–827. doi:10.1007/s10597-020-00714-4 PMID:33052548

Gelencsér, M., Szabó-Szentgróti, G., Kőmüves, Z., & Hollósy-Vadász, G. (2023). The holistic model of labour retention: The impact of workplace wellbeing factors on employee retention. *Administrative Sciences, 13*(5), 121. doi:10.3390/admsci13050121

Genrich, M., Angerer, P., Worringer, B., Gündel, H., Kröner, F., & Müller, A. (2022). Managers' action-guiding mental models towards mental health-related organizational interventions—A systematic review of qualitative studies. *International Journal of Environmental Research and Public Health, 19*(19), 12610. doi:10.3390/ijerph191912610 PMID:36231909

Guarino, V., Zuppolini, S., Borriello, A., & Ambrosio, L. (2016). Electro-active polymers (EAPs): A promising route to design bio-organic/bioinspired platforms with on-demand functionalities. *Polymers, 8*(5), 185. doi:10.3390/polym8050185 PMID:30979278

Joyce, A., Moussa, B., Elmes, A., Campbell, P., Suchowerska, R., Buick, F., Barraket, J., & Carey, G. (2022). Organizational structures and processes for health and wellbeing: Insights from work integration social enterprise. *BMC Public Health, 22*(1), 1624. Advance online publication. doi:10.1186/s12889-022-13920-4 PMID:36030204

Kelloway, E. K. (2017). Mental health in the workplace: Towards evidence-based practice. *Canadian Psychology, 58*(1), 1–6. doi:10.1037/cap0000084

Khalid, A., & Syed, J. (2024). Mental health and wellbeing at work: A systematic review of literature and directions for future research. *Human Resource Management Review, 34*(1), 100998. doi:10.1016/j.hrmr.2023.100998

Kundi, Y. M., Aboramadan, M., Elhamalawi, E. M., & Shahid, S. (2020). Employee psychological wellbeing and job performance: Exploring mediating and moderating mechanisms. *The International Journal of Organizational Analysis, 29*(3), 736–754. doi:10.1108/IJOA-05-2020-2204

Kupcová, I., Danišovič, Ľ., Klein, M., & Harsanyi, S. (2023). Effects of the COVID-19 pandemic on mental health, anxiety, and depression. *BMC Psychology*, *11*(1), 108. Advance online publication. doi:10.1186/s40359-023-01130-5 PMID:37041568

Li, F., Luo, S., Mu, W., Li, Y., Ye, L., Zheng, X., Xu, B., Ding, Y., Ling, P., Zhou, M., & Chen, X. (2021). Effects of sources of social support and resilience on the mental health of different age groups during the COVID-19 pandemic. *BMC Psychiatry*, *21*(1), 16. Advance online publication. doi:10.1186/s12888-020-03012-1 PMID:33413238

Loch, A. A., Díaz, A. P., Pacheco-Palha, A., Wainberg, M. L., Da Silva, A. G., & Malloy-Diniz, L. F. (2021). Editorial: Stigma's impact on people with mental illness: Advances in understanding, management, and prevention. Frontiers in Psychology, p. 12. doi:10.3389/fpsyg.2021.715247

Lub, V. (2015). Validity in qualitative evaluation. *International Journal of Qualitative Methods*, *14*(5), 160940691562140. doi:10.1177/1609406915621406

Maulana, H., & Khawaja, N. G. (2022). A cultural perspective of wellbeing. In S. Deb & B. A. Gerrard (Eds.), *Handbook of Health and Wellbeing*. Springer. doi:10.1007/978-981-16-8263-6_2

Nimmi, P. M., Zakkariya, K. A., & Philip, A. V. (2022). Enhancing employee wellbeing – An employability perspective. *Benchmarking*, *30*(1), 102–120. doi:10.1108/BIJ-03-2021-0116

Ott, D. L., Tolentino, J. L., & Michailova, S. (2018). Effective talent retention approaches. *Human Resource Management International Digest*, *26*(7), 16–19. doi:10.1108/HRMID-07-2018-0152

Prescott, J. (2022). Digital technology to support mental health: A brief introduction to what it is and why it is important. *Mental Health and Social Inclusion*, *26*(2), 103–106. Advance online publication. doi:10.1108/MHSI-02-2022-0010

Ruggeri, K., García-Garzón, E., Maguire, Á., Matz, S., & Huppert, F. A. (2020). Wellbeing is more than happiness and life satisfaction: A multidimensional analysis of 21 countries. *Health and Quality of Life Outcomes*, *18*(1), 192. Advance online publication. doi:10.1186/s12955-020-01423-y PMID:32560725

Taubman, D. S., & Parikh, S. V. (2023). Understanding and addressing mental health disorders: A workplace imperative. *Current Psychiatry Reports*, *25*(10), 455–463. doi:10.1007/s11920-023-01443-7 PMID:37589777

Tortia, E., Sacchetti, S., & Arceiz, F. J. L. (2022). A human growth perspective on sustainable HRM practices, worker wellbeing and organizational performance. *Sustainability (Basel)*, *14*(17), 11064. doi:10.3390/su141711064

Troup, J., Fuhr, D. C., Woodward, A., Sondorp, E., & Roberts, B. (2021). Barriers and facilitators for scaling up mental health and psychosocial support interventions in low- and middle-income countries for populations affected by humanitarian crises: A systematic review. *International Journal of Mental Health Systems*, *15*(1), 5. Advance online publication. doi:10.1186/s13033-020-00431-1 PMID:33413526

Tsen, M. K., Gu, M., Tan, C. M., & Goh, S. K. (2021). Do flexible work arrangements decrease or increase turnover intention? A comparison between the social exchange theory and border theory. *The International Journal of Sociology and Social Policy*, *42*(11–12), 962–983. doi:10.1108/IJSSP-08-2021-0196

Van Der Voordt, D., & Jensen, P. A. (2021). The impact of healthy workplaces on employee satisfaction, productivity and costs. *Journal of Corporate Real Estate, 25*(1), 29–49. doi:10.1108/JCRE-03-2021-0012

Wasil, A. R., Franzen, R. E., Gillespie, S., Steinberg, J. S., Malhotra, T., & DeRubeis, R. J. (2021). Commonly reported problems and coping strategies during the COVID-19 crisis: A survey of graduate and professional students. *Frontiers in Psychology, 12*, 598557. Advance online publication. doi:10.3389/fpsyg.2021.598557 PMID:33716864

Wijngaards, I., King, O. C., Burger, M., & Van Exel, J. (2021). Worker wellbeing: What it is, and how it should be measured. *Applied Research in Quality of Life, 17*(2), 795–832. doi:10.1007/s11482-021-09930-w

Yang, Z. (2023). Bridging the mental health gap: Unveiling and mitigating the hidden toll of workplace behaviours on diverse populations. Frontiers in Public Health, 11. doi:10.3389/fpubh.2023.1308099

Zhang, Z. (2023). Early warning model of adolescent mental health based on big data and machine learning. *Soft Computing, 28*(1), 811–828. doi:10.1007/s00500-023-09422-z

KEY TERMS AND DEFINITIONS

Employee Wellbeing: The holistic state of health, happiness, and fulfilment experienced by individuals in the workplace, encompassing physical, emotional, and social aspects.

Global Practices: Organizations adopt strategies, policies, and approaches to address challenges and leverage opportunities across diverse geographic regions and cultural contexts.

Mental Health: The psychological wellbeing of individuals, encompassing emotions, thoughts, and behaviours, and their ability to cope with stress and function effectively.

Retention Strategies: Initiatives and practices implemented by organizations to enhance employee satisfaction, engagement, and loyalty, thereby reducing turnover and retaining top talent.

Talent Acquisition: Attracting, identifying, and recruiting skilled individuals to fulfil organizational needs and objectives.

Workplace Wellness: Programs, policies, and initiatives designed to promote and support the physical, mental, and emotional health of employees within the work environment.

Chapter 20
Talent Acquisition and Retention in Hospitality Industry:
Current Skill Gaps and Challenges

Amrik Singh
https://orcid.org/0000-0003-3598-8787
Lovely Professional University, India

Supina Supina
https://orcid.org/0000-0002-1183-0734
Bunda Mulia University, Indonesia

ABSTRACT

The process of acquiring, developing, and retaining high-potential people is the primary emphasis of talent management, which is a strategic approach to managing human capital. Retaining talent comprehending the socio-demographic characteristics of an organization's workforce can assist in formulating tactics that are more successful in retaining people. The hospitality sector relies heavily on its employees, making talent management procedures vital to its success. As a service industry, the hospitality sector delivers a positive customer experience. Effective talent management practices are crucial for a hotel's performance because the quality of its personnel is directly proportional to the hotel's service level to greater success. The objective of the study is to explore the factors associated with talent management and evaluate the impact of the identified factors on employee productivity in the hospitality industry.

DOI: 10.4018/979-8-3693-1938-3.ch020

BACKGROUND OF THE STUDY

Given the constant twists of development and opportunity, the value and accomplishment of every company's premises are considered key objectives for hospitality institutions (Ghani et al., 2022). Talent management is the most recent technique and strategy planning for starting the position of Talent, focusing on processes and management changes, selecting expert executives, supervisors and employees at all levels and building the HR nature for high performance (Al-Dalhmeh, 2020). In related situations, Claus (2019) declared that Talent Acquisition, through trying to match the working skills of employees with existing and potential company requirements, is working to develop necessary human capital to achieve the strategic goals of the institutions. In addition to the initial aim of registration, identification, and preparation of the Talent discovery, the fundamental assignment of the human resources departments is considered. When competition now increases by one day, HR speculation has become a major part of strategic ideology. The evolution of the talent management strategy is one of the unrivalled origins of strength, ensuring growth and continuing consistency in the modern hospitality industry (TMS). According to Thunnissen (2016), TM's scope is restricted to the results of organisations' minimal human resources practises. While HR operations have received much coverage, the recognition of the experiences, objectives, wishes and ambitions of individual staff and the development of their own profession has received little attention (Supina, 2020; Singh and Bathla, 2023; Sharma and Singh, 2024; Singh and Singh, 2024; Singh and Hassan, 2024a; Singh, 2024a; Singh, 2024b; Singh and Kumar, 2022; Singh and Hassan, 2024b, Singh and Kumar, 2021; Sharma and Singh, 2024; Ansari and Singh, 2023; Ansari et al., 2023; Ambardar and singh, 2017; Ambardar et al., 2022). Most research investigated the factors of employee expectations, discovering that personal interests, activities and history, schooling and gender all play a role (Tabassum & Nayak, 2021). Some research in the major TM literature, however, recognises the value of recognising the work aspirations of particular workers, their perspectives and the results of TM's activities (Sudarji et al., 2022; Singh and Bathla, 2023; Sharma and Singh, 2024; Singh and Singh, 2024; Singh and Hassan, 2024a; Singh, 2024a; Singh, 2024b; Singh and Kumar, 2022; Singh and Hassan, 2024b, Singh and Kumar, 2021; Sharma and Singh, 2024; Ansari and Singh, 2023; Ansari et al., 2023; Ambardar and singh, 2017; Ambardar et al., 2022). This research seeks to assess the effect on employee productivity of Talent Management Practices. In the hotel sector, where the level of customer care provided to our customers drives continued growth that is especially relevant. Employee's ability to be repeated clients or refer the hotel to others has a large impact. The turnover of employees was incredibly large in the hotel sector, and that this high turnover may be attributed to the absence of talent retention activities. Setting up talent acquisition practises to build a community built on results in the increasingly competitive hotel industry will contribute to employee loyalty, minimize employee morale and ensure high quality of service for customers. The consistency of employees and facilities in the hotel industry has clear implications. The efficiency of the employee thus leads to real competitive advantages for organisations and to success, management needs to recruit, cultivate and maintain capable, exciting and accountable staff to keep them committed and empowered.

As a result, the researcher advocates for expanding the scope of the study, moving away from a narrow focus on HR activities to a broader perspective that considers the unique needs, aspirations, and goals of hotel employees. Individuals with unique personal histories, interests, viewpoints, and ambitions for career progression within the hotel sector comprise the workforce (Singh, 2024a; Singh, 2024b; Singh and Kumar, 2022; Singh and Hassan, 2024b, Singh and Kumar, 2021; Sharma and Singh, 2024; Ansari and Singh, 2023; Ansari et al., 2023; Ambardar and singh, 2017; Ambardar et al., 2022).. Gaining insight into the factors that attract individuals to this sector, as well as how they perceive their own professional development, could assist hotels in improving their talent management practices would be the main objectives of this study. When McKinsey Consulting coined the term "battle for talent" in the 1990s, its political significance became apparent. People refer to the competition for a limited number of highly skilled individuals in the job market as the "talent war." The recognition of talent scarcity as a major concern for human professionals in worldwide enterprises also impacted the competition for skilled individuals. Therefore, based on the earlier studies that have established the fundamental principles for this field of investigation, which leads to further analysis that was carried out in this study. The objectives of the study are: (1) Identifying talent management strategies' value and significance, (2) Evaluate the effect on the satisfaction level of TM practises of the socio-economic context of respondents, (3) To study the effect on employee engagement of talent management activities.

LITERATURE REVIEW

Numerous obstacles have beset hospitality organisations, including the COVID-19 pandemic-induced decline in performance, which prompted the majority of management to retrench talent through drastic measures; these decisions have resulted in a lack of discretionary work behaviour and emotional labour display among the workforce. The study by Edeh et al. (2022) reaches the conclusion that talent retention, talent development, and talent attraction, which are all components of talent management, have substantial impacts on the indicators of discretionary work behaviour, which suggests talent management as a method for organisational executives and human resource professionals to enhance discretionary work behaviour within their respective organisations. Rafaqat et al. (2022) concluded that the inclusion in the workforce of multiple generational features may be of benefit to the diversity of organisations. On the other side, several generations of people in the workplace will often pose problems. The inevitability of tackling tension between individuals and classes of individuals from various types of generations are major management problems.Job satisfaction among various generations of staff in the hospitality sector is extremely important, which directly affects their experiences and invites guests to stay (Supina et al., 2022; Singh and Bathla, 2023; Sharma and Singh, 2024; Singh and Singh, 2024; Singh and Hassan, 2024a; Singh, 2024a; Singh, 2024b; Singh and Kumar, 2022; Singh and Hassan, 2024b, Singh and Kumar, 2021; Sharma and Singh, 2024; Ansari and Singh, 2023; Ansari et al., 2023; Ambardar and singh, 2017; Ambardar et al., 2022). The morale of employees is motivated by extrinsic and intrinsic awards. Extrinsic incentives include wage bonuses, promotional activities and workplace environments, while intrinsic rewards are dependent on the importance workers attach to their jobs. For employees' self-esteem and general motivation, the second form of recompense is extremely significant. Employees that are respected are increasing morale and achieving workplace targets and priorities more quickly than others that are disregarded, unhappy and unmotivated (Singh, 2024a; Singh, 2024b; Singh and Kumar, 2022; Singh and Hassan, 2024b, Singh and Kumar, 2021; Sharma and Singh, 2024; Ansari and Singh, 2023; Ansari et al., 2023; Ambardar and singh, 2017; Ambardar et al., 2022). Incentives are important for organizations growth and promotion. There are a variety of explanations. This are linked to an evaluation mechanism that tracks and produces positive input on talented employees. The accuracy of assessments is of interest to managers at all stages. The results of assessments have an important effect on the company's decision to award incentives and inspire its best talent.The movement towards a more respectable status, i.e. advancement, within the company is part of a compensation scheme. Promotion is used to acknowledge excellent results to enable creative people to feel appreciated and involved in the growth of the organisation. More progress opportunities contribute to work satisfaction and long-term loyalty. Award: a promotion mechanism allows administration to search for the best applicant, the best skills, to occupy most senior vacancies. The method of compensation shows that the most skilled employees have reached a high level and are respected by colleagues (Davidescu et al., 2020; Singh, 2024a; Singh, 2024b; Singh and Kumar, 2022; Singh and Hassan, 2024b, Singh and Kumar, 2021; Sharma and Singh, 2024; Ansari and Singh, 2023; Ansari et al., 2023; Ambardar and singh, 2017; Ambardar et al., 2022). Along with success, there are financial incentives that can motivate employees and help keep creativity inside the organisation. Okioga (2013) therefore states that the churn tendency is greatly diminished where an appropriate incentive system is in operation. The attrition, both for employees and employers, is deemed expensive; thus both parties make financial profits. Conservation is a necessity in order to minimize risks and expenses for profitable companies. Ardiansyah & Iskandar (2021) as an HRM invention with specific features and a focus on the growth, development and retention of high performers in the enterprise. There may be tensions when this strategy is considered morally wrong, and contradicts the concept of fair opportunities, by concentrating on top-class performers. However, in order to eliminate labour scarcity and competed with competitors of skilled human capital, Gardner (2002) argued that it is more necessary to investigate how companies and businesses changed their HR practises in the recent crisis.Swailes (2013) claims that a question of ethics should be included in the TM definition. He states that HRM has become an ethical challenge for a while with the issue of dehumanization. There is fear that assessment of human resources and accounting of human capital is being dehumanized when workers are being reduced to accounting assets. In addition, there are risks if managers mark workers as skilled or untalented. Swailes (2013) claims that marking induces an abstraction and a relational barrier between staff. When a community of elites may be selected, an employer may be suspected of favouring one party over the other. In fact, where identified skill markets, organisations and management teams must take account of the ethics of TM in order to implement TM programmes, with all workers at each stage, managers can optimise the positive to maximize and prevent damage to others.For hospitality organisations, in order to maintain competition, are investing their money in attracting skilled workers (Singh, 2024a; Singh, 2024b; Singh and Kumar, 2022; Singh and Hassan, 2024b, Singh and Kumar, 2021; Sharma and Singh, 2024; Ansari and Singh, 2023; Ansari et al., 2023; Ambardar and singh, 2017; Ambardar et al., 2022). The need for skilled employees in the United States and the United Kingdom is incredibly strong, since it is the key economic motive for a profitable business growth.Talent management strategy (Ambardar & Singh, 2017; Singh & Kumar, 2022) Younger people are unmistakably in need and negotiate with their director the psychological contracts. During the next 5 years the holding and establishment of important people in the membership would be a major achievement aspect. The value of talent acquisition is one of the challenges facing association. This investigation has been established to propel these discourses. The complete variety of the paper's discrete components is the commonly integrated structure utilized and used in this analysis for private banks in India to represent and explain talent acquisition methods this review examines areas of best practises and challenges facing affiliates for the real purpose of understanding the realities of talent acquisition strategies.The Talent management idea started by the work of a group of McKinsey advisors who had spotlighted the concept of "war of talent" during 1990s. This real examination demonstrated the critical job of workers for management' extraordinary presentation that can build up competitive benefits (Khilji, Tarique& Schuler, 2015). From that point forward, not only the truth, also the awareness of such real talent wars has strengthened because of the absence of talented workers (Latukha et al., 2019). Regardless of how the overall state of the economy; for example positive or negative, talent the board remains as a basic worry for all organizations in all occasions.

Management of Talents

Talent management is an interconnected system of corporate HR mechanisms aimed at attracting, motivating and retaining committed and active workers. The aim of talent management is to build a viable, high-level enterprise that fulfils its strategic and organisational aims.McKinsey & Company invented the word during a report in 1997. Later, the book was titled by Ed Michaels, Helen Handfield-Jones and Beth Axelrod, but since the 1970s, a connection has been formed between the growth of human resources and the efficiency of the organisation. Talent marketing profession in the early 2000s has been more and more organised.

The problem today for many corporations is that their organisations are making enormous efforts to recruit their workers but investing less time on preserving and building talent. The corporate plan would have a talent acquisition framework to be applied across the entire enterprise in everyday operations (Singh, 2024a; Singh, 2024b; Singh and Kumar, 2022; Singh and Hassan, 2024b, Singh and Kumar, 2021; Sharma and Singh, 2024; Ambardar and singh, 2017; Ambardar et al., 2022). It cannot be left to recruit and maintain workers exclusively in the Human Resources Department, but must be practised at all levels. In order to improve their subordinates' talents, line managers should have roles within the company plan. In order for the corporation to achieve awareness of the general organizational goals, divisions must freely share details with other departments.

Table 1. Talent management definitions

S.NO.	NAME OF AUTHOR AND YEAR	TALENT MANAGEMENT DEFINATIONS
1	Listwan 2005	TM means a host of activities relating to exceptionally gifted persons, taken up with a view to development of their skills and achievement of corporate goals.
2	E Blass 2007	The additional management processes and opportunities that are made available to people in the organization who are considered to be "talent "
3	Armstrong 2011	TM is more complicated and integrated set of activities aimed at securing the flow of talents within an organization, remembering that talent is one of the main resources of a company.

Since the 90s, talent management has been a favorite idea among both companies and the university world. But the strategic revolution states that talent management rehearsal is essential because skilled people have the tactical capabilities to increase management's profits, regulation and competitive advantages in all industries. Thus, the word 'talent' should first be fully discovered, in order to comprise talent management. The 'Talent' theory assimilates various explications, which are capable, insightful and capable of making such calls that enable explicit actions. In broad terms, 'talent' often avoids the degree of experience or capabilities that empower a campaign with ease and expertise. About the fact that creativity is usually related to ability, it may often be generated through practice, training and preparation (Singh, 2024a; Singh, 2024b; Singh and Kumar, 2022; Singh and Hassan, 2024b, Singh and Kumar, 2021; Sharma and Singh, 2024; Ansari and Singh, 2023; Ansari et al., 2023; Ambardar and singh, 2017; Ambardar et al., 2022). Though qualified employees in the various fields have comparable critical implications for the presentations and strength of organizations, the proof of the main skills where "who will be the professional workers" is quite special in any industry. By directing a subjective examination, the current investigation intends to recognize vital capabilities that portray the principle characteristics of skilled workers in cordiality area inside J&K business condition.

DISCUSSION AND IMPLICATIONS

Talent management procedure is correlated with recognizable proof, enchant, creating, fulfilling and holding workers with critical traits by which they can bolster manage talent of authoritative accomplishment just as hierarchical turn of events (Yuwono et al., 2021; Singh and Kumar, 2022; Singh and Hassan, 2024b, Singh and Kumar, 2021; Sharma and Singh, 2024; Ansari and Singh, 2023; Ansari et al., 2023).

Global Perspective

Management of talented employees at a global pace irrespective of country is a challenging data complex task for all the organizations Gardner (2002). Moreover, scarcity of talented employees is biggest concern. Different kinds of organizations all around the world compete for the same employee pool as a globalized talent labor market. Global convergence trends reflect the standardization of organizations in procurement and talent acquisition data creation to ensure the longevity of their strategic role. The organization achieves strategic advantages not primarily through the formulation of evidence applying best practices in the field of talent management, but in many respects through an appropriate inner integration of the various elements of a talent management regime (Singh, 2024a; Singh, 2024b; Singh and Kumar, 2022; Singh and Hassan, 2024b, Singh and Kumar, 2021; Sharma and Singh, 2024; Ansari and Singh, 2023; Ansari et al., 2023; Ambardar and singh, 2017; Ambardar et al., 2022). Hence the organizations need to adapt the global best practices of TM (talent management) including the local data domestic requirements of local labor marketplace.

Process Perspective

This process comprises all the processes which are needed to optimize the people inside a company. According to this perspective, the future success data growth of a company is based upon having the right talent. Therefore management data nourishment of talent is a part of everyday process of an organization's life.

Cultural Perspective

According to this approach of TM, for the success of an organization, it should be believed that talent mind set is the necessity data due to the fiercely competitive marketplace, for the survival data success, each data every person depend on his/her talent. On the other hand data it becomes an organizations work culture where the development of each data every employee's talent is uppermost data gets appreciated. People are allowed to explore data flourish their talent.

Competitive Perspective

Under this approach, talent management is all round accelerating the progress pathways for the high budding employees. Therefore, the focal point is the development of high potential employees.

Human Resource Planning Perspective

Perspective on human resources management says that personnel management has the best employees to have the right positions at the right moment, evidence that performs the right things. In this perspective, succession planning is very prominent for organizations.

Outlook for Change Management

Through this viewpoint, talent management in every institution in which talent management as part of the huge strategic human resources initiative is used for the corporate transformation of data is known as the catalyst of change. Perhaps it can be considered as an opportunity to integrate the talent management mechanism within an organization as part of a major transformation plan or it can place more pressure on the talent management framework if the opposition against reform is overwhelmed.

Principles of Talent Management

According to Cappelli (2008), there are four principles of talent management are needs to be followed by the organizations to gain a competitive advantage in this fiercely competitive era. These principles are based upon the supply chain perspective.

Figure 1. Principles of talent management

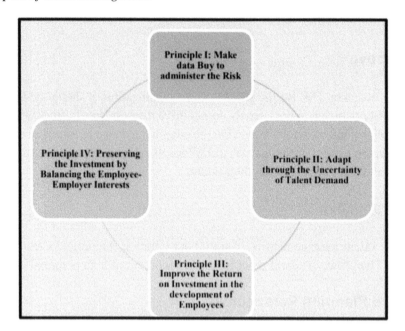

Principle I: Make Data Buy to Administer the Risk

According to this principle, companies should forecast wisely about the needs data requirements of the talent in the organization. Nowadays, a deep bench of talented employees is becoming an expensive inventory for the organization. Data it becomes more expensive when these inventories of talents walk out from the organization. People trained by the organizations, are leaving for better learning opportunities. But still growing the talent inside, makes a deep sense as hiring the talented employees from outside is faster data responsive. Therefore, an organization should estimate its requirements properly data follow the mediocre approach i.e. combination of both (Singh, 2024a; Singh, 2024b; Singh and Kumar, 2022; Singh and Hassan, 2024b, Singh and Kumar, 2021; Sharma and Singh, 2024; Ambardar and singh, 2017).

Principle II: Adapting Talent Demand Uncertainty

Uncertainty of talent demand is a universal fact but the smart organization finds a way to adapt through it. The companies should develop a talent pool which is organization wise. The allocation of talent can be done to the industry units whenever the needs arise. Another way to deal through the uncertainties is to break the long-term developmental programs in short units.

Principle III: Enhance Investment Return on Employee Growth

According to this principle, to increase the payoff, the organizations should share the cost of development through the employees. They may ask to participate in additional stretch work assignments on volunteer basis. A relationship should be maintained through the former talented employees in the hope that someday they will return back to the organization.

Principle IV: Preserving the Investment by Balancing the Employee-Employer Interests

The reason for the employees to exit from an organization is mainly the more desirable opportunities somewhere else which makes the development of talent, a short-lived commodity. The shared advancement decisions between employee data employers may help the organizations in preserving their investments.

Requirement of 'Talent' in the Hotel Industry

The hotel industry is customer-centric and relies heavily on agents to ensure that visitors are happy. There is a clear grasp of the importance of employees' performance in meeting guests' demands in this manner (Park et al., 2015). Hiring a competent employee is one of the most important aspects of running a successful company. To influence visitors' desire and self-confidence, this appears in plenty. Guest familiarity with service in the hotel industry is heavily based on employee-guest relationships. Amenities and facilities might be the same amongst hotels, but the pleasant attitude and conduct of personnel will contribute to a favorable impression of the establishment. Because the hotel industry is heavily dependent on human assets, it becomes clear that they must devote an enormous amount of attention to the problem of employees and, particularly, the value of their employees. Recruiting, recognizing, and retaining great employees is a certain approach. In the hotel industry, where staff turnover is frequent, the recruiting and firing of competent employees play a role in meeting the needs and wishes of employees.

Results in Talent Management

Talent management is linked both to managerial indices that become obvious by the effects of the jobs of the workers and to economic and organizational metrics for businesses. Worker attrition is one of talent management's primary symbolic outcomes. In the study of Saeed et al. (2023) the most important variables on the workforce turnover standards were test work, learning based organizational interactions and viable award frameworks. In terms of the general working environments of the testing work, studying and the grants, these elements thus affect the turnover rates of the two associations and branches. In terms of worker sales and job performance, for example, the effect of talent management on staff outcomes can be seen. Talent management often rehearses hierarchical results such as performance, quality of items and management, the organizational growth, the results related to the organizational money, which are visible from ROA, ROE and profit estimates, as well as capital market outcomes, such as stock cost results. and capital market results. In the event that an individual feels that the activity or occupation position doesn't fit with his/her talent, needs, and qualities, at that point he/she would go into a pessimistic mind- set that likewise associates with individual's confidence. In addition, pioneers are the principle drivers of authoritative accomplishment by being the sole vital chiefs. So as to create pioneers inside associations talent management rehearses become pivotal. Branham claims that 20% of the staff can include esteem 80% of the business result dependent on the Pareto Principle. In like manner, so as to make sure about 80% of all out organization result, we have to put resources into to the most skilled workers.

Talent Management Practices

There can be different talent management rehearses with alternate points of view. By and large, the most widely recognized talent management practice is creating talent pools by making progression arrangements for each characterized activity and position by choosing workers as per their presentation levels. Another point of view relies upon humanistic and segment perspectives (Lewis and Heckman, 2006). Since every single skilled worker have and a claim to fame that significant for the accomplishment of the organization, it is difficult to group and allot them into severe positions. Additionally, in the wake of characterizing or making the capable workers, it is a lot simpler to make some advancement arrangements for those skilled staff. Talent the board rehearses in Chipotle Restaurants as probably the best model for recognizable proof and making stars in associations. Chipotle Restaurants concentrated on rewarding workers reasonably, and allowing staffs to advance dependent on their exhibition. Making a reasonable and straightforward advancement process turns into the principle driver of their prosperity (Singh, 2024a; Singh, 2024b; Singh and Kumar, 2022; Singh and Hassan, 2024b, Singh and Kumar, 2021; Sharma and Singh, 2024; Ansari and Singh, 2023; Ansari et al., 2023; Ambardar and singh, 2017; Ambardar et al., 2022). Advancements dependent on representative exertion and execution turns out to be exceptionally helpful for talent management program. Each staff in association direct significant activities that merit installment; yet in various sums which is connected with unpredicted talent of the activity and talent of worker. The best model for such an application referred to by Bill Gates, "An incredible machine administrator orders a few times the pay of a normal machine administrator; however an extraordinary essayist of programming code is worth multiple times the cost of a normal programming author" (Aguinis et al., 2014). Some activity positions require increasingly explicit abilities which are elusive and create. The administration of vital HR, that is top supervisors and high expected capable workers, has been acknowledged as a key job for the HR capacity of the organization, particularly in the global organizations. Key places of an organization ought to be satisfied with key specialists with talent. These talent management rehearses have been normal in created nations and MNC's. Be that as it may, in creating nations, for example, India, Brazil, Turkey and so forth and in little and medium measured undertakings (SME's) these practices have not been organized and generally applied at this point. In addition, uses of talent management vary from locale to district just as association to association. Talent management rehearses deliberately chose and applied by worldwide firms essentially include position arranging and reposition the executives, HR arranging and anticipating, staffing, preparing and advancement, execution count, and compensating components; anyway these practices may not be straightforwardly appropriate for SME's. There are various techniques to be applied for talent the board (Singh, 2024a; Singh, 2024b; Singh and Kumar, 2022; Singh and Hassan, 2024b, Singh and Kumar, 2021; Sharma and Singh, 2024; Ansari and Singh, 2023; Ansari et al., 2023; Ambardar and singh, 2017; Ambardar et al., 2022). Organizations can deftly set their own talent the board needs. Taking into account that, talent the board should be viewed as a drawn out speculation changing with the particular states of the division, district, and friends. If a company would want to recruit the best talents and even wish to keep workers at all stages of the organization, the talent acquisition method has to be developed by the various activities which can be carried out in an organization. Talent management itself is a rather broad concept in its entirety. The most fascinating aspects of skill management can be the success of talent review meetings, by talking about the talented employees in an organization, and when trying to inform the other managers about their knowledge, skills and potential in other parts of the organization about their potential use and development. In any phase of the talent acquisition procedure, talent management practices are carried out. For company to be successful, it is extremely necessary to develop a set of instruments and methods to manage their employees' talents and abilities. In these organizations, the proposed method model should be used. The framework for talent management must be integrated into the business system and implemented daily across the whole company. Rather than relying just on the HR department to attract and retain people, it should be taught at every company level. Line supervisors must be held accountable for developing their immediate subordinates' abilities as part of the company strategy. In order for employees to understand the company's overall mission, divisions within the business should be openly disseminating information. Businesses now compete in two markets: one for their products and services and for those who can deliver or execute them. The success of an organization in its business marketplaces is largely determined by its performance in the ability showcase. When it comes to every area, the market for talent has all the signs of contracting. As the amount of data needed to create and distribute products and services grows, retaining skilled employees becomes more important to enhancing productivity and allowing for more time to publicize (Ansari and Singh, 2023; Ansari et al., 2023; Ambardar and singh, 2017; Ambardar et al., 2022; Zhenjing et al., 2022; Singh, 2024a; Singh, 2024b; Singh and Kumar, 2022; Singh and Hassan, 2024b, Singh and Kumar, 2021; Sharma and Singh, 2024). It is becoming more and more imperative for organizations to keep an eye out for exceptional talent in a market where demand outstrips supply, which necessitates that the right people, with the right aptitudes and knowledge, be in the right jobs. Increasing competition, tightening budgets, and more corporate supervision, among other factors, have made it more important than ever to find, cultivate, communicate, convince, and retain top-tier employees. It is always a challenge to find the appropriate individuals with the right skills for the right job. All hard-to-fill jobs are affected by talent management's focus on organizations and highly specialized roles. This has made personnel management one of the most important challenges for top corporate executives to address. Today, an organization's focus is on aligning HRM with the company's strategic goals and corporate objectives, creating an authoritative culture that fosters advancement and adaptability, and finally gaining the overhand. According to Gardner (2002), "talent" All companies face new management challenges due to the country's globalization. In addition, there is concern over a global skill shortage. Talented people are hard to come by for any business. Human capital is more vital than land or money to any organization's ability to compete in today's market. Consequently, businesses go to great lengths to hire and retain top-notch staff to accomplish their objectives. Fifty-seven percent of firms surveyed by the Aberdeen Group and Human Capital Institute (2005) said that their main priority in the next five years would be finding and retaining the right personnel, as well as addressing talent shortages. The difficulty of implementing succession planning is cited as the top problem of 79% of enterprises. 71% of firms examined had formal maintenance plans for leadership and 65% for mid-level administrative workers, according to the report.

The fight for talent is not only about enticing brilliant people with cash incentives and material rewards; it is also about building procedures and processes to ensure that competent individuals emerge and contribute to the firm. To paraphrase Williams (2000), "in the struggle for talent, there are champions and washouts, just as in business, there is accomplishment and failure" There are more winners in this fight for talent when the organization employs talent management tactics. Best practices for talent management should ensure that organizations can create local gifts in a manner that is consistent with local norms while also being fully institutionalized so that all segments of the organization may draw upon varied and appropriate professional talents. Organizations are increasingly using global leadership competence profiles and performance evaluation systems to improve their performance. Talent management systems are unique to every organization. Whatever the situation may be, organizations have a broad understanding of the steps they should take to improve their personnel management. A study by Poorhosseinzadeh & Subramaniam (2012) on Malaysian multinational companies found that 67.3 percent of organizations have implemented talent management practices and that there is a significant relationship between different talent management variables, including talent identification, attraction, training, and retention.

TM starts through industry strategy. It is one of the trendy words thrown about in human resource today; but we should know the meaning of it to an organization data to recognize the meaning of talent management, first data foremost, we should know about its historical background or how it becomes talent management from the personnel department. In a study by Bersin (2006), the genesis of talent management from personnel department is described as follows:

Figure 2. Phases of talent management

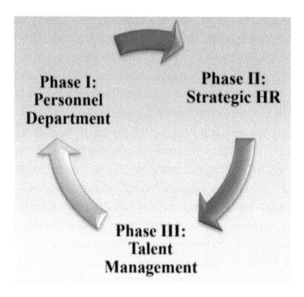

Phase I: Personnel Department

In early 1980s, the industry function, responsible for the people was called "Personnel Department." The role played by this department was to recruit people, reward them; data ascertain that they are availing the obligatory benefits. To fortify this system, the batch payroll system has grown up. Under this character ——Personnel Department was a well agreed industry gathering.

Phase II: Strategic HR

Design of — In the 1980s and the 90s, strategic HR was developed as the organization recognized that the role of human resources was more important. In this period the industrial organization recognized the position of vice president of human resources, i.e. recruiting of the right employees, preparation of them, supporting business in the creation of organizational work positions, developing packages of 'complete pay' with additional incentive rewards data incentives the industry played. It also tried to serve a key point for communication for health data bliss of the employees. The "Head of Personnel" converted in to the "VP of HR". The systems which were made to fortify this incipient role consist of recruiting, applicant tracking systems (ATS), total compensation systems, portals data management of learning systems (Ansari and Singh, 2023; Ansari et al., 2023; Ambardar and singh, 2017; Ambardar et al., 2022). HR department is now known as an industry partner, which is developed to aid data serve the lines of industry.

Phase III: Talent Management

In spite of the fact that, ——Strategic HR propagates to be a noteworthy undertaking, still human asset information learning information advancement associations are as of now accentuating on an incipient arrangement of vital issues viz. How to make the selecting procedure more methodical, efficient information solid by utilizing "competency based" enrollment in lieu of grouping through resumes, each one in turn? How might we better enroot the regulates information pioneers to help culture, impart the qualities, information cause a manageable "administration pipeline?" How would we intensely distinguish information perceive competency holes with the goal that we can give preparing, e-learning, or other advancement programs to fill these holes? How might we function through these holes to enlist information select only the perfect individuals? How would we oversee those individuals in more sane information quantifiable way so that everybody feel adjusted considered responsible information committed, information remunerated reasonably? How would we distinguish information perceive the superior workers information successors to linchpin positions all through the business association to ensure that we have a profoundly adaptable information responsive association? How would we give discovering that is adaptable, significant, advantageous, information convenient? These contemporary information testing issues are fundamental information new. The imperative higher incorporation between the distinctive HR storehouses information coordinate combination into line of industry the executives forms(Singh and Bathla, 2023; Sharma and Singh, 2024; Singh and Singh, 2024; Singh and Hassan, 2024a; Singh, 2024a; Singh, 2024b; Singh and Kumar, 2022; Singh and Hassan, 2024b, Singh and Kumar, 2021; Sharma and Singh, 2024; Ansari and Singh, 2023; Ansari et al., 2023; Ambardar and singh, 2017; Ambardar et al., 2022). Talent Management is considered as conventional information does not underline on particular positions or the limits since individuals may have more to pick up by creating information utilizing their normal aptitudes than by endeavoring to restore their weaknesses. Changing dynamics of the workforce marketplace, shortage of skills, employee's demands for balance in work data personal life data growth opportunities are creating a burning obsession to the organizations to identify, develop, deploy, administer, retain data replace the valuable assets. Assets in any organization can be divided into two major parts viz. its human capital data everything else. In this increasingly complex global era, there is a decline in the value of hard assets in comparison to intangible assets namely name recognition, reputation, data, knowhow etc. Talent as a critical resource is increasingly scarce; therefore the organizations need to administer it through their fullest efforts. Hence, in order to administer talent for industry success, the term talent management is becoming one of the most significant buzzwords among the industry world.

REFERENCES

Aguinis, H., & O'Boyle, E. Jr. (2014). Star performers in twenty-first century organizations. *Personnel Psychology*, *67*(2), 313–350. doi:10.1111/peps.12054

Al-Dalahmeh, M. L. (2020). Talent management: A systematic review. *Oradea Journal of Business and Economics*, *5*(Special), 115–123. doi:10.47535/1991ojbe102

Ambardar, A., & Singh, A. (2017). Quality of work life practices in Indian hotel industry. *International Journal of Hospitality and Tourism Systems*, *10*(1), 22–33.

Ambardar, A., Singh, A., & Singh, V. (2023). Barriers in Implementing Ergonomic Practices in Hotels-A Study on five star hotels in NCR region. *International Journal of Hospitality and Tourism Systems*, *16*(2), 11–17.

Ansari, A. I., & Singh, A. (2023). Application of Augmented Reality (AR) and Virtual Reality (VR) in Promoting Guest Room Sales: A Critical Review. In Impact of Industry 4.0 on Sustainable Tourism. Emerald Publishing Limited. doi:10.1108/978-1-80455-157-820231006

Ansari, A. I., Singh, A., & Singh, V. (2023). The impact of differential pricing on perceived service quality and guest satisfaction: An empirical study of mid-scale hotels in India. *Turyzm/Tourism*, 121–132. doi:10.18778/0867-5856.33.2.10

Ardiansyah, I., & Iskandar, H. (2021). Implementation of Green Hotel Management 5-star hotel in Jakarta, case study: The dharmawangsa hotel Jakarta. *IOP Conference Series. Earth and Environmental Science*, *704*(1), 012034. doi:10.1088/1755-1315/704/1/012034

Bhalla, A., Singh, P., & Singh, A. (2023). Technological Advancement and Mechanization of the Hotel Industry. In R. Tailor (Ed.), *Application and Adoption of Robotic Process Automation for Smart Cities* (pp. 57–76). IGI Global. doi:10.4018/978-1-6684-7193-7.ch004

Claus, L. (2019a). HR disruption—Time already to reinvent talent management. *Business Research Quarterly*, *22*(3), 207–215. doi:10.1016/j.brq.2019.04.002

Collings, D. G., & Mellahi, K. (2009). Strategic talent management: A review and research agenda. *Human Resource Management Review*, *19*(4), 304–313. doi:10.1016/j.hrmr.2009.04.001

Davidescu, A. A., Apostu, S.-A., Paul, A., & Casuneanu, I. (2020). Work flexibility, job satisfaction, and job performance among Romanian employees—Implications for Sustainable Human Resource Management. *Sustainability (Basel)*, *12*(15), 6086. doi:10.3390/su12156086

Edeh, F. O., Zayed, N. M., Perevozova, I., Kryshtal, H., & Nitsenko, V. (2022). Talent management in the hospitality sector: Predicting discretionary work behaviour. *Administrative Sciences*, *12*(4), 122. doi:10.3390/admsci12040122

Gardner, T. M. (2002). In the trenches at the talent wars: Competitive interaction for scarce human resources. *Human Resource Management, 41*(2), 225-237.

Ghani, B., Zada, M., Memon, K. R., Ullah, R., Khattak, A., Han, H., Ariza-Montes, A., & Araya-Castillo, L. (2022). Challenges and strategies for employee retention in the Hospitality Industry: A Review. *Sustainability (Basel)*, *14*(5), 2885. doi:10.3390/su14052885

Gupta, V. (2020). Talent management dimensions and its relationship with Generation Y employee's intention to quit: An Indian hotel perspective. *International Journal of Tourism Cities*, *6*(3), 583–600. doi:10.1108/IJTC-02-2019-0018

Khilji, S. E., Tarique, I., & Schuler, R. S. (2015). Incorporating the macro view in global talent management. *Human Resource Management Review*, *25*(3), 236–248. doi:10.1016/j.hrmr.2015.04.001

Latukha, M., Lisina, P., & Panibratov, Y. (2019). Developing sustainable competitive advantage of a firm through human resource management practices: A competence-based approach. *Global Business and Economics Review*, *21*(1), 96–119. doi:10.1504/GBER.2019.096855

Lewis, R. E., & Heckman, R. J. (2006). Talent management: A critical review. *Human Resource Management Review*, *16*(2), 139–154. doi:10.1016/j.hrmr.2006.03.001

Mellahi, K., & Wilkinson, A. (2010). Slash and burn or nip and tuck? Downsizing, innovation and human resources. *International Journal of Human Resource Management*, *21*(13), 2291–2305. doi:10.1080/09585192.2010.516584

Narzary, P. K., Rai, A. K., Sarkar, S., Shekhar, S., & Mahata, D. (2019). Demographic And Morphological Changes In Kolkata City, India During 1951-2014. *European Journal of Geography*, *10*(3).

Okioga, C. K. (2013). The contribution of Human Resource strategies to the Organizational Success; a case of Commercial Banks in Kisii County. *European Journal of Business and Management*, *5*(6), 181–191.

Park, J., Shin, S. Y., Lee, S., & No, S. R. (2015). Human resource management practices and organizational creativity: The role of chief executive officer's learning goal orientation. *Social Behavior and Personality*, *43*(6), 899–908. doi:10.2224/sbp.2015.43.6.899

Poorhosseinzadeh, M., & Subramaniam, I. D. (2012). Determinants of successful talent management in MNCs in Malaysia. *Journal of Basic Applied Science Research, 2*(12), 12524-12533.

Rafaqat, S., Rafaqat, S., Rafaqat, S., & Rafaqat, D. (2022). The impact of workforce diversity on Organizational Performance: A Review. *Journal of Economics and Behavioral Studies*, *14*(2(J)), 39–50. doi:10.22610/jebs.v14i2(J).3301

Saeed, F., Mir, A., Hamid, M., Ayaz, F., & Iyyaz, U. (2023). Employee salary and employee turnover intention: A key evaluation considering job satisfaction and job performance as mediators. *International Journal of Management Research and Emerging Sciences*, *13*(1). Advance online publication. doi:10.56536/ijmres.v13i1.234

Sharma, M., & Singh, A. (2024). Enhancing Competitive Advantages Through Virtual Reality Technology in the Hotels of India. In S. Kumar, M. Talukder, & A. Pego (Eds.), *Utilizing Smart Technology and AI in Hybrid Tourism and Hospitality* (pp. 243–256). IGI Global. doi:10.4018/979-8-3693-1978-9.ch011

Sharma, R., & Singh, A. (2024). Use of Digital Technology in Improving Quality Education: A Global Perspectives and Trends. In V. Nadda, P. Tyagi, R. Moniz Vieira, & P. Tyagi (Eds.), *Implementing Sustainable Development Goals in the Service Sector* (pp. 14–26). IGI Global. doi:10.4018/979-8-3693-2065-5.ch002

Singh, A. (2024a). Quality of Work-Life Practices in the Indian Hospitality Sector: Future Challenges and Prospects. In M. Valeri & B. Sousa (Eds.), *Human Relations Management in Tourism* (pp. 208–224). IGI Global. doi:10.4018/979-8-3693-1322-0.ch010

Singh, A. (2024b). Virtual Research Collaboration and Technology Application: Drivers, Motivations, and Constraints. In S. Chakraborty (Ed.), *Challenges of Globalization and Inclusivity in Academic Research* (pp. 250–258). IGI Global. doi:10.4018/979-8-3693-1371-8.ch016

Singh, A., & Bathla, G. (2023). Fostering Creativity and Innovation: Tourism and Hospitality Perspective. In P. Tyagi, V. Nadda, V. Bharti, & E. Kemer (Eds.), Embracing Business Sustainability through Innovation and Creativity in the Service Sector (pp. 70-83). IGI Global. doi:10.4018/978-1-6684-6732-9.ch005

Singh, A., & Hassan, S. C. (2024a). Service Innovation Through Blockchain Technology in the Tourism and Hospitality Industry: Applications, Trends, and Benefits. In S. Singh (Ed.), *Service Innovations in Tourism: Metaverse, Immersive Technologies, and Digital Twin* (pp. 205–214). IGI Global. doi:10.4018/979-8-3693-1103-5.ch010

Singh, A., & Hassan, S. C. (2024b). Identifying the Skill Gap in the Workplace and Their Challenges in Hospitality and Tourism Organisations. In Contemporary Challenges in Social Science Management: Skills Gaps and Shortages in the Labour Market (Contemporary Studies in Economic and Financial Analysis, Vol. 112B). Emerald Publishing Limited. doi:10.1108/S1569-375920240001112B006

Singh, A., & Kumar, S. (2021). Identifying Innovations in Human Resources: Academia and Industry Perspectives. In A. Pathak & S. Rana (Eds.), *Transforming Human Resource Functions With Automation* (pp. 104–120). IGI Global. doi:10.4018/978-1-7998-4180-7.ch006

Singh, A., & Kumar, S. (2022). Identifying Innovations in Human Resources: Academia and Industry Perspectives. In I. Management Association (Ed.), Research Anthology on Human Resource Practices for the Modern Workforce (pp. 219-231). IGI Global. doi:10.4018/978-1-6684-3873-2.ch013

Singh, V., & Singh, A. (2024). Digital Health Revolution: Enhancing Well-Being Through Technology. In V. Nadda, P. Tyagi, R. Moniz Vieira, & P. Tyagi (Eds.), *Implementing Sustainable Development Goals in the Service Sector* (pp. 213–219). IGI Global. doi:10.4018/979-8-3693-2065-5.ch016

Stahl, G. K., Björkman, I., & Morris, S. (Eds.). (2012). *Handbook of research in international human resource management*. Edward Elgar Publishing.

Sudarji, S., Panggabean, H., & Marta, R. F. (2022). Challenges of the sandwich generation: Stress and coping strategy of the multigenerational care. *Indigenous: Jurnal Ilmiah Psikologi, 7*(3), 263–275. doi:10.23917/indigenous.v7i3.19433

Supina, S. (2020). Generation Z career options in the government sector in the tourism sector with the presence of the generation X minister as a moderating variable. *Journal of Indonesia Tourism and Policy Studies, 5*(1). Advance online publication. doi:10.7454/jitps.v5i1.169

Supina, S., Marta, R. F., & Karolina, C. M. (2022). Comparison of the influence of motivation for foreign tourists' visits to Bali with the inauguration of the Garuda Wisnu Kencana statue. *International Journal of Applied Sciences in Tourism and Events*, *6*(1), 42–51. doi:10.31940/ijaste.v6i1.42-51

Swailes, S. (2016). The cultural evolution of talent management: A memetic analysis. *Human Resource Development Review*, *15*(3), 340–358. doi:10.1177/1534484316664812

Tabassum, N., & Nayak, B. S. (2021). Gender stereotypes and their impact on women's career progressions from a managerial perspective. *IIM Kozhikode Society & Management Review*, *10*(2), 192–208. doi:10.1177/2277975220975513

Taylor, S. (2007). Creating social capital in MNCs: The international human resource management challenge. *Human Resource Management Journal*, *17*(4), 336–354. doi:10.1111/j.1748-8583.2007.00049.x

Thunnissen, M. (2016). Talent management: For what, how and how well? An empirical exploration of talent management in practice. *Employee Relations*, *38*(1), 57–72. doi:10.1108/ER-08-2015-0159

Yuwono, I. A., Suroso, A. I., & Hubeis, A. V. (2021). *The effect of talent management on employee performance with corporate culture as a mediating variable*. Jurnal Aplikasi Bisnis Dan Manajemen. doi:10.17358/jabm.7.1.212

Zhenjing, G., Chupradit, S., Ku, K. Y., Nassani, A. A., & Haffar, M. (2022). Impact of employees' workplace environment on employees' performance: A multi-mediation model. *Frontiers in Public Health*, *10*, 890400. Advance online publication. doi:10.3389/fpubh.2022.890400 PMID:35646787

Chapter 21
Talented Engineer Acquisition and Retention in the Global Textile Industry

Radostina A. Angelova

https://orcid.org/0000-0002-6943-7695

R&D Services, Bulgaria

ABSTRACT

This chapter examines the acquisition and retention of talented engineers within the global textile industry. It explores the multifaceted definition of a "talented engineer" and highlights key attributes such as technical proficiency, problem-solving skills, and adaptability. Emphasis is placed on the importance of ongoing learning, effective communication, leadership qualities, and ethical integrity in retaining talent. Additionally, the chapter underscores the necessity of aligning HR practices with the global talent landscape to meet the diverse needs of the industry.

INTRODUCTION

International textiles industry is an excellent example of dynamic nature and strong competition that encompasses the global market. Based on a stubborn innovativeness, quality and resilience to the dynamism of consumer needs, it is at that axis of creativity, technology and management. In this setting, talent acquisition and retention emerges as the paramount factor of success, shaping the journey of businesses towards success or failure in a context of dynamic changes and fierce competition.

The Textile Industry as a Global Industry

The textile industry is considered as a global industry due to certain interrelated factors. These factors go beyond the boundaries of a particular country and influence the structure and development of the textile industry worldwide (Atkar et al., 2021).

DOI: 10.4018/979-8-3693-1938-3.ch021

First, the textile industry is characterised by highly integrated global supply chain (Cao et al., 2008). Cotton, wool, and synthetic fibres are sourced from various regions of the world. The raw materials pass through several stages of processing in various countries before finally getting to the end user. These complex networks of production and distribution include several nations coming together to produce the final textile product (Islam, 2020).

Despite the fact that the production of textiles is international, there are countries that specialize in specific operations (Boussemart & De Bandt, 1993). For example, certain countries focus on spinning and weaving technologies or are centre points of garment processing or textile printing. Some others focus on technical textiles or hi-tech technologies. This specialization and interdependence give rise to a global system of which each participant contributes to the overall process of production (Coe & Yeung, 2015).

International trade is prevalent in the textile industry, as much of the production is geared towards export (Pickles et al., 2015). Countries with developed textile sectors export their products to satisfy global consumers. This transcontinental trade does not only stimulate economic progress but also increases the industrial interdependence globally (Amin, 2017). Actually, consumer preferences and markets are limitless. Fashion trends, the influence of international events (Oscar Awards, for example), media, and cultural exchanges, can spread worldwide rapidly (Pieterse, 2019). Therefore, the textile industry must be flexible and dynamic to accommodate a varying and dynamic market (Guarnieri & Trojan, 2019).

The textile industry benefits from global technological development and improvement (Huang, Yan, & Yang, 2021). Many research activities or breakthroughs in the field of textile technology are shared and get used in different parts of the world. This concept of the alliance with respect to innovation helps the industry not only to remain competitive but also to be a leader in the field of technological development.

However, the textile industry is a sector heavily regulated, and standardised internationally (Desore & Narula, 2018). Standards and regulations operate on different facets of the production chain including quality assurance, environmental stability, or safety. Organizations and agreements, such as the World Trade Organization (WTO), play a role in establishing guidelines that globally influence the textile manufacturing practices (Qureshi, 2022).

The issues concerning the environment and sustainability, as well as the recognized global challenges, affect the textile industry as well. Different aspects like water usage (Hasanbeigi & Price, 2015), waste management (Yacout & Hassouna, 2016), and the environmental effects of textile manufacturing (Toprak & Anis, 2017) are continuously concerned. Initiatives are instituted and practices evolved in order to provide more sustainable future to the industry. In addition, world occurrences including economic swings, geopolitical fluctuations and trade arrangements have both regional and macro impact on the textile sector. These global events influence production costs, market availability, and overall stability of the production chains.

In essence, the classification of the textile industry as a global industry is a result of the vast and interdependent system of production, trade, innovativeness, and market dynamics that transcend state boundaries. Thus, this global implication suggests the versatility of the industry and its importance as one of the actors in the world trade and cultural medium.

The Requirement for Talented Engineers' Acquisition and Retention

The term a "talented engineer" is not defined universally and there are multiple interpretations of it based on talent being a subjective concept (Gallardo-Gallardo, 2018). Yet the talented engineer for a textile industry or any engineering field could be defined as compound of technical background, problem-solving skills and genius creativity coupled with working quality patience (Blockley, 2020).

First of all, the excellent engineers are well-versed in the engineering concepts related to their field. They are aware of new tools and latest techniques that they need (Milton et al., 1999). Talented engineers are resourceful individuals trained to use their intuition to solve problems. They are good at thinking creatively, developing new approaches, and solving complex technical problems. They derive satisfaction from unearthing ways of doing things better either concerning the processes, products or the (Beecham et al., 2008).

Analytical skills are typical for the talented engineers. They can cut distinctly through the problems and acquire observation of facts from which critical conclusions may be drawn (Brophy et al., 2008). They can decompose problems into tractable parts and identify requisite conditions/causes and construct appropriate remedial approaches founded on evidence and rationality.

Undoubtedly, very good communication and collaboration skills are also crucial for the behaviour of the talented engineers (Wong et al., 2021). They need to deal well with teamwork and translate technical ideas appropriately among different stakeholders (Van den Beemt et al., 2020). The talented engineers have to present their ideas cogently both in written reports, oral communication and interpersonal relationship (Humphrey & Holmes, 2023).

The engineering field is very dynamic since there are new technologies, methodologies as well as promising industrial ideas (Potkonjak et al., 2016). The talented engineers are eager to learn, staying updated on industry developments. Being adaptable, they are able to acquire new skills and remain competitive in their professional field (Ktoridou, Doukanari & Karayiannis, 2019).

Steering projects is undoubtedly a significant task for the engineers (Rodriguez et al., 2018). Excellent engineers often show leadership qualities and proactive behaviour. At the same time, they recognise and analyse opportunities for optimisation and inspire the others to achieve the foreseen goals.

Integrity is a fundamental characteristic for any engineer (Zhang et al. 2023). Talented engineers uphold ethical standards, prioritize safety and sustainability. They conduct themselves with professionalism and reliability in all aspects of their work.

An important element of this discussion is the understanding of the role that global perceptions play in talent management strategies. By definition, the global textiles industry is not limited to national borders and serves a wide range of markets that each have their own distinct needs and cultures. In the context of an effective acquisition and retention of talent, it is important to be aware of the global talent landscape which involves cultural differences, legalities and global challenges brought about by dispersed workforce. This chapter will reveal the significance of creating a global mindset in the leadership and HR teams, promoting intercultural understanding and customizing talent strategies depending on the requirements of specific areas.

THE CULTURAL DIFFERENCES IN THE TEXTILE WORLD

The textile industry's talent pool should extend beyond local borders. Companies must adopt practices to attract and source talent from a global perspective.

However, this raises the question of the adaptability of the "global textile engineer" in relation to cultural differences. Needless to say, the existence of national and even regional cultural differences can prove to be a significant obstacle to the recruitment and especially the retention of textile specialists from foreign cultural backgrounds. Ethnic, religious and even generational differences are no less important, but in the context of the global movement of people and goods, national cultural differences and regional peculiarities within a country/culture are of paramount importance.

Let's look at the largest producers and exporters of textiles in the world according to data from 2022 (Statista, 2022). It can be assumed that these are the countries with the greatest need for engineering personnel as well. China is the largest textile exporter with a share of 48% of the total amount produced by the top ten textile exporters. It is followed by the European Union with 23% of exports, India (6%) and Turkey (5%).

The situation in the production and export of clothing (for year 2021) is very similar – Fig. 2. Again, China is the largest exporter with a 39% share of the eight largest producers in the world, followed by the European Union (33%). Bangladesh (8%) and Vietnam (7%) have an almost equal share. Türkiye and India are also in the group of the largest exporters of clothing, as well as in the group of the largest exporters of textiles (Figure 1).

Figure 1. Top 10 textile exporting countries in 2022 (data from Statista, 2024)

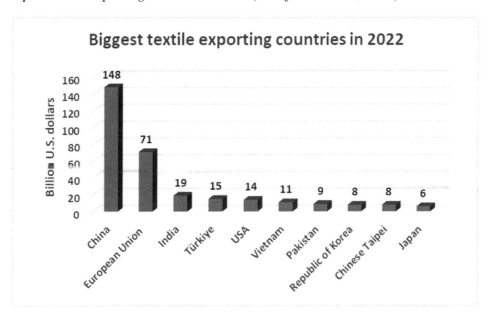

Figure 2. Top clothes exporting countries in 2021 (data from Statista, 2023)

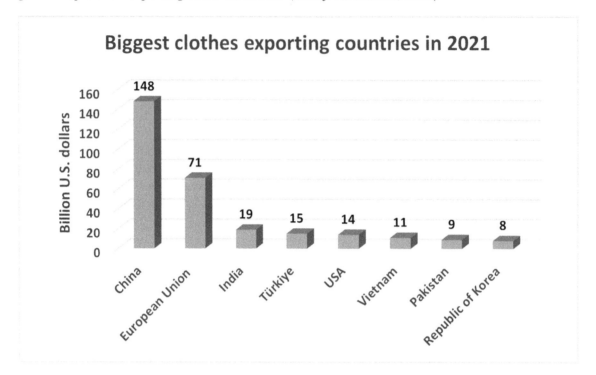

It is interesting to compare these countries in terms of their national cultures. Hofstede's criteria, used in our other studies regarding the influence of national culture on the development of textiles as a global industry (Angelova, 2018), are particularly relevant. The comparison covers the largest textile exporters of Figure 1 (more than half overlapping with the leaders in apparel exports, Figure 2).

Geert Hofstede developed a six-dimensional model of cultural differences between nations that includes the following criteria (Hofstede, 2011):

- Individualism vs. Collectivism: Determines how much the emphasis is on individual achievement versus group interests.
- Power Distance: Reflects society's tolerance for power and status inequality.
- Uncertainty Avoidance: Reflects society's willingness to deal with uncertainty and risks.
- Masculinity vs. Femininity: Indicates the extent to which a culture incorporates traditional masculine or feminine characteristics.
- Long-Term vs. Short-Term Orientation: Determines how future-oriented or present-oriented the culture is.
- Indulgence vs. Restraint: Shows the measures that a society allows its members to gratify their basic and natural human drives related to enjoying life and having fun.

Individualism vs. Collectivism

Individualism and collectivism are two opposite cultural characteristics to measure national cultural differences in Hofstede's model. In individualistic cultures, people are perceived as autonomous and independent entities who strive to achieve personal goals and successes. In such cultures, individual rights, freedom of choice, and self-realization are highly valued. The personal identity and dignity of the individual are considered important (Hofstede, Hofstede & Minkov, 2010).

In collectivist cultures, group interests, communal values, and solidarity are valued more than individual goals. Individuals perceive themselves as part of a group (e.g., family, community, company) and often make decisions that align with group interests. Cooperation and responsibility towards the community are especially important. Individual desires (if any) are subordinated to group norms (Darwish & Huber, 2003).

The analysis of the countries shown in Fig. 1, shows that the following groups can be distinguished:

- Cultures with high collectivism. These are the export leader China, Republic of Korea, Chinese Taipei and Japan. They place great importance on group interests over individual interests and promote solidarity and community. The ties between the workers and the company are strong, everyone obeys the interests of the group (family, company, community).
- Cultures with a medium to high level of collectivism. This definition includes India, Turkey, Vietnam and Pakistan. Community ties and family ties matter greatly, and group interests trump individual interests. The importance of group harmony and solidarity is emphasized.
- Cultures with a low to medium level of individualism. Differences between individual European Union (EU) member states are significant, but the general pattern of cultures includes low to medium individualism for the EU as a whole. People's individual rights, freedom of choice and self-realization are usually valued.
- Cultures with a medium to high level of individualism. The representative of this culture in the ranking of Figure 1 is the United States. American culture generally places individual rights and persona

The presence of eight countries with a medium to high level of collectivist relationships in the Top 10 of textile production and export is not a coincidence. A strong sense of community and cooperation is encouraged in these cultures (Koch & Koch, 2007). Thus, the textile industry, which involves mass production and a large number of workers, can be seen as part of the wider community. Workers work together to achieve common goals, in conditions of social harmony and coherence. In the production of textiles, consistency and coordination between the various stages of production are key to the successful operation of production, especially in high volume (Burki & Buvik, 2017). The negation of individual needs and goals is of particular importance when large groups of workers work together.

Workers are usually organized into separate groups (crews, workshops), with the group having a leader and a common goal. The production process is closely controlled and coordinated. The group complies with the instructions of its supervisor and interacts with other groups to ensure smooth and efficient production (Jackson et al., 2006). Workers work closely with each other, sharing information, resources, and efforts to achieve a common goal. The group leader, in turn, acts as a leader who not only gives instructions but also looks after the welfare of his workers. He maintains good relations with them and tries to solve current problems in talks and special meetings.

Power Distance

Power Distance describes the extent to which members of a culture accept and expect inequality in the distribution of power and status (Hofstede, Hofstede & Minkov, 2010). In the analysis of Fig. 1 two groups of countries differ on this dimension:

- Countries with a low to medium Power Distance index. These are the US and the EU (with possible index fluctuations between member states). Greater equality between people is encouraged (Bochner & Hesketh, 1994). The ideal for these cultures is to reduce differences in power and status. Social hierarchies are not so important, alienation from authority is often felt. People are expected to be treated equally and have the right to express their opinions and ideas.
- Countries with a high-Power Distance index. These are all the remaining eight countries that are leaders in textile exports. Inequality in the distribution of power and wealth is considered normal. Power is often assumed to be an integral part of society and expected to be exercised smoothly (Hofstede, 1984). Employees in companies, students in universities, family or group members generally obey authority, social hierarchies are clearly defined and respected. In general, individuals are comfortable with inequality in society.

Linking the high index of Power distance to China's role as the largest textile producer can be done through several important aspects. Factories and other manufacturing establishments inevitably reflect ideas of hierarchy and authority. High Power distance can lead to more efficient organisation of work and greater control over processes (Zagladi, Hadiwidjojo & Rahayu, 2015). This is important in textile and apparel manufacturing because accuracy, quality standards and high-volume production are essential.

Not only in China, but also in the other seven countries with a high-Power distance index, workers generally agree to the authority of their supervisors. They carry out their assigned tasks without question and are particularly suited to performing monotonous, repetitive work such as running garment production lines. Managers are usually educated in the field of engineering or technology and represent an unquestioned authority for their subordinates.

The high index of Power Distance allows to maintain the low cost of labour and relatively low production costs (Hofstede, 1984). This in turn reinforces and maintains structures of social inequality in businesses and in society. This is how social and economic contexts are created, which help to develop and maintain the textile industry in the country.

Uncertainty Avoidance

This Hofstede's index shows the degree to which members of a given culture feel uncomfortable with or try to avoid uncertainty and ambiguity in various aspects of life (Hofstede, Hofstede & Minkov, 2010). Countries that fall into the group of Top 10 textile exporters can be defined as:

- Cultures with a high index of Uncertainty Avoidance. These are China, India, Pakistan, Korea, and Japan. With slightly lower indicators, but with levels above the average, are Turkey, Vietnam, and Chinese Taipei. These cultures are characterized by a strong desire for stability and security. Uncertainty and risks are met with dissatisfaction and tried to be avoided through clearly defined rules and procedures. Change and the unknown can be perceived as a threat. The educational system and business tend to be more formal and bureaucratic (Kreiser et al., 2010). The same applies to the custody administration and regulatory organizations.

- Cultures with a low index of Uncertainty Avoidance. In the EU, there is a greater tolerance for uncertainty and risk. Change and innovation are welcomed, and institutions are more flexible. In American culture, change and risk are seen as part of life and as opportunities for growth and development (Tavanti, 2012).

Having a strict organization, clear rules, and procedures, allows the Chinese textile industry to become the largest and most efficient producer in the world. High uncertainty avoidance leads to the creation of stable and secure production environments (Qu & Yang, 2015). In the textile industry, this is essential, as the stability of the production process and quality assurance are crucial. Along with this, clear rules and orderly structures are created that facilitate the organization and management of production.

High uncertainty avoidance makes China an attractive place for investment and business partnerships (Shao, Kwok & Zhang, 2013). Enterprises investing in China's textile sector can have more confidence in the stability of their business and in their relationships with suppliers and partners.

Masculinity vs. Femininity

The dimension describes differences in values and behaviors related to sexual identity and gender roles in a particular culture (Hofstede, 1998). It is important to note that no culture is entirely masculine or entirely feminine, but rather can have various combinations and shades of both poles. Of those shown in Fig. 2 countries, the substantial part is in the high masculinity index group. These are China, India, Turkey, US, Pakistan, Republic of Korea, Chinese Taipei and Japan. In these cultures, strength, ambition and success are highly valued (Hofstede, 1996). Work is often central to an individual's identity and self esteem. At the same time, there is a clear distinction between the roles of the two sexes in society: men are expected to be decisive, ambitious and successful, while women are encouraged to take on more traditional roles such as looking after the home and family (Hofstede, Hofstede & Minkov, 2010).

In feminine-dominant cultures, compassion, interpersonal cooperation, and quality of life are valued more than ambition and success. Relationships between people, nature and harmony are important. It should be noted that Scandinavian countries are an example of cultures with a high femininity index (Warner-Søderholm, 2012). In this sense, the EU countries have a great diversity regarding this criterion.

Long-Term vs. Short-Term Orientation

This dimension of national cultural differences covers the approaches of different cultures to the future, time and traditions (Hofstede, 1998). In short-term oriented cultures, people focus on the present and the past instead of the future. Quick wins, short-term successes and results are more important. Such cultures are prone to change and may be less traditional.

In long-term oriented cultures, people are focused on the future. They are distinguished by long-term planning, sustainability, and attention to traditions. Such cultures may value efforts made today to achieve success in the future. Most cultures in the world have both orientations (Venaik, Zhu, & Brewer, 2013).

It is no coincidence, however, that more countries in Figure 1 and Figure 2 belong to cultures with a long-term orientation. These are China, India, Pakistan, Republic of Korea, Chinese Taipei and Japan.

Japan is the culture known for its extreme long-term orientation, whose fundamental values are tradition, long-term plans and sustainability (Park & Lemaire, 2011).

The EU tends to be more long-term oriented, with values such as sustainability, innovation and long-term planning held high. However, different member states may have different shades of this orientation. Turkey has aspects of long-term orientation, but in business it is oriented more toward short-term goals and rapid growth.

The US and Vietnam are usually associated with a short-term orientation, especially in an economic context (Park & Lemaire, 2011). Individualism and capitalism often encourage quick results and innovation.

Long-term orientation is a criterion that allows to analyse the success of the largest textile and clothing exporters in the world. The long-term strategy of investment in development technologies, infrastructure and innovation leads to constant improvement of the quality and efficiency of production. This, for example, makes Chinese textile products competitive in the world market. Long-term oriented countries also build a wide network of suppliers who can provide raw materials, materials and other resources needed for textile production.

Training is also part of the long-term orientation of countries that are leaders in textile and clothing exports (he & Sun, 2020). They develop their high-quality workforce through education and training. Thus, in the long term, they have more competitive and productive workers who contribute to economic growth and innovation. Investments in the training of specialists in various technologies, engineering sciences and research activities are particularly significant.

Indulgence vs. Restraint

Indulgence vs. Restraint describes the degree to which members of a culture are controlled or restricted from expressing their desires and pursuit of pleasure (Hofstede, Hofstede & Minkov, 2010). Among the largest exporters of textiles and apparel (Figs. 1 and 2), China, India Pakistan, Republic of Korea, Chinese Taipei and Japan are with high levels of restraint. Traditional values in these cultures include self-discipline, moderation, and control in everyday life. Some countries in the EU (e.g., France, Italy and Spain) as well as the US have a more indulgent approach to life that encourages self-fulfilments, individualism and freedom of choice. But other EU countries (Germany and the Scandinavian countries) are distinguished by a higher degree of restraint (Nyström, 2017).

Restraint can explain the leadership positions of countries such as China, India and others in the production of textiles and clothing (Huang, 2022). In these countries, the textile sector is known for its low labour costs, often due to strict management practices and moderate wages. These restraint practices allow textile firms to maintain competitive prices for their products in the world market. Chinese textile firms generally adhere to stable and sustainable business models that focus on long-term success instead of quick profits. This includes investments in product quality, optimisation of production processes and maintaining reliable partnerships with customers and suppliers (Scott, 2017). At the same time, countries with a high degree of restraint invest significantly in technology and innovation in the textile sector.

GLOBAL TEXTILE ENGINEERS EDUCATION

The above-mentioned requirement that textile companies have to source talent from a global perspective includes building partnerships with educational institutions worldwide and engaging in talent exchange programs. Let's track down which universities are the leaders in textile education in the world. Figure 3 summarizes the data reported by Textile Engineering (2023).

Figure 3. Top 10 textile universities in the world (data from Textile Engineering, 2023)

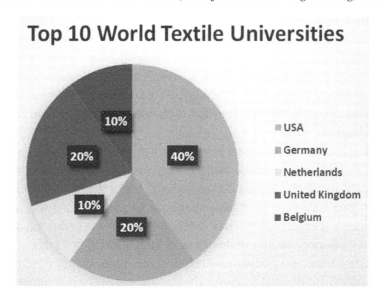

Forty per cent of the top universities are located in the US. These are the Massachusetts Institute of Technology (MIT), North Carolina State University, University of Nebraska-Lincoln, and South Carolina University. Twenty per cent of the leading universities are in Germany: Technical University of Munich (TUM) and Dresden University of Technology. Another twenty per cent are in the UK: the University of Leeds and the University of Manchester. One of the top 10 universities is in the Netherlands (Technical University of Delft) and one in Belgium (Ghent University, Belgium).

It can be assumed that the US and the EU train personnel not only for their textile industry but also attract talented students from all over the world. Some of these students probably come from countries whose cultural metrics are quite different from those of the US and the EU: e.g., China, India, Pakistan, and Turkey. During their studies, these students inevitably absorb elements of the new culture, especially in terms of management practices, communication, and financial behaviour (Marginson, 2010).

It is an indisputable fact, that US and EU universities tend to be multicultural, with students from all over the world (Delic, Vidacek-Hains & Adarve, 2011). This experience provides an opportunity to become familiar with different cultural and social perspectives, which can enrich their understanding and provide them with opportunities for international mobility and careers. The new knowledge can improve their chances of employment in the global textile industry and encourage them to acquire cross-cultural skills and experience.

Education systems themselves encourage active student participation, critical thinking and teamwork. These training methods are different from the traditional methods, used in Eastern countries (Fang & Gopinathan, 2009). Students from these countries may face the challenge of adapting to new learning methods and developing new skills. Moreover, the US and the EU are often leaders in the development of new technologies and innovations in the textile industry (Schäfer, 2018). Thus, students from China and India, for example, who study in these countries can access the latest technological advances and learn how to apply them to their work.

Despite the potential benefits, training textile engineers in countries such as the US or the European Union may present some challenges and issues related to cultural differences. Differences in language, customs, food and social structures can be a source of stress and difficulties in adjustment (Sam & Berry, 2010). Moving away from family and friends and cutting off normal social contacts can lead to feelings of isolation and loneliness. This can worsen students' mental health and lead to depression and stress (Aldwin & Greenberger, 1987).

Contrasts in culture and communication styles between East and West can lead to misunderstandings and conflicts in academic and work environments (Ting-Toomey & Dorjee, 2018). For example, different notions of hierarchy, authority, and conflict resolution can create tension between students and faculty or between colleagues.

A separate question is how textile engineers from Eastern countries will apply what they have learned in their own cultures. In their own cultures, students may encounter different business practices and strategies than those they are taught in countries such as the US or the EU. For example, in China and India, business models and approaches to management can be more hierarchical and based on family ties or personal connections (Berger, 2014). Thus, textile engineers who graduated in Western countries may face challenges in managing conflict situations or communicating in a team.

Implementation of new ideas and practices will be difficult if they do not fit into social and cultural expectations. For example, in traditional Eastern cultures, the role of the individual and the family may be more significant than innovation and personal initiative. While the US and EU often encourage individualism and initiative at work, in China and India more traditional collectivistic structures may prevail (Hofstede, Hofstede & Minkov, 2010).

Of course, the importance of cultural differences would be greatly reduced if future textile engineers were trained in their own country. Leading universities for textile training in China, for example, are:

- Shanghai University of Engineering Science, which offers a variety of programs in textile engineering, including textile materials, textile technology, and fashion design.
- Donghua University, one of China's leading universities specializing in textile engineering and fashion design.
- North China University of Textile Engineering specialised in manufacturing technology and sustainable textile materials.

Among the leaders in training textile engineers in India are:

- Indian Institute of Technology Delhi, with programs in textile engineering, including advanced technology and research in the textile industry.
- Indian Institute of Technology Bombay, known for its educational opportunities in textile engineering.
- National Institute of Technology Calcutta, which in addition to programs in textile engineering also offers numerous research opportunities in the field of textile materials and manufacturing technology.

The advantages of recruiting talented personnel not from the "world banks" for textile engineers, but from one's own country, are many and varied. First, it is the common language and communication both horizontally (with those on the same level of hierarchy) and vertically - with subordinate workers and superiors. Textile engineers trained in their own country usually have a better understanding of the workplace culture. This ensures more effective communication and better collaboration in carrying out daily production tasks.

The trained "at home" engineers often have a better understanding of the local market and industry context (Saxeniean, 2002). This can be useful in the design and development of textiles, traditional clothing, and textile accessories that are tailored to the specific needs and preferences of local consumers.

Training in one's own country can allow textile engineers to gain a better knowledge of local textile traditions. It is especially important for traditional technologies, raw materials and design in countries such as China, India, Japan, Turkey, and some European countries. To mention just the traditional kimonos, sarees, woven wall tapestries, and tartans, which, apart from being important to the modern culture of the respective countries, are also part of the global tourism business.

Last but not least, during their training "at home", students can make local connections and networks in the industry. This can help them find job opportunities and develop their career in the local textile sector (Meyer, 2001).

Despite these advantages, it is important to note that there may still be cultural differences and challenges in the work environment, even if textile engineers are trained in their own country. The larger the country, the more significant regional cultural differences appear. There are also always differences in terms of generation, ethnicity or religious affiliation (Hofstede, 1984). Therefore, in multinational companies and in companies with a large scale of operations, it is important to provide an appropriate training program and cultural adaptation for new employees to ensure their successful integration (Briscoe, Schuler & Tarique, 2012).

STRATEGIES AND METHODS FOR ATTRACTING TALENTED ENGINEERS

Researching strategies and methods to attract talented engineers is essential for textile companies that need highly skilled personnel for development and innovation. In today's competitive job market, it is a challenge to find and retain talented engineers in any field (Whysall, Owtram & Brittain, 2019).

There are different methods of attracting talented employees to a certain company, but here three of the most used at the moment will be discussed: employer branding, direct attraction from educational institutions and the use of social job platforms.

Building a Strong Employer Brand

Building a strong employer brand, also known as "employer branding", is the process of creating and maintaining an attractive and unique company identity as an employer (Mandhanya & Shah, 2010). This includes communicating the values, culture and benefits of working within the particular organisation to attract and retain talented employees and textile engineers in particular.

First of all, a company needs to have its own identity that makes them different from other employers. This may include vision, mission, values, corporate culture, work environment and other aspects to be presented as attractive to talented textile engineers (Sokro, 2012). Patagonia, for example, is known for its commitment to environmental protection and sustainable practices in the textile industry. It builds its brand as an employer by emphasizing the importance of environmental responsibility and social justice in all aspects of its business management.

Communication of the employer brand is also particularly important. The use of various channels, mainly those that are popular among the younger generation, makes it possible not only to expand consumer demand but also to attract talented engineering personnel (Gaddam, 2008). Communication through various channels such as websites, social media, events, media, print materials and others should be consistent and attractive to attract the attention of talented candidates. Companies like Nike and Adidas use social media and various marketing campaigns to communicate their values, culture, and benefits as employers. They share success stories; career opportunities and the employee benefit they offer.

Creating an attractive - stimulating and pleasant - work environment is one of the main aims of the leaders in global production (Abrudan & Conea-Simiuc, 2019). This may include providing flexible working hours, professional development opportunities, seminars and training, bonuses and other benefits (Esau, 2010). One such example is Lululemon, a multinational sportswear retailer. In addition to creating modern and comfortable workplaces, they offer flexible working hours, opportunities for sports and fitness activities, as well as programs for personal and professional development.

Sharing success stories and examples of current and former employees can convince potential candidates that the company offers a stimulating work environment (Smith, 2012). This is especially important for young textile engineers, who are attracted by the development prospects even more than the attractive salary. H&M often shares success stories of its designers and employees on social media and its website. They represent their contributions to the brand and the industry, which inspires others to join the company.

Positive reviews and testimonials from current and former employees are generally powerful tool for attracting talent (Sujansky & Ferri-Reed, 2009). Under Armour, for example, supports feedback and interaction with its employees. They encourage their employees to share their stories and experiences about working for the company through social media and other channels.

Active participation in community initiatives and events is also a method of strengthening the textile company's image as a socially responsible employer (Andersen, 2005; Smith, 2012). Levi Strauss & Co. is a similarly active participant in community initiatives related to sustainability and social responsibility. The company organizes events and programs to engage employees in charitable activities and projects, which is also a way to. and attract the attention of potential candidates.

Attracting the Best Students Directly From Universities

Attracting the best students from educational institutions is an important method for companies looking for talented engineers and other professionals with specific skills and education (Barrena-Martínez et al. 2015).

It is the practice of many universities and colleges to organise career forums and exhibitions. Companies can participate there to present their career opportunities, the availability of internships and other recruitment programs (Florea, 2010). A similar opportunity is the special information sessions and presentations to majors, faculties or student clubs. Detailed information about the company, career opportunities and job requirements can be shared there. Even large companies such as Adidas and Nike carry out similar activities.

Offering internship programs (P. Maertz Jr, Stoeberl & Marks, 2014) is another way to attract young talent from universities teaching textile . These programs provide an opportunity for students not only to get to know the company but also to apply their knowledge in a real work environment. In the summer of 2024, for example, such programs are offered by Victoria's Secret & Co., Medline Industries Inc. and others.

Other means of cooperation with universities can be also found to make a textile company more attractive or recognizable among students. Sponsoring student competitions and projects, establishing partnerships with faculties or individual scientists, and working closely with university career centres and others, are among them.

Use of Professional Social Networks and Work Platforms

Professional social networks and job search platforms are effective means of attracting talented textile engineers (Ollington, Gibb & Harcourt, 2013). LinkedIn is the most famous professional social network and is a good place to attract talent in the textile industry. Regularly posting content on the dedicated company page attracts the attention of potential talented candidates. It can be information about culture, achievements, projects and career opportunities (Constantinov & Mocanu, 2021). Thus, a virtual "showcase" of the company is created to attract the attention of potential candidates.

Along with this, direct job postings on job platforms like LinkedIn, Indeed, and Glassdoor are an excellent working tool. Through them, companies can connect with possible candidates who meet their requirements. The job platforms also allow active networking with potential candidates, commenting on their posts and participating in professional groups and discussions (Rehman & Mazhar, 2016).

The use of professional social networks and job search platforms increases the chances of textile companies to attract the attention of talented textile engineers. The reason is the large scale of attendance of these networks and the presence of potential job candidates who may not be currently looking for work but would consider a well-made offer. There is also an opportunity for direct communication through social networks to establish a quick and effective connection with talented textile engineers (Jue, Marr & Kassotakis, 2009).

Larger and smaller textile brands and companies use LinkedIn actively to post job ads and share information about their projects. Examples of this are Nike, its competitor Adidas, Patagonia, H&M, Levi Strauss & Co. They also actively share information about their sustainability and innovation efforts in the textile industry.

STRATEGIES AND METHODS FOR RETAINING TALENTED ENGINEERS

The success and prospective development of textile companies in the world are impossible without the retention of talented engineers in their workplace. The professional development opportunities, the competitive payment, friendly and inspiring work environment as well as challenging tasks and project developments are among the strategies and methods for retaining the talents "at home".

Providing Opportunities for Professional Development

Providing professional development opportunities is essential to retaining talented engineers in the textile industry. The feeling that the company invests in improving existing skills, and developing new competencies, helps talented engineers to realise their importance to the company (Guo, 2014). As they progress in their careers, of course.

Different channels can be used in this direction. The most common are the organization of various trainings and seminars on current topics and technologies in the textile industry (Cao et al., 2012). These trainings can be internal, local to the company, or external, provided by experts in the field. Examples are workshops on innovations in the textile industry, new materials or production processes, as well as opportunities for the integration of smart technologies. A common example is quality management courses that help engineers understand and apply best practices for quality control and optimization of manufacturing processes.

The opportunity to participate in refresher courses and certifications is another way to ensure professional development. Courses in project management, technology management, and communication skills are common. Professional training is also essential: training in product design and development, working with CAD/CAM systems, statistical processing software, 3D design systems, and more (Nafz et al., 2022). Courses focusing on environmental and sustainable practices in the textile industry, including methods to reduce the carbon footprint, recycling materials, and using biodegradable materials, are particularly relevant (Piwowar-Sulej, 2021). Of course, training for working with new types of machines for spinning, weaving, knitting or assembly, is always relevant.

Teamwork is another means of retaining talented engineers by nurturing their professional development. Companies can offer mentors and mentoring programs where more experienced employees can share their knowledge and experience with their new/younger colleagues. This is an effective way to develop professional career and accelerate professional development (Finkelstein & Poteet, 2007). Providing opportunities to participate in group projects and initiatives, both internal and external to the company, is an important way to develop the skills and knowledge of engineers.

Offering a Competitive Salary and Work Environment

The salary is an important factor in retaining talent. Offering competitive pay, bonuses and other financial incentives is a way to motivate engineers to stay with the company (Msengeti & Obwogi, 2015).

One of the important prerequisites is that companies take into account the average salary for the relevant position. This is particularly important for large markets such as the EU, where the movement of labour is in most cases from countries with lower to higher wages for the same type of work. Both attracting and retaining talented engineers can only be done with competitive salaries (Keller & Meaney, 2017). In addition, bonuses and premiums can be used to achieve goals and results. Thus, engineers are motivated to work hard and achieve excellent results.

Despite the base salary and bonuses, companies can offer various forms of fringe benefits and compensation that are almost mandatory in the corporate world: health insurance, retirement plans, and days off (Dizaho, Salleh, & Abdullah, 2017). Flexible working hours and occasional work from home, while not applicable in the essential part of textile productions, can be a surprising bonus to the work of designers, for example. Supporting work-life balance is important for retaining talent. Any initiative to help engineers manage stress and maintain work-life balance is beneficial.

An important point in retaining talented staff is clarity in determining the salary. Companies with transparent procedures for negotiating remuneration are preferred (Brütt & Yuan, 2022). Thus, employees can express their expectations and agree on adequate remuneration following their skills and contribution to the company. The retention of talented engineers is also closely related to the prospect of career development: the employer can offer a clear structure of the career path, incl. wage growth over time.

Stimulating Projects and Tasks

Having stimulating projects and tasks is a key aspect of a strategy to retain talented engineers. Working with new or leading technologies can be inspiring and beneficial for both parties. Talented young people should be involved in projects to develop new products, improve existing lines or develop innovative technical solutions (Morgan, 2014). Project work usually requires collaboration and synergy between different teams, which is also stimulating for engineers' creativity. In such situations, they actively share knowledge and experience.

Working on customer projects and requirements is an inevitable production task. It may involve developing customized products or solutions. Involving talented engineers in such challenges is an excellent motivation and assessment of their capabilities (Alves et al., 2007). Creativity and innovation can also be manifested in projects to improve the company's technology or production efficiency (Anderson, Potočnik & Zhou, 2014). These projects may include the implementation of new technologies, process automation or workflow optimization, thus motivating them to find solutions to optimize work and increase productivity.

CONCLUSION

In the global textile industry, acquiring and retaining talented engineers requires a comprehensive approach that encompasses a variety of strategies and methods. Companies must offer a stimulating work environment, competitive pay and bonuses, and professional development opportunities to attract and retain the best engineers. Creating interesting and challenging projects and tasks is a key element in motivating engineers, and this can include working in teams, client projects, research projects, and process and efficiency improvement projects.

Furthermore, the introduction of adaptive approaches that take cultural differences into account is essential, as the global textile industry is global in scale and involves diverse cultural contexts. Understanding and respecting different cultural perspectives and practices can foster better understanding and collaboration between teams from different cultural backgrounds, thus supporting the successful acquisition and retention of talented engineers in the industry.

By addressing and accommodating cultural differences, companies in the global textile industry can create an inspiring and innovative work environment. This environment can attract and retain the best talent in the industry, thereby supporting its growth and development on a global scale.

REFERENCES

Abrudan, D., & Conea-Simiuc, I. (2019). How Managers Can Create Happy Working Environment. *Revista de Management Comparat International, 20*(3), 286–296. doi:10.24818/RMCI.2019.3.286

Aldwin, C., & Greenberger, E. (1987). Cultural differences in the predictors of depression. *American Journal of Community Psychology, 15*(6), 789–813. doi:10.1007/BF00919803 PMID:3439551

Alves, C., & De Sousa, J. H. F. S. (2021). Creativity and Innovation to Improve Processes in a Textile Industry. *International Journal of Engineering and Management Sciences, 6*(3). Advance online publication. doi:10.21791/IJEMS.2021.3.7.

Alves, J., Marques, M. J., Saur, I., & Marques, P. (2007). Creativity and innovation through multi-disciplinary and multisectoral cooperation. *Creativity and Innovation Management, 16*(1), 27–34. doi:10.1111/j.1467-8691.2007.00417.x

Amin, A. (2017). An institutionalist perspective on regional economic development. In *Economy* (pp. 59–72). Routledge. doi:10.4324/9781351159203-3

Andersen, P. H. (2005). Relationship marketing and brand involvement of professionals through web-enhanced brand communities: The case of Coloplast. *Industrial Marketing Management, 34*(3), 285–297. doi:10.1016/j.indmarman.2004.07.007

Anderson, N., Potočnik, K., & Zhou, J. (2014). Innovation and creativity in organizations: A state-of-the-science review, prospective commentary, and guiding framework. *Journal of Management, 40*(5), 1297–1333. doi:10.1177/0149206314527128

Angelova, R. A. (2018). Cross-Cultural Management of the European Textile and Clothing Industries: Application of Hofstede's Cultural Dimensions. In Fashion and Textiles: Breakthroughs in Research and Practice (pp. 386-407). IGI Global.

Atkar, A., Pabba, M., Sekhar, S. C., & Sridhar, S. (2021). Current limitations and challenges in the global textile sector. In *Fundamentals of Natural Fibres and Textiles* (pp. 741–764). Woodhead Publishing. doi:10.1016/B978-0-12-821483-1.00004-8

Barrena-Martínez, J., López-Fernández, M., Márquez-Moreno, C., & Romero-Fernández, P. M. (2015). Corporate social responsibility in the process of attracting college graduates. *Corporate Social Responsibility and Environmental Management, 22*(6), 408–423. doi:10.1002/csr.1355

Beecham, S., Baddoo, N., Hall, T., Robinson, H., & Sharp, H. (2008). Motivation in Software Engineering: A systematic literature review. *Information and Software Technology, 50*(9-10), 860–878. doi:10.1016/j.infsof.2007.09.004

Berger, R. (2014). Mastering the art of Jugaad and Guanxi: A western guide to business practices in India and China. [IJABIM]. *International Journal of Asian Business and Information Management, 5*(4), 14–22. doi:10.4018/ijabim.2014100102

Blockley, D. (2020). *Creativity, problem solving, and aesthetics in engineering.* Springer International Publishing. doi:10.1007/978-3-030-38257-5

Bochner, S., & Hesketh, B. (1994). Power distance, individualism/collectivism, and job-related attitudes in a culturally diverse work group. *Journal of Cross-Cultural Psychology*, 25(2), 233–257. doi:10.1177/0022022194252005

Boussemart, B., & De Bandt, J. (1993). The textile industry: widely varying structures. In *Progress in Intercalation Research* (pp. 203–235). Springer Netherlands.

Briscoe, D., Schuler, R., & Tarique, I. (2012). *International human resource management: Policies and practices for multinational enterprises*. Routledge. doi:10.4324/9780203816189

Brophy, S., Klein, S., Portsmore, M., & Rogers, C. (2008). Advancing engineering education in P-12 classrooms. *Journal of Engineering Education*, 97(3), 369–387. doi:10.1002/j.2168-9830.2008.tb00985.x

Brütt, K., & Yuan, H. (2022). *Pitfalls of pay transparency: Evidence from the lab and the field* (No. TI 2022-055/I). Tinbergen Institute Discussion Paper.

Burki, U., & Buvik, A. (2017). Manufacturing complexity and inter-firm coordination: Evidence from the textile-exporting firms of Pakistan. *International Journal of Procurement Management*, 10(2), 227–247. doi:10.1504/IJPM.2017.082790

Cao, J., Huang, L., Xue, Y., & Yi, H. (2012). The Establishment and Practice of Textile Engineering Applied Professionals Training Model. In *Engineering Education and Management: Vol 2, Results of the 2011 International Conference on Engineering Education and Management (ICEEM2011)* (pp. 611-616). Springer Berlin Heidelberg. 10.1007/978-3-642-24820-7_98

Cao, N., Zhang, Z., Man To, K., & Po Ng, K. (2008). How are supply chains coordinated? An empirical observation in textile-apparel businesses. *Journal of Fashion Marketing and Management*, 12(3), 384–397. doi:10.1108/13612020810889326

Coe, N. M., & Yeung, H. W. C. (2015). *Global production networks: Theorizing economic development in an interconnected world*. Oxford University Press. doi:10.1093/acprof:oso/9780198703907.001.0001

Constantinov, C., & Mocanu, M. L. (2021). A comprehensive review of professional network impact on education and career. *Challenges and Applications of Data Analytics in Social Perspectives*, 1-26.

Darwish, A. F. E., & Huber, G. L. (2003). Individualism vs collectivism in different cultures: A cross-cultural study. *Intercultural Education*, 14(1), 47–56. doi:10.1080/1467598032000044647

Delic, A., Vidacek-Hains, V., & Adarve, L. (2011). Perceptions of Multicultural College Students: Case-Studies of European, American and Australian Universities. In *Central European Conference on Information and Intelligent Systems* (p. 89). Faculty of Organization and Informatics Varazdin.

Desore, A., & Narula, S. A. (2018). An overview on corporate response towards sustainability issues in textile industry. *Environment, Development and Sustainability*, 20(4), 1439–1459. doi:10.1007/s10668-017-9949-1

Dizaho, E. K., Salleh, R., & Abdullah, A. (2017). Achieveing Work Life Balance Through Flexible Work Schedules and Arrangements. *Global Business and Management Research*, ●●●, 9.

Esau, K. A. (2010). *The relationship between career development, flexible work arrangements, job roles, and employee engagement within a non-profit organization* (Doctoral dissertation, Argosy University, Tampa).

Fang, Y., & Gopinathan, S. (2009). Teachers and teaching in Eastern and Western schools: A critical review of cross-cultural comparative studies. International handbook of research on teachers and teaching, 557-572.

Finkelstein, L. M., & Poteet, M. L. (2007). Best practices in workplace formal mentoring programs. The Blackwell handbook of mentoring: A multiple perspectives approach, 345-367.

Florea, N. (2010). Linking marketing and human resources recruitment to obtain organizational efficiency. *Management & Marketing-Craiova*, (2), 352–364.

Gaddam, S. (2008). Modeling Employer Branding Communication: The Softer Aspect of HR Marketing Management. *The IUP Journal of Soft Skills*, 2(1).

Gallardo-Gallardo, E. (2018). The meaning of talent in the world of work. *Global talent management*, 33-58.

Guarnieri, P., & Trojan, F. (2019). Decision making on supplier selection based on social, ethical, and environmental criteria: A study in the textile industry. *Resources, Conservation and Recycling, 141*, 347–361. doi:10.1016/j.resconrec.2018.10.023

Guo, S. (2014). Developing effective professional development programs: A case study. *New Library World, 115*(11/12), 542–557. doi:10.1108/NLW-05-2014-0048

Hasanbeigi, A., & Price, L. (2015). A technical review of emerging technologies for energy and water efficiency and pollution reduction in the textile industry. *Journal of Cleaner Production, 95*, 30–44. doi:10.1016/j.jclepro.2015.02.079

He, J., & Sun, L. (2020). Does continuity matter? Developing a new long-term orientation structure in a cross-cultural context: A study on supply chain relationships. *Industrial Marketing Management, 88*, 186–194. doi:10.1016/j.indmarman.2020.05.003

Hofstede, G. (1984). *Culture's consequences: International differences in work-related values* (Vol. 5). Sage.

Hofstede, G. (1996). Gender stereotypes and partner preferences of Asian women in masculine and feminine cultures. *Journal of Cross-Cultural Psychology, 27*(5), 533–546. doi:10.1177/0022022196275003

Hofstede, G. (1998). *Masculinity and femininity: The taboo dimension of national cultures* (Vol. 3). Sage.

Hofstede, G. (2011). Dimensionalizing cultures: The Hofstede model in context. *Online Readings in Psychology and Culture, 2*(1), 8. doi:10.9707/2307-0919.1014

Hofstede, G., Hofstede, G. J., & Minkov, M. (2010). Cultures and Organizations: Software of the Mind. Academic Press.

Huang, C. H. (2022). *Power and Restraint in China's Rise*. Columbia University Press. doi:10.7312/huan20464

Huang, R., Yan, P., & Yang, X. (2021). Knowledge map visualization of technology hotspots and development trends in China's textile manufacturing industry. *IET Collaborative Intelligent Manufacturing*, *3*(3), 243–251. doi:10.1049/cim2.12024

Humphrey, J. D., & Holmes, J. W. (2023). *Style and ethics of communication in science and engineering*. Springer Nature.

Islam, S. (2020). Sustainable raw materials: 50 shades of sustainability. In *Sustainable technologies for fashion and textiles* (pp. 343–357). Woodhead Publishing. doi:10.1016/B978-0-08-102867-4.00015-3

Jackson, C. L., Colquitt, J. A., Wesson, M. J., & Zapata-Phelan, C. P. (2006). Psychological collectivism: A measurement validation and linkage to group member performance. *The Journal of Applied Psychology*, *91*(4), 884–899. doi:10.1037/0021-9010.91.4.884 PMID:16834512

Jue, A. L., Marr, J. A., & Kassotakis, M. E. (2009). *Social media at work: How networking tools propel organizational performance*. John Wiley & Sons.

Keller, S., & Meaney, M. (2017). Attracting and retaining the right talent. McKinsey & Company, 24.

Koch, B. J., & Koch, P. T. (2007). Collectivism, individualism, and outgroup cooperation in a segmented China. *Asia Pacific Journal of Management*, *24*(2), 207–225. doi:10.1007/s10490-006-9004-5

Kreiser, P. M., Marino, L. D., Dickson, P., & Weaver, K. M. (2010). Cultural influences on entrepreneurial orientation: The impact of national culture on risk taking and proactiveness in SMEs. *Entrepreneurship Theory and Practice*, *34*(5), 959–984. doi:10.1111/j.1540-6520.2010.00396.x

Ktoridou, D., Doukanari, E., & Karayiannis, A. (2019, April). Educating the New Generation of Engineering Managers to Stay Relevant in the 21st Century Workforce. In *2019 IEEE Global Engineering Education Conference (EDUCON)* (pp. 1547-1551). IEEE. 10.1109/EDUCON.2019.8725177

Maertz, P. Jr, C., A. Stoeberl, P., & Marks, J. (. (2014). Building successful internships: Lessons from the research for interns, schools, and employers. *Career Development International*, *19*(1), 123–142. doi:10.1108/CDI-03-2013-0025

Mandhanya, Y., & Shah, M. (2010). Employer branding-A tool for talent management. *Global Management Review, 4*(2).

Marginson, S. (2010). Higher education in the global knowledge economy. *Procedia: Social and Behavioral Sciences*, *2*(5), 6962–6980. doi:10.1016/j.sbspro.2010.05.049

Meyer, J. B. (2001). Network approach versus brain drain: Lessons from the diaspora. *International Migration (Geneva, Switzerland)*, *39*(5), 91–110. doi:10.1111/1468-2435.00173

Milton, N., Shadbolt, N., Cottam, H., & Hammersley, M. (1999). Towards a knowledge technology for knowledge management. *International Journal of Human-Computer Studies*, *51*(3), 615–641. doi:10.1006/ijhc.1999.0278

Morgan, J. (2014). *The future of work: Attract new talent, build better leaders, and create a competitive organization*. John Wiley & Sons.

Msengeti, D. M., & Obwogi, J. (2015). *Effects of pay and work environment on employee retention: A study of hotel industry in Mombasa county.* Academic Press.

Nafz, R., Schinle, C., Kaiser, C., & Kyosev, Y. K. (2022). Digital transformation of the textile process chain–state-of-the-art. *Communications in Development and Assembling of Textile Products, 3*(2), 79–89. doi:10.25367/cdatp.2022.3.p79-89

Nyström, J. (2017). *Leadership and Culture: A comparison between Finland and Germany.* Academic Press.

Ollington, N., Gibb, J., & Harcourt, M. (2013). Online social networks: An emergent recruiter tool for attracting and screening. *Personnel Review, 42*(3), 248–265. doi:10.1108/00483481311320390

Park, S., & Lemaire, J. (2011). Culture matters: Long-term orientation and the demand for life insurance. *Asia-Pacific Journal of Risk and Insurance, 5*(2).

Pickles, J., Plank, L., Staritz, C., & Glasmeier, A. (2015). Trade policy and regionalisms in global clothing production networks. *Cambridge Journal of Regions, Economy and Society, 8*(3), 381–402. doi:10.1093/cjres/rsv022

Pieterse, J. N. (2019). *Globalization and culture: Global mélange.* Rowman & Littlefield.

Piwowar-Sulej, K. (2021). Human resources development as an element of sustainable HRM–with the focus on production engineers. *Journal of Cleaner Production, 278,* 124008. doi:10.1016/j.jclepro.2020.124008 PMID:32901179

Potkonjak, V., Gardner, M., Callaghan, V., Mattila, P., Guetl, C., Petrović, V. M., & Jovanović, K. (2016). Virtual laboratories for education in science, technology, and engineering: A review. *Computers & Education, 95,* 309–327. doi:10.1016/j.compedu.2016.02.002

Qu, W. G., & Yang, Z. (2015). The effect of uncertainty avoidance and social trust on supply chain collaboration. *Journal of Business Research, 68*(5), 911–918. doi:10.1016/j.jbusres.2014.09.017

Qureshi, A. (2022). *The World Trade Organization: implementing international trade norms.* Academic Press.

Rehman, S., & Mazhar, S. S. (2016). A Study On New Hiring Strategies To Manage Talent Crisis At Entry Level From The Perspective Of Recruiters And Fresh Graduate Engineer Job Seekers. *International Journal of Research-GRANTHAALAYAH, 4*(9), 14–29. doi:10.29121/granthaalayah.v4.i9.2016.2530

Rodriguez, A. A., Pradhan, P. A., Puttannaiah, K., Das, N., Mondal, K., Sarkar, A., . . . Waggoner, T. (2018, October). A Comprehensive ASAP Framework that uses Career-Steering/Shaping Projects to Train Engineering Students & Develop Critical Life/Professional Skills: Part II–Case Studies from Students Working on Funded Projects. In *2018 IEEE Frontiers in Education Conference (FIE)* (pp. 1-9). IEEE.

Sam, D. L., & Berry, J. W. (2010). Acculturation: When individuals and groups of different cultural backgrounds meet. *Perspectives on Psychological Science, 5*(4), 472–481. doi:10.1177/1745691610373075 PMID:26162193

Saxenian, A. (2002). Transnational communities and the evolution of global production networks: The cases of Taiwan, China and India. *Industry and Innovation*, 9(3), 183–202. doi:10.1080/1366271022000034453

Schäfer, M. (2018). The fourth industrial revolution: How the EU can lead it. *European View*, *17*(1), 5–12. doi:10.1177/1781685818762890

Schweyer, A. (2004). *Talent management systems: Best practices in technology solutions for recruitment, retention and workforce planning*. John Wiley & Sons.

Scott, J. T. (2017). *The sustainable business: A practitioner's guide to achieving long-term profitability and competitiveness*. Routledge. doi:10.4324/9781351276603

Shao, L., Kwok, C. C., & Zhang, R. (2013). National culture and corporate investment. *Journal of International Business Studies*, *44*(7), 745–763. doi:10.1057/jibs.2013.26

Smith, P. (2012). *Lead with a story: A guide to crafting business narratives that captivate, convince, and inspire*. Amacom.

Sokro, E. (2012). Impact of employer branding on employee attraction and retention. *European Journal of Business and Management*, *4*(18), 164–173.

Statista. (2023, April 25). *The World's Biggest Exporters of Clothes*. Retrieved February 8, 2024, from https://www.statista.com/chart/29845/worlds-biggest-exporters-of-clothes/

Statista. (2024). *Top textile exporting countries worldwide 2022*. Retrieved February 8, 2024, from https://www.statista.com/statistics/265064/leading-10-textile-exporters-worldwide-by-country/

Sujansky, J., & Ferri-Reed, J. (2009). *Keeping the Millennials: Why companies are losing billions in turnover to this generation-and what to do about it*. John Wiley & Sons.

Tavanti, M. (2012). The cultural dimensions of Italian leadership: Power distance, uncertainty avoidance and masculinity from an American perspective. *Leadership*, *8*(3), 287–301. doi:10.1177/1742715012441876

Textile Engineering. (2023, February 13). *Top 10 Textile Universities in the World*. Retrieved February 9, 2024, from https://textileengineering.net/top-10-textile-universities-in-the-world/

Ting-Toomey, S., & Dorjee, T. (2018). *Communicating across cultures*. Guilford Publications.

Toprak, T., & Anis, P. (2017). Textile industry's environmental effects and approaching cleaner production and sustainability, an overview. *Journal of Textile Engineering & Fashion Technology*, *2*(4), 429–442. doi:10.15406/jteft.2017.02.00066

Van den Beemt, A., MacLeod, M., Van der Veen, J., Van de Ven, A., Van Baalen, S., Klaassen, R., & Boon, M. (2020). Interdisciplinary engineering education: A review of vision, teaching, and support. *Journal of Engineering Education*, *109*(3), 508–555. doi:10.1002/jee.20347

Venaik, S., Zhu, Y., & Brewer, P. (2013). Looking into the future: Hofstede long term orientation versus GLOBE future orientation. *Cross Cultural Management*, *20*(3), 361–385. doi:10.1108/CCM-02-2012-0014

Vickers, J. N. (2011). Skill acquisition: Designing optimal learning environments. *Performance psychology: A practitioner's guide*, 191-206.

Warner-Søderholm, G. (2012). Culture matters: Norwegian cultural identity within a Scandinavian context. *SAGE Open*, *2*(4), 2158244012471350. doi:10.1177/2158244012471350

Whysall, Z., Owtram, M., & Brittain, S. (2019). The new talent management challenges of Industry 4.0. *Journal of Management Development*, *38*(2), 118–129. doi:10.1108/JMD-06-2018-0181

Wong, S. S., Cross, J. A., & Burton, C. M. (2021). A quantitative analysis of knowledge collaboration enablers for practicing engineers. *Engineering Management Journal*, *33*(3), 174–186. doi:10.1080/10 429247.2020.1780840

Yacout, D. M., & Hassouna, M. S. (2016). Identifying potential environmental impacts of waste handling strategies in textile industry. *Environmental Monitoring and Assessment*, *188*(8), 1–13. doi:10.1007/ s10661-016-5443-8 PMID:27372905

Zagladi, A. N., Hadiwidjojo, D., Rahayu, M., & Noermijati. (2015). The Role of job satisfaction and power distance in determining the influence of organizational justice toward the turnover intention. *Procedia: Social and Behavioral Sciences*, *211*, 42–48. doi:10.1016/j.sbspro.2015.11.007

Zhang, P., Ma, S. G., Zhao, Y. N., & Cao, X. Y. (2023). Analyzing Core Competencies and Correlation Paths of Emerging Engineering Talent in the Construction Industry—An Integrated ISM–MICMAC Approach. *Sustainability (Basel)*, *15*(22), 16011. doi:10.3390/su152216011

Chapter 22
The Soft Power of Talent:
Comparative Analysis of China's Talent Acquisition and Retention Strategies in the Middle East

Mohamad Zreik

https://orcid.org/0000-0002-6812-6529

Sun Yat-sen University, China

ABSTRACT

In the midst of a global competition for talent, it is crucial to grasp China's distinctive strategy for attracting and retaining top talent in countries as culturally and geographically varied as the Middle East and East Asia. This chapter tries to provide a holistic examination of China's talent initiatives, which are a key component of the country's soft power diplomacy and, by extension, its geopolitical impact. This chapter compares and contrasts the ways in which China's southern, eastern, and northern regions handle talent management by analyzing empirical data and case studies. The findings not only provide insight into how soft power techniques may be improved for talent acquisition and retention, but also provide a road map for long-term, cross-cultural HR practices. Talent management in today's geopolitically complicated world can benefit greatly from such new viewpoints, especially as the future of work becomes more globalized and competitive.

1. INTRODUCTION

In today's fast-paced, linked world, a nation's place on the international arena is determined by more than military strength, economic might, and political influence. This is where 'soft power,' a term coined by Joseph Nye, comes into play; it describes a country's ability to influence and sway the opinions of others by allure rather than threat or monetary compensation (Nye, 2008). Culture, diplomacy, ideology, and the ability to attract and keep talented people are all examples of how a country might exert its soft power. When compared to "hard power," which tends to incite hostility and opposition, "soft power" paves the way for countries to form bonds predicated on mutual admiration and respect (Nye, 2021).

DOI: 10.4018/979-8-3693-1938-3.ch022

The globalization of international relations has made the use of soft power increasingly important in the field of talent acquisition and retention. Human capital, or talent, is an invaluable asset that knows no national boundaries. In a worldwide "brain race" that has implications for economic growth and scientific discovery, countries compete for the best and brightest workers, thinkers, entrepreneurs, and academic visionaries (Zweig & Wang, 2013). In this way, countries are able to staff their own projects and initiatives with top-tier talent while simultaneously indirectly influencing the global distribution of skills and experience by employing soft power.

This is especially true in the scientific, medical, financial, and academic communities, where a single discovery can alter the worldwide pecking order (Wang et al., 2020). The availability of talented individuals is now a major factor in determining a country's international standing. Countries can increase their "soft power," or influence over other nations, by becoming centers of global talent (Shambaugh, 2015).

A noteworthy illustration of how soft power and talent management may be integrated to promote geopolitical goals is the rise of China as a global superpower (Zreik, 2023a). China has been able to create an image of opportunity and innovation thanks to the coordination of its educational, cultural, and commercial platforms with its global diplomacy activities (Nye, 2012). Taking into account cultural, historical, and geopolitical differences, the country's initiatives in the Middle East and East Asia demonstrate its flexible and sophisticated approach to global talent management.

The importance of leveraging soft power and attracting top personnel will only grow as we get further into the 21st century. The globe has shrunk to the size of a town, and the winner of the talent war will also control a significant portion of the future (Hall & Pfeiffer, 2013). Therefore, it is vital for both international relations and global human resource management to comprehend how countries like China navigate this complex landscape.

The rise of China as the world's second largest economy is both remarkable and instructive. China's development is characterized not just by its economic and military muscle, but also by its purposeful use of soft power. China's grand geopolitical strategy includes a focus on "talent management," which includes "talent acquisition," "talent development," and "talent retention," as a multifaceted method for expanding China's worldwide influence (Vaiman et al., 2018).

China's strategy for managing its human capital is firmly ingrained in the country's overarching plans and objectives. The country's "Thousand Talents Plan" and "Double First-Class" program demonstrate its aspiration to attract and develop the best and brightest minds in a variety of fields, including research, development, and business (Shambaugh, 2015). These initiatives aren't just about fostering homegrown talent; they're also geared at bringing in foreign expertise, including that of Chinese citizens who have worked abroad. Not only is the economy attractive, but so is China's cultural diversity, technological innovation, and expanding research ecosystems (Parente, Geleilate, & Rong, 2018).

In the realm of international talent acquisition and retention, the concept of 'soft power' extends far beyond the borders of any single nation, encompassing a global landscape where diverse strategies lead to varying degrees of success. A prime example of soft power in action is seen in Canada, known for its welcoming immigration policies and emphasis on cultural diversity, which have collectively positioned it as a hub for international talent, particularly in the technology sector. Canada's approach contrasts yet complement China's, offering a comparative perspective on the use of soft power in talent management.

Canada's Global Skills Strategy, for instance, streamlines visa processing for skilled workers, making it an attractive destination for talent in fields like information technology, green energy, and biotechnology. Cities like Toronto and Vancouver have become melting pots of innovation, drawing experts from around the world, thanks to an environment that not only values diversity but actively integrates it into the socio-economic fabric. The success of this strategy is evident in the growth of Canada's tech sector, which has seen a surge in cutting-edge startups and investment from major global tech companies.

This Canadian example serves as a lens through which we can examine and understand the soft power of talent management from a global perspective. It highlights the effectiveness of inclusive, welcoming policies in attracting international talent, contrasting with China's more strategic and targeted talent acquisition approach. The comparative analysis of these diverse methodologies provides a comprehensive understanding of how nations can leverage their unique attributes to attract and retain the global talent necessary for economic and technological advancement.

China stands out because of its capacity to adapt its talent management tactics to different local conditions. For instance, it might use the Middle East's natural riches and rising aspirations in tech innovation by focusing its operations there on collaborations in the energy and technology industries. Meanwhile, China uses East Asian countries' common cultural and historical ground to boost scholarly and technical collaboration. China's adaptability has allowed it to draw from a wider variety of talent pools and strengthen regional ties, both of which have contributed to the country's soft power.

China's worldwide infrastructure development initiative, the Belt and Road Initiative (BRI), is also a venue for exchanging expertise (Benabdallah, 2019). By employing engineers, planners, and businesspeople from all over the world, China is not only advancing its geopolitical objectives but also engaging in a type of talent diplomacy. China is able to not only import human capital but also incorporate it into the very fabric of its rising global influence because to its complicated, multi-layered strategy towards talent management (Yang & Modell, 2012).

Therefore, China has emerged as a rising powerhouse because to its unique talent management tactics and soft power skills. When it comes to China's global ambitions, talent management is about more than just meeting labor demands or closing skill gaps. The country is a great example of how talent management can be both a byproduct and an instrument of soft power, demonstrating that influencing others is as much about who you know as it is about what you have accomplished (Zweig & Wang, 2013).

Both the Middle East and East Asia bring unique geopolitical and cultural opportunities and threats. China has also made substantial investments in these fields through its diplomatic efforts, economic alliances, and the recruitment of top people (Clinton, 2014). As a result, learning about the unique techniques China employs in these areas can shed light on its grander plans for global influence and soft power.

China's talent management methods in the Middle East and East Asia are being compared primarily to investigate the malleability and versatility of China's soft power techniques. Even while both regions have promising job markets in fields like technology, academia, and energy, they are very distinct from one another culturally, politically, and economically. China's global soft power agenda is multifaceted and nuanced, and studying the country's adaptation of techniques across various contexts could offer further insight into the matter.

These areas are centers of political tension and power struggles on a global scale. The Middle East is a resource-rich region with many competing factions for power, making it a difficult geopolitical riddle (Eibl, 2020). However, East Asia is home to some of the world's most advanced economies and technological powers, like Japan and South Korea (Wong, 2004). Since China's larger geopolitical goals and global adaptability are reflected in its interactions with these regions.

The comparison also provides a useful framework for analyzing the concept of "regional soft power." China's actions present an ideal setting in which to examine the theory that soft power methods may be adapted to meet the needs of different regions. The means China uses to align its talent strategy with its soft power goals are instructive for other countries seeking to do the same. These include educational partnerships, R&D collaborations, and entrepreneurial initiatives (Lahtinen, 2015).

There are implications for global human resource management in the comparative study as well. Learning from China's approach to people management in a variety of cultural and geopolitical settings is important as more and more businesses and organizations go global. Considerations might range from the tactical, like tailoring HR policies and procedures to local circumstances, to the strategic, such ensuring that talent management is in line with overarching business goals.

China's talent management activities in the Middle East and East Asia will be analyzed in detail in the next section. The most important results show that China successfully modifies its strategies to match the cultural, economic, and political conditions of each region. Because of the Middle East's strategic location and abundance of natural resources, China has been investing heavily in the region through educational and technological ties. China, on the other hand, uses its cultural and historical ties to the East Asian region to forge closer partnerships in the fields of education and technology. China's comprehensive comprehension of how soft power dynamics can be fine-tuned for maximum impact is on display in these region-specific measures.

These results have far-reaching implications for the study of international human resource management. How talent management may be effectively woven into larger geopolitical and organizational agendas is demonstrated by China's approach. China's willingness to change and focus on specific regions has much to teach the world in terms of contextualizing HR policies and procedures. It's become abundantly evident that a cookie-cutter strategy is insufficient in today's complex, globalized environment, and this is true across the board: from building incentive packages to crafting organizational culture to strategizing for talent retention. To not only recruit but also retain top-tier talent in today's competitive global landscape, it is essential to understand local customs, connect with regional prospects, and develop strategies accordingly. Therefore, international human resource professionals can learn from China's initiatives and use them as a guide to improve the effectiveness and local relevance of their own talent management plans.

2. CONCEPTUAL FRAMEWORK

2.1. Definition of "Soft Power"

In the late 1980s, political scientist Joseph Nye created the term "soft power" to describe a country's ability to influence other nations without resorting to force or coercion (Nye, 1990). "Soft power," in contrast to "hard power," is the capacity to influence another person's choices and values without resorting to force or economic consequences (Nye, 2008). Cultural relevance, ideological congruence, diplomatic skill, and moral authority are all crucial. There are several manifestations of soft power, including the popularity of a country's culture, values, and political ideas on a global scale; international collaborations in the fields of education and research; and the worldwide impact of a country's media and entertainment (Paradise, 2009).

This chapter defines soft power to include a nation's ability to attract, develop, and retain its human capital as a strategic asset. A country's potential to influence global trends and perceptions improves as it becomes a magnet for talented workers, innovators, and thought leaders. Thus, soft power is not limited to the realm of diplomacy but extends into new areas such as talent management to have a far-reaching impact.

2.2. The Linkage Between Talent Acquisition, Talent Retention, and Soft Power

With the world becoming increasingly interdependent, competition for talent has reached new heights. Countries, like large firms, are always on the lookout for top talent to add to their workforces and further their economic, social, and geopolitical agendas (Shenkar, Luo, & Chi, 2021). This is where soft power and talent acquisition and retention tactics meet, forming a mutually beneficial partnership that increases a country's global clout.

The first stage of these three interrelated processes is talent acquisition. Not only does a country benefit immediately from the addition of highly skilled professionals, scholars, and creatives to its workforce, but it also begins to establish itself as an attractive destination for human potential (Sennett, 2007). This is an example of soft power, the capacity to persuade and influence others without resorting to violence. Examples include innovation centers that attract global firms, fast-track visa programs for talented workers, and scholarships for international students (Robertson, 2013). It is via these channels that a country's soft power flows, shaping the image of the country as a center of opportunity and progress.

The capacity to keep this new talent for the long term, known as talent retention, is also crucial (Iqbal, Guohao, & Akhtar, 2017). A country's soft power is displayed when it fosters communities where its citizens can thrive intellectually, culturally, and socially. Creating environments that encourage innovation, creativity, and individual development is more important than simply providing competitive pay or job prospects (Kagermann, 2014). Strategies for retaining top talent can take many forms, such as facilitating legal permanent residency, investing in local communities, encouraging professional development programs, and providing tax breaks for innovative research and development (Robertson, 2013). Retention of skilled workers is thus a potent indicator of a country's high quality of life, social stability, and general attractiveness, all of which contribute to its soft power.

There are numerous ramifications. First, a country's ability to attract and retain talent has far-reaching consequences. The country's economic, scientific, and cultural development all benefit from the accumulated human capital. Second, a nation that is widely regarded for its talent management techniques gets geopolitical leverage and is better able to bargain for favorable terms when forming international alliances. Finally, a country with a large pool of skilled people can leverage this group to advocate on its behalf internationally, with its soft power increased as a result.

2.3. The Significance of Regional Focus (Middle East and East Asia) in Talent Management

It is impossible to overestimate the significance of concentrating on certain regions in the worldwide search for talent. Talent management techniques need to be adapted to each region's unique set of advantages, disadvantages, and possibilities. For China, a rising giant with global aspirations, this is especially true. China is a great example of how a sophisticated, region-specific approach to talent management may increase soft power and geopolitical influence, since it has focused on two dissimilar but equally important regions: The Middle East and East Asia (Lahtinen, 2015).

The Middle East is rich in oil and gas, among other natural resources, and offers a rare and exciting opportunity. Talent acquisition and partnership opportunities in STEM sectors are especially fruitful in nations like the United Arab Emirates and Saudi Arabia, which are placing a greater emphasis on technology and innovation (Young, 2014). China's strategy here often involves using its technology superiority and investment prowess to create mutually beneficial alliances (Heath & Thompson, 2018). China solidifies its position as a long-term player in the region by investments in education, training, and technical partnerships (Zreik, 2021). This develops a broader, non-economic sort of soft power that can exert longer lasting effect.

In contrast, East Asia is notable for its innovative technologies, thriving economies, and shared cultural values with China (Rozman, 2014). Academic exchanges, research collaborations, and new business starts are all common forms of talent management in this area. China gains access to a large pool of talented individuals and strengthens its ties with its partners via the development of common cultural and historical traditions (Weiming, 2017). This strategy fosters a distinct flavor of soft power, one that is based on shared values, common history, and intellectual exchange.

Having a regional focus in talent management is important because it allows for strategies to be adapted and optimized based on local conditions and opportunities. China's adaptability and insight in today's competitive global economy are on full display in the country's decision to tailor its policies to certain regions. Attracting the finest and brightest is only half the battle; the other half is figuring out how to incorporate this talent into a bigger geopolitical plan by defining what "best and brightest" means in each specific situation (Zhong, 2021).

Additionally, a country can develop a more versatile portfolio of talents, skills, and collaborations by concentrating on different regions. The talent ecosystem in China benefits from the combined efforts of many different regions, each of which brings its own unique set of skills to the table (Li et al., 2019). The country's own path to progress and its standing in the world are both improved by this diversity.

3. HISTORICAL BACKGROUND

3.1. China's Historical Relationships With the Middle East and East Asia

3.1.1. China and the Middle East: A Silk Road Legacy

The historic Silk Road connected China and the Middle East and allowed for the free flow of goods as well as ideas, beliefs, and even religions and technologies (Millward, 2013). Connecting China to ancient Middle Eastern civilizations like the Persians and subsequently the Islamic Caliphates, the Silk Road was an important trade route in antiquity (Rezakhani, 2010). The present Chinese connection with the region is built on this tradition and has expanded from a focus on trade to include political, economic, and cultural contacts (Zreik, 2022).

With China's expanding demand for oil and other natural resources to support its robust economy, the modern era has seen a diversification and deepening of the connection. China's energy security plan relies heavily on countries like Saudi Arabia, Iran, and the United Arab Emirates (Zhao et al., 2019). The resulting increased interdependence across regions is a direct result of Chinese investment in infrastructure projects across the Middle East, many of which fall under the Belt and Road Initiative.

3.1.2. China and East Asia: Proximity and Complexity

The proximity of East Asia to China and the common cultural and historical settings between the two regions make China's connection with East Asia more nuanced (Rozman, 2014). China's history is intricately entangled with that of other countries, including Japan and South Korea (Weiming, 2017).

China's influence spread over East Asia in the form of Confucianism, written characters, and governance styles, and the region was once known as the "Middle Kingdom," or the cultural and intellectual epicenter (Borthwick, 2018). However, the twentieth century was marked by a time of rising tensions and battles, such as the two Sino-Japanese wars and the ideological divide that arose during the Cold War (Chen, 2010).

Economic dependency and sometimes delicate diplomacy have defined the relationship in recent decades. Some of the world's most advanced economies are located in East Asia, and China has taken advantage of this fact. Despite underlying political difficulties that occasionally boil up, trade relations, technical exchanges, and intellectual cooperation remain robust (Dent, 2016).

3.1.3. Synthesis: Historical Context in Modern Interactions

China's modern talent management tactics in the Middle East and East Asia require an appreciation of these antecedent connections. In the Middle East, educational and technological collaborations that recall the Silk Road's heyday are a common way to tell the story of the region's historical connections and mutual benefits. East Asian countries have a more nuanced approach, prioritizing economic and scientific cooperation among a complicated historical and political backdrop.

China uses its longstanding relationships to both regions as a foundation for its contemporary methods of attracting and retaining top personnel. As a result of these longstanding connections, China is able to employ soft power strategies that are uniquely tailored to each area of the world. China's talent management tactics are exceptionally effective and robust because of these long-standing links, which are being used in a variety of ways, from tapping into the high-tech labor market of East Asia to forging educational alliances in the Middle East.

The deep-seated historical connections between China and the Middle East and East Asia are vividly illustrated by the legacy of the ancient Silk Road. This network of trade routes, established more than 2,000 years ago, not only facilitated the exchange of goods like silk and spices but also served as a conduit for cultural and intellectual exchange. A poignant example of this historic intertwining can be seen in the exchange of scientific knowledge and practices between China and the Islamic world during the Golden Age of Islam.

During the Tang dynasty, when the Silk Road was at its zenith, Chinese scholars and traders journeyed to the Middle East, bringing with them knowledge of gunpowder, papermaking, and printing. In return, Middle Eastern innovations in mathematics, astronomy, and medicine traveled back to China, enriching its scientific landscape. One notable instance was the introduction of the astrolabe, an astronomical instrument developed by Islamic scholars, which profoundly influenced Chinese navigation and celestial studies.

This ancient interplay of knowledge and culture set the foundation for modern collaborations. Today, these historical ties have evolved into robust educational and technological partnerships. For example, several Chinese universities have established Confucius Institutes in Middle Eastern countries, promoting not only the Chinese language but also technological and scientific collaboration. In return, Middle

Eastern universities have become centers for the study of China's development model, offering courses and research opportunities focused on Chinese politics, economy, and society.

This enduring connection, from the Silk Road to contemporary educational and technological collaborations, underscores the deep-rooted and evolving nature of China's relationship with these regions. It illustrates how historical ties can be leveraged to foster modern partnerships, a testament to the enduring impact of cultural and intellectual exchanges across centuries.

3.2. Evolution of China's Talent Acquisition and Retention Initiatives

There has been a sea change in China's approach to attracting and retaining top people. Earlier in its contemporary growth, especially in the latter part of the 20th century, China was more frequently considered as an exporter of talent (Scullion & Collings, 2011). There has been a "brain drain" in China since so many students and professionals have left the country in quest of better possibilities (Dodani & LaPorte, 2005).

China, with its booming economy and rising global weight, began taking steps to reverse this tendency around the turn of the 21st century. The "Thousand Talents Plan" was created to entice Chinese citizens who had travelled abroad to return to their home country and put their newly acquired skills and knowledge to good use (Vogel & Ouagrham-Gormley, 2023). These programs provided not just generous compensation packages, but also seed money for new businesses, money for research, and accelerated advancement paths. The goal was quite clear: reverse the brain drain and experience a "brain gain" (Hartley & Jarvis, 2022).

Launched in 2013, China's Belt and Road Initiative (BRI) revolutionized the country's approach to talent management. The BRI, an infrastructure and investment initiative spanning the Middle East and East Asia, among others, necessitated a wide range of professionals with specialized knowledge and experience. China's efforts to achieve its grand strategy shifted from simply retraining its own citizens to also luring top talent from around the world (Benabdallah, 2019).

China has made significant investments in recent years to position itself as a technological and innovative leader on a global scale. Shenzhen, Beijing, and Shanghai are now recognized as global IT centers that draw top professionals in AI, biotech, and clean energy from all over the world (Jolly, 2022). These urban centers offer cutting-edge labs, incubators for new ideas, and supportive government policies to bring in and keep local and global experts (Tang et al., 2021).

China's policies for attracting and retaining top personnel are becoming increasingly region-specific, as seen by the country's tailored approaches to markets in East Asia and the Middle East. China's efforts to manage its talent pool have become increasingly nuanced as a result of this regional focus, making them responsive to the opportunities, difficulties, and demands of certain regions.

China appears to be headed in the direction of developing a more robust ecosystem for talent management. Plans are in the works to make it easier for qualified employees to obtain visas, strengthen educational collaborations with premier universities across the world, and provide even more incentives for the best and brightest in a wide range of areas (Vaiman et al., 2018). The overarching goal of this strategy is to make the entire process of talent identification, evaluation, and eventual assimilation into the Chinese labor and society as smooth as possible for the individuals involved.

The transformation in China's approach to talent acquisition and retention is best illustrated by the evolution and impact of the "Thousand Talents Plan." Initially launched in 2008, this program aimed to reverse the trend of Chinese 'brain drain' by attracting high-level overseas Chinese and foreign experts to contribute to China's development. A prime example of the plan's success is found in Shenzhen's burgeoning technology sector. Consider the story of Dr. Lin Wei, a Chinese-born, US-educated artificial intelligence expert. Dr. Wei, a leading researcher in machine learning, had spent over a decade in Silicon Valley, contributing to significant advancements in AI technologies. In 2012, drawn by the opportunities presented by the Thousand Talents Plan, Dr. Wei decided to return to China, specifically choosing Shenzhen for its dynamic tech environment.

Upon his return, Dr. Wei established an AI research lab in collaboration with Shenzhen University. The lab, initially funded through the Thousand Talents Plan, quickly became a nexus for AI innovation in China. Dr. Wei's team developed a series of groundbreaking AI algorithms that significantly enhanced image recognition technologies, a key component in Shenzhen's smart city initiatives. This contribution not only elevated Shenzhen's status as a global tech hub but also demonstrated China's growing capability in cutting-edge AI research. Moreover, the presence of talents like Dr. Wei attracted further international attention and investment. Major tech corporations, intrigued by the innovations coming out of Shenzhen, began to establish their R&D centers in the city, further consolidating its status as a technology powerhouse.

The impact of Dr. Wei's return and subsequent contributions exemplifies the broader implications of China's strategic approach to talent acquisition and retention. The Thousand Talents Plan not only helped reverse the brain drain but also fostered an environment of innovation and intellectual growth within China. By attracting high-caliber talents like Dr. Wei, China was able to catalyze advancements in key sectors, spurring economic growth and enhancing its global competitiveness. This case also illustrates the importance of aligning talent management strategies with broader economic and developmental goals. Dr. Wei's expertise, coupled with China's focused investment in AI and technology, created a synergy that propelled both the nation's and the individual's aspirations.

3.3. The Rise of China's Global Soft Power Agenda

China spent the majority of the last century tending to its own matters at home, prioritizing domestic reforms and social stability over expanding its global footprint. However, as China rose to prominence on the world stage economically, its leaders realized the value of soft power to supplement the country's expanding military and economic might. Chinese skills were on full display at the 2008 Olympics in Beijing, marking a turning point in the country's rise to global prominence (Giulianotti, 2015).

China's cultural influence has been one of the country's most effective forms of soft power. Confucius Institutes are opening up all over the world to spread Chinese language and culture, while Chinese cinema and television have begun to break into international markets (Zreik, 2021). China has a wide range of cultural exports, from ancient components like Chinese medicine and food to more contemporary elements like pop culture and technical items (Ding & Saunders, 2006).

The Belt and Road Initiative (BRI), which China launched in 2013, is its most extensive use of soft power to date. The BRI is more than just a plan to build infrastructure and invest in countries across Asia, Europe, Africa, and the Middle East; it is also a vehicle for China to strengthen its ties to those regions (Zreik, 2023b). China increases both its hard might and its soft power by helping developing countries with much-needed finance and expertise (Grix & Brannagan, 2016).

China swiftly used technology advancement into its soft power objectives as the world entered the digital age. Companies like Huawei, Alibaba, and Tencent have helped establish China as a global leader in the technology industry (Lundvall & Rikap, 2022). The export of technology, especially in fields like fifth-generation (5G), artificial intelligence (AI), and electronic commerce (e-commerce), has become another channel through which China's soft power influences global norms and tastes (Keane et al., 2020).

China's emphasis on talent acquisition and retention is another part of its growing soft power in a world that places a higher importance on intellectual and creative contributions. China aspires to establish itself as a global hub for innovation and research by offering lucrative salaries, research funding, and access to state-of-the-art facilities to attract the world's best and brightest minds (Hillman, 2020). The influence of China's soft power is increased as these individuals promote the country's advantages (Lahtinen, 2015).

The United Nations, the World Health Organization, and the World Trade Organization are just a few of the international organizations in which China actively participates, all of which help to increase its soft power (Gauttam, Singh, & Kaur, 2020). China presents itself as a responsible global actor by participating in global policymaking and taking on leadership responsibilities. Its latest measures in environmental sustainability, such as carbon neutrality commitments, match with global interests and contribute to its soft power (Qi & Dauvergne, 2022).

The strategic importance of regional focus in China's talent management is exemplified through its collaborative initiatives with Middle Eastern universities, particularly in the STEM (Science, Technology, Engineering, and Mathematics) fields. A prime example of this is the partnership between Tsinghua University in China and King Abdullah University of Science and Technology (KAUST) in Saudi Arabia. This collaboration, established to foster innovation and research in areas such as renewable energy and environmental sciences, reflects a blend of China's technological prowess and the Middle East's rich natural resources and commitment to technological advancement.

Under this joint venture, students and researchers from both institutions engage in exchange programs, working on projects that address regional and global challenges like water scarcity and sustainable energy solutions. One notable outcome of this collaboration is the development of a novel solar-powered water desalination technique, which has the potential to significantly benefit arid regions in both China and the Middle East. This technology not only showcases the innovative capabilities of the joint team but also addresses a critical environmental challenge common to both regions.

This partnership extends beyond research and development; it also includes the establishment of innovation hubs and incubators to nurture future talent in the STEM fields. These hubs provide students and young professionals from both China and the Middle East with the resources, mentorship, and network to transform their ideas into viable solutions and start-ups. The success of the Tsinghua-KAUST collaboration underscores the importance of regionally focused talent management strategies. It highlights how tailored approaches, which consider the unique strengths and needs of each region, can lead to significant breakthroughs in research and development, while also nurturing a new generation of global talent equipped to handle the challenges of a rapidly changing world.

4. REGIONAL APPROACHES TO TALENT MANAGEMENT

4.1. Southern China

Talent programs focused at attracting and keeping technology and entrepreneurial talents have become a hot topic in southern China, particularly in regions like Guangdong and its pioneering metropolis Shenzhen (Gu et al., 2020). These regions are not just the driving forces behind China's economic growth, but also the incubators for new ideas and businesses. They are a special combination of government support, market forces, and private initiative that foster a thriving environment for creative problem solving (Wang & Bao, 2015).

Talent management in Guangdong and Shenzhen is fascinating in part because of the ways in which technological and entrepreneurial pursuits are intertwined there. Consider the city of Shenzhen as an illustration. A large number of engineers, data scientists, and tech aficionados have relocated to the city during the past two decades, helping it become a center of technological innovation (Lindtner & Lin, 2017). However, this technical knowledge is only a piece of the puzzle. Shenzhen's distinguishing feature is the city's pervasive spirit of enterprise. It's a hub for technological innovation, providing its residents with not only the means to develop their skills but also the venues in which to commercialize them (Stevens, 2019).

Here, Guangdong's overarching strategy becomes relevant. Because of Guangdong's pioneering role in China's economic reforms, the province's policies and frameworks are a good fit for the dynamic city of Shenzhen. Industrial parks and hubs of innovation in various fields, including as green technology, artificial intelligence development, and software engineering, may be found all around the province (Xue et al., 2022). There is a remarkable efficiency to the cycle of conception, development, and commercialization made possible by the presence of these specialized zones, which allow for a smooth transfer from technological invention to entrepreneurial execution.

The dynamic between the many players is the real engine that drives these changes. The government, the academic community, and the business sector have all worked together to foster an environment where exceptional individuals can thrive. As an example, universities in Guangdong have taken the initiative to adapt their coursework to the needs of the local economy (Huang & Tsai, 2021). On the other side, Shenzhen has seen a rise in the number of venture capital firms that are prepared to put their money into potential new businesses and offer them both financial backing and expert business advice (Pan, Zhao, & Wójcik, 2016).

Technological and entrepreneurial abilities find a supportive community in which to develop professionally and make meaningful contributions to economic and social goals. The case studies of Guangdong and Shenzhen provide useful information for optimizing regional plans in order to foster the kinds of environments where technological innovation and entrepreneurial zeal can flourish. They are models for how regions might focus on developing a specific type of talent and give that talent opportunities for sustained growth and widespread effect.

4.2. Eastern China

Shanghai, the financial center of Eastern China, and Jiangsu, an educational powerhouse, offer a distinctly different but no less fascinating narrative in China's talent strategy (Cheung, Chung, & Lin, 2016). It's true that southern provinces like Guangdong and Shenzhen are leading lights in IT and entrepreneurship, but northern provinces like Shanghai and Jiangsu have carved out their own unique markets in banking and education (Zhaojin, 2016).

Shanghai is China's financial center, on par with New York City and London (Wójcik et al., 2019). The city's skyscrapers attract a global pool of financial experts who conduct business, create new products and services, and influence China's and the world's economies. Intentional changes to regulations, creation of incentive programs, and the launch of new financial institutions have all contributed to this global melting pot (Liang et al., 2016). Therefore, Shanghai has gathered a pool of experts in the fields of investment banking, asset management, and financial technology, giving rise to a thriving and ever-evolving ecosystem.

Jiangsu, home to major cities like Nanjing and Suzhou, on the other hand, has made education one of its top priorities. Many of China's top educational and scientific institutes are located in this region (Ye et al., 2017). Not only have these institutions become magnets for bright minds, but they have also become testing grounds for new approaches to education. Jiangsu has become a hub for the development of innovative approaches to curricular planning, pedagogical study, and tech-enhanced learning. The province has made tremendous efforts to integrate its educational institutions into local communities and international educational movements (Zhou, 2021).

Attracting and retaining specialized individuals in fields with far-reaching ramifications for China's national development goals is what makes the talent initiatives in Shanghai and Jiangsu particularly exciting. Shanghai's financial experts are not simply helping the city prosper; they are also shaping national and international financial policy and instrument. Just as the quality of a country's human capital is essential to its long-term prosperity, so too are the educational skills in Jiangsu essential to pushing that quality in China.

Strategic policymaking and investment led to the emergence of a mutually beneficial relationship between these areas and the talents they had in demand. Shanghai has a strong regulatory environment that encourages financial innovation and a cosmopolitan atmosphere that attracts top financial talent (Liang et al., 2016). Jiangsu, on the other hand, has used its educational relevance and history to become known as a hub for research and development in the field of education (Zhou et al., 2021).

Shanghai and Jiangsu's specialized approaches teach us about how to target certain industries while yet incorporating regional differences into a national talent plan. They show that different regions have different types of talent, but that the ideas of building hospitable ecosystems, coordinating the efforts of many different parties, and making a direct impact on the achievement of overarching strategic goals are universal. The sophistication and success of China's personnel management programs may be seen in their multifaceted yet cohesive approach.

4.3. Northern China

Beijing and Tianjin, two of Northern China's most prominent cities, add another layer of complexity to China's already rich tapestry of talent management techniques. Beijing and Tianjin have carved out their own niche by cultivating political and cultural skills, just like Guangdong and Shenzhen are known for their technological and entrepreneurial vigor and Shanghai and Jiangsu are known for their financial and educational savvy (Li & Jonas, 2023).

Beijing, as the political center of China, attracts people who want to make a difference in the country's policymaking, diplomatic, and governing processes. Policy innovation and political conversation are fostered through the region's many nongovernmental organizations (NGOs), academic institutions, and think tanks (Xue, Zhu, & Han, 2018). Beijing's approach to talent stands out because of its emphasis on integrating heritage with modernity (Zeng et al., 2020). There is a clear appreciation for China's traditional approaches to government, but also a palpable readiness to change in the face of new difficulties. The city's outlook is seen in the types of people it attracts: thinkers steeped in Chinese political philosophy but interested in international affairs.

Tianjin, on the other hand, has emerged as a hub for creatives despite its proximity to Beijing. Tianjin may not have the global recognition of Beijing, but it does have a thriving cultural scene with a wide range of artistic expressions (Keane, 2013). Many cultural festivals, exhibitions, and events have been held in the city over the years, attracting artists, writers, and performers from all over China and the world. Investment in Tianjin's cultural institutions, art schools, and creative spaces has come from both the public and private sectors, providing a stage for the city's budding artists (Keane & Chen, 2019).

Beijing and Tianjin's talent efforts are richer than may be seen through the narrow lens of either city's particular expertise. What binds these urban centers together is their recognition of the inextricable connection between a nation's political and cultural talents. Artists and creatives in Tianjin actively participate in conversations regarding the city's development and governance, while policymakers in Beijing frequently contact cultural specialists to understand the societal repercussions of their actions (Keane, 2013).

Northern China, led by Beijing and Tianjin, highlights the need for skilled individuals who can negotiate China's political and cultural landscape. These metropolitan areas demonstrate the potential for holistic talent development when policymakers prioritize the requirements of the country as a whole. Together with Southern and Eastern China, they form a trio that sheds light on how sophisticated China's talent acquisition and retention strategies are.

The adaptability and emphasis on personal growth are what make this method so brilliant. China is developing a wide range of experts across the country, from technologists in the south to bankers in the east to policy-makers and artists in the north (Gallagher, 2014). This demonstrates a broad and nuanced national plan. Beijing and Tianjin's efforts are illustrative of how developing expertise in the fields of politics and culture can advance national goals and strengthen the country's standing abroad in a world where talent is increasingly prized.

5. COMPARATIVE ANALYSIS: MIDDLE EAST

The United Arab Emirates (UAE) and Saudi Arabia, two prominent Middle Eastern nations, will be singled out for this comparative research because of their demonstrable interest in China's talent efforts. These nations are not only the economic and political backbones of the Middle East, but they are also examples of how hungry the area is to join international talent pools, especially those affected by China.

China's move to attract and retain top talent in the Middle East is a complex one, influenced by regional customs and international politics. China's involvement is, on the one hand, culturally harmonious because of similar values and longstanding trading connections (Zreik, 2021). However, China's talent strategy in the region is made more complicated by geopolitical variables such as energy resources, political alliances, and economic investments (Eibl, 2020).

Such a huge infrastructure and investment project as China's Belt and Road Initiative (BRI) has a significant impact on talent development programs in the Middle East (Hoh, 2019). Incorporating talent exchange into larger geopolitical goals, China often sends engineers and project managers to the United Arab Emirates and Saudi Arabia to work on projects related to the BRI (Fulton, 2020). This talent exchange is more likely to succeed in the long run if participants are aware of and respectful of local cultures and diplomatic etiquette.

China's collaborations in higher education and research have made a significant impact on the UAE's educational scene. Several UAE universities have begun collaborative initiatives with their Chinese counterparts in the form of joint degree programs, research initiatives, and student exchanges (Zhao,

2021). Importing Chinese teachers has helped raise the profile of STEM disciplines like engineering and computer science in the United Arab Emirates (Aydarova, 2013).

A distinct but no less intriguing scenario unfolds in Saudi Arabia. Here, China's impact on technology is more obvious, especially in fields like alternative energy, telecommunications, and AI (Fulton, 2020). As part of its Vision 2030 ambition to diversify the economy and lessen reliance on oil exports, Saudi Arabia is actively recruiting Chinese experts in these fields (Yamada, 2023). Chinese experts in technology help Saudi Arabia speed up its ambitious development plans.

China's talent programs have found common ground with those of the United Arab Emirates and Saudi Arabia through a convergence of shared values, mutual respect, and pragmatic foreign policy. By adapting its talent policies to the unique characteristics of each region, China is able to not only increase the effectiveness of its soft power but also create long-lasting partnerships that support its diplomatic and economic goals. This serves as an example of how a country's foreign relations can have a significant impact on its ability to attract and retain top people, offering lessons for effective global talent management in today's linked world.

6. COMPARATIVE ANALYSIS: EAST ASIA

Two countries in East Asia, South Korea and Japan, deserve special consideration when considering China's talent ambitions. While these countries share many cultural and historical affinities with China, their geopolitical and economic profiles couldn't be more different. South Korea and Japan, as close neighbors with centuries of historical ties, provide interesting contexts in which to study the flexibility and influence of China's talent policies.

China's approach to talent management in South Korea and Japan is shaped by different geopolitical pressures, despite the fact that the two countries share cultural similarities including Confucian principles and a common historical narrative (Buzan & Goh, 2020). China's policies strike a careful balance between respecting the similarities between countries and adjusting to their unique geopolitical situations. This duality is made clear when we look at the foci in question: cultural exchanges with Japan and research and development collaborations with South Korea (Chun, 2017).

When it comes to South Korea, the field of research and development (R&D) has been a hotspot for the sharing of expertise. China has put a lot of money into joint R&D projects with South Korea because of the country's technological and innovative prowess, especially in the fields of semiconductors, bioengineering, and green technology (Walcott, 2017). Mutual dedication to technological advancement is at the heart of these partnerships. In a virtuous cycle, South Korean talent is expanding its horizons in China's burgeoning digital economy, while Chinese talent is enriching Korea's innovative ecosystem (Rozman, 2014).

In Japan, however, the emphasis shifts to the mutual appreciation of other cultures. The genuine richness of talent exchange has been more obvious in cultural sectors, like the arts, language studies, and even gastronomic exchanges, even though technical cooperation do exist. Artists and traditional craftspeople from Japan have found a receptive audience in China (Brandt, 2007). On the flip side, Japanese audiences have been captivated by Chinese authors and philosophers (Suzuki, 2019). Both countries benefit from this exchange of ideas, and the improved understanding and appreciation that results is a powerful diplomatic soft power tool.

China's talent management policies in East Asia are an example of the country's strategic acumen and its capacity to be a good neighbor. China has adapted its talent efforts to provide mutual benefits by taking into account the respective capabilities and needs of each country involved, such as South Korea's technological innovation and Japan's rich cultural legacy. China's adaptability and holistic approach to foreign talent acquisition and retention are on display in the case studies from South Korea and Japan, which show how talent management techniques can accommodate cultural similarities and geopolitical complexities.

Not only as an HR function, but also as an essential part of international diplomacy and cooperation, the success of these programs in East Asia demonstrates the transformative power of well-designed talent strategies.

7. COMPARATIVE ANALYSIS: MIDDLE EAST VS. EAST ASIA

China's approach to talent management methods in the Middle East and East Asia demonstrates both similarity and difference, indicating a complex matrix of factors beyond sheer proximity. China's approach to both regions, at a high level, has a lot in common because of how flexible and adaptable it is. China has a remarkable knack for adapting its talent policies to the specific requirements of various countries, such as the United Arab Emirates and South Korea.

But the distinctions are just as illuminating. Practical issues like energy security and political alliances have a huge impact on China's talent programs in the Middle East, which are generally implemented within wider geopolitical frameworks like the Belt and Road Initiative. East Asian methods, on the other hand, appear to be influenced more by shared cultural heritage and the economic rewards of trade and other forms of cooperation.

China's endeavors to cultivate talent in the Middle East have been shaped in unique ways by the region's religious and cultural traditions (Fulton, 2020). China treads cautiously in areas like education and technology because the largely Islamic countries in the region have distinct norms and beliefs. Educational exchanges and joint research often involve cultural and religious sensitivity, demonstrating an emphasis on tolerance and understanding for one another.

Talent management solutions in East Asia appear to be implemented against a cultural backdrop of shared historical narratives and Confucian principles (Weiming, 2017). In fields that reflect traditional East Asian values, such as academic brilliance and technical innovation, there is frequently a more natural exchange of talent because of the shared cultural background.

However, both regions are being overshadowed by geopolitical concerns. The delicate nature of the talent exchange is heightened in the Middle East due to the intricate network of alliances, wars, and power struggles that permeate the region. Given the global ramifications of its agreements with countries like Saudi Arabia and the United Arab Emirates, China must tread carefully in its interpersonal dealings. Regional competition in East Asia, especially in technological and commercial spheres, is a common manifestation of geopolitical concerns. In this context, talent initiatives are used not just to attract and keep top employees, but also to cement the company's position as a leader in the region.

8. KEY FINDINGS

The speed with which China has adapted its talent management tactics to meet local demands stands out as one of the study's most interesting discoveries. Focusing on industries like engineering and project management that are directly related to infrastructure and development projects, China has carefully weaved its talent efforts into bigger geopolitical frameworks like the Belt and Road Initiative in the Middle East. This exemplifies a holistic strategy to soft power, which integrates talent strategies with diplomatic and economic goals.

China displays a special kind of finesse in the East Asian region. Its strategies are still in line with larger national goals, but the emphasis is on culture and academia, which reflects the commonalities in the past and present of China, South Korea, and Japan. China's R&D collaborations in South Korea and cultural interactions with Japan are focused on areas that not only benefit from but also deeply resonate with the respective cultures.

China's talent programs in these locations provide instructive examples of how to increase soft power through strategic talent management in a competitive global environment. First, there is no way to adequately stress the significance of a focused, detailed strategy. China's capacity to adapt its talent tactics to varied regional cultural and political contexts highlights the need of learning about and respecting such contexts.

Second, it is essential that talent efforts be in sync with larger geopolitical or national goals. China's talent management isn't just an HR duty; it's also an integral part of the country's diplomatic efforts, helping to expand its global sway. This multi-pronged strategy gives talent initiatives more clout and helps them advance a variety of goals, from diplomatic ties to business collaborations.

To sum up, every talent program aiming at boosting soft power should prioritize the value of mutual benefit. The best talent strategies offer mutual benefits, such as helping advance technology in South Korea or increasing awareness of Japanese culture. By making sure that everyone involved in a talent exchange benefits, China strengthens its bonds and boosts its standing as an influential power on the international stage.

9. IMPLICATIONS AND RECOMMENDATIONS

Talent management may be a very powerful tactic in soft power diplomacy, as the instance of China's talent efforts in the Middle East and East Asia shows. One implication for other countries is that improving diplomatic relations and national interests through talent management that is tailored to a given region is possible. The importance of soft power, especially in the form of talent acquisition and retention, cannot be overstated in a geopolitical setting where hard power often fails to solve complicated issues satisfactorily. Crafting talent strategies that are both culturally sensitive and strategically integrated with broader national and regional goals is essential for countries seeking to improve their global status.

The importance of mutual benefit in international relations is also highlighted. Relationships can be strengthened and long-term trust can be built through talent efforts that benefit both parties. Countries might foster this by organizing mutually beneficial exchange programs, research collaborations, and vocational training programs.

In light of these findings, numerous suggestions are made for companies and nations that want to become leaders in cross-cultural HR policies and procedures. To begin, it is not a luxury but a need to have a firm grasp of cultural nuances. To help steer their personnel management strategy, companies should invest in cultural sensitivity training and either recruit or consult with experts knowledgeable with the targeted locations.

Second, companies are no different from countries when it comes to the importance of connecting talent programs with overarching goals. Whether the overarching objective is to expand into new markets, encourage creative problem-solving, or build a stronger brand image, talent management should be viewed as a strategic function. Thus, HR should collaborate closely with strategy or policy teams to achieve harmony.

Finally, flexibility is a must. Even if two countries or regions share many characteristics, what works in one may not in the other. Therefore, long-term strategies should be malleable enough to adjust to shifting geopolitical and economic environments as well as advances in technology. Organizations may maintain their responsiveness and effectiveness in today's fast-paced global economy by regularly reviewing and updating their talent management strategies.

10. CONCLUSION

Given the linked and complicated nature of the modern world, talent management has emerged as an essential facet of foreign policy and soft power diplomacy. The focus of this chapter has been on China's unique talent initiatives in the Middle East and East Asia, illuminating how a country can use a complex, comprehensive approach to talent management to bolster diplomatic ties, mutual advantages, and international status.

This research shows that China's strategies are highly varied. Instead, they are developed with the local cultural, economic, and political situations in mind. China's talent management acts as a strategic tool that is both adaptable and directive, from the political nerve centers of Beijing and Tianjin in the north to the tech hubs of Shenzhen and Guangdong in the south; from the educational and technological sectors in the Middle East to R&D and cultural exchanges in East Asia.

Beyond the scope of Chinese endeavors, this research has far-reaching ramifications. The major learnings stress the importance of a culturally sensitive, strategically aligned, and adaptive approach to people management for countries and organizations around the world. As the nature of work changes around the world, these guidelines provide a road map for attracting and maintaining top people, as well as for using human resources as a strategic asset.

Finally, in terms of international sway, talent management represents a vast untapped resource. As we negotiate the complexities of contemporary geopolitics, this soft power approach offers a balanced blend of cultural appreciation, mutual gain, and strategic alignment, thereby creating fresh opportunities for diplomatic ties and global cooperation. China's experiences provide us vital lessons about how soft power and talent management may work together to establish a world in which collaboration and mutual respect are prioritized.

REFERENCES

Aydarova, O. (2013). If not "the best of the West," then "look East" Imported teacher education curricula in the Arabian Gulf. *Journal of Studies in International Education, 17*(3), 284–302. doi:10.1177/1028315312453742

Benabdallah, L. (2019). Contesting the international order by integrating it: The case of China's Belt and Road initiative. *Third World Quarterly, 40*(1), 92–108. doi:10.1080/01436597.2018.1529539

Borthwick, M. (2018). *Pacific century: The emergence of modern Pacific Asia.* Routledge. doi:10.4324/9780429494895

Brandt, K. (2007). *Kingdom of Beauty: Mingei and the politics of folk art in Imperial Japan.* Duke University Press.

Buzan, B., & Goh, E. (2020). *Rethinking Sino-Japanese alienation: history problems and historical opportunities.* Oxford University Press. doi:10.1093/oso/9780198851387.001.0001

Chen, J. (2010). *Mao's China and the cold war.* University of North Carolina Press.

Cheung, P. T., Chung, J. H., & Lin, Z. (2016). *Provincial strategies of economic reform in Post-Mao China: leadership, politics, and implementation.* Routledge.

Chun, A. (2017). *Forget Chineseness: On the geopolitics of cultural identification.* Suny Press. doi:10.1515/9781438464732

Clinton, H. R. (2014). *Hard choices.* Simon and Schuster.

Dent, C. M. (2016). *East Asian Regionalism.* Routledge. doi:10.4324/9781315717258

Ding, S., & Saunders, R. A. (2006). Talking up China: An analysis of China's rising cultural power and global promotion of the Chinese language. *East Asia (Piscataway, N.J.), 23*(2), 3–33. doi:10.1007/s12140-006-0021-2

Dodani, S., & LaPorte, R. E. (2005). Brain drain from developing countries: How can brain drain be converted into wisdom gain? *Journal of the Royal Society of Medicine, 98*(11), 487–491. doi:10.1177/014107680509801107 PMID:16260795

Eibl, F. (2020). *Social dictatorships: The political economy of the welfare state in the Middle East and North Africa.* Oxford University Press. doi:10.1093/oso/9780198834274.001.0001

Fulton, J. (2020). China-Saudi Arabia Relations Through the '1+ 2+ 3' Cooperation Pattern. *Asian Journal of Middle Eastern and Islamic Studies, 14*(4), 516–527. doi:10.1080/25765949.2020.1841991

Gallagher, K. S. (2014). *The globalization of clean energy technology: Lessons from China.* MIT press. doi:10.7551/mitpress/9805.001.0001

Gauttam, P., Singh, B., & Kaur, J. (2020). COVID-19 and Chinese global health diplomacy: Geopolitical opportunity for China's hegemony? *Millennial Asia, 11*(3), 318–340. doi:10.1177/0976399620959771

Giulianotti, R. (2015). The Beijing 2008 Olympics: Examining the interrelations of China, globalization, and soft power. *European Review (Chichester, England)*, *23*(2), 286–296. doi:10.1017/S1062798714000684

Grix, J., & Brannagan, P. M. (2016). Of mechanisms and myths: Conceptualising states'"soft power" strategies through sports mega-events. *Diplomacy and Statecraft*, *27*(2), 251–272. doi:10.1080/09592296.2016.1169791

Gu, H., Meng, X., Shen, T., & Wen, L. (2020). China's highly educated talents in 2015: Patterns, determinants and spatial spillover effects. *Applied Spatial Analysis and Policy*, *13*(3), 631–648. doi:10.1007/s12061-019-09322-6

Hall, P., & Pfeiffer, U. (2013). *Urban future 21: a global agenda for twenty-first century cities*. Routledge. doi:10.4324/9781315011523

Hartley, K., & Jarvis, D. S. (2022). Let nine universities blossom: Opportunities and constraints on the development of higher education in China. *Higher Education Research & Development*, *41*(5), 1542–1556. doi:10.1080/07294360.2021.1915963

Heath, T. R., & Thompson, W. R. (2018). Avoiding US-China competition is futile: Why the best option is to manage strategic rivalry. *Asia Policy*, *13*(2), 91–120. doi:10.1353/asp.2018.0027

Hillman, J. E. (2020). *The emperor's new road: China and the project of the century*. Yale University Press.

Hoh, A. (2019). China's belt and road initiative in Central Asia and the Middle East. *Domes*, *28*(2), 241–276. doi:10.1111/dome.12191

Huang, J., & Tsai, K. S. (2021). Upgrading Big Brother: Local Strategic Adaptation in China's Security Industry. *Studies in Comparative International Development*, *56*(4), 560–587. doi:10.1007/s12116-021-09342-9 PMID:34629564

Iqbal, S., Guohao, L., & Akhtar, S. (2017). Effects of job organizational culture, benefits, salary on job satisfaction ultimately affecting employee retention. *Review of Public Administration and Management*, *5*(3), 1–7. doi:10.4172/2315-7844.1000229

Jolly, D. (2022). The Chinese national system of innovation. In *The New Threat: China's Rapid Technological Transformation* (pp. 29–57). Springer International Publishing. doi:10.1007/978-3-031-08690-8_3

Kagermann, H. (2014). Change through digitization—Value creation in the age of Industry 4.0. In *Management of permanent change* (pp. 23–45). Springer Fachmedien Wiesbaden.

Keane, M. (2013). *China's new creative clusters: Governance, human capital and investment*. Routledge. doi:10.4324/9780203124505

Keane, M., & Chen, Y. (2019). Entrepreneurial solutionism, characteristic cultural industries and the Chinese dream. *International Journal of Cultural Policy*, *25*(6), 743–755.

Keane, M., Yu, H., Zhao, E. J., & Leong, S. (2020). *Chinas digital presence in the asia-pacific: Culture, technology and platforms*. Anthem Press. doi:10.2307/j.ctv20pxxzt

Lahtinen, A. (2015). China's soft power: Challenges of Confucianism and Confucius Institutes. *Journal of Comparative Asian Development*, *14*(2), 200–226. doi:10.1080/15339114.2015.1059055

Li, L., Du, K., Zhang, W., & Mao, J. Y. (2019). Poverty alleviation through government-led e-commerce development in rural China: An activity theory perspective. *Information Systems Journal, 29*(4), 914–952. doi:10.1111/isj.12199

Li, Y., & Jonas, A. E. (2023). Small cities and towns in global city-centred regionalism: Observations from Beijing-Tianjin-Hebei region, China. *Transactions in Planning and Urban Research, 2*(1), 103–114. doi:10.1177/27541223231157225

Liang, X., Kidwai, H., Zhang, M., & Zhang, Y. (2016). *How Shanghai does it: Insights and lessons from the highest-ranking education system in the world.* World Bank Publications. doi:10.1596/978-1-4648-0790-9

Lindtner, S., & Lin, C. (2017). Making and its promises. *CoDesign, 13*(2), 70–82. doi:10.1080/15710882.2017.1308518

Lundvall, B. Å., & Rikap, C. (2022). China's catching-up in artificial intelligence seen as a co-evolution of corporate and national innovation systems. *Research Policy, 51*(1), 104395. doi:10.1016/j.respol.2021.104395

Millward, J. A. (2013). *The Silk Road: A very short introduction.* Oxford University Press. doi:10.1093/actrade/9780199782864.001.0001

Nye, J. S. (1990). Soft power. *Foreign Policy, 80*(80), 153–171. doi:10.2307/1148580

Nye, J. S. Jr. (2008). Public diplomacy and soft power. *The Annals of the American Academy of Political and Social Science, 616*(1), 94–109. doi:10.1177/0002716207311699

Nye, J. S. (2012). China and soft power. *South African Journal of International Affairs, 19*(2), 151–155. doi:10.1080/10220461.2012.706889

Nye, J. S. (2021). Soft power: The evolution of a concept. *Journal of Political Power, 14*(1), 196–208. doi:10.1080/2158379X.2021.1879572

Pan, F., Zhao, S. X., & Wójcik, D. (2016). The rise of venture capital centres in China: A spatial and network analysis. *Geoforum, 75*, 148–158. doi:10.1016/j.geoforum.2016.07.013

Paradise, J. F. (2009). China and international harmony: The role of Confucius Institutes in bolstering Beijing's soft power. *Asian Survey, 49*(4), 647–669. doi:10.1525/as.2009.49.4.647

Parente, R. C., Geleilate, J. M. G., & Rong, K. (2018). The sharing economy globalization phenomenon: A research agenda. *Journal of International Management, 24*(1), 52–64. doi:10.1016/j.intman.2017.10.001

Qi, J. J., & Dauvergne, P. (2022). China's rising influence on climate governance: Forging a path for the global South. *Global Environmental Change, 73*, 102484. doi:10.1016/j.gloenvcha.2022.102484

Rezakhani, K. (2010). The road that never was: The Silk Road and trans-Eurasian exchange. *Comparative Studies of South Asia, Africa and the Middle East, 30*(3), 420–433. doi:10.1215/1089201X-2010-025

Robertson, S. (2013). *Transnational student-migrants and the state: The education-migration nexus.* Springer. doi:10.1057/9781137267085

Rozman, G. (Ed.). (2014). *The East Asian region: Confucian heritage and its modern adaptation* (Vol. 1179). Princeton University Press.

Scullion, H., & Collings, D. G. (2011). Global talent management: Introduction. In *Global talent management* (pp. 19–32). Routledge. doi:10.4324/9780203865682

Sennett, R. (2007). *The culture of the new capitalism.* Yale University Press.

Shambaugh, D. (2015). China's soft-power push: The search for respect. *Foreign Affairs, 94*(4), 99–107.

Shenkar, O., Luo, Y., & Chi, T. (2021). *International business.* Routledge. doi:10.4324/9781003034315

Stevens, H. (2019). The quotidian labour of high tech: Innovation and ordinary work in Shenzhen. *Science, Technology & Society, 24*(2), 218–236. doi:10.1177/0971721819841997

Suzuki, D. T. (2019). *Zen and Japanese culture* (Vol. 334). Princeton University Press. doi:10.2307/j.ctvc77449

Tang, M., Walsh, G. S., Li, C., & Baskaran, A. (2021). Exploring technology business incubators and their business incubation models: Case studies from China. *The Journal of Technology Transfer, 46*(1), 90–116. doi:10.1007/s10961-019-09759-4

Vaiman, V., Sparrow, P., Schuler, R., & Collings, D. G. (Eds.). (2018). *Macro talent management in emerging and emergent markets: A global perspective.* Routledge. doi:10.4324/9780429469527

Vogel, K. M., & Ouagrham-Gormley, S. B. (2023). Scientists as spies?: Assessing US claims about the security threat posed by China's Thousand Talents Program for the US life sciences. *Politics and the Life Sciences, 42*(1), 32–64. doi:10.1017/pls.2022.13 PMID:37140223

Walcott, S. M. (2017). *Chinese science and technology industrial parks.* Routledge. doi:10.4324/9781315198170

Wang, H., & Bao, Y. (2015). *Reverse migration in contemporary China: Returnees, entrepreneurship and the Chinese economy.* Springer. doi:10.1057/9781137450609

Wang, K., Shen, Z., Huang, C., Wu, C. H., Dong, Y., & Kanakia, A. (2020). Microsoft academic graph: When experts are not enough. *Quantitative Science Studies, 1*(1), 396–413. doi:10.1162/qss_a_00021

Weiming, T. (2017). Implications of the rise of "Confucian" East Asia. In Multiple modernities (pp. 195-218). Routledge. doi:10.4324/9781315124872-8

Wójcik, D., Pažitka, V., Knight, E., & O'Neill, P. (2019). Investment banking centres since the global financial crisis: New typology, ranking and trends. *Environment and Planning A. Environment & Planning A, 51*(3), 687–704. doi:10.1177/0308518X18797702

Wong, J. (2004). The adaptive developmental state in East Asia. *Journal of East Asian Studies (Seoul), 4*(3), 345–362. doi:10.1017/S1598240800006007

Xue, L., Zhang, Q., Zhang, X., & Li, C. (2022). Can digital transformation promote green technology innovation? *Sustainability (Basel), 14*(12), 7497. doi:10.3390/su14127497

Xue, L., Zhu, X., & Han, W. (2018). Embracing scientific decision making: The rise of think-tank policies in China. *Pacific Affairs*, *91*(1), 49–71. doi:10.5509/201891149

Yamada, M. (2023). Japan's Relations with Saudi Arabia: The Evolution of Energy Diplomacy in Response to the Developmental Shift in the Rentier State. In *Japan and the Middle East: Foreign Policies and Interdependence* (pp. 27–55). Springer Nature Singapore. doi:10.1007/978-981-19-3459-9_2

Yang, C., & Modell, S. (2012). Power and performance: Institutional embeddedness and performance management in a Chinese local government organization. *Accounting, Auditing & Accountability Journal*, *26*(1), 101–132. doi:10.1108/09513571311285630

Ye, C., Chen, M., Duan, J., & Yang, D. (2017). Uneven development, urbanization and production of space in the middle-scale region based on the case of Jiangsu province, China. *Habitat International*, *66*, 106–116. doi:10.1016/j.habitatint.2017.05.013

Young, K. E. (2014). *The political economy of energy, finance and security in the United Arab Emirates: between the Majilis and the market*. Springer. doi:10.1057/9781137021977

Zeng, M., Wang, F., Xiang, S., Lin, B., Gao, C., & Li, J. (2020). Inheritance or variation? Spatial regeneration and acculturation via implantation of cultural and creative industries in Beijing's traditional compounds. *Habitat International*, *95*, 102071. doi:10.1016/j.habitatint.2019.102071

Zhao, H. (2021). *Internationalization of Regional Higher Education in China: A Critical Policy Case Study of A Transnational Double-Degree Program* (Doctoral dissertation, The University of Western Ontario (Canada)).

Zhao, Y., Liu, X., Wang, S., & Ge, Y. (2019). Energy relations between China and the countries along the Belt and Road: An analysis of the distribution of energy resources and interdependence relationships. *Renewable & Sustainable Energy Reviews*, *107*, 133–144. doi:10.1016/j.rser.2019.03.007

Zhaojin, J. (2016). *A History of Modern Shanghai Banking: The Rise and Decline of China's Financial Capitalism: The Rise and Decline of China's Financial Capitalism*. Routledge. doi:10.4324/9781315706849

Zhong, Z. (2021). Opening-up as entrepreneurial internationalisation in Chinese higher education. *International Journal of Comparative Education and Development*, *23*(3), 175–192. doi:10.1108/IJCED-04-2021-0035

Zhou, S. (2021). The Role of China's Teaching Research System in Promoting Evidence-Based Reform in Education: A Case Study of Jiangsu Province. *Best Evidence in Chinese Education*, *9*(2), 1227–1241. doi:10.15354/bece.21.or067

Zreik, M. (2021). Academic Exchange Programs between China and the Arab Region: A Means of Cultural Harmony or Indirect Chinese Influence? *Arab Studies Quarterly*, *43*(2), 172–188. doi:10.13169/arabstudquar.43.2.0172

Zreik, M. (2022). The Chinese presence in the Arab region: Lebanon at the heart of the Belt and Road Initiative. *International Journal of Business and Systems Research*, *16*(5-6), 644–662. doi:10.1504/IJBSR.2022.125477

Zreik, M. (2023a). Navigating the Dragon: China's Ascent as a Global Power Through Public Diplomacy. In Global Perspectives on the Emerging Trends in Public Diplomacy (pp. 50-74). IGI Global.

Zreik, M. (2023b). The Integration of China's Belt and Road Initiative Into Global Supply Chains: New Pathways for Social and Environmental Responsibility. In *Government Impact on Sustainable and Responsible Supply Chain Management* (pp. 74–94). IGI Global. doi:10.4018/978-1-6684-9062-4.ch005

Zweig, D., & Wang, H. (2013). Can China bring back the best? The Communist Party organizes China's search for talent. *The China Quarterly*, *215*, 590–615. doi:10.1017/S0305741013000751

KEY TERMS AND DEFINITIONS

Cross-Cultural HR Practices: Human Resource Management techniques that are mindful of the cultural variances across different countries and regions. These practices are crucial for managing talent in a diverse global landscape.

Geopolitical Impact: The influence that one country's politics, economy, and culture can have on its relations with other nations. In the context of this study, it's the global influence China gains by successfully attracting and retaining talent from different regions.

Soft Power Diplomacy: This refers to the ability of a country to shape the preferences of others through appeal and attraction, rather than coercion. In the context of talent acquisition and retention, it means using cultural, educational, and societal attributes to attract high-skilled individuals.

Southern, Eastern, and Northern Regions: Refers to the geographical segments of China where various approaches to talent management are observed and analyzed. These regions may employ different strategies due to cultural or economic differences.

Talent Acquisition: The process of finding and attracting skilled human capital, either domestically or internationally, to meet organizational needs. For China, this would include recruiting from the Middle East and East Asia to enhance its workforce.

Talent Retention: The strategies and tactics an organization uses to keep high-value employees from leaving. In China's case, these strategies may vary depending on the cultural and geographic considerations of the regions involved.

Chapter 23
Workforce Diversity Management and Organizational Effectiveness

Doris Esinam Afi Ahiawodzi
Knutsford University College, Accra, Ghana

Peace Kumah
Knutsford University College, Accra, Ghana

ABSTRACT

This study examined the impact of workforce diversity on organizational effectiveness. It aimed to evaluate the level of commitment to diversity management within organizations, identify challenges in diversity management, and explore the relationship between diversity and effectiveness. To gather data, a quantitative approach was used, with respondents rating their views on a 5-point Likert scale question-naire. The sample size consisted of 150 employees and data analysis was conducted using IBM SPSS. Both descriptive and inferential statistics were utilized. The results revealed that while organizations were highly committed to diversity management, they struggled to provide equal treatment to all staff due to outdated diversity policies. Nevertheless, the study showed that diversity had a positive effect on organizational effectiveness. The study suggests that organizations should establish updated workforce diversity policies that address current trends in employees' work culture.

INTRODUCTION

In modern organizations, workplace diversity is a key factor that affects overall efficiency, competency, and growth (Goel, 2019). Workforce diversity refers to the variety of differences among people in an organization (Chua et al., 2023). These differences include age, gender, race, ethnicity, sexual orienta-tion, physical abilities, religious beliefs, educational background, and work experience (Eboh et al., 2018). Workforce diversity encompasses both the visible or surface-level characteristics (demographic) and the deeper psychological characteristics of individuals (Chua et al., 2023). These characteristics are

DOI: 10.4018/979-8-3693-1938-3.ch023

divided into two categories: primary and secondary dimensions. In the primary dimension, individuals possess fundamental characteristics such as age, race, gender, physical and mental abilities, and sexual orientation, which are interdependent and contribute significantly to self-image (Li et al., 2020). Conversely, the secondary dimension comprises a person's health practices, religious convictions, education and training, appearance, relationship status, ethnicity, communication style, and income level (Gunjan, 2022). They are factors that can be altered or adjusted in some way.

The importance of workforce diversity cannot be overemphasized (Balanay & Richards, 2022). Workforce diversity brings a wide range of perspectives, experiences, and skills to the organization, which can lead to increased creativity, innovation, and better problem-solving (Kuknor et al., 2023). Therefore, workforce diversity needs to be properly managed. Diversity management aims to create a diverse and inclusive workforce by recognizing and valuing employee differences (Köllen, 2019). It involves implementing policies and practices that promote diversity, equity, and inclusion in the workplace, such as targeted diversity recruiting, diversity training, mentoring programs, and creating an inclusive organizational culture (Chua et al., 2023). The goal of diversity management is to leverage the benefits of a diverse workforce while addressing the challenges that can arise from managing a diverse group of employees (Köllen, 2019). Research suggests that a diverse workforce can lead to improved efficiency, effectiveness, and innovation (Nyako, 2017). Moreover, a more diverse workforce can contribute to building high-performing teams, fostering inclusive cultures, and providing excellent customer service (Borry et al., 2021). Likewise, diversity can bring unique perspectives and experiences to the organization, which can lead to better problem-solving and decision-making (Ahiawodzi, 2018).

Workforce diversity has both positive and negative implications on organizational effectiveness. It can increase the chances of dissatisfaction, lack of identification (Durga, 2017), and conflict among employees (Ahiawodzi, 2018). Consequently, diversity should be managed effectively by establishing policies and training programs that promote understanding and provide employment opportunities to various groups in the workforce. It is important to consider cultural and legislative factors when implementing diversity programs and policies. Cross-national diversity management should consider the cultural and legislative factors applicable to different countries. Ultimately, diversity should be viewed as a helpful attribute that promotes the attainment of the corporate mission and objectives of the organization (Omotayo et al, 2020). Sanyang and Othman (2019) note that to achieve profitability, productivity, and a competitive edge, organizations must not only embrace diversity but also implement effective strategies to attract and retain the best talent. Managing a diverse workforce presents unique challenges for organizations. Despite the potential threats to performance, various strategies have been proposed to help organizations navigate this complex issue (Suleman, 2017). Properly managing diversity in the workplace can increase productivity, though there is some conflicting evidence on its effects.

As mentioned earlier, the primary demographic characteristics of employees of age, gender, education, and experience and the secondary demographic characteristics of ethnicity, race, religion, and sexual orientation can affect organizational performance in various ways. For example, age diversity has been found to have both positive and negative effects on performance, while gender diversity has not been found to have a significant impact (Abir et al., 2022). Education and experience can also impact performance, with higher levels of education and experience leading to better performance. However, it is important to note that the relationship between demographic characteristics and performance can be complex and may depend on various contextual factors (Abir et al., 2022). Therefore, exploring workforce diversity and organizational effectiveness within the context of a developing country is essential (Ahiawodzi, 2018). The extent of workforce diversity management in organizations in developing countries and the relationship between diversity and organizational effectiveness is still a subject of debate, with differing results from various studies. While some argue that diversity can improve productivity, others suggest it may have adverse effects (Sanyang & Othman, 2019) such as increased conflicts due to diverse opinions and ideas (Gunjan, 2022). Moreover, previous studies may not provide a comprehensive understanding of workforce diversity. For instance, some studies have focused solely on multi-ethnic diversity (Suleman, 2017).

Therefore, this chapter aims to explore the extent of workforce diversity management, the challenges of workforce diversity management practices, and the impact of workforce diversity on organizational effectiveness in power-generation companies in Ghana with employees from various nationalities, ethnicities, ages, and cultural backgrounds. The specific objectives of the chapter are to:

a)   Evaluate the level of commitment organizations have towards managing workforce diversity.
b)   Identify the obstacles that are encountered in managing workforce diversity.
c)   Analyze the relationship between workforce diversity and organizational effectiveness.

Significantly, this chapter provides valuable insights for organizations on how to effectively manage workforce diversity to improve their overall effectiveness. This is essential for organizations, having similar contexts, seeking to understand and effectively manage diversity in the workplace.

BACKGROUND

Workforce Diversity and Organizational Leadership

Managing a diverse workforce has significant implications for management, as management must adopt a more inclusive approach to treat all workers with dignity and respect. This may improve productivity, reduce labor turnover, boost employee morale, and improve communication (Gunjan, 2022). A diverse workforce can lead to positive outcomes such as larger networks, and broad prospects in the decision-making process that will further lead to employee commitment. Additionally, it can lead to increased creativity, innovation, and problem-solving abilities within teams (Kuknor et al., 2023). Organizational inclusion contributes to employee commitment and productivity by creating a work environment where employees feel valued, involved, and engaged. For example, when employees feel included, they are more likely to be committed to their work and the organization, leading to higher productivity. Inclusive environments also allow employees to contribute their authentic selves without fear of discrimination, resulting in increased job satisfaction and motivation. This, in turn, can positively impact employee performance and overall productivity (Kuknor et al., 2023).

Therefore, it is important to recognize and manage diversity based on religion, race, caste, language, gender, sexual orientation, ethnic heritage, physical abilities, disabilities, and other factors within the workforce (Gunjan, 2022). Workforce diversity management should address issues related to bullying behavior by offering a mechanism for solving job issues related to equality, justice, inclusion, and bullying behavior, which are based on gender, age, and ethnicity (Li et al., 2020). By managing all differences such as race, gender, age, ethnicity, education, experience, interest, status, and functional diversity, organizations can create an environment where discrimination will not take place based on age, gender, ethnicity, functions, skills, and knowledge. This inclusive approach to diversity management can help in controlling discrimination, ultimately leading to employees' job satisfaction and job performance (Li et al., 2020).

Despite the numerous benefits of having a diverse workforce, many organizations fail to realize how they can benefit from it (Gunjan, 2022). An important factor is leadership, which plays a crucial role in fostering an inclusive work environment. Engaged leaders who understand the importance of inclusion and promote an inclusive climate can contribute to improved group productivity (Kuknor et al., 2023). Leaders who demonstrate genuine concern and care for their followers can increase trust and foster psychological safety among their colleagues. Additionally, inclusive leadership focuses on stimulating and valuing distinctiveness and ensuring the belongingness of team members, which sets it apart from other leadership styles (Kuknor et al., 2023). Therefore, recognizing leaders as essential contributors to sustaining and developing an inclusive climate is crucial.

Besides, organizations can promote workforce diversity by managing all differences such as differences in race, gender, age, ethnicity, education, experience, interest, status, and functional diversity. This can be achieved through effective workforce diversity management, which includes practices such as performance appraisal, employee development, recruitment, reward, and individual self-leadership behavior to produce competitive employee performance and develop interpersonal skills to work in a group (Li et al., 2020). Moreover, organizations can manage diversity based on skills, knowledge, functions, interests, and preferences, which is rare but can lead to productive job outcomes. It is also important to create a positive working environment through diversity management, which can lead to positive changes in employees and the organization, ultimately increasing employees' and organizational performance (Li et al., 2020).

Likewise, Zhao et al. (2023) proposed inclusive human resource management (IHRM) as an approach to managing human resources that emphasizes the importance of diversity and inclusion in the workplace. It involves creating a work environment that values and respects the differences among employees and utilizes those differences to achieve organizational goals. It involves implementing policies and practices that promote fairness, equity, and inclusion, and that address the unique needs and challenges of diverse employees (Zhao et al., 2023). Zhao et al. (2023) found affective leadership as a moderator of the relationship between IHRM and employee well-being. Affective leaders know how to motivate and retain employees through affective concern and emotion management, which complements the economic and social resources provided by IHRM. Moreover, affective leaders understand how to motivate individuals by caring about their welfare and are attentive to employees' changing moods and unique needs. In addition, affective leaders demonstrate adequate affective concern for employees by proactively supporting those who encounter problems at work and regulating their negative emotions. This creates a supportive and inclusive work environment that enhances the positive effects of IHRM on employee well-being (Zhao et al., 2023).

Lastly, Chua et al. (2023) proposed three dimensions of leadership's role in effective diversity management:

- Leadership's approach to diversity management: This dimension addresses how leadership approaches managing the cultural diversity in their organization, ranging from a surface approach that focuses on visible diversity demographic characteristics to a deep approach that acknowledges the complexity of deep-level psychological characteristics.
- Leadership's accountability: This dimension involves implicit internal drivers influenced by leaders' integrity, values, and convictions to do what is best for the organization. It also considers

leadership's beliefs and values that influence the priority and commitment to implementing the organization's diversity management strategy.

- Leadership's focus on diversity management: This dimension considers the range of cultural diversity characteristics that leadership chooses to focus on within their organization, whether narrow (focusing on one or two characteristics) or broad (involving multiple characteristics).

Challenges of Workforce Diversity Management

Notwithstanding its benefits, organizations face several challenges when implementing diversity management (Köllen, 2019). Thus, incorporating a diverse workforce can present several challenges for organizations (Abir et al., 2022), including:

- Resistance to Change: Some employees may resist the changes associated with incorporating a diverse workforce, leading to resistance and potential conflicts (Abir et al., 2022). This resistance can be due to a lack of understanding of the benefits of diversity or fear of losing power or status (Köllen, 2019).
- Communication Barriers: Differences in language, communication styles, and cultural norms can create barriers to effective communication and collaboration (Abir et al., 2022).
- Stereotyping and Bias: Stereotyping and bias can lead to discrimination and exclusion of certain groups, which can undermine diversity management efforts (Köllen, 2019).
- Bias and Discrimination: Prejudice, stereotypes, and discrimination can hinder the integration of diverse employees and create a hostile work environment (Abir et al., 2022).
- Lack of Inclusivity: Failure to create an inclusive culture where all employees feel valued and respected can lead to feelings of exclusion and disengagement (Abir et al., 2022).
- Cultural Clashes: Differences in values, beliefs, and work practices among employees from diverse backgrounds can lead to misunderstandings and conflicts (Abir et al., 2022).
- Lack of Diversity in Leadership: A lack of diversity in leadership can hinder diversity management efforts, as leaders may not fully understand the experiences and perspectives of diverse employees (Köllen, 2019).
- Inadequate Resources: Implementing diversity management initiatives can require significant resources, including time, money, and personnel (Köllen, 2019).

Overcoming Workforce Diversity Challenges

Trenerry et al. (2023) proposed a strategy for addressing discriminatory attitudes and practices at both the interpersonal and institutional levels through multi-level organizational policies. The strategies emphasized the need for interventions that target individual attitudes and behaviours as well as organizational structures, policies, and cultures by advocating for a comprehensive approach that addresses discriminatory attitudes and practices at multiple levels within the organization, recognizing the interconnectedness of individual and institutional factors in perpetuating or mitigating workplace racism (Trenerry et al., 2023). The key proposals include:

1.   Micro-level Strategies (Interpersonal/Group Level):

- Implement training programs aimed at addressing individual attitudes and behaviours, such as cultural awareness, cultural competency, implicit bias, and anti-racism training.
- Recognize the importance of targeting anti-racism strategies in local contexts, considering the variations like racism and racist attitudes in different places.

2. Meso-level Strategies (Organizational Level):
    - Assess and alter organizational structures, policies, and practices, including human resource policies, recruitment/hiring practices, anti-discrimination complaints and grievance policies, and diversity plans.
    - Implement changes to hiring practices, such as alternative recruitment methods and greater flexibility to meet diversity targets and consider doing away with practices that disadvantage under-represented groups, such as lengthy selection criteria.
    - Establish accountability for commitments to diversity and anti-racism practice, both externally through legislation and policies and internally through leadership and management support.

3. Macro-structural Factors:
    - Consider the influence of macro-structural factors, such as equal opportunity and anti-discrimination laws and regulations, on micro and meso-level practices and processes.

According to Manoharan et al. (2021), implementing appropriate HR practices can minimize workforce diversity challenges. Organizations can modify their culture to promote greater diversity among employees through several strategies (Abir et al., 2022), including:

- Implementing Diversity Training: Providing training programs that raise awareness about diversity issues, unconscious bias, and inclusive behaviors can help employees understand the value of diversity and create a more inclusive environment.
- Establishing Diversity and Inclusion Initiatives: Developing specific initiatives and programs focused on diversity and inclusion, such as employee resource groups, mentorship programs, and diversity councils, can foster a more inclusive culture.
- Diverse Hiring Practices: Implementing diverse hiring practices, such as using diverse interview panels, ensuring job descriptions are inclusive, and actively seeking diverse candidates, can help create a more diverse workforce.
- Encouraging Open Communication: Creating an environment where employees feel comfortable discussing diversity-related issues and sharing their experiences can help promote understanding and inclusivity.
- Leadership Commitment: Having visible support and commitment from organizational leaders to diversity and inclusion efforts is crucial for creating a culture that values diversity.
- Evaluating and Addressing Biases: Regularly evaluating and addressing biases in policies, procedures, and decision-making processes can help mitigate the impact of biases on diversity and inclusion.

Furthermore, to overcome these challenges, organizations can take several steps (Köllen, 2019). By addressing these challenges and implementing the best practices, organizations can create a more diverse and inclusive workplace that benefits both employees and the organization. These steps include:

- Communicating the Benefits of Diversity: Organizations can communicate the benefits of diversity to employees, including increased creativity, innovation, and problem-solving.
- Addressing Stereotyping and Bias: Organizations can implement training programs to address stereotyping and bias and promote inclusive behaviors.
- Promoting Diversity in Leadership: Organizations can promote diversity in leadership by implementing policies that encourage diversity in hiring and promotion decisions.
- Allocating Adequate Resources: Organizations can allocate adequate resources to diversity management initiatives, including funding, personnel, and time.

Related Works

In today's globalized and uncertain world, cultural diversity has become a crucial factor impacting all aspects of an organization, both internally and externally (Mousa & Alas, 2016).

Similarly, Akey et al. (2016) studied the relationship between diversity management and competitive advantage in multinational firms located in sub-Saharan Africa (Ghana). The study was conducted by selecting a few multinational organizations. The study found that effective management of diversity can help create a competitive advantage by increasing innovation, enhancing brand quality and customer loyalty, and lowering buyer propensity to customer loyalty. The study also suggested that for a company to gain the acceptance of customers, it must reflect on the diversity of its customer base. In a related study, Suleman (2017) investigated the impact of diversity management on the overall performance of organizations in the telecommunication industry in Ghana. The target population for the study was made up of top and middle management teams, and ten respondents were selected using the purposive sampling technique. The study found that diversity management has a positive influence on the performance of the organization. However, the findings also suggest that though diversity management is present in the company, management of it is improperly undertaken.

According to Mohammed (2019), many Human Resource departments are now focusing on workforce diversity as a key factor in achieving organizational success. This is because having a diverse workforce can provide access to new markets through the unique perspectives of multicultural employees. Mohammed (2019) specifically examined the impact of workforce diversity on job performance in hotels operating in Jordan, with a focus on four areas of diversity: gender, age, nationality, and educational background. Job performance was measured by two dimensions: task performance and contextual performance. The study population included 389 managers from various managerial levels in hotels in Jordan. Based on the study's findings, the study recommends that managers and decision-makers in Jordanian hotels establish better diversity management plans to better adapt to the changing business landscape. Additionally, it is widely acknowledged that diversity in the workforce, whether in business, government, or society at large, can have a significant impact on organizational performance.

In a recent study, Eboh et al. (2018) examined the critical issues impacting workforce diversity in modern-day organizations. The study revealed that diversity in the workplace enhances the critical thinking, problem-solving, and professional skills of employees. It also enables organizations to attract talent and improve corporate attractiveness and productivity. However, workforce diversity is hampered by hostility, disrespect, and discrimination toward people with diverse backgrounds. These factors can negatively affect morale, teamwork, profitability, and the organization's attractiveness. To exploit the benefits of workforce diversity, modern organizations need to address the causes of these issues through strategies that promote an empowerment culture and build communication and teamwork. These efforts will promote acceptance, productivity, and profits in the future. Also, Khan et al. (2019) assessed the impact of demographic factors - namely age, gender, and educational background diversity - on employee performance within the Higher Education sector in Pakistan. The results indicate that there is a favorable association between the independent variables (age, gender, educational background, and ethnic diversity) and the dependent variable (employee performance).

Moreover, Li et al. (2020) explored the effects of diversity management on job match, job satisfaction, and job performance, and the mediating role of job match in the relationship between workforce diversity management and employees' outcomes. The study revealed that workforce diversity management has a positive correlation with job satisfaction and job performance. Furthermore, job matching is also positively associated with job satisfaction and job performance, and it serves as a mediator for the link between workforce diversity management and employee outcomes. In a related study, Saif (2020) explored the impact of diversity management on employees' intention to quit. The study surveyed 121 individuals to identify factors that influence turnover intention and employee motivation, and to analyze how diversity management can improve work performance. Results showed a significant negative correlation between employee intention to resign and diversity management, with possible mediation in the relationship. The study also found that diversity management practices can reduce turnover intention and help manage diversity, leading to better employee retention.

The study found that the organization's workforce consists mostly of young individuals, with a healthy mix of fresh and experienced talent. Inference findings also highlighted the correlation between demographic, cultural, diversity management programs, and diversity managerial roles with the implementation of HRM practices. The researcher ultimately recommends that global companies provide instruction, preparation, and mentoring to the incoming generations to mitigate future problems for top executives and continue pursuing business in the age of globalization and evolving technology and culture (Goel, 2019). Moreover, Otike et al. (2022) conducted a study to determine the impact of demographic and social-cultural diversity on the effectiveness of organizations. The study examined the management of diversity across five East African countries. The study found that diversity affects the cohesion of the organization. Although diversity issues are not a constant problem in most organizations, they occur frequently in less than 20% of organizations.

Research Design

The study focused on employees of large power generation companies in Ghana where there is various diverse workforce. While it would be ideal to study every element of a population, this is often not practical. For this reason, the study employed non-probability sampling techniques. Convenience sampling was used to select employees who were readily available, willing, and able to provide the necessary information. The population of the accessible population was 242 individuals, with 22 of them being contract workers. For the study, a sample size of 150 respondents was purposefully chosen. Respondents were selected from various departments within the selected companies, including information technology, administration and finance, operations, customer and relationship officers, drivers, security, and technical teams.

To gather primary data, the researchers created a structured questionnaire with clear questions to solicit information from the respondents. The questionnaire contained both close-ended questions, which enhanced the ease and speed with which respondents could complete it, as well as a few open-ended questions to gather further clarification and information on the opinions of respondents on the subject.

The questionnaire was designed in line with the research objectives and divided into four sections for easy analysis and understanding. The first section of the questionnaire focused on the demographic of respondents, while the second section assessed the extent to which the companies subscribe to diversity commitment. The third section gathered information on the challenges that confront management in managing diversity, and the fourth section collected data on the relationship between workforce diversity and organizational effectiveness. The questionnaires were administered in person by the researchers, who took care to explain the purpose of the study and obtain the necessary permissions from respondents. To analyze the data collected from the questionnaires, a quantitative approach was employed, which allowed for statistical representation and facilitated the interpretation of the findings. SPSS was used as the analytical tool to process the data gathered from the field.

RESULTS

This section presents the analysis of responses collected from the sample population. The aim was to answer the research questions by examining the various responses provided by the respondents.

Demographic Characteristics of Respondents

The gender distribution of respondents is depicted in Figure 1, with 90 (60%) male respondents and 57 (38%) female respondents. Three (2%) respondents did not provide gender information. Notably, there were more male respondents than female respondents. Figure 2 displays the age distribution of the employees surveyed. Only 2 (1.3%) respondents did not disclose their age. Most respondents, 52 (34.7%), were between 21-30 years old, while 51 (34%) were between 31-40 years old. Respondents aged 41-50 years old accounted for 34 (22.7%) of the total, and 11 (7.3%) respondents were 50 years old or above.

Figure 1. Demonstrating gender of respondents

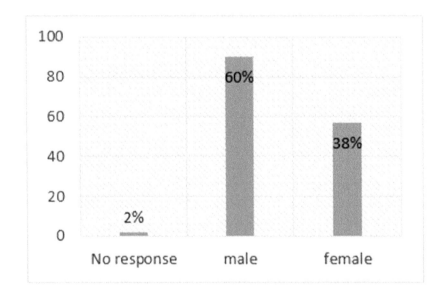

Figure 2. Demonstrating the age of respondents

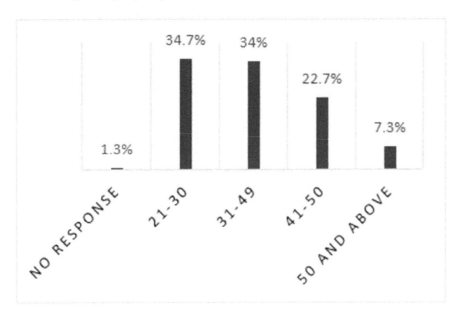

The data in Figure 3 displays the marital status of the participants. Out of the respondents, 12 did not provide a response, which accounts for 8% of the total. Sixty-one respondents, representing 40.7%, indicated they were married, while 14 indicated they were divorced, accounting for 9.3%. The majority, 63 respondents or 42%, indicated that they were single. Moreover, Figure 4 shows the educational status of the participants. Twenty-five of the respondents, or 16.7%, hold a diploma, while 64 respondents, representing 42.7%, hold a first degree. Fifty-one respondents, or 34%, hold masters-level qualifications, and 9 respondents have post-graduate degrees, accounting for 6%. The results highlight that all participants have attained tertiary education, indicating a high level of understanding of the subject matter.

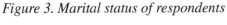

Figure 3. Marital status of respondents

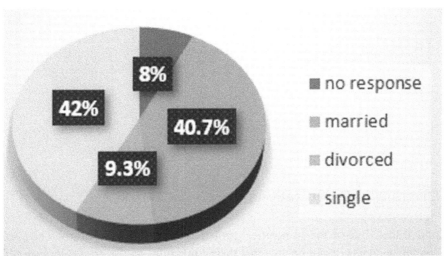

Figure 4. Educational status of respondents

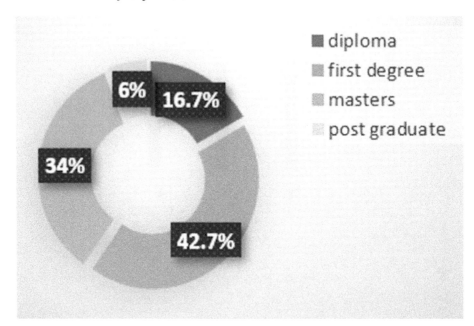

Figure 5 shows the distribution of organizational positions among employees. Notably, 2% of respondents did not respond, while 38.7% held lower-level positions, 41.3% held middle-level status, and 18% held top-level positions. These findings suggest that the surveyed employees possess a commendable level of comprehension and regard for the intricacies of workforce diversity within the organization.

Figure 5. Organizational status/position of respondents

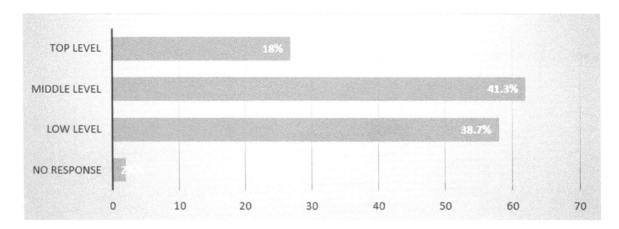

Workforce Diversity in Organizations

Table 1 and Figure 6 shed light on the companies' approach to workforce diversity. The average score of 2.15 indicates that respondents do not believe that their companies have a zero-tolerance policy towards employee discrimination. Respondents hold a neutral view (mean=3.26, SD=1.165) on whether their companies are dedicated to ensuring equal performance criteria for success. Additionally, the mean scores of 3.31 and 3.30 suggest that respondents are also neutral on whether there is gender balance in employment policy and whether growth opportunities exist for women in the organization. The mean scores of 3.24 and 3.42 indicate that respondents are neutral on whether women are equally involved in decision-making and whether their companies currently lack diversity in terms of race.

On the other hand, the mean scores of 3.56 and 3.58 demonstrate that respondents agree that people from different ethnic backgrounds are treated with respect and that management pays attention to diversity challenges. The corresponding standard deviation reveals that the responses vary widely across the mean. Overall, the analysis suggests that respondents hold a neutral view on how much their companies subscribe to workforce diversity. However, they do disagree that their companies have a zero-tolerance policy towards employee discrimination. Respondents agree that people from different ethnic backgrounds are treated with respect and that management is attentive to diversity challenges. This indicates that the companies studied are committed to effectively managing workforce diversity.

Table 1. Subscription to workforce diversity

Items	Mean	SD	Interpretation
1. My company has zero tolerance for employee discrimination.	2.15	1.34	Disagree
2. My company is committed to ensuring equal performance criteria for success.	3.26	1.17	Neutral
3. There is a gender balance according to my company's employment policy.	3.31	1.18	Neutral
4. Growth opportunities exist for women in our organization.	3.30	1.09	Neutral
5. Women are involved in the organization's decision-making as much.	3.24	1.17	Neutral
6. Currently there are no diverse races in my company.	3.42	1.24	Neutral
7. People from different ethnic groups are treated with respect.	3.56	1.22	Agree
8. In my company, management pays particular attention to diversity challenges.	3.58	1.16	Agree

N = 149. Mean Scale: 1= Strongly Disagree 2= Disagree 3=Neutral 4= Agree 5= Strongly Agree

Figure 6. Workforce diversity best practices

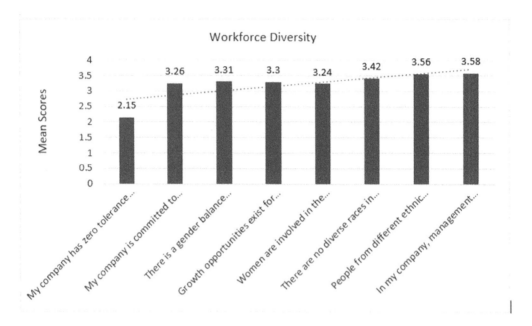

Challenges of Managing Workforce Diversity

In Table 2, management challenges related to diversity are explored. The average score of 2.44 indicates that respondents do not believe higher health costs are associated with managing employee diversity. Respondents were neutral about whether there are increased contributions to pension schemes and the difficulty of creating work schemes for diverse employees. Additionally, respondents were neutral about the financial resources allocated for diversity management. However, many respondents agreed that blending the diverse cultures of employees can be challenging due to their varying backgrounds. Some respondents felt the company's workforce diversity policy was outdated and ineffective for managing current employees. Finally, respondents agreed that providing equal treatment to employees with diverse backgrounds can be difficult.

Table 2. Challenges managing workforce diversity

Items	Mean	SD	Interpretation
1. Higher health cost is involved in managing employees' diversity.	2.44	1.35	Disagree
2. There are higher contributions made toward pension schemes.	3.01	1.23	Neutral
3. Difficulty in blending diverse cultures of employees.	4.00	1.32	Agree
4. It is a challenge to build work schemes for employees.	2.70	1.09	Neutral
5. It is difficult to provide equal treatment when it comes to diversity.	4.3	1.36	Agree
6. Outmoded workforce diversity policy.	3.91	1.27	Agree
7. There are high financial resources Committed to diversity management.	2.85	1.22	Neutral

N = 149. Mean Scale: 1= Strongly Disagree 2= Disagree 3=Neutral 4= Agree 5= Strongly Agree

Figure 7. Challenges of workforce diversity management

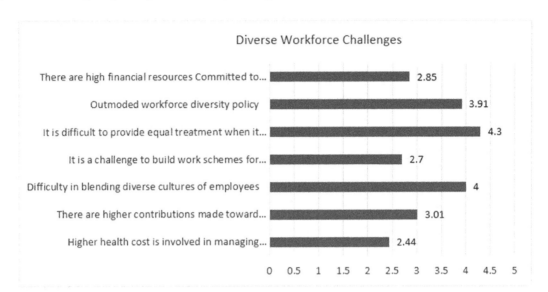

Workforce Diversity and Organizational Effectiveness

Regression analysis was conducted to examine the correlation between workforce diversity and organizational effectiveness. The study utilized workforce diversity and organizational effectiveness as independent and dependent variables, respectively. The model summary indicates a positive correlation between the two. As presented in Table 3, the results demonstrate that workforce diversity has a significant and positive impact on organizational effectiveness ($R^2 = .465$, sig=.000). These findings suggest that an increase in workforce diversity is associated with increased organizational effectiveness. The R-value of 0.465 indicates a strong correlation between the variables. Furthermore, the coefficient of determination suggests that 21.6% of the variations in organizational effectiveness can be explained by workforce diversity, while other factors account for the remaining 78.4%.

The analysis of the variance (ANOVA) reveals that workforce diversity has a significant impact on organizational effectiveness, with a P-value of less than 0.05 (see Table 4). This supports the finding that an increase in diversity has a proportionally positive effect on organizational effectiveness. Specifically, workforce diversity has a positive effect of 0.341 on organizational effectiveness, as indicated by the Beta value of 0.465 (refer to Table 5). The regression analysis confirms that workforce diversity is significantly associated with organizational effectiveness and has a strong positive correlation.

Table 3. Model summary of workforce diversity and effectiveness

R	R Square	Adjusted R Square	Std. Error of the Estimate
.465[a]	.216	.211	4.11174

a. Predictors: (Constant), Workforce Diversity.

Table 4. Analysis of variance (ANOVA) of workforce diversity and effectiveness

Model	Sum of Squares	df	Mean Square	F	Sig.
Regression	684.400	1	684.400	40.482	.000^b
Residual	2485.237	147	16.906		
Total	3169.638	148			

a. Dependent Variable: Organizational Effectiveness
b. Predictors: (Constant), Workforce Diversity

Table 5. Coefficients of regression of workforce diversity on effectiveness

Model	Unstandardized Coefficients		Standardized Coefficients	T	Sig.
	B	Std. Error	Beta		
(Constant)	15.810	1.423		11.114	.000
Workforce	.341	.054	.465	6.363	.000

a. Dependent Variable: Organizational Effectiveness

DISCUSSION AND RECOMMENDATIONS

Summary of Findings

The findings of the study on workforce diversity management and organizational effectiveness are as follows:

- The first objective was to assess power-generation companies' commitment to workforce diversity management. It was discovered that power generation companies are highly committed to this.
- The second objective aimed to identify challenges with workforce diversity management at power generation companies. It was found that companies struggle to blend the diverse cultures of their employees due to variations in their backgrounds. Additionally, the current workforce diversity policy is outdated and poses difficulty in providing equal treatment to employees.
- Lastly, the study revealed a positive and significant correlation between workforce diversity and organizational effectiveness. In other words, the higher the level of diversity, the higher the effectiveness of the organization.

Discussion

Our primary objective was to evaluate the degree to which power-generating companies in Ghana are dedicated to managing diversity in the workplace. Our findings indicate that survey respondents believe that individuals from diverse ethnic backgrounds are treated with respect and that management is actively addressing diversity-related challenges. These results suggest that companies are committed to effectively managing workforce diversity, a conclusion that is supported by previous research (Bano et al., 2013).

Studies have shown that a well-managed diverse workforce can improve organizational performance, making it crucial for companies to prioritize diversity and inspire employee loyalty.

Furthermore, the study aimed to identify the obstacles that are faced in managing workforce diversity. The results showed that management struggles with integrating the diverse cultures of its employees, likely due to the varying cultural backgrounds of the workforce. The study also found that the companies' current diversity policy is outdated and ineffective in managing the current workforce, leading to difficulty in providing equal treatment to employees from diverse backgrounds. Ebohet al. (2018) identified additional challenges, such as hostility, disrespect, and discrimination toward individuals from diverse backgrounds in the workplace. These behaviors were attributed to prejudices and biases towards people with different lifestyles, ethnicities, cultures, disabilities, and generational gaps. Both sets of findings highlight the numerous challenges that organizations must address to promote organizational effectiveness in managing workforce diversity.

The final objective was to examine the relationship between workforce diversity and organizational effectiveness. The analysis showed that there is a positive and significant effect of workforce diversity on effectiveness. This indicates that higher levels of diversity lead to higher organizational effectiveness. This finding is consistent with the research of Nyako (2017) and Suleman (2017), who both confirmed a positive correlation between workforce diversity and organizational performance. Other scholars from around the world have also reported similar findings. For example, Odita and Egbule (2015) found a positive connection between workforce diversity and organizational effectiveness in the Nigerian brewery, while Prasad (2015) observed the same impact in some selected banks in Ethiopia. These findings suggest that organizations must effectively manage their diverse workforce to optimize value creation, as it is a necessary component of organizational performance.

Recommendations

The study offers several recommendations for organizations looking to improve their effectiveness through diversity management.

- Improving diversity policies to promote positive relationships between workforce diversity and organizational effectiveness.
- Organizations should create new policies to address current trends in employees' work culture.
- It also recommends raising awareness about diversity management and its impact on the organization.
- Education and training programs should be implemented to help employees navigate the complexities of diversity.
- Management should enforce sanctions against discrimination, stereotyping, and ethnocentrism, and effectively use the Equal Employment Opportunity policy.
- Organizations should prioritize utilizing the strengths of workforce diversity and implementing measures to increase employee commitment to improving organizational performance.

FUTURE RESEARCH DIRECTIONS

The research direction of workforce diversity is focused on understanding the complex nature of diversity in the workplace and identifying strategies to promote diversity, inclusion, and organizational performance. Specifically, future research direction may include the following:

- Intersectionality: Intersectionality refers to the interconnected nature of social categories such as race, gender, and sexuality, and how they interact to shape individuals' experiences. Current research on workforce diversity explores the intersectionality of different social categories and how they impact individuals' experiences in the workplace (Köllen, 2019).
- Inclusion: Inclusion refers to creating a workplace culture that values and respects individual differences. Current research on workforce diversity explores how organizations can create an inclusive workplace culture and the impact of inclusion on employee well-being and organizational performance (Köllen, 2019).
- Leadership: Leadership plays a critical role in promoting diversity and inclusion in the workplace. Current research on workforce diversity explores the role of leadership in promoting diversity and inclusion, including the impact of diverse leadership teams on organizational performance (Köllen, 2019).
- Globalization: Globalization has led to an increasingly diverse workforce, and current research on workforce diversity explores the challenges and opportunities of managing diversity in a global context (Köllen, 2019).
- Technology: Technology has the potential to promote diversity and inclusion in the workplace, but it can also perpetuate bias and exclusion. Current research on workforce diversity explores the impact of technology on diversity and inclusion in the workplace (Köllen, 2019).
- Leveraging Business Benefits: There is a need to understand how to leverage the business benefits of diversity and inclusion, especially for global companies operating in multiple geographies (Sangwan & Garg, 2020).
- Customization of Initiatives: It is important to design and customize diversity and inclusion initiatives according to specific situations and local needs, as the same set of practices may not apply to all organizations (Sangwan & Garg, 2020).
- Linkage with Organizational Characteristics: Research is required to explore how diversity and inclusion are linked with other important organizational characteristics such as leadership, top management composition, and organizational culture (Sangwan & Garg, 2020).
- Inclusion of LGBT Communities: There is a need for organizational research to examine well-known metaphors such as the 'glass ceiling' and 'glass cliff' with context to LGBT communities, to provide useful insights for addressing the barriers faced by minorities at the workplace (Sangwan & Garg, 2020).
- Theoretical Development in Inclusion: While more studies have been conducted in the field of diversity and its outcomes, there is a need for more theoretical development in the area of inclusion and its related outcomes (Sangwan & Garg, 2020).
- Practices for Uniqueness and Belongingness Needs**: Future research should focus on practices that satisfy uniqueness and belongingness needs, contributing to the creation of an inclusive environment in the workplace (Sangwan & Garg, 2020).

CONCLUSION

This study has revealed a positive and significant correlation between workforce diversity and organizational performance. This suggests that effective management of diversity issues among employees can greatly enhance the organization's productivity. For example, if employees perceive a consistent relationship between diversity and a committed work environment in their workplace, a positive response can be expected from them. Proper implementation of diverse workforce practices can lead to employee satisfaction and commitment. Negative attitudes are only expressed by employees when they are treated unfairly. Organizations that embrace workforce diversity could attract new employees and welcome their creativity, resulting in a more flexible system that improves quality.

Conversely, a lack of diversity and ethical work practices can lead to behavioral issues that cause great concern for organizations. It is crucial to address these underlying problems as a top priority to ensure the organization's survival in a competitive market. Moreover, it is important to maintain a positive work culture to prevent more aggressive and harmful behaviors that have negatively impacted organizations. Consequently, this study concludes that a diverse workforce and committed work environment have a positive impact on organizational performance and employee attitudes. It is recommended that organizations prioritize leveraging the strength of diversity in their workforce and implement measures to enhance employee commitment to improve organizational effectiveness.

REFERENCES

Abrir, Farmanesh, & Zargar. (2022). An Examination of the Relationship Between Levels Diversity-Organizational Performance: Does Innovative Culture Matter? *SAGE Open*, *12*(1).

Ahiawodzi, D. F. (2018). *The impact of workforce diversity on organizational effectiveness*. University of Professional Studies.

Akey, B., Jiang, X., Antwi, E., & Torku, E. (2016). Diversity Management and Competitive Advantage in Multinational Firms in Sub-Saharan Africa. Institute of Medical Insurance and Healthcare Management Journal, 481-488.

Balanay, J. A. G., & Richards, S. L. (2022). Insights into Diversity in the Environmental Health Science Workforce. *Environmental Health Insights*, *16*, 1–2. doi:10.1177/11786302221077513 PMID:35153487

Bano, S., Khan, M. F., Butt, N. A., & Ullah, H. (2013). Analysis of Workforce Diversity, Commitment of Employees and its Effects on Organizational Performance: Corporate Sector in Islamabad Pakistan. *International Review of Basic and Applied Sciences*.

Borry, E. L., Getha-Taylor, H., & Holmes, M. H. (2021). Promoting Diversity and Inclusion in the Federal Workforce: Executive Order 13583 and Demographic Trends. *Public Administration Quarterly*, *45*(4), 392–417. doi:10.37808/paq.45.4.3

Chua, R. Y. J., Morris, M. W., & Mor, S. (2023). Making sense of cultural diversity's complexity: Addressing an emerging challenge for leadership. *International Journal of Cross Cultural Management*, *23*(3), 643–662. doi:10.1177/14705958231214623

Durga, P. (2017). The Impact of Workforce Diversity on Organizational Effectiveness: (A Study of Selected Banks in Tigray Region of Ethiopia). *International Journal of Scientific Research*, 427.

Eboh, H. C., Asiah, M. N., Umar, A., & Doko, I. A. (2018). Prospects and Challenges of Workplace Diversity in Modern Day Prospects and Challenges of Workplace Diversity in Modern Day. *Journal of Business and Public Administration*.

Goel, R. (2019). Diversity At Workplace: Performance Of Human Resource Management Practices in IT sector in NCR, India. *International Journal Of Scientific & Technology Research, 8*(12).

Gunjan, S. (2022, March 11). *Workforce Diversity*. Retrieved from Business Management ideas: /www.businessmanagementideas.com/human-resource-management-2/workforce-diversity/20385

Khan, F., Sohail, A., Sufyan, M., Uddin, M., & Basit, A. (2019). The effect of Workforce Diversity on Employee Performance in the Higher Education Sector. *Journal of Management Info*.

Köllen, T. (2019). Diversity Management: A Critical Review and Agenda for the Future. *Journal of Management Inquiry, 30*(3), 259–272. doi:10.1177/1056492619868025

Kuknor, S., Kumar, A., & Bhattacharya, S. (2023). Organizational inclusion and OCB: The moderating role of inclusive leadership. *FIIB Business Review, 12*(1), 1–14. doi:10.1177/23197145231183859

Li, W., Wang, X., Haque, M. J., Shafique, M. N., & Nawaz, M. Z. (2020). Impact of workforce diversity management on employees' outcomes: Testing the mediating role of a person's job match. *SAGE Open, 10*(1), 1–16. doi:10.1177/2158244020903402

Manoharan, S., Chelliah, J., & Sardeshmukh, S. R. (2021). Antecedents and outcomes of a culturally diverse workforce in hotels. *Journal of Hospitality & Tourism Research (Washington, D.C.), 45*(8), 1383–1416. Advance online publication. doi:10.1177/1096348020986906

Mohammed, A. (2019). Effect of Workforce Diversity on Job Performance of Hotels Working in Jordan. *international. Journal of Business and Management*.

Nyako, I. Z. (2017). *Impact of Workforce Diversity on Organizational Performance in Calabar, Cross-River State*. American University of Nigeria.

Omotayo, O., Anthonia, A., Hezekia, F., Opeyemi, O., & Odion, E. (2020). Diversity management and organisational performance in deposit money banks in Nigeria. *Cogent Business & Management*, 3-4.

Otike, W. F., Omboi, M. B., & Mwalekwa, F. K. (2022, Feb 25). *Effects of Workplace Diversity Management on Organizational Effectiveness*. www.iiste.org

Saif, R. (2020). The Effects of Diversity Management on Employee Intention to Quit: Mediating Role of Employee Motivation. *Journal of Health, Medicine and Nursing*.

Sangwan, S., & Garg, P. (2020). Literature review on diversity and inclusion at the workplace (2010-2017). Vision. *The Journal of Business Perspective, 25*(1), 1–11.

Sanyang, L., & Othman, K. (2019). Workforce diversity and its impact on Organisational Performance. *Journal of Islamic Social Sciences and Humanities*, 25.

Suleman, B. A. (2017). *Diversity Management for improving performances in Mobile telephone.* University of Professional Studies.

Trenerry, B., Dunn, K., & Paradies, Y. (2023). Productive disruptions: Supporting diversity and anti-racism in the workplace through multi-level organisational strategies. *Australian Journal of Management*, 1–28. doi:10.1177/03128962231175182

Zhao, H., Guan, Y., Liu, Y., Jiang, P., & Zhou, X. (2023). How and when inclusive human resource management promotes employee well-being: The roles of ambidextrous fit and affective leadership. *Journal of Business and Psychology*, *38*(1), 1–16. doi:10.1007/s10869-022-09789-1 PMID:36373110

Compilation of References

Aaker, J. (2009). The problems of brand definition. *Sustainable Management and Marketing. Australian and New Zealand Marketing Academy Conference 2009*, 1–10.

Aaker, J. L. (1997). Dimensions of Brand Personality. *JMR, Journal of Marketing Research, 34*(3), 347–356. doi:10.1177/002224379703400304

Aaker, J., & Fournier, S. (1995). Brand as a character, a partner and a person: Three perspectives on the question of brand personality. *Advances in Consumer Research. Association for Consumer Research (U. S.), 22*, 391–395.

Ababneh, O. M. A. (2021). How do green HRM practices affect employees' green behaviors? The role of employee engagement and personality attributes. *Journal of Environmental Planning and Management, 64*(7), 1204–1226. doi:10.1080/09640568.2020.1814708

Abdelhay, S. (2023). How Artificial Intelligence can affect the process of recruitment and improve the quality of new hired employees. *Resmilitaris, 13*(3), 2517-2533.

Abdelmotaleb, M. (2023). Exploring the effect of perceived fun at work on hospitality employees' behaviors in and out of work. *International Journal of Contemporary Hospitality Management*. Advance online publication. doi:10.1108/IJCHM-02-2023-0139

Abdelwahed, N. A. A., & Al Doghan, M. A. (2023). Developing Employee Productivity and Performance through Work Engagement and Organizational Factors in an Educational Society. *Societies (Basel, Switzerland), 13*(3), 65. Advance online publication. doi:10.3390/soc13030065

Abdul, C., Wang, W., & Li, Y. (2020). The impact of technology on recruitment process. *Issues in Information Systems, 21*(4).

Abdullahi, M. S., Raman, K., & Solarin, S. A. (2022). Talent management practices on employee performance among academic staff of Malaysian private universities: Employee engagement as a mediator. *Journal of Applied Research in Higher Education, 14*(1), 135–158. doi:10.1108/JARHE-08-2020-0283

Abhilasha & Pathak, S. (2014). Managing multigenerational workforce: An Indian perspective. *Asian Journal of Research in Business Economics and Management, 4*, 29-37.

Aboramadan, M. (2020). The effect of green HRM on employee green behaviors in higher education: The mediating mechanism of green work engagement. *The International Journal of Organizational Analysis, 30*(1), 7–23. doi:10.1108/IJOA-05-2020-2190

Abraham, M., Kaliannan, M., Avvari, M., & Thomas, S. (2023). Reframing talent acquisition, retention practices for organisational commitment in Malaysian SMEs: A managerial perspective. *Journal of General Management*. Advance online publication. doi:10.1177/03063070231184336

Abrir, Farmanesh, & Zargar. (2022). An Examination of the Relationship Between Levels Diversity-Organizational Performance: Does Innovative Culture Matter? *SAGE Open*, *12*(1).

Abrudan, D., & Conea-Simiuc, I. (2019). How Managers Can Create Happy Working Environment. *Revista de Management Comparat International*, *20*(3), 286–296. doi:10.24818/RMCI.2019.3.286

Aczél, B., Kovács, M., Van Der Lippe, T., & Szászi, B. (2021). Researchers working from home: Benefits and challenges. *PLoS One*, *16*(3), e0249127. doi:10.1371/journal.pone.0249127 PMID:33765047

Adam, A. K. (2020). Modern challenges of human resource management practice in job placement and recruitment within organisations in the African continent. *Journal of Human Resource Management*, *8*(2), 69–75. doi:10.11648/j.jhrm.201200802.14

Ada, N., Korolchuk, M., & Yunyk, I. (2023). The Role of Employer Branding Practices on Management of Employee Attraction and Retention. *Economics Ecology Socium*, *7*(1), 46–60. doi:10.31520/2616-7107/2023.7.1-5

Adeosun, O. T., & Ohiani, A. S. (2020). Attracting and recruiting quality talent: Firm perspectives. *Rajagiri Management Journal*, *14*(2), 107–120. doi:10.1108/RAMJ-05-2020-0016

Aftab, J., Abid, N., Cucari, N., & Savastano, M. (2023). Green human resource management and environmental performance: The role of green innovation and environmental strategy in a developing country. *Business Strategy and the Environment*, *32*(4), 1782–1798. doi:10.1002/bse.3219

Agarwal, S., Gupta, A., & Roshani, P. (2023). Redefining HRM with artificial intelligence and machine learning. In The Adoption and Effect of Artificial Intelligence on Human Resources Management, Part A (pp. 1-13). Emerald Publishing Limited. doi:10.1108/978-1-80382-027-920231001

Aggarwal, I., Schilpzand, M. C., Martins, L. L., Woolley, A. W., & Molinaro, M. (2022). The Benefits of Cognitive Style Versatility for Collaborative Work. *The Journal of Applied Psychology*, *108*(4), 647–659. doi:10.1037/apl0001035 PMID:35901407

Aggarwal, R., Lee, M., & Midhac, V. (2023). Differential Impact of Content in Online Communication on Heterogeneous Candidates: A Field Study in Technical Recruitment. *Information Systems Research*, *34*(2), 609–628. doi:10.1287/isre.2022.1120

Aggerholm, H. K., & Andersen, S. E. (2018). Social Media Recruitment 3.0. *Journal of Communication Management (London)*, *22*(2), 122–137. doi:10.1108/JCOM-11-2017-0131

Aguinis, H., & O'Boyle, E. Jr. (2014). Star performers in twenty-first century organizations. *Personnel Psychology*, *67*(2), 313–350. doi:10.1111/peps.12054

Aguirre, T. M., Koehler, A. E., Joshi, A., & Wilhelm, S. L. (2018). Recruitment and retention challenges and successes. *Ethnicity & Health*, *23*(1), 111–119. doi:10.1080/13557858.2016.1246427 PMID:27764955

Ahamad, F., Saini, G., & Jawahar, I. M. (2023). Interactive influence of work-life balance benefits, employee recommendation, and job attributes on employer attractiveness and job pursuit intentions: Two experiments. *Asian Business & Management*, *22*(4), 1215–1242. doi:10.1057/s41291-022-00184-4

Ahiawodzi, D. E. (2018). *The impact of workforce diversity on organizational effectiveness*. University of Professional Studies.

Ahmad, S. (2015). Green human resource management: Policies and practices. *Cogent Business & Management*, *2*(1), 1030817. doi:10.1080/23311975.2015.1030817

Ahmed, R. R., Azam, M., Qureshi, J. A., & Hashem, E. (2022). The Relationship Between Internal Employer Branding and Talent Retention: A Theoretical Investigation for the Development of a Conceptual Framework. *Frontiers in Psychology*, *13*, 859614. doi:10.3389/fpsyg.2022.859614 PMID:35369242

Aitken, P. P., Leathar, D. S., O'Hagan, F. J., & Squair, S. I. (1987). Children's awareness of cigarette advertisements and brand imagery. *British Journal of Addiction*, *82*(6), 615–622. doi:10.1111/j.1360-0443.1987.tb01523.x PMID:3475100

Ajzen, I. (1991). The theory of planned behavior. *Organizational Behavior and Human Decision Processes*, *50*(2), 179–211. doi:10.1016/0749-5978(91)90020-T

Akay, V. (2006). Business is the people and people are the business. Humanizing the corporation, iUniverse.

Akey, B., Jiang, X., Antwi, E., & Torku, E. (2016). Diversity Management and Competitive Advantage in Multinational Firms in Sub-Saharan Africa. Institute of Medical Insurance and Healthcare Management Journal, 481-488.

Akour, I. A., & Dwairi, M. A. (2011). Testing technology acceptance model in developing countries: The case of Jordan. *International Journal of Business and Social Science, 2*(14).

Al Omoush, K. S., Yaseen, S. G., & Atwah Alma'aitah, M. (2012). The impact of Arab cultural values on online social networking: The case of Facebook. *Computers in Human Behavior*, *28*(6), 2387–2399. doi:10.1016/j.chb.2012.07.010

Alburo, J., Bradshaw, A. K., Santiago, A. E., Smith, B. L., & Vinopal, J. (2020). Looking beyond libraries for inclusive recruitment and retention practices: Four successful approaches. In Advances in library administration and organization (pp. 85–109). doi:10.1108/S0732-067120200000041009

Al-Dalahmeh, M. L. (2020). Talent management: A systematic review. *Oradea Journal of Business and Economics*, *5*(Special), 115–123. doi:10.47535/1991ojbe102

Aldwin, C., & Greenberger, E. (1987). Cultural differences in the predictors of depression. *American Journal of Community Psychology*, *15*(6), 789–813. doi:10.1007/BF00919803 PMID:3439551

Algner, M., & Lorenz, T. (2022). You're Prettier When You Smile: Construction and Validation of a Questionnaire to Assess Microaggressions Against Women in the Workplace. *Frontiers in Psychology*, *13*, 809862. Advance online publication. doi:10.3389/fpsyg.2022.809862 PMID:35369207

Ali, M., Grabarski, M. K., & Baker, M. (2023). An exploratory study of benefits and challenges of neurodivergent employees: Roles of knowing neurodivergents and neurodiversity practices. *Equality, Diversity and Inclusion*. Advance online publication. doi:10.1108/EDI-03-2023-0092

Al-Khiami, M. I., & Jaeger, M. (2023). Safer Working at Heights: Exploring the Usability of Virtual Reality for Construction Safety Training among Blue-Collar Workers in Kuwait. *Safety (Basel, Switzerland)*, *9*(3), 63. Advance online publication. doi:10.3390/safety9030063

Allal-Chérif, O., Aranega, A. Y., & Sánchez, R. C. (2021). Intelligent recruitment: How to identify, select, and retain talents from around the world using artificial intelligence. *Technological Forecasting and Social Change*, *169*, 120822. doi:10.1016/j.techfore.2021.120822

Allden, K., Jones, L., Weissbecker, I., Wessells, M. G., Bolton, P., Betancourt, T. S., Hijazi, Z., Galappatti, A., Yamout, R., Patel, P., & Sumathipala, A. (2009). Mental health and psychosocial support in crisis and conflict: Report of the mental health working group. *Prehospital and Disaster Medicine*, *24*(S2), s217–s227. doi:10.1017/S1049023X00021622 PMID:19806544

Allen, D. G., Bryant, P. C., & Vardaman, J. M. (2010). Retaining talent: Replacing misconceptions with evidence-based strategies. *The Academy of Management Perspectives*, *24*(2), 48–64. https://www.jstor.org/stable/25682398

Allen, T. D., Eby, L. T., Chao, G. T., & Bauer, T. N. (2017). Taking stock of two relational aspects of organizational life: Tracing the history and shaping the future of socialization and mentoring research. *The Journal of Applied Psychology*, *102*(3), 324–337. doi:10.1037/apl0000086 PMID:28125264

Alniacik, E., Alniacik, U., Erat, S., & Akcin, K. (2014). Attracting Talented Employees to the Company: Do We Need Different Employer Branding Strategies in Different Cultures? *10th International Strategic Management Conference*, *150*, 336-344. 10.1016/j.sbspro.2014.09.074

AlQudah, N. F., Anjum, M. A., Naeem, K., Ajloun, M. M. A., Ahmed, A., & Shtnaoui, H. (2023). Examining the antecedents of employee retention among Jordanian private Universities: The moderating role of knowledge sharing. *Cogent Business & Management*, *10*(2), 2208429. Advance online publication. doi:10.1080/23311975.2023.2208429

Alshehhi, K., Zawbaa, S. B., Abonamah, A. A., & Tariq, M. U. (2021). Employee retention prediction in corporate organizations using machine learning methods. *Academy of Entrepreneurship Journal*, *27*, 1–23.

Alshurideh, D. M. (2019). Do electronic loyalty programs still drive customer choice and repeat purchase behavior? *International Journal of Electronic Customer Relationship Management*, *12*(1), 40–57. doi:10.1504/IJECRM.2019.098980

Al-Somali, S. A., Gholami, R., & Clegg, B. (2009). An investigation into the acceptance of online banking in Saudi Arabia. *Technovation*, *29*(2), 130–141. doi:10.1016/j.technovation.2008.07.004

Alves, C., & De Sousa, J. H. F. S. (2021). Creativity and Innovation to Improve Processes in a Textile Industry. *International Journal of Engineering and Management Sciences*, *6*(3). Advance online publication. doi:10.21791/IJEMS.2021.3.7.

Alves, J., Marques, M. J., Saur, I., & Marques, P. (2007). Creativity and innovation through multidisciplinary and multisectoral cooperation. *Creativity and Innovation Management*, *16*(1), 27–34. doi:10.1111/j.1467-8691.2007.00417.x

Alwahaishi, S., & Snásel, V. (2013). Consumers' Acceptance and Use of Information and Communications Technology: A UTAUT and Flow Based Theoretical Model. *Journal of Technology Management & Innovation*, *8*(2), 9–10. doi:10.4067/S0718-27242013000200005

Amankwah-Amoah, J. (2015). An integrative review of the antecedents and consequences of lateral hiring. *Journal of Management Development*, *34*(7), 754–772. doi:10.1108/JMD-01-2014-0007

Amaro, S., & Duarte, P. (2013). Online travel purchasing: A literature review. *Journal of Travel & Tourism Marketing*, *30*(8), 755–785. doi:10.1080/10548408.2013.835227

Ambardar, A., & Singh, A. (2017). Quality of work life practices in Indian hotel industry. *International Journal of Hospitality and Tourism Systems*, *10*(1), 22–33.

Ambardar, A., Singh, A., & Singh, V. (2023). Barriers in Implementing Ergonomic Practices in Hotels- A Study on five star hotels in NCR region. *International Journal of Hospitality and Tourism Systems*, *16*(2), 11–17.

Ambler, T., & Barrow, S. (1996, December). The employer brand. *Journal of Brand Management*, *4*(3), 185–206. doi:10.1057/bm.1996.42

Amin, A. (2017). An institutionalist perspective on regional economic development. In *Economy* (pp. 59–72). Routledge. doi:10.4324/9781351159203-3

Andersen, P. H. (2005). Relationship marketing and brand involvement of professionals through web-enhanced brand communities: The case of Coloplast. *Industrial Marketing Management*, *34*(3), 285–297. doi:10.1016/j.indmarman.2004.07.007

Andersen, T. S., & Wellen, H. (2023). Being a mentor in the digital era: An exploratory study of the benefits under-graduate student mentors derived from providing virtual mentoring to youth. *Journal of Community Psychology*, 51(7), 2635–2651. doi:10.1002/jcop.23051 PMID:37148560

Anderson, G., Di Nota, P. M., Groll, D., & Carleton, R. N. (2020). Peer support and crisis-focused psychological interventions designed to mitigate post-traumatic stress injuries among public safety and frontline healthcare personnel: A systematic review. *International Journal of Environmental Research and Public Health*, 17(20), 7645. doi:10.3390/ijerph17207645 PMID:33092146

Anderson, J., Smith, L., & Johnson, R. (2020). Exploring remote mentoring in the digital age. *The Journal of Applied Psychology*, 25(4), 567–584.

Anderson, N., Potočnik, K., & Zhou, J. (2014). Innovation and creativity in organizations: A state-of-the-science review, prospective commentary, and guiding framework. *Journal of Management*, 40(5), 1297–1333. doi:10.1177/0149206314527128

Angelova, R. A. (2018). Cross-Cultural Management of the European Textile and Clothing Industries: Application of Hofstede's Cultural Dimensions. In Fashion and Textiles: Breakthroughs in Research and Practice (pp. 386-407). IGI Global.

Angulo-Jiménez, H., & DeThorne, L. (2019). Narratives about autism: An analysis of YouTube videos by individuals who self-identify as autistic. *American Journal of Speech-Language Pathology*, 28(2), 569–590. doi:10.1044/2018_AJSLP-18-0045 PMID:30995116

Annell, S., Lindfors, P., Kecklund, G., & Sverke, M. (2018). Sustainable Recruitment: Individual Characteristics and Psychosocial Working Conditions Among Swedish Police Officers. *Nordic Journal of Working Life Studies*, 8(4), 3–24.

Ansar, N., & Baloch, A. (2018). Talent and talent management: definition and issues. *IBT Journal of Business Studies (JBS)*, 1(2).

Ansari, A. I., & Singh, A. (2023). Application of Augmented Reality (AR) and Virtual Reality (VR) in Promoting Guest Room Sales: A Critical Review. In Impact of Industry 4.0 on Sustainable Tourism. Emerald Publishing Limited. doi:10.1108/978-1-80455-157-820231006

Ansari, A. I., Singh, A., & Singh, V. (2023). The impact of differential pricing on perceived service quality and guest satisfaction: An empirical study of mid-scale hotels in India. *Turyzm/Tourism*, 121–132. doi:10.18778/0867-5856.33.2.10

Ansari, M. S. A., & Khan, S. A. (2023). FDI, disinvestment and growth: An appraisal of Bhutanese economy. *Journal of Chinese Economic and Foreign Trade Studies. Journal of Chinese Economic and Foreign Trade Studies*, 16(1), 64–82. Advance online publication. doi:10.1108/JCEFTS-05-2022-0031

Antons, D., Piening, E. P., & Salge, T. O. (2023). The Elites-Mutual-Attraction Effect: How Relative Reputation Influences Employee Flows between Organizations. *Journal of Management Studies*. Advance online publication. doi:10.1111/joms.12935

Anwar, N., Mahmood, N. H. N., Yusliza, M. Y., Ramayah, T., Faezah, J. N., & Khalid, W. (2020). Green human resource management for organisational citizenship behaviour towards the environment and environmental performance on a university campus. *Journal of Cleaner Production*, 256, 120401. doi:10.1016/j.jclepro.2020.120401

Appels, M. (2023). CEO Sociopolitical Activism as a Signal of Authentic Leadership to Prospective Employees. *Journal of Management*, 49(8), 2727–2765. doi:10.1177/01492063221110207

Ardiansyah, I., & Iskandar, H. (2021). Implementation of Green Hotel Management 5-star hotel in Jakarta, case study: The dharmawangsa hotel Jakarta. *IOP Conference Series. Earth and Environmental Science*, 704(1), 012034. doi:10.1088/1755-1315/704/1/012034

Arif, S., Johnston, K. A., Lane, A., & Beatson, A. (2023). A strategic employee attribute scale: Mediating role of internal communication and employee engagement. *Public Relations Review*, *49*(2), 102320. Advance online publication. doi:10.1016/j.pubrev.2023.102320

Arifuzzaman, M., Islam, M. S., Masum, M. Y., & Anonna, J. S. (2023). The Use of E-Recruitment Process with the Comparison of Traditional Recruitment Process in Bangladesh: A Case Study on BRAC Bank Ltd. Journal of Education. *Management and Development Studies*, *3*(2), 15–25. doi:10.52631/jemds.v3i2.191

Ariss, A. A. (2014). Global talent management: An introduction and a review. In Management for Professionals (pp. 3–13). doi:10.1007/978-3-319-05125-3_1

Armstrong, M. (2006). *A handbook of human resource management practice* (10th ed.). Kogan Page.

Armstrong, M. (2006). *A handbook of human resources management practice*. Kogan Page.

Armstrong, T. (2015). The myth of the normal brain: Embracing neurodiversity. *AMA Journal of Ethics*, *17*(4), 348–352. doi:10.1001/journalofethics.2015.17.4.msoc1-1504 PMID:25901703

Arora, M., Prakash, A., Mittal, A., & Singh, S. (2021, December). HR analytics and artificial intelligence-transforming human resource management. In *2021 International Conference on Decision Aid Sciences and Application (DASA)* (pp. 288-293). IEEE. 10.1109/DASA53625.2021.9682325

Arora, R., & Stoner, C. (2009). A mixed method approach to understanding brand personality. *Journal of Product and Brand Management*, *18*(4), 272–283. doi:10.1108/10610420910972792

Arshadi, N., & Damiri, H. (2013). The Relationship of Job Stress with Turnover Intention and Job Performance: Moderating Role of OBSE. *Procedia: Social and Behavioral Sciences*, *84*, 706–710. doi:10.1016/j.sbspro.2013.06.631

Arulrajah, A. A., & Opatha, H. H. D. N. P. (2016). Analytical and Theoretical Perspectives on Green Human Resource Management: A Simplified Underpinning. *International Business Research*, *9*(12), 153. doi:10.5539/ibr.v9n12p153

Arulrajah, A. A., Opatha, H. H. D. N. P., & Nawaratne, N. N. J. (2015). Green human resource management practices: A review. *Sri Lankan Journal of Human Resource Management*, *5*(1), 1–16. doi:10.4038/sljhrm.v5i1.5624

Askari, M. R. (2023). *Retention Strategies for Managers of Generation Y Employees* (Doctoral dissertation, Walden University).

Atkar, A., Pabba, M., Sekhar, S. C., & Sridhar, S. (2021). Current limitations and challenges in the global textile sector. In *Fundamentals of Natural Fibres and Textiles* (pp. 741–764). Woodhead Publishing. doi:10.1016/B978-0-12-821483-1.00004-8

Attridge, M. (2009). Employee assistance programs: A research-based primer. In C. L. Cooper, J. C. Quick, & M. J. Schabracq (Eds.), *International handbook of work and health psychology* (3rd ed., pp. 383–407). Wiley Blackwell. doi:10.1002/9780470682357.ch17

Austin, R. D., & Pisano, G. P. (2017). Neurodiversity as a competitive advantage. *Harvard Business Review*, *95*(3), 96–103.

Aydarova, O. (2013). If not "the best of the West," then "look East" Imported teacher education curricula in the Arabian Gulf. *Journal of Studies in International Education*, *17*(3), 284–302. doi:10.1177/1028315312453742

Backhaus, K., & Tikoo, S. (2004, August). Conceptualizing and researching employer branding. *Career Development International*, *9*(5), 501–517. doi:10.1108/13620430410550754

Badri, S. K. Z., Yung, C. T. M., Wan Mohd Yunus, W. M. A., & Seman, N. A. A. (2023). The perceived effects of spirituality, work-life integration and mediating role of work passion to millennial or gen Y employees' mental health. *Management Research Review, 46*(9), 1278–1295. doi:10.1108/MRR-04-2021-0275

Bagai, R., & Mane, V. (2023). Designing an AI-Powered Mentorship Platform for Professional Development: Opportunities and Challenges. *International Journal of Computer Trends and Technology, 71*(4), 108–114. doi:10.14445/22312803/IJCTT-V71I4P114

Bagatell, N. (2010). From cure to community: Transforming notions of autism. *Ethos, 38*(1), 33-55. Burnett, E. R. (2021). 'Different, not less': pastoral care of autistic adults within Christian churches. *Practical Theology, 14*(3), 211–223.

Bagley, E. A., & Shaffer, D. W. (2015). Stop talking and type: Comparing virtual and face-to-face mentoring in an epistemic game. *Journal of Computer Assisted Learning, 31*(6), 606–622. doi:10.1111/jcal.12092

Bahri-Ammari, N., Soliman, M., & Salah, O. B. (2022). The impact of employer brand on job seekers' attitudes and intentions: The moderating role of value congruence and social media. *Corporate Reputation Review*. Advance online publication. doi:10.1057/s41299-022-00154-8

Bahuguna, P. C., Srivastava, R., & Tiwari, S. (2023). Two-decade journey of green human resource management research: A bibliometric analysis. *Benchmarking, 30*(2), 585–602. doi:10.1108/BIJ-10-2021-0619

Baker, D. L. (2011). *The Politics of Neurodiversity: Why Public Policy Matters.* Lynne Rienner Publishers. doi:10.1515/9781685851224

Baker, E. K. (2021). Mentorship in a virtual world. *The Journal of Nursing Education, 60*(5), 277–278. PMID:34039141

Baker, J. D. (2021). Virtual mentoring: Tips and techniques for finding and providing support in online environments. *Journal of Online Learning Research, 7*(1), 5–24.

Balanay, J. A. G., & Richards, S. L. (2022). Insights into Diversity in the Environmental Health Science Workforce. *Environmental Health Insights, 16*, 1–2. doi:10.1177/11786302221077513 PMID:35153487

Balconi, M., Fronda, G., Cassioli, F., & Crivelli, D. (2022). Face-to-face vs. remote digital settings in job assessment interviews: A multilevel hyperscanning protocol for investigating interpersonal attunement. *PLoS One, 17*(2), e0263668. doi:10.1371/journal.pone.0263668 PMID:35130314

Bambacas, M., & Kulik, T. C. (2013). Job embeddedness in China: How HR practices impact turnover intentions. *International Journal of Human Resource Management, 24*(10), 1933–1952. doi:10.1080/09585192.2012.725074

Banaji, M. R., & Greenwald, A. G. (1995). Implicit gender stereotyping in judgments of fame. *Journal of Personality and Social Psychology, 68*(2), 181–198. doi:10.1037/0022-3514.68.2.181 PMID:7877095

Bandari, V. (2019). Exploring the Transformational Potential of Emerging Technologies in Human Resource Analytics: A Comparative Study of the Applications of IoT, AI, and Cloud Computing. *Journal of Humanities and Applied Science Research, 2*(1), 15–27.

Bandyopadhyay, G. (2017). Determinants of psychological wellbeing and its impact on mental health. In India, studies in business and economics (pp. 53–95). doi:10.1007/978-981-10-6104-2_5

Bangwal, D., & Tiwari, P. (2015). Green HRM – A way to greening the environment. *IOSR Journal of Business and Management, 17*(12), 43–53.

Bano, S., Khan, M. F., Butt, N. A., & Ullah, H. (2013). Analysis of Workforce Diversity, Commitment of Employees and its Effects on Organizational Performance: Corporate Sector in Islamabad Pakistan. *International Review of Basic and Applied Sciences*.

Baporikar, N. (2016). Talent Management Integrated Approach for Organizational Development. In Strategic Labor Relations Management in Modern Organizations (pp. 22-48). IGI Global. doi:10.4018/978-1-5225-0356-9.ch002

Baporikar, N. (2017b). Sustainable framework to attract, develop, and retain global talent. In Driving multinational enterprises through effective global talent management (pp. 50-74). IGI Global. doi:10.4018/978-1-5225-2557-8.ch003

Baporikar, N. (2013). Understanding Talent Management in Borderless World. *Management Today*, *3*(4), 10–16. doi:10.11127/gmt.2013.12.02

Baporikar, N. (2017a). Global perspective on talent management: The South African experience. In *Effective talent management strategies for organizational success* (pp. 283–300). IGI Global. doi:10.4018/978-1-5225-1961-4.ch018

Baporikar, N. (2020). Human Resource Management for Managing Cultural Diversity. *International Journal of Applied Management Sciences and Engineering*, *7*(1), 74–99. doi:10.4018/IJAMSE.2020010104

Baporikar, N. (2021). Post-Pandemic Restorative Talent Management Strategy for SME Development. In *Cases on Small Business Economics and Development During Economic Crises* (pp. 80–96). IGI Global. doi:10.4018/978-1-7998-7657-1.ch004

Barbu, S. J., McDonald, K. A., Brazil-Cruz, L., Sullivan, L., & Bisson, L. F. (2021). Data-driven decision-making. In Springer eBooks (pp. 47–59). doi:10.1007/978-3-030-85668-7_3

Barnes, J., Hall, J. B., & Grubb, B. (2023). Cultural humility and inclusion: Transformation to a culture of belonging. In Building Leadership Bridges (pp. 25–38). doi:10.1108/S2058-880120230000009003

Barr, D. A. (2019). *Health disparities in the United States: Social class, race, ethnicity, and the social determinants of health*. JHU Press. doi:10.56021/9781421432571

Barrena-Martínez, J., López-Fernández, M., Márquez-Moreno, C., & Romero-Fernández, P. M. (2015). Corporate social responsibility in the process of attracting college graduates. *Corporate Social Responsibility and Environmental Management*, *22*(6), 408–423. doi:10.1002/csr.1355

Barron, P. (2008). Education and talent management: Implications for the hospitality industry. *International Journal of Contemporary Hospitality Management*, *20*(7), 730–742. doi:10.1108/09596110810897583

Barry, M. M. (2012). Promoting positive mental health and wellbeing: Practice and policy. In Springer eBooks (pp. 355–384). doi:10.1007/978-94-007-5195-8_16

Basford, T. E., Offermann, L. R., & Behrend, T. S. (2013). Do You See What I See? Perceptions of Gender Microaggressions in the Workplace. *Psychology of Women Quarterly*, *38*(3), 340–349. doi:10.1177/0361684313511420

Bashynska, I., Prokopenko, O., & Sala, D. (2023). Managing Human Capital with AI: Synergy of Talent and Technology. *Zeszyty Naukowe Wyższej Szkoły Finansów i Prawa w Bielsku-Białej*, *27*(3), 39–45.

Baumgartl, C. (2019). *Employer brand experience. Theoretical foundations and empirical findings on how employees experience the employer brand*. MERKUR - Writings on Innovative Marketing Management.

Baum, T. (2007). Skills, training and development within an insular labour market: The changing role of catering managers in the healthcare environment. *Journal of Management Development*, *26*(2), 132–147. doi:10.1108/02621710710726044

Baum, T. (2008). Implications of hospitality and tourism labour markets for talent management strategies. *International Journal of Contemporary Hospitality Management, 20*(7), 720–729. doi:10.1108/09596110810897574

Beattie, G., & Johnson, P. (2012). Possible unconscious bias in recruitment and promotion and the need to promote equality. Perspectives. *Policy and Practice in Higher Education, 16*(1), 7–13.

Bechtoldt, M. N. (2015). Wanted: Self-doubting employees- Managers scoring positively on impostorism favor insecure employees in task delegation. *Personality and Individual Differences, 86*, 482–486. doi:10.1016/j.paid.2015.07.002

Beecham, S., Baddoo, N., Hall, T., Robinson, H., & Sharp, H. (2008). Motivation in Software Engineering: A systematic literature review. *Information and Software Technology, 50*(9-10), 860–878. doi:10.1016/j.infsof.2007.09.004

Beechler, S., & Woodward, I. (2009). The Global War for Talent. *Journal of International Management, 15*(3), 273–285. doi:10.1016/j.intman.2009.01.002

Bella, K. M. J. (2023). The power of employee well-being: A catalyst for organizational success. *International Journal of Scientific Research in Modern Science and Technology, 2*(4), 20–26.

Benabdallah, L. (2019). Contesting the international order by integrating it: The case of China's Belt and Road initiative. *Third World Quarterly, 40*(1), 92–108. doi:10.1080/01436597.2018.1529539

Bendick, M. Jr, & Nunes, A. P. (2012). Developing the research basis for controlling bias in hiring. *The Journal of Social Issues, 68*(2), 238–262. doi:10.1111/j.1540-4560.2012.01747.x

Benedict, C., Hahn, A., Diefenbach, M. A., & Ford, J. S. (2019). Recruitment via social media: Advantages and potential biases. *Digital Health, 5*. doi:10.1177/2055207619867223 PMID:31431827

Benevene, P., & Buonomo, I. (2020). Green Human Resource Management: An EvidenceBased Systematic Literature Review. *Sustainability (Basel), 12*(15), 1–25. doi:10.3390/su12155974

Benuyenah, V. (2023, August). Rethinking recruitment ethically through the lens of corporate social responsibility (CSR). In *Evidence-based HRM: a Global Forum for Empirical Scholarship* (Vol. 11, No. 3, pp. 372-376). Emerald Publishing Limited.

Berger, R. (2014). Mastering the art of Jugaad and Guanxi: A western guide to business practices in India and China. [IJABIM]. *International Journal of Asian Business and Information Management, 5*(4), 14–22. doi:10.4018/ijabim.2014100102

Berraies, S., Lajili, R., & Chtioui, R. (2020). Social capital, employees' well-being and knowledge sharing: Does enterprise social networks use matter? Case of Tunisian knowledge-intensive firms. *Journal of Intellectual Capital, 21*(6), 1153–1183. doi:10.1108/JIC-01-2020-0012

Berthon, P., Ewing, M., & Hah, L. L. (2005, January). Captivating company: Dimensions of attractiveness in employer branding. *International Journal of Advertising, 24*(2), 151–172. doi:10.1080/02650487.2005.11072912

Bewley, H., & George, A. (2016). *Neurodiversity at work*. National Institute of Social and Economic Research.

Bhalla, A., Singh, P., & Singh, A. (2023). Technological Advancement and Mechanization of the Hotel Industry. In R. Tailor (Ed.), *Application and Adoption of Robotic Process Automation for Smart Cities* (pp. 57–76). IGI Global. doi:10.4018/978-1-6684-7193-7.ch004

Bhanumathi & Pragalapati. (2022). To Study the Impact of Artificial Intelligence on Recruitment in the IT sector. *Journal of Management & Entrepreneurship*.

Bhutto, S., & Auranzeb. (2016). Effects of Green Human Resources Management on Firm Performance: An Empirical Study on Pakistani Firms. *European Journal of Business and Management, 8*(16), 119–125.

Bibi, P., Ahmad, A., & Majid, A. H. A. (2018). HRM Practices and Employee Retention: The Moderating Effect of Work Environment. In Applying Partial Least Squares in Tourism and Hospitality Research. Emerald Publishing Limited. doi:10.1108/978-1-78756-699-620181007

Bibi, N., Bin Saeed, B., & Afridi, M. A. (2022). An Integrated Approach to Linking Job Love with Contextual Factors and Performance: An Empirical Study from Pakistan. *Journal of Asian FinanceEconomics and Business*, *9*(5), 157–169. doi:10.13106/jafeb.2022.vol9.no5.0157

Bierema, L. L. (2020). Virtual mentoring: Navigating online professional relationships. *New Directions for Adult and Continuing Education*, *168*, 37–46.

Bijja Vishwanath, D. S. V. (2023). The Future of Work: Implications of Artificial Intelligence on Hr Practices. *Tuijin Jishu/Journal of Propulsion Technology, 44*(3), 1711-1724.

Bissola, R., & Imperatori, B. (2014). Recruiting Gen Yers Through Social Media: Insights from the Italian Labor Market. doi:10.1108/S1877-6361(2013)0000012007

Blackston, M. (1993). Beyond brand personality: Building brand relationships. In D. A. Aaker & A. L. Biel (Eds.), *Brand equity and advertising: Advertising's role in building strong brands* (pp. 113–124). Lawrence Erlbaum and Associates.

Blashfield, R. K., Keeley, J. W., Flanagan, E. H., & Miles, S. R. (2014). The cycle of classification: DSM-I through DSM-5. *Annual Review of Clinical Psychology*, *10*(1), 25–51. doi:10.1146/annurev-clinpsy-032813-153639 PMID:24679178

Blockley, D. (2020). *Creativity, problem solving, and aesthetics in engineering*. Springer International Publishing. doi:10.1007/978-3-030-38257-5

Bocar, A. C., Khan, S. A., & Epoc, F. (2022). COVID-19 Work from Home Stressors and the Degree of its Impact: Employers and Employees Actions. *International Journal of Technology Transfer and Commercialisation*, *19*(2), 270–291.

Bochner, S., & Hesketh, B. (1994). Power distance, individualism/collectivism, and job-related attitudes in a culturally diverse work group. *Journal of Cross-Cultural Psychology*, *25*(2), 233–257. doi:10.1177/0022022194252005

Bodet-Contentin, L., Letourneur, M., & Ehrmann, S. (2023). Virtual reality during work breaks to reduce fatigue of intensive unit caregivers: A crossover, pilot, randomised trial. *Australian Critical Care*, *36*(3), 345–349. doi:10.1016/j.aucc.2022.01.009 PMID:35246356

Boehncke, G. A. (2023). The role of CSR in high Potential recruiting: Literature review on the communicative expectations of high potentials. *Corporate Communications*, *28*(2), 249–273. doi:10.1108/CCIJ-02-2022-0021

Boekhorst, J. A. (2015). The role of authentic leadership in fostering workplace inclusion: A social information processing perspective. *Human Resource Management*, *54*(2), 241–264. doi:10.1002/hrm.21669

Boeri, T., Garnero, A., & Luisetto, L. G. (2023). *Non-compete agreements in a rigid labor market: The case of Italy*. Academic Press.

Bogathy, Z., Ilin, C., Virga, D., Palos., R., Erdei. I., Sava, P.A., & Zoborila, C.A. (2004). Manual de psihologia muncii şi organizaţională, Editura Polirom.

Bohlander, G., & Snell, S. (2010). *Managing human resources* (15th ed.). Cengage Learning.

Boiko, J., Volianska-Savchuk, L., Bazaliyska, N., & Zelena, M. (2021, September). Smart recruiting as a modern tool for HR hiring in the context of business informatization. In *2021 11th International Conference on Advanced Computer Information Technologies (ACIT)* (pp. 284-289). IEEE. 10.1109/ACIT52158.2021.9548558

Boksberger, P., Dolnicar, S., Laesser, C., & Randle, M. (2011). Self-congruity theory: To what extent does it hold in tourism? *Journal of Travel Research, 50*(4), 454–464. doi:10.1177/0047287510368164

Bondarouk, T., Ruël, H., Axinia, E., & Arama, R. (2014). What Is the Future of Employer Branding Through Social Media? Results of the Delphi Study into the Perceptions of HR Professionals and Academics. doi:10.1108/S1877-6361(2013)0000012006

Bongard, A. (2019). Automating talent acquisition: Smart recruitment, predictive hiring algorithms, and the data-driven nature of artificial intelligence. *Psychosociological Issues in Human Resource Management, 7*(1), 36–41.

Boonbumroongsuk, B., & Rungruang, P. (2022). Employee perception of talent management practices and turnover intentions: A multiple mediator model. *Employee Relations, 44*(2), 461–476. doi:10.1108/ER-04-2021-0163

Borowiec, A. A., & Drygas, W. (2022). Work–Life Balance and Mental and Physical Health among Warsaw Specialists, Managers and Entrepreneurs. *International Journal of Environmental Research and Public Health, 20*(1), 492. doi:10.3390/ijerph20010492 PMID:36612813

Borry, E. L., Getha-Taylor, H., & Holmes, M. H. (2021). Promoting Diversity and Inclusion in the Federal Workforce: Executive Order 13583 and Demographic Trends. *Public Administration Quarterly, 45*(4), 392–417. doi:10.37808/paq.45.4.3

Borthwick, M. (2018). *Pacific century: The emergence of modern Pacific Asia.* Routledge. doi:10.4324/9780429494895

Bosco, S. M., Wang, Y., Chen, P. Y., & Sharma, P. N. (2017). The role of mentoring functions on mentor commitment and mentee turnover intentions. *Journal of Business Research, 78*, 124–132.

Bostjancic, E., & Slana, Z. (2018). The Role of Talent Management Comparing Medium-Sized and Large Companies - Major Challenges in Attracting and Retaining Talented Employees. *Frontiers in Psychology, 9*, 1750. Advance online publication. doi:10.3389/fpsyg.2018.01750 PMID:30283391

Boussemart, B., & De Bandt, J. (1993). The textile industry: widely varying structures. In *Progress in Intercalation Research* (pp. 203–235). Springer Netherlands.

Bowen, D., & Schneider, B. (1985). Boundary-spanning-role employees and the service encounter: Some guidelines for management and research. In J. A. Czepiel, M. R. Solomon, & C. Surprenant (Eds.), *The service encounter* (pp. 127–147). D. C. Heath.

Bower, P., Brueton, V., Gamble, C., Treweek, S., Smith, C. T., Young, B., & Williamson, P. (2014). Interventions to improve recruitment and retention in clinical trials: A survey and workshop to assess current practice and future priorities. *Trials, 15*(1), 399. Advance online publication. doi:10.1186/1745-6215-15-399 PMID:25322807

Brandt, K. (2007). *Kingdom of Beauty: Mingei and the politics of folk art in Imperial Japan.* Duke University Press.

Bratton, J., & Watson, S. (2018). Talent management, emotional labour and the role of line managers in the Scottish hospitality industry: A roundtable discussion. *Worldwide Hospitality and Tourism Themes, 10*(1), 57–68. doi:10.1108/WHATT-10-2017-0063

Bravata, D. M., Watts, S. A., Keefer, A. L., Madhusudhan, D. K., Taylor, K. H., Clark, D., Nelson, R., Cokley, K., & Hagg, H. (2020). Prevalence, Predictors, and Treatment of Impostor Syndrome: A Systematic Review. *Journal of General Internal Medicine, 35*(4), 1252–1275. doi:10.1007/s11606-019-05364-1 PMID:31848865

Brega, C., Briones, S., Javornik, J., León, M., & Yerkes, M. A. (2023). Flexible work arrangements for work-life balance: A cross-national policy evaluation from a capabilities perspective. *The International Journal of Sociology and Social Policy, 43*(13/14), 278–294. doi:10.1108/IJSSP-03-2023-0077

Briscoe, D., Schuler, R., & Tarique, I. (2012). *International human resource management: Policies and practices for multinational enterprises*. Routledge. doi:10.4324/9780203816189

Brockman, S. L. (2023). Can nudging mentors weaken student support? experimental evidence from a virtual communication intervention. *Journal of Research on Educational Effectiveness*, 1–33. doi:10.1080/19345747.2023.2186291

Brody, G. H., Yu, T., Chen, E., Ehrlich, K. B., & Miller, G. E. (2018). Racial discrimination, body mass index, and insulin resistance: A longitudinal analysis. *Health Psychology*, *37*(12), 1107–1114. doi:10.1037/hea0000674 PMID:30307274

Brohan, E., & Thornicroft, G. (2010). Stigma and discrimination of mental health problems: Workplace implications. *Occupational Medicine*, *60*(6), 414–415. doi:10.1093/occmed/kqq048 PMID:20719967

Brondolo, E., Beatty, D. L., Cubbin, C., Pencille, M., Saegert, S., Wellington, R., Tobin, J., Cassells, A., & Schwartz, J. (2009). Sociodemographic Variations in Self-Reported Racism in a Community Sample of Blacks and Latino(a)s. *Journal of Applied Social Psychology*, *39*(2), 407–429. doi:10.1111/j.1559-1816.2008.00444.x

Brondolo, E., Brady, N., Thompson, S., Tobin, J. N., Cassells, A., Sweeney, M., McFarlane, D. J., & Contrada, R. J. (2008). Perceived Racism and Negative Affect: Analyses of Trait and State Measures of Affect in a Community Sample. *Journal of Social and Clinical Psychology*, *27*(2), 150–173. doi:10.1521/jscp.2008.27.2.150 PMID:19079772

Brophy, S., Klein, S., Portsmore, M., & Rogers, C. (2008). Advancing engineering education in P-12 classrooms. *Journal of Engineering Education*, *97*(3), 369–387. doi:10.1002/j.2168-9830.2008.tb00985.x

Brown, D. (2018). Virtual mentoring: A popular option in talent development. *Talent Development*, *72*(5), 28–33.

Brown, T. J. (1998). Corporate Associations in Marketing: Antecedents and Consequences. *Corporate Reputation Review*, *1*(3), 215–233. doi:10.1057/palgrave.crr.1540045

Brütt, K., & Yuan, H. (2022). *Pitfalls of pay transparency: Evidence from the lab and the field* (No. TI 2022-055/I). Tinbergen Institute Discussion Paper.

Brymer, R. A., & Rocha, V. (2023). Affiliation-based hiring in startups and the origins of organizational diversity. *Personnel Psychology*. Advance online publication. doi:10.1111/peps.12612

Bubonya, M., Cobb-Clark, D. A., & Wooden, M. (2017). Mental health and productivity at work: Does what you do matter? *Labour Economics*, *46*, 150–165. doi:10.1016/j.labeco.2017.05.001

Buckley, E., Pellicano, E., & Remington, A. (2020). The real thing I struggle with is other people's perceptions: The experiences of autistic performing arts professionals and attitudes of performing arts employers in the UK. *Journal of Autism and Developmental Disorders*, *51*(1), 45–59. doi:10.1007/s10803-020-04517-0 PMID:32356080

Bui, L. T. T., & Chang, Y. (2018). Talent management and turnover intention: Focus on Danang city government in Vietnam. *International Review of Public Administration*, *23*(4), 219–236. doi:10.1080/12294659.2018.1552403

Buitek, E. K., Kaliyeva, S. A., Turginbayeva, A. N., Meldakhanova, M. K., & Shaikh, A. A. (2023). How much does an employer's attractiveness matter to youth employment? Evidence from a developing country. *Asia-Pacific Journal of Business Administration*. Advance online publication. doi:10.1108/APJBA-02-2023-0086

Burki, U., & Buvik, A. (2017). Manufacturing complexity and inter-firm coordination: Evidence from the textile-exporting firms of Pakistan. *International Journal of Procurement Management*, *10*(2), 227–247. doi:10.1504/IJPM.2017.082790

Burmeister, M. (2009). It's all about me becomes a cross generational conversation. *Training & Development*, *63*(5), 92–93.

Burnett, K., & Trerise, M. (2019). Embracing neurodiversity in the workplace. *Train. J*, 28-29.

Burnham Riosa, P., Greenblatt, A., & Muskat, B. (2017). An online ASD learning module for pediatric health care professionals. *Advances in Autism*, *3*(3), 154–162. doi:10.1108/AIA-03-2017-0007

Buzan, B., & Goh, E. (2020). *Rethinking Sino-Japanese alienation: history problems and historical opportunities*. Oxford University Press. doi:10.1093/oso/9780198851387.001.0001

Byrd, M. Y. (2022). Employee resource groups: Enabling developmental relationships to support socially just and morally inclusive organizations. In Springer eBooks (pp. 219–237). doi:10.1007/978-3-030-85033-3_10

Cadorette, M., & Agnew, J. (2017). Mental health in the workplace. *Workplace Health & Safety*, *65*(9), 448. doi:10.1177/2165079917716188 PMID:28703037

Calderón-Fajardo, V., Molinillo, S., Anaya-Sánchez, R., & Ekinci, Y. (2023). Brand personality: Current insights and future research directions. *Journal of Business Research*, *166*, 114062. doi:10.1016/j.jbusres.2023.114062

Callaci, B., Gibson, M., Pinto, S., Steinbaum, M., & Walsh, M. (2023). *The Effect of Franchise No-poaching Restrictions on Worker Earnings*. Working Paper.

Cao, J., Huang, L., Xue, Y., & Yi, H. (2012). The Establishment and Practice of Textile Engineering Applied Professionals Training Model. In *Engineering Education and Management: Vol 2, Results of the 2011 International Conference on Engineering Education and Management (ICEEM2011)* (pp. 611-616). Springer Berlin Heidelberg. 10.1007/978-3-642-24820-7_98

Cao, N., Zhang, Z., Man To, K., & Po Ng, K. (2008). How are supply chains coordinated? An empirical observation in textile-apparel businesses. *Journal of Fashion Marketing and Management*, *12*(3), 384–397. doi:10.1108/13612020810889326

Cappelli, P., & Keller, J. (2014). Talent Management: Conceptual Approaches and Practical Challenges. *Annual Review of Organizational Psychology and Organizational Behavior*, *1*(1), 305–331. doi:10.1146/annurev-orgpsych-031413-091314

Carbajal-Cribillero, M., Javier-Niño, G., Mäckelmann, M., & Gallardo-Echenique, E. (2022). Employer branding on social media to engage Generation Z. In Smart innovation, systems and technologies (pp. 469–478). doi:10.1007/978-981-16-9272-7_38

Cardenas-Munoz, M., & Ramon Campos-Blazquez, J. (2023). Towards an integrated definition of job crafting. *Intangible Capital*, *19*(1), 42–54. doi:10.3926/ic.2107

Cardon, M. S., Wincent, J., Singh, J., & Drnovsek, M. (2009). The nature and experience of entrepreneurial passion. *Academy of Management Review*, *34*(3), 511–532. doi:10.5465/amr.2009.40633190

Carlsson, C., Carlsson, J., Hyvonen, K., Puhakainen, J., & Walden, P. (2006). Adoption of Mobile Devices/Services — Searching for Answers with the UTAUT. *Proceedings of the 39th Annual Hawaii International Conference on System Sciences (HICSS'06)*, 132a–132a. 10.1109/HICSS.2006.38

Cassidy, C., & Kreitner, R. (2010). *Supervision: setting people up for success*. South-Western Cengage Learning.

Cennamo, L., & Gardner, D. (2008). Generational differences in work values, outcomes and person organization values fit. *Journal of Managerial Psychology*, *23*(8), 891–906. doi:10.1108/02683940810904385

Centers for Disease Control and Prevention. (2019). *Attention-Deficit / Hyperactivity Disorder (ADHD)*. Retrieved at https://www.cdc.gov/ncbddd/adhd/facts.html

Chaminade, B. (2010). *Attirer et fidéliser les bonnes competences. Créer votre marque d'employeur*. AFNOR Editions, St. Denis Cedex.

Chan, D. K., Lam, C. B. I., Chow, S. Y., & Cheung, S. F. (2008). Examining The Job-Related, Psychological, and Physical Outcomes of Workplace Sexual Harassment: A Meta-Analytic Review. *Psychology of Women Quarterly*, *32*(4), 362–376. doi:10.1111/j.1471-6402.2008.00451.x

Chang, D. C., Chang, N., Saw, D. G., Lomel'ı-Carrillo, U., Zhi, D. M., Romano, D. K., & Culbertson, R. (2021). Electronic Mentoring During the COVID-19 Pandemic: Effects on Engineering Graduate Students' Academic, Career, and Mental Health Outcomes. *ASEE Virtual Annual Conference, ASEE 2021*. 10.18260/1-2--37018

Charlton, J. (1998). *Nothing about Us without Us: Disability, Oppression and Empowerment.* University of California Press.

Chaudhary, R. (2020). Green human resource management and employee green behavior: An empirical analysis. *Corporate Social Responsibility and Environmental Management*, *27*(2), 630–641. doi:10.1002/csr.1827

Chaudhry, I. S., Paquibut, R. Y., & Tunio, M. N. (2021). Do workforce diversity, inclusion practices, and organizational characteristics contribute to organizational innovation? Evidence from the U.A.E. *Cogent Business & Management*, *8*(1), 1947549. Advance online publication. doi:10.1080/23311975.2021.1947549

Cheese, P., Thomas, R. T., & Craig, E. (2008). *The talent powered organization: Strategies for globalization, talent management and high performance*. Kogan Page.

Chen, J. (2010). *Mao's China and the cold war*. University of North Carolina Press.

Chen, K. P., Chen, H., & Wang, Y. (2024). The moderating effect of safety image on guests' perceived risk and revisit intentions in luxury hotels. *International Journal of Tourism Research*, *26*(1), e2614. doi:10.1002/jtr.2614

Chen, P., & Choi, Y. (2008). Generational differences in work values: A study of hospitality management. *International Journal of Contemporary Hospitality Management*, *20*(6), 595–615. doi:10.1108/09596110810892182

Chen, Z. (2022). Collaboration among recruiters and artificial intelligence: Removing human prejudices in employment. *Cognition Technology and Work*, *25*(1), 135–149. doi:10.1007/s10111-022-00716-0 PMID:36187287

Cherri Ho, C. Y. (2010). Intergenerational learning between generation x and y families – a narrative inquiry. *International Education Studies*, *3*(4), 60–61.

Cheung, P. T., Chung, J. H., & Lin, Z. (2016). *Provincial strategies of economic reform in Post-Mao China: leadership, politics, and implementation*. Routledge.

Chiaburu, D. S., & Lindsay, D. R. (2008). Virtual mentoring and career outcomes: Evidence from a field study. *Journal of Vocational Behavior*, *73*(3), 330–341.

Chiang, J. K.-H., & Suen, H.-Y. (2015). Self-presentation and hiring recommendations in online communities: Lessons from LinkedIn. *Computers in Human Behavior*, *48*, 516–524. doi:10.1016/j.chb.2015.02.017

Chiranmai, I., Rajesh, S. M., Meghana, G., Rose, S., & Jayapandian, N. (2023). Post covid scenario effective e-mentoring system in higher education. *2023 International Conference on Innovative Data Communication Technologies and Application (ICIDCA)*. 10.1109/ICIDCA56705.2023.10100176

Chowdhury, S., Dey, P., Joel-Edgar, S., Bhattacharya, S., Rodriguez-Espindola, O., Abadie, A., & Truong, L. (2023). Unlocking the value of artificial intelligence in human resource management through AI capability framework. *Human Resource Management Review*, *33*(1), 100899. doi:10.1016/j.hrmr.2022.100899

Chua, R. Y. J., Morris, M. W., & Mor, S. (2023). Making sense of cultural diversity's complexity: Addressing an emerging challenge for leadership. *International Journal of Cross Cultural Management*, *23*(3), 643–662. doi:10.1177/14705958231214623

Chun, A. (2017). *Forget Chineseness: On the geopolitics of cultural identification.* Suny Press. doi:10.1515/9781438464732

Cizmic, E., & Ahmic, A. (2021). The Influence of Talent Management on Organisational Performance in Bosnia & Herzegovina as a Developing Country. *Management*, *26*(1), 129–147. doi:10.30924/mjcmi.26.1.8

Clance, P. R., & Imes, S. A. (1978). The impostor phenomenon in high achieving women: Dynamics and therapeutic intervention. *Psychotherapy: Theory, Research &Amp. Practice*, *15*(3), 241–247. doi:10.1037/h0086006

Clarke, N., Mondisa, J.-L., & Gosha, K. (2021). The Role of E-Mentoring in the African American Higher Education Experience (Work in Progress). *2021 ASEE Virtual Annual Conference.* Retrieved from https://par.nsf.gov/biblio/10296096

Clark, E. (2021). Building trust in virtual mentoring relationships. *Journal of Career Development*, *48*(5), 512–526.

Clark, M. (2021). Virtual mentoring: Strategies for building rapport and trust. *Journal of Mentoring & Tutoring: Partnership in Learning*, *29*(4), 369–383.

Clark, R., Anderson, N. B., Clark, V. R., & Williams, D. R. (1999). Racism as a stressor for African Americans: A biopsychosocial model. *The American Psychologist*, *54*(10), 805–816. doi:10.1037/0003-066X.54.10.805 PMID:10540593

Claus, L. (2019a). HR disruption—Time already to reinvent talent management. *Business Research Quarterly*, *22*(3), 207–215. doi:10.1016/j.brq.2019.04.002

Clauss-Ehlers, C. S. (2019). Virtual mentoring and cross-generational mentoring in the 21st century. In *The Wiley Handbook of Global Workplace Learning* (pp. 595–607). Wiley.

Clinton, H. R. (2014). *Hard choices.* Simon and Schuster.

Cobb, M., Branson, N., McGreevy, P., Lill, A., & Bennett, P. (2015). The advent of canine performance science: Offering a sustainable future for working dogs. *Behavioural Processes*, *110*, 96–104. doi:10.1016/j.beproc.2014.10.012 PMID:25444772

Coculova, J., & Tomcikova, L. (2021). Innovative Human Resource Management Practices for the Talent Management Implementation. *Marketing and Management of Innovations*, *4*(4), 47–54. doi:10.21272/mmi.2021.4-04

Coe, N. M., & Yeung, H. W. C. (2015). *Global production networks: Theorizing economic development in an interconnected world.* Oxford University Press. doi:10.1093/acprof:oso/9780198703907.001.0001

Cohen, J. (2013). *Statistical Power Analysis for the Behavioral Sciences.* Routledge., doi:10.4324/9780203771587

Cole, G. A. (2000). *Personnel management.* Editura CODECS.

Coles, A. (2021). Diversity and inclusion in talent acquisition. In Springer eBooks (pp. 171–183). doi:10.1007/978-3-030-60060-0_12

Collings, D. G., & Isichei, M. (2017). Global talent management: What does it mean for expatriates? In Research Handbook of Expatriates (pp. 148–159). Edward Elgar Publishing. doi:10.4337/9781784718183.00016

Collings, D. G., McDonnell, A., & McMackin, J. (2017). *Talent management. A Research agenda for human resource management.* Academic Press.

Collings, D. G., & Mellahi, K. (2009). Strategic talent management: A review and research agenda. *Human Resource Management Review*, *19*(4), 304–313. doi:10.1016/j.hrmr.2009.04.001

Collins, C. J., & Stevens, C. K. (2002). The relationship between early recruitment-related activities and the application decisions of new labor-market entrants: A brand equity approach to recruitment. *The Journal of Applied Psychology*, *87*(6), 1121–1133. doi:10.1037/0021-9010.87.6.1121 PMID:12558218

Compeau, D., Higgins, C. A., & Huff, S. (1999). Social Cognitive Theory and Individual Reactions to Computing Technology: A Longitudinal Study. *Management Information Systems Quarterly*, *23*(2), 145. doi:10.2307/249749

Compton, R., Morrissey, W., & Nankervis, A. (2009). Effective recruitment and selection practices, CCH a Wolters, Australia

Constantinov, C., & Mocanu, M. L. (2021). A comprehensive review of professional network impact on education and career. *Challenges and Applications of Data Analytics in Social Perspectives*, 1-26.

Coppens, E., Hogg, B., Greiner, B. A., Paterson, C., De Winter, L., Mathieu, S., Cresswell-Smith, J., Aust, B., Leduc, C., Van Audenhove, C., Pashoja, A. C., Kim, D., Reich, H., Fanaj, N., Dushaj, A., Thomson, K., O'Connor, C., Moreno-Alcázar, A., Amann, B. L., & Arensman, E. (2023). Promoting employee wellbeing and preventing non-clinical mental health problems: A preparatory consultation survey. *Journal of Occupational Medicine and Toxicology (London, England)*, *18*(1), 17. Advance online publication. doi:10.1186/s12995-023-00378-2 PMID:37582790

Cornescu, V., Mihăilescu, I., & Stanciu, S. (2001). *Management general*. Editura Actami.

Corple, D. J. (2023). Empowerment at Work?: Examining Employment-Based Economic Empowerment Initiatives for Survivors of Commercial Sexual Exploitation. *Violence Against Women*. Advance online publication. doi:10.1177/10778012231181047 PMID:37321818

Cortina, L. M., Magley, V. J., Williams, J. M., & Langhout, R. D. (2001). Incivility in the workplace: Incidence and impact. *Journal of Occupational Health Psychology*, *6*(1), 64–80. doi:10.1037/1076-8998.6.1.64 PMID:11199258

Cox, T. Jr, & Blake, S. (1991). Managing cultural diversity: Implications for organizational competitiveness. *The Academy of Management Executive*, *5*(3), 45–56.

Cox, W. T. L. (2022). Developing scientifically validated bias and diversity training that work: Empowering agents of change to reduce bias, create inclusion, and promote equity. *Management Decision*, *61*(4), 1038–1061. doi:10.1108/MD-06-2021-0839 PMID:37090785

Cresswell-Smith, J., Kauppinen, T., Laaksoharju, T., Rotko, T., Solin, P., Suvisaari, J., Wahlbeck, K., & Tamminen, N. (2022). Mental health and mental wellbeing impact assessment frameworks—A systematic review. *International Journal of Environmental Research and Public Health*, *19*(21), 13985. doi:10.3390/ijerph192113985 PMID:36360865

Creswell, J. W., & Plano Clark, V. L. (2018). *Designing and conducting mixed methods research*. Sage Publications.

Crumpacker, M., & Crumpacker, J. D. (2007). Succession planning and generational stereotypes: Should HR consider age-based values and attitudes- a relevant factor or a passing fad? *Public Personnel Management*, *36*(4), 349–369. doi:10.1177/009102600703600405

Curtis, L., Edwards, C., Fraser, K. L., Gudelsky, S., Holmquist, J., Thornton, K., & Sweetser, K. D. (2010). Adoption of social media for public relations by nonprofit organizations. *Public Relations Review*, *36*(1), 90–92. doi:10.1016/j.pubrev.2009.10.003

Daft, R., & Lengel, R. (1986). Organizational Information Requirements, Media Richness and Structural Design. *Management Science*, *32*(5), 554–571. doi:10.1287/mnsc.32.5.554

Daileyl, R. C., & Kirk, D. J. (1992). Distributive and Procedural Justice as Antecedents of Job Dissatisfaction and Intent to Turnover. *Human Relations*, *45*(3), 305–317. doi:10.1177/001872679204500306

Dai, X., & Si, K. (2023). The Fundamental Recruitment Error: Candidate-Recruiter Discrepancy in Their Relative Valuation of Innate Talent vs. Hard Work. *Organization Science*. Advance online publication. doi:10.1287/orsc.2023.1667

Dana, L. P., Gautam, O., Gupta, A., & Sharma, N. (2023). *Indian SMEs and start-ups.* World Scientific Publishing. doi:10.1142/13239

Dancza, K. M., Choi, Y. M., Amalia, K., Wong, P. S., Hu, J. H., & Yap, L. W. (2022). An Appreciative Inquiry Approach to Understanding What Attracts and Retains Early-Career Therapists to Work in Community Organizations. *The Internet Journal of Allied Health Sciences and Practice, 20*(1). Advance online publication. doi:10.46743/1540-580X/2022.2002

Dardenne, B., Dumont, M., & Bollier, T. (2007). Insidious dangers of benevolent sexism: Consequences for women's performance. *Journal of Personality and Social Psychology, 93*(5), 764–779. doi:10.1037/0022-3514.93.5.764 PMID:17983299

Darwish, A. F. E., & Huber, G. L. (2003). Individualism vs collectivism in different cultures: A cross-cultural study. *Intercultural Education, 14*(1), 47–56. doi:10.1080/1467598032000044647

Dauth, T., Schmid, S., Baldermann, S., & Orban, F. (2023). Attracting talent through diversity at the top: The impact of TMT diversity and firms' efforts to promote diversity on employer attractiveness. *European Management Journal, 41,* 9-20. doi:10.1016/j.emj.2021.10.007

Davenport, L. J., Allisey, A., Page, K. M., LaMontagne, A. D., & Reavley, N. (2016). How can organizations help employees thrive? The development of guidelines for promoting positive mental health at work. *International Journal of Workplace Health Management, 9*(4), 411–427. doi:10.1108/IJWHM-01-2016-0001

Davidescu, A. A., Apostu, S.-A., Paul, A., & Casuneanu, I. (2020). Work flexibility, job satisfaction, and job performance among Romanian employees—Implications for Sustainable Human Resource Management. *Sustainability (Basel), 12*(15), 6086. doi:10.3390/su12156086

Davies, B., & Davies, B. J. (2010). Talent management in academies. *International Journal of Educational Management, 24*(5), 418–426. doi:10.1108/09513541011055983

Davies, G. (2008, May 30). Employer branding and its influence on managers. *European Journal of Marketing, 42*(5/6), 667–681. doi:10.1108/03090560810862570

Davies, S. W., Putnam, H. M., Ainsworth, T. D., Baum, J. K., Bove, C. B., Crosby, S. C., Côté, I. M., Duplouy, A., Fulweiler, R. W., Griffin, A., Hanley, T. C., Hill, T. M., Humanes, A., Mangubhai, S., Metaxas, A., Parker, L. M., Rivera, H. E., Silbiger, N. J., Smith, N. S., ... Bates, A. E. (2021). Promoting inclusive metrics of success and impact to dismantle a discriminatory reward system in science. *PLoS Biology, 19*(6), e3001282. doi:10.1371/journal.pbio.3001282 PMID:34129646

De Chernatony, L., & Dall'Olmo Riley, F. (1998). Defining a "brand": Beyond the literature with experts' interpretations. *Journal of Marketing Management, 14*(5), 417–443. doi:10.1362/026725798784867798

de Falco, H. (2011). *Maitriser ses recrutements. 7 etapes clés pour faire le bon choix* (4th ed.). Dunod.

De Janasz, S. C., & Godshalk, M. V. (2013). The role of e-mentoring in protégés'. Learning and satisfaction. *Group & Organization Management, 38*(6), 743–774. doi:10.1177/1059601113511296

De Munck, B. (2020). Apprenticeship, guilds, and craft knowledge. In Springer eBooks (pp. 1–7). doi:10.1007/978-3-319-20791-9_247-1

De Oliveira, C. M., Almeida, C. R. S., & Giacomoni, C. H. (2022). School-based positive psychology interventions that promote wellbeing in children: A systematic review. *Child Indicators Research, 15*(5), 1583–1600. doi:10.1007/s12187-022-09935-3 PMID:35637709

De Silva, K. D., Punsith, H., Damayanthi, H. N. P., Perera, R., Chandrasiri, S., & De Silva, H. (2023). Promoting Remote Employee Well-being: Role of Emotion Detection, Social Media Analysis, Mental Health Monitoring, and Performance Tracking. *International Research Journal of Innovations in Engineering and Technology*, 7(10), 42.

De StAubin, D., & Carlsen, B. J. (2008). *Attract, engage and retain top talent: 50 plus one strategies used by the best*. AuthorHouse.

Deckop, J. R. (2006). *Human resources management ethics*. Information Age Pub.Inc.

Deckop, J. R., Merriman, K. K., & Gupta, S. (2006). The Effects of CEO Pay Structure on Corporate Social Performance. *Journal of Management*, 32(3), 329–342. doi:10.1177/0149206305280113

Decramer, A., Smolders, C., & Vanderstraeten, A. (2013). Employee performance management culture and system features in higher education: Relationship with employee performance management satisfaction. *International Journal of Human Resource Management*, 24(2), 352–371. doi:10.1080/09585192.2012.680602

Deery, M., & Jago, L. (2015). Revisiting talent management, work-life balance and retention strategies. *International Journal of Contemporary Hospitality Management*, 27(3), 453–472. doi:10.1108/IJCHM-12-2013-0538

Dejoux, C., & Thevenet, M. (2010). *La gestion des talents. La GRH d 'apres- crise*. Dunod.

Delic, A., Vidacek-Hains, V., & Adarve, L. (2011). Perceptions of Multicultural College Students: Case-Studies of European, American and Australian Universities. In *Central European Conference on Information and Intelligent Systems* (p. 89). Faculty of Organization and Informatics Varazdin.

Dell, D., Ainspan, N., Bodenberg, T., Troy, K., & Hickey, J. (2001). *Engaging employees through your brand* (Research Report 1288-01-RR). New York: The Conference Board.

Demir, M., & Günaydın, Y. (2022). A digital job application reference: How do social media posts affect recruitment? *Employee Relations*, 45(2), 457–477. doi:10.1108/ER-05-2022-0232

Dent, C. M. (2016). *East Asian Regionalism*. Routledge. doi:10.4324/9781315717258

Deshmukh, S., Shmelev, K., Vassilades, L., Kurumety, S., Agarwal, G., & Horowitz, J. M. (2022). Impostor phenomenon in radiology: Incidence, intervention, and impact on wellness. *Clinical Imaging*, 82, 94–99. doi:10.1016/j.clinimag.2021.11.009 PMID:34801842

Deshwal, S. (2015). Employee retention-perspective of employees. *International Journal of Applied Research*, 1(6), 344–345.

Desore, A., & Narula, S. A. (2018). An overview on corporate response towards sustainability issues in textile industry. *Environment, Development and Sustainability*, 20(4), 1439–1459. doi:10.1007/s10668-017-9949-1

Dessler, G. (2007). *Human resource management*. Prentice Hall of India Private Limited.

Dhiraj, A., & Kumar, P. D. S. (2023). Impact of E-learning on the Higher Education Sector during the COVID-19 pandemic through Pedagogy tools: An observational Study. *Revista de Educación y Derecho*, 27(27). Advance online publication. doi:10.1344/REYD2023.27.40935

Diba, H. (2023). Employer Branding: The Impact of COVID-19 on New Employee Hires in IT Companies. *IT Professional*, 25(5), 4–9. doi:10.1109/MITP.2023.3321926

Diehl, A. B., Stephenson, A. L., Dzubinski, L. M., & Wang, D. (2020). Measuring the invisible: Development and multi-industry validation of the Gender Bias Scale for Women Leaders. *Human Resource Development Quarterly*, 31(3), 249–280. doi:10.1002/hrdq.21389

Dikshit, S., Grover, Y., Shukla, P., Mishra, A., Sahu, Y., Kumar, C., & Gupta, M. (2024). Empowering Employee Wellness and Building Resilience in Demanding Work Settings Through Predictive Analytics. *EAI Endorsed Transactions on Internet of Things*, 10.

DiMatteo-Gibson, D. (2023). Remote engagement through Cohort mentors. *Advances in Social Networking and Online Communities*, 254–268. doi:10.4018/978-1-6684-5190-8.ch013

Din-Dzietham, R., Nembhard, W. N., Collins, R., & Davis, S. K. (2004). Perceived stress following race-based discrimination at work is associated with hypertension in African–Americans. The metro Atlanta heart disease study, 1999–2001. *Social Science & Medicine*, *58*(3), 449–461. doi:10.1016/S0277-9536(03)00211-9 PMID:14652043

Ding, S., & Saunders, R. A. (2006). Talking up China: An analysis of China's rising cultural power and global promotion of the Chinese language. *East Asia (Piscataway, N.J.)*, *23*(2), 3–33. doi:10.1007/s12140-006-0021-2

Dinnen, M., & Alder, M. (2017). *Exceptional talent. How to attract, acquire, and retain the very best employees*. Kogan Page.

DiRenzo, M. S., Linnehan, F., Shao, P., & Rosenberg, W. L. (2010). A moderated mediation model of e-mentoring. *Journal of Vocational Behavior*, *76*(2), 292–305. doi:10.1016/j.jvb.2009.10.003

Dixit, C. K., Somani, P., Gupta, S. K., & Pathak, A. (2023). Data-Centric Predictive Modeling of Turnover Rate and New Hire in Workforce Management System. In *Designing Workforce Management Systems for Industry 4.0* (pp. 121–138). CRC Press. doi:10.1201/9781003357070-8

Dixon-Fyle, S., Dolan, K., Hunt, D. V., & Prince, S. (2019). Diversity wins: How inclusion matters. In *McKinsey & Company*. Retrieved December 29, 2022, from https://www.mckinsey.com/featured-insights/diversity-and-inclusion/diversity-wins-how-inclusion-matters

Dizaho, E. K., Salleh, R., & Abdullah, A. (2017). Achieveing Work Life Balance Through Flexible Work Schedules and Arrangements. *Global Business and Management Research*, ●●●, 9.

Dodani, S., & LaPorte, R. E. (2005). Brain drain from developing countries: How can brain drain be converted into wisdom gain? *Journal of the Royal Society of Medicine*, *98*(11), 487–491. doi:10.1177/014107680509801107 PMID:16260795

Dögl, C., & Holtbrügge, D. (2014). Corporate environmental responsibility, employer reputation and employee commitment: An empirical study in developed and emerging economies. *International Journal of Human Resource Management*, *25*(12), 1739–1762. doi:10.1080/09585192.2013.859164

Dolezalek, H. (2007). X-Y Vision - Generation X is all grown up, and Generation Y is coming into its own. What does this mean for companies' training efforts today and tomorrow? *Training: The Magazine of Manpower and Management Development*, *44*(6), 22–29.

Donaldson, A. L., Krejcha, K., & McMillin, A. (2017). A strengths-based approach to autism: Neurodiversity and partnering with the autism community. *Perspectives of the ASHA Special Interest Groups*, *2*(1), 56–68. doi:10.1044/persp2.SIG1.56

Doyle, N. (2020). Neurodiversity at work: A biopsychosocial model and the impact on working adults. *British Medical Bulletin*, *135*(1), 108–125. doi:10.1093/bmb/ldaa021 PMID:32996572

Doyle, N., & McDowall, A. (2021). Diamond in the rough? An 'empty review' of research into 'neurodiversity' and a road map for developing the inclusion agenda. *Equality, Diversity and Inclusion*, *41*(3), 352–382. doi:10.1108/EDI-06-2020-0172

Drazic, I., Schermuly, C. C., & Buesch, V. (2023). Empowered to Stay Active: Psychological Empowerment, Retirement Timing, and Later Life Work. *Journal of Adult Development*. Advance online publication. doi:10.1007/s10804-023-09453-8 PMID:37361380

Dubey, A., Maheshwari, I., & Mishra, A. (2018). Predict Employee Retention Using Data Science. *Journal of Diversity Management (JDM), 5*.

Du, F., & Wang, Q. (2017). New teachers' perspectives of informal mentoring: Quality of mentoring and contributors. *Mentoring & Tutoring. Mentoring & Tutoring, 25*(3), 309–328. doi:10.1080/13611267.2017.1364841

Duffield, C., Baldwin, R., Roche, M., & Wise, S. (2014). Job enrichment: Creating meaningful career development opportunities for nurses. *Journal of Nursing Management, 22*(6), 697–706. doi:10.1111/jonm.12049 PMID:23463905

Dunn, D., de la Garza, J. D., Jones, D. R., & Sasson, N. J. (2023). Awkward but so what: Differences in social trait preferences between autistic and non-autistic adults. *Neurodiversity, 1*. doi:10.1177/27546330231203833

Durai, K., & Viji, R. (2022). Impact of Talent Management Practices on Organisational Engagement in Start- Ups in India. *Polish Journal of Management Studies, 25*(2), 138–156. doi:10.17512/pjms.2022.25.2.09

Durga, P. (2017). The Impact of Workforce Diversity on Organizational Effectiveness: (A Study of Selected Banks in Tigray Region of Ethiopia). *International Journal of Scientific Research*, 427.

Dutraj, R., & Sengupta, P. R. (2022). Employee Well-Being and Influences of its various Factors. *Asian Journal of Management, 13*(4), 335–344. doi:10.52711/2321-5763.2022.00055

Dutta, D., & Vedak, C. (2023). Determining quality of hire, the holy grail of recruitment: A structuration perspective. *Human Resources Management and Services, 5*(2).

Dutta, S. (2010). What's Your Personal Social Media Strategy? *Harvard Business Review, 88*(11), 127–130. PMID:21049685

Dwertmann, D. J., & Boehm, S. A. (2016). Status matters: The asymmetric effects of supervisor–subordinate disability incongruence and climate for inclusion. *Academy of Management Journal, 59*(1), 44–64. doi:10.5465/amj.2014.0093

Dwivedi, S. (2015). Turnover Intentions: Scale Construction & Validation. *Indian Journal of Industrial Relations, 50*(3), 452.

Eboh, H. C., Asiah, M. N., Umar, A., & Doko, I. A. (2018). Prospects and Challenges of Workplace Diversity in Modern Day Prospects and Challenges of Workplace Diversity in Modern Day. *Journal of Business and Public Administration*.

Eby, L. T., Allen, T. D., Evans, S. C., Ng, T., & DuBois, D. L. (2008). Does mentoring matter? A multidisciplinary meta-analysis comparing mentored and non-mentored individuals. *Journal of Vocational Behavior, 72*(2), 254–267. doi:10.1016/j.jvb.2007.04.005 PMID:19343074

Edeh, F. O., Zayed, N. M., Perevozova, I., Kryshtal, H., & Nitsenko, V. (2022). Talent management in the hospitality sector: Predicting discretionary work behaviour. *Administrative Sciences, 12*(4), 122. doi:10.3390/admsci12040122

Edwards, M. R. (2009). An integrative review of employer branding and OB theory. *Personnel Review, 39*(1), 5–23. doi:10.1108/00483481011012809

Eger, L., Micik, M., Gangur, M., & Rehor, P. (2019). Employer Branding: Exploring Attractiveness Dimensions in a Multicultural Context. *Technological and Economic Development of Economy, 25*(3), 519–541. doi:10.3846/tede.2019.9387

Eibl, F. (2020). *Social dictatorships: The political economy of the welfare state in the Middle East and North Africa.* Oxford University Press. doi:10.1093/oso/9780198834274.001.0001

Eisner, S. P. (2005). Managing generation Y. *S.A.M. Advanced Management Journal*, *70*(4), 4–15.

Ekinci, Y., & Hosany, S. (2006). Destination Personality: An Application of Brand Personality to Tourism Destinations. *Journal of Travel Research*, *45*(2), 127–139. doi:10.1177/0047287506291603

Elgharbawy, H. (2021). *Understanding Mentoring Relationships during and after COVID-19 Restrictions from the Perspective of Mentors: A Community-Engaged Participatory Approach.* Master of Science Thesis. University of Victoria, Canada.

Elias, R., & White, S. W. (2018). Autism goes to college: Understanding the needs of a student population on the rise. *Journal of Autism and Developmental Disorders*, *48*(3), 732–746. doi:10.1007/s10803-017-3075-7 PMID:28255760

Ellahi, A., Javed, Y., Jan, M. F., & Sultan, Z. (2024). Determining the Effect of Software Project Managers' Skills on Work Performance. *International Journal of Information Technology Project Management*, *15*(1), 1–20. doi:10.4018/IJITPM.333620

Elsamani, Y., Mejía, C., & Kajikawa, Y. (2023). Employee wellbeing and innovativeness: A multi-level conceptual framework based on citation network analysis and data mining techniques. *PLoS One*, *18*(1), e0280005. doi:10.1371/journal.pone.0280005 PMID:36608048

El-Sherbeeny, A. M., Al-Romeedy, B. S., Abd Elhady, M. H., Sheikhelsouk, S., Alsetoohy, O., Liu, S., & Khairy, H. A. (2023). How Is Job Performance Affected by Ergonomics in the Tourism and Hospitality Industry? Mediating Roles of Work Engagement and Talent Retention. *Sustainability (Basel)*, *15*(20), 14947. Advance online publication. doi:10.3390/su152014947

Ensher, E. A., Heun, C., & Blanchard, A. (2003). Online mentoring and computer-mediated communication: New directions in research. *Journal of Vocational Behavior*, *63*(2), 264–288. doi:10.1016/S0001-8791(03)00044-7

Esau, K. A. (2010). *The relationship between career development, flexible work arrangements, job roles, and employee engagement within a non-profit organization* (Doctoral dissertation, Argosy University, Tampa).

Fagnani, J., & Letablier, M.-T. (2004). Work and Family Life Balance: The Impact of the 35-Hour laws in France. *Work, Employment and Society*, *18*(3), 551–572. doi:10.1177/0950017004045550

Faisal, S. (2023). Green human resource management—A synthesis. *Sustainability (Basel)*, *15*(3), 2259. doi:10.3390/su15032259

Fang, Y., & Gopinathan, S. (2009). Teachers and teaching in Eastern and Western schools: A critical review of cross-cultural comparative studies. International handbook of research on teachers and teaching, 557-572.

Fan, P., Zhang, H., Yang, S., Yu, Z., & Guo, M. (2023). Do Illegitimate Tasks Lead to Work Withdrawal Behavior among Generation Z Employees in China? The Role of Perceived Insider Status and Overqualification. *Behavioral Sciences (Basel, Switzerland)*, *13*(9), 702. Advance online publication. doi:10.3390/bs13090702 PMID:37753980

Faragher, J. (2018). Are employers losing out on skills of people with autism? *Occupational Health & Wellbeing*, *70*(5), 16–17.

Farrukh, K., & Hoor, T. (2022). Online mentoring session during COVID-19: Experiences of mentees and mentors -A phenomenology. *The Professional Medical Journal*, *29*(12), 1886–1891. doi:10.29309/TPMJ/2022.29.12.7126

Fatima, F., Oba, P., & Sony, M. (2022). Exploring employee wellbeing during the COVID-19 remote work: Evidence from South Africa. *European Journal of Training and Development*, *47*(10), 91–111. doi:10.1108/EJTD-06-2022-0061

Fattoracci, E. S. M., & King, D. D. (2022). The Need for Understanding and Addressing Microaggressions in the Workplace. *Perspectives on Psychological Science*. Advance online publication. doi:10.1177/17456916221133825 PMID:36379041

Faulkner, D. (2002). *Strategy: critical perspectives on business and management*. Routledge.

Fawehinmi, O., Yusliza, M. Y., Mohamad, Z., Faezah, J. N., & Muhammad, Z. (2020). Assessing the green behaviour of academics: The role of green human resource management and environmental knowledge. *International Journal of Manpower*, *41*(7), 879–900. doi:10.1108/IJM-07-2019-0347

Fernandes, A. B. A., & Machado, C. (2022). E-Recruitment and the impact of the digital age on recruitment: A critical literature review. In Springer eBooks (pp. 199–209). doi:10.1007/978-3-030-98183-9_8

Fernandes, C.A., Kanan, L.A., Mayer, A.B., & Lopes, F.N.C. (2023). Demotivation for work: the lack of attraction for existing vacancies in industries in the metallurgy and mechanics segment in serra catarinense. *Revista de Gestao e Secretariato- GESEC, 14*(3), 4022-4042. doi:10.7769/gesec.v14i3.1867

Fernlund, P. (2013). *Competence Visualisation-Prerequisites and guidelines for visualising competence*. Academic Press.

FerrésD.KankanhalliG.MuthukrishnanP. (2023). Anti-Poaching Agreements, Innovation, and Corporate Value: Evidence from the Technology Industry. Available at SSRN 4552393. doi:10.2139/ssrn.4552393

Ferri-Reed, J. (2010). The keys to engaging millennials. *Journal for Quality and Participation, 33*(1), 1–33.

Figueroa, O. (2017). Virtual Mentoring: Practitioner Strategies for Students Underrepresented in Industry. *Journal of Management and Sustainability, 7*(2), 2. doi:10.5539/jms.v7n2p144

Finkelstein, L. M., & Poteet, M. L. (2007). Best practices in workplace formal mentoring programs. The Blackwell handbook of mentoring: A multiple perspectives approach, 345-367.

Fischer, M., Rilke, R. M., & Yurtoglu, B. B. (2023). When, and why, do teams benefit from self-selection? *Experimental Economics*, *26*(4), 749–774. doi:10.1007/s10683-023-09800-2

Fishman, A. A. (2016). How generational differences will impact America's aging workforce: Strategies for dealing with aging Millennials, Generation X, and Baby Boomers. *Strategic HR Review*, *15*(6), 250–257. doi:10.1108/SHR-08-2016-0068

Florea, N. (2010). Linking marketing and human resources recruitment to obtain organizational efficiency. *Management & Marketing-Craiova*, (2), 352–364.

Ford, D. G. (2017). Talent Management and Its Relationship to Successful Veteran Transition Into the Civilian Workplace: Practical Integration Strategies for the HRD Professional. *Advances in Developing Human Resources*, *19*(1), 36–53. doi:10.1177/1523422316682736

Fornell, C., & Larcker, D. F. (1981). Evaluating Structural Equation Models with Unobservable Variables and Measurement Error. *JMR, Journal of Marketing Research*, *18*(1), 39–50. doi:10.1177/002224378101800104

Fournier, S. (1998). Consumers and their brands: Developing relationship theory in consumer research. *The Journal of Consumer Research*, *24*(4), 343–373. doi:10.1086/209515

Frampton, G. K., Shepherd, J., Pickett, K., Griffiths, G., & Wyatt, J. C. (2020). Digital tools for recruiting and retaining participants in randomized controlled trials: A systematic map. *Trials*, *21*(1), 478. Advance online publication. doi:10.1186/s13063-020-04358-3 PMID:32498690

Franklin, A. J. (1999). Invisibility Syndrome and Racial Identity Development in Psychotherapy and Counseling African American Men. *The Counseling Psychologist*, *27*(6), 761–793. doi:10.1177/0011000099276002

Freitas, F. B. (2023). *Talent management practices for the future of work: How can artificial intelligence reconcile recruitment tensions in organizations?* (Doctoral dissertation, Nova School of Business and Economics).

Fujimoto, Y., & Uddin, M. J. (2021). Inclusive leadership for reduced inequality: Economic–social–economic cycle of inclusion. *Journal of Business Ethics, 181*(3), 563–582. doi:10.1007/s10551-021-04920-2

Fulton, J. (2020). China-Saudi Arabia Relations Through the '1+ 2+ 3'Cooperation Pattern. *Asian Journal of Middle Eastern and Islamic Studies, 14*(4), 516–527. doi:10.1080/25765949.2020.1841991

Gaddam, S. (2008). Modeling Employer Branding Communication: The Softer Aspect of HR Marketing Management. *The IUP Journal of Soft Skills, 2*(1).

Gaiha, S. M., Gulfam, F. R., Siddiqui, I., Kishore, R., & Krishnan, S. (2020). Pilot community mental health awareness campaign improves service coverage in India. *Community Mental Health Journal, 57*(5), 814–827. doi:10.1007/s10597-020-00714-4 PMID:33052548

Gallagher, K. S. (2014). *The globalization of clean energy technology: Lessons from China.* MIT press. doi:10.7551/mitpress/9805.001.0001

Gallardo-Gallardo, E. (2018). The meaning of talent in the world of work. *Global talent management*, 33-58.

Gangwar, V., & Khan, S. (2022). Analyzing the Role of Micro-Entrepreneurship and Self-Help Groups (SHGs) in Women Empowerment and Development: A Bottom-of-Pyramid Perspective. Driving Factors for Venture Creation and Success in Agricultural Entrepreneurship. In Driving Factors for Venture Creation and Success in Agricultural Entrepreneurship. IGI-Global. doi:10.4018/978-1-6684-2349-3.ch011

Gardas, B. B., Mangla, S. K., Raut, R. D., Narkhede, B., & Luthra, S. (2019). Green talent management to unlock sustainability in the oil and gas sector. *Journal of Cleaner Production, 229*, 850–862. doi:10.1016/j.jclepro.2019.05.018

Gardner, T. M. (2002). In the trenches at the talent wars: Competitive interaction for scarce human resources. *Human Resource Management, 41*(2), 225-237.

Gardner, T. M., Stansbury, J., & Hart, D. (2010). The ethics of lateral hiring. *Business Ethics Quarterly, 20*(3), 341–369. doi:10.5840/beq201020326

Garelnabi, M., Cowdin, M. A., Fang, Y., Shrestha, B., Ushio–Fukai, M., Aikawa, E., Graham, G., Molema, G., Yanagisawa, H., & Aikawa, M. (2022). Embracing diversity, equity, and inclusion in the scientific community—Viewpoints of the North American vascular biology organization's diversity, equity, and inclusion committee. *Frontiers in Cardiovascular Medicine, 9*. Advance online publication. doi:10.3389/fcvm.2022.863256 PMID:35463765

Garrison, M. J., & Wendt, J. T. (2015). Employee Non-competes and Consideration: A Proposed Good Faith Standard for the Afterthought Agreement. *U. Kan. L. Rev., 64*, 409.

Gauttam, P., Singh, B., & Kaur, J. (2020). COVID-19 and Chinese global health diplomacy: Geopolitical opportunity for China's hegemony? *Millennial Asia, 11*(3), 318–340. doi:10.1177/0976399620959771

Ge, C., Shi, H., Jiang, J., & Xu, X. (2023). Investigating the Demand for Blockchain Talents in the Recruitment Market: Evidence from Topic Modeling Analysis on Job Postings. *Information & Management, 59*(7), 103513. Advance online publication. doi:10.1016/j.im.2021.103513

Gelencsér, M., & Szabó-Szentgróti, G. (2023, June). Analysis of the determinants of employee well-being and retention through a sample of Hungarian employees. In *Proceedings of FEB Zagreb International Odyssey Conference on Economics and Business* (Vol. 5, No. 1, pp. 178-192). University of Zagreb, Faculty of Economics and Business.

Gelencser, M., Szabo-Szentgroti, G., Komuves, Z. S., & Hollosy-Vadasz, G. (2023). The Holistic Model of Labour Retention: The Impact of Workplace Wellbeing Factors on Employee Retention. *Administrative Sciences*, *13*(5), 121. Advance online publication. doi:10.3390/admsci13050121

Genrich, M., Angerer, P., Worringer, B., Gündel, H., Kröner, F., & Müller, A. (2022). Managers' action-guiding mental models towards mental health-related organizational interventions—A systematic review of qualitative studies. *International Journal of Environmental Research and Public Health*, *19*(19), 12610. doi:10.3390/ijerph191912610 PMID:36231909

George, E., & Chattopadhyay, P. (2022). Like Attracts Like? The Effects of Anxiety, Implicit Bias, and Perception of Diversity Culture on Team Attraction. *Makara Hubs- Asia, 26*(2), 114-131. doi:10.7454/hubs.asia.1270622

Gernsbacher, M. A., Stevenson, J. L., & Dern, S. (2017). Specificity, contexts, and reference groups matter when assessing autistic traits. *PLoS One*, *12*(2), e0171931. doi:10.1371/journal.pone.0171931 PMID:28192464

Ghani, B., Zada, M., Memon, K. R., Ullah, R., Khattak, A., Han, H., Ariza-Montes, A., & Araya-Castillo, L. (2022). Challenges and strategies for employee retention in the Hospitality Industry: A Review. *Sustainability (Basel)*, *14*(5), 2885. doi:10.3390/su14052885

Gilani, H., & Cunningham, L. (2017). Employer branding and its influence on employee retention: A literature review. *The Marketing Review*, *17*(2), 239–256. doi:10.1362/146934717X14909733966209

Gilch, P. M., & Sieweke, J. (2020). Recruiting digital talent: The strategic role of recruitment in organizations' digital transformation. *Zeitschrift Fur Personalforschung*, *35*(1), 53–82. doi:10.1177/2397002220952734

Gillespie-Lynch, K., Kapp, S. K., Brooks, P. J., Pickens, J., & Schwartzman, B. (2017). Whose expertise is it? Evidence for autistic adults as critical autism experts. *Frontiers in Psychology*, *8*, 438. doi:10.3389/fpsyg.2017.00438 PMID:28400742

Girard, A., Fallery, B., & Rodhain, F. (2014). *Integration of Social Media in Recruitment: A Delphi Study*. doi:10.1108/S1877-6361(2013)0000012009

Gitman, L. J., & McDaniel, C. (2009). *The future of business: the essentials*. South-Western.

Giulianotti, R. (2015). The Beijing 2008 Olympics: Examining the interrelations of China, globalization, and soft power. *European Review (Chichester, England)*, *23*(2), 286–296. doi:10.1017/S1062798714000684

Glavas, A., Hahn, T., Jones, D. A., & Willness, C. R. (2023). Predisposed, Exposed, or Both? How Prosocial Motivation and CSR Education Are Related to Prospective Employees' Desire for Social Impact in Work. *Business & Society*. Advance online publication. doi:10.1177/00076503231182665

Glen, J., Hilson, C., & Lowitt, E. (2009). The emergence of green talent. *Business Strategy Review*, *20*(4), 52–56. doi:10.1111/j.1467-8616.2009.00631.x

Glenn, T. (2012). The state of talent management in Canada's public sector: Talent Management in Canada's Public Sector. *Canadian Public Administration*, *55*(1), 25–51. doi:10.1111/j.1754-7121.2012.00204.x

Glick, P., & Fiske, S. T. (2001). An ambivalent alliance: Hostile and benevolent sexism as complementary justifications for gender inequality. *The American Psychologist*, *56*(2), 109–118. doi:10.1037/0003-066X.56.2.109 PMID:11279804

Goel, R. (2019). Diversity At Workplace: Performance Of Human Resource Management Practices in IT sector in NCR, India. *International Journal Of Scientific & Technology Research, 8*(12).

Golden, T., Veiga, J., & Dino, R. (2008). The Impact of Professional Isolation on Teleworker Job Performance and Turnover Intentions: Does Time Spent Teleworking, Interacting Face-to-Face, or Having Access to Communication-Enhancing Technology Matter? *The Journal of Applied Psychology*, *93*(6), 1412–1421. doi:10.1037/a0012722 PMID:19025257

Gomez Vasquez, L. M., & Soto Velez, I. (2011). *Social Media as a strategic tool for Corporate Communication. Los Medios Sociales como una Herramienta Estratégica para la Comunicación Corporativa.* doi:10.5783/RIRP-2-2011-09-157-174

Gorde, S. (2019). A Study of Employee Retention. *Journal of Emerging Technologies and Innovative Research*, *6*(6), 331–337.

Gourova, N., & Gourova, E. (2017). Attracting Talents, Book Group Author Assoc Comp Machinery, *Proceedings of the Vikingplop 2017 Conference on Pattern Languages of Program.* 10.1145/3158491.3158497

Gravett, L., & Throckmorton, R. (2007). *Bridging the generation gap.* Career Press.

Green, M. S. (2008). The Significance of Self-Expression. *Self-Expression*, 1–20. doi:10.1093/acprof:oso/9780199283781.003.0001

Gregory, A., & Milner, S. (2009). Editorial: Work-life Balance: A Matter of Choice? *Gender, Work and Organization*, *16*(1), 1–13. doi:10.1111/j.1468-0432.2008.00429.x

Griffeth, R. W., Tenbrink, A., & Robinson, S. M. (2013). Recruitment sources. In Oxford University Press eBooks. doi:10.1093/oxfordhb/9780199756094.013.0013

Griffeth, R. W., Hom, P. W., & Gaertner, S. (2000). A Meta-Analysis of Antecedents and Correlates of Employee Turnover: Update, Moderator Tests, and Research Implications for the Next Millennium. *Journal of Management*, *26*(3), 463–488. doi:10.1177/014920630002600305

Grix, J., & Brannagan, P. M. (2016). Of mechanisms and myths: Conceptualising states'"soft power" strategies through sports mega-events. *Diplomacy and Statecraft*, *27*(2), 251–272. doi:10.1080/09592296.2016.1169791

Grove, K., & Strudler, N. (2001). 1 Cooperating Teacher Practice in Mentoring Student Teachers Toward Technology Use. *Journal of Research on Technology in Education*, 37.

Grzesiuk, K., & Wawer, M. (2018, September 6). Employer branding through social media: The case of largest polish companies. *10th International Scientific Conference "Business and Management 2018."* 10.3846/bm.2018.42

Guan, J., Wang, W., Guo, Z., Chan, J. H., & Qi, X. (2021). Customer experience and brand loyalty in the full-service hotel sector: The role of brand affect. *International Journal of Contemporary Hospitality Management*, *33*(5), 1620–1645. doi:10.1108/IJCHM-10-2020-1177

Guarino, V., Zuppolini, S., Borriello, A., & Ambrosio, L. (2016). Electro-active polymers (EAPs): A promising route to design bio-organic/bioinspired platforms with on-demand functionalities. *Polymers*, *8*(5), 185. doi:10.3390/polym8050185 PMID:30979278

Guarnieri, P., & Trojan, F. (2019). Decision making on supplier selection based on social, ethical, and environmental criteria: A study in the textile industry. *Resources, Conservation and Recycling*, *141*, 347–361. doi:10.1016/j.resconrec.2018.10.023

Guest, D. E. (2017). Human resource management and employee well-being: Towards a new analytic framework. *Human Resource Management Journal*, *27*(1), 22–38. doi:10.1111/1748-8583.12139

Gu, H., Meng, X., Shen, T., & Wen, L. (2020). China's highly educated talents in 2015: Patterns, determinants and spatial spillover effects. *Applied Spatial Analysis and Policy*, *13*(3), 631–648. doi:10.1007/s12061-019-09322-6

Gulati, C., Mathur, G., & Upadhyay, Y. (2023). Internal Branding: Connecting Links to Establish Employees' Brand Behaviour in Hospitality Sector. *FIIB Business Review*. Advance online publication. doi:10.1177/23197145221143831

Gunjan, S. (2022, March 11). *Workforce Diversity*. Retrieved from Business Management ideas: /www.businessmanagementideas.com/human-resource-management-2/workforce-diversity/20385

Gunuc, S. (2015). Implementation and Evaluation of Technology Mentoring Program Developed for Teacher Educators: A 6M-Framework. *Qualitative Research in Education, 4*(2), 164–191. doi:10.17583/qre.2015.1305

Guo, S. (2014). Developing effective professional development programs: A case study. *New Library World, 115*(11/12), 542–557. doi:10.1108/NLW-05-2014-0048

Gupta, P. (2021, December 27). *[Year in Review 2021] Times are changing as women in tech reach new heights*. YourStory.com. https://yourstory.com/herstory/2021/12/women-technology-leader-gender-diversity

Guptan, S. U. (2018). *Mentoring 2.0: A Practitioner's Guide to Changing Lives*. SAGE Publishing India.

Gupta, S. K., Bhatia, N., & Bhagat, M. (2022). A review of employee turnover models and their role in the evolution of turnover literature. *The Indian Journal of Labour Economics : the Quarterly Journal of the Indian Society of Labour Economics, 65*(1), 185–214. doi:10.1007/s41027-022-00366-w

Gupta, V. (2020). Talent management dimensions and its relationship with Generation Y employee's intention to quit: An Indian hotel perspective. *International Journal of Tourism Cities, 6*(3), 583–600. doi:10.1108/IJTC-02-2019-0018

Gürlek, M., Düzgün, E., & Uygur, S. M. (2017). How does corporate social responsibility create customer loyalty? The role of corporate image. *Social Responsibility Journal, 13*(3), 409–427. doi:10.1108/SRJ-10-2016-0177

Gurusinghe, R. N., Arachchige, B. J. H., & Dayarathna, D. (2021). Predictive HR analytics and talent management: A conceptual framework. *Journal of Management Analytics, 8*(2), 195–221. doi:10.1080/23270012.2021.1899857

Gutner, T. (2002). A Balancing Act for Gen X Women. *Business Week, 3766*, 82. Retrieved from: https://eruralfamilies.uwagec.org/ERFLibrary/Readings/ABalancingActForGenXWomen.pdf

Haegele, J. A., & Hodge, S. (2016). Disability discourse: Overview and critiques of the medical and social models. *Quest, 68*(2), 193–206. doi:10.1080/00336297.2016.1143849

Hair, J. F., Black, W. C., Anderson, R. E., & Babin, B. J. (2018). *Multivariate Data Analysis*. Cengage.

Hair, J. F., Black, W. C., & Babin, B. J. (2010). *Multivariate Data Analysis: A Global Perspective*. Pearson.

Hair, J. F. Jr, Howard, M. C., & Nitzl, C. (2020). Assessing measurement model quality in PLS-SEM using confirmatory composite analysis. *Journal of Business Research, 109*, 101–110. doi:10.1016/j.jbusres.2019.11.069

Hair, J. F., Risher, J. J., Sarstedt, M., & Ringle, C. M. (2019). When to use and how to report the results of PLS-SEM. *European Business Review, 31*(1), 2–24. doi:10.1108/EBR-11-2018-0203

Hall, P., & Pfeiffer, U. (2013). *Urban future 21: a global agenda for twenty-first century cities*. Routledge. doi:10.4324/9781315011523

Hammadi, H. A. A., & Noor, M. A. B. M. (2020). The Role of Leadership in the Talent Management and Employee Retention of Education in Abu Dhabi. *European Journal of Multidisciplinary Studies, 5*(1), 68. doi:10.26417/301nxi33o

Hammond, J., Davies, N., Morrow, E., Ross, F., Vandrevala, T., & Harris, R. (2022). "Raising the curtain on the equality theatre": A study of recruitment to first healthcare job post-qualification in the UK National Health Service. *Human Resources for Health, 20*(1), 57. Advance online publication. doi:10.1186/s12960-022-00754-9 PMID:35804352

Hand, M. C., & Reid, A. (2022). Men in Nursing Academia Factors Associated with Recruitment and Retention. *Nurse Educator, 47*(4), 246–251. doi:10.1097/NNE.0000000000001150 PMID:35113054

Han, J. W., Kok, S. K., & McClelland, R. (2023). The impact of green training on employee turnover intention and customer satisfaction: An integrated perspective. *Corporate Social Responsibility and Environmental Management, 30*(6), 3006–3019. doi:10.1002/csr.2534

Hankinson, G. (2001). Brand orientation in the hotel industry. *International Journal of Contemporary Hospitality Management, 13*(5), 204–214.

Harisha, B. S., Venkataswamy, K. P., Devi, R. M., Govindaraj, G. S., & Bhandwalkar, S. S. (2023). The Role Of Artificial Intelligence In Hr: Transforming Recruitment And Hr Operations. *Boletin de Literatura Oral-The Literary Journal, 10*(1), 1374–1384.

Harper, T. (2022). *How To Hire And Retain Neurodivergent Employees.* https://www.forbes.com/sites/forbeshumanresourcescouncil/2022/08/22/how-to-hire-and-retain-neurodivergent-employees/?sh=61763be7264e

Harris, C., van der Vloodt, R., & Maddocks, J. (2020). *Championing neurodiversity and emotional intelligence in the workplace.* Available at: https://content.psionline.com/whitepaperchampioning-neurodiversity-and-emotional-intelligence-in-the-workplace

Harris, M. (1996). Aggressive Experiences and Aggressiveness: Relationship to Ethnicity, Gender, and Age. *Journal of Applied Social Psychology, 26*(10), 843–870. doi:10.1111/j.1559-1816.1996.tb01114.x

Harrison, J. S., Boivie, S., & Withers, M. C. (2023). Executives' prior employment ties to interlocking directors and interfirm mobility. *Organization Science, 34*(4), 1602–1625. doi:10.1287/orsc.2022.1638

Harrisr, L., & Foster, C. (2010). Aligning talent management with approaches to equality and diversity. *Equality, Diversity and Inclusion, 29*(5), 422–435. doi:10.1108/02610151011052753

Härtel, C. E. J., & Fujimoto, Y. (2000). Diversity is not the problem – openness to perceived dissimilarity is. *Journal of Management and & Organization, 6*(1), 14–27. doi:10.1017/S1833367200005484

Hartley, K., & Jarvis, D. S. (2022). Let nine universities blossom: Opportunities and constraints on the development of higher education in China. *Higher Education Research & Development, 41*(5), 1542–1556. doi:10.1080/07294360.2021.1915963

Hasanbeigi, A., & Price, L. (2015). A technical review of emerging technologies for energy and water efficiency and pollution reduction in the textile industry. *Journal of Cleaner Production, 95*, 30–44. doi:10.1016/j.jclepro.2015.02.079

Hausmann, R., Tyson, L. D., & Zahidi, S. (2006). The global gender gap report 2006. *World Economic Forum.*

Hawkins, A. H., Ouellette, J. A., & Hadley, W. S. (2020). Reverse mentoring as an intergenerational exchange: A review and practical implications. *Human Resource Development Review, 19*(4), 455–480.

Heath, T. R., & Thompson, W. R. (2018). Avoiding US-China competition is futile: Why the best option is to manage strategic rivalry. *Asia Policy, 13*(2), 91–120. doi:10.1353/asp.2018.0027

Heijnen, J., De Reuver, M., Bouwman, H., Warnier, M., & Horlings, H. (2013). Are social media data relevant for measuring key performance Indicators? A content analysis approach. In Lecture Notes in Business Information Processing (pp. 74–84). doi:10.1007/978-3-642-39808-7_7

He, J., & Sun, L. (2020). Does continuity matter? Developing a new long-term orientation structure in a cross-cultural context: A study on supply chain relationships. *Industrial Marketing Management, 88*, 186–194. doi:10.1016/j.indmarman.2020.05.003

Henderson, K., & Welsh, E. T. (2023). Potential bias when using social media for selection: Differential effects of candidate demographic characteristics, race match, perceived similarity, and profile detail. *International Journal of Selection and Assessment*. Advance online publication. doi:10.1111/ijsa.12454

Hendrick, R. Z., & Raspiller, E. E. (2011). Predicting employee retention through pre-employment assessment. *Community College Journal of Research and Practice*, *35*(11), 895–908. doi:10.1080/10668920802421561

Hennekam, S., & Follmer, K. (2024). Neurodiversity and HRM: a practice-based review and research agenda. Equality, Diversity and Inclusion. doi:10.1108/EDI-12-2023-0424

Henseler, J., Hubona, G., & Ray, P. A. (2016). Using PLS path modeling in new technology research: Updated guidelines. *Industrial Management & Data Systems*, *116*(1), 2–20. doi:10.1108/IMDS-09-2015-0382

Henseler, J., Ringle, C. M., & Sarstedt, M. (2015). A new criterion for assessing discriminant validity in variance-based structural equation modeling. *Journal of the Academy of Marketing Science*, *43*(1), 115–135. doi:10.1007/s11747-014-0403-8

Henseler, J., & Sarstedt, M. (2013). Goodness-of-fit indices for partial least squares path modeling. *Computational Statistics*, *28*(2), 565–580. doi:10.1007/s00180-012-0317-1

Herring, C. (2009). *Does diversity pay? Race, gender, and the business case for diversity*. American. doi:10.1177/000312240907400203

Hew, J.-J., Lee, V.-H., Ooi, K.-B., & Wei, J. (2015). What catalyses mobile apps usage intention: An empirical analysis. *Industrial Management & Data Systems*, *115*(7), 1269–1291. doi:10.1108/IMDS-01-2015-0028

Higgins, E. T. (1998). Promotion and Prevention: Regulatory Focus as A Motivational Principle. In Advances in Experimental Social Psychology. Elsevier. doi:10.1016/S0065-2601(08)60381-0

Hillen, J. (2021). Psychological pricing in online food retail. *British Food Journal*, *123*(11), 3522–3535. doi:10.1108/BFJ-09-2020-0847

Hillman, J. E. (2020). *The emperor's new road: China and the project of the century*. Yale University Press.

Hilton, J. L., & Von Hippel, W. (1996). Stereotypes. *Annual Review of Psychology*, *47*(1), 237–271. doi:10.1146/annurev.psych.47.1.237 PMID:15012482

Hinton, K. G. (2001). *The experiences of African American women administrators at predominantly white institutions of higher education* [Unpublished PhD dissertation]. Indiana University, Bloomington, IN.

Hofstede, G. (1984). *Culture's consequences: International differences in work-related values* (Vol. 5). Sage.

Hofstede, G., Hofstede, G. J., & Minkov, M. (2010). Cultures and Organizations: Software of the Mind. Academic Press.

Hofstede, G. (1996). Gender stereotypes and partner preferences of Asian women in masculine and feminine cultures. *Journal of Cross-Cultural Psychology*, *27*(5), 533–546. doi:10.1177/0022022196275003

Hofstede, G. (1998). *Masculinity and femininity: The taboo dimension of national cultures* (Vol. 3). Sage.

Hofstede, G. (2011). Dimensionalizing cultures: The Hofstede model in context. *Online Readings in Psychology and Culture*, *2*(1), 8. doi:10.9707/2307-0919.1014

Hoh, A. (2019). China's belt and road initiative in Central Asia and the Middle East. *Domes*, *28*(2), 241–276. doi:10.1111/dome.12191

Holbeche, L., & Mayo, A. (2012). *Motivating people in Lean organizations*. Butterworth-Heineman.

Holgersson, S., Gottschalk, P., & Dean, G. (2008). Knowledge Management in Law Enforcement: Knowledge Views for Patrolling Police Officers. *International Journal of Police Science & Management, 10*(1), 76–88. doi:10.1350/ijps.2008.10.1.76

Holmes, T. H., & Rahe, R. H. (1967). The social readjustment rating scale. *Journal of Psychosomatic Research, 11*(2), 213–218. doi:10.1016/0022-3999(67)90010-4 PMID:6059863

Homans, G. C. (1958). Social behavior as exchange. *American Journal of Sociology, 63*(6), 597–606. doi:10.1086/222355

Hosdey, A. (2010). *Pour des entretiens d'evaluation efficaces*. Edi.Pro.

Hossin, M. S., Ulfy, M. A., & Karim, M. W. (2021). Challenges in adopting artificial intelligence (AI) in HRM practices: A study on Bangladesh perspective. *International Fellowship Journal of Interdisciplinary Research, 1*.

Howaniec, H., Karyy, O., & Pawliczek, A. (2022). The Role of Universities in Shaping Talents-The Case of the Czech Republic, Poland and Ukraine. *Sustainability, 14*. doi:10.3390/su14095476

Howe, A. S., Lo, J., Jaiswal, S., Bani-Fatemi, A., Chattu, V. K., & Nowrouzi-Kia, B. (2023). Engaging Employers in Apprentice Training: Focus Group Insights from Small-to-Medium-Sized Employers in Ontario, Canada. *International Journal of Environmental Research and Public Health, 20*(3), 2527. doi:10.3390/ijerph20032527 PMID:36767893

Huang, C. H. (2022). *Power and Restraint in China's Rise*. Columbia University Press. doi:10.7312/huan20464

Huang, C.-Y., Weng, R.-H., & Chen, Y.-T. (2016). Investigating the relationship among transformational leadership, interpersonal interaction and mentoring functions. *Journal of Clinical Nursing, 25*(15-16), 2144–2155. doi:10.1111/jocn.13153 PMID:27108764

Huang, J., & Tsai, K. S. (2021). Upgrading Big Brother: Local Strategic Adaptation in China's Security Industry. *Studies in Comparative International Development, 56*(4), 560–587. doi:10.1007/s12116-021-09342-9 PMID:34629564

Huang, R., Yan, P., & Yang, X. (2021). Knowledge map visualization of technology hotspots and development trends in China's textile manufacturing industry. *IET Collaborative Intelligent Manufacturing, 3*(3), 243–251. doi:10.1049/cim2.12024

Hu, L., & Bentler, P. M. (1999). Cutoff criteria for fit indexes in covariance structure analysis: Conventional criteria versus new alternatives. *Structural Equation Modeling, 6*(1), 1–55. doi:10.1080/10705519909540118

Humphrey, J. D., & Holmes, J. W. (2023). *Style and ethics of communication in science and engineering*. Springer Nature.

Humphrey, S. (2014). Recruiters and applicants: An exchange of words. *Journal of Financial Services Marketing, 19*(2), 94–103. doi:10.1057/fsm.2014.8

Hunkenschroer, A. L., & Luetge, C. (2022). Ethics of AI-enabled recruiting and selection: A review and research agenda. *Journal of Business Ethics, 178*(4), 977–1007. doi:10.1007/s10551-022-05049-6

Huntley, R. (2006). *The world according to Y: Inside the new adult generation*. Allen and Unwin.

Hupfer, S., Mazumder, S., Bucaille, A., & Crossan, G. (2021, November 30). *Women in the tech industry: Gaining ground, but facing new headwinds*. Deloitte Insights. https://www2.deloitte.com/us/en/insights/industry/technology/technology-media-and-telecom-predictions/2022/statistics-show-women-in-technology-are-facing-new-headwinds.html.html.html

Hurley-Hanson, A. E., & Giannantonio, C. M. (2017). *LMX and autism: Effective working relationships*. Academic Press.

Hurley-Hanson, A. E., Giannantonio, C. M., Griffiths, A. J., Hurley-Hanson, A. E., Giannantonio, C. M., & Griffiths, A. J. (2020). Leadership and Autism. *Autism in the Workplace: Creating Positive Employment and Career Outcomes for Generation A*, 215-236.

Ilies, R., Bono, J. E., & Bakker, A. B. (2024). Crafting Well-Being: Employees Can Enhance Their Own Well-Being by Savoring, Reflecting upon, and Capitalizing on Positive Work Experiences. *Annual Review of Organizational Psychology and Organizational Behavior*, *11*(1), 63–91. doi:10.1146/annurev-orgpsych-110721-045931

Iqbal, S., Guohao, L., & Akhtar, S. (2017). Effects of job organizational culture, benefits, salary on job satisfaction ultimately affecting employee retention. *Review of Public Administration and Management*, *5*(3), 1–7. doi:10.4172/2315-7844.1000229

Ishikawa, T., & Yamazaki, Y. (2021). Atmosphere Sharing System by Lighting and Fragrance to Enhance Quality of Work in Telework. *2021 IEEE 3rd Global Conference on Life Sciences and Technologies*, 416-418. 10.1109/LifeTech52111.2021.9391858

Islam, M.A., Hack-Polay, D., Rahman, M., Hosen, M., Hunt, A., & Shafique, S. (2022). Work environment, HR practices and millennial employee retention in hospitality and tourism in Bangladesh. *International Journal of Emerging Markets*. . doi:10.1108/IJOEM-06-2021-0859

Islam, S. (2020). Sustainable raw materials: 50 shades of sustainability. In *Sustainable technologies for fashion and textiles* (pp. 343–357). Woodhead Publishing. doi:10.1016/B978-0-08-102867-4.00015-3

Ivaldi, S., Scaratti, G., & Fregnan, E. (2021). Dwelling within the fourth industrial revolution: Organizational learning for new competencies, processes and work cultures. *Journal of Workplace Learning*, *34*(1), 1–26. doi:10.1108/JWL-07-2020-0127

Jaarsma, P., & Welin, S. (2012). Autism as a natural human variation: Reflections on the claims of the neurodiversity movement. *Health Care Analysis*, *20*(1), 20–30. doi:10.1007/s10728-011-0169-9 PMID:21311979

Jabbour, C. J. C. (2013). Environmental training in organisations: From a literature review to a framework for future research. *Resources, Conservation and Recycling*, *74*, 144–155. doi:10.1016/j.resconrec.2012.12.017

Jackson, C. L., Colquitt, J. A., Wesson, M. J., & Zapata-Phelan, C. P. (2006). Psychological collectivism: A measurement validation and linkage to group member performance. *The Journal of Applied Psychology*, *91*(4), 884–899. doi:10.1037/0021-9010.91.4.884 PMID:16834512

Jacobs, S., & Quinn, J. (2022). Cultural reproduction of mental illness stigma and stereotypes. *Social Science & Medicine*, *292*, 114552. doi:10.1016/j.socscimed.2021.114552 PMID:34802779

Jain, N., & Maitri. (2018). Big data and predictive analytics: A facilitator for talent management. In *Studies in big data* (pp. 199–204). doi:10.1007/978-981-10-7515-5_14

Jain, S., & Lobo, R. (2012). Diversity and inclusion: a business imperative in global professional services. *Globalization of Professional Services: Innovative Strategies, Successful Processes, Inspired Talent Management, and First-Hand Experiences*, 181-187.

Jansen, B. J., Jansen, K. J., & Spink, A. (2005). Using the web to look for work. *Internet Research*, *15*(1), 49–66. doi:10.1108/10662240510577068

Janta, H., & Ladkin, A. (2013). In search of employment: Online technologies and Polish migrants. *New Technology, Work and Employment*, *28*(3), 241–253. doi:10.1111/ntwe.12018

Japheth, O., Rahab, M., & Albert, K. (2023). The Efficacy of Talent Selection Approaches on the Competitiveness among Five Star Hotels in Nairobi City County, Kenya. *Journal of Human Resource and Sustainability Studies*, *11*(3), 736–758. doi:10.4236/jhrss.2023.113041

Jaskyte, K., Hunter, A., & Mell, A. C. (2023). Predictors of Interdisciplinary Team Innovation in Higher Education Institutions. *Innovative Higher Education*. Advance online publication. doi:10.1007/s10755-023-09676-3

Jatobá, M. N., Fernandes, C., Gunkel, M., & Kraus, S. (2022). Innovation and human resource management: A systematic literature review. *European Journal of Innovation Management*, *25*(6), 1–18. doi:10.1108/EJIM-07-2021-0330

Jayasinghe, S., Suraweera, T., & Samarasinghe, D. (2022). Job seeker value proposition conceptualised from the perspective of the job choice theory. *Sri Lanka Journal of Social Sciences*, *45*(2), 107–126. doi:10.4038/sljss.v45i2.8341

Jena, L., & Nayak, U. (2023). Organizational career development and retention of millennial employees: The role of job engagement and organizational engagement. *Asia-Pacific Journal of Business Administration*. Advance online publication. doi:10.1108/APJBA-07-2022-0323

Jerrold, L. (2018). Poaching employees. *American Journal of Orthodontics and Dentofacial Orthopedics*, *153*(5), 755–756. doi:10.1016/j.ajodo.2018.02.003 PMID:29706224

Jiang, S., Ling, F. Y. Y., & Ma, G. (2024). Fostering Resilience in Project Teams: Adaptive Structuration Perspective. *Journal of Management Engineering*, *40*(1), 04023047. Advance online publication. doi:10.1061/JMENEA.MEENG-5615

Jimoh, L. A., & Kee, D. M. H. (2022). Talent management: The way out of poor task performance. *Industrial and Commercial Training*, *54*(4), 623–636. doi:10.1108/ICT-03-2022-0016

Jirawuttinunt, S., & Limsuwan, K. (2019). The Effect of Green Human Resource Management on Performance of Certified ISO 14000 Businesses in Thailand. *UTCC International Journal of Business and Economics*, *11*(1), 168–185.

Johansson, J., & Herranen, S. (2019). *The application of artificial intelligence (AI) in human resource management: Current state of AI and its impact on the traditional recruitment process*. Academic Press.

Johnson, W. B., & Kram, K. E. (2020). Mentoring in the digital age. The Oxford Handbook of Workplace Mentoring, 295-314.

Johnson, R. D., Stone, D. L., & Lukaszewski, K. M. (2021). The benefits of eHRM and AI for talent acquisition. *Journal of Tourism Futures*, *7*(1), 40–52. doi:10.1108/JTF-02-2020-0013

Johnson, T. D., & Joshi, A. (2016). Dark clouds or silver linings? A stigma threat perspective on the implications of an autism diagnosis for workplace well-being. *The Journal of Applied Psychology*, *101*(3), 430–449. doi:10.1037/apl0000058 PMID:26595753

Jolly, D. (2022). The Chinese national system of innovation. In *The New Threat: China's Rapid Technological Transformation* (pp. 29–57). Springer International Publishing. doi:10.1007/978-3-031-08690-8_3

Jones, B., Brown, S. P., Zoltners, A. A., & Weits, B. A. (2005). The changing environment of selling and sales management. *Journal of Personal Selling & Sales Management*, *25*(2), 105–111.

Jones, K. P., Peddie, C. I., Gilrane, V. L., King, E. B., & Gray, A. L. (2016). Not So Subtle. *Journal of Management*, *42*(6), 1588–1613. doi:10.1177/0149206313506466

Jones, M. R. (2019). *Communication in the digital age: Understanding the impact of technology on human interaction*. Routledge.

Jones, S. M., & Johnson, M. A. (2020). The future of mentoring: How remote work is reshaping mentorship. *Catalyst : Feminism, Theory, Technoscience, 32*(3), 55–59.

Joyce, A., Moussa, B., Elmes, A., Campbell, P., Suchowerska, R., Buick, F., Barraket, J., & Carey, G. (2022). Organizational structures and processes for health and wellbeing: Insights from work integration social enterprise. *BMC Public Health, 22*(1), 1624. Advance online publication. doi:10.1186/s12889-022-13920-4 PMID:36030204

Judd, K., & McKinnon, M. (2021). A systematic map of inclusion, equity and diversity in science communication research: Do we practice what we preach? *Frontiers in Communication, 6*, 744365. Advance online publication. doi:10.3389/fcomm.2021.744365

Jue, A. L., Marr, J. A., & Kassotakis, M. E. (2009). *Social media at work: How networking tools propel organizational performance*. John Wiley & Sons.

Kagermann, H. (2014). Change through digitization—Value creation in the age of Industry 4.0. In *Management of permanent change* (pp. 23–45). Springer Fachmedien Wiesbaden.

Kalev, A., Dobbin, F., & Kelly, E. (2006). Best practices or best guesses? Assessing the efficacy of corporate affirmative action and diversity policies. *American Sociological Review, 71*(4), 589–617. doi:10.1177/000312240607100404

Kalia, P., Singla, M., & Kaushal, R. (2023). Human resource management practices and employee retention in the Indian textile industry. *International Journal of Productivity and Performance Management, 73*(11), 96–121. Advance online publication. doi:10.1108/IJPPM-01-2022-0057

Kamal, S., Naim, A., Magd, H., Khan, S. A., & Khan, F. M. (2022). The Relationship Between E-Service Quality, Ease of Use, and E-CRM Performance Referred by Brand Image. In *Building a Brand Image Through Electronic Customer Relationship Management* (pp. 84–108). IGI Global. doi:10.4018/978-1-6684-5386-5.ch005

Kambur, E., & Yildirim, T. (2022). Changes in Human Resources Management with Artificial Intelligence. In *Handbook on Artificial Intelligence-Empowered Applied Software Engineering: Vol. 2: Smart Software Applications in Cyber-Physical Systems* (pp. 89–102). Springer International Publishing. doi:10.1007/978-3-031-07650-3_6

Kang, M., Lee, E., Kim, Y., & Yang, S. U. (2023). A Test of a Dual Model of Positive and Negative EORs: Dialogic Employee Communication Perceptions Related to Employee-Organization Relationships and Employee Megaphoning Intentions. *Journal of Public Relations Research, 35*(3), 182–208. Advance online publication. doi:10.1080/106272 6X.2023.2194025

Kang, S. (2014). Factors influencing intention of mobile application use. *International Journal of Mobile Communications, 12*(4), 360. doi:10.1504/IJMC.2014.063653

Kanter, J. W., Williams, M. T., Kuczynski, A. M., Manbeck, K. E., Debreaux, M., & Rosen, D. C. (2017). A Preliminary Report on the Relationship Between Microaggressions Against Black People and Racism Among White College Students. *Race and Social Problems, 9*(4), 291–299. doi:10.1007/s12552-017-9214-0

Kaoud, M., & ElBolok, M. (2022). The effect of employer branding through social media on employee engagement and employer attractiveness: A case study research. In Studies in systems, decision and control (pp. 451–463). doi:10.1007/978-3-031-10212-7_38

Kapferer, J.-N. (2008). The new strategic brand management: creating and sustaining brand equity, Les editions d'Organization.

Kapferer, J. N. (2008). *The New Strategic Brand Management: Advanced Insights and Strategic Thinking*. Kogan Page.

Kaplan, A. M., & Haenlein, M. (2010). Users of the world, unite! The challenges and opportunities of Social Media. *Business Horizons*, *53*(1), 59–68. doi:10.1016/j.bushor.2009.09.003

Kapoor, S. (2020). HR Trends in the Era of Artificial Intelligence. In Transforming Management Using Artificial Intelligence Techniques (pp. 51-61). CRC Press. doi:10.1201/9781003032410-4

Kapoor, V. (2010). Employer Branding: A Study of Its Relevance in India. *IUP Journal of Brand Management, 7*.

Kapp, S. K., Steward, R., Crane, L., Elliott, D., Elphick, C., Pellicano, E., & Russell, G. (2019). 'People should be allowed to do what they like': Autistic adults' views and experiences of stimming. *Autism*, *23*(7), 1782–1792. doi:10.1177/1362361319829628 PMID:30818970

Karkhanis, G. V., Chandnani, S. U., & Chakraborti, S. (2023). Analysis of employee perception of employer brand: A comparative study across business cycles using structural topic modelling. *Journal of Business Analytics*, *6*(2), 95–111. doi:10.1080/2573234X.2022.2104663

Karyamsetty, H. J., Khan, S. A., & Nayyar, A. (2023). Envisioning Towards Modernization of Society 5.0- A Prospective Glimpse on Status, Opportunities, and Challenges With XAI. In F. Al-Turjman, A. Nayyar, M. Naved, A. K. Singh, & M. Bilal (Eds.), *XAI Based Intelligent Systems for Society 5.0* (pp. 223–267). Elsevier. doi:10.1016/B978-0-323-95315-3.00005-X

Kasapakis, V., Dzardanova, E., Nikolakopoulou, V., & Vosinakis, S. (2022). Evaluation of a virtual reality learning enviroment testbed and non-verbal cue integration. *2022 International Conference on Interactive Media, Smart Systems and Emerging Technologies (IMET)*. 10.1109/IMET54801.2022.9929618

Kaskan, E. R., & Ho, I. K. (2014). Microaggressions and Female Athletes. *Sex Roles*, *74*(7–8), 275–287. doi:10.1007/s11199-014-0425-1

Kasprisin, C. A., Single, P. B., Single, R. M., & Muller, C. B. (2003). Building a better bridge: Testing e-training to improve e-mentoring programmes in higher education. *Mentoring & Tutoring*, *11*(1), 67–78. doi:10.1080/1361126032000054817

Kasprowicz, V., Waddilove, K. D., Chopera, D., Khumalo, S. B., Harilall, S., Wong, E., Karita, E., Sanders, E. J., Kilembe, W., Gaseitsiwe, S., & Ndung'u, T. (2023). Developing a diversity, equity and inclusion compass to guide African scientific capacity-strengthening efforts. *PLOS Global Public Health*, *3*(12), e0002339. doi:10.1371/journal.pgph.0002339 PMID:38117812

Kaufman, B. E. (2022). The academic-practitioner gap: Past time to bring in the practitioner perspective. *Human Resource Management Review*, *32*(2), 100895. doi:10.1016/j.hrmr.2022.100895

Kaushik, N., Sharma, A., & Kumar Kaushik, V. (2014). Equality in the workplace: A study of gender issues in Indian organisations. *Journal of Management Development*, *33*(2), 90–106. doi:10.1108/JMD-11-2013-0140

Keane, M. (2013). *China's new creative clusters: Governance, human capital and investment*. Routledge. doi:10.4324/9780203124505

Keane, M., & Chen, Y. (2019). Entrepreneurial solutionism, characteristic cultural industries and the Chinese dream. *International Journal of Cultural Policy*, *25*(6), 743–755.

Keane, M., Yu, H., Zhao, E. J., & Leong, S. (2020). *Chinas digital presence in the asia-pacific: Culture, technology and platforms*. Anthem Press. doi:10.2307/j.ctv20pxxzt

Kelan, E. K. (2008). Gender fatigue — Camouflaging gender discrimination in organizations. *Proceedings - Academy of Management*, *2008*(1), 1–6. doi:10.5465/ambpp.2008.33645060

Keller, S., & Meaney, M. (2017). Attracting and retaining the right talent. McKinsey & Company, 24.

Kelloway, E. K. (2017). Mental health in the workplace: Towards evidence-based practice. *Canadian Psychology, 58*(1), 1–6. doi:10.1037/cap0000084

Kerslake, P. (2005). Words from the Ys. *New Zealand Management, 52*(4), 44–46.

Khairy, H. A., Agina, M. F., Aliane, N., & Hashad, M. E. (2023). Internal Branding in Hotels: Interaction Effects of Employee Engagement, Workplace Friendship, and Organizational Citizenship Behavior. *Sustainability (Basel), 15*(5), 4530. doi:10.3390/su15054530

Khalid, A., & Syed, J. (2024). Mental health and wellbeing at work: A systematic review of literature and directions for future research. *Human Resource Management Review, 34*(1), 100998. doi:10.1016/j.hrmr.2023.100998

Khan, F., Sohail, A., Sufyan, M., Uddin, M., & Basit, A. (2019). The effect of Workforce Diversity on Employee Performance in the Higher Education Sector. *Journal of Management Info.*

Khan, S. A., Magd, H., & Epoc, F. (2022). Application of Data Management System in Business to Business Electronic Commerce. In Competitive Trends and Technologies in Business Management. (pp. 109-124). Nova Science Publishers.

Khan, S. A., Magd, H., Bhuyan, U., Jonathan, H., & Naim, A. (2024). Digital Marketing (DM): How are Small Business Enterprises (SBEs) of Bhutan and Sikkim (India) Responding to it? In Digital Influence on Consumer Habits: Marketing Challenges and Opportunities (pp. 135-145). Emerald Publishing Limited. doi:10.1108/978-1-80455-342-820241008

Khan, S.A, Epoc, F., Gangwar, V.P., Ligori T.A.A, & Ansari, Z.A. (2021). Will Online banking sustain in Bhutan post Covid – 19? A quantitative analysis of the customer e-satisfaction and e-loyalty in the Kingdom of Bhutan. *Transnational Marketing Journal, 9*(3), 607-624. doi:10.33182/tmj.v9i3.1288

Khan, S. A. (2023). E-Marketing, E-Commerce, E-Business, and Internet of Things: An Overview of Terms in the Context of Small and Medium Enterprises (SMEs). In A. Naim & V. Devi (Eds.), *Global Applications of the Internet of Things in Digital Marketing* (pp. 332–348). IGI Global. doi:10.4018/978-1-6684-8166-0.ch017

Khan, S. A., & Magd, H. (2021). Empirical Examination of MS Teams in Conducting Webinar: Evidence from International Online Program conducted in Oman. *Journal of Content. Community and Communication, 7*(1), 159–175. doi:10.31620/JCCC.12.21/13

Khan, S. A., & Magd, H. (2023). New Technology Anxiety and Acceptance of Technology: An Appraisal of MS Teams. In *Advances in Distance Learning in Times of Pandemic* (pp. 105–134). CRC Press, Taylor and Francis. doi:10.1201/9781003322252-5

Khan, S. A., Magd, H., Ansari, M. S. A., Sharma, P. P., Tirwa, I. P., & Bhuyan, U. (2022). Analysis of Regional Tourists in Bhutan before Covid-19. *Anusandhan-NDIM's Journal of Business and Management Research, 4*(1), 39–58. doi:10.56411/anusandhan.2022.v4i1.39-58

Khan, S. A., Magd, H., Khatri, B., Arora, S., & Sharma, N. (2023). Critical Success Factors of Internet of Things and Digital Marketing. In A. Naim & V. Devi (Eds.), *Global Applications of the Internet of Things in Digital Marketing* (pp. 233–253). IGI Global. doi:10.4018/978-1-6684-8166-0.ch012

Khan, S. A., & Naim, A. (2023). XAI in Society 5.0 through the lens of Marketing and HRM. In F. Al-Turjman, A. Nayyar, M. Naved, A. K. Singh, & M. Bilal (Eds.), *XAI Based Intelligent Systems for Society 5.0* (pp. 327–363). Elsevier. doi:10.1016/B978-0-323-95315-3.00004-8

Khan, S. A., Narula, S., Kansra, P., Naim, A., & Kalra, D. (2024). Should Marketing and Public Relations be Part of the Institutional Accreditation Criterion of Business Schools? An Appraisal of Accreditation Criterion of Selected Accreditation Agencies. In A. Naim (Ed.), *Accreditation Processes and Frameworks in Higher Education* (pp. 349–375). Nova Science Publishers. doi:10.52305/QUVJ6658

Khare, K., Singhal, S., Singhal, S., & Singh, D. Rajendra, Employee Poaching - Why? & Whom? (November 3, 2014). IJRSS, Vol. 4, Issue 4, November 2014, Available at SSRN: https://ssrn.com/abstract=2956777

Khatri, B., Shrimali, H., Khan, S. A., & Naim, A. (2023). Role of HR Analytics in Ensuring Psychological Wellbeing and Job Security: Learnings From COVID-19. In R. Yadav, M. Sinha, & J. Kureethara (Eds.), *HR Analytics in an Era of Rapid Automation* (pp. 36–53). IGI Global. doi:10.4018/978-1-6684-8942-0.ch003

Khatri, B., Singh, R. K., Arora, S., Khan, S. A., & Naim, A. (2024). Optimizing Supply Chain Management Indicators for Sustainable Supply Chain Integration and Customer Loyalty: Potential Role of Environmentally Responsible Practices. In Y. Ramakrishna & B. Srivastava (Eds.), *Strategies for Environmentally Responsible Supply Chain and Production Management* (pp. 156–181). IGI Global. doi:10.4018/979-8-3693-0669-7.ch008

Khatri, C., Chapman, S. J., Glasbey, J., Kelly, M. E., Nepogodiev, D., Bhangu, A., & Fitzgerald, J. E. (2015). Social media and Internet driven study recruitment: Evaluating a new model for promoting collaborator engagement and participation. *PLoS One*, *10*(3), e0118899. doi:10.1371/journal.pone.0118899 PMID:25775005

Khilji, S. E., Tarique, I., & Schuler, R. S. (2015). Incorporating the macro view in global talent management. *Human Resource Management Review*, *25*(3), 236–248. doi:10.1016/j.hrmr.2015.04.001

Kichuk, A., Brown, L., & Ladkin, A. (2019). Talent pool exclusion: The hotel employee perspective. *International Journal of Contemporary Hospitality Management*, *31*(10), 3970–3991. doi:10.1108/IJCHM-10-2018-0814

Kim, J. H. (2014). Employee poaching: Why it can be predatory. *MDE. Managerial and Decision Economics*, *35*(5), 309–317. doi:10.1002/mde.2637

Kincaid, R., & Reynolds, J. (2023). *Unconventional Work, Conventional Problems: Gig Microtask Work, Inequality, and the Flexibility Mystique*. Soxiological Quarterly. doi:10.1080/00380253.2023.2268679

King, R. (2022). *Microaggressions, Impostor Phenomenon, and People of Color: A Quantitative Analysis* (Order No. 29258450). Available from ProQuest Dissertations & Theses Global. (2705775654). https://christuniversity.knimbus.com/loginAndLaunch?docUrl=?url=https://www.proquest.com/dissertations-theses/microaggressions-impostor-phenomenon-people-color/docview/2705775654/se-2

King, E. B., & Cortina, J. M. (2010). The Social and Economic Imperative of Lesbian, Gay, Bisexual, and Transgendered Supportive Organizational Policies. *Industrial and Organizational Psychology: Perspectives on Science and Practice*, *3*(1), 69–78. doi:10.1111/j.1754-9434.2009.01201.x

King, E. B., Hebl, M. R., George, J. M., & Matusik, S. F. (2010). Understanding Tokenism: Antecedents and Consequences of a Psychological Climate of Gender Inequity. *Journal of Management*, *36*(2), 482–510. doi:10.1177/0149206308328508

King, K. A. (2015). Global talent management: Introducing a strategic framework and multiple-actors model. *Journal of Global Mobility*, *3*(3), 273–288. doi:10.1108/JGM-02-2015-0002

King, K. R. (2005). Why Is Discrimination Stressful? The Mediating Role of Cognitive Appraisal. *Cultural Diversity & Ethnic Minority Psychology*, *11*(3), 202–212. doi:10.1037/1099-9809.11.3.202 PMID:16117588

Kişescu, R. (2017). *Autism, big data and innovation. About neurodiversity at work*. Retrieved at https://ralucakisescu.ro/autismul-big-data-si-inovatia-despre-neurodiversitate-locul-de-munca-0

Kissel, P., & Büttgen, M. (2015). Using social media to communicate employer brand identity: The impact on corporate image and employer attractiveness. *Journal of Brand Management*, *22*(9), 755–777. doi:10.1057/bm.2015.42

Kluemper, D. H., & Rosen, P. A. (2009). Future employment selection methods: Evaluating social networking web sites. *Journal of Managerial Psychology*, *24*(6), 567–580. doi:10.1108/02683940910974134

Knouse, S. B. (2001). Virtual mentors: Mentoring on the internet. *Journal of Employment Counseling*, *38*(4), 162–169. doi:10.1002/j.2161-1920.2001.tb00498.x

Koch, B. J., & Koch, P. T. (2007). Collectivism, individualism, and outgroup cooperation in a segmented China. *Asia Pacific Journal of Management*, *24*(2), 207–225. doi:10.1007/s10490-006-9004-5

Koch, J. L., Tung, R., Gmelch, W., & Swent, B. (1982). Job stress among school administrators: Factorial dimensions and differential effects. *The Journal of Applied Psychology*, *67*(4), 493–499. doi:10.1037/0021-9010.67.4.493 PMID:7130071

Koch, T., Gerber, C., & De Klerk, J. J. (2018). The impact of social media on recruitment: Are you LinkedIn? *SA Journal of Human Resource Management*, *16*(1), 1–14. doi:10.4102/sajhrm.v16i0.861

Koivunen, S., Olsson, T., Olshannikova, E., & Lindberg, A. (2019). Understanding decision-making in recruitment: Opportunities and challenges for information technology. *Proceedings of the ACM on Human-Computer Interaction*, *3*(GROUP), 1-22.

Köllen, T. (2019). Diversity Management: A Critical Review and Agenda for the Future. *Journal of Management Inquiry*, *30*(3), 259–272. doi:10.1177/1056492619868025

Komeda, H. (2015). Similarity hypothesis: Understanding of others with autism spectrum disorders by individuals with autism spectrum disorders. *Frontiers in Human Neuroscience*, *9*, 124. doi:10.3389/fnhum.2015.00124 PMID:25852514

Kondaiah, B. V., & Varshney, P. K. (2022). A Comparative Study (Engineering) on Employer Branding Practices to Retain Talent in Professional Engineering Colleges in A.P. W.R.T West Godavarir (DT). *International Journal of Early Childhood Speacial Education*, *14*(2), 7657–7665. doi:10.9756/INTJECSE/V14I2.875

Koster, K. (2013). *Communication and engagement*. Employee Benefit News. https://www.highbeam.com/ publications/ employee-benefit-news-p4839/april-2013

Kovarik, M. (2008). How to engage Gen Y. *Inside Supply Management*, 10-12.

Kramar, R. (2014). Beyond strategic human resource management: Is sustainable human resource management the next approach? *International Journal of Human Resource Management*, *25*(8), 1069–1089. doi:10.1080/09585192.2013.816863

Kram, K. E. (1983). Phases of the mentor relationship. *Academy of Management Journal*, *26*(4), 608–625. doi:10.2307/255910

Kram, K. E., & Isabella, L. A. (2020). Virtual mentoring: The state of the art. *Journal of Management*, *46*(8), 1228–1254.

Krcek, T. E. (2012). Deconstructing disability and neurodiversity: Controversial issues for autism and implications for social work. *Journal of Progressive Human Services*, *24*(1), 4–22. doi:10.1080/10428232.2013.740406

Kreiser, P. M., Marino, L. D., Dickson, P., & Weaver, K. M. (2010). Cultural influences on entrepreneurial orientation: The impact of national culture on risk taking and proactiveness in SMEs. *Entrepreneurship Theory and Practice*, *34*(5), 959–984. doi:10.1111/j.1540-6520.2010.00396.x

Kriss, M., Te, H. S., Elizabeth, C., VanWagner, L. B., Scott, F. I., & Lai, J. C. (2021). National Early Career Transplant Hepatologist Survey: Compensation, Burnout, and Job Satisfaction. *Hepatology Communications*, *5*(4), 701–712. doi:10.1002/hep4.1666 PMID:33860127

Krzeminska, A., Austin, R. D., Bruyere, S. M., & Hedley, D. (2019). The advantages and challenges of neurodiversity employment in organizations. *Journal of Management & Organization*, *25*(4), 453–463. doi:10.1017/jmo.2019.58

Ktoridou, D., Doukanari, E., & Karayiannis, A. (2019, April). Educating the New Generation of Engineering Managers to Stay Relevant in the 21st Century Workforce. In *2019 IEEE Global Engineering Education Conference (EDUCON)* (pp. 1547-1551). IEEE. 10.1109/EDUCON.2019.8725177

Kucherov, D., & Zavyalova, E. (2012). HRD practices and talent management in the companies with the employer brand. *European Journal of Training and Development*, *36*(1), 86–104. doi:10.1108/03090591211192647

Kuknor, S., Kumar, A., & Bhattacharya, S. (2023). Organizational inclusion and OCB: The moderating role of inclusive leadership. *FIIB Business Review*, *12*(1), 1–14. doi:10.1177/23197145231183859

Kuknor, S., & Kumar, V. (2023). Impact of training and development interventions for diversity & inclusion: Proposing an organizational schema. *Development and Learning in Organizations*, *38*(1), 16–19. doi:10.1108/DLO-11-2022-0233

Kumar Betchoo, N. (2022, September). Data-Driven Decision Management from a Dashboard Perspective. In *Proceedings of the 6th International Conference on Advance Computing and Intelligent Engineering: ICACIE 2021* (pp. 509-519). Singapore: Springer Nature Singapore.

Kumar, K. K., Mishra, S. K., & Budhwar, P. (2021). Employee turnover in India: insights from the public–private debate. In D. G. Allen & J. M. Vardaman (Eds.), *Global Talent Retention: Understanding Employee Turnover Around the World* (pp. 213–238). Emerald Publishing. doi:10.1108/978-1-83909-293-020211011

Kumar, R. S., & Peter, H. (2020). A study on talent stalk with the support of employee poaching in automobile sector with particular reference to Krishnagiri District, Tamilnadu, India. *Editorial Board*, *9*(4), 29.

Kumar, S., Kapoor, B., & Shah, M. A. (2024). Contemporary Issues and Challenges Facing the Hospitality Industry. In N. Kumar, K. Sood, E. Özen, & S. Grima (Eds.), *The Framework for Resilient Industry: A Holistic Approach for Developing Economies* (pp. 55–64). Emerald Publishing Limited. doi:10.1108/978-1-83753-734-120241004

Kumar, S., Savani, K., Sanghai, A., Pochkhanawalla, S., Dhar, S., Ramaswami, A., & Rose Markus, H. (2015). Indian employees' attitudes toward poaching. *Business Perspectives and Research*, *3*(2), 81–94. doi:10.1177/2278533715578553

Kumar, S., Tiwari, P., & Zymbler, M. (2019). Internet of Things is a revolutionary approach for future technology enhancement: A review. *Journal of Big Data*, *6*(1), 1–21. doi:10.1186/s40537-019-0268-2

Kundi, Y. M., Aboramadan, M., Elhamalawi, E. M., & Shahid, S. (2020). Employee psychological wellbeing and job performance: Exploring mediating and moderating mechanisms. *The International Journal of Organizational Analysis*, *29*(3), 736–754. doi:10.1108/IJOA-05-2020-2204

Kundu, S. C., & Lata, K. (2017). Effects of supportive work environment on employee retention: Mediating role of organizational engagement. *The International Journal of Organizational Analysis*, *25*(4), 703–722. doi:10.1108/IJOA-12-2016-1100

Kupcová, I., Danišovič, Ľ., Klein, M., & Harsanyi, S. (2023). Effects of the COVID-19 pandemic on mental health, anxiety, and depression. *BMC Psychology*, *11*(1), 108. Advance online publication. doi:10.1186/s40359-023-01130-5 PMID:37041568

Lafontaine, F., & Slade, M. (2023). *No-Poaching Clauses in Franchise Contracts, Anticompetitive or Efficiency Enhancing?* Anticompetitive or Efficiency Enhancing. doi:10.2139/ssrn.4404155

Lahtinen, A. (2015). China's soft power: Challenges of Confucianism and Confucius Institutes. *Journal of Comparative Asian Development*, *14*(2), 200–226. doi:10.1080/15339114.2015.1059055

Lakhdar, S. (2001). *Gestion de ressources humaines*. Universite de Boeck.

Landers, R. N., & Schmidt, G. B. (2016). Social media in employee selection and recruitment: An overview. In Springer eBooks (pp. 3–11). doi:10.1007/978-3-319-29989-1_1

Langenegger, P. B., Mahler, P., & Staffelbach, B. (2011). Effectiveness of talent management strategies. *European Journal of International Management*, *5*(5), 524. doi:10.1504/EJIM.2011.042177

Lassleben, H., & Hofmann, L. (2023). Attracting Gen Z talents: Do expectations towards employers vary by gender? *Gender in Management*, *38*(4), 545–560. doi:10.1108/GM-08-2021-0247

Lathabhavan, R. (2023). Mental well-being through HR analytics: Investigating an employee supportive framework. *Personnel Review*. Advance online publication. doi:10.1108/PR-11-2022-0836

Latukha, M., Lisina, P., & Panibratov, Y. (2019). Developing sustainable competitive advantage of a firm through human resource management practices: A competence-based approach. *Global Business and Economics Review*, *21*(1), 96–119. doi:10.1504/GBER.2019.096855

Latukha, M., Zhang, Y., Panibratov, A., Arzhanykh, K., & Rysakova, L. (2023). Talent management practices for firms' absorptive capacity in a host country: A study of the Chinese diaspora in Russia. *Critical Perspectives on International Business*, *19*(2), 181–205. doi:10.1108/cpoib-07-2020-0099

Le, D. A., Le-Hoai, L., Le, V. H., & Dang, C. N. (2022, September). Factors Affecting Employee Retention in Construction: Empirical Study in the Mekong Delta Region. In *ICSCEA 2021: Proceedings of the Second International Conference on Sustainable Civil Engineering and Architecture* (pp. 263-277). Singapore: Springer Nature Singapore.

Leach, P. K., Nygaard, R. M., Chipman, J. G., Brunsvold, M. E., & Marek, A. P. (2019). Impostor Phenomenon and Burnout in General Surgeons and General Surgery Residents. *Journal of Surgical Education*, *76*(1), 99–106. doi:10.1016/j.jsurg.2018.06.025 PMID:30122638

Lee, H. F., & Chang, Y.-J. (2022). The Effects of Work Satisfaction and Work Flexibility on Burnout in Nurses. *The Journal of Nursing Research*, *30*(6), e240. Advance online publication. doi:10.1097/jnr.0000000000000522 PMID:36166364

Lee, H., Operario, D., Yi, H., Choo, S., Kim, J. H., & Kim, S. S. (2022). Does Discrimination Affect Whether Transgender People Avoid or Delay Healthcare?: A Nationwide Cross-sectional Survey in South Korea. *Journal of Immigrant and Minority Health*, *24*(1), 170–177. doi:10.1007/s10903-021-01193-9 PMID:33881679

Lee, I., Lin, C., & Lin, T. (2017). The creation of national intellectual capital from the perspective of Hofstede's national culture. *Journal of Intellectual Capital*, *18*(4), 807–831. doi:10.1108/JIC-11-2016-0117

Lee, J. J., Bell, L. F., & Shaulskiy, S. L. (2017). Exploring mentors' perceptions of mentees and the mentoring relationship in a multicultural service-learning context. *Active Learning in Higher Education*, *18*(3), 243–256. doi:10.1177/1469787417715203

Leekha Chhabra, N., & Sharma, S. (2014, March 4). Employer branding: Strategy for improving employer attractiveness. *The International Journal of Organizational Analysis*, *22*(1), 48–60. doi:10.1108/IJOA-09-2011-0513

Lee, L., & Yu, H. (2023). Socioeconomic diversity in the hospitality industry: The relationship between social class background, family expectations and career outcomes. *International Journal of Contemporary Hospitality Management*, *35*(11), 3844–3863. Advance online publication. doi:10.1108/IJCHM-11-2022-1356

Lee, S., Kim, S., Lee, K., & Choi, Y. (2022). The role of digital technologies in online mentoring: An analysis of mentoring platforms and applications. *Interactive Learning Environments*, *30*(2), 235–250.

Lee, Y., & Kim, K. H. (2020). Enhancing employee advocacy on social media: The value of internal relationship management approach. *Corporate Communications*, *26*(2), 311–327. doi:10.1108/CCIJ-05-2020-0088

Lee, Y., & Lim, K. (2021). A Case Study on the University Freshman Adaptation Program Using an Online Mentoring Program during the COVID-19 Pandemic. *Korean J Gen Edu*, *15*(4), 217–231. doi:10.46392/kjge.2021.15.4.217

LeFevre-Levy, R., Melson-Silimon, A., Harmata, R., Hulett, A. L., & Carter, N. T. (2023). Neurodiversity in the workplace: Considering neuroatypicality as a form of diversity. *Industrial and Organizational Psychology: Perspectives on Science and Practice*, *16*(1), 1–19. doi:10.1017/iop.2022.86

Lei, N. (2022). Research on Job Preference in China's Internet Industry Through the Conjoint Analysis. *Journal of Industrial Integration and Management-Innovation and Entrepreneurship*, *07*(03), 273–309. doi:10.1142/S2424862222500142

Lemmetty, S., & Billet, S. (2023). Employee-driven learning and innovation (EDLI) as a phenomenon of continuous learning at work. *Journal of Workplace Learning*, *35*(9), 162–176. doi:10.1108/JWL-12-2022-0175

Levy, S. J. (1959). Symbols for sale. *Harvard Business Review*, *37*(4), 117–124.

Lewis, L. (2019). Organizational Change. In Origins and Traditions of Organizational Communication. Academic Press.

Lewis, J. A., & Neville, H. A. (2015). Construction and initial validation of the Gendered Racial Microaggressions Scale for Black women. *Journal of Counseling Psychology*, *62*(2), 289–302. doi:10.1037/cou0000062 PMID:25867696

Lewis, R. E., & Heckman, R. J. (2006). Talent management: A critical review. *Human Resource Management Review*, *16*(2), 139–154. doi:10.1016/j.hrmr.2006.03.001

Liang, X., Kidwai, H., Zhang, M., & Zhang, Y. (2016). *How Shanghai does it: Insights and lessons from the highest-ranking education system in the world.* World Bank Publications. doi:10.1596/978-1-4648-0790-9

Li, F., Luo, S., Mu, W., Li, Y., Ye, L., Zheng, X., Xu, B., Ding, Y., Ling, P., Zhou, M., & Chen, X. (2021). Effects of sources of social support and resilience on the mental health of different age groups during the COVID-19 pandemic. *BMC Psychiatry*, *21*(1), 16. Advance online publication. doi:10.1186/s12888-020-03012-1 PMID:33413238

Ligori, T. A. A., Suresh, N., Khan, S. A., Rabgay, T., & Yezer, K. (2022). The mediating effect of university image on the relationship between curriculum and student satisfaction: An empirical study of the Royal University of Bhutan. *International Journal of Pluralism and Economics Education*, *13*(2), 192–208. doi:10.1504/IJPEE.2022.127218

Li, L., Du, K., Zhang, W., & Mao, J. Y. (2019). Poverty alleviation through government-led e-commerce development in rural China: An activity theory perspective. *Information Systems Journal*, *29*(4), 914–952. doi:10.1111/isj.12199

Li, M., Malik, M. S., Ijaz, M., & Irfan, M. (2023). Employer Responses to Poaching on Employee Productivity: The Mediating Role of Organizational Agility in Technology Companies. *Sustainability (Basel)*, *15*(6), 5369. doi:10.3390/su15065369

Lim, S., & Cortina, L. M. (2005). Interpersonal Mistreatment in the Workplace: The Interface and Impact of General Incivility and Sexual Harassment. *The Journal of Applied Psychology*, *90*(3), 483–496. doi:10.1037/0021-9010.90.3.483 PMID:15910144

Lindley, L. D. (2005). Perceived Barriers to Career Development in the Context of Social Cognitive Career Theory. *Journal of Career Assessment*, *13*(3), 271–287. doi:10.1177/1069072705274953

Lindsay, S., Osten, V., Rezai, M., & Bui, S. (2021). Disclosure and workplace accommodations for people with autism: A systematic review. *Disability and Rehabilitation*, *43*(5), 597–610. doi:10.1080/09638288.2019.1635658 PMID:31282214

Lindtner, S., & Lin, C. (2017). Making and its promises. *CoDesign*, *13*(2), 70–82. doi:10.1080/15710882.2017.1308518

Ling, L. M. (2023). Prevalence Of Mental Health and Its Impact on Employee Productivity. *Reviews of Contemporary Business Analytics*, 6(1), 1–13.

Liu, R., & Tan, J. (2022). A review of talent management research at home and abroad. *Journal of Chinese Human Resource Management*, 13(1), 39–58. doi:10.47297/wspchrmWSP2040-800502.20221301

Li, W., Wang, X., Haque, M. J., Shafique, M. N., & Nawaz, M. Z. (2020). Impact of workforce diversity management on employees' outcomes: Testing the mediating role of a person's job match. *SAGE Open*, 10(1), 1–16. doi:10.1177/2158244020903402

Li, X., Yen, C.-L. A., & Liu, T. (2020). Hotel brand personality and brand loyalty: An affective, conative and behavioral perspective. *Journal of Hospitality Marketing & Management*, 29(5), 550–570. doi:10.1080/19368623.2019.1654961

Li, Y., & Jonas, A. E. (2023). Small cities and towns in global city-centred regionalism: Observations from Beijing-Tianjin-Hebei region, China. *Transactions in Planning and Urban Research*, 2(1), 103–114. doi:10.1177/27541223231157225

Loch, A. A., Díaz, A. P., Pacheco-Palha, A., Wainberg, M. L., Da Silva, A. G., & Malloy-Diniz, L. F. (2021). Editorial: Stigma's impact on people with mental illness: Advances in understanding, management, and prevention. Frontiers in Psychology, p. 12. doi:10.3389/fpsyg.2021.715247

Logan, G. (2008). Anatomy of a Gen Y- er. *Personnel Today*, 24-25.

Lombardo, M. V., Lai, M. C., & Baron-Cohen, S. (2019). Big data approaches to decomposing heterogeneity across the autism spectrum. *Molecular Psychiatry*, 24(10), 1435–1450. doi:10.1038/s41380-018-0321-0 PMID:30617272

Long, C. S., Xuan, S. S., Wan Ismail, W. K., Abd Rasid, S. Z., & Kowang, T. O. (2014). An analysis on academicians' job satisfaction in the perspective of HRD practices. *International Education Studies*, 7(7), 85–95. doi:10.5539/ies.v7n7p85

Lopamudra & Acharya, S. K. (2015). Case Study on Culture of Recruiting Rewarding and Retaining Strategy for Talent Management. *Adarsh Journal of Management Research, 8*(2), 42. doi:10.21095/ajmr/2015/v8/i2/88214

Love, S. (2019). *Offices are a hell for people whose brains work differently*. Retrieved at https://www.vice.com/ro/article/wjvd9q/de-ce-e-sanatos-sa-lucrezi-de-acasa

Love, K. L. (2009). An emancipatory study with African -American women in predominantly White nursing schools. *Dissertation Abstracts International*.

Lowe, D., Levitt, K., & Wilson, T. (2008). Solutions for retaining generation Y employees in the workplace. *Business Renaissance Quarterly*, 3(3), 43–57.

Lub, V. (2015). Validity in qualitative evaluation. *International Journal of Qualitative Methods*, 14(5), 160940691562140. doi:10.1177/1609406915621406

Luc, K. (2024). *Neurodiversity in the workplace: Why it matters*. https://www.cultureamp.com/blog/neurodiversity-in-the-workplace

Ludviga, I., Sennikova, I., & Kalvina, A. (2016). Turnover of Public Sector Employees and the Mediating Role of Job Satisfaction: An Empirical Study in Latvia. Society, Integration, Education, 4, 364-378. doi:10.17770/sie2016vol4.1577

Luna-Arocas, R. (2023). The key role played by innovation in the talent management and organizational performance relationship. *Employee Relations*, 45(6), 1347–1370. doi:10.1108/ER-09-2022-0430

Luna-Arocas, R., & Danvila-del-Valle, I. (2022). The impact of talent management on ethical behavior and intention to stay in the organization. *Journal of Management & Organization*, 1–16. Advance online publication. doi:10.1017/jmo.2022.64

Lundvall, B. Å., & Rikap, C. (2022). China's catching-up in artificial intelligence seen as a co-evolution of corporate and national innovation systems. *Research Policy*, *51*(1), 104395. doi:10.1016/j.respol.2021.104395

Luo, X., Li, H., Zhang, J., & Shim, J. P. (2010). Examining multi-dimensional trust and multi-faceted risk in initial acceptance of emerging technologies: An empirical study of mobile banking services. *Decision Support Systems*, *49*(2), 222–234. doi:10.1016/j.dss.2010.02.008

Lyons, S. T. (2003). *An exploration of generational values in life and at work* [PhD Thesis]. Carleton University.

Madore, M. R., & Byrd, D. (2022). Optimizing mentoring relationships with persons from historically marginalized communities through the use of difficult dialogues. *Journal of Clinical and Experimental Neuropsychology*, *44*(5–6), 441–449. doi:10.1080/13803395.2022.2108770 PMID:35924945

Maertz, P. Jr, C., A. Stoeberl, P., & Marks, J. (. (2014). Building successful internships: Lessons from the research for interns, schools, and employers. *Career Development International*, *19*(1), 123–142. doi:10.1108/CDI-03-2013-0025

Mafrachi, A. M., Abed, H., & Mohammed, M. (2020). Assessing the Role of Green Human Resources Management and Environmental Cooperation: A Case Study on Food Industries Sector in Iraq. *"Ovidius" University Annals. Economic Sciences Series*, *20*(1), 14–23.

Magd, H., & Khan, S. A. (2022). Strategic Framework for Entrepreneurship Education in Promoting Social Entrepreneurship in GCC Countries During and Post COVID-19. In International Perspectives on Value Creation and Sustainability Through Social Entrepreneurship (pp. 61-75). IGI Global.

Magd, H., Jonathan, H., & Khan, S. A. (2023b). Education Situation in Online Education before the Pandemic and in the Time of Pandemic. In Advances in Distance Learning in Times of Pandemic. CRC Press, Taylor and Francis. doi:10.1201/9781003322252-3

Magd, H., Ansari, M. S. A., & Khan, S. A. (2023a). Need for Explainable Artificial Intelligence Ethnic Decision Making in Society 5.0. In F. Al-Turjman, A. Nayyar, M. Naved, A. K. Singh, & M. Bilal (Eds.), *XAI Based Intelligent Systems for Society 5.0* (pp. 103–127). Elsevier. doi:10.1016/B978-0-323-95315-3.00010-3

Magd, H., & Khan, S. A. (2022). Effectiveness of using online teaching platforms as communication tools in higher education institutions in Oman: Stakeholders perspectives. *Journal of Content. Community and Communication*, *16*, 148–160. doi:10.31620/JCCC.12.22/13

Mahto, M., Hogan, S. K., & Sniderman, B. (2022). *A rising tide lifts all boats: Creating a better work environment for all by embracing neurodiversity*. Deloitte Insights.

Maier, L., Baccarella, C. V., Wagner, T. F., Meinel, M., Eismann, T., & Voigt, K. I. (2022). Saw the office, want the job: The effect of creative workspace design on organizational attractiveness. *Journal of Environmental Psychology*, *80*, 101773. Advance online publication. doi:10.1016/j.jenvp.2022.101773

Malär, L., Krohmer, H., Hoyer, W. D., & Nyffenegger, B. (2011). Emotional brand attachment and brand personality: The relative importance of the actual and the ideal self. *Journal of Marketing*, *75*(4), 35–52. doi:10.1509/jmkg.75.4.35

Malik, S. Y., Cao, Y., Mughal, Y. H., Kundi, G. M., Mughal, M. H., & Ramayah, T. (2020). Pathways towards sustainability in organizations: Empirical evidence on the role of green human resource management practices and green intellectual capital. *Sustainability (Basel)*, *12*(8), 3228. doi:10.3390/su12083228

Mandhanya, Y., & Shah, M. (2010). Employer branding-A tool for talent management. *Global Management Review, 4*(2).

Mangi, R. A., Soomro, H. J., Ghumro, I., Abidi, A. R., & Jalbani, A. A. (2011). A study of job satisfaction among non-PhD faculty in universities. *Australian Journal of Business and Management Research*, *1*(7), 83–90. doi:10.52283/NSWRCA.AJBMR.20110107A09

Manoharan, S., Chelliah, J., & Sardeshmukh, S. R. (2021). Antecedents and outcomes of a culturally diverse workforce in hotels. *Journal of Hospitality & Tourism Research (Washington, D.C.)*, *45*(8), 1383–1416. Advance online publication. doi:10.1177/1096348020986906

Manolescu, A. (2006). *Managementul resurselor umane*. Ed. Economica.

Marginson, S. (2010). Higher education in the global knowledge economy. *Procedia: Social and Behavioral Sciences*, *2*(5), 6962–6980. doi:10.1016/j.sbspro.2010.05.049

Marinaş, C. (2006). *Managementul comparat al resurselor umane*. Teză de doctorat. ASE Bucureşti.

Martin, C. A. (2005). From High Maintenance to High Productivity: What Managers Need to Know about Generation Y. *Industrial and Commercial Training*, *37*(1), 39–44. doi:10.1108/00197850510699965

Martin, M., & Jackson, T. (2008). *Practica de personal*. Editura CODECS.

Martins, P. S., & Thomas, J. (2023). *Employers' associations, worker mobility, and training*. Nova SBE Working Paper Series, (653).

Martins, P. S., & Thomas, J. P. (2018). Employer collusion and employee training. *New York Times*, 2.

Martins, C., Oliveira, T., & Popovič, A. (2014). Understanding the Internet banking adoption: A unified theory of acceptance and use of technology and perceived risk application. *International Journal of Information Management*, *34*(1), 1–13. doi:10.1016/j.ijinfomgt.2013.06.002

Martins, N., Dominique-Ferreira, S., & Lopes, C. (2022). Design and development of a digital platform for seasonal jobs: Improving the hiring process. *Journal of Global Scholars of Marketing Science*, *32*(3), 452–469. doi:10.1080/21639159.2020.1808851

MartinsP. S.ThomasJ. (2022). Training, Worker Mobility, and Employer Coordination. Battiston, D., Espinosa, M., & Liu, S. (2021). Talent poaching and job rotation. Available at SSRN 3778068.

Mashaba, N., & Botha, D. (2023). Factors affecting the attraction of women to technical mining positions in South Africa. *SA Journal of Human Resource Management*, *21*(1). Advance online publication. doi:10.4102/sajhrm.v21i0.2227

Mashala, Y. L. (2018). Green Human Resource Management and Environmental Sustainability in Tanzania: A Review and Research Agenda. *International Journal of Academic Multidisciplinary Research*, *2*(12), 60–68.

Masoom, K., Rastogi, A., & Khan, S. A. (2024). Impact of AI on Knowledge-based Marketing: A Study of B2B Markets. In N. Singh, P. Kansra, & S. L. Gupta (Eds.), *Digital Influence on Consumer Habits: Marketing Challenges and Opportunities* (pp. 147–158). Emerald Publishing Limited. doi:10.1108/978-1-80455-342-820241009

Masri, H. A., & Jaaron, A. A. (2017). Assessing green human resources management practices in Palestinian manufacturing context: An empirical study. *Journal of Cleaner Production*, *143*, 474–489. doi:10.1016/j.jclepro.2016.12.087

Mastari, L., Spruyt, B., & Siongers, J. (2019). Benevolent and Hostile Sexism in Social Spheres: The Impact of Parents, School and Romance on Belgian Adolescents' Sexist Attitudes. *Frontiers in Sociology*, *4*, 47. Advance online publication. doi:10.3389/fsoc.2019.00047 PMID:33869370

Mathimaran, K. B., & Kumar, A. A. (2017). Employee retention strategies: An empirical research. *Global Journal of Management and Business Research*, *17*(1), 17–19.

Mathur, S., & Mathur, S. (2019). *Artificial intelligence: redesigning human resource management, functions and practices*. ResearchGate.

Matthews, G., & Clance, P. R. (1985). Treatment of the impostor phenomenon in psychotherapy clients. *Psychotherapy in Private Practice*, *3*(1), 71–81. doi:10.1300/J294v03n01_09

Mattone, J., & Xavier, L. F. (2013). *Talent leadership: A proven method for identifying and developing high-potential employees*. Amacom.

Maulana, H., & Khawaja, N. G. (2022). A cultural perspective of wellbeing. In S. Deb & B. A. Gerrard (Eds.), *Handbook of Health and Wellbeing*. Springer. doi:10.1007/978-981-16-8263-6_2

Maurya, K. K., & Agarwal, M. (2018). Organisational talent management and perceived employer branding. *The International Journal of Organizational Analysis*, *26*(2), 312–330. doi:10.1108/IJOA-04-2017-1147

Ma, X., Bashir, H., & Ayub, A. (2023). Cultivating green workforce: The roles of green shared vision and green organizational identity. *Frontiers in Psychology*, *14*, 1041654. doi:10.3389/fpsyg.2023.1041654 PMID:37008862

Maxwell, J. C. (2007). *Talent is never enough: Discover the choices that will take you beyond your talent*. HarperCollins Leadership.

McCartney, S., & Fu, N. (2022). Bridging the gap: Why, how and when HR analytics can impact organizational performance. *Management Decision*, *60*(13), 25–47. doi:10.1108/MD-12-2020-1581

McChesney, J., Campbell, C., Wang, J., & Foster, L. (2022). What is in a name? Effects of game-framing on perceptions of hiring organizations. *International Journal of Selection and Assessment*, *30*(1), 182–192. doi:10.1111/ijsa.12370

McDowall, A., Doyle, N. & Kiseleva, M. (2022). *Neurodiversity at Work 2023: Demand, Supply and a Gap Analysis*. Academic Press.

Mehta, K., & Chugan, K. P. (2015). Green HRM in Pursuit of Environmentally Sustainable Business. *Universal Journal of Industrial and Business Management*, *3*(3), 74–81. doi:10.13189/ujibm.2015.030302

Mellahi, K., & Wilkinson, A. (2010). Slash and burn or nip and tuck? Downsizing, innovation and human resources. *International Journal of Human Resource Management*, *21*(13), 2291–2305. doi:10.1080/09585192.2010.516584

Mellifont, D. (2019). DESerting clients? A study investigating evidence-based measures supporting the long-term employment of neurodiverse Australians. *Management and Labour Studies*, *44*(4), 455–466. doi:10.1177/0258042X19882519

Mer, A. (2023). Artificial Intelligence in Human Resource Management: Recent Trends and Research Agenda. *Digital Transformation, Strategic Resilience. Cyber Security and Risk Management*, *111*, 31–56.

Mesthrige Jayantha, W., & Sze Man, W. (2013). Effect of green labelling on residential property price: A case study in Hong Kong. *Journal of Facilities Management*, *11*(1), 31–51. doi:10.1108/14725961311301457

Metro, K., Bogus, S. M., & Harper, C. (2022). Hiring for the New Age: Job Advertisements and the Transportation Workforce. *Construction Research Congress 2022: Health and Safety, Workforce, and Education*, 501-509. 10.1061/9780784483985.051

Meyer, J. B. (2001). Network approach versus brain drain: Lessons from the diaspora. *International Migration (Geneva, Switzerland)*, *39*(5), 91–110. doi:10.1111/1468-2435.00173

Meyer, J. P., & Maltin, E. R. (2010). Employee commitment and well-being: A critical review, theoretical framework and research agenda. *Journal of Vocational Behavior*, *77*(2), 323–337. doi:10.1016/j.jvb.2010.04.007

Meyers, M. C., van Woerkom, M., & Dries, N. (2013). Talent — Innate or acquired? Theoretical considerations and their implications for talent management. *Human Resource Management Review, 23*(4), 305–321. doi:10.1016/j.hrmr.2013.05.003

Michael, N., Michael, I., & Fotiadis, A. K. (2023). The role of human resources practices and branding in the hotel industry in Dubai. *Journal of Human Resources in Hospitality & Tourism, 22*(1), 1–25. doi:10.1080/15332845.2023.2126927

Michaels, E., Handfield-Jones, H., & Axelrod, B. (2001). *The war for talent.* Harvard Business School Press.

Mihalca, L., Mengelkamp, C., Brendea, G., & Metz, D. (2022). Job Attribute Preferences of Incoming University Students and Newly-Hired Employees in the Context of the Romanian Labour Market. *Journal for East European Management Studies, 27*(1), 31–63. doi:10.5771/0949-6181-2022-1-31

Mijakoski, D., Atanasovska, A., Bislimovska, D., Brborovic, H., Brborovic, O., Cvjeanov, K. L., Milosevic, M., Minov, J., Onal, B., & Pranjic, N. (2023). Associations of burnout with job demands/resources during the pandemic in health workers from Southeast European countries. *Frontiers in Psychology, 14*, 1258226. Advance online publication. doi:10.3389/fpsyg.2023.1258226 PMID:37954180

Miller, A. J., & Smith, K. L. (2021). *Communicating in a digital world: Principles, practices, and perspectives.* Oxford University Press.

Miller-Kuhlmann, R., Sasnal, M., Gold, C. A., Nassar, A. K., Korndorffer, J. R. Jr, Van Schaik, S., Marmor, A., Williams, S., Blankenburg, R., & Rassbach, C. E. (2024). Tips for developing a coaching program in medical education. *Medical Education Online, 29*(1), 2289262. Advance online publication. doi:10.1080/10872981.2023.2289262 PMID:38051864

Millward, J. A. (2013). *The Silk Road: A very short introduction.* Oxford University Press. doi:10.1093/actrade/9780199782864.001.0001

Milton, D. E. (2014). Autistic expertise: A critical reflection on the production of knowledge in autism studies. *Autism, 18*(7), 794–802. doi:10.1177/1362361314525281 PMID:24637428

Milton, N., Shadbolt, N., Cottam, H., & Hammersley, M. (1999). Towards a knowledge technology for knowledge management. *International Journal of Human-Computer Studies, 51*(3), 615–641. doi:10.1006/ijhc.1999.0278

Mimoun, L., & Gruen, A. (2021). Customer Work Practices and the Productive Third Place. *Journal of Service Research, 24*(4), 563–581. doi:10.1177/10946705211014278

Min, J. (2023). A Symbolic Framing of Exploitative Firms: Evidence from Japan. *Journal of Business Ethics.* Advance online publication. doi:10.1007/s10551-023-05404-1

Mobley, W. C. (1977). Intermediate linkages in the relationship between job satisfaction and employee turnover. *The Journal of Applied Psychology, 62*(2), 237–240. doi:10.1037/0021-9010.62.2.237

Mofokeng, M. (2018). Future-Proofing Talent for the Bank of the Future: A Study of Employees in a Bank Operating in Africa. *Proceedings of the 6th International Conference on Management, Leadership and Governance*, 453-461.

Mohammed, A. (2019). Effect of Workforce Diversity on Job Performance of Hotels Working in Jordan. *international. Journal of Business and Management.*

Mohsin, A., Lengler, J., & Kumar, B. (2013). Exploring the antecedents of intentions to leave the job: The case of luxury hotel staff. *International Journal of Hospitality Management, 35*, 48–58. doi:10.1016/j.ijhm.2013.05.002

Moncarz, E., Zhao, J., & Kay, C. (2009). An exploratory study of US lodging properties' organizational practices on employee turnover and retention. *International Journal of Contemporary Hospitality Management, 21*(4), 437–458. doi:10.1108/09596110910955695

Monteiro, E., & Joseph, J. (2023). A Review on the Impact of Workplace Culture on Employee Mental Health and Well-Being. *International Journal of Case Studies in Business IT and Education*, 7(2), 291–317.

Montvelisky, J. (2021). *Neurodiversity as a Strengthening Point for Your Team and Our Society*. Available https://www.forbes.com/sites/forbestechcouncil/2021/08/13/neurodiversity-as-a-strengthening-point-for-your-team-and-our-society/?sh=4f2b186228f9

Moore, J., & Hanson, W. R. (2022). Improving leader effectiveness: Impact on employee engagement and retention. *Journal of Management Development*, 41(7/8), 450–468. doi:10.1108/JMD-02-2021-0041

Morgan, M. (2018). *Four ways employers can support neurodiversity at work*. Retrieved at https://www.personneltoday.com/hr/four-ways-employers-can-support-neurodiversity-at-work/

Morgan, J. (2014). *The future of work: Attract new talent, build better leaders, and create a competitive organization*. John Wiley & Sons.

Morgan, N., Pritchard, A., & Pride, R. (2011). Destination branding and the role of the stakeholders: The case of New Zealand. *Journal of Vacation Marketing*, 17(3), 205–217.

Morley, T. (2018). Making the business case for diversity and inclusion. *Strategic HR Review*, 17(1), 58–60. doi:10.1108/SHR-10-2017-0068

Morrison, T. G., & Morrison, T. G. (2003). Development and Validation of a Scale Measuring Modern Prejudice Toward Gay Men and Lesbian Women. *Journal of Homosexuality*, 43(2), 15–37. doi:10.1300/J082v43n02_02 PMID:12739696

Mosley, R. W. (2007, October 9). Customer experience, organisational culture and the employer brand. *Journal of Brand Management*, 15(2), 123–134. doi:10.1057/palgrave.bm.2550124

Msengeti, D. M., & Obwogi, J. (2015). *Effects of pay and work environment on employee retention: A study of hotel industry in Mombasa county*. Academic Press.

Mukherjee, B., Chandra, B., & Singh, S. (2020). Talent retention in Indian public sector units (PSUs): An empirical investigation. *Kybernetes*, 49(6), 1783–1810. doi:10.1108/K-03-2019-0165

Munde, G. (2010). Considerations for managing an increasingly intergenerational workforce in libraries. *Library Trends*, 59(1/2), 89. doi:10.1353/lib.2010.a407808

Munn, G. (2019). *Thinking diversity*. Retrieved at https://thewellbeingpulse.com/neurodiversity-atwork/.

Munyon, T. P., Summers, J. K., Thompson, K. M., & Ferris, G. R. (2015). Political skill and work outcomes: A theoretical extension, meta-analytic investigation, and agenda for the future. *Personnel Psychology*, 68(1), 143–184. doi:10.1111/peps.12066

Mustika, M. I., & Martdianty, F. (2023). Factors Influencing Employee's Well-Being and Job Performance: The Perspective of State-Owned Enterprise Employee. *IJHCM*, 7(1), 86–103. doi:10.21009/IJHCM.07.01.7

Mwita, M. K. (2019). Conceptual Review of Green Human Resource Management Practices. *East African Journal of Social and Applied Sciences*, 1(2), 13–20.

Myers, V. L., & Dreachslin, J. L. (2007). Recruitment and retention of a diverse workforce: Challenges and opportunities. *Journal of Healthcare Management*, 52(5), 290–298. doi:10.1097/00115514-200709000-00004 PMID:17933185

Nabawanuka, H., & Ekmekcioglu, E. B. (2022). Millennials in the workplace: Perceived supervisor support, work–life balance and employee well–being. *Industrial and Commercial Training*, 54(1), 123–144. doi:10.1108/ICT-05-2021-0041

Nadal, K. L. (2011). The Racial and Ethnic Microaggressions Scale (REMS): Construction, reliability, and validity. *Journal of Counseling Psychology*, *58*(4), 470–480. doi:10.1037/a0025193 PMID:21875180

Nadal, K. L., & Haynes, K. (2012). *The effects of sexism, gender microaggressions, and other forms of discrimination on women's mental health and development*. Women and Mental Disorder.

Nafz, R., Schinle, C., Kaiser, C., & Kyosev, Y. K. (2022). Digital transformation of the textile process chain–state-of-the-art. *Communications in Development and Assembling of Textile Products*, *3*(2), 79–89. doi:10.25367/cdatp.2022.3.p79-89

Naim, A., Khan, S. A., Malik, P. K., Hussain, M. R., & Dildar, M. S. (2023). Internet of things support for Marketing Sports and Fitness Products. *2023 3rd International Conference on Advancement in Electronics & Communication Engineering (AECE)*, 215-219. 10.1109/AECE59614.2023.10428323

Naim, A., Mohammed, A. B., Fatima, N., Khan, S. A., Alnfiai, M. M., & Malik, P. K. (2024b). Applications of Artificial Intelligence in Environmental Resource Business Management and Sustainability. In AI Applications for Business, Medical, and Agricultural Sustainability (pp. 1-22). IGI Global. doi:10.4018/979-8-3693-5266-3.ch001

Naim, A., & Khan, S. A. (2023). Impact and Assessment of Electronic Commerce on Consumer Buying Behaviour. In A. Naim & V. Devi (Eds.), *Global Applications of the Internet of Things in Digital Marketing* (pp. 264–289). IGI Global. doi:10.4018/978-1-6684-8166-0.ch014

Naim, A., Khan, S. A., Mohammed, A. B., & Malik, P. K. (2024a). Applications of High Performance Computing and AI in Green Digital Marketing. In A. Naim (Ed.), *AI Applications for Business, Medical, and Agricultural Sustainability* (pp. 47–67). IGI Global. doi:10.4018/979-8-3693-5266-3.ch003

Najmaei, A., & Sadeghinejad, Z. (2019). Inclusive leadership: A scientometric assessment of an emerging field. In Advanced series in management (pp. 221–245). doi:10.1108/S1877-636120190000022012

Namin, B. H., Øgaard, T., & Røislien, J. (2021). Workplace Incivility and Turnover Intention in Organizations: A Meta-Analytic Review. *International Journal of Environmental Research and Public Health*, *19*(1), 25. doi:10.3390/ijerph19010025 PMID:35010292

Narendra, U. P., Jain, R. R., Rao, N. S., Shreesha, H. R., Udith, D., & Prashanth, S. (2022). An intelligent ubiquitous online application for mentoring system. *International Journal of Multidisciplinary Research and Analysis*, *05*(06). Advance online publication. doi:10.47191/ijmra/v5-i6-30

Narzary, P. K., Rai, A. K., Sarkar, S., Shekhar, S., & Mahata, D. (2019). Demographic And Morphological Changes In Kolkata City, India During 1951-2014. *European Journal of Geography*, *10*(3).

Nayak, S., & Budhwar, P. (2023). Social networking sites and employer branding: A qualitative study of Indian organizations. *Asian Business & Management*. Advance online publication. doi:10.1057/s41291-023-00245-2

Neely, A. R., Cotton, J., & Neely, A. D. (2017). E-mentoring: A Model and Review of the Literature. *AIS Transactions on Human-Computer Interaction*, *9*(3), 220–242.

Nelke, A. (2021). Impact of the COVID-19 pandemic on corporate employer branding. *Technium Social Sciences Journal*, *16*, 388–393. doi:10.47577/tssj.v16i1.2436

Nemțeanu, M. S., Dinu, V., Pop, R. A., & Dabija, D. C. (2022). Predicting Job Satisfaction and Work Engagement Behavior in the COVID-19 Pandemic: A Conservation of Resources Theory Approach. *E&M Economics and Management*, *25*(2), 23–40. doi:10.15240/tul/001/2022-2-002

Neurodiversity in the workplace. (2023). https://mydisabilityjobs.com/statistics/neurodiversity-in-the-workplace

Ngo-Henha, P. E. (2018). A Review of Existing Turnover Intention Theories. Zenodo *(CERN European Organization for Nuclear Research)*. doi:10.5281/zenodo.1316263

Ngo, L. V., Nguyen, N. P., Huynh, K. T., Gregory, G., & Cuong, P. H. (2020). Converting internal brand knowledge into employee performance. *Journal of Product and Brand Management, 29*(3), 273–287. doi:10.1108/JPBM-10-2018-2068

Nikolaou, I. (2021). What is the role of technology in recruitment and selection? *The Spanish Journal of Psychology, 24*, e2. Advance online publication. doi:10.1017/SJP.2021.6 PMID:33536110

Nimisha, N. (2019). Employee Poaching and Career Advancement: A study on CUSAT Alumni. *International Journal of Scientific Research and Review, 8*(2), 235–243.

Nimmi, P. M., Zakkariya, K. A., & Philip, A. V. (2022). Enhancing employee wellbeing – An employability perspective. *Benchmarking, 30*(1), 102–120. doi:10.1108/BIJ-03-2021-0116

Nocker, M., & Sena, V. (2019). Big data and human resources management: The rise of talent analytics. *Social Sciences (Basel, Switzerland), 8*(10), 273. doi:10.3390/socsci8100273

Noh, S., & Kaspar, V. (2003). Perceived Discrimination and Depression: Moderating Effects of Coping, Acculturation, and Ethnic Support. *American Journal of Public Health, 93*(2), 232–238. doi:10.2105/AJPH.93.2.232 PMID:12554575

Norlander, P. (2023). *New Evidence on Employee Non-compete, No-Poach, and No Hire Agreements in the Franchise Sector*. Academic Press.

Nuankaew, P., & Temdee, P. (2014). Determining of compatible different attributes for online mentoring model. In *Information Theory and Aerospace & Electronics Systems (VITAE)*. IEEE. doi:10.1109/VITAE.2014.6934434

Nyako, I. Z. (2017). *Impact of Workforce Diversity on Organizational Performance in Calabar, Cross-River State*. American University of Nigeria.

Nye, J. S. (1990). Soft power. *Foreign Policy, 80*(80), 153–171. doi:10.2307/1148580

Nye, J. S. (2012). China and soft power. *South African Journal of International Affairs, 19*(2), 151–155. doi:10.1080/10220461.2012.706889

Nye, J. S. (2021). Soft power: The evolution of a concept. *Journal of Political Power, 14*(1), 196–208. doi:10.1080/2158379X.2021.1879572

Nye, J. S. Jr. (2008). Public diplomacy and soft power. *The Annals of the American Academy of Political and Social Science, 616*(1), 94–109. doi:10.1177/0002716207311699

Nyström, J. (2017). *Leadership and Culture: A comparison between Finland and Germany*. Academic Press.

O'Neill, D. K., Wagner, R., & Gomez, L. M. (1996). Online Mentors: Experimenting in science class. *Educational Leadership, 54*(3), 39–42.

Odugbesan, J. A., Aghazadeh, S., Al Qaralleh, R. E., & Sogeke, O. S. (2023). Green talent management and employees' innovative work behavior: The roles of artificial intelligence and transformational leadership. *Journal of Knowledge Management, 27*(3), 696–716. doi:10.1108/JKM-08-2021-0601

Ohlrich, K. (2011). *Analyzing Corporate Social Responsibility's Impact on Employee Attraction and Retention with a Focus on Generation Y*. Fielding Graduate University.

Okeyika, K. O., Ibeto, V. C., Okere, A. I., & Umoh, B. (2023). The applicastion of Artificail Intelligence (AI) ioj Human Resource Management: Current state of AI and its impact on the traditional recruitment process. *AKU: An African Journal of Contemporary Research, 4*(3).

Okioga, C. K. (2013). The contribution of Human Resource strategies to the Organizational Success; a case of Commercial Banks in Kisii County. *European Journal of Business and Management, 5*(6), 181–191.

Okolie, U. C., & Irabor, I. E. (2017). E-recruitment: Practices, opportunities and challenges. *European Journal of Business and Management, 9*(11), 116–122.

Ollington, N., Gibb, J., & Harcourt, M. (2013). Online social networks: An emergent recruiter tool for attracting and screening. *Personnel Review, 42*(3), 248–265. doi:10.1108/00483481311320390

Omer, I. (2003). *Psihologia muncii.* F. România de Mâine, Ed.

Omotayo, O., Anthonia, A., Hezekia, F., Opeyemi, O., & Odion, E. (2020). Diversity management and organisational performance in deposit money banks in Nigeria. *Cogent Business & Management*, 3-4.

Oosthuizen, N., & Perks, S. (2019). The enabling conditions necessary for effective online mentoring: A proposed model. *International Journal of Academic Research in Business & Social Sciences, 9*(6). Advance online publication. doi:10.6007/IJARBSS/v9-i6/5975

Opatha, H. H. D. N. P. (2013). Green human resource management: A simplified introduction. *Proc. HR Dialogue, 1*, 11–21.

Opatha, H. H. P., & Arulrajah, A. A. (2014). Green human resource management: Simplified general reflections. *International Business Research, 7*(8), 101–112. doi:10.5539/ibr.v7n8p101

Oprea, B., Păduraru, L., & Iliescu, D. (2022). Job crafting and intent to leave: The mediating role of meaningful work and engagement. *Journal of Career Development, 49*(1), 188–201. doi:10.1177/0894845320918666

Orlova, M. V., & Aleksandrova, I. Yu. (2022). Distributed teams: Challenges and opportunities. *Vestnik Universiteta*, (2), 33–40. doi:10.26425/1816-4277-2022-2-33-40

Ormeno, M. (2007). *Managing corporate brands- a new approach to corporate communication.* GWV Fachverlage GmbH.

Ortega, F. (2009). The cerebral subject and the challenge of neurodiversity. *Biosocieties, 4*(4), 425–446. doi:10.1017/S1745855209990287

Oswald, D. L., Baalbaki, M., & Kirkman, M. S. (2019). Experiences with Benevolent Sexism: Scale Development and Associations with Women's Well-Being. *Sex Roles, 80*(5–6), 362–380. doi:10.1007/s11199-018-0933-5

Otike, W. F., Omboi, M. B., & Mwalekwa, F. K. (2022, Feb 25). *Effects of Workplace Diversity Management on Organizational Effectiveness.* www.iiste.org

Ott, D. L., Tolentino, J. L., & Michailova, S. (2018). Effective talent retention approaches. *Human Resource Management International Digest, 26*(7), 16–19. doi:10.1108/HRMID-07-2018-0152

Ovaska-Few, S. (2018). Promoting neurodiversity. *Journal of Accountancy, 225*(1), 46–49.

Paludi, M. (2012). Managing Diversity in Today's Workplace: Strategies for Employees and Employers [4 volumes] (Women and Careers in Management). Praeger.

Panda, S., & Sahoo, C. K. (2015). Strategic talent development interventions: An analysis. *Industrial and Commercial Training, 47*(1), 15–22. doi:10.1108/ICT-05-2014-0031

Pandey, A., Balusamy, B., & Chilamkurti, N. (Eds.). (2023). *Disruptive artificial intelligence and sustainable human resource management: Impacts and innovations-The future of HR*. CRC Press. doi:10.1201/9781032622743

Pandiya, B., Tewari, V., & Upadhyay, C. K. (2023). An empirical assessment of antecedents able to attract the prospective talented workforce for information technology industry across borders. *European Journal of International Management*, *19*(4), 491–517. doi:10.1504/EJIM.2023.129531

Pan, F., Zhao, S. X., & Wójcik, D. (2016). The rise of venture capital centres in China: A spatial and network analysis. *Geoforum*, *75*, 148–158. doi:10.1016/j.geoforum.2016.07.013

Pânişoară, G., & Pânişoară, I.-O. (2007). *Managementul resurselor umane: ghid practic*. Editura Polirom.

Panopoulos, A., & Sarri, K. (2013). E-mentoring: The adoption process and innovation challenge. *International Journal of Information Management*, *33*(1), 217–226. doi:10.1016/j.ijinfomgt.2012.10.003

Pantelimon, F.-V., Bologa, R., Toma, A., & Posedaru, B.-S. (2021). The Evolution of AI-Driven Educational Systems during the COVID-19 Pandemic. *Sustainability (Basel)*, *13*(23), 13501. doi:10.3390/su132313501

Papasolomou, I., & Vrontis, D. (2006, September). Using internal marketing to ignite the corporate brand: The case of the UK retail bank industry. *Journal of Brand Management*, *14*(1–2), 177–195. doi:10.1057/palgrave.bm.2550059

Paradise, J. F. (2009). China and international harmony: The role of Confucius Institutes in bolstering Beijing's soft power. *Asian Survey*, *49*(4), 647–669. doi:10.1525/as.2009.49.4.647

Parente, R. C., Geleilate, J. M. G., & Rong, K. (2018). The sharing economy globalization phenomenon: A research agenda. *Journal of International Management*, *24*(1), 52–64. doi:10.1016/j.intman.2017.10.001

Parida, S., Ananthram, S., Chan, C., & Brown, K. (2021). Green office buildings and sustainability: Does green human resource management elicit green behaviors? *Journal of Cleaner Production*, *329*, 129764. doi:10.1016/j.jclepro.2021.129764

Park, J. (2014). *Retaining talented employees in the hotel industry in Stavanger: An interview-based qualitative research* (Master's dissertation). Norwegian School of Hotel Management, University of Stavanger.

Park, S., & Lemaire, J. (2011). Culture matters: Long-term orientation and the demand for life insurance. *Asia-Pacific Journal of Risk and Insurance, 5*(2).

Park, H. M., Patel, P., Varma, A., & Jaiswal, A. (2022). The challenges for macro talent management in the mature emerging market of South Korea: A review and research agenda. *Thunderbird International Business Review*, *64*(5), 393–404. doi:10.1002/tie.22260

Park, J., Shin, S. Y., Lee, S., & No, S. R. (2015). Human resource management practices and organizational creativity: The role of chief executive officer's learning goal orientation. *Social Behavior and Personality*, *43*(6), 899–908. doi:10.2224/sbp.2015.43.6.899

Parlinska, A., & Stawicka, E. (2018). Corporate Social Responsibility: Measuring And Reporting the Effectiveness of Community Involvement on the Basis of the LBG Model. Economic Science for Rural Development, 48, 313-320. doi:10.22616/ESRD.2018.100

Parment, A., Anna, D., & Lutz. (2017). *Employer branding: Employer branding: how employers build strong brands*. Academic Press.

Parr, A. D., & Hunter, S. T. (2014). Enhancing work outcomes of employees with autism spectrum disorder through leadership: Leadership for employees with autism spectrum disorder. *Autism*, *18*(5), 545–554. doi:10.1177/1362361313483020 PMID:23886575

Parr, A. D., Hunter, S. T., & Ligon, G. S. (2013). Questioning universal applicability of transformational leadership: Examining employees with autism spectrum disorder. *The Leadership Quarterly*, 24(4), 608–622. doi:10.1016/j.leaqua.2013.04.003

Patton, D., Johnston, J., Gamble, K., Milham, L., Townsend, L., Riddle, D., & Phillips, H. (2019). Training for readiness and resilience. In *Advances in Human Error, Reliability, Resilience, and Performance: Proceedings of the AHFE 2018 International Conference on Human Error, Reliability, Resilience, and Performance, July 21-25, 2018, Loews Sapphire Falls Resort at Universal Studios, Orlando, Florida, USA 9* (pp. 292-302). Springer International Publishing.

Patton, E. (2019). Autism, attributions and accommodations. *Personnel Review*, 48(4), 915–934. doi:10.1108/PR-04-2018-0116

Patton, E. (2022). To disclose or not disclose a workplace disability to coworkers: Attributions and invisible health conditions in the workplace. *Equality, Diversity and Inclusion*, 41(8), 1154–1180. doi:10.1108/EDI-09-2021-0228

Pavlou & Fygenson. (2006). Understanding and Predicting Electronic Commerce Adoption: An Extension of the Theory of Planned Behavior. *MIS Quarterly*, 30(1), 115. doi:10.2307/25148720

Pawar, A., Cahyono, B. T., Indrati, K., Siswati, E., & Loupias, H. (2022). Validating the effect of talent management on organisational outcomes with mediating role of job empowerment in business. *International Journal of Learning and Intellectual Capital*, 19(6), 527–547. doi:10.1504/IJLIC.2022.126297

Payambarpour, S. A., & Hooi, L. W. (2015). The impact of talent management and employee engagement on organisational performance. *International Journal of Management Practice*, 8(4), 311. doi:10.1504/IJMP.2015.073483

Pelczarski, K. (2013). Dealing with non-compete agreements. *Tribology & Lubrication Technology*, 69(11), 98.

Penny, C., & Bolton, D. (2010). Evaluating the outcomes of an eMentoring program. *Journal of Educational Technology Systems*, 39(1), 17–30. doi:10.2190/ET.39.1.c

Perusso, A., & Wagenaar, R. (2023). Electronic work-based learning (eWBL): A framework for trainers in companies and higher education. *Studies in Higher Education*, 1–17. Advance online publication. doi:10.1080/03075079.2023.2280193

Peterson, J. R. (2023). Employee bonding and turnover efficiency. *Journal of Economics & Management Strategy*, 32(1), 223–244. doi:10.1111/jems.12499

Philip, J. (2021). A perspective on embracing emerging technologies research for organizational behaviour. *Organizational Management Journal*, 19(3), 88–98. doi:10.1108/OMJ-10-2020-1063

Pickles, J., Plank, L., Staritz, C., & Glasmeier, A. (2015). Trade policy and regionalisms in global clothing production networks. *Cambridge Journal of Regions, Economy and Society*, 8(3), 381–402. doi:10.1093/cjres/rsv022

Pierli, G., Murmura, F., & Bravi, L. (2023). Digital transformation and sustainability. A systematic literature review. Lecture notes on information systems and organization (pp. 83–99). doi:10.1007/978-3-031-30351-7_8

Pieterse, J. N. (2019). *Globalization and culture: Global mélange*. Rowman & Littlefield.

Pillai, R., & Sivathanu, B. (2020). Adoption of artificial intelligence (AI) for talent acquisition in IT/ITeS organizations. *Benchmarking*, 27(9), 2599–2629. doi:10.1108/BIJ-04-2020-0186

Pincus, J. D. (2022). Employee engagement as human motivation: Implications for theory, methods, and practice. *Integrative Psychological & Behavioral Science*, 57(4), 1223–1255. doi:10.1007/s12124-022-09737-w PMID:36577907

Pivateau, G. T. (2011). Preserving Human Capital: Using the Non-compete Agreement to Achieve Competitive Advantage. The Journal of Business. *Entrepreneurship & the Law*, 4(2), 3.

Piwowar-Sulej, K. (2021). Human resources development as an element of sustainable HRM–with the focus on production engineers. *Journal of Cleaner Production, 278*, 124008. doi:10.1016/j.jclepro.2020.124008 PMID:32901179

Plummer, J. T. (1985). *Brand personality: A strategic concept for multinational advertising*. Paper presented at the Marketing Educator's Conference, New York.

Polden, D. J. (2023). *Restrictions on Worker Mobility and the Need for Stronger Policies on Anticompetitive Employment Contract Provisions*. Academic Press.

Pollard, R., & Kumar, S. (2021). Mentoring graduate students online: Strategies and challenges. *International Review of Research in Open and Distance Learning, 22*(2), 267–284. doi:10.19173/irrodl.v22i2.5093

Polyakova-Norwood, V., Creed, J., Patterson, B., & Heiney, S. (2023). Making group work gratifying: Implementing and evaluating a three-stage model of group processes in an online nursing course. *Journal of Professional Nursing, 46*, 13–18. doi:10.1016/j.profnurs.2023.02.004 PMID:37188401

Pooley, E. (2005). Kids these days. *Canadian Business, 78*(12), 67–68.

Poorhosseinzadeh, M., & Subramaniam, I. D. (2012). Determinants of successful talent management in MNCs in Malaysia. *Journal of Basic Applied Science Research, 2*(12), 12524-12533.

Potkonjak, V., Gardner, M., Callaghan, V., Mattila, P., Guetl, C., Petrović, V. M., & Jovanović, K. (2016). Virtual laboratories for education in science, technology, and engineering: A review. *Computers & Education, 95*, 309–327. doi:10.1016/j.compedu.2016.02.002

Praslova, L. N. (2021). *Autism Doesn't Hold People Back at Work. Discrimination Does*. Available on: https://hbr.org/2021/12/autism-doesnt-hold-people-back-at-work-discrimination-does

Preece, D., Iles, P., & Chuai, X. (2011). Talent management and management fashion in Chinese enterprises: Exploring case studies in Beijing. *International Journal of Human Resource Management, 22*(16), 3413–3428. doi:10.1080/09585192.2011.586870

Prescott, J. (2022). Digital technology to support mental health: A brief introduction to what it is and why it is important. *Mental Health and Social Inclusion, 26*(2), 103–106. Advance online publication. doi:10.1108/MHSI-02-2022-0010

Price Waterhouse Coopers. (2008). *Managing tomorrow's people: millennials at work – perspectives from a new generation*. Retrieved from www.pwc.com/managingpeople2020

Price, A. (2000). *Priciples of human resources management: an active learning approach*. Blackwell Business.

Prowse, P., & Prowse, J. (2010). Whatever happened to human resource management performance? *International Journal of Productivity and Performance Management, 59*(2), 145–162. doi:10.1108/17410401011014230

Qi, J. J., & Dauvergne, P. (2022). China's rising influence on climate governance: Forging a path for the global South. *Global Environmental Change, 73*, 102484. doi:10.1016/j.gloenvcha.2022.102484

Qin, Y. S., & Men, L. R. (2023). Exploring the impact of internal communication on employee psychological well-being during the COVID-19 pandemic: The mediating role of employee organizational trust. *International Journal of Business Communication, 60*(4), 1197–1219. doi:10.1177/23294884221081838

Qureshi, A. (2022). *The World Trade Organization: implementing international trade norms*. Academic Press.

Qu, W. G., & Yang, Z. (2015). The effect of uncertainty avoidance and social trust on supply chain collaboration. *Journal of Business Research, 68*(5), 911–918. doi:10.1016/j.jbusres.2014.09.017

Radler, V. M. (2018). 20 Years of brand personality: A bibliometric review and research agenda. *Journal of Brand Management*, *25*(4), 370–383. doi:10.1057/s41262-017-0083-z

Radu, E., Tigu, G., & State, O. (2004). *Conducerea resurselor umane*. Editura ASE.

Rafaqat, S., Rafaqat, S., Rafaqat, S., & Rafaqat, D. (2022). The impact of workforce diversity on Organizational Performance: A Review. *Journal of Economics and Behavioral Studies*, *14*(2(J)), 39–50. doi:10.22610/jebs.v14i2(J).3301

Rafiq, M., & Ahmed, P. K. (2000, November 1). Advances in the internal marketing concept: Definition, synthesis and extension. *Journal of Services Marketing*, *14*(6), 449–462. doi:10.1108/08876040010347589

Rafique, M. A., Hou, Y., Chudhery, M. A. Z., Gull, N., & Ahmed, S. J. (2023). The dimensional linkage between public service motivation and innovative behavior in public sector institutions; the mediating role of psychological empowerment. *European Journal of Innovation Management*, *26*(1), 207–229. doi:10.1108/EJIM-02-2021-0098

Ragins, B., & Kram, K. (2007). The Handbook of Mentoring at Work. Academic Press.

Ragins, B. R., Singh, R., & Cornwell, J. M. (2007). Making the invisible visible: Fear and disclosure of sexual orientation at work. *The Journal of Applied Psychology*, *92*(4), 1103–1118. doi:10.1037/0021-9010.92.4.1103 PMID:17638468

Rahimian, S., ShamiZanjani, M., Manian, A., & Esfidani, M. R. (2021). A framework of customer experience management for hotel industry. *International Journal of Contemporary Hospitality Management*, *33*(5), 1413–1436. doi:10.1108/IJCHM-06-2020-0522

Rai, A., & Singh, L. B. (2023). Artificial Intelligence-based People Analytics Transforming Human Resource Management Practices. In The Adoption and Effect of Artificial Intelligence on Human Resources Management, Part A (pp. 229-244). Emerald Publishing Limited. doi:10.1108/978-1-80382-027-920231012

Raimi, L., Kah, J. M., & Tariq, M. U. (2022). The Discourse of Blue Economy Definitions, Measurements, and Theories: Implications for Strengthening Academic Research and Industry Practice. In L. Raimi & J. Kah (Eds.), *Implications for Entrepreneurship and Enterprise Development in the Blue Economy* (pp. 1–17). IGI Global. doi:10.4018/978-1-6684-3393-5.ch001

Raimi, L., Tariq, M. U., & Kah, J. M. (2022). Diversity, Equity, and Inclusion as the Future Workplace Ethics: Theoretical Review. In L. Raimi & J. Kah (Eds.), *Mainstreaming Diversity, Equity, and Inclusion as Future Workplace Ethics* (pp. 1–27). IGI Global. doi:10.4018/978-1-6684-3657-8.ch001

Raj, S., & Paliwal, M. (2022). Higher Education Dashboard Implementation Using Data Mining and Data Warehouse: A Review Paper. *International Journal of Innovative Research in Computer Science & Technology*, *10*(1), 107–111. doi:10.55524/ijircst.2022.10.1.19

Raman, G., Ramendran, C., Beleya, P., Nodeson, S., & Arokiasamy, L. (2011). Generation Y in institution of higher learning. *International Journal of Economics and Business Modelling*, *2*(2), 142–148.

Ramesh, S., & Das, S. (2022). Adoption of AI in talent acquisition: A conceptual framework. In Lecture notes in networks and systems (pp. 12–20). doi:10.1007/978-3-031-01942-5_2

Rana, G., Agarwal, S., & Ravindra, S. (2021). *Employer branding for competitive advantage*. CRC Press.

Rao, B., & Polepeddi, J. (2019). Neurodiverse workforce: Inclusive employment as an HR strategy. *Strategic HR Review*, *18*(5), 204–209. doi:10.1108/SHR-02-2019-0007

Rasoolimanesh, S. M., Taheri, B., Gannon, M., Vafaei-Zadeh, A., & Hanifah, H. (2019). Does living in the vicinity of heritage tourism sites influence residents' perceptions and attitudes? *Journal of Sustainable Tourism*, *27*(9), 1295–1317. doi:10.1080/09669582.2019.1618863

Rehman, S., & Mazhar, S. S. (2016). A Study On New Hiring Strategies To Manage Talent Crisis At Entry Level From The Perspective Of Recruiters And Fresh Graduate Engineer Job Seekers. *International Journal of Research-GRANTHAALAYAH*, *4*(9), 14–29. doi:10.29121/granthaalayah.v4.i9.2016.2530

Reich, R. (2002). *The company of the future. Fast company 19*, 1998, 124, from Sims R.R. In *Organizational success through effective human resources management*. Greenwood Pub. Inc.Group.

Reilly, P. (2018). Building customer centricity in the hospitality sector: The role of talent management. *Worldwide Hospitality and Tourism Themes*, *10*(1), 42–56. doi:10.1108/WHATT-10-2017-0068

Renwick, D., Redman, T., & Maguire, S. (2008). Green HRM: A review, process model, and research agenda. *University of Sheffield Management School Discussion Paper*, *1*(1), 1-46.

Rezakhani, K. (2010). The road that never was: The Silk Road and trans-Eurasian exchange. *Comparative Studies of South Asia, Africa and the Middle East*, *30*(3), 420–433. doi:10.1215/1089201X-2010-025

Richards, J. (2012). Examining the exclusion of employees with Asperger syndrome from the workplace. *Personnel Review*, *41*(5), 630–646. doi:10.1108/00483481211249148

Rios, I. C., de Medeiros, M. E. Jr, de Almeida Fernandes, M. T., & Zombini, E. V. (2021). Virtual mentoring for medical students in the Covid-19 times. *Revista Brasileira de Educação Médica*, *45*(3), e170. doi:10.1590/1981-5271v45.3-20200419.ing

Roberson, L., Kulik, C. T., & Tan, R. Y. (2013). Effective diversity training. In Oxford University Press eBooks (pp. 341–365). doi:10.1093/oxfordhb/9780199736355.013.0019

Robertson, S. (2013). *Transnational student-migrants and the state: The education-migration nexus*. Springer. doi:10.1057/9781137267085

Robinson, R. N. S., Solnet, D. J., & Breakey, N. (2014). A phenomenological approach to hospitality management research: Chefs' occupational commitment. *International Journal of Hospitality Management*, *43*, 65–75. doi:10.1016/j.ijhm.2014.08.004

Robison, J. E. (2013). What is neurodiversity? *Psychology Today*. https://www.psychologytoday.com/us/blog/my-life-aspergers/201310/what-is-neurodiversity

Rodrigues, D., & Martinez, L. F. (2020). The influence of digital marketing on recruitment effectiveness: A qualitative study. *The European Journal of Management Studies*, *25*(1), 23–44. doi:10.1108/EJMS-09-2020-002

Rodriguez, A. A., Pradhan, P. A., Puttannaiah, K., Das, N., Mondal, K., Sarkar, A., . . . Waggoner, T. (2018, October). A Comprehensive ASAP Framework that uses Career-Steering/Shaping Projects to Train Engineering Students & Develop Critical Life/Professional Skills: Part II–Case Studies from Students Working on Funded Projects. In 2018 IEEE Frontiers in Education Conference (FIE) (pp. 1-9). IEEE.

Rollnik-Sadowska, E., Glińska, E., & Ryciuk, U. (2022). Model of communication effectiveness in the mentoring process. *WSEAS Transactions on Business and Economics*, *19*, 1–12. doi:10.37394/23207.2022.19.1

Rosales, R., León, I. A., & León-Fuentes, A. L. (2022). Recommendations for recruiting and retaining a diverse workforce: A report from the field. *Behavior Analysis in Practice*, *16*(1), 346–361. doi:10.1007/s40617-022-00747-z PMID:36212634

Rose, E. (2015). Temporal Flexibility and its Limits: The Personal Use of ICTs at Work. *Sociology*, *49*(3), 505–520. doi:10.1177/0038038514542121

Ross-Sheriff, F. (2012). Microaggression, Women, and Social Work. *Affilia*, *27*(3), 233–236. doi:10.1177/0886109912454366

Roth, P. L., Bobko, P., Van Iddekinge, C. H., & Thatcher, J. B. (2016). Social Media in Employee-Selection-Related Decisions. *Journal of Management*, *42*(1), 269–298. doi:10.1177/0149206313503018

Roux, A. M., Shattuck, P. T., Rast, J. E., Rava, J. A., & Anderson, K. A. (2015). *National autism indicators report: Transition into young adulthood. Life Course Outcomes Research Program.* AJ Drexel Autism Institute, Drexel University. doi:10.17918/NAIRTransition2015

Roy, M. (2021). AI-Powered Workforce Management and Its Future in India. In Artificial Intelligence-Latest Advances, New Paradigms and Novel Applications. IntechOpen. doi:10.5772/intechopen.97817

Rozman, G. (Ed.). (2014). *The East Asian region: Confucian heritage and its modern adaptation* (Vol. 1179). Princeton University Press.

Ruggeri, K., García-Garzón, E., Maguire, Á., Matz, S., & Huppert, F. A. (2020). Wellbeing is more than happiness and life satisfaction: A multidimensional analysis of 21 countries. *Health and Quality of Life Outcomes*, *18*(1), 192. Advance online publication. doi:10.1186/s12955-020-01423-y PMID:32560725

Rurkkhum, S. (2023). A bundle of human resource practices and employee resilience: The role of employee well-being. *Asia-Pacific Journal of Business Administration*. Advance online publication. doi:10.1108/APJBA-01-2022-0050

Rynes-Weller, S. L., Reeves, C. J., & Darnold, T. C. (2013). The history of recruitment research. In Oxford University Press eBooks. doi:10.1093/oxfordhb/9780199756094.013.020

Saad, H., & Mayouf, M. (2018). Talent Management Strategies and Practices in Five Star Hotels: An Exploratory Study. *International Journal of Heritage. Tourism and Hospitality*, *12*(2), 32–49. doi:10.21608/ijhth.2019.31649

Saeed, F., Mir, A., Hamid, M., Ayaz, F., & Iyyaz, U. (2023). Employee salary and employee turnover intention: A key evaluation considering job satisfaction and job performance as mediators. *International Journal of Management Research and Emerging Sciences*, *13*(1). Advance online publication. doi:10.56536/ijmres.v13i1.234

Sagnak, H., & Baran, E. (2021). Faculty members' planned technology integration behaviour in the context of a faculty technology mentoring programme. *Australasian Journal of Educational Technology*, 1–21. doi:10.14742/ajet.5912

Saif, R. (2020). The Effects of Diversity Management on Employee Intention to Quit: Mediating Role of Employee Motivation. *Journal of Health, Medicine and Nursing*.

SakkaF.GhadiM. Y.GoldmanA. (2022). Talent Management and Professional Development of Employees using Digital Technologies. *TEM Journal- Technology Education Management Informatics, 11*(4), 1612-1619. DOI doi:10.18421/TEM114-23

Saks, A. M. (2006). Antecedents and consequences of employee engagement. *Journal of Managerial Psychology*, *21*(7), 600–619. doi:10.1108/02683940610690169

Saleem, M., Khan, S. A., & Magd, H. (2022). Content Marketing Framework for Building Brand Image: A Case Study of Sohar International School, Oman. In Building a Brand Image Through Electronic Customer Relationship Management (pp. 64-83). IGI Global.

Saleem, I., Qureshi, T. M., & Verma, A. (2023). Task Challenge and Employee Performance: A Moderated Mediation Model of Resilience and Digitalization. *Behavioral Sciences (Basel, Switzerland)*, *13*(2), 119. Advance online publication. doi:10.3390/bs13020119 PMID:36829348

Saleem, M., Khan, S. A., Al Shamsi, I. R., & Magd, H. (2023). Digital Marketing Through Social Media Best Practices: A Case Study of HEIs in the GCC Region. In A. Naim & V. Devi (Eds.), *Global Applications of the Internet of Things in Digital Marketing* (pp. 17–30). IGI Global. doi:10.4018/978-1-6684-8166-0.ch002

Salunkhe, T. P. (2018). *Improving employee retention by predicting employee attrition using machine learning techniques* (Doctoral dissertation, Dublin Business School).

Sam, D. L., & Berry, J. W. (2010). Acculturation: When individuals and groups of different cultural backgrounds meet. *Perspectives on Psychological Science*, *5*(4), 472–481. doi:10.1177/1745691610373075 PMID:26162193

Sam, D., Ganesan, M., Ilavarasan, S., & Victor, T. J. (2023, January). Hiring and Recruitment Process Using Machine Learning. In *2023 International Conference on Artificial Intelligence and Knowledge Discovery in Concurrent Engineering (ICECONF)* (pp. 1-4). IEEE. 10.1109/ICECONF57129.2023.10084133

Samudra, S., Walters, C., Williams-Dobosz, D., Shah, A., & Brickman, P. (2024). Try Before You Buy: Are There Benefits to a Random Trial Period before Students Choose Their Collaborative Teams? *CBE Life Sciences Education*, *23*(1), ar2. Advance online publication. doi:10.1187/cbe.23-01-0011 PMID:38085687

San Martín, H., & Herrero, Á. (2012). Influence of the user's psychological factors on the online purchase intention in rural tourism: Integrating innovativeness to the UTAUT framework. *Tourism Management*, *33*(2), 341–350. doi:10.1016/j.tourman.2011.04.003

Sangwan, S., & Garg, P. (2020). Literature review on diversity and inclusion at the workplace (2010-2017). Vision. *The Journal of Business Perspective*, *25*(1), 1–11.

Sanyang, L., & Othman, K. (2019). Workforce diversity and its impact on Organisational Performance. *Journal of Islamic Social Sciences and Humanities*, 25.

SAP. (n.d.). *SAP's Autism at Work Program Provides Meaningful Employment for People on the Autism Spectrum*. Retrieved at http://www.accessibleemployers.ca/wpcontent/uploads/2017/10/SAP-Case-Study-FINAL.pdf

Sarkiunaite, I., & Sciukauske, I. (2021). The Assessment of Employer Brand Impact on the Attraction of Employees in International Organization. *Transformations in Business & Economics*, *20*(3C), 387–404.

Savov, R., Kozakova, J., & Tluchor, J. (2022). Talent Retention In Slovak Companies: Explorative Study. *E+M. Ekonomie a Management*, *25*(1), 77–95. doi:10.15240/tul/001/2022-1-005

Saxenian, A. (2002). Transnational communities and the evolution of global production networks: The cases of Taiwan, China and India. *Industry and Innovation*, *9*(3), 183–202. doi:10.1080/1366271022000034453

Sayers, R. (2007). The right staff from X to Y. *Library Management*, *28*(8/9), 474–487. doi:10.1108/01435120710837765

Scarbrough, H., Sanfilippo, K. R. M., Ziemann, A., & Stavropoulou, C. (2024). Mobilizing pilot-based evidence for the spread and sustainability of innovations in healthcare: The role of innovation intermediaries. *Social Science & Medicine*, *340*, 116394. Advance online publication. doi:10.1016/j.socscimed.2023.116394 PMID:38000177

Schäfer, M. (2018). The fourth industrial revolution: How the EU can lead it. *European View*, *17*(1), 5–12. doi:10.1177/1781685818762890

Scharfenkamp, K., Wicker, P., & Frick, B. (2023). Female representation at the national level and women sport volunteering in European countries. *Nonprofit Management & Leadership*, *33*(4), 783–806. doi:10.1002/nml.21550

Schaufeli, W. B., & Bakker, A. B. (2004). Job demands, job resources, and their relationship with burnout and engagement: A multi-sample study. *Journal of Organizational Behavior*, *25*(3), 293–315. doi:10.1002/job.248

Scheid, T. L. (2005). Stigma as a barrier to employment: Mental disability and the Americans with Disabilities Act. *International Journal of Law and Psychiatry*, *28*(6), 670–690. doi:10.1016/j.ijlp.2005.04.003 PMID:16112732

Schlager, T., Bodderas, M., Maas, P., & Luc Cachelin, J. (2011, October 11). The influence of the employer brand on employee attitudes relevant for service branding: An empirical investigation. *Journal of Services Marketing*, *25*(7), 497–508. doi:10.1108/08876041111173624

Schlechter, A., Hung, A., & Bussin, M. (2014). Understanding talent attraction: The influence of financial rewards elements on perceived job attractiveness. *SA Journal of Human Resource Management*, *12*(1). Advance online publication. doi:10.4102/sajhrm.v12i1.647

Schmitt, M. T., Branscombe, N. R., Postmes, T., & Garcia, A. (2014). The consequences of perceived discrimination for psychological well-being: A meta-analytic review. *Psychological Bulletin*, *140*(4), 921–948. doi:10.1037/a0035754 PMID:24547896

Schoon, I., & Parsons, S. (2002). Teenage Aspirations for Future Careers and Occupational Outcomes. *Journal of Vocational Behavior*, *60*(2), 262–288. doi:10.1006/jvbe.2001.1867

Schroeder, J. E., & Salzer-Morling, M. (2005). Brand culture. In Corporates brand cultures and communities. Routledge.

Schuler, R. S., Jackson, S. E., & Tarique, I. (2011, October). Global talent management and global talent challenges: Strategic opportunities for IHRM. *Journal of World Business*, *46*(4), 506–516. doi:10.1016/j.jwb.2010.10.011

Schuller, R. S., & Jackson, S. E. (2005). *Strategic human resources management*. Blackwell Pub.

Schultz, M., Antorini, Y. M., & Csaba, F. F. (2005). Corporate branding- an evolving concept, from Corporate branding: purpose, people, process- towards the second wave of corporate branding. Copenhagen Business School Press.

Schumann, M., & Sartain, L. (2009). *Brand for talent*. Wiley.

Schur, L., Nishii, L., Adya, M., Kruse, D., Bruyère, S. M., & Blanck, P. (2014). Accommodating employees with and without disabilities. *Human Resource Management*, *53*(4), 593–621. doi:10.1002/hrm.21607

Schwartz, S. E. O., Rhodes, J. E., Liang, B., Sánchez, B., Spencer, R., Kremer, S., & Kanchewa, S. (2014). Mentoring in the digital age: Social media use in adult-youth relationships. *Children and Youth Services Review*, *47*, 205–213. doi:10.1016/j.childyouth.2014.09.004

Schweyer, A. (2018). Predictive analytics and artificial intelligence in people management. *Incentive Research Foundation*, 1-18.

Schweyer, A. (2004). *Talent management systems: Best practices in technology solutions for recruitment, retention and workforce planning*. John Wiley & Sons.

Scott, C., Sackmaster, S., Schembre, D., Rice, G. M., & Vicari, J. (2023). *Best practice recommendation: advanced practice providers contract terms and negotiations*. iGIE.

Scott, J. T. (2017). *The sustainable business: A practitioner's guide to achieving long-term profitability and competitiveness*. Routledge. doi:10.4324/9781351276603

Scott, M., Falkmer, M., Girdler, S., & Falkmer, T. (2015). Viewpoints on factors for successful employment for adults with autism spectrum disorder. *PLoS One*, *10*(10), e0139281. doi:10.1371/journal.pone.0139281 PMID:26462234

Scott, P. R., & Jacka, J. M. (2011). *Auditing Social Media: A Governance and Risk Guide*. Willey.

Scullion, H., & Collings, D. G. (2011). Global talent management: Introduction. In *Global talent management* (pp. 19–32). Routledge. doi:10.4324/9780203865682

Sekiguchi, T., Mitate, Y., & Yang, Y. (2023). Internship Experience and Organizational Attractiveness: A Realistic Job Fit Perspective. *Journal of Career Development*, *50*(2), 353–371. doi:10.1177/08948453221094311

Sennett, R. (2007). *The culture of the new capitalism*. Yale University Press.

Seppälä, P., Mauno, S., Feldt, T., Hakanen, J., Kinnunen, U., Tolvanen, A., & Schaufeli, W. (2008). The Construct Validity of the Utrecht Work Engagement Scale: Multisample and Longitudinal Evidence. *Journal of Happiness Studies*, *10*(4), 459–481. doi:10.1007/s10902-008-9100-y

Šerić, M., & Mikulić, J. (2020). Building brand equity through communication consistency in luxury hotels: An impact-asymmetry analysis. *Journal of Hospitality and Tourism Insights*, *3*(4), 451–468. doi:10.1108/JHTI-11-2019-0119

Shahbaz, U. (2022). *Towards automating the recruitment process* (Doctoral dissertation, Macquarie University).

Shah, M. (2019). Green human resource management: Development of a valid measurement scale. *Business Strategy and the Environment*, *28*(5), 771–785. doi:10.1002/bse.2279

Shah, P., Singh Dubey, R., Rai, S., Renwick, D. W., & Misra, S. (2023). Green human resource management: A comprehensive investigation using bibliometric analysis. *Corporate Social Responsibility and Environmental Management*.

Shakespeare, T., & Watson, N. (1997). Defending the social model. *Disability & Society*, *12*(2), 293–300. doi:10.1080/09687599727380

Shambaugh, D. (2015). China's soft-power push: The search for respect. *Foreign Affairs*, *94*(4), 99–107.

Shao, L., Kwok, C. C., & Zhang, R. (2013). National culture and corporate investment. *Journal of International Business Studies*, *44*(7), 745–763. doi:10.1057/jibs.2013.26

Sharma, M., & Singh, A. (2024). Enhancing Competitive Advantages Through Virtual Reality Technology in the Hotels of India. In S. Kumar, M. Talukder, & A. Pego (Eds.), *Utilizing Smart Technology and AI in Hybrid Tourism and Hospitality* (pp. 243–256). IGI Global. doi:10.4018/979-8-3693-1978-9.ch011

Sharma, N., Khatri, B., & Khan, S. A. (2023b). Do e-WOM Persuade Travelers Destination Visit Intentions? An investigation on how Travelers Adopt the Information from the Social Media Channels. *Journal of Content. Community and Communication*, *17*(9), 147–161. doi:10.31620/JCCC.06.23/11

Sharma, N., Khatri, B., & Khan, S. A. (2024). Exploring the Past and Identifying the Future Research Agenda for Social Media and Tourist Behavior: A Bibliometric Analysis. In C. Ramos, T. Costa, F. Severino, & M. Calisto (Eds.), *Social Media Strategies for Tourism Interactivity* (pp. 261–284). IGI Global. doi:10.4018/979-8-3693-0960-5.ch011

Sharma, N., Khatri, B., Khan, S. A., & Shamsi, M. S. (2023a). Extending the UTAUT Model to Examine the Influence of social media on Tourists' Destination Selection. *Indian Journal of Marketing*, *53*(4), 47–64. doi:10.17010/ijom/2023/v53/i4/172689

Sharma, P., & Khan, W. A. (2022). Revolutionizing Human Resources Management with Big Data: From Talent Acquisition to Workforce Optimization. *International Journal of Business Intelligence and Big Data Analytics*, *5*(1), 35–45.

Sharma, R., & Singh, A. (2024). Use of Digital Technology in Improving Quality Education: A Global Perspectives and Trends. In V. Nadda, P. Tyagi, R. Moniz Vieira, & P. Tyagi (Eds.), *Implementing Sustainable Development Goals in the Service Sector* (pp. 14–26). IGI Global. doi:10.4018/979-8-3693-2065-5.ch002

Sheahan, P. (2005). *Generation Y: thriving and surviving with Generation Y at work*. Hardie Gran Books.

Shein, E. (2020). Hiring from the autism spectrum. *Communications of the ACM, 63*(6), 17–19. doi:10.1145/3392509

Shen, J., Dumont, J., & Deng, X. (2018). Employees' Perceptions of Green HRM and Non-Green Employee Work Outcomes: The Social Identity and Stakeholder Perspectives. *Group & Organization Management, 43*(4), 594–622. doi:10.1177/1059601116664610

Shenkar, O., Luo, Y., & Chi, T. (2021). *International business*. Routledge. doi:10.4324/9781003034315

Shi, J., Wang, J., Kang, L., & Sun, J. (2023). How to poach the talents? Role of social capital and contextual knowledge base. *Technological Forecasting and Social Change, 197*, 122905. doi:10.1016/j.techfore.2023.122905

Shikweni, S., Schurink, W., & van Wyk, R. (2019). Talent management in the South African construction industry. *SA Journal of Human Resource Management, 17*. Advance online publication. doi:10.4102/sajhrm.v17i0.1094

Shi, X., Chen, Y., Xia, M., & Zhang, Y. (2022). Effects of the Talent War on Urban Innovation in China: A Difference-in-Differences Analysis. *Land (Basel), 11*(9), 1485. Advance online publication. doi:10.3390/land11091485

SHRM. (2009). *Global diversity and inclusion: Perceptions, practices and attitudes*. Report for the Economic Intelligence Unit – The Economist. Society for Human Resource Management.

Shukla, A., & Srivastava, R. (2016). Development of short questionnaire to measure an extended set of role expectation conflict, coworker support and work-life balance: The new job stress scale. *Cogent Business &Amp. Management, 3*(1), 1. doi:10.1080/23311975.2015.1134034

Shuler, H., Cazares, V., Marshall, A., Garza-Lopez, E., Hultman, R., Francis, T.-K., Rolle, T., Byndloss, M. X., Starbird, C. A., Hicsasmaz, I., AshShareef, S., Neikirk, K., Johnson, P. E. C., Vue, Z., Beasley, H. K., Williams, A., & Hinton, A. Jr. (2021). Intentional mentoring: Maximizing the impact of underrepresented future scientists in the 21st Century. *Pathogens and Disease, 79*(6), ftab038. Advance online publication. doi:10.1093/femspd/ftab038 PMID:34283236

Signore, C., Della Piana, B., & Di Vincenzo, F. (2023). Digital job searching and recruitment platforms: A semi-systematic literature review. In Lecture Notes in Networks and Systems (pp. 313–322). doi:10.1007/978-3-031-42134-1_31

Sills, M. (2014). *E-recruitment: A comparison with traditional recruitment and the influences of social media: A qualitative and quantitative review*. Academic Press.

Silva, N. C. S., & Machado, C. F. (2023). A glance at recruitment and selection in the digital age. In Springer eBooks (pp. 115–124). doi:10.1007/978-3-031-26232-6_6

Silva, A. J., & Dias, H. (2022). The relationship between employer branding, corporate reputation and intention to apply to a job offer. *The International Journal of Organizational Analysis, 31*(8), 1–16. doi:10.1108/IJOA-01-2022-3129

Sims, R. R. (2002). *Organizational success through effective human resources management*. Greenwood Pub. Inc.Group. doi:10.5040/9798400693953

Singer, J. (1998) *Odd People In: The Birth of Community Amongst People on the Autism Spectrum: A personal exploration of a New Social Movement based on Neurological Diversity*. An Honours Thesis presented to the Faculty of Humanities and Social Science, the University of Technology, Sydney.

Singer, J. (1999). Why can't you be normal for once in your life? From a "Problem with No Name" to a new category of disability. Sociological Review, 74(2), 208-224.

Singh, A., & Bathla, G. (2023). Fostering Creativity and Innovation: Tourism and Hospitality Perspective. In P. Tyagi, V. Nadda, V. Bharti, & E. Kemer (Eds.), Embracing Business Sustainability through Innovation and Creativity in the Service Sector (pp. 70-83). IGI Global. doi:10.4018/978-1-6684-6732-9.ch005

Singh, A., & Hassan, S. C. (2024b). Identifying the Skill Gap in the Workplace and Their Challenges in Hospitality and Tourism Organisations. In Contemporary Challenges in Social Science Management: Skills Gaps and Shortages in the Labour Market (Contemporary Studies in Economic and Financial Analysis, Vol. 112B). Emerald Publishing Limited. doi:10.1108/S1569-37592024000112B006

Singh, A., & Kumar, S. (2022). Identifying Innovations in Human Resources: Academia and Industry Perspectives. In I. Management Association (Ed.), Research Anthology on Human Resource Practices for the Modern Workforce (pp. 219-231). IGI Global. doi:10.4018/978-1-6684-3873-2.ch013

Singh, A. (2024a). Quality of Work-Life Practices in the Indian Hospitality Sector: Future Challenges and Prospects. In M. Valeri & B. Sousa (Eds.), *Human Relations Management in Tourism* (pp. 208–224). IGI Global. doi:10.4018/979-8-3693-1322-0.ch010

Singh, A. (2024b). Virtual Research Collaboration and Technology Application: Drivers, Motivations, and Constraints. In S. Chakraborty (Ed.), *Challenges of Globalization and Inclusivity in Academic Research* (pp. 250–258). IGI Global. doi:10.4018/979-8-3693-1371-8.ch016

Singh, A., & Hassan, S. C. (2024a). Service Innovation Through Blockchain Technology in the Tourism and Hospitality Industry: Applications, Trends, and Benefits. In S. Singh (Ed.), *Service Innovations in Tourism: Metaverse, Immersive Technologies, and Digital Twin* (pp. 205–214). IGI Global. doi:10.4018/979-8-3693-1103-5.ch010

Singh, A., & Kumar, S. (2021). Identifying Innovations in Human Resources: Academia and Industry Perspectives. In A. Pathak & S. Rana (Eds.), Advances in Human Resources Management and Organizational Development. IGI Global. doi:10.4018/978-1-7998-4180-7.ch006

Singha, R. (2024). Stress, Resilience, and brain performance. In S. Saluja, J. Kukreja, & S. Sharma (Eds.), *Building Organizational Resilience With Neuroleadership* (Vol. 1, pp. 14–29). IGI Global., doi:10.4018/979-8-3693-1785-3.ch002

Singh, P., & Kumar, K. (2019). E-mentoring Alternative Paradigm for Entrepreneurial Aptitude Development. *Academy of Entrepreneurship Journal, 25*, 1–12.

Singh, V., & Singh, A. (2024). Digital Health Revolution: Enhancing Well-Being Through Technology. In V. Nadda, P. Tyagi, R. Moniz Vieira, & P. Tyagi (Eds.), *Implementing Sustainable Development Goals in the Service Sector* (pp. 213–219). IGI Global. doi:10.4018/979-8-3693-2065-5.ch016

Single, P. B., & Single, R. M. (2005). E-mentoring for social equity: Review of research to inform program development. *Mentoring & Tutoring. Mentoring & Tutoring, 13*(2), 301–320. doi:10.1080/13611260500107481

Sivertzen, A.-M., Nilsen, E. R., & Olafsen, A. H. (2013). Employer branding: Employer attractiveness and the use of social media. *Journal of Product and Brand Management, 22*(7), 473–483. doi:10.1108/JPBM-09-2013-0393

Smedley, A., & Smedley, B. D. (2005). Race as biology is fiction, racism as a social problem is real: Anthropological and historical perspectives on the social construction of race. *The American Psychologist, 60*(1), 16–26. doi:10.1037/0003-066X.60.1.16 PMID:15641918

Smit, B. W., & Lawson, K. M. (2023). Growth mindsets increase flexible work arrangement attractiveness: A policy-capturing study. *Personnel Review*, *52*(1), 342–362. doi:10.1108/PR-10-2020-0793

Smitha, C. (2023). Effectiveness Of Virtual Recruitment–A Study On Commerce And Managment Students' Perspective. *Journal of Namibian Studies: History Politics Culture*, *35*, 330–341.

Smith, E. (2019). Virtual mentoring: Mentoring across the digital divide. *Journal of Community Practice*, *27*(1-2), 5–26.

Smith, J. A. (2019). Virtual mentoring: Expanding the boundaries of traditional mentoring relationships. *Journal of Leadership & Organizational Studies*, *26*(2), 261–273.

Smith, J., & Johnson, M. (2018). Social Exchange Theory: Its Structure and Influence in the Social Sciences. In D. Byrne & J. M. Ragin (Eds.), *The SAGE Handbook of Case-Based Methods* (pp. 255–270). Sage.

Smith, J., Roberts, D., & Petrie, N. (2021). Virtual mentoring in the remote workplace: A systematic review and research agenda. *Journal of Career Development*, *48*(2), 116–133.

Smith, M. V. A., Grohmann, D., & Trivedi, D. (2023). Use of social media in recruiting young people to mental health research: A scoping review. *BMJ Open*, *13*(11), e075290. doi:10.1136/bmjopen-2023-075290 PMID:38016791

Smith, P. (2012). *Lead with a story: A guide to crafting business narratives that captivate, convince, and inspire*. Amacom.

Smith, P. A., & Cockburn, T. (2016). *Developing and Leading Emergence Teams: A new approach for identifying and resolving complex business problems*. Routledge. doi:10.4324/9781315576800

Sokro, E. (2012). Impact of employer branding on employee attraction and retention. *European Journal of Business and Management*, *4*(18), 164–173.

Solnet, D., & Hood, A. (2008). Generation Y as hospitality employees: Framing a research agenda. *Journal of Hospitality and Tourism Management*, *15*(1), 59–68. doi:10.1375/jhtm.15.1.59

Solorzano, D. G., Ceja, M., & Yosso, T. J. (2000). Critical Race Theory, Racial Microaggressions, and Campus Racial Climate: The Experiences of African American College Students. *The Journal of Negro Education*, *69*, 60–73.

Song, M., & Xie, Q. (2020). How does green talent influence China's economic growth? *International Journal of Manpower*, *41*(7), 1119–1134. doi:10.1108/IJM-08-2019-0378

Sop, S. A., & Kozak, N. (2019). Effects of brand personality, self-congruity and functional congruity on hotel brand loyalty. *Journal of Hospitality Marketing & Management*, *28*(8), 1–31. doi:10.1080/19368623.2019.1577202

Špoljarić, A., & Došen, Đ. O. (2023). Employer brand and international employer brand: A literature review. *Corporate Communications*, *28*(4), 671–682. doi:10.1108/CCIJ-11-2022-0141

Stahl, C., & Unkelbach, C. (2009). Evaluative learning with single versus multiple unconditioned stimuli: The role of contingency awareness. *Journal of Experimental Psychology. Animal Behavior Processes*, *35*(2), 286–291. doi:10.1037/a0013255 PMID:19364238

Stahl, G. K., & Bjorkman, I. (2006). *Handbook of research in international HRM*. Edward E. Pub.Ltd.

Stahl, G. K., Björkman, I., Farndale, E., Morris, S. P. J., & Stiles, P. (2007). *Global talent management: How leading multinationals build and sustain their talent pipeline*. INSEAD Faculty and Research Papers.

Stahl, G. K., Björkman, I., & Morris, S. (Eds.). (2012). *Handbook of research in international human resource management*. Edward Elgar Publishing.

Statista. (2023, April 25). *The World's Biggest Exporters of Clothes.* Retrieved February 8, 2024, from https://www.statista.com/chart/29845/worlds-biggest-exporters-of-clothes/

Statista. (2024). *Top textile exporting countries worldwide 2022.* Retrieved February 8, 2024, from https://www.statista.com/statistics/265064/leading-10-textile-exporters-worldwide-by-country/

Stevens, H. (2019). The quotidian labour of high tech: Innovation and ordinary work in Shenzhen. *Science, Technology & Society, 24*(2), 218–236. doi:10.1177/0971721819841997

Stevens, R. E., Loudon, D. L., & Cole, H. (2013). *Concise encyclopedia of church and religious organization marketing.* Routledge. doi:10.4324/9780203725443

Strelnikova, Y. Y., & Goncharova, N. A. (2023). Psychological Features of Professional Demand and Motivation of Law-Enforcement Officers. *Psychology and Law, 13*(1), 27–39. doi:10.17759/psylaw.2023130102

Stumpf, S. A., Tymon, W. G. Jr, & van Dam, N. H. M. (2013). Felt and behavioral engagement in workgroups of professionals. *Journal of Vocational Behavior, 83*(3), 255–264. doi:10.1016/j.jvb.2013.05.006

Stuss, M. M. (2020). Talent Management - War for Talents. *Proceedings of the 11th Business & Management Conference*, 198-212. 10.20472/BMC.2020.011.013

Suar, D. (2014). Antecedents and Consequences of Employer Branding. *Journal of Business Ethics.* https://doi.org/doi:10.1007/s10551-014-2502

Sudarji, S., Panggabean, H., & Marta, R. F. (2022). Challenges of the sandwich generation: Stress and coping strategy of the multigenerational care. *Indigenous: Jurnal Ilmiah Psikologi, 7*(3), 263–275. doi:10.23917/indigenous.v7i3.19433

Sue, D. W. (2010). *Microaggressions in Everyday Life: Race, Gender, and Sexual Orientation* (1st ed.). Wiley.

Sue, D. W., Capodilupo, C. M., & Holder, A. M. B. (2008). Racial microaggressions in the life experience of Black Americans. *Professional Psychology, Research and Practice, 39*(3), 329–336. doi:10.1037/0735-7028.39.3.329

Sue, D. W., Capodilupo, C. M., Torino, G. C., Bucceri, J. M., Holder, A. M. B., Nadal, K. L., & Esquilin, M. (2007). Racial microaggressions in everyday life: Implications for clinical practice. *The American Psychologist, 62*(4), 271–286. doi:10.1037/0003-066X.62.4.271 PMID:17516773

Sufrin, R. L. (2014). *The role of multicultural competence, privilege, attributions, and team support in predicting positive youth mentor outcomes.* Master's Thesis. DePaul University, USA.

Sujansky, (2002). The critical care and feeding of generation Y. *Workforce, 81*(5), 15.

Sujansky, J., & Ferri-Reed, J. (2009). *Keeping the Millennials: Why companies are losing billions in turnover to this generation-and what to do about it.* John Wiley & Sons.

Suleman, B. A. (2017). *Diversity Management for improving performances in Mobile telephone.* University of Professional Studies.

Sumner, K. E., & Brown, T. J. (2015). Neurodiversity and human resource management: Employer challenges for applicants and employees with learning disabilities. *The Psychologist Manager Journal, 18*(2), 77–85. doi:10.1037/mgr0000031

Su, N., & Reynolds, D. (2017). Effects of brand personality dimensions on consumers' perceived self-image congruity and functional congruity with hotel brands. *International Journal of Hospitality Management, 66*, 1–12. doi:10.1016/j.ijhm.2017.06.006

Su, N., & Reynolds, D. (2019). Categorical differences of hotel brand personality: Identifying competition across hotel categories. *International Journal of Contemporary Hospitality Management*, *31*(4), 1801–1818. Advance online publication. doi:10.1108/IJCHM-05-2018-0354

Suomi, A., Schofield, T., & Butterworth, P. (2022). Does receipt of unemployment benefits change recruiter perceptions of candidates' personality, work relevant skills and employability? *Work (Reading, Mass.)*, *71*(4), 1029–1041. doi:10.3233/WOR-205048 PMID:35253667

Supardi, A. M., Salehah, M., & Komalasari, S. (2023, March). The Role of Workplace Well-Being on Employee Work Satisfaction. In Conference of Psychology and Flourishing Humanity (PFH 2022) (pp. 318-327). Atlantis Press. doi:10.2991/978-2-38476-032-9_33

Supina, S. (2020). Generation Z career options in the government sector in the tourism sector with the presence of the generation X minister as a moderating variable. *Journal of Indonesia Tourism and Policy Studies*, *5*(1). Advance online publication. doi:10.7454/jitps.v5i1.169

Supina, S., Marta, R. F., & Karolina, C. M. (2022). Comparison of the influence of motivation for foreign tourists' visits to Bali with the inauguration of the Garuda Wisnu Kencana statue. *International Journal of Applied Sciences in Tourism and Events*, *6*(1), 42–51. doi:10.31940/ijaste.v6i1.42-51

Sutter, P.-E. (2007). *Comment… recruter ou se faire recruter*. Editions de Boeck Universite.

Suzuki, D. T. (2019). *Zen and Japanese culture* (Vol. 334). Princeton University Press. doi:10.2307/j.ctvc77449

Swailes, S. (2016). The cultural evolution of talent management: A memetic analysis. *Human Resource Development Review*, *15*(3), 340–358. doi:10.1177/1534484316664812

Swartz, T. H., Palermo, A. S., Masur, S. K., & Aberg, J. A. (2019). The science and value of diversity: Closing the gaps in our understanding of inclusion and diversity. *The Journal of Infectious Diseases*, *220*(Supplement_2), S33–S41. doi:10.1093/infdis/jiz174 PMID:31430380

Swim, J. K., Aikin, K. J., Hall, W. S., & Hunter, B. A. (1995). Sexism and racism: Old-fashioned and modern prejudices. *Journal of Personality and Social Psychology*, *68*(2), 199–214. doi:10.1037/0022-3514.68.2.199

Szulc, J. M., Davies, J., Tomczak, M. T., & McGregor, F. L. (2021). AMO perspectives on the well-being of neurodivergent human capital. *Employee Relations*, *43*(4), 858–872. doi:10.1108/ER-09-2020-0446

Tabassum, N., & Nayak, B. S. (2021). Gender stereotypes and their impact on women's career progressions from a managerial perspective. *IIM Kozhikode Society & Management Review*, *10*(2), 192–208. doi:10.1177/2277975220975513

Tagliaro, C., Migliore, A., Mosca, E. I., & Capolongo, S. (2023). Room for diversity: A review of research and industry approaches to inclusive workplaces. *Journal of Corporate Real Estate*. Advance online publication. doi:10.1108/JCRE-04-2023-0017

Tajfel, H., & Turner, J. C. (1986). The social identity theory of intergroup behavior. In S. Worchel, & W. G. Austin (Eds.), Psychology of Intergroup Relations (pp. 7-24). Nelson-Hall.

Tang, M., Walsh, G. S., Li, C., & Baskaran, A. (2021). Exploring technology business incubators and their business incubation models: Case studies from China. *The Journal of Technology Transfer*, *46*(1), 90–116. doi:10.1007/s10961-019-09759-4

Tanova, C., & Bayighomog, S. W. (2022). Green human resource management in service industries: The construct, antecedents, consequences, and outlook. *Service Industries Journal*, *42*(5–6), 412–452. doi:10.1080/02642069.2022.2045279

Tansley, C. (2011). What do we mean by the term "talent" in talent management? *Industrial and Commercial Training*, *43*(5), 266–274. doi:10.1108/00197851111145853

Tansley, C., Harris, L., Stewart, J., & Turner, P. (2006). *Talent Management: Understanding the Dimensios*. CIPD.

Tapscott, D. (2009). *Grown up digital: how the net generation is changing your world*. McGraw Hill.

Tarhini, A., Hone, K., & Liu, X. (2013). User Acceptance Towards Web-based Learning Systems: Investigating the Role of Social, Organizational and Individual Factors in European Higher Education. *Procedia Computer Science*, *17*, 189–197. doi:10.1016/j.procs.2013.05.026

Tarhini, A., Hone, K., & Liu, X. (2014). The effects of individual differences on e-learning users' behaviour in developing countries: A structural equation model. *Computers in Human Behavior*, *41*, 153–163. doi:10.1016/j.chb.2014.09.020

Tariq, M. U. (2024a). Equity and Inclusion in Learning Ecosystems. In F. Al Husseiny & A. Munna (Eds.), *Preparing Students for the Future Educational Paradigm* (pp. 155–176). IGI Global. doi:10.4018/979-8-3693-1536-1.ch007

Tariq, M. U. (2024b). Empowering Educators in the Learning Ecosystem. In F. Al Husseiny & A. Munna (Eds.), *Preparing Students for the Future Educational Paradigm* (pp. 232–255). IGI Global. doi:10.4018/979-8-3693-1536-1.ch010

Tariq, M. U. (2024c). Revolutionizing Health Data Management With Blockchain Technology: Enhancing Security and Efficiency in a Digital Era. In M. Garcia & R. de Almeida (Eds.), *Emerging Technologies for Health Literacy and Medical Practice* (pp. 153–175). IGI Global. doi:10.4018/979-8-3693-1214-8.ch008

Tariq, M. U. (2024d). Emerging Trends and Innovations in Blockchain-Digital Twin Integration for Green Investments: A Case Study Perspective. In S. Jafar, R. Rodriguez, H. Kannan, S. Akhtar, & P. Plugmann (Eds.), *Harnessing Blockchain-Digital Twin Fusion for Sustainable Investments* (pp. 148–175). IGI Global. doi:10.4018/979-8-3693-1878-2.ch007

Tariq, M. U. (2024e). Emotional Intelligence in Understanding and Influencing Consumer Behavior. In T. Musiolik, R. Rodriguez, & H. Kannan (Eds.), *AI Impacts in Digital Consumer Behavior* (pp. 56–81). IGI Global. doi:10.4018/979-8-3693-1918-5.ch003

Tariq, M. U. (2024f). Fintech Startups and Cryptocurrency in Business: Revolutionizing Entrepreneurship. In K. Kankaew, P. Nakpathom, A. Chnitphattana, K. Pitchayadejanant, & S. Kunnapapdeelert (Eds.), *Applying Business Intelligence and Innovation to Entrepreneurship* (pp. 106–124). IGI Global. doi:10.4018/979-8-3693-1846-1.ch006

Tarique, I. (2022). *Contemporary talent management. A research companion*. Routledge.

Tarique, I., & Schuler, R. S. (2010). Global talent management: Literature review, integrative framework, and suggestions for further research. *Journal of World Business*, *45*(2), 122–133. doi:10.1016/j.jwb.2009.09.019

Taubman, D. S., & Parikh, S. V. (2023). Understanding and addressing mental health disorders: A workplace imperative. *Current Psychiatry Reports*, *25*(10), 455–463. doi:10.1007/s11920-023-01443-7 PMID:37589777

Tavanti, M. (2012). The cultural dimensions of Italian leadership: Power distance, uncertainty avoidance and masculinity from an American perspective. *Leadership*, *8*(3), 287–301. doi:10.1177/1742715012441876

Taylor, C. (2019). *A third of the world's female entrepreneurs face gender bias from investors, HSBC claims*. Academic Press.

Taylor, S. (2007). Creating social capital in MNCs: The international human resource management challenge. *Human Resource Management Journal*, *17*(4), 336–354. doi:10.1111/j.1748-8583.2007.00049.x

Terjesen, S., Vinnicombe, S., & Freeman, C. (2007). Attracting generation Y graduates. *Career Development International*, *12*(6), 504–522. doi:10.1108/13620430710821994

Terrés Molina, P. (2023). *The impact of artificial intelligence on human talent management: attraction, retention and motivation.* Academic Press.

Tett, R. P., & Meyer, J. P. (2006). Job satisfaction, organizational commitment, turnover intention, and turnover: Path analyses based on meta-analytic findings. *Personnel Psychology, 46*(2), 259–293. doi:10.1111/j.1744-6570.1993.tb00874.x

Tetzlaff, J., Lomberk, G., Smith, H. M., Agrawal, H., Siegel, D. H., & Apps, J. N. (2022). Adapting Mentoring in Times of Crisis: What We Learned from COVID-19. *Academic Psychiatry, 46*(6), 774–779. doi:10.1007/s40596-022-01589-1 PMID:35217939

Textile Engineering. (2023, February 13). *Top 10 Textile Universities in the World.* Retrieved February 9, 2024, from https://textileengineering.net/top-10-textile-universities-in-the-world/

Thangaraja, T. (2023). Challenges Faced by HR on Recruitment Process. *MET Management Review, 10*(2), 19–24. doi:10.34047/MMR.2020.10203

Theurer, C. P., Tumasjan, A., Welpe, I. M., & Lievens, F. (2018). Employer Branding: A Brand Equity-based Literature Review and Research Agenda. *International Journal of Management Reviews, 20*(1), 155–179. doi:10.1111/ijmr.12121

Theys, N. A., & Barkhuizen, E. N. (2022). The development of an employee value proposition framework for the South African water board sector. *SA Journal of Human Resource Management, 20.* Advance online publication. doi:10.4102/sajhrm.v20i0.1944

Thompson, G. L. (2020). Technology and virtual mentoring: Challenges and opportunities. *Journal of Human Behavior in the Social Environment, 30*(8), 988–1003.

Thunnissen, M. (2016). Talent management: For what, how and how well? An empirical exploration of talent management in practice. *Employee Relations, 38*(1), 57–72. doi:10.1108/ER-08-2015-0159

Thunnissen, M., Boselie, P., & Fruytier, B. (2013). A review of talent management: 'infancy or adolescence?'. *International Journal of Human Resource Management, 24*(9), 1744–1761. doi:10.1080/09585192.2013.777543

Thunnissen, M., Boselie, P., & Fruytier, B. (2013). Talent management and the relevance of context: Towards a pluralistic approach. *Human Resource Management Review, 23*(4), 326–336. doi:10.1016/j.hrmr.2013.05.004

Ting-Toomey, S., & Dorjee, T. (2018). *Communicating across cultures.* Guilford Publications.

Tinoco-Giraldo, H., Torrecilla Sánchez, E. M., & García-Peñalvo, F. J. (2020). E-Mentoring in Higher Education: A Structured Literature Review and Implications for Future Research. *Sustainability (Basel), 12*(11), 4344. doi:10.3390/su12114344

Toprak, T., & Anis, P. (2017). Textile industry's environmental effects and approaching cleaner production and sustainability, an overview. *Journal of Textile Engineering & Fashion Technology, 2*(4), 429–442. doi:10.15406/jteft.2017.02.00066

Tortia, E., Sacchetti, S., & Arceiz, F. J. L. (2022). A human growth perspective on sustainable HRM practices, worker wellbeing and organizational performance. *Sustainability (Basel), 14*(17), 11064. doi:10.3390/su141711064

Tortora, E. M., & Strohbehn, X. S. (2023). *Embracing and Accommodating Neurodiversity: Equitable and Legal Considerations for Neurodiverse Employees in the Workplace.* https://www.venable.com/insights/publications/2023/11/embracing-and-accommodating-neurodiversity

Tosun, C., Parvez, M. O., Bilim, Y., & Yu, L. (2022). Effects of green transformational leadership on green performance of employees via the mediating role of corporate social responsibility: Reflection from North Cyprus. *International Journal of Hospitality Management, 103,* 103218. doi:10.1016/j.ijhm.2022.103218

Tracey, J. B., & Hinkin, T. R. (2008). Contextual Factors and Cost Profiles Associated with Employee Turnover. *Cornell Hospitality Quarterly*, *49*(1), 12–27. doi:10.1177/0010880407310191

Tracy, B. (2008). *Cum să angajaţi şi să păstraţi cei mai buni oameni*. Meteor Press.

Trenerry, B., Dunn, K., & Paradies, Y. (2023). Productive disruptions: Supporting diversity and anti-racism in the workplace through multi-level organisational strategies. *Australian Journal of Management*, 1–28. doi:10.1177/03128962231175182

Trevor, C. O., & Nyberg, A. J. (2008). Keeping Your Headcount When All About You Are Losing Theirs: Downsizing, Voluntary Turnover Rates, and The Moderating Role of HR Practices. *Academy of Management Journal*, *51*(2), 259–276. doi:10.5465/amj.2008.31767250

Trost, A. (2014). An overview of talent relationship management. In Management for Professionals (pp. 11–15). doi:10.1007/978-3-642-54557-3_3

Troup, J., Fuhr, D. C., Woodward, A., Sondorp, E., & Roberts, B. (2021). Barriers and facilitators for scaling up mental health and psychosocial support interventions in low- and middle-income countries for populations affected by humanitarian crises: A systematic review. *International Journal of Mental Health Systems*, *15*(1), 5. Advance online publication. doi:10.1186/s13033-020-00431-1 PMID:33413526

Trunfio, M., & Rossi, S. (2021). Conceptualizing and measuring social media engagement: A systematic literature review. *Italian Journal of Marketing*, *2021*(3), 267–292. doi:10.1007/s43039-021-00035-8

Tsen, M. K., Gu, M., Tan, C. M., & Goh, S. K. (2021). Do flexible work arrangements decrease or increase turnover intention? A comparison between the social exchange theory and border theory. *The International Journal of Sociology and Social Policy*, *42*(11–12), 962–983. doi:10.1108/IJSSP-08-2021-0196

Tulgan, B. (2000). *Managing generation X: how to bring out the best in young talent*. W. W. Norton & Company.

Turban, D. B., Forret, M. L., & Hendrickson, C. L. (1998, February). Applicant Attraction to Firms: Influences of Organization Reputation, Job and Organizational Attributes, and Recruiter Behaviors. *Journal of Vocational Behavior*, *52*(1), 24–44. doi:10.1006/jvbe.1996.1555

Turnea, E. S., Prodan, A., Boldureanu, G., Ciulu, R., Arustei, C. C., & Boldureanu, D. (2020). The Importance of Organizational Rewards on Attracting and Retaining Students at Work. *Transformations in Business & Economics*, *19*(2B), 923–943.

Uddin, M. A., Azim, M. T., & Haque, M. M. (2021). Does Compliance to the Prescribed Standards in Readymade Garments Sector Predict Employee Turnover Intention? The Mediating Role of Job Satisfaction and Organizational Attraction. *Iim Kozhikode Society & Management Review*, *10*(2), 209–221. doi:10.1177/2277975221989109

Ujlayan, A., Bhattacharya, S., & Sonakshi. (2024). A machine learning-based AI framework to optimize the recruitment screening process. *International Journal of Global Business and Competitiveness*. doi:10.1007/s42943-023-00086-y

Ulrich, D. (1996). *Human resource champions: The next agenda for adding value and delivering results*. Harvard Business Press.

Ulrich, D. (2007). *The Talent Trifecta*. Workforce Management.

Uma, V. R., Velchamy, I., & Upadhyay, D. (2023). Recruitment Analytics: Hiring in the Era of Artificial Intelligence. In The Adoption and Effect of Artificial Intelligence on Human Resources Management, Part A (pp. 155-174). Emerald Publishing Limited.

Umair, S., Waqas, U., Mrugalska, B., & Al Shamsi, I. R. (2023). Environmental Corporate Social Responsibility, Green Talent Management, and Organization's Sustainable Performance in the Banking Sector of Oman: The Role of Innovative Work Behavior and Green Performance. *Sustainability (Basel)*, *15*(19), 14303. doi:10.3390/su151914303

Umrani, W. A., Channa, N. A., Ahmed, U., Syed, J., Pahi, M. H., & Ramayah, T. (2022). The laws of attraction: Role of green human resources, culture and environmental performance in the hospitality sector. *International Journal of Hospitality Management*, *103*, 103222. Advance online publication. doi:10.1016/j.ijhm.2022.103222

Unurlu, C., & Uca, S. (2017). The effect of culture on brand loyalty through brand performance and brand personality. *International Journal of Tourism Research*, *19*(6), 672–681. doi:10.1002/jtr.2139

Vaiman, V., Cascio, W. F., Collings, D. G., & Swider, B. W. (2021). The shifting boundaries of talent management. *Human Resource Management*, *60*(2), 253–257. doi:10.1002/hrm.22050

Vaiman, V., Scullion, H., & Collings, D. (2012). Talent management decision making. *Management Decision*, *50*(5), 925–941. doi:10.1108/00251741211227663

Vaiman, V., Sparrow, P., Schuler, R., & Collings, D. G. (Eds.). (2018). *Macro talent management in emerging and emergent markets: A global perspective*. Routledge. doi:10.4324/9780429469527

Valentin-Welch, M. (2016). Evaluation of a National E-Mentoring Program for Ethnically Diverse Student Nurse-Midwives and Student Midwives. *Journal of Midwifery & Women's Health*, *61*(6), 759–767. doi:10.1111/jmwh.12547 PMID:27926807

Van den Beemt, A., MacLeod, M., Van der Veen, J., Van de Ven, A., Van Baalen, S., Klaassen, R., & Boon, M. (2020). Interdisciplinary engineering education: A review of vision, teaching, and support. *Journal of Engineering Education*, *109*(3), 508–555. doi:10.1002/jee.20347

Van Der Voordt, D., & Jensen, P. A. (2021). The impact of healthy workplaces on employee satisfaction, productivity and costs. *Journal of Corporate Real Estate*, *25*(1), 29–49. doi:10.1108/JCRE-03-2021-0012

Vandy, J. F. (2023). Revolutionizing the HR Functions for future work–the Critical Role of Technology and AI. *TIJER-International Research Journal*, *10*(3), 758–764.

Vanhala, S., & Tuomi, K. (2006). HRM, company performance and employee well-being. *Management Revue*, 241-255.

Veena, K., & Sharma, D. P. (2018). HR Transformation through artificial intelligence. In *International Conference on Digital Innovation: Meeting the Business Challenges* (pp. 199-207). Academic Press.

Veglianti, E., Trombin, M., Pinna, R., & De Marco, M. (2023). Customized Artificial Intelligence for Talent Recruiting: A Bias-Free Tool? In *Smart Technologies for Organizations: Managing a Sustainable and Inclusive Digital Transformation* (pp. 245–261). Springer International Publishing. doi:10.1007/978-3-031-24775-0_15

Venaik, S., Zhu, Y., & Brewer, P. (2013). Looking into the future: Hofstede long term orientation versus GLOBE future orientation. *Cross Cultural Management*, *20*(3), 361–385. doi:10.1108/CCM-02-2012-0014

Venkataramani, V., & Tang, C. (2023). When Does External Knowledge Benefit Team Creativity? The Role of Internal Team Network Structure and Task Complexity. *Organization Science*. Advance online publication. doi:10.1287/orsc.2023.1661

Venkatesh, M., Morris, Davis, & Davis. (2003). User Acceptance of Information Technology: Toward a Unified View. *Management Information Systems Quarterly*, *27*(3), 425. doi:10.2307/30036540

Venkatesh, T., Thong, & Xu. (2012). Consumer Acceptance and Use of Information Technology: Extending the Unified Theory of Acceptance and Use of Technology. *Management Information Systems Quarterly, 36*(1), 157. doi:10.2307/41410412

Venkatesh, V., & Zhang, X. (2010). Unified Theory of Acceptance and Use of Technology: U.S. Vs. China. *Journal of Global Information Technology Management, 13*(1), 5–27. doi:10.1080/1097198X.2010.10856507

Vickers, J. N. (2011). Skill acquisition: Designing optimal learning environments. *Performance psychology: A practitioner's guide*, 191-206.

Vik, Å. S., Nørbech, B. C., & Jeske, D. (2018). Virtual career fairs: Perspectives from Norwegian recruiters and exhibitors. *Future Internet, 10*(2), 19. doi:10.3390/fi10020019

Vivek, R. (2023). Enhancing diversity and reducing bias in recruitment through AI: a review of strategies and challenges. *Информатика. Экономика. Управление-Informatics. Economics. Management, 2*(4), 101-118.

Vogel, K. M., & Ouagrham-Gormley, S. B. (2023). Scientists as spies?: Assessing US claims about the security threat posed by China's Thousand Talents Program for the US life sciences. *Politics and the Life Sciences, 42*(1), 32–64. doi:10.1017/pls.2022.13 PMID:37140223

Vogel, R., & Satzger, M. (2023). What Drives the Attractiveness of Public and Private Employers? Comparative Evidence from an Online Employer Review Platform. *American Review of Public Administration*. Advance online publication. doi:10.1177/02750740231206805

Von Karolyi, C., Winner, E., Gray, W., & Sherman, G. F. (2003). Dyslexia linked to talent: Global visual-spatial ability. *Brain and Language, 85*(3), 427–431. doi:10.1016/S0093-934X(03)00052-X PMID:12744954

Wagner, B., & Koob, C. (2022). The relationship between leader-member exchange and work engagement in social work: A mediation analysis of job resources. *Heliyon, 8*(1), e08793. Advance online publication. doi:10.1016/j.heliyon.2022.e08793 PMID:35128097

Waheed, S., Zaim, A., & Zaim, H. (2012). Talent Management in Four Stages. The USV Annals of Economics and Public Administration, 130-137.

Walcott, S. M. (2017). *Chinese science and technology industrial parks*. Routledge. doi:10.4324/9781315198170

Walker, N. (2014). *Neurodiversity: Some basic terms & definitions*. Available on: https://neuroqueer.com/neurodiversity-terms-and-definitions/https://neuroqueer.com/neurodiversity-terms-and-definitions/

Walumbwa, F. O., Avolio, B. J., Gardner, W. L., Wernsing, T. S., & Peterson, S. J. (2008). Authentic leadership: Development and validation of a theory-based measure. *Journal of Management, 34*(1), 89–126. doi:10.1177/0149206307308913

Wang, H., & Bao, Y. (2015). *Reverse migration in contemporary China: Returnees, entrepreneurship and the Chinese economy*. Springer. doi:10.1057/9781137450609

Wang, H., Sha, H., Wang, Y., Cheng, L., Yu, Q., Jia, D., & Lu, L. (2023). How Does Friendship Motivate Frontline Employees to Exhibit Brand Ambassador Behavior: The Important Role of Well-Being and Helping Behavior. *Sustainability (Basel), 15*(8), 6859. Advance online publication. doi:10.3390/su15086859

Wang, K., Shen, Z., Huang, C., Wu, C. H., Dong, Y., & Kanakia, A. (2020). Microsoft academic graph: When experts are not enough. *Quantitative Science Studies, 1*(1), 396–413. doi:10.1162/qss_a_00021

Wang, X., Cheng, M., Wong, I. K. A., Teah, M., & Lee, S. (2021). Big-five personality traits in P2P accommodation platforms: Similar or different to hotel brands? *Current Issues in Tourism*, 24(23), 3407–3419. doi:10.1080/13683500.2021.1884205

Wang, Y., & Shi, Y. (2023). Evolvement of international mobility of talents: A complex network perspective. *International Journal of Innovation Science*, 15(2), 317–328. doi:10.1108/IJIS-02-2021-0029

Wanous, J. P., & Lawler, E. E. (1972). Measurement and meaning of job satisfaction. *The Journal of Applied Psychology*, 56(2), 95–105. doi:10.1037/h0032664

Warner-Søderholm, G. (2012). Culture matters: Norwegian cultural identity within a Scandinavian context. *SAGE Open*, 2(4), 2158244012471350. doi:10.1177/2158244012471350

Warshaw, J., Whittaker, S., Matthews, T., & Smith, B. A. (2016). When distance doesn't really matter. *Proceedings of the 19th ACM Conference on Computer-Supported Cooperative Work & Social Computing*. 10.1145/2818048.2835237

Washington, E. F. (2022, May 10). Recognizing and Responding to Microaggressions at Work. *Harvard Business Review*. https://hbr.org/2022/05/recognizing-and-responding-to-microaggressions-at-work

Wasil, A. R., Franzen, R. E., Gillespie, S., Steinberg, J. S., Malhotra, T., & DeRubeis, R. J. (2021). Commonly reported problems and coping strategies during the COVID-19 crisis: A survey of graduate and professional students. *Frontiers in Psychology*, 12, 598557. Advance online publication. doi:10.3389/fpsyg.2021.598557 PMID:33716864

Wassan, S. (2021). How artificial intelligence transforms the experience of employees. *Turkish Journal of Computer and Mathematics Education*, 12(10), 7116–7135.

Weber, C. (2004). Breaking the circle: How do you say goodbye to a partnership and reinvent a practice? *Residential Architect*, 8(9), 39–45.

Weber, C., Krieger, B., Häne, E., Yarker, J., & McDowall, A. (2022). Physical workplace adjustments to support neurodivergent workers: A systematic review. *Applied Psychology*.

Wei, M., Ku, T. Y., Russell, D. W., Mallinckrodt, B., & Liao, K. Y. H. (2008). Moderating effects of three coping strategies and self-esteem on perceived discrimination and depressive symptoms: A minority stress model for Asian international students. *Journal of Counseling Psychology*, 55(4), 451–462. doi:10.1037/a0012511 PMID:22017552

Weiming, T. (2017). Implications of the rise of "Confucian" East Asia. In Multiple modernities (pp. 195-218). Routledge. doi:10.4324/9781315124872-8

Weller, I., Hymer, C. B., Nyberg, A., & Ebert, J. (2019). How Matching Creates Value: Cogs and Wheels for Human Capital Resources Research. *The Academy of Management Annals*, 13(1), 188–214. doi:10.5465/annals.2016.0117

Wells, C., Malik, R. F., & Edmondson, V. C. (2021). The Influence of Diversity Climate on Employer Branding: 2020 and Beyond. *IUP Journal of Brand Management*, 18(1).

Wey Smola, K., & Sutton, C. D. (2002). Generational differences: Revisiting generational work values for the new millennium. *Journal of Organizational Behavior*, 23(4), 363–382. doi:10.1002/job.147

Weyland, A. (2011). Engagement and talent management of Gen Y. *Industrial and Commercial Training*, 43(7), 439–445. doi:10.1108/00197851111171863

Whysall, Z., Owtram, M., & Brittain, S. (2019). The new talent management challenges of Industry 4.0. *Journal of Management Development*, 38(2), 118–129. doi:10.1108/JMD-06-2018-0181

Wijngaards, I., King, O. C., Burger, M., & Van Exel, J. (2021). Worker wellbeing: What it is, and how it should be measured. *Applied Research in Quality of Life, 17*(2), 795–832. doi:10.1007/s11482-021-09930-w

Wikimedia Foundation. (2022, October 25). *Employee retention*. Wikipedia. Retrieved February 6, 2023, from https://en.wikipedia.org/wiki/Employee_retention

Willett, J. F., LaGree, D., Shin, H., Houston, J. B., & Duffy, M. (2023). The role of leader communication in fostering respectful workplace culture and increasing employee engagement and well-being. *International Journal of Business Communication*. doi:10.1177/23294884231195614

Williams, A. C., Iqbal, S., Kiseleva, J., & White, R. W. (2023). Managing Tasks across the Work-Life Boundary: Opportunities, Challenges, and Directions. *ACM Transactions on Computer-Human Interaction, 30*(3), 1–31. Advance online publication. doi:10.1145/3582429

Williams, D. R., Neighbors, H. W., & Jackson, J. S. (2003). Racial/Ethnic Discrimination and Health: Findings From Community Studies. *American Journal of Public Health, 93*(2), 200–208. doi:10.2105/AJPH.93.2.200 PMID:12554570

Williams, L. M. (2021). Creating connections: The role of structured activities in virtual mentoring. *Journal of Youth Development, 16*(3), 79–93.

Williams, M. T., Skinta, M. D., & Martin-Willett, R. (2021). After Pierce and Sue: A Revised Racial Microaggressions Taxonomy. *Perspectives on Psychological Science, 16*(5), 991–1007. doi:10.1177/1745691621994247 PMID:34498518

Wilton, N. (2019). *An introduction to human resource management* (4th ed.). SAGE.

Wisker, Z. L. (2022, November 25). Managing Employee-Based Brand Equity and Firm Performance in the Hospitality Industry: The Role of an Employer's Symbolic Brand Image and Work Environment. *Proceedings: 2021 ITP Research Symposium*. 10.34074/proc.2205019

Wójcik, D., Pažitka, V., Knight, E., & O'Neill, P. (2019). Investment banking centres since the global financial crisis: New typology, ranking and trends. *Environment and Planning A. Environment & Planning A, 51*(3), 687–704. doi:10.1177/0308518X18797702

Women, Business, and the Law. (2022). International Bank for Reconstruction and Development. doi:10.1596/978-1-4648-1817-2

Wong, J. (2004). The adaptive developmental state in East Asia. *Journal of East Asian Studies (Seoul), 4*(3), 345–362. doi:10.1017/S1598240800006007

Wong, M., Gardiner, E., Lang, W., & Coulon, L. (2008). Generational differences in personality and motivation: Do they exist and what are the implications for the workplace? *Journal of Managerial Psychology, 23*(8), 878–890. doi:10.1108/02683940810904376

Wong, S. S., Cross, J. A., & Burton, C. M. (2021). A quantitative analysis of knowledge collaboration enablers for practicing engineers. *Engineering Management Journal, 33*(3), 174–186. doi:10.1080/10429247.2020.1780840

Wong, Y. N. (2012). World Development Report 2012: Gender equality and development. *Forum for Development Studies, 39*(3), 435–444. doi:10.1080/08039410.2012.722769

Wright, A. J. (2022). Deliberate context-driven conceptualization in psychological assessment. *Journal of Personality Assessment, 104*(5), 700–709. doi:10.1080/00223891.2021.1942024 PMID:34227917

Xiao, Q., & Khan, M. S. (2024). Exploring factors influencing supply chain performance: Role of supply chain resilience with mixed method approach empirical evidence from the Chinese healthcare Sector. *Cogent Business & Management*, *11*(1), 2287785. Advance online publication. doi:10.1080/23311975.2023.2287785

Xue, L., Zhang, Q., Zhang, X., & Li, C. (2022). Can digital transformation promote green technology innovation? *Sustainability (Basel)*, *14*(12), 7497. doi:10.3390/su14127497

Xue, L., Zhu, X., & Han, W. (2018). Embracing scientific decision making: The rise of think-tank policies in China. *Pacific Affairs*, *91*(1), 49–71. doi:10.5509/201891149

Yacout, D. M., & Hassouna, M. S. (2016). Identifying potential environmental impacts of waste handling strategies in textile industry. *Environmental Monitoring and Assessment*, *188*(8), 1–13. doi:10.1007/s10661-016-5443-8 PMID:27372905

Yadav, P. V., Kollimath, U. S., Giramkar, S. A., Pisal, D. T., Badave, S. S., & Swamy, S. M. (2023, October). HR 4.0: Role of AI in transforming HRM. In *2023 3rd International Conference on Emerging Smart Technologies and Applications (eSmarTA)* (pp. 1-9). IEEE.

Yadav, S., Jain, A., & Singh, D. (2018, December). Early prediction of employee attrition using data mining techniques. In *2018 IEEE 8th International Advance Computing Conference (IACC)* (pp. 349-354). IEEE. 10.1109/IADCC.2018.8692137

Yadav, U. S., Tripathi, R., Rena, R., Khan, S. A., & Ghosal, I. (2025). Use and Effect of Fintech Awareness in Women for Sustainable Development in Small Industry during COVID-19 Pandemic: An Empirical Analysis with UTUAT model. *International Journal of Electronic Finance*. Advance online publication. doi:10.1504/IJEF.2025.10062118

Yakubovich, V., & Lup, D. (2006). Stages of the recruitment process and the referrer's performance effect. *Organization Science*, *17*(6), 710–723. doi:10.1287/orsc.1060.0214

Yamada, M. (2023). Japan's Relations with Saudi Arabia: The Evolution of Energy Diplomacy in Response to the Developmental Shift in the Rentier State. In *Japan and the Middle East: Foreign Policies and Interdependence* (pp. 27–55). Springer Nature Singapore. doi:10.1007/978-981-19-3459-9_2

Yang, Z. (2023). Bridging the mental health gap: Unveiling and mitigating the hidden toll of workplace behaviours on diverse populations. Frontiers in Public Health, 11. doi:10.3389/fpubh.2023.1308099

Yang, C.-L., Matsumoto, K., Yu, S., Sawada, L., Arakawa, K., Yamada, D., & Kuzuoka, H. (2023). Understanding the effect of a virtual moderator on people's perception in remote discussion using social VR. *Frontiers in Virtual Reality*, *4*, 1198024. Advance online publication. doi:10.3389/frvir.2023.1198024

Yang, C., & Modell, S. (2012). Power and performance: Institutional embeddedness and performance management in a Chinese local government organization. *Accounting, Auditing & Accountability Journal*, *26*(1), 101–132. doi:10.1108/09513571311285630

Yarbrough, S., Martin, P., Alfred, D., & McNeill, C. (2017). Professional values, job satisfaction, career development, and intent to stay. *Nursing Ethics*, *24*(6), 675–685. doi:10.1177/0969733015623098 PMID:26811397

Ye, C., Chen, M., Duan, J., & Yang, D. (2017). Uneven development, urbanization and production of space in the middle-scale region based on the case of Jiangsu province, China. *Habitat International*, *66*, 106–116. doi:10.1016/j.habitatint.2017.05.013

Yildiz, D., Temur, G. T., Beskese, A., & Bozbura, F. T. (2020). Evaluation of positive employee experience using hesitant fuzzy analytic hierarchy process. *Journal of Intelligent & Fuzzy Systems*, *38*(1), 1043–1058. doi:10.3233/JIFS-179467

Yilmaz, G. (2023). *Silence and Focus: Noise-Canceling Headphones as Assistive Tools for Cognitive Disabilities.* Available https://blogs.perficient.com/2023/10/05/silence-and-focus-noise-canceling-headphones-as-assistive-tools-for-cognitive-disabilities/

Yimsai, T., & Booranapong, N., Nhomuang, P., Boonthaim, H., Wongpinpech, P., & Chunin, M. (2022). Work Flexibility and Self-Regulation Predicting the Success in Work of Private Company Employees. *International Journal of Early Childhood Special Education, 14*(2), 3028–3035. doi:10.9756/INT-JECSE/V14I2.298

Yoon, D. J., Bono, J. E., Yang, T., Lee, K., Glomb, T. M., & Duffy, M. K. (2022). The balance between positive and negative affect in employee well-being. *Journal of Organizational Behavior, 43*(4), 763–782. doi:10.1002/job.2580

Young, N. C. J. (2022). Adapting a New Inclusive Mindset in the Hiring Process. In Now Hiring (pp. 29-42). Emerald Publishing Limited.

Young, K. E. (2014). *The political economy of energy, finance and security in the United Arab Emirates: between the Majilis and the market.* Springer. doi:10.1057/9781137021977

Young, S. J., Sturts, J. R., Ross, C. M., & Kim, K. T. (2013). Generational differences and job satisfaction in leisure services. *Managing Leisure, 18*(2), 152–170. doi:10.1080/13606719.2013.752213

Yu, L., Zhong, J., Lam, W., Wang, Y., & Chen, H. (2023). Healthy lifestyle is a signal: How applicants' healthy lifestyle information affects recruiter judgments. *Journal of Business Research, 167,* 114148. Advance online publication. doi:10.1016/j.jbusres.2023.114148

Yu, R., Gan, Q., Bian, J., Chen, R., Sun, X., & Ling, H. (2023). The mediating role of psychological empowerment in perceptions of decent work and work immersion among Chinese nurses: A cross-sectional study. *International Nursing Review,* inr.12883. Advance online publication. doi:10.1111/inr.12883 PMID:37647225

Yusuf, J. E. W., Saitgalina, M., & Chapman, D. W. (2022). Work-life balance and well-being of graduate students. In *Work-Life Balance in Higher Education* (pp. 63–88). Routledge. doi:10.4324/9781003314868-8

Yuwono, I. A., Suroso, A. I., & Hubeis, A. V. (2021). *The effect of talent management on employee performance with corporate culture as a mediating variable.* Jurnal Aplikasi Bisnis Dan Manajemen. doi:10.17358/jabm.7.1.212

Zagladi, A. N., Hadiwidjojo, D., Rahayu, M., & Noermijati. (2015). The Role of job satisfaction and power distance in determining the influence of organizational justice toward the turnover intention. *Procedia: Social and Behavioral Sciences, 211,* 42–48. doi:10.1016/j.sbspro.2015.11.007

Zaid, A. A., Bon, A. T., & Jaaron, A. A. (2018). Green human resource management bundle practices and manufacturing organizations for performance optimization: a conceptual model. *International Journal of Engineering & Technology, 7*(3.20), 87-91.

Zareen, S., & Khan, S. A. (2023). Exploring Dependence of Human Resource Management (HRM) on Internet of Things (IoT) and Digital Marketing in the Digital Era. In A. Naim & V. Devi (Eds.), *Global Applications of the Internet of Things in Digital Marketing* (pp. 51–66). IGI Global. doi:10.4018/978-1-6684-8166-0.ch004

Zehir, C., Karaboğa, T., & Başar, D. (2020). The transformation of human resource management and its impact on overall business performance: big data analytics and AI technologies in strategic HRM. *Digital Business Strategies in Blockchain Ecosystems: Transformational Design and Future of Global Business,* 265-279.

Zeithaml, V. A., Rajan Varadarajan, P., & Zeithaml, C. P. (1988, July 1). The Contingency Approach: Its Foundations and Relevance to Theory Building and Research in Marketing. *European Journal of Marketing, 22*(7), 37–64. doi:10.1108/EUM0000000005291

Zemke, R., Raines, C., & Filipczak, B. (2000). *Generations at work: managing the clash of veterans, boomers, xers, and nexters in your workplace*. AMACOM.

Zeng, H. (2020). Adaptability of artificial intelligence in human resources management in this era. *International Journal of Sciences*, *7*(1), 271–276.

Zeng, M., Wang, F., Xiang, S., Lin, B., Gao, C., & Li, J. (2020). Inheritance or variation? Spatial regeneration and acculturation via implantation of cultural and creative industries in Beijing's traditional compounds. *Habitat International*, *95*, 102071. doi:10.1016/j.habitatint.2019.102071

Zeytinoglu, I. U., & Denton, M. (2005). Satisfied workers, retained workers: Effects of work and work environment on homecare workers' job satisfaction, stress, physical health, and retention. Canadian Health Services Research Foundation (CHSRF).

Zhang, P., Ma, S. G., Zhao, Y. N., & Cao, X. Y. (2023). Analyzing Core Competencies and Correlation Paths of Emerging Engineering Talent in the Construction Industry—An Integrated ISM–MICMAC Approach. *Sustainability (Basel)*, *15*(22), 16011. doi:10.3390/su152216011

Zhang, X., Yang, H., & Huang, Q. (2019). Examining the impacts of hotel employees' compensation fairness on turnover intention. *International Journal of Contemporary Hospitality Management*, *31*(2), 947–965.

Zhang, Y. C., Shum, C., & Belarmino, A. (2023). "Best Employers": The Impacts of Employee Reviews and Employer Awards on Job Seekers' Application Intentions. *Cornell Hospitality Quarterly*, *64*(3), 298–306. doi:10.1177/19389655221130741

Zhang, Z. (2023). Early warning model of adolescent mental health based on big data and machine learning. *Soft Computing*, *28*(1), 811–828. doi:10.1007/s00500-023-09422-z

Zhao, H. (2021). *Internationalization of Regional Higher Education in China: A Critical Policy Case Study of A Transnational Double-Degree Program* (Doctoral dissertation, The University of Western Ontario (Canada)).

Zhao, H., Guan, Y., Liu, Y., Jiang, P., & Zhou, X. (2023). How and when inclusive human resource management promotes employee well-being: The roles of ambidextrous fit and affective leadership. *Journal of Business and Psychology*, *38*(1), 1–16. doi:10.1007/s10869-022-09789-1 PMID:36373110

Zhaojin, J. (2016). *A History of Modern Shanghai Banking: The Rise and Decline of China's Financial Capitalism: The Rise and Decline of China's Financial Capitalism*. Routledge. doi:10.4324/9781315706849

Zhao, Y., Liu, X., Wang, S., & Ge, Y. (2019). Energy relations between China and the countries along the Belt and Road: An analysis of the distribution of energy resources and interdependence relationships. *Renewable & Sustainable Energy Reviews*, *107*, 133–144. doi:10.1016/j.rser.2019.03.007

Zhenjing, G., Chupradit, S., Ku, K. Y., Nassani, A. A., & Haffar, M. (2022). Impact of employees' workplace environment on employees' performance: A multi-mediation model. *Frontiers in Public Health*, *10*, 890400. Advance online publication. doi:10.3389/fpubh.2022.890400 PMID:35646787

Zhong, Z. (2021). Opening-up as entrepreneurial internationalisation in Chinese higher education. *International Journal of Comparative Education and Development*, *23*(3), 175–192. doi:10.1108/IJCED-04-2021-0035

Zhou, S. (2021). The Role of China's Teaching Research System in Promoting Evidence-Based Reform in Education: A Case Study of Jiangsu Province. *Best Evidence in Chinese Education*, *9*(2), 1227–1241. doi:10.15354/bece.21.or067

Zorlenţan, T., Burduş, E., & Căprărescu, G. (1996). *Managementul organizaţiei*. H. Reporter, Ed.

Zreik, M. (2023a). Navigating the Dragon: China's Ascent as a Global Power Through Public Diplomacy. In Global Perspectives on the Emerging Trends in Public Diplomacy (pp. 50-74). IGI Global.

Zreik, M. (2021). Academic Exchange Programs between China and the Arab Region: A Means of Cultural Harmony or Indirect Chinese Influence? *Arab Studies Quarterly*, *43*(2), 172–188. doi:10.13169/arabstudquar.43.2.0172

Zreik, M. (2022). The Chinese presence in the Arab region: Lebanon at the heart of the Belt and Road Initiative. *International Journal of Business and Systems Research*, *16*(5-6), 644–662. doi:10.1504/IJBSR.2022.125477

Zreik, M. (2023b). The Integration of China's Belt and Road Initiative Into Global Supply Chains: New Pathways for Social and Environmental Responsibility. In *Government Impact on Sustainable and Responsible Supply Chain Management* (pp. 74–94). IGI Global. doi:10.4018/978-1-6684-9062-4.ch005

Zubair, S. S., & Khan, A. M. (2019). Sustainable development: The role of green HRM. *International Journal of Research in Human Resource Management*, *1*(2), 1-6.

Zweig, D., & Wang, H. (2013). Can China bring back the best? The Communist Party organizes China's search for talent. *The China Quarterly*, *215*, 590–615. doi:10.1017/S0305741013000751

Петитта, Л., & Ghezzi, V. (2023). Remote, disconnected, or detached? Examining the effects of psychological disconnectedness and cynicism on employee performance, wellbeing, and work–family interface. *International Journal of Environmental Research and Public Health*, *20*(13), 6318. doi:10.3390/ijerph20136318 PMID:37444165

About the Contributors

Bryan Christiansen is an Adjunct Professor at Southern New Hampshire University where he teaches undergraduate business courses entirely online. Christiansen is also the Chief Executive Officer of the Idaho-based management consultancy, CYGERA, LLC. He is fluent in Chinese, Japanese, and Spanish with extensive exposure to Russian and Turkish. Christiansen has given presentations on his field of expertise at numerous universities in Europe, the Middle East, and North America.

* * *

Neeta Baporikar is currently a Professor/Director (Business Management) at Harold Pupkewitz Graduate School of Business, Namibia University of Science and Technology, Namibia. Prior to this, she was Head-Scientific Research, with the Ministry of Higher Education CAS-Salalah, Sultanate of Oman, Professor (Strategy and Entrepreneurship) at IIIT Pune and BITS India. With a decade-plus of experience in the industry, consultancy, and training, she made a lateral switch to research and academics in 2000. Prof Baporikar holds D.Sc. (Management Studies) USA, Ph.D. (Management), SP Pune University, INDIA with MBA (Distinction) and Law (Hons.) degrees. Apart from this, she is an external reviewer, Oman Academic Accreditation Authority, an Accredited Management Teacher, a Qualified Trainer, an FDP from EDII, a Doctoral Guide, and a Board Member of Academic Advisory Committee in accredited B-Schools. She has to her credit many conferred doctorates, 350+ scientific publications, and authored 30+ books in the areas of Strategy, Entrepreneurship, Management, and Higher Education. She is also a member of the international and editorial advisory board, and reviewer for Emerald, IGI, Inderscience, Wiley, etc.

P. Bhanumathi is an Associate Professor and Head Academics at M S Ramaiah Institute of Management, Bangalore. She completed her Ph.D. in Knowledge management from the University of Mysore. She has qualified in UGC NET and AMT certification from AIMA and has over 19+ years of teaching and eleven years of research experience. Ph.D. Guide ship @ Ramaiah University of Applied Sciences and the University of Mysore. Best Capstone Project Award 2023 on "Leadership Style Prediction Using Data Science & ML models from Boston -RVCE Centre of Excellence in AI research and Business solutions, RVCE, Bengaluru. She has four patent publications to her credit. Her thesis identified knowledge management enablers and processes for select SMEs in and around Bangalore and suggested a feasible model for improving organizational performance. She has published research papers in peer-reviewed journals, including UGC-listed and ABDC journals and a few reputed conferences. She handles courses in HR, Operations, Entrepreneurship, and General Management. She is a reviewer of the Journal of Human Resource Management, the University of Kelaniya, Sri Lanka, and many other top universities.

Nazlı Ece Bulgur received a BA in Economics from Yıldız Technical University, Türkiye (2019), and completed her Master's degree in Human Resources Management of the Business Administration Department from Yıldız Technical University, Türkiye (2021). She is currently a Ph.D. candidate in Organizational Behaviour at Yıldız Technical University. Her research interests include career management, career sustainability, kaleidoscope career, network behaviors, and generational studies. She is currently involved in two international projects and has 26 publications (a total of congress participations and articles).

Gabriel Croitoru is a professor and PhD supervisor with an academic career over 25 years in Management. Promoter and president of the Association of Young Entrepreneurs in the Virtual Environment and of the Student Center for Entrepreneurship and Business Administration. Author of university books, participant in international conferences and reviewer of ISI journals. Since 2020, director of the Marketing Management Department and director of the Center for Research and Applied Studies in Management and Marketing.

Mihai Bogdan Croitoru is a student at Academy of Economic Studies in Bucharest, Management Faculty but also at "Valahia" University of Targoviste, Marketing section, with a rich student career manifested through involvement in academic research. The activity carried out in school and extracurricular activities has substantiated an interdisciplinary accumulation on managerial and entrepreneurial skills by collaborating in writing articles, participating in international conferences and obtaining awards.

Daria Florea has graduated the National College of Pedagogy, Philology section, bilingual English section. Now is in the first year as a student at Valahia University of Targoviste, Section Business Administration- Commerce, Tourism and Services in Economy. She is the beneficiary of a performance scholarship and she is interested in team work, and collaboration in publishing articles, book chapters and books in the field of Management, Business Simulation, and Communication.

Alphonsa Haokip is currently the Headmistress of Christ King High School, Chingjaroi Khullen, Manipur. She has completed her doctorate entitled, "Attitude, Problem Solving Ability, and Achievement in Mathematics Learning among the Secondary School Students of Thadou Kuki Tribe in Manipur". Her areas of interest are Mathematics Learning of Secondary School Students, their problem-solving ability, their academic achievement, mathematics teachers and their concerns, paradigm shift in higher education, and gender issues. Orcid: 0000-0003-2578-0114

Zidan Kachhi is a Counselling Psychologist and is currently associated with the Department of Psychology as an Assistant Professor at PES University, RR Campus, Bengaluru. His research interests include Gender and Sexuality Studies, Diversity and Inclusion, Behavioral Finance and Sustainability.

Fehmina Khalique, Professor OB & HR, Lloyd Business School, Greater Noida, is a Ph.D. and MBA in human resource management and also Editor for Lloyd Business Review Journal. She is associated with academics for the past 17 years with 4 years of industry experience and enjoys being a corporate trainer, counsellor, and consultant. Her research interest lies in cross-cultural management, international management, human resource management, and human capital management. She has several high-quality research papers to her credit and has co-authored a book with a reputed publisher. In her free time, she likes to do some social work and deliver free career counselling sessions for students.

Nusrat Khan is an expert in the area of HR and OB. She has worked with national and International NGOs. She also worked as a researcher for projects with an internationally recognized Distinguished Professor of Western Kentucky University, Kentucky, USA. She has also worked for the corporates both nationally and internationally. She has taught in several well-known universities. While working in these universities she had held several administrative duties as well. She is presently working as a Professor at GD Goenka University in the School of Management. At GD Goenka University she has also been serving as Head Post Graduate Programmes, MBA Admission head, HR Area Head, Teaching various management subjects, also served as a class teacher, handling mentees, had been a member of the Internal Quality Assurance Cell (IQAC) as prescribed by National Assessment and Accreditation Council (NAAC), Member of the Departmental Research Committee for Doctor of Philosophy (Ph.D.) program of G.D. Goenka University, Member of the Examination Moderation Committee, served as an Associate editor of GD Goenka Journal. She is also a Mendeley Advisor from Mendeley (Elsevier UK).

Shad Ahmad Khan is serving as Assistant Professor in College of Business, University of Buraimi in Sultanate of Oman. He is an active researcher who has a professional strength in the area of Business Management and Marketing. He has a vast experience of organizing international events like conferences and seminars. His area of interest is Data Sciences, green practices, entrepreneurship, administration sciences and marketing.

Peace Kumah holds a doctorate degree in Business Administration and MBA (Human Resource Management) degree from Wisconsin International University College, Accra, Ghana. She has several years of teaching experience and occupies leadership positions in various educational institutions. Her research interest includes strategic management, organizational leadership and motivation, change management, and employment relations.

Sanjeev Kumar is an accomplished expert in Food and Beverage. He currently holds the positions of Professor in Lovely Professional University, Punjab, India. With over a decade of experience in the field, food Service Industry, his research focuses on Alcoholic beverages, Event management and Sustainable Management Practices, Metaverse and Artificial Intelligence. He has published more than 40 research papers, articles and chapters in Scopus Indexed, UGC Approved and peer reviewed Journals and books. Dr. Sanjeev Kumar participated and acted as resource person in various National and International conferences, seminars, research workshops and industry talks and his work has been widely cited.

Melita Stephen Natal is an Assistant Professor at Amity Business School, Amity University, Greater Noida, India. With a wealth of academic expertise, she brings dedication and passion to her role in shaping the minds of future business leaders. Her commitment to fostering a dynamic learning environment is reflected in her contributions to the academic realm. Melita's professional journey is characterized by a steadfast dedication to education and a firm commitment to the growth and development of her students. Orcid: 0009-0004-1240-7817

Florea Nicoleta Valentina is a PhD Associate Professor and a PhD supervisor, Valahia University of Targoviste, Romania. She published 94 articles, 14 books and 6 book chapters in the fields she is teaching: HRM, CRM, Communication, Business simulation, and Marketing. She is a member of AVES, CRMMS, and EUMMAS. In 2018 and 2023 she received Erasmus+ teaching scholarships in Poland and Hungary. From 2018 she is a trainer, teaching HRM, Communication, CRM, and Antrepreneurial competencies.

Lijeesh P. is working as an Assistant professor in CHRIST (Deemed to be University), Bengaluru, India from the year 2017. Completed M Phil from Bharathiar University and Ph D from Mahatma Gandhi University, Kottayam, Kerala. Areas of interest/teaching includes law (Business Law, Company Law and Tax Laws), Human Resource Management and Organisation Behaviour. Also published articles and chapters in reputed UGC-listed and Scopus journals. Currently pursuing the Professional level of CS (Company Secretary).

Ana Pinto Borges is PhD in Economics, Faculty of Economics, University of Porto. She is Coordinating Professor (since 2010), President of the Pedagogical Council (since 2015), Coordinator of the Master in Business Management (since 2015) and of the Executive MBA (since 2016) at ISAG - European Business School. Scientific Coordinator of Research Center in Business Sciences and Tourism (CICET – FCVC) since 2021 and coordinated the ISAG Research Center (NIDISAG) between 2015 and 2021. She has published several articles and book chapters indexed in highly recognized international scientific journals. She also publishes books of international distribution, namely "Building Consumer-Brand Relationship in Luxury Brand Management" and "New Techniques for Brand Management in the Healthcare Sector". Participation in presentations in various national and international congresses and member of the Scientific Committees in academic events. Editor and one of the founding members of the European Journal of Applied Business and Management (EJABM). Former Accenture consultant in the financial area. Economist at the Health Regulatory Entity since 2010.

Valentina Ofelia Robescu is an Associate professor, Ph.D., and Ph.D. supervisor in Management. Personal experience in Entrepreneurship, Bio-economy, Environmental Management, and Innovation Management. Editor-in-chief of the VJES, president of the Association of Graduates of VUT, and Vice-president of the Virtual Environment Young Entrepreneurs Association. She has a huge scientific research activity, publishing books, and articles representing original scientific contributions.

V. Muthu Ruben is a distinguished Associate Professor at the School of Law, Christ University, situated in Bengaluru, Karnataka, India. Driven by an extensive scholarly foundation and a steadfast dedication to legal education, Dr. Ruben makes substantial contributions to both the academic community and the domain of law. His proficiency transcends numerous spheres within the realm of law, and he significantly influences the educational journeys of students enrolled at Christ University. Motivated by an ardent interest in legal research, he actively participates in scholarly endeavors, thereby making significant contributions to the ongoing legal dialogue. In addition to his scholarly responsibilities, Dr. V. Muthu Ruben is renowned for his commitment to cultivating an atmosphere that encourages intellectual engagement. His mentorship and counsel motivate pupils to explore into the complexities of the law, fostering the development of critical thinking skills and a profound comprehension of legal principles. In his role as an Associate Professor, Dr. Ruben provides the School of Law with an abundance of expertise, experience, and a forward-thinking perspective, thereby enhancing the institution's dedication to providing superior legal education. Orcid: 0009-0006-7723-8596

Kartikay Saini, an ex Naval Commander of the Indian Navy, is the Chairman of Scottish High International School, India. He is the former Chairman of Special Olympics of India and Board Member of Special Olympics Worldwide, Washington. With more than 36 years of experience in the Corporate, Defence and the Education world, Cdr Saini had been recognised worldwide and felicitated at House of Commons London, the President of Mauritius,, the Govt of Sri Lanka, the Presient of Dominican Republic, Education world, Forbes Magazine among others.Presently he is a research scholar at GD Goenka University.

Shilpi Sarna is working as Professor, (UG Management) Lloyd Group of Institutions, Greater Noida. She has done Ph.D. in Labour Laws from Jiwaji University, Gwalior and having 20 years of experience. She is HR Analytics certified by IIM Rohtak. and expert in the areas of organizational Behavior, HRM, Performance Management, Strategic HR and Stress Management and Labour Laws. She has a keen interest and expertise in HR and organized, workshops, seminar, Conference, FDP and various management development programs for students and faculties. She has numerous publications in national, international, and Scopus indexed Journals.

Rohit Shaji is a student pursuing a BSc Psychology (Hons) degree at PES University, Bangalore.

Nidhi Sharma is currently working as a research scholar at Chandigarh University, Mohali, India. Her research interest includes social media, destination marketing, travel and ecotourism. She has published several papers and book chapters in reputed journals and books.

Amrik Singh is working as Professor in the School of Hotel Management and Tourism at Lovely Professional University, Punjab, India. He obtained his Ph.D. degree in Hotel Management from Kurukshetra University, Kurukshetra. He started his academic career at Lovely Professional University, Punjab, India in the year 2007. He has published more than 40 research papers in UGC and peer-reviewed and Scopus/Web of Science) journals. He has published 12 patents and 01 patent has been granted in the inter-disciplinary domain. Dr. Amrik Singh participated and acted as a resource person in various national and international conferences, seminars, research workshops, and industry talks. His area of research interest is accommodation management, ergonomics, green practices, human resource management in hospitality, waste management, AR VR in hospitality, etc. He is currently guiding 8Ph.D. scholars and 2 Ph.D. scholars have been awarded Ph.D.

Ranjit Singha is a doctoral research fellow at Christ (Deemed to be a university) and a distinguished member of the American Psychological Association (APA). His expertise lies in research and development across various domains, including Mindfulness, Addiction Psychology, Women Empowerment, UN Sustainable Development Goals, and Data Science. With an impressive track record, Mr Ranjit serves as an Editor for TNT (Publication). He has earned certifications in mindfulness from renowned institutions, including IBM and The University of Oxford Mindfulness Centre, UK. Additionally, he holds certifications as a Microsoft Innovative Educator, Licensed Yoga Professional, Certified Mindfulness Teacher, and CBCT Teachers Training from Emory University, USA. Mr Ranjit's educational qualifications include PGDBA (GM), MBA (IB), MSc in Counseling Psychology, and completion of a Senior Diploma in Tabla (Musical Instrumentation). His dedication to continuous learning is evident through his involvement in the SEE Learning® (Social, Emotional, and Ethical) Learning program. As a committed researcher and educator, Mr Ranjit focuses on mindfulness and compassion-based interventions. He has an impressive publication record, having authored twenty-three research papers, ten chapters, four books, and five edited books. His research interests encompass various aspects of mindfulness, such as assessment, benefits of mindfulness-based programs, change mechanisms, professional training, mindfulness ethics, cognitive and neuropsychology, and studies related to high-risk behaviours. Apart from his research endeavours, Mr Ranjit has extensive teaching experience, instructing courses in diverse subjects like Forensic Psychology, Positive Psychology, Organizational Planning, Strategic Management, Psycho Metric Tests, Counseling Skills, Disaster Management, Basic Computer Science, Business Planning, Business Law, and Auditing. He has mentored numerous graduate and undergraduate research projects, demonstrating his commitment to nurturing young minds in psychology. Furthermore, Mr Ranjit actively provides personal counselling services, showcasing his genuine concern for his students' well-being and academic success. His unwavering dedication to research and education has solidified his position as a valuable contributor to psychology. Orcid: 0000-0002-3541-8752

Surjit Singha is an academician with a broad spectrum of interests, including UN Sustainable Development Goals, Organizational Climate, Workforce Diversity, Organizational Culture, HRM, Marketing, Finance, IB, Global Business, Business, AI, K12 & Higher Education, Gender and Cultural Studies. Currently a faculty member at Kristu Jayanti College, Dr. Surjit also serves as an Editor, reviewer, and author for prominent global publications and journals, including being on the Editorial review board of Information Resources Management Journal and contributor to various publications. With over 13 years of experience in Administration, Teaching, and Research, Dr. Surjit is dedicated to imparting knowledge and guiding students in their research pursuits. As a research mentor, Dr. Surjit has nurtured young minds and fostered academic growth. Dr. Surjit has an impressive track record of over 75 publications, including articles, book chapters, and textbooks, holds two US Copyrights, and has successfully completed and published two fully funded minor research projects from Kristu Jayanti College. Orcid: 0000-0002-5730-8677

Deepti Sinha has an overall experience of 22 years and is presently associated with Christ (Deemed to be University), Delhi NCR. Her specialization is in Human Resource Management and she has carried out her doctoral work in the area of Quality of Work Life. She is presently on the editorial and review board of a few journals and has published about 25+ research papers in various national and international journals and one book. She is also on the panel of evaluators of NMIMS Global Access School of Continuing Education, Mumbai and is certified as Accredited Management Teacher in the area of Organizational Behaviour by All India Management Association, New Delhi.

Sachin Sinha has taught at different business schools and also worked in the field of corporate communications. His areas of teaching interest include consumer psychology and marketing communications. He is also a literature and cinema enthusiast, and, in addition to his academic publications, he has two literary books to his credit.

Supina is working as an Assistant Professor in Bunda Mulia University, Indonesia.

Muhammad Usman Tariq has more than 16+ year's experience in industry and academia. He has authored more than 200+ research articles, 100+ case studies, 50+ book chapters and several books other than 4 patents. He has been working as a consultant and trainer for industries representing six sigma, quality, health and safety, environmental systems, project management, and information security standards. His work has encompassed sectors in aviation, manufacturing, food, hospitality, education, finance, research, software and transportation. He has diverse and significant experience working with accreditation agencies of ABET, ACBSP, AACSB, WASC, CAA, EFQM and NCEAC. Additionally, Dr. Tariq has operational experience in incubators, research labs, government research projects, private sector startups, program creation and management at various industrial and academic levels. He is Certified Higher Education Teacher from Harvard University, USA, Certified Online Educator from HMBSU, Certified Six Sigma Master Black Belt, Lead Auditor ISO 9001 Certified, ISO 14001, IOSH MS, OSHA 30, and OSHA 48. He has been awarded Principal Fellowship from Advance HE UK & Chartered Fellowship of CIPD.

Mary Rani Thomas is presently serving as an Assistant Professor at CHRIST (Deemed to be University) in Bengaluru, India since 2010. She holds an MPhil and a PhD from the same university. Her expertise lies in the domains of Marketing, Management, Human Resource Management, and Organizational Behavior. Dr. Thomas has dedicated her research endeavors to consumer behavior and organizational behavior, with publications featured in esteemed UGC-listed and Scopus journals.

Elvira Vieira is a PhD in Applied Economics, University of Santiago de Compostela. Professor, member of the Scientific Council at Institute of Marketing Management between 2007-2009 and Invited Professor at Minho University between 2009-2012. Professor at Polytechnic Institute of Viana do Castelo and Coordinating Professor at ISAG - European Business School since 2009. General Director at ISAG - European Business School since 2012, researcher in UNIAG, scientific coordinator of NIDISAG Research Center (between 2014 - 2021) and of Center in Business Sciences and Tourism (CICET - FCVC) since 2021. Author of several publications (papers and book chapters) indexed to the main bibliographic databases. Editor and one of the founding members of the European Journal of Applied Business and Management (EJABM). 2009 1st prize winner for research of the "Catedra da Euroregión Galicia – Norte of Portugal" and President of the European Grouping of Territorial Cooperation Galicia – North of Portugal, from 2010-2012.

Mohamad Zreik, a Postdoctoral Fellow at Sun Yat-sen University, is a recognized scholar in International Relations, specializing in China's Arab-region foreign policy. His recent work in soft power diplomacy compares China's methods in the Middle East and East Asia. His extensive knowledge spans Middle Eastern Studies, China-Arab relations, East Asian and Asian Affairs, Eurasian geopolitics, and Political Economy, providing him a unique viewpoint in his field. Dr. Zreik is a proud recipient of a PhD from Central China Normal University (Wuhan). He's written numerous acclaimed papers, many focusing on China's Belt and Road Initiative and its Arab-region impact. His groundbreaking research has established him as a leading expert in his field. Presently, he furthers his research on China's soft power diplomacy tactics at Sun Yat-sen University. His significant contributions make him a crucial figure in understanding contemporary international relations.

526

Index

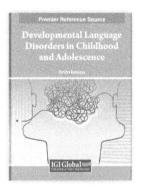

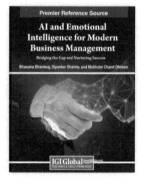

 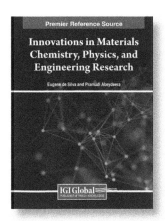 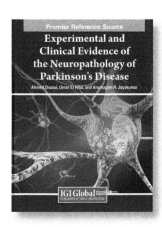 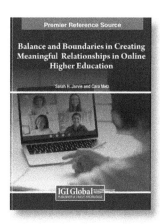

Milton Keynes UK
Ingram Content Group UK Ltd.
UKHW020125150624
444031UK00007B/127

9 798369 319383